Hegel stands out for having expressly linked the logic of singularity with the autonomy of thought that can liberate reason from the given and enable philosophy to be self-determining and fully self-responsible. Few subsequent commentators on Hegel's work have focused on this connection, obscuring how Hegel develops a foundation free metaphysics in which the logic of freedom coincides with the logic of the concept. Gregory Moss' *Hegel's Foundation Free Metaphysics* is an ambitious exception to this neglect. Moss offers us a comprehensive and enlightening journey through the seminal turning points in the history of Western Philosophy, exposing how the recurring efforts to overcome dogmatic presuppositions has dovetailed with the attempts to unravel the relation between the universal and the singular.

—**Richard Dien Winfield**, *University of Georgia, USA*

One does not have to leaf through the pages of Hegel's *Logic* at great length to see that Hegel regularly appears to endorse explicit contradictions. Of course, most commentators, inspired by an Aristotle-derived *horror contradictionis*, have had to maintain that he did not mean these things literally, for fear of making him appear irrational. Contemporary dialetheism has shown that endorsing contradictions is not the bogeyman that it has been cracked up to be. Moss' book is the first commentary on Hegel's metaphysics that draws on developments in contemporary dialetheism. As such, it shows us Hegel in a very new and—it seems to me—much more authentic light.

—**Graham Priest**, the CUNY Gradate Center and the University of Melbourne

Gregory Moss offers us a challenging and mature reflection on the metaphysical implications of Hegel's claim to offer a foundation-free philosophy. The seriousness of its overall argument asks for our attentive consideration of its praiseworthy illumination of Hegel's intentions. The book is written with impressive intelligence, wide ranging reference and in a thoughtful manner that philosophically engages the reader. Arguing against the evacuation of Hegel's thought of metaphysical significance, Gregory Moss invites us to take seriously dimensions of that thought that are underplayed by, or written out of, recent influential commentary in Anglo-American treatments of Hegel. This book takes leave of the beige Hegelianism that perhaps has become too common. Very warmly recommended.

—**William Desmond**, *David Cook Chair in Philosophy, Villanova University, USA*

Hegel's Foundation Free Metaphysics

Contemporary philosophical discourse has deeply problematized the possibility of Absolute Existence. *Hegel's Foundation Free Metaphysics* demonstrates that by reading Hegel's *Doctrine of the Concept* in his *Science of Logic* as a form of Absolute Dialetheism, Hegel's logic of the concept can account for the possibility of Absolute Existence. Through a close examination of Hegel's concept of self-referential universality in his *Science of Logic*, Moss demonstrates how Hegel's concept of singularity is designed to solve a host of metaphysical and epistemic paradoxes central to this problematic. He illustrates how Hegel's revolutionary account of universality, particularity, and singularity offers solutions to six problems that have plagued the history of Western philosophy: the problem of Nihilism, the problem of Instantiation, the problem of the Missing Difference, the problem of Absolute Empiricism, the problem of Onto-theology, and the Third Man regress. Moss shows that Hegel's affirmation and development of a revised ontological argument for God's existence is designed to establish the necessity of Absolute Existence. By adopting a metaphysical reading of Richard Dien Winfield's foundation free epistemology, Moss critically engages dominant readings and contemporary debates in Hegel scholarship. *Hegel's Foundation Free Metaphysics* will appeal to scholars interested in Hegel, German Idealism, 19th- and 20th-century European philosophy, metaphysics, epistemology, and contemporary European thought.

Gregory S. Moss has been Assistant Professor of Philosophy at the Chinese University of Hong Kong since 2016. Dr. Moss was a lecturer in philosophy at Clemson University from 2014 to 2016. Dr. Moss earned his PhD in philosophy in August 2014 at the University of Georgia, before which he was a Fulbright Fellow (2013–2014) at the University of Bonn.

Routledge Studies in Nineteenth-Century Philosophy

The Kantian Foundation of Schopenhauer's Pessimism
Dennis Vanden Auweele

Nietzsche's Constructivism
A Metaphysics of Material Objects
Justin Remhof

Hegel and Ancient Philosophy
A Re-Examination
Edited by Glenn Alexander Magee

Hegel's Metaphysics and the Philosophy of Politics
Edited by Michael J. Thompson

Reassessing Marx's Social and Political Philosophy
Freedom, Recognition and Human Flourishing
Edited by Jan Kandiyali

Logic from Kant to Russell
Laying the Foundations for Analytic Philosophy
Edited by Sandra Lapointe

Hegel's Civic Republicanism
Integrating Natural Law with Kant's Moral Constructivism
Kenneth R. Westphal

Hegel's Foundation Free Metaphysics
The Logic of Singularity
Gregory S. Moss

For a full list of titles in this series, visit www.routledge.com/Routledge-Studies-in-Nineteenth-Century-Philosophy/book-series/SE0508

Hegel's Foundation Free Metaphysics
The Logic of Singularity

Gregory S. Moss

Routledge
Taylor & Francis Group

NEW YORK AND LONDON

First published 2020
by Routledge
605 Third Avenue, New York, NY 10017

and by Routledge
2 Park Square, Milton Park, Abingdon, Oxon OX14 4RN

First issued in paperback 2022

Routledge is an imprint of the Taylor & Francis Group, an informa business

Copyright © 2020 Taylor & Francis

The right of Gregory S. Moss to be identified as author of this work has been asserted by him in accordance with sections 77 and 78 of the Copyright, Designs and Patents Act 1988.

Publisher's Note
The publisher has gone to great lengths to ensure the quality of this reprint but points out that some imperfections in the original copies may be apparent.

Library of Congress Cataloging-in-Publication Data
Names: Moss, Gregory S., 1983– author.
Title: Hegel's foundation free metaphysics : the logic of
    singularity / Gregory S. Moss.
Description: New York and London : Routledge, 2020. | Series:
    Routledge studies in nineteenth-century philosophy | Includes
    bibliographical references and index.
Identifiers: LCCN 2020006610 (print) | LCCN 2020006611
    (ebook) | ISBN 9781138737464 (hardback) | ISBN
    9781315185347 (ebook)
Subjects: LCSH: Hegel, Georg Wilhelm Friedrich, 1770–1831. |
    Hegel, Georg Wilhelm Friedrich, 1770–1831. Wissenschaft der
    Logik.
Classification: LCC B2948 .M65 2020 (print) | LCC B2948
    (ebook) | DDC 193—dc23
LC record available at https://lccn.loc.gov/2020006610
LC ebook record available at https://lccn.loc.gov/2020006611

ISBN: 978-0-367-50306-2 (pbk)
ISBN: 978-1-138-73746-4 (hbk)
ISBN: 978-1-315-18534-7 (ebk)

DOI: 10.4324/9781315185347

Typeset in Sabon
by Apex CoVantage, LLC

For Valerie and Isla

Contents

Acknowledgments   xi
Abbreviations   xii
Foreword   xiii
RICHARD DIEN WINFIELD

Introduction   1

PART I
The Problem of Absolute Knowledge

1 The Problem of Nihilism in Early German Idealism   11

2 The Problem of Emanation in Neo-Platonism   73

3 Dual Principles of Truth and the Problem
   of Instantiation   92

4 The Logic of the Finite Concept   134

5 The Problem of the Missing Difference and
   Absolute Empiricism   159

6 The Problem of Onto-Theology   189

7 From the Third Man Regress to Absolute
   Dialetheism   226

PART II
Hegel's Absolute Dialetheism

8 Hegel's Logic of the Concept: The Concept of
   Self-Particularization   255

 9 Relative Dialetheism: The No-World View   286

10 Hegel's Solution to the Problem of Absolute
    Knowledge   307

11 Hegel's Ontological Argument: The Existence of
    the Absolute   329

12 Forms of Ideality in Hegel's Logic: Being, Essence,
    and Concept   359

13 The Logic of Singularity   381

14 Relativizing the Absolute: Empiricism, Judgment,
    and Inference   445

15 The Singular Absolute   482

    References   492
    Index   504

Acknowledgments

It goes without saying that without the generous support of family, friends, colleagues, students, institutional bodies, and philosophical societies, this book would never have been completed. I would like to thank the following persons and institutions for supporting the writing of this book and for contributing to the development of the ideas contained therein: my family (most especially Valerie Anne Moss), Richard Dien Winfield, Markus Gabriel, the International Centre for Philosophy NRW, Jens Rometsch, Graham Priest, William Desmond, Edward Halper, Elizabeth Brient, Bradley O. Bassler, all of my colleagues in the Philosophy Department at the Chinese University of Hong Kong (especially Saulius Geniusas, Kwok-ying Lau, Chong-fuk Lau, and Qingjie Wang), the Faculty of Arts at CUHK, the University Grants Committee in Hong Kong, Wesley Bergen, Samuel Lee, Leonard Ip, Janice Ching Lam Law, Philipp Schwab, Alexander Bilda, Christoph Asmuth, Friedemann Barniske, Héctor Ferraro, Marcela Garcia, Jakub Kloc-Konkołowicz, Steve Palmquist, Eric Nelson, Nahum Brown, Anthony Bruno, Jesper Rasmussen, Andrew Weckenmann, Eric Helelloid, Robert Scott, Joseph P. Carter, Jason Carter, A. J. Tiarsmith, Daniel and Larry Bloom, Chad Wiener, Graham Schuster, Emre Ebeturk, the Philosophy Departments of the University of Georgia, Oglethorpe University, and Clemson University, the Metaphysical Society of America, the North American Schelling Society, and the Internationales Forschungsnetzwerk für Transzendentalphilosophie und Deutschen Idealismus. Last but not least I would like to thank the following publishers and journals for their permission to reproduce previously published articles (either in whole or in part): Routledge, *SATS* (*Northern European Journal of Philosophy*), *Social Imaginaries*, and *Frontiers of Philosophy in China* (Brill).

Abbreviations

Kant, *Critique of Pure Reason* = CPR
Fichte, *Science of Knowledge* = SK
Schelling, *System of Transcendental Idealism* = STI
Hegel, *Science of Logic* = SL
Hegel, *Encyclopedia Logic* = EL
Hegel, *Phenomenology of Spirit* = PS
Jacobi, *The Main Philosophical Writings and the Novel Allwill* = MPW

Foreword

From the very beginning, philosophy has inevitably grappled with two seemingly unconnected, yet ultimately inseparable challenges: how to free philosophical inquiry of given foundations and how to think singularity.

The first problem, of securing the autonomy of reason by overcoming any dependence upon unexamined assumptions, has generated two successive strategies. The first consists in the pursuit of ontology as the foundation of philosophical investigation, where some first principle of being is sought as the fulcrum beyond all assumption on which reality and knowledge can rest. Doubt about the authority of reason to make any immediate claims about being has fostered a second strategy, abandoning *foundational* ontology for the turn to *foundational* epistemology, which seeks to uncover the ultimate conditions of knowing so as thereupon to determine what we can legitimately know about what is.

In conjunction with these foundational investigations, philosophers have been compelled to consider how concepts can lay hold of the singularity perennially acknowledged to be intrinsic to objective reality. Under successive rubrics of the problems of the One and many, of emanation from the absolute, of the participation of the forms in particulars, and of the relation of universal, particular, and singular, philosophers have grappled with whether thinking is an empty scaffold that must be supplied with content from elsewhere or whether thinking can be *pregnant* with content and conceive the singularity so basic to actual existence.

Hegel stands out for having expressly linked the logic of singularity with the autonomy of thought that can liberate reason from the given and enable philosophy to be self-determining and fully self-responsible. Few subsequent commentators on Hegel's work have focused on this connection, which allows the universal to be concrete and the singular to lose its opposition to thought. As a result, thinkers today have generally failed to notice, let alone take advantage of, the philosophical breakthrough lying in how Hegel develops a foundation free metaphysics in which the logic of freedom coincides with the logic of the concept.

Gregory S. Moss' *Hegel's Foundation Free Metaphysics: The Logic of Singularity* is an ambitious exception to this neglect. Moss here offers us a revelatory journey through the seminal turning points in the history of Western philosophy, exposing how the recurring efforts to overcome dogmatic presuppositions have dovetailed with the attempts to unravel the relation between the universal and the singular. Be prepared for a riveting reconstruction of how the greatest thinkers of ancient and modern Western philosophy have grappled with the challenge of liberating thought from empty formality, of securing the synthetic *a priori* that lies within reason itself. Time and again, as Moss documents, the advocates of fundamental ontology and foundational epistemology have foundered on perplexities whose solution will only come when German Idealism unveils the resources for thinking how concept, freedom, and singularity go together. Moss has done us the service of laying out the itinerary, pioneered by Hegel, by which philosophy secures the objectivity of thought and liberates itself from foundations.

Richard Dien Winfield

Introduction

Independently of Absolute Existence *nothing* else can be. Indeed, today nothing may seem to be more anachronistic to contemporary philosophy than such a claim to Absolute Knowledge. For a century (or more), on both sides of the Atlantic, the claim to Absolute Knowledge generated immense suspicion. It appeared certain that the situation could not worsen for the friends of the Absolute. And yet, this certainty proved itself to be completely illusory, for today, while the existence of relative and contextual existence is affirmed and enjoys much recognition, the existence of the non-contextual Absolute is increasingly looked upon with grave suspicion, if not outright disdain.

Many of us, however, remember the lessons of our Christian heritage and continue to believe that the *death* of the Absolute may only be a prelude to its *resurrection*. While Post-Modernism might be justly characterized by its tendency to flee the Absolute, the New Realism that stands on the ashes of Post-Modernism has declared that there is nothing at all from which to flee. After all, the Absolute cannot die (or be resurrected) if it never lived in the first place.

In *Hegel's Foundation Free Metaphysics: The Logic of Singularity*, dear reader, you will find a defense of the existence of the Absolute against its detractors. Although the term 'Absolute' itself undergoes much scrutiny in what follows, for the sake of these preliminary reflections, the 'Absolute' should be understood as that which is all-encompassing—the *One and All* of the Tübingen three, or more simply: the world. What is more, *Hegel's Foundation Free Metaphysics* will problematize any view that attempts to separate relative and contextual existence from Absolute Existence, namely existence that is absolutely *independent of* all contexts. The defense of Absolute Existence is nothing less than a defense of what stands alone—*itself by itself*—to use a phrase from our esteemed Greek ancestors. The Absolute is the singular existence, in the sense that it is *the One and only*.

Such a defense of the Absolute cannot find success without first seriously considering the philosophical ground(s) upon which its denial is grounded. As Chapter 4, *The Logic of the Finite Concept*, discusses in great detail, a dominant and influential tradition in the West takes for granted the assumption that the concept, or the universal, cannot achieve truth *in virtue of itself* alone. Because the universal cannot achieve truth on its own, a separate principle of particularity must be presupposed as the ultimate arbiter of the truth of the universal. Disabled by the separation of principles of universality and particularity, we traditionally conceive of the universal as a mere *possibility to be*. Because of this, we traditionally conceive of actuality as external and other to the universal. The question of whether the universal *exists* (naturally as more than a mere possibility to be), so it is supposed, is a question that cannot be answered by merely consulting the concept alone. I call this the 'finite' or 'relative' concept because it exists and is true *in virtue of something else*. Despite the great variety of conceptions of universality in the Western tradition, such as the genus, the abstract universal, and class-membership, all of these conceptions are species of finite universality and instantiate its features, such as the fundamental principle that universality is *insufficient* for the differentiation of its particulars. In the very same chapter, I contend that the separation of the principles of universality and particularity is ultimately indebted to *the PNC*.

Many problems await the advocate of the finite universal, however. Many of these can be formulated independently of any concern for Absolute Knowledge. Part I of *Hegel's Foundation Free Metaphysics* is devoted to explicating these paradoxes. The separation of the principles of universality and particularity, as established by the PNC, engenders (at least) six aporias: the problem of Nihilism (Chapters 1 and 2), the problem of Instantiation (Chapter 3), the problems of the Missing Difference and Absolute Empiricism (Chapter 5), the problem of Onto-theology (Chapter 6), and finally the problem of the Third Man Regress (Chapter 7).

Part I of *Hegel's Foundation Free Metaphysics* presents the argument that as long as the principle of non-contradiction is presumed to have a privileged, absolute status, the Absolute can neither exist nor be known. Although the reasons for this must be worked out in the course of the text, the general problem can be briefly indicated in advance. The Absolute ought to be what is all-encompassing and therefore ought to exclude nothing. In order to conceive of the Absolute by means of concepts, the Absolute must abide by the very same principles of finite universality, including, most fundamentally, the principle of non-contradiction (PNC). Accordingly, by employing the PNC to know the Absolute, the Absolute must be restrained to *one side* of a contradictory opposition. Because it is supposed to abide by the PNC, the Absolute cannot be what is *not* Absolute. But since the Absolute is forced to occupy only one side of an opposition, everything relative must then be conceived of as *other* to the Absolute. Because it is known by finite or relative conceptuality, and thereby *reduced* to one side of an opposition, the Absolute becomes *one relative being* that exists relative to other relative beings. Thus, the Absolute is *not* Absolute—it is relative to another and is not the all-encompassing One and All. Since any attempt to think the Absolute by means of concepts transforms the concept into that which is *not* Absolute, every attempt to conceptualize the Absolute leads to a contradiction. Since the PNC precludes the truth of all contradiction, *no conceptualization of the Absolute can be true*. By this line of reasoning, it is not unreasonable at all to infer either that the Absolute cannot be known or that it simply does not exist. Because the Absolute seems to disappear every time we attempt to know it by means of finite and relative concepts governed by the PNC, at the close of Part I argue that the Absolute can only exist and be known by *denying* that the PNC is a principle governing truth and existence.

Fittingly, Part I concludes with an endorsement and formulation of the generic solution to the problem of Absolute Existence: *Absolute Dialetheism*. 'Dialetheism,' a term coined by Graham Priest, signifies that there are *true contradictions*. 'Absolute Dialetheism' is the more specific thesis that the world, or the *singular* One and All, exists and can only be known as a true contradiction. Further, I argue that of this generic type there are (at least) two species of Absolute Dialetheism: mystical and rationalist, each of which has its own sub-divisions.

The mystical type of Absolute Dialetheism affirms the existence of the Absolute but denies that it can be known or encapsulated by concepts. Apophatic, or negative, theology is a good example of this tendency in knowing. Because this species of Absolute Dialetheism allows that the domain of concepts (and thereby philosophical knowing) is governed by the PNC and the other features of finite universality, it must posit the contradictory Absolute as that which *transcends* all conceptual determinacy. Because this transcendence cannot itself be explicated conceptually, the mystical solution finds itself saddled with a singularity that lies beyond its concepts, and for this reason, it cannot even conceptually explicate the transcendence of the world. Because there is no way to reconcile the Absolute with the concept, philosophy is transformed into a ritual or *practice* of revealing the non-conceptuality of the Absolute. Here, the failure itself becomes revelatory: the philosopher *experiences* the *ecstatic* and non-eidetic character of the Absolute in virtue of consistently failing to capture the Absolute with concepts.

Hegel's *Science of Logic*, on the contrary, forges a unique path. By denying that the PNC is an ultimate principle of conceptual determination, Hegel enables the concept to know the Absolute Singularity. Unlike the mystical response, Hegel's Absolute Dialetheism proclaims the Absolute to be conceptually explicable. Chapters 8 and 9 of Part II develop Hegel's dialetheism and bring it into conversation with more contemporary philosophical work, work that attempts to problematize Absolute Being and Knowing.

The perennial appeal to the PNC in the Western tradition, as is evident enough in Aristotle and Kant, for example, has obscured the truth of Absolute Dialetheism. This disposition to insist on the PNC and the structures that it engenders certainly constitutes one disposition or tendency in the tradition. But it would be a grave error to suppose that the Western tradition has been oblivious to the problems that arise in any effort to achieve Absolute Knowledge. Indeed, it is the Western tradition that provides the sources from which these various problems have been here uncovered and discussed. As is obvious, any student of the Western tradition will discover more than the two possibilities mentioned earlier. Usually, whenever the problem (or problems) of Absolute Knowledge is acknowledged, an appeal is subsequently made to theoretical maneuvers that protect the very assumptions that generated the problem in the first place. For example, while Aristotle famously recognizes that *any attempt to think the genus of Being leads to contradiction*, neither does he conclude therefrom that it does not exist, nor that it exists as contradictory. Instead, he argues that the genus of Being is *pros hen*. Despite the profundity of such solutions, I will argue that all such compromised positions *fail*. Generally, one discovers that such maneuvers do more to obscure the truly dialetheic character of Being than reveal its true nature. Although it is my contention that it is in the tradition of German Idealism where the tradition becomes fully self-conscious of the fundamentally dialethic character of Absolute Existence, this dialetheic character of the Absolute has been intimated from the beginning. In addition to that disposition of Western thinkers to cling to self-identity, there is another disposition (sometimes on the margins of the tradition) that draws thinkers to endorse the truth of contradiction. Arguably, thinkers as diverse as Heraclitus, Meister Eckhart, and Schlegel (among others) all endorse some form of dialetheism. It is with the Neo-Platonic and early German Romantic and Idealist traditions that the dialetheic disposition of the Western tradition bubbles to the surface.

Although there are other ways of integrating contradiction into the form of conceptual determination besides Hegel's, it is Hegel who, in his preface to the *Phenomenology of Spirit*, uncovers the two species of Absolute Dialetheism and polemically advances his own account of Absolute Science against the mysticism that was so popular in his own time. For a long time we have stood at an impasse, for which we have our own tradition to thank. Either the Absolute stands before us as an ineffable singularity that transcends conceptual articulation, or we are confronted with the Herculean task of drawing the contradiction into the very being of the concept. If Absolute thinking has a future, it will not be because we have ceased to think historically. To the contrary, it will only have a future because we will have creatively developed the possibilities given over to us from our own past.

Part II of *Hegel's Foundation Free Metaphysics* explores this second species of Absolute Dialetheism through a close textual analysis and reconstruction of Hegel's *Lehre Vom Begriff*. In the second part, I give special attention to the structural reforms demanded by Hegel in his *Doctrine of the Concept*. Thus, it is my contention that Hegel's *Science of Logic*, in particular his logic of subjectivity, has very significant metaphysical ambitions. Hegel means to demonstrate to us, via his famed and oft-maligned dialectic, *why the world exists*. Or better: Hegel means to show why the world's non-existence is *absolutely impossible*.

Given that Hegel's efforts to re-think the concept are motivated by the aim of achieving knowledge of the Absolute, one might reasonably suppose that Hegel's reformation of philosophical thought would proceed by modeling conceptual determinacy and philosophical thinking on the contradictory character of the Absolute Singularity. To the contrary, Hegel's reformation of conceptual determinacy does not proceed from any *presupposition*. Rather, Hegel establishes the dialetheic character of Absolute thinking by allowing finite universality to *annihilate itself*. As that which has its own internal limit, finite universality comes to an end in virtue of itself. By restricting the Absolute to the finite form of universality, the finite universal relativizes the Absolute and thereby brings *the finite* conception of the Absolute to contradiction. Having absolutized the finite concept, the finite concept shows itself to be contradictory and thereby unable to consistently abide by its own principles. Because it draws finite universality and its underlying PNC into a contradiction, the finite concept *transforms itself* into an absolute contradiction. Rather than show that the Absolute does not exist, or cannot be known, the self-destruction of finite universality establishes the *non-being of finite universality* on its *own* terms and thereby resurrects the *Absolute*, though now in a *dialetheic form*. In short, the Absolute establishes itself as dialetheic—free and without presupposition. Rather than flee from what is revealed, Hegel simply calls us to confront, boldly and without hesitation, the truth of contradiction that manifests itself in the death throes of relativity and finitude.

Naturally, a sufficient description of Hegel's self-overcoming of finite being and knowing requires more than an acknowledgment of the role of contradiction. In Chapter 10, I investigate the various structural forms initiated by Hegel's solution to the problem, some of which I can briefly indicate here in advance. In virtue of the self-destruction of finite conceptuality, Hegel re-conceives the concept as *infinite*. Since the finite universal is true in virtue of another, and it eliminates itself, Hegel presents the universal as *true in virtue of itself*. Because the overcoming of the PNC also engenders the elimination of the separation between the principles of universality and particularity, Hegel construes the universal as the principle of its own particularization, or as *self-particularizing*. As self-particularizing, the universal becomes endowed with the power to instantiate itself, without the need to appeal to external principles. This power of self-instantiation is nothing less than the power of *existential implication*, whereby the concept *exists* in virtue of itself alone. This alone indicates that Hegel's Absolute Idealism is not opposed to Realism, but is an Absolute or Total *Realism*. Because the concept is no longer a mere possibility to be, existence is no longer contingently connected to the concept. To the contrary, the modality of the concept is transformed such that it becomes endowed with new life and power to *actualize itself*. What is more, the synthetic, conceptual power that amplifies itself into existence is achieved by means of *self-referential predication*. Although an absolutely ubiquitous and indispensable feature of Hegel's categories, self-referential predication has traditionally been rejected as a fundamental feature of the categories of knowing in being by thinkers of the Aristotelian and Kantian traditions.

Strikingly, Hegel characterizes the self-particularizing aspect of the universal in explicitly metaphysical terms. More specifically, Hegel describes the self-particularizing power of the universal as a novel formulation of the *ontological argument* for God's existence. In the debate over the status of Hegel as a metaphysician, this dimension of Hegel's metaphysics has been significantly underplayed. In order to lay bare the metaphysical and theological contribution of Hegel's logic of the concept, Chapter 12 investigates Hegel's critically revised version of the ontological argument and his further identification of the concept with *God*. Hegel's concept takes the place of God, for the truth of the concept is established by means of the concept alone—*auto kath auto*. This version of Hegel may be the metaphysical bogyman some recent scholars of Hegel mean to avoid, but this version is nevertheless the real Hegel; this Hegel is the only one who can salvage the existence of the Absolute without forsaking the Absolute Being of reason. By declawing Hegel's metaphysics, we also fail to see the power of his account to solve what have traditionally appeared to be intractable metaphysical problems.

Because Hegel's solution to the problem of the disappearance of the Absolute is developed by re-thinking the *concept of the concept*, Hegel's *Science of Logic*, and in particular his *Lehre Von Begriff*, contains the most important resources for gleaning systematic insights into the categorial structure of his solution. Accordingly, the majority of the textual exegesis of Part II focus on this text. In the *Science of Logic*, however, the self-overcoming of finitude is what Hegel calls *ideality*, and this ideality is *not* univocal. Given the importance of ideality to the discourse on Absolute Knowledge, Chapter 11 focuses exclusively on parsing out these various ways that ideality (the overcoming of finitude and otherness) is conceived in Hegel's work. In the *Science of Logic*, Hegel develops different forms of ideality. Finitude is overcome in different ways according to different categories of the *Logic*. In the logic of Being, ideality takes the form of *transition*, while in the logic of Essence, ideality takes the form of *positing*. In the *Doctrine of the Concept*, ideality manifests itself as a development characterized by self-particularization. Since the Logic of the Concept is the truth and unity of the logic of Being and Essence, I give special attention to the development of the categories there. In particular, by reconstructing the logical development of universality, particularity, and singularity (Chapter 13), I reconstruct how Hegel's concept of the universal singularizes itself and thereby imbues itself with Absolute Significance. Part II concludes with a discussion of how Hegel's account of the singular concept can integrate empirical determinations, judgment, and inference in his thinking, since all of these do not appear to instantiate the general features of the concept discussed in the previous chapters. This chapter also provides an opportunity to employ Hegel's insights on the singularity of universality as a way to critique the Pittsburgh school's tendency to *overlook* the singularity of the concept and *absolutize the particular*.

Given our special focus on these categories of the *Science of Logic*, by no means do I claim that my analysis constitutes a sufficient explication of Hegel's concept of Absolute Being and Knowing. Such an endeavor would require a complete explication of the totality of Hegel's system—encompassing all three volumes of the *Encyclopedia*. My aim is less ambitious than this. I mean to indicate, in outline, *the logical form* of Hegel's solution to the problem of the existence of Absolute Being and Knowing.

In the final chapters, I investigate the relation of Absolute Knowledge to Absolute Being, the contours of which I can only briefly indicate in advance. Because there is no standpoint beyond the Absolute from which the Absolute might be known, the defense of the existence of Absolute Being and Knowing cannot be achieved from any standpoint outside of the Absolute. Rather, the overcoming of the limits of contextual, relative, and finite knowing and existence can only take place from *within* the Absolute itself. In addition, because the Absolute is constituted by the self-negation of its own relative being, it is nothing other than the power of the Absolute itself, in virtue of which relative being is overcome. Moreover, were the Absolute not to exist in knowledge, then it would exclude knowledge and would be relative to the knowing that exists beyond it. Accordingly, in order for *the Absolute to exist absolutely*, and to correspond to what it *truly* is, the Absolute must also exist in knowing. Since it falls to the philosopher to know the Absolute, the Absolute overcomes its alienation in relative being and comes to exist absolutely in *philosophical knowledge*. Since the philosopher is the means by which the Absolute comes to exist absolutely, Absolute Dialetheism must transform philosophical knowledge into an indispensable vehicle by which the Absolute can overcome the threat of non-existence.

Because Absolute Knowledge is dialetheic, one cannot plausibly make a claim to Absolute Knowledge while simultaneously precluding the negation of the position. Accordingly, Hegel's Absolute Dialetheism, as one species of Absolute Dialetheism, must make a place for the ineffable and the mystical in his account of the concept in his system of philosophy. For the same reason, Hegel's dialetheism demands that he also make a place for finite universality and its underlying PNC in his system of philosophy. Without doing so, his own system would be one sided, a criticism he levies against others. Accordingly, one of the great challenges of this book is to show, by means of his dialectic, how Hegel integrates, while simultaneously transcends, the limits of relative knowing. Likewise, the mystical species of Absolute Dialetheism, which proclaims the Absolute to be a non-conceptual singularity, cannot plausibly make *this* claim to Absolute Knowledge without making a place for concepts in its system of thought. Accordingly, each species of Absolute Dialetheism must integrate its negation, and each must thereby mirror the other. On the one hand, although for mysticism the conceptual exists, it nevertheless exists as an alienated form of non-conceptual singularity. On the other hand, the rationalist species of Absolute Dialetheism, of which Hegel is the most profound representative, must integrate the non-conceptual, ecstatic, and mystical approach to the Absolute as a form of self-alienation, a form in which the Absolute has become relative and has lost its absolute character.

Ironically, however, for the Absolute Dialetheist, the self-alienation or error is a necessity. For without error the Absolute would not be Absolute; it would be a one-sided determination. In this extra-ordinary charity that animates the spirit of Hegelian philosophy, Hegel proclaims the abstract universal to be *the soul of singularity*. Having recognized the necessity of the error, those who have led us into believing that the world does not exist, or that the Absolute is unknowable, become our teachers too, and even those principles we mean to overcome become essential to our discourse. In *Hegel's Foundation Free Metaphysics*, I do not wish to impel the reader to accept any particular species of Absolute Dialetheism at the expense of any other. Indeed, I only mean to impress upon the reader the dire need to confront the truth of contradiction that exists at the heart of the Absolute, without which nothing else could exist or could be known.

Part I

The Problem of Absolute Knowledge

1 The Problem of Nihilism in Early German Idealism

The Contingency of Categorial Self-Consciousness

The Ancients, having perceived that anything that can be known must *be* in some way, construed the inquiry into the Absolute as an inquiry into Being, an inquiry thematized again by Heidegger in the early 20th century. The task of metaphysics is to provide a science of Being *qua* Being. Since metaphysics is the science of first principles, all other forms of knowing depend upon metaphysics for their being. Since metaphysics exists, or is actual at least as a practice, it is also possible. Given that metaphysics is possible as a practice, we can ask 'what makes metaphysics possible?' In addition, we can also ask whether metaphysics is possible as a science, or *Wissenschaft*. Without inquiring into the possibility of metaphysics, metaphysics runs the risk of falling victim to dogmatism. Since all other forms of knowing depend upon metaphysics, no other science or form of knowing can demonstrate how metaphysics is possible. Since it is metaphysics that constitutes the inquiry into first principles, it must fall to metaphysics to inquire into how metaphysics is possible. Hence, metaphysics is not only an inquiry into Being *qua* Being, but it is also an inquiry into its own knowing of Being *qua* Being. Insofar as this inquiry is characterized as knowledge, it can be construed as the knowledge of knowledge of Being. For this reason, the metaphysical inquiry into first principles can equally be construed as epistemology, since it is an inquiry into the very possibility of the knowledge of first principles.

Meta-metaphysics is the discipline that constitutes the knowledge of metaphysics itself and thereby takes metaphysics as its object. We should note at the outset that meta-metaphysics is not a discipline distinct from metaphysics, but belongs to the activity and content of metaphysics proper. By inquiring into whether metaphysics is possible as a science, as well as the inquiry into the condition for the possibility of metaphysics as a practice, metaphysical inquiry takes itself as its own object. Naturally, this makes metaphysics an inherently reflexive discipline. As a reflexive discipline inquiring into the possibility of metaphysics as a science, meta-metaphysical inquiry aims to uncover how the relationship between knowing and Being ought to be construed. For this reason, meta-metaphysical inquiry is not only interested in the discipline of metaphysics, namely the knowing of Being, but by virtue of its inquiry into the knowing of Being it aims to establish some truth about Being itself, namely whether Being, as the object of metaphysics, is itself structured in such a way as to be an object of philosophical knowing. Accordingly, meta-metaphysics also aims to establish whether Being as it is in itself is amenable to the structure of knowing. Therefore, within the meta-metaphysical aspects of metaphysics alone, one discovers an identity of subject and object, for meta-metaphysics itself contains the two sides of metaphysical inquiry: an inquiry into both the activity of the subject, or (i) the knowing of Being, as well as (ii) the object of that inquiry, Being itself. Most generally, we have established two theses: metaphysics is meta-metaphysics, and meta-metaphysics is metaphysics. For the Ancient Greeks, the inquiry into knowledge of Being are *not* two separate disciplines.

As an inquiry into wisdom, the classical injunction of philosophy, as the love of wisdom, is to inquire into what is *universal*: that in virtue of which any particular instance of wisdom counts as wise. For this very reason, it must inquire into its own wisdom. Following the famous injunction on the temple at the oracle of Delphi, philosophy aims at self-knowledge. Philosophy seeks to draw the limit between itself and its other, namely between philosophical and non-philosophical knowing. As an inquiry into the principles of all wisdom, philosophy means to inquire into not only what is universal but that which is not conditional upon anything: it wants to know that upon which all wisdom depends. Accordingly, since philosophy aims at knowledge that is unconditionally universal, and the Absolute is what is unconditionally universal, philosophy aims at knowledge of the Absolute, Absolute Knowing. Of course, Absolute Knowing must know the *being* of knowledge *in itself*—what it is to know as such. Thus, the inquiry into the knowledge of knowledge is also a metaphysical inquiry into the *being* of knowing.

Further, in order to know what it is to know, one must be able to distinguish kinds of Being—namely the being that consists in knowing from that which does not. What is more, if this Absolute Knowing, which is the aim of epistemology, were to exclude knowledge of any being, then its knowledge would only be relative to some beings and would not be absolute. Accordingly, Absolute Knowing cannot be a knowledge of some beings to the exclusion of others, but ought to entail knowledge of all beings. Absolute Knowing is not just epistemological (knowledge of knowing), but it is inherently metaphysical (knowledge of Being). Thus, the epistemic inquiry into the first principles of knowledge can equally be construed as metaphysics. In short, whether one takes Being as the object of first philosophy, or Absolute Knowledge, metaphysics is an epistemic inquiry just as much as epistemology is a metaphysical inquiry.

The fundamental question for ancient Greek philosophy is the question concerning the what it is to be of Being. Kant's Copernican revolution in philosophy re-directed the focus of inquiry towards an assumption that ancient philosophy takes for granted. By immediately inquiring into the *what it is to be* of Being, ancient thought fails to ask whether the subject is capable of knowing what it is to be and under what *subjective* conditions that knowing is made possible. This is not to claim that the ancients were not critical in their metaphysics. For sure, any philosophy that makes a claim to be first philosophy must inquire into its own possibility, since there are no prior sciences that could establish that for it. But the ancients inquired into the possibility of first philosophy from *the side of the object*. Instead of asking under what conditions *subjectivity* must be construed in order to know its object, they inquired into how the object must be construed in order for it to conform to structures of knowledge. For example, Aristotle argues that in order for Being to be knowable, it must be governed by the PNC. The thing must conform to the principles of knowledge in order for it to be graspable.

Although Kant may have gained a new method and critical perspective on knowledge, his critique also initiated a fundamental break between the knowing of Being and Being itself, a break quite foreign to the spirit of Greek thinking. Nonetheless, it would be the fate of German Idealism to heal this divide and *critically return* the knowing of Being to Being itself. This critical return to the spirit of Greek thinking re-introduced the unity of Idealism and Realism enjoyed by Greek philosophical thought. Perhaps there is no better illustration of the contrast between the Kantian and Aristotelian approaches to knowledge than their accounts of the relation between mind and world. Despite their differences, we will discover that on either model of philosophical thinking, the categorial determinations posited by both Aristotle and Kant have trouble escaping the challenge of rhapsodic contingency.[1]

Aristotle, for example, assumes that the subject is a transparent vessel that takes on the Form of what it knows.[2] In *On the Soul* Aristotle takes the position that the self can only have mediated self-knowledge. Aristotle argues that the thinking self only knows itself by way of knowledge of some Form. Since knowledge is of a Form, and the mind itself is not a Form, but that which takes on some Form, the mind cannot immediately know itself. As Aristotle states:

> It is necessary, then, since it thinks of everything, for the mind to be un-mixed with anything, so that, as Anaxagoras says, it may have control, that is, so that it may recognize things. For any alien element that appears in it is a hindrance and impediment; it follows that it cannot have any nature other than that of being capable of doing what it does. That part of the soul that is called the mind (and by

mind I mean that with which the soul thinks and believes) is not a thing that exists in actuality at all before it thinks.[3]

For Aristotle, the mind can only know itself in virtue of knowing a Form, something distinct from itself. By taking on Forms it comes to know itself *as that which takes on Forms*.[4]

As is evident, Aristotle argues that we come to see what the mind is by knowing a Form distinct from it. Aristotle has good motivation to deny Form to the mind. The basic idea is that the mind takes the Form of what it thinks. For this reason, the mind could not know anything other than itself if it had its own Form. The mind, for this reason, must be a *pure potential* that is able to take on the various Forms of the entities that it thinks.[5] By contrast, the mind of God is pure Form, or Being at Work, and for this reason only ever thinks itself. Aristotle is clear that God, or pure self-thinking-thought, can only think itself. Otherwise, it would admit of some potency, and in God there is no potency whatever.

Unlike Plato's account of learning, Aristotle provides an account of the origin of the universal in which it is not the failure of the object of perception that gives insight into Form, but a *psychological* process that brings the universal to the purview of thinking. As usual, Aristotle gives a *military* metaphor to illuminate this process: 'It is like a rout in battle stopped by first one man making a stand and then another, until the original formation has been restored.'[6] Put in terms of universality and particularity, Aristotle elucidates the meaning of the metaphor:

> What we have just said but not said clearly, let us say again: when one of the undifferentiated things makes a stand, there is a primitive universal in the mind (for though one perceives the particular, perception is of the universal—e.g. of man but not of Callias the man); again a stand is made in these, until what has no parts and is universal stands—e.g. such and such an animal stands, until animal does, and in this a stand is made in the same way.[7]

Universals arise by particulars 'taking a stand.' What does Aristotle mean by 'take a stand?' Sense-perception has the particular as its object, for example, the man 'Callias,' not 'man.' For this reason, sense-perception cannot differentiate universals. In this sense, it is logically indiscriminate. Particulars may be remembered, or they may not. The human being is able to remember particulars sensed in the past. This *persistence* of the particular in the mind long after sensation has ceased, or the *recollection* of the particular, is what it means for particulars to 'take a stand.' Instead of fleeing from the mind, as in a *rout*, they remain in memory. Without taking a stand, the particulars are forever lost to the mind, and there is no way to re-identify particulars. In virtue of the particulars taking a stand, one can recognize the *common* feature of one's recollected perception and one's *occurrent* perception. Since the universal is the common feature of the particulars, universals first become identified only on condition of the persistence of the particular in memory. The universals 'man' and 'woman' are established in just this way. From these more universal genera may be formed. Of course, this method is inductive, since we are inferring the universal case *from the particular* case. By running through a group of particulars, we infer that there *is* some common feature. Since the categories are the highest or most universal genera, the categories are the ultimate result of this process of induction. Thus, for Aristotle the categories are *collected empirically*. We should note that for Aristotle the categories can apply to all beings even though they are collected empirically. There is, as a result, the problem that the universality of the categories appears *contingent*, and this is a problem that Fichte will take up again in his critique of Kant.

This process of discovery cumulates in an act of *intuitive induction* and ought not be conflated with the modern sense of *empirical* induction. In intuitive induction, we do *not construct* the universal, since we *discover* it in a flash of insight, or 'intuition,' in which we see the 'what it is to be' of something. But we do infer the universal from the particular cases, and for this reason the process deserves the name 'induction.' Henceforth, we *abstract* out that *given* feature, for example 'man' and think it separately from the particular, for example 'Callias.' For Aristotle, induction is the process by which distinct subjects and attributes are first identified.

Because the mind itself has no Form, the mind can only know itself *indirectly*. Were it to directly know itself, it would imbue itself with a Form that it does not possess. If we *directly* think the mind as that *which takes on Forms*, then we have contradicted ourselves, for the mind cannot grasp itself directly. Thus, we must admit that we never grasp the Form of the mind as 'that which takes on Forms.' Yet, if upon turning to think the mind as 'that which takes on Forms,' we are not thinking ourselves, yet by necessity some other Form, then we are not thinking the mind as 'that which takes on Forms.' Therefore, we never encounter the mind as such and are unjustified in positing the mind as anything, including 'that which takes on Forms.' If the mind is nothing, we cannot know that it is such. It appears that mediated self-knowing, as it appears in Aristotle, may indeed provide transparent access to what is distinct from the mind. Surely, that is the power of Aristotle's account, though it unfortunately denies us any access to what the mind itself is. Indeed, it appears that we must admit that the mind can only know itself directly.

Any philosophy which does not inquire into the knowing of Being, but instead immediately inquiries into Being itself is *dogmatic*, since it fails to be critical of the knowing that underlies the scientific appropriation of the object. Kant's philosophy is critical exactly in this respect: he attempts to lay bare the conditions under which the knowing of an object is possible from the side of subjectivity. Reason must set the limits of its own knowing, in order to know what it is and is not capable of grasping. For this reason, Kant's methodology takes *epistemology as first philosophy*, since knowing is the primary object of philosophy, not Being. Being can be an object of philosophy only once we have determined what reason is capable of grasping—that is—only after reason thinks itself.

One essential assumption of Kant's methodology is the separation of knowing from Being. The very turn from Being to the knowing of Being as the object of the inquiry implies that *the object of metaphysics is distinct from the object of epistemology*. Indeed, that the inquiry into Being characteristic of Ancient Greek philosophy is deemed separate from the inquiry into the knowing of Being implies this difference. Fichte, following Kant, argues that transcendental philosophy 'abstracts from existence':

> The question proposed, namely: How is an existent possible for us? . . . It inquires as to the ground of the predicate of existence in general. . . . The answer, if it is to be an answer to this question . . . must similarly abstract from all existence.[8]

Following Kant's understanding of the concept of existence, Fichte identifies existence with having sensory determination or in other terminology, with having *intuitive* fulfillment:

> All existence, for us, is necessarily sensory in character.[9]

Thus, for Fichte and Kant the abstraction from existence is an *abstraction from sensory intuition*. Fichte's claim that transcendental philosophy *abstracts from existence* can be further clarified by reading Kant's method in terms of *analysis*.

Kant is a logician whose method is fundamentally *analytical*. His question takes the *concept of experience* as the object. The transcendental investigator asks: what is it for experience to be what it is? Or more exactly: what are the universal and necessary conditions for experience as such? Understood this way, Kant is asking about the *logical structure* of experience as experience. In order for any knowledge to be derived from the content of experience, experience itself must be given. Of course, all knowledge derived from experience is empirical or *a posteriori*. Thus, our question may be formulated another way: what is the condition for the possibility of empirical knowledge? Since the ingredients constitutive of experience cannot be derived from experience, we must inquire into those elements that are independent of all experience, the *a priori* conditions for any empirical knowledge, or the *a priori* conditions for the synthetic *a posteriori*.

Accordingly, Kant's arguments in the *Transcendental Aesthetic* and the *Transcendental Analytic* constitute separate acts of *abstraction from empirical existence*, for each means to uncover the *a priori* conditions that make that empirical consciousness possible. Since the transcendental inquirer is not interested in what is derived from the content of experience, but instead is interested in what is necessary for any content, Kant proceeds by investigating what structures constitutive of consciousness are necessary for *empirical consciousness*. In the *Transcendental Doctrine of the Elements*, Kant *analyzes* two faculties necessary for experience: Sensibility and the Understanding. The analysis of the former is called the *Transcendental Aesthetic*, while the latter is called the *Transcendental Analytic*. In each division of the *Transcendental Doctrine of the Elements*, Kant gives two types of arguments: the Metaphysical and the Transcendental Deduction. The *Metaphysical Deduction* analyzes what is contained in the faculty *a priori*. The *Transcendental Deduction* takes the result of the *Metaphysical Deduction* as an assumption and shows how the elements deduced in that deduction make synthetic, *a priori* judgments possible.[10] Indeed, Kant's critique of Aristotle's account of the categories is contingent upon his endorsement of the *transcendental* method. More specifically, Kant rejects the derivation of the categories from experience. A brief overview of Kant's *analytic* method will indicate the way he means to improve upon Aristotle's empirical account of the categories.

In order to proceed in the analytic of Sensibility, Kant first thinks *Sensibility by itself* apart from the Understanding. Secondly, he thinks what Sensibility *qua* Sensibility is if one were to remove all sensuous, empirical content from the faculty. Likewise, in the analytic of the Understanding, Kant shall think the *Understanding by itself* and remove all that is sensuous and empirical from the faculty. More generally, Kant's aim is to separate out the matter of the appearance and think the form of the appearance, that by which appearance is ordered.

Sensibility is our capacity to receive representations in virtue of being affected by objects. *Qua* receptive, Sensibility is a passive faculty in which one simply finds representations given. Thus, Sensibility is that faculty in which representations (*Vorstellungen*) are given. In contrast, Understanding is the faculty in virtue of which given representations are thought. In sensation, Sensibility relates to the object intuitively—that is, it has an *immediate relation to its object*. An immediate relation is one in which there is no mediating factor standing between the subject and the object.

Following the same pattern of reasoning in the *Transcendental Aesthetic*, Kant's metaphysical deduction of the categories *isolates the Understanding* from Sensibility in order to *analyze* what is pure in that faculty, that is what is contained in the faculty *a priori*. A leading claim of this analysis is Kant's basic principles that 'concepts without intuitions are empty' while 'intuitions without concepts are blind.' Since intuition is only given in Sensibility, we know that the Understanding, the faculty of concepts, is *not intuitive*. As a non-intuitive faculty, Understanding is not receptive. That the faculty of concepts is not intuitive is expressed in the proposition that 'concepts without intuitions are empty.' Since intuition is an immediate relation to an object, and concepts are not intuitive, concepts cannot relate to their objects immediately. Given that the concept relates to the object, the non-immediate relation to an object cannot be anything more than a *mediated relation*. Thus, in themselves concepts are opposed to intuitions in their relation to the object.[11]

Kant's *Metaphysical Deduction*—an analysis of the *a priori* content of the faculty of Understanding—deduces the 12 categories from the 12 forms of judgment. For Kant, the attribution of the concept to the object is reducible to the act of judgment, for judgment is nothing more than the attribution of the universal to the singular, for example 'the singular is universal.' For this reason, no representation is subsumed under a concept except in a judgment. It is in a judgment that different representations are ordered under a common one, for example different bodies are ordered under 'body.' Kant calls the unity of action that orders different representations under a common one a *function*. Since judgment is just the application of a concept, each distinct form of judgment contains its own distinct concept. Each form of judgment, simply as a form of judgment, is formal, for it *abstracts from what is being judged*, or the content of judgment. Given that concepts only apply to objects in the act of judgment, Kant postulates that the *a priori* concepts inherent in Understanding, the categories or unifying functions in acts of judgment, can be discovered by enumerating every form of judgment *per se*. For example, in the universal judgment, the category of 'unity' is the operative concept. However, simply specifying what category is operative in the judgment does *not* specify what is unified. By itself, the category, like the judgment, is also formal, for if the category, simply as the category, specified what it unified, it would not be a concept, since concepts without intuitions are *empty*. In sum, we may say that it is through the study of *formal judgment*, and *formal reasoning* in general, that Kant finds his clue to discovering the *a priori* categories inherent in the Understanding.

Kant argues that Aristotle did not possess a singular principle for the deduction of his categories. Because he lacked a principle, Aristotle collected them haphazardly, or what is the same, via empirical description. Kant is systematic insofar as he derives his categories from a *single* principle: *the table of judgments*. To put it briefly, Kant *analyzes the categories* out of the 12 forms of judgment in which they are given and thereby means to avoid the contingent dimension of Aristotle's empirical account.

As Anthony Bruno points out, Fichte both (i) critiques Kant's metaphysical deduction of the categories and (ii) sets out to provide an absolute foundation for Kant's account of the categories.[12] Fichte critiques this method as an *unscientific* procedure, since for Fichte Kant advances the categories as *brute contingent facts* from which the transcendental deduction proceeds:[13]

> For the peculiarity of our understanding, that it is able to bring about the unity of apperception *a priori* only by means of categories and only through precisely this kind and number of them, a further ground may be offered just as little as one can be offered for why we have precisely these and no other functions for judgments or for why space and time are the sole forms of our possible intuition.[14]

Because Kant thinks one cannot give an account of the plurality of the forms of judgment, neither can an account be given of the *plurality* of the functions of judgment. Thus, the deduction is grounded in the mere *stipulation* that the 12 forms of judgment and their correlative functions *truly* reflects the *a priori* forms of formal judgment and that it *exhaustively explicates* the varieties of that *a priori* form. Because the necessity of these forms of judgment and their correlative functions are not established by any rational ground or principle, Kant's deduction depends upon a *contingent stipulation*. In order to be scientific, and avoid the charge of being just as *rhapsodic* as Aristotle's derivation of his categories, Kant's table of categories must be grounded in a more fundamental principle. To put it simply: despite some fundamental differences in their method and their conception of the primary object of philosophical knowledge, both Aristotle and Kant have the same problem: their categories are contingent, when they ought to be necessary. The *Wissenschaftslehre* aims to secure that single fundamental scientific principle upon which the scientific deduction and the necessity of Kant's categories depends. For Fichte this is one reason that

> Nowhere did Kant consider the foundation of all philosophy.[15]

Because transcendental philosophy is an inquiry of the subject into its own knowing, the I must not only be able to think the *Mannigfaltigkeit* given in sensible intuition by means of categories, but the I must also be able to *think the I* that thinks the manifold. Indeed, since categories only apply *to possible objects of experience*, categories would not mediate between the I and its knowledge of itself, for they only apply to possible objects of experience, that is phenomena given in sensible intuition. Indeed, categories only apply to possible objects of sensible intuition, and since the transcendental subject itself is not an object of intuition, categories cannot apply to the self-knowing of the transcendental subjectivity by which the results of transcendental analysis are secured. Accordingly, for Fichte the intellectual self-apprehension of the I *cannot be mediated* by means of categories, but must be *immediate*. Indeed, were the self-knowledge of the I initially mediated by categories, then it would not account for them, but would *presuppose* them from the outset. Thus, transcendental analysis has its ground in an *immediate intellectual act* that takes itself as its own object. Since immediate self-knowledge has no intermediaries, it is thereby *a simple* identity of subject and object.[16] As Hegel writes:

> In the transcendental intuition all opposition is suspended, all distinction between the universe as constructed by and for the intelligence, and the universe as an organization intuited as objective and appearing independent, is nullified.[17]

To summarize, for Fichte it is only from *immediate* self-knowledge that one could have any mediated knowledge, whether that be mediated *a priori* or *a posteriori* knowledge.

In order to know what it is to know, philosophy must achieve self-knowledge. Since 'intellectual intuition' is an immediate relation to an object that is not sensory,[18] but intellectual, the immediate thinking of oneself constitutes an act of *intellectual intuition*. In his *Versuch einer Neuen Darstellung*, Fichte explicitly characterizes this self-knowledge as intellectual intuition:

> This intuiting of himself that is required of the philosopher, in performing the act whereby the self arises for him, I refer to as intellectual intuition.[19]

Although Fichte's introduction of intellectual intuition is distinct from Kant's definition of the same term, it is nonetheless a deviation from Kant, who only acknowledges sensible intuition, the immediate consciousness of an object given in time and space.[20] Fichte acknowledges that he and Kant are in disagreement over the use of the term.[21] For instance, Fichte acknowledges that Kant repudiates the use of intellectual intuition for accounting for self-knowledge in the following passage:

> Just because it can and must teach us immediately, we ought not to confuse the pure active self-consciousness . . . with the faculty of intuition, or maybe conclude therefrom that we possess a nonsensory, intellectual power of intuition.[22]

Because both Kant and Aristotle understand self-knowledge as fundamentally mediated experiences (either indirectly through the knowledge of Form or via categories), self-knowledge is just as problematic in the case of Kant as it is in the case of Aristotle. Each system of thought, despite their profound differences, share common limits: each ultimately finds itself saddled with contingent categories and problems accounting for self-knowledge. Unlike Kant, for Fichte self-consciousness comes 'solely' from intellectual intuition.[23] Because intellectual intuition estab-lishes the truth of categorical determinations, it cannot itself be *proven from concepts*. As Fichte writes,

We cannot prove from concepts that Intellectual Intuition exists.[24]

This does not mean that intellectual intuition is completely divorced from sensory intuition. Fichte claims that although it is not sensory it is con-nected with sensory intuition and that the latter would be impossible without it.[25] Following Kant, Fichte argues that intellectual intuition is discovered by *an act of analysis*. By resolving the whole of experience into its parts, for example categories, intuitions, and so on, the transcen-dental investigator arrives by such analysis at the ultimate condition of all experience: intellectual intuition.[26]

Having arrived at intellectual intuition by having abstracted away from existence or sensory intuition, Fichte consistently proclaims that 'existence is not primary.'[27] Because intellectual intuition is constituted by an immediate relation of subject to object, there is no mediating prin-ciple that could differentiate the subject from its object. As a simple and non-differentiated knowing, intellectual intuition does not contain any limitation, for all limitation requires some distinction. As infinite, it is not a finite object, or a thing. Fichte is clear that it is an *act* of self-consciousness.[28] As the first principle it produces objects, but cannot itself be reduced to one. Having abstracted from existence, intellectual intuition 'refers not to existence at all, but to action.'[29] Since the ground is always beyond what it grounds, and intellectual intuition is the ground of existence, transcendental philosophy inquires as to the ground of the predicate of existence.[30]

Naturally, this raises an important question: is the act of intellectual intuition completely non-existent? If intellectual intuition is the ground of existence, then ought it not follow that *intellectual intuition does not exist*? Fichte's consistently Kantian procedure on this point indicates a point of trouble in Kant's philosophy, which leads Fichte to introduce another kind of existence distinct from the kind employed in Kant's criti-cal philosophy.

In order for transcendental subjectivity to be subject to transcendental *analysis* by the transcendental philosopher, transcendental subjectivity must *exist*. Markus Gabriel raises one of the central questions of German Idealism in his book *Transcendental Ontology*: what are the *ontological conditions* for the possibility of subjectivity?[31] Given that the transcen-dental subject must be, it is not evident that transcendental subjectivity possesses the resources for elucidating its own being. If we take 'being' in the sense of *sein*, we know from Kant's famous critique of the ontological argument that 'being' is not a predicate.[32] When we say of some concept that it is (or has being), we mean that it is given in *intuition*. The concept of $100 has being because it is given in intuition. But transcendental subjectivity as such is not given *as a whole* in intuition. If it were, it would be an object contained within another transcendental consciousness, which would engender an infinite regress. Still less can we say of transcendental subjectivity that it 'exists' or 'possibly exists' or 'necessarily exists,' for these are modalities which are contained in the Understanding. Since the categories of the Understanding apply to intuition, and not to themselves, we cannot say of the Understanding or transcendental subjectivity as a whole that it 'exists,' 'is possible,' or 'is necessary.' To put the problem yet another way, we might also ask whether transcendental subjectivity is itself a phenomenon or Noumenon. If transcendental subjectivity were a mere phenomenon, any analysis into the structure of subjectivity would be an appearance of what it is rather than what it is simpliciter. What is more, it would be contained within itself, which would initiate an infinite regress, and an infinite series of transcendental subjectivities would be presupposed in which it could appear. But if transcendental subjectivity were a Noumenon, its structure and contents ought to remain utterly inscrutable to the transcendental philosopher.[33]

Thus, Fichte must introduce another sense of existence in order to be able to account for the very *existence of intellectual intuition*. Indeed, in order for reason to know itself, it must know what it really is. Although transcendental philosophy abstracts from existence, it does not abstract from its own existence. Fichte calls the ground of existence *existence for itself*.[34] Accordingly, there is 'existence' and 'existence for itself':

> Reason is absolutely independent; it exists only for itself; but for it, too, is all that exists.[35]

What is absolutely independent only exists *in relation to itself*, and is therefore not relative to another, but only relative to itself. Because it thinks itself, it is that which is simultaneously subject and object—it is *for itself* in addition to being *by itself*. Through intellectual intuition, the self does not think the self as it appears, but as it *truly is*. Thus, the intellectual intuition of the I is the self-grounding of the *Self-in-Itself*.[36] The Self-in-Itself is not a 'thing-in-itself,' since for Fichte, nothing can be said to 'exist' that is not conditioned by self-thinking thought, and in this sense no thing in itself can be said to 'exist' since it could only be independently of self-thinking reason. What is more, appealing to a 'thing-in-itself' is the mode of explanation in dogmatism, a kind of appeal that cannot account for the *existence of representations*. Nonetheless, intellectual intuition still exists 'in itself' as the *noumenal object of Nous—intellectual intuition*. In short, by introducing the concept of existence *for itself*, Fichte can account for the existence of the transcendental subjectivity that cannot be the subject of the predicate of existence in a merely empirical sense. For this reason, it seems to me that Fichte's use of the

Although a close reading of the tradition shows that the various figures within the tradition all grapple with this problem, it is *not* a new problem. In fact, the problem already shows up in the attempt of Neo-Platonism to derive the whole of existence, including that of plurality, from *the One*. While Fichte and the early Schelling attempt to ground all knowledge on one single first *epistemic* principle—the I—Plotinus attempts to ground *all being* on one *metaphysical* principle—the One. In order to demonstrate that this systematic problem affecting the program of German Idealism is a perennial problem in philosophy, I will begin by explicating the problem in the context of German Idealism and thereafter show how an *analogous* problem affects the prospects of the Neo-Platonic account of emanation. Indeed, their first principles are not the same, and among other important differences, their philosophical programs are distinguished by the difference in the *primary* object of knowledge. Although each is beset by its *own* set of systematic problems and accompanying historical context, a similar *systematic* problem undermines the prospects of both programs.

Because the very *same* objection can be raised against both programs of philosophy, it follows that the difference in the object of knowing— the knowing of Being or the knowing of knowing—does not in any way affect the problem at hand. Thus, the source of the problem cannot lie in the difference constituted by their epistemic or metaphysical orientation *per se*. Instead, the problem must lie in common principles advanced by both programs of philosophy, namely that each attempts to derive philosophical knowledge from a *single* and *undifferentiated* foundation, while also maintaining that *discursive* knowledge is structured by a complete separation of the principles of identity and difference. Thus, the advantage of this comparative approach to the problem highlights what is essential and accidental to the formulation of the problem.

Accordingly, our analysis will show that the problem of the disappearance of the Absolute in the tradition of German Idealism as well as Neo-Platonism is grounded in a fundamental *incongruity* between the structure of logical or *conceptual* determination (or in older language, the form of the *universal*) and any philosophical program that demands the derivation of all Being or knowledge from one self-identical principle that is completely devoid of plurality and difference. Hegel's radical solution to the problem of the possibility of the Absolute—the *One and All*—will hinge upon his refutation of the possibility of a *first principle* of all knowledge, as well as any commitment to the *absolute separation* of principles of identity and difference.

Kant's Critique of a General Criterion of Truth

Schelling's uncontroversial claim that all knowledge is of what is *true* entails that false knowledge is a contradiction in terms. And truth, according to Schelling, is the *correspondence* of the subjective with the objective, or the correspondence of the presentation with its proper object. Hence, *knowledge depends upon the correspondence of subjective with the objective*, the presentation of the object with the object itself. From the very outset, Schelling identifies subjectivity with the self, consciousness, and intelligence, while objectivity is identified with unconsciousness and nature.

Since the philosopher aims to give an *account of* or *reason for* knowledge, this would also demand an account for the *fact* of truth. In order to give a *reason* for truth, one cannot *begin with the fact of truth*. As Schelling states, in order to give an account of the identity of subject and object, one must *separate* the subject from the object. Given that any account of truth must begin from the *separation* of the presentation from the object, one can account for the possibility of truth in two ways. Either one can begin from the subject alone, and from it derive an object, or one can begin from the object alone, and from it derive the subject. Accordingly, Schelling divides the whole of philosophy into *two sciences*, according to the method by which each attempts to account for *truth*. While transcendental philosophy begins from *thought alone*, philosophy of nature begins from nature alone.[53]

Rather than focus on the (albeit very important) dispute between Schelling and Fichte regarding the (putatively) autonomous character of Schelling's philosophy of nature, I mention the division between the two sciences in order to demonstrate that each is primarily concerned with establishing *Truth itself*. Because Schelling's system of 1800 demonstrates the unity of the subject and object from the side of the subject, our focus will concern the relation of *transcendental philosophy* to *Absolute Truth* itself. The project of *accounting for truth* raises a significant methodological demand and a series of impasses.

Early German Idealism, from Fichte's 1794 *Grundlage der Gesamten Wissenschaftslehre* to Schelling's *System des Transzendentalen Idealismus*, attempts to ground all knowledge on a *single* principle. In *STI*, Schelling's argument for a first principle of knowledge is derived from an argument *against* the possibility of the existence of *multiple principles of truth*. Schelling writes:

> There can only be one such principle. For all truth is absolutely on a par. There may certainly be degrees of probability, but there are no degrees of truth; one truth is as true as another. But that the truth of all propositions of knowledge is absolutely equal is impossible, if they derive their truth from different principles (or mediating factors); so there can only be one (mediating) principle in all knowledge.[54]

Schelling's argument is simple but effective. Because truth is the *correspondence* of a presentation with its object, a presentation either corresponds with its object or it does not—it cannot correspond *more or less* with its object. To put it simply: a presentation (of some state of affairs) is *either* true or false. If 'S is P' is true, then it corresponds with its object. If 'S is Q' is true, it corresponds with its object. Insofar as *both* are true (both correspond with their respective objects), neither is *truer* than the other. As Schelling puts it, 'the truth of all proposition of knowledge is absolutely equal.' It may be *more likely to be true* that 'S is P' rather than that 'S is Q', but from this it does not follow that 'S is P' is truer than 'S is Q.' Were it possible for truths to derive their truth or (their property of *being true*) from multiple principles of truth, then it would be possible for one truth to be more true than another. Since it is impossible for one truth to be more true than another, it follows that there cannot be multiple principles of truth.

Truth would be *multi-vocal* were there many principles of truth. Given that there are not many principles, the equality of all truths entails that truth is meant *univocally*. When one predicates 'true' of a proposition, one is attributing *one sense* of truth to the true proposition. The single principle of all truth is that (univocal sense) *in virtue of which* presentations of the object are true. Such a principle of truth would not simply be one truth among others, but *Truth* itself: that *in virtue of which* any true proposition would be true. In short: each truth is just as true as any other truth, because each is true in virtue of the very same principle of truth: Truth itself. Because all knowledge is *true*, all knowledge depends upon the very same principle.

Since transcendental philosophy is a knowing of knowledge, the principle of knowledge cannot be outside knowledge, otherwise it would be *un*knowable. Were the principle of knowledge beyond the domain of knowledge, then the principle of knowledge could not be known. Rather, the principle of knowledge—that in virtue of which there is knowledge—must itself be an *instance* of knowledge. Indeed, were the principles of knowledge not themselves known, then knowledge would rest upon something unknown. Were this the case, then all knowing would depend upon unknowing, and therefore *nothing would be known*.

Since Schelling's argument for the first principle of knowledge here depends upon an argument for a *first principle of truth*, the very same claim ought to be made for the latter. Given that transcendental philosophy attempts to ground truth in *subjectivity alone*, subjectivity must be the principle of truth. Were the components of truth *not themselves true*, then truth *would not be true*. Were subjectivity not itself a unity of subject (presentation and object), then subjectivity would be *false*. Were this the case, then truth would depend upon the truth of falsehood—which would be absurd. Accordingly, just as in the case of knowledge, the principle of truth in transcendental philosophy, namely subjectivity, *must itself be an instance of truth*. The principle of truth cannot exist beyond truth.

Likewise, in the case of the philosophy of nature, objectivity is posited as the principle of truth (namely, that in virtue of which the object corresponds with the subject). Were objectivity (a condition for truth) itself untrue—were it lacking the correspondence of subjectivity with objectivity—then the unity of subject and object would depend upon a falsehood. In short: *the components of truth*, subjectivity and objectivity, must themselves be true in order for truth, the correspondence of subjectivity and objectivity, to itself be true.

Philosophy aims to be a science of knowledge. Schelling defines *science* as a body of propositions that is structured by a determinate form. Science is a *body* of knowledge that has *content* and *form*. Moreover, insofar as *systematic* knowing derives the truth of the propositions in science from the truth of *one fundamental principle*, the characteristic form of philosophy is that of a system of knowledge such that the content of the system (the true propositions) are structured by their *mutual dependence* upon the single, first principle. Given that no other discipline can determine the form of science for philosophy, philosophy must itself be what the form of systematic science ought to be. Hence, philosophy is a *science of science.*[55]

In his *Differenzschrift*, Hegel affirms Schelling's philosophy as an advance over Fichte because Fichte only acknowledges subjectivity as a unity of subject and object. In his philosophy of nature, Schelling acknowledges that *the object too* must be a unity of the subject and the object:

> For absolute identity to be the principle of an entire system it is necessary that both subject and object be posited as Subject-Object. In Fichte's system identity constitutes itself only as subjective Subject-Object. [But] this subjective Subject-Object needs an objective Subject-Object to complete it.[56]

Of course, by doing so Schelling raised the object to an Absolute status—for alongside transcendental philosophy—it contains the *whole of truth* (both subject and object and their identity). Schelling's philosophy of nature constitutes his so-called *Objective Idealism*, the complementary and completing science to Fichte's Subjective Idealism.

This argument in Part I of *STI* appears to contradict Schelling's division of philosophy into two autonomous sciences that is programmatically outlined in the introduction. If there are two principles in virtue of which there is truth (nature and the self), then there is more than one mediating principle of truth, neither of which is reducible to the other. Yet, Schelling argues that there cannot be more than one principle of truth. Thus, either it is false that there is only one principle of truth or each of the two sciences must be reducible to a higher principle. It seems to me that the principle of Absolute Identity in his *Presentation of*

My System of Philosophy (1801) means to alleviate this tension within the *STI* by appealing to a *higher* principle beyond both transcendental philosophy and the philosophy of nature. Ironically, Hegel will follow Schelling's insight in his identity philosophy that transcendental philosophy (of mind) and philosophy of nature requires a ground beyond themselves. But this incongruity endemic to Schelling's early reflections on the systematic unity of philosophy is not the main problem of the *STI*. Rather—at the outset Schelling considers *two objections* to the possibility of a first principle of philosophy.

The first objection stems from the inherent *circularity* of philosophical knowledge. If the science of knowledge seeks the *underlying* principle of truth, yet this underlying principle must itself be a unity of subjectivity and objectivity, in order to be *a true ground of truth*, one can only account for truth by *assuming truth* from the very beginning. Rather than begin with the separation of subject from object, the subject must always already be in agreement with its object. Whether this principle of truth be subjectivity or objectivity (self or nature), every attempt to give a reason for truth begs the question. Accordingly, in order to give an account of truth, one must embark upon not only a *science* of knowledge but also a *science of the science* of knowledge. But since the *principle of the principle* of truth ought also be *true*, to arrive at the ground of truth one must embark upon another science in order to discover the ultimate principle of truth: the science of the science of the science of knowledge, *ad infinitum*.[57] Truth—it appears—is either not true at all—for it is grounded on falsehoods, or it should have no ground whatsoever.

Having committed himself to a first principle, and rejecting the possibility that truth could be grounded on falsehood, Schelling calls for a *self-mediating* first principle that *generates form and content*. On the one hand, because the principle of knowledge is the principle of *all* knowledge, it is not true in virtue something else. Thus, it is *immediately* true. On the other hand, because it is an *instance of truth*, it appears to depend upon the correspondence of given, *antecedent* principles: namely subjectivity and objectivity. Thus, it is also a mediated truth: a truth that is the result of a process of unification. But because it is first, it cannot depend upon antecedent principles of mediation. Thus, the principle of knowledge must be *self-mediated*, and is constituted by a unity of opposition.[58] The principle must both be responsible for the *content* that it unifies as well as the *form* of the unification. Thus, Schelling infers that

> For this purpose we should require to discover in the intellect a point at which, by one and the same indivisible act of primordial cognition, both content and form are generated.[59]

By establishing subjectivity as a self-mediating first principle, it becomes possible for Schelling to show how subjectivity could give rise to objectivity *by itself*. The *self-mediated* character of the first principle that philosophy aims to know reflects the structure of philosophical knowing itself. Since philosophy is that science of first principles that *knows* knowledge itself, philosophy must also know its own knowing.[60] Thus, philosophy is a science that is constituted by *self-knowing*. The transcendental philosopher, she who is herself a (non-empirical) subject, knows knowing by knowing her *own subjectivity* as the principle of knowing. Schelling famously writes that transcendental philosophy—as a philosophical knowing of subjective knowing, is the 'lamp of the whole system of knowledge, but it only casts its light ahead only, not behind.'[61] By means of self-knowledge, philosophical knowing must ground its own claims to know. Since philosophy proceeds by way of self-knowledge, the very method of philosophy already indicates what the content of the first principle of transcendental philosophy ought to be: *self-consciousness*. Nonetheless, given the problematic nature of self-consciousness for both Aristotle and Kant, Schelling's approach to self-consciousness invokes fundamental deviations from their accounts.

Before proceeding to explicate *Section Two, The Deduction of the Principle Itself*, Schelling raises *the second fundamental impasse* that appears to undermine any attempt to uncover a single principle of Truth and Knowledge: the problem of the *general criterion* of truth. This second impasse is a reformulation of the initial Kantian critique of dialectic as the *logic of illusion*, which he formulates in his *Doctrine of Elements*, Part III, *On the Division of General Logic into Analytic and Dialectic*.[62] Schelling formulates the problem in two different ways. Consider the second formulation:

> Let us consider any formal proposition, A=A, as the highest; the logical element in this proposition is merely the form of identity between A and A; but where, then, do I get A itself from? This question can assuredly be answered, not from the proposition itself, but only from a higher one. The analysis A=A presupposes the synthesis A. So it is evident that no formal principle can be thought without presupposing a material principle, or a material principle without presupposing a formal one.[63]

All thinking of an object is governed by the *principle of identity*. Whatever thought I have of an object, the thought must be self-identical. Were it *possible* for the thought to be different from itself, then it would be possible for the very same 'A' to be 'not A,' which would be a contradiction. Given that contradictions cannot be true,[64] the very *possibility* of the *truth of* any thought of an object depends upon its adherence to the principle of identity.

As a principle of *identity*, it imposes the self-same universal form on all thoughts: each is self-identical. But the fact that each thought is self-identical does not specify *what* the thoughts themselves are. Because it only imposes one universal form of self-identity, it cannot *differentiate* the self-identical contents from one another. Thus, in order to know the content of thinking, one must appeal to a principle that is completely independent of the principle of identity: the principle of difference. Given the fact that all thinking of an object must be self-identical in order to be true (it is a *necessary* condition for its truth), and from the mere self-identity of thinking one cannot derive the content of what is thought, one must always presuppose *two separate principles* in order to account for the form and content of thought: a principle of identity and a principle of difference.

How does this argument directly problematize the ambitions of transcendental philosophy? Transcendental philosophy aims to show how Intelligence can produce truth *by itself*. Since truth is the *agreement* of the thought with its object, transcendental philosophy must show how thinking *can produce its own object*. In Schelling's words, transcendental philosophy concerns the 'passing from the world of presentation into the real world or a determining of the objective by a presentation.' Indeed, transcendental philosophy proceeds from the subject, and has the 'objective arise from' it.[65] But if the thinking of the object *only* contains the form of identity, then thinking *by itself* is necessarily *insufficient* to deduce the content of the thought. Thus, one cannot in principle proceed from *thinking alone* to knowledge of the truth of its object. As Schelling points out, we cannot simply posit a material or *non-formal* principle as the *first* principle, for all thinking of an object appears to presuppose the laws of thinking, such as the principle of identity.[66] Thus, just as much as we cannot derive the material from the formal, we cannot derive the formal from the material without always already presupposing the formal principle from the outset.

Although Kant does not formulate the impasse in terms of first principles, he does employ a very similar impasse in order to motivate the *duality of principles* that is constitutive of his transcendental logic of truth that he develops directly thereafter in Part IV of the *Transcendental Logic*. Kant claims that a 'general and certain criterion of truth' mistakenly treats logic as an *organon* rather than as a mere *canon* for judging.[67] General logic that is employed as an *organon* for the *production of objective assertions* is 'dialectic' and a logic of illusion. Schelling's argument for a first principle of Knowledge attempts to establish a *single* principle of all truth in virtue of which presentations of the object are true. Accordingly, Schelling's investigation into the first principle is an inquiry into the 'general and certain criterion of truth,' which Kant derides as an illusionary dialectic. Since Schelling's transcendental logic is an attempt to show how the subjective thinking of an object is sufficient for producing objective assertions, for Kant Schelling's transcendental philosophy would be a logic of illusion.

Kant argues that there cannot be *one principle* of the truth of all knowledge:

> If truth consists in the agreement of a cognition with its object, then this object must thereby be distinguished from the others; for a cognition is false if it does not agree with the object to which it is related even if it contains something that could well be valid of other objects. Now a general criterion of truth would be that which was valid of all cognitions without any distinction among their objects. But it is clear that with such a criterion one abstracts from all content of cognition (relation to its object), yet truth concerns precisely this content, it would be completely impossible and absurd to ask for a mark of truth of this content of cognition, and thus it is clear that a sufficient and yet at the same time general sign of truth cannot possibility be provided. Since above we have called the content of a cognition its matter, one must therefore say that no general sign of the truth of the matter of cognition can be demanded, because it is self-contradictory.[68]

The *content* of any particular thought of an object expresses that *something is the case* about a specific object (or set of objects). In order to evaluate *the truth* of that content, namely whether the presentation agrees with the object, one *must* be able to *differentiate* among the various objects to which the content of the thought refers. A thought is true if it agrees with its object—and false if it does not. Were one to attempt to develop one universal criterion of truth, this criterion would necessarily apply to *every possible object* of thought. Because it would apply to every possible object of thought, it could not in principle *differentiate* among the various objects of thought. If such a universal criterion of truth could *not* in principle differentiate among the possible objects of thought, and differentiating the possible objects is a necessary condition for differentiating (what is stated in) the content of the thought, a universal criterion of truth could not in principle differentiate the contents of one thought from another. As Kant writes, such a criterion would necessarily 'abstract from all contents of cognition.' Since the evaluation of the truth of some content of thought requires differentiating the objects of cognition from each other (as well as the contents of the thoughts about them), and a general criterion of truth abstracts from the content of thought, it *could not in principle* evaluate the truth of any thought about an object.

Because a general criterion of truth abstracts from the content of the thought, it could only specify a *common form of thinking*. To sum up: since truth concerns the *relation of thought to its object*, while a general criterion of truth abstracts from the content of thought (and could thereby *only* specify a *common form* of the thought about the object), a general criterion of truth abstracts from the relation of thought to the object. Such a criterion would only be able to evaluate the truth of a thought in virtue of its *form alone, independently* of its relation to the object. But if truth is the *agreement* of the thought with its object, then a universal criterion of truth would be *contradictory*, for it would evaluate the *relation of the thought* to its object in a way that is *independent of the relation* to the object.[69]

On the one hand, there can only be one principle of truth. On the other hand, such a principle seems impossible. Schelling recognizes that in order to transform the logic of illusion into a *logic of truth*, he must rescue the general criterion of truth from Kant's objection.

Fichte will proclaim with Kant that the self-thinking thought of transcendental philosophy must account for existence after having abstracted from the question of existence:

> The question proposed, namely: How is an existent possible for us? . . . It inquires as to the ground of the predicate of existence in general. . . . The answer, if it is to be an answer to this question . . . must similarly abstract from all existence.[70]

Since self-thinking thought grounds all existence, Fichte must give an account of the predicate of existence after having abstracted it away. To put it simply, even if 'existence' is always to be qualified as existence for a subjectivity (as is formulated in the synthetic unity of apperception), Fichte, like Schelling after him, intends to *ground existence in one principle*.

For Schelling in his *STI*, the first principle of all knowing is also the principle of all *forms of existence*. Indeed, Schelling is clear that it is the principle of *nature itself*. Schelling claims to deduce matter as well as organic existence from the self-knowing of the I.[71] Of course, his ambition here is insatiable, for it ultimately means to account not only for nature but also culture, such as human history.[72] Indeed, for Schelling philosophical knowing is a re-construction in time of an eternal act of the self, such that the process whereby the objective comes to be is certainly not to be understood as a creation in time—rather it is an eternal creation:

> For if it is through self-consciousness that all limitation originates, and thus all time as well, this original act cannot itself occur in time; hence, of the rational being as such, one can no more say that it has begun to exist, than that it has existed for all time; the self as self is absolutely eternal, that is, outside time altogether. But now our secondary act necessarily occurs at a particular moment in time.[73]

Here it is obvious enough that Schelling's account of truth is not indifferent to metaphysics. Rather, he portrays the epistemic project of philosophy as a temporal, though rational, re-construction of the eternal (non-temporal) production of reason from a first principle. For both thinkers, even if transcendental philosophy requires that thought be initially separated from existence, the system can only be completed once thought has accounted for that existence from which it had initially withdrawn itself.

Beyond Analytic Thinking: Towards a Synthetic First Principle

As is obvious, Fichte and Schelling's pursuit of a first principle of truth is in fundamental conflict with the fundamental duality of principles in Kant's philosophy. But the conceptual problem raised by Schelling in *STI* (and Kant in his *CPR*) requires deeper scrutiny in terms of the concepts of analysis and synthesis. Indeed, it is by reflecting on the way that these terms appear in the problem that Schelling arrives at his solution to the Kantian-style critique. Not only does an investigation into these concepts bear fruit for Schelling, but it also illuminates Jacobi's critique of Fichte as *nihilism*.

Given that formal logic cannot produce truth on its own, Kant famously posits *two* separate *principles*, whose *co-operation* can produce truth. In addition to the *Understanding*—by which one conceives the object, consciousness is also determined by *Sensibility*—by which one *intuits* the object. The former relates to the object in a *mediated* way, while the latter constitutes an *immediate* relation to the object. Kant overtly rejects the proposition that the categories of the Understanding could *produce* the very manifold of intuition that is given in the *a priori* forms of space and time. Rather, truth is constructed from *two* principles, neither of which is reducible to the other. The duality of principles is explicit in Kant's famous formulation that 'concepts without intuitions are empty, and intuitions without concepts are blind.' Schelling's *System of Transcendental Idealism* is on the search for what Kant calls *intellectual intuition*: a thinking that *produces its object* in virtue of thinking it. In the *Elucidations* section following his deduction of the first principle, Schelling is explicit that the first principle intuits itself intellectually in *Kant's sense* of the term.[74] The object of such an intellectual intuition would be the noumenal *thing-in-itself*. Since consciousness is not endowed with intellectual intuition, it always requires a separate faculty in which the content of intuition is given, for the categories of the Understanding (as categories) do not already contain any intuitive content within themselves.

Analytic judgments are true in *virtue of identity*. 'S is P' is an analytic judgment if the predicate is *contained* in the concept of the subject. 'All bodies are extended' is an analytic judgment.[75] The connection between the predicate and the subject is achieved by *identity*: the concept of the body conceptually entails the concept of extension. Synthetic judgments, by contrast, connect a predicate to a subject that is *not already contained* in the concept of the subject. In such judgments, 'reason adds something alien' to what is already present in the subject. To put it in other terms: the predicate is connected to the subject by means of a *third* term. All empirical judgments are of this sort: 'all crows are black' predicates 'black' to 'crow.' 'Black' is not entailed in the concept of 'crow,' but is attributed to the subject 'crow' by means of experience as the *mediating principle*. Rather than an immediate identity with the subject, synthetic judgments depend upon a mediating principle. Kant's main interest of course is the possibility of synthetic, *a priori* judgments such as 'everything that happens has a cause.'[76] The concept of 'causality' is not entailed analytically in the concept of an event; it must be *added* from without.

For our purposes, the more helpful mark that distinguishes such judgments is the difference between *clarification* and *amplification*. In an analytic judgment, 'P' does not add anything to 'S' that is not already there: they are *judgments of clarification*—one merely makes explicit what was already there, but in a covert way. Synthetic judgments, by contrast, are judgments of *amplification*. Because the predicate of the synthetic judgment is not already present in the subject of the judgment, the predicate *adds* something to my knowledge of the subject. Indeed, the judgment that 'all crows are black' augments the knowledge of the subject. Even if *my* knowledge may not be augmented, the knowledge expressed in the judgment *cannot be gleaned* merely from an analysis of the subject.

In his *Deduction of the Principle Itself*, Schelling adds the helpful qualification that analytic judgments or *judgments of identity*, on the one hand, compare the thought to itself, or in another formulation, they compare *the concept with the concept*. On the other hand, synthetic judgments compare the predicate *with an object* that is distinct from itself.[77] In order to discover whether it is true that 'all bodies are extended' one must compare the judgment to the concept of the body—such a comparison investigates whether the *claim about the concept* agrees with the concept itself, which in this case constitutes the *object* of the presentation. Thus, in any attempt to assess the truth of the statement of identity, the truth is determined by comparing one's conception of the concept with the concept itself. But for synthetic judgments such as 'all crows are black,' I can only determine the truth of the predicate by comparing it *with the object itself*—in this case, the crows themselves. In the case of such *a posteriori* judgments, I must consult *experience* in order to judge whether the concept corresponds to the object or not. Whether the synthetic judgment is *a priori* or *a posteriori*, the truth of the predicate is not attained by merely comparing a concept with a concept.

Given this distinction between synthetic and analytic judgments, we can better *analyze* the objection against the possibility of the first principle. Since transcendental philosophy must demonstrate how *thinking alone* can posit not only an object but also *truth*, the *unity of concept and object*, it cannot achieve this end as long as it conceives of thinking as only *analytic*. As long as the form of presentation of the Intellect is only analytic, it cannot produce new knowledge, for no analytic thinking is ampliative. Since the principle of identity, A=A, is an analytic truth, and appears to *only* to contain identity, one could *never* discover difference in the self-identical form of thought; one could only deduce more *identity*. Hence, in order for thinking to *produce an object* to which it corresponds, its thinking must be *ampliative*—thinking which can produce *novel* truth. Accordingly, in order for the first principle to produce its object, its thinking must be synthetic in form. This is nothing other than an affirmation of *intellectual intuition* in Kant's sense. Hegel is not wrong that

> Intellectual Intuition is the absolute principle of philosophy, the one real ground and firm standpoint in Fichte as well as in Schelling.[78]

Nonetheless, Fichte overtly rejects the concept of intellectual intuition in Kant's sense. Concerning Kant's sense of intellectual intuition, he writes that

> We recognize it to be the utmost perversion of reason, and a concept perfectly absurd.[79]

Fichte does not appear to acknowledge that grounding all truth in *one* principle demands the affirmation of intellectual intuition in Kant's sense. For Fichte, this would entail recognition of the existence of the *thing-in-itself* as well as knowledge of it, which for him is a complete impossibility:

> In the Kantian terminology, all intuition is directed to existence of some kind (a posited or permanent); intellectual intuition would thus be the immediate consciousness of a nonsensuous entity; the immediate consciousness of the thing-in-itself, and that by way of pure thought; hence a creation of the thing in itself, and that by way of pure thought; hence a creation of the thing-in-itself by means of the concept (much as those who prove the existence of God from the mere concept are obliged to regard God's existence as a mere consequence of their thinking.)[80]

Fichte's intellectual intuition is the immediate self-knowledge of the I. Such an immediate self-knowledge is *not synthetic* for it is *simple* and therefore has nothing to synthesize. Unlike Schelling *who recognizes the need* to read synthesis into the formulation of the first principle, Fichte does not appear to explicitly read synthesis in to the first principle. Schelling's initial advance upon Fichte is to recognize that the first principle must be synthetic—it must amplify itself into objectivity—in order to successfully ground truth in one principle. Whereas Fichte holds the first principle *apart* from the synthesis for which it will give an account, Schelling appears to recognize that intellectual intuition must already be conceived *synthetically from the very beginning* in order to successfully account for existence.

The kind of knowing at which transcendental philosophy aims is that which goes beyond the limits of its own *subjectivity* and *becomes objective*, thereby knowing something *different* from itself as mere subjectivity.[81] Transcendental philosophy must *amplify itself into objectivity*—an act for which analysis alone is utterly inept. Schelling himself claims that

> the whole of our knowledge consists of nothing but synthetic propositions, and only therein do we find true knowledge, that is, a knowing that has its object outside itself.[82]

Because we cannot account for *synthetic truth* by means of an analytic principle, the logic of the Intellect must become synthetic—otherwise the first principle cannot give rise to a *second*. By elevating thinking to a synthetic principle, a general criterion of truth may be possible. For this reason, Schelling claims that the argument *against* a first principle of knowledge (and a general criterion of truth) rests upon the false assumption that the purely formal laws of logic are unconditioned. He writes:

> The first mistaken assumption of the above argument consists, therefore, in taking the principles of logic to be unconditioned, that is, derivative from no higher presuppositions.[83]

Since laws of logic, such as the principle of identity, A=A, are *analytic* judgments and at best analytic *truths*, positing such principles as unconditioned undermines the possibility of a first principle.

The Dominance of Identity: Kant, Jacobi, and Fichte

On its face, it appears that Kant does privilege *synthesis over analysis*. This, of course, is true as concerns the relationship between the synthetic and analytic unities of apperception. In his *Critique of Pure Reason*, Kant makes is clear that the analytic unity of apperception presupposes the synthetic unity of apperception:

> the analytical unity of apperception is only possible under the presupposition of some synthetic one.[84]

In order to analyze consciousness into the separate representations that are given in it, the representations must first be *combined into one consciousness*. In order to give an account of knowledge and conceptual determinations that constitute its material, empirical consciousness must presuppose the *givenness* of psychological content to consciousness. Because empiricism must assume the fact of some psychological content, it cannot account for the very fact that it is given. The fact of givenness—and the forms in which it is given—most fundamentally the form of consciousness itself—remains unaccounted for. Kant introduces the transcendental question exactly at the point where empirical thinking ends: what is the condition for the possibility of the givenness of the contents of consciousness? In Kant's terms, in order for there to be an awareness of an object, the various contents of consciousness must be combined into *one* awareness. Only once the contents are combined or synthesized into *one* awareness, is it possible for one to isolate any particular object and be conscious of it.

Kant's appeal to the synthetic unity of apperception marks a turning point in the history of Western philosophy. Not only does it undermine any naïve empiricism that uncritically takes consciousness of the particular for granted, but it also reverses the traditional order of the categories. For Aristotle, Thinghood is the primary category and relations only exist because things exist that can stand in relations with one another. Kant reverses the priority. Rather than privilege Thinghood, Kant prioritizes the *relation* of all material constituents over the givenness of any thing. In order for any material to be given at all, it must stand in a *relationship* with other material in one consciousness. The combination of all contents into one consciousness via the synthetic unity of apperception raises relation to a priority over things. To use Kant's language, no object or objectivity for that matter is possible without the universal combination and relatedness of all material in one consciousness. Indeed, the object itself becomes constituted by the kinds of relationships that it exhibits.

Nonetheless, the very *possibility* of the synthesis of all content into one consciousness presupposes an *analytic* principle: *the I think must be able to accompany all of my representations*. Kant writes:

> The principle of the necessary unity of apperception is itself, indeed, an identical, and therefore analytic proposition; nevertheless it reveals the necessity of a synthesis of the manifold given in intuition, without which the thoroughgoing identity of self-consciousness cannot be thought. For through the 'I', as simple representation, nothing manifold is given; and only through combination in one consciousness can it be thought. An understanding in which through self-consciousness all the manifold would *eo ipso* be given, would be intuitive; our understanding can only think, and for intuition must look to the senses.[85]

That the I think must accompany all of my representations is the fundamental principle that makes possible the synthesis of the manifold.

Thus, exactly because it is the principle of synthesis, it cannot be *synthesized itself*; otherwise it would be some content brought to the unity of consciousness and would necessarily presuppose itself. Rather, Kant proceeds *analytically*. From the very concept of *the experience of a representation*, one can abstract the 'I think' as a common feature of every possible representation. Reflection upon the concept of the experience of a representation entails that the representation must be *mine*—otherwise it could not be. Since this principle is analytic, as Kant points out, it specifies the universal form of all content of experience, namely that it must be mine. But *what representations* (what contents) are thought by the 'I think' are not specified. Because it has no intuitive content of its own, one can only discover the 'I think' because *there are representations* which it accompanies. Indeed—although it makes the synthesis of all manifold of intuition possible, because it is analytic, the intuitive content that it synthesizes must be derived from elsewhere: from sensibility. Thus, the *duality* of the Kantian principles—Understanding and Sensibility—is motivated by the *analytic* character of the principle of synthetic unity. As Kant states, in order to arrive at a principle that is in itself synthetic, one must transform the I think into *intellectual intuition* in which the thinking of the manifold is transformed into the very principle in virtue of which the manifold is given. For Kant, synthesis is always a result, for every synthesis is the *result* of a *more primitive mediating principle*.

The merely analytic character of the principle of synthesis in Kant is further illuminated by the way in which the synthetic unity is affected. In his deduction, Kant argues that since it is the categories—the logical functions of judgment—which bring various representations under a common one, they are the *principles of synthesis* by which all contents of consciousness are combined into one awareness. Independently of the manifold which they combine, the categories do not themselves contain intuition—they are formal, for they are completely *empty of intuitive content*. Thus, they do not already contain truth, the correspondence of subject and object. We can only say that the logical forms of judgment contain *analytic judgments*. They acquire a transcendental function and thereby a place in transcendental logic by bringing representations into one consciousness and making the *cognition of objectivity* possible.

Because the categories are *a priori*, and the content of sensible intuition *a posteriori*, and truth is the agreement of the concept with the object, the *a priori* character of the categories fails to correspond with the *a posteriori* content of the sensible intuition. Indeed—Kant's solution to the problem, the schematism, is to posit an *a priori* manifold of intuition (an *a priori* content) that is given in the forms of intuition in advance of the synthesis of the categories. Categories can apply to sensible intuition, since Sensibility contains an *a priori* content. In virtue of their synthesis of the a priori content of intuition, the categories give form to the *a priori* manifold. Accordingly, Kant could confidently assert the truth of the categories, because the intuition is brought to the unity of consciousness by taking on categorial form. The categorial form immanent in the intuition agrees with the categorial form in the Understanding. A category is *true* only because *it corresponds with its own form* in the *a priori* intuition. Just as consciousness of the object is self-consciousness, truth is not just the correspondence of the concept with the object, but it is the *correspondence of the concept with itself in the object*. As Hegel will later announce in the *Encyclopedia*, *truth is self-correspondence* or the agreement of the thought content with itself.[86]

Kant implicitly employs this concept of truth in his argument that being (*sein*) is not a predicate. If being were a predicate, then the reality of the concept would be incongruous with the concept as a mere possibility. For example, in addition to the concept of 'being unmarried,' the concept of bachelor, insofar as it is realized in a person, would entail the additional predicate 'being.' In this case, the concept of a bachelor, understood as a mere possibility, would not entail the predicate 'being,' while the concept (insofar as it is actual) would contain that predicate. Since the concept as a mere possibility would not contain the predicate, but the concept as a reality would contain the predicate, the concept as possibility could not agree with the very same concept in its actuality. Thus, one could not say that the concept 'bachelor' corresponds with the actual bachelor, for the latter would contain a predicate that does not obtain in the former. Fichte rejects Kant's concept of intellectual intuition for the same reason that he rejects the ontological argument. For both, thinking alone would be *sufficient* for producing the *intuitive realization of the thought*.[87] Yet, if self-thinking is *not* sufficient for producing its own intuitive realization, then there cannot be one principle of truth.

Besides all appearances to the contrary, both in his *Second Introduction* to the (1794) *Wissenschaftslehre* and Parts I and II of the same text, Fichte conceives of synthesis as a result—*never as an absolute beginning*. Both Fichte and early Schelling agree that although Kant's philosophy contained *the true results*, the grounds and premises upon which those results were deduced were problematic.[88] In particular, following Reinhold, both recognize that the Kantian philosophy must be grounded in a single *first principle*. Fichte—a self-described Kantian—follows Kant's lead by grounding synthesis in a *principle of identity*. Fichte draws upon Kant to denounce the possibility that the first principle could be synthetic:

> 'This principle of the necessary unity of apperception,' says Kant (C. P. R., B 1 3 5), 'is itself, indeed, an identical, and therefore analytic, proposition.' This is equivalent to what I was just saying: the self arises, not through any synthesis whose manifold could be further dissected, but through an absolute thesis.[89]

Following Kant, Fichte denies that the first principle of the self is a synthesis. Rather, Fichte posits what he calls an absolute thesis. This absolute thesis is formulated in terms of a *thetic* judgment. Fichte defines a thetic judgment in the following way:

> A thetic judgment, however, would be one in which something is asserted, not to be like anything else or opposed to anything else, but simply to be identical with itself: thus it could presuppose no ground of conjunction or distinction at all.[90]

As Fichte makes absolutely clear, the thetic judgment does not presuppose a 'ground of distinction.' The Absolute Thesis, the 'I am,' is the first principle of Fichte's system of philosophy and exemplifies this form of thetic judgment:

> The first and foremost judgment of this type is 'I am', in which nothing whatever is affirmed of the self.[91]

Because synthesis is always only ever result, it cannot be the first principle. The first principle, the thesis 'I am,' is formulated as a thetic judgment that is *free of all distinction*. According to Fichte, all synthetic judgments depend upon the third principle of the *Science of Knowledge*:

> The celebrated question which Kant placed at the head of the *Critique of Pure Reason*: How are synthetic judgments a priori possible? is now answered in the most universal and satisfactory manner. In the third principle we have established a *synthesis between the two opposites*, self and not-self, by *postulating them each to be divisible*; there can be no further question as to the possibility of this, nor can any ground for it be given; it is absolutely possible, and we are entitled to it without further grounds of any kind. All other syntheses, if they are to be valid, must be rooted in this one, and must have been established in and along with it. And once this has been demonstrated, we have the most convincing proof that they are valid as well.[92]

All other syntheses are rooted in the third principle. Accordingly, all the rules governing synthesis must be grounded in the third principle as well:

> The logical rules governing all antithesis and synthesis are derived from the third principle of the *Science of Knowledge*, and from this, therefore, all command over antithesis and synthesis is in general is derived.[93]

Since the third principle depends upon the first principle, the 'I am' which can only be formulated as a thetic judgment, all synthetic knowing depends upon a thetic judgment:

> Just as there can be no antithesis without synthesis, no synthesis without antithesis, *so there can be neither without a thesis*—an absolute positing, whereby an A (the self) is neither equated nor opposed to any other, but is just absolutely posited. This, as applied to our system, is what gives strength and completeness to the whole; it must be a system, and it must be one; the opposites must be united, so long as opposition remains, until absolute unity is erected; a thing, indeed—as will appear in due course—which could be brought about only by a completed approximation to infinity, which in itself is impossible. The necessity of opposing and uniting in the manner prescribed rests directly *on the third principle*; the necessity of combination in general, on the first, highest, absolutely unconditioned principle. The form of the system is based on the *highest synthesis*; that there should be a system at all, on the absolute thesis.[94]

According to Fichte, although synthesis and anti-thesis condition each other, *both* synthesis and antithesis *depend upon* the thesis I=I, or 'I am I'—the absolute self-positing of the self that is independent and free of all opposition.[95] Because the I am I is a condition for the highest synthesis (the third principle), *the first principle cannot itself be a synthesis*. Whereas all syntheses depends upon the third principle, the 'highest synthesis' that synthesizes 'self' and 'not self' *in the self*,[96] the fact of the system itself depends upon the *non-synthetic* and *thetic self-identity* of the first principle. Following Kant, Fichte argues that synthesis is only possible on the presupposition of a *non-synthetic* principle. But Fichte goes further: by means of the self-positing 'I' he attempts to account for all synthetic *a priori* truth, the constituents of which are the system of categories and *a priori* intuitions.

Although in these texts Fichte does not appear to ground all knowledge on a synthetic principle, his first principle is not a *formal principle*. The first principle is unconditioned, but it has *content*. The principle of identity, A=A, expresses the formal self-identity of the non-formal first principle,[97] I is I, whose content is the I itself. As Fichte writes:

> If we abstract from 'I am' the specific content, namely the self, and are left with the mere form that is given with this content, the form of an inference from being posited to being, as for purposes of logic we are compelled to do, we then obtain 'A = A' as the basic proposition of logic.[98]

Accordingly, the thetic judgment 'I am I' is not synthetic, but it is not merely a formal principle, as is the case with the principle of identity.

Indeed, Fichte recognizes that one could not produce a system of philosophy *from analysis*. Regarding analytic judgments, Fichte follows Kant's insight.[99] Although the first principle I=I is not a formal, analytic principle, it is just as much impossible for it to be synthetic. The first principle must be simple. For were it manifold, then it would require *another mediating principle* in virtue of which it would be unified into a systematic whole. Were the 'I am' an internally differentiated synthetic principle, then it would require a mediating principle in virtue of which its manifold parts would be unified into a unified whole. The I must be simple—otherwise it could not be the first principle. The I simply *is*; it has *no predicates* that could in principle demand a mediating principle. Like Kant's 'I,' Fichte's first principle must be simple, without any manifold given within it.[100] Because nothing limits the first principle, *the I is infinite*—only once the absolute and infinite I has posited the not I, and is limited thereby, does the I posit itself as finite. For Fichte, the I is responsible both for the positing of *the antithesis* between the finite I, as well as the finite not-I, in addition to their *synthesis* as is expressed in the self. Fichte wants a self-identical first principle *without the Kantian dualism*—but this seems impossible.

Given the simplicity of the first principle, the fundamental problem of German Idealism arises: how can difference and plurality arise from what is simple and indivisible? Although the first principle has content, namely the I, the I is self-identical, whose self-identical form is truly expressed in the abstract form of the principle of identity. Thus, just as no difference can follow from the abstract identity of the principle of identity, *nothing different* from the I, namely the not-self, can follow from the pure self-identity of the self. Indeed, as we have put the problem, Fichte cannot account for the possibility of the second principle because he denies that the first principle could be synthetic. In order for the first principle to become *ampliative*, it must first attain the status of an ampliative judgment. It must become *synthetic*. Because the first principle is not synthetic, it cannot move beyond itself. Schwab puts the problem in the following way:

> Zunächst ist unklar, warum überhaupt ein zweiter Grundsatz nötig wird; in der reinen Identität des absolut-anfänglichen Ich selbst liegt keine Notwendigkeit, aus sich herauszugehen oder sich etwas entgegenzusetzen.[101]

Accordingly, Fichte raises the fundamental problem facing his philosophy in a letter to Reinhold from 1795:

> Wenn das Ich ursprünglich nur sich selbst sezt, wie kommt es denn dazu, noch etwas anderes zu setzen, als ihm entgegengesezt? aus sich selbst herauszugehen?[102]

Indeed, insofar as everything is posited by the I, and the I is infinite, if the I cannot posit anything different from itself, then the infinite I can just as little account for the existence of finitude. Schelling in his *Philosophical Letters*, as well as Schlegel and Hegel, ask the same question. Schlegel and Hegel put the same question formulated by Fichte in terms of the possibility of finitude (for which difference is obviously a necessary condition). During the Winter semester of 1800–1801 in Jena, Schlegel puts the question in the following way:

Why has the infinite gone out of itself and made itself finite?[103]

Indeed, Hegel asks the very same question in his first remark under the heading of affirmative infinity in his *Science of Logic*, a text in which he means to have fully resolved that question. As he puts it:

The essence of philosophy has often been located by those already adept in the things of thought in the task of answering the question: *how does the infinite go forth out of itself and come to finitude?*— This, as opinion would have it, escapes *conceptual comprehension*. In the course of this exposition, the infinite at whose concept we have arrived will *further determine* itself, and the desideratum—*how* the infinite (if one can so express oneself) *comes to finitude*—will be manifested in it in the full manifold of forms.[104]

Hegel's formulation of the question is a variation on the very same question asked by Fichte and Schlegel. Fichte posits that the first principle is self-identical: I am I, whose logical form is A=A. Given that the first principle is an absolute identity, how is difference possible? Given that the One is, how is the All possible? The Ἐν καὶ Πᾶν, the holy grail of the Tubingen three: Hölderlin, Schelling, and Hegel appears out of reach. If we cannot answer this question, then philosophy itself is endangered. No one made this clearer than the oft-maligned Jacobi, who—as I read him—employed this problem against Fichte to accuse him of *nihilism*. Indeed, the full impact of Jacobi's critique of Fichte in the tradition can only be fully appreciated when we understand not only the epistemic but also the full-blooded metaphysical implications of the program of early German Idealism as a whole.[105]

Jacobi had charged Spinoza's philosophy, and his followers, with *Atheism* and *Fatalism*. Jacobi levelled his criticism beyond Spinoza and extended them to philosophy itself. As Giovanni has pointed out, although Fichte himself attempts to develop a *philosophy of freedom* in order to respond to Jacobi's charge against philosophy, Fichte himself incurred the ire of Jacobi. Jacobi's accusation that Fichte's philosophy leads to nihilism[106] draws upon the primarily *ontological* sense of the term:

Yet, as I explore the mechanism of the nature of the I as well as of the not-I, I attain only to the nothing in-itself; . . . I have nothing

confronting me, after all, except nothingness; and even chimeras
are a good match for that. . . . Truly, my dear Fichte, I would not
be vexed if you, or anyone else, were to call Chimerism the view
I oppose to the Idealism that I chide for Nihilism.[107]

Hegel discusses Jacobi's charges in various places. In his *Encyclopedia*,
Hegel addresses Jacobi in the section entitled *Third Approach to Objectivity*.[108] In his earlier *Faith and Knowledge* from 1802, he analyzes and
critiques Jacobi in much detail. In his discussion of Fichte, Hegel explicitly discusses Jacobi's charge of nihilism. Hegel sometimes puts it quite
poetically:

> Jacobi, who focused his reflection on the one side of the antithesis, on
> infinity, on formal identity, felt that this nihilism of the transcenden-
> tal philosophy would tear the heart out of his breast.[109]

In his prefatory note to the first edition of *David Hume on Faith*, Jacobi
lays down his assumptions about the structure of reason.[110] Jacobi's accusation that Fichte's philosophy leads to nihilism is grounded on important classical assumptions about reason. If we abstract from all *contents*
thought *by* reason, the content of reason understood *by itself* that remains
is the *self-identity* of what is thought. Reason by itself can judge whether
the content that is thought is *consistent* with the principle of identity and
non-contradiction by comparing it to the *a priori* form of self-identity.
From these assumptions, Jacobi is right that reason alone is a power of
'formulating the principle of identity' and 'judging in accordance with it.'
    Jacobi levels the charge of nihilism against the speculative Idealism of
Fichte because Fichte, according to Jacobi, posits the I as the principle
of philosophy. Fichte postulates that the I is the principle from which all
content of experience and existence for us must be derived. The thinking
subjectivity must abstract away from *all content of what is thought* and
deduce experience and existence for us from *the empty* knowing of the I.
According to Fichte:

> The question proposed, namely: How is an existent possible for
> us? . . . It inquires as to the ground of the predicate of existence
> in general. . . . The answer, if it is to be an answer to this ques-
> tion . . . *must similarly abstract from all existence.* [my emphasis][111]

For Jacobi, since one cannot deduce *the existence* of any finite, determinate being from the mere identity of the I in the thetic expression, I=I,
Fichte's philosophy must deny the *existence of all finite being*. Fichte's
thought is a form of *nihilism*, a philosophy of *nothing* in which the world
disappears. The world cannot be deduced from the formal self-identity
of thinking. *Nothing* further is thought in the self-identity of I=I except
the I.[112] After having abstracted all existence away, one cannot *regain*

existence again out of the empty identity of the thinking. Accordingly, Jacobi endorses *Realism* as a way to avoid nihilism. Note that Jacobi's critique is not in any way weakened or undermined if existence is conceived in explicitly Fichtean terms (rather than on overtly 'dogmatic terms'). For the force of the critique lies in *the inability to derive difference from pure identity*, so that even if the only difference that exists is 'for consciousness' that existence for consciousness cannot itself be accounted for. To put the problem in terms of Kant's concept of intellectual intuition, without re-thinking the first principle as a *concept that produce its own intuitive realization*, the Idealist cannot account for the existence of the world.

Thus, all knowledge of all finite and differentiated contents, or of all finite *particulars*, must be given *independently of reason*. In order to discover these contents, the philosopher must appeal to *the Given* in some form or another. If faith is the acceptance of a truth that is not inferred from rational principles,[113] or if 'every cognition that does not originate in rational sources is faith,'[114] then the fact that there are particulars or that there is a content for reason to know must be given by faith. For Jacobi, the existence of *finite* entities upon which we reflect depends upon faith.[115]

Jacobi argues that the self-identical form of reason is an *abstraction* from given content.[116] We only arrive at science by means of abstracting away content from what is given. Accordingly, the bare self-identity of reflection by which it judges contents given to it from the outside is not one of two principles, but it is wholly *derivative*. Since the contents given to reflection and abstraction are only given in faith, the *whole of philosophy is contingent upon faith*. Jacobi writes:

> For man knows only in that he comprehends, only in that, by changing the real thing into mere shape, he turns the shape into the thing, and the thing into nothing.[117]

This critique is devastating, for it is not just the finite but the infinite that also disappears upon the approach of reason. By applying the finite category onto the infinite, the infinite fails to appear as infinite. Instead, the infinite appears as that which is opposed to the finite. Accordingly, the infinite itself becomes finite, for when it is treated as a finite conceptual form, it functions as the mere negation of finitude and thereby excludes finitude from itself, rendering it finite. Indeed—insofar as the I is infinite, but cannot account for finitude, it becomes finite. But this finitude cannot be, for the I is I cannot account for it. Thus, Fichte's philosophy is *self-annihilating*. Not even the I can be.[118]

For Jacobi, the rationalist confuses the conditions of *explanation* for the conditions of *existence*. Here Jacobi tends to view nature as the totality of all conditions. The totality of all conditions cannot itself *be* conditioned, yet if the conditions of explanation are the conditions of explanation, then it must have some particular condition, and the whole complex of nature would thereby 'disappear.' The only cognition that reason can have is of some *element* of the whole. Jacobi is insistent that the fact of *nature's existence* must be taken on *faith*, and all acts of reasoning about nature must take nature, as the unconditioned, as an assumption. The *unconditioned conditioned* cannot be established naturally; it must be established *super-naturally*.[119] Philosophy becomes nihilistic when it projects its own form onto the form of all things. The world itself, as an *infinite* totality, *disappears into nothingness* when reason applies its finite categories.

In the *Spinoza Letters* of 1785, Jacobi writes that the greatest service of the investigator is to reveal that which cannot be explained.[120] Jacobi famously argued that the metaphysicians confused the conditions of existence with the conditions of explanation.[121] Far from *intending* to advocate for irrationalism, Jacobi argues that rationalistic metaphysics, such as that of Spinoza, inverted the natural order of knowledge by substituting the requirements of reflection for those of existence.[122] Indeed, in his 1815 preface to *David Hume on Faith* Jacobi compares his own methodology on par with Kant. Both aim to expose a 'false' and 'self-deceiving' rationalism.[123] By offering a critique of metaphysics in which the Absolute is posited as something that is knowable by means of *rational demonstration*, Jacobi attempts to employ philosophy in order to reveal the need for faith. Explanation *points beyond itself to what cannot be explained*: *das Unauflösissche, das Unmittelbare.*

In a supplement to his 1789 edition of the *Spinoza Letters*, Jacobi writes that philosophy tears the world apart rather than thinking it as it is:

> We appropriate the universe by tearing it apart, and creating a world of pictures, ideas, and words, which is proportionate to our powers, but quite unlike the real one. . . . Our philosophical understanding does not reach beyond its own creation. All understanding comes about, however, by the fact that we posit distinctions, and then supersede them.[124]

Ultimately all demonstration must rely upon something which cannot be demonstrated. Through positing distinctions and superseding them, Jacobi attempts to show the need for faith. Through Jacobi's demonstration, one comes to recognize that all demonstration relies on what *transcends all possible demonstration*. According to Giovanni, for Jacobi, faith is the assent given to a stated truth even though the said truth does not admit of proof.[125] As he writes in his *Prefatory Note* to the first edition of *David Hume*:

> For the assumption [in the *Spinoza Letters*] was that every cognition that does not originate in rational sources is faith.[126]

In the following, he defines faith in a similar way:

> The definition of certainty is translated [from Spinoza] verbatim, and
> the whole first paragraph almost verbatim, he just does not use the
> word 'faith' which I, for my part, use because, as I go on to explain
> explicitly, it is common practice to call any acceptance of a truth not
> inferred from principles faith.[127]

As Jacobi himself later admitted in the 1815 *Preface to David Hume*,
one of the main problems with Jacobi's conception of philosophy in his
Spinoza Letters is the fact that he seems to fail to distinguish between
the faculties of Understanding and Reason. Indeed, it appears that
Jacobi tends to identify philosophy as such with the former. If philosophy is only demonstrative knowing, then philosophy cannot think the
Absolute, and the only recourse to the Absolute is to faith. Indeed, as
Giovanni points out, there are arguably a number of inconsistencies
in Jacobi's work.[128] One of the most glaring problems is the status of
philosophy itself.

Hamman famously criticized Jacobi for failing to stand on his Christianity alone. As Giovanni points out, Jacobi attacks philosophy by
means of philosophy. And what is even more problematic, Jacobi did
not seem to be aware that he was doing this.[129] If philosophy is some
kind of demonstrative knowing, and it cannot ground itself, then Jacobi cannot use philosophy to ground philosophy. Yet, Jacobi employs
philosophy to ground philosophy on faith. If the requirement of faith
is established by means of philosophical demonstration, then the first
principles have been demonstrated. Or what is the same: if philosophy cannot know the *un*conditioned Absolute, but Jacobi knows this
fact about the Absolute by means of philosophy, then philosophy can
know the Absolute. Jacobi's failure to differentiate various modes
of philosophical thought appears to have fundamentally stymied his
appeal to faith.

Hamman, whom Isaiah Berlin calls the *father of modern irrationalism*,[130] poses an important challenge. It appears that we are forced into
one of two positions: either we withdraw back from the position that the
Absolute cannot be known, or we give up on any demonstration that it
is unknowable and stand on irrationalism alone. The former is deeply
problematic, for our experience of our attempt to know the Absolute
leads us back into non-knowing. Fittingly, Hamman offers an attractive
view: abandon philosophy and have the courage to stand on irrationalism alone. Yet of course, even proposing this as the conclusion of an
argument is already a preposterous endeavor and betrays the spirit of the
position.

However seduced one may feel by Hamman, I think he cannot be
right, for there is a third way. Jacobi himself seems to have recognized

this later in his career, when he makes the distinction between the faculties of Understanding and intuitive Reason. In the preface to the 1815 version of *David Hume*, Jacobi admits that he called something that is not reason 'reason.' Rather than a critique of reason, the *Spinoza Letters* were truly a critique of the Understanding, or an attempt to construe the Absolute as structured by the Understanding. What Jacobi called the 'power of faith' is nothing less than *the restoration of reason*.[131] As Jacobi writes:

> Just as there is an intuition of the senses, an intuition through the sense, so is there a *rational intuition* through reason. . . . No demonstration counts against *rational intuition*, or the intuition of reason, which gives objects that transcend nature for our cognition, i.e. it makes us certain of their actuality and truth.[132]

Here Jacobi identifies faith with rational intuition, which gives objects which transcend nature and understanding, such as the *un*conditioned Absolute. He goes on to clarify the significance of intuitive Reason in the following passage:

> We have to make use of the expression 'intuition of reason' because language does not possess any other way to signify how something that the senses cannot reach is given to the Understanding in feelings of rapture and yet given as something truly objective, and not merely imaginary.[133]

In his late work, it appears that Jacobi recognized the need for a *third way* between discursive thinking and faith. Jacobi is clear that *Intuitive Reason* is his way of signifying the feeling of rapture before that which transcends demonstration. Nonetheless, Jacobi does not clarify how this term exactly overcomes the problem posed by Hamman. Despite his aggressive critique of Fichte, Jacobi too eventually realizes that he cannot truly philosophize without a concept of reason that is *also* intuitive. Of course, unlike Fichte's intellectual intuition, Jacobi's Intuitive Reason is deployed against Idealism, namely to illuminate the truth of Realism through the self-destruction of discursive thinking. From a purely systematic point of view, Jacobi has an insight: in order to conceptualize what transcends concepts, *conceptual thinking must transcend itself*—it must become 'ecstatic' so to speak.

Fichte's attempt to ground categorial thinking in a principle that *transcends* categorial thinking undergirds the Romantic impetus at the turn of the 19th century in the thought of figures such as Hölderlin, Schlegel, and Novalis.[134] Schelling too was affected by this impulse in thinking. Indeed, although Schelling is no *mystic*, as late as Schelling's late Berlin lectures on *The Grounding of Positive Philosophy*, Schelling claims that mysticism has not yet been refuted. Regarding mysticism, Schelling claims that

> This system formed, at the very least, a powerful opposition to rationalism—a system that at no time, and even now, has ever really been overcome. This could only have happened if a true philosophy had been put in opposition to it.[135]

Although the context in this passage clearly indicates that the type of mysticism to which Schelling is here referring is not that of Jacobi but *Jakob Boehme*, and his theosophy, once popular with the Jena Romantics around the same time that Schelling was completing the *STI*, the attraction of mysticism can be understood given our current problematic. The reasoning is simple: if the laws of logic cannot be unconditioned, then the laws of logic ought to be grounded by an appeal to that which *transcends* logic and philosophy.

The early Romantics, such as Schlegel and Novalis, would describe their own philosophy as *mystical*.[136] Indeed, Schelling—inspired by early German Romanticism—will himself famously proclaim in the *STI* that *philosophy is incomplete* independently of the genius of aesthetic creation, who creates by means of the fact that he is possessed by an Absolute power whom it *cannot fully comprehend*. Despite the profound differences in thinkers as diverse as Jacobi, Schelling, Hölderlin, Schlegel, and Novalis, they all share a certain *family resemblance* in one respect: all of them at various points in their thinking acknowledge that the Absolute cannot be fully grasped by *discursive reason*, and appeal to principles that transcend conceptual determination. Indeed, in order to fully come to terms with the problem of the existence of the Absolute, philosophy must systematically confront the resolution of the problem posed by such varieties of mysticism. Indeed, the problematizing of the unconditional status of the laws of logic invites *mysticism to the table*—irrespective of how unappealing it may be to philosophical consciousness.

Although Fichte appears to laud the simplicity and non-synthetic character of the first principle at the outset of his *Wissenschaftslehre*, in the fifth Section of the *Grundlage der Wissenschaft der Praktiken*, he appears to argue that the first principle contains diversity. In order for difference and diversity to be possible, it must already be posited in the first principle:

> Demnach müßte schon ursprünglich im Ich selbst eine Verschiedenheit seyn, wenn jemals eine darein kommen sollte; und zwar müsste diese Verschiedenheit im absoluten Ich, als solchem, gegründet seyn.[137]

Indeed—without positing the diversity of directions in the Absolute I (inwardly toward the self and outwardly toward the not-self), the

Absolute I could not in principle determine itself to be finite. Yet, with this qualification, Fichte must contradict his earlier claim that the first principle cannot be synthetic. For if the Absolute, the I=I, were to contain any difference, then the differences would require a mediating principle in virtue of which those differences would be unified into the principle. Since the unity of the differences in the principle would thereby be *synthetic*, the first principle would be synthetic. But the first principle cannot be synthetic. For according to Fichte's earlier argument, the mediating principle in virtue of which synthesis is possible cannot itself be a synthesis. Rather, it is a *thetic*, not a synthetic principle. Thus, whatever I contains differences cannot be the primordial I, for it is a synthesis. Accordingly, there must be a higher I, *I**, a pure thesis that transcends all synthesis. If I* were a synthesis of differences, then it too could not be the highest principle, *ad infinitum*. As Fichte himself proclaims:

> Hence it would have to have the ground for its non-self-positing within itself; it would have to contain the principle of self-positing, and also that of non-self-positing. And thus the self would be essentially opposed to, and in conflict with, itself; it would contain a doubly opposed principle, which is itself a self-contradictory assumption, for then there would be no principle in it at all. The self would be nothing whatever, for it would eliminate itself.[138]

Every time one attempts to conceive of the Absolute, one fails and only discovers a relative principle. Or what is the same, every time one attempts to locate the *point at which the difference originates*, one only finds the fallen—downgraded I—not the Absolute. Thus, the highest that can be achieved is an *infinite approximation* towards the Absolute. But notice—this also entails that one can never fully arrive at the principle of difference. Rather, one *approaches it without end*—a bad infinity that is never resolved. The first principle—the point at which difference originates—is never what it *ought to be*—it is not true in the sense that it *fails to correspond with itself*. Indeed, Fichte writes that *for us* thetic judgments (those judgments that are subsumed under the Absolute positing of the self), insofar as they are *positive judgments* in which some concept is *predicated of the Absolute I*, cannot help but appear as a contradiction:

> For all that, the logical form of the judgment, which is positive, requires that both concepts should be united; yet they cannot be combined in any concept whatever, but only the Idea of a self whose consciousness has been determined by nothing outside itself, it being rather its own mere consciousness which determines everything outside it. Yet this Idea is itself unthinkable, since for us it contains a contradiction.[139]

Accordingly—Fichte famously proclaims that the highest practical goal of the human being is to 'approximate, ad infinitum, to a freedom he can never, in principle, attain.'[140]

Hence, Hegel is not wrong when he claims that both Jacobi and Fichte *absolutize* finitude.[141] Hegel further claims that because Fichte's infinite is negated into a form of finitude from which it cannot recover, Fichte could never fully overcome the limitation of the infinite by the finite. Thus, according to Hegel, Fichte actually took the negation of finitude, what Hegel here calls *nihilism*, *as a goal* to be accomplished:[142]

> We have already shown why Jacobi so violently abhors the nihilism he finds in Fichte's philosophy. As far as Fichte is concerned, nihilism is certainly implicit in pure thought as a task [to be accomplished.][143]

According to Hegel, while Jacobi aims to preserve the finite against Idealism, Fichte's philosophy takes the *nullification* of the finite as a goal to be achieved, which it cannot accomplish. Nihilism in this sense is the annihilation of finitude and the resurrection of the infinite. Since for Hegel both thinkers posit an *absolute difference* between form and content, Jacobi and Fichte continue to think of the infinite under the *guise* of finitude.[144]

Schelling appears to notice the tension in the *Wissenschaftslehre*. Were the highest principle a unity of differences, then it would not be the first principle—since no first principle is synthetic. But if there is a first—purely self-identical or thetic—principle, then there would be no differences and no system either. The thetic principle in virtue of which the fact of the system as such is possible is the very thing that appears to undermine its possibility. As we've already indicated, Schelling claims that philosophy 'makes the real world vanish before our eyes.'[145] Despite this, philosophy can indeed make it re-appear again by *thinking synthesis into the first principle*. By raising synthesis into the first principle, Schelling lays bare the necessary conditions that must be fulfilled for a principle to be *first*: it must be both *self-identical* and *synthetic*. These requirements are themselves demanded by Fichte's system. Schelling's new method in the *STI* means to give an account of how the first principle can both be the first principle of all knowledge while at the same time give rise to difference and finitude.

The Identity of Synthesis and Analysis in Schelling's System of Transcendental Idealism[146]

Having uncovered the problematic assumption underlying the argument against the possibility of a first principle, Schelling has cleared the way for his deduction of the first principle. Schelling notes that this deduction 'can be carried out in many different ways.' Indeed—Schelling makes room for other deductions, such as Fichte's deduction from the 1794

Wissenscaftslehre which proceeds from the 'empirical certainty of logical principles.'[147] His deduction is the 'easiest' proof that offers the most
'immediate insight into the meaning of the first principle.' Because
Schelling's proof for the first principle draws upon the insights of the
Wissenschaftslehre for its formulation of the identity of synthesis and
analysis, in *STI* Schelling claims that he does not mean to offer a new
account of first principles. Following Fichte, Schelling posits the freedom
constituted by *self-consciousness*, the I, as the first principle. In the *foreword*
Schelling writes that

> in regard to basic enquiries nothing can be found here that has not
> already been said long since, either in the writings of the origina-
> tor of the Science of Knowledge [*Fichte*], or in those of the present
> author.[148]

Schelling acknowledges that the 1800 system was dependent upon
Fichte's Idealism. Although it is not a completely *new* account, it nonetheless offers an *improvement* of Fichte's account.[149]

Indeed, this humble self-presentation covers over what Schelling will
later acknowledge contained a more decisive methodological innova-
tion. Indeed, by integrating synthesis into the first principle, Schelling reformulates the way that synthesis must be accounted for. Just as
Schelling proclaims that all real knowing (and real truth) is synthetic,
by raising synthesis to a first principle, *synthesis must account for itself*.
The first principle must be the synthesis upon which all others rely, as
well as a synthesis, just as the first principle of knowledge is *Truth itself
and a truth*. By raising synthesis to the status of a first principle, the
self-identical thesis ought no longer ground the synthetic. Put more
starkly: one cannot account *for the possibility of the system of philosophy* without unifying the thetic with the synthetic in the first principle.
The system can only be posited if it is ampliative (not just potentially
ampliative) from the outset. Although Fichte acknowledges the necessity of building difference into the first principle, this does not appear to
undermine his prioritization of the thetic over the synthetic, as it should.
Likewise, despite the fact that in Kant's late *Opus Postumum*, Kant
will (quite darkly and obliquely) at times refer to self-consciousness
as 'simultaneously synthetic and analytic,' the *Opus Postumum* was
meant to complete, not *undermine*, the insights laid bare in the *Critique
of Pure Reason*. In short: the whole of German philosophy from Kant
through Fichte seems to point to the identity of synthesis and analysis,
an identity Schelling first makes *absolutely explicit* in his deduction of
the first principle.

Schelling notes that the 'deduction of the first principle' cannot proceed from a more fundamental principle. For were it to proceed from a
more fundamental principle, then the first principle would be assumed,

rather than deduced. Thus, it would appear that proceeding in such a manner could only establish a derivative principle. Rather, the proof must proceed by establishing the *distinguishing characteristics* of the first principle and therefrom investigating what could in principle *instantiate* those characteristics:

> The proof can proceed only upon the dignity of this principle, or upon proving that it is the highest, and possesses all of those characteristics which appertain thereto.[150]

Schelling, of course, argues that only self-consciousness has the characteristics required of the first principle. But were one to show that something other than self-consciousness could fulfill such conditions, then one could generate a *dilemma*.

Given that knowledge in general is possible, knowledge is either conditioned or unconditioned: if knowledge depends upon more fundamental principles, it is conditioned. But conditioned knowledge is only knowledge because it depends upon a first principle. Such a principle *cannot be conditioned* upon anything else—thus it must be *unconditioned*. Schelling further qualifies the unconditioned principle as necessarily *subjective*—no objective principle can be unconditioned. The form of my thinking of the object is the form of identity, A=A. Irrespective of what object I think, my thinking of that object is *conditioned* by the identical principle A=A. As an analytic judgment or identical proposition, it is a certain and evident judgment whose *certainty* can be established by *thought* alone. Because in analytic judgments the predicate is contained in the subject by *identity*, the certainty of the proposition never requires comparing the proposition with an object outside itself. Instead, its certainty can be established *by thought alone*. By comparing thought with itself, thought can establish the certainty of the analytical proposition, or proposition of identity. Because the certainty of the analytical proposition, A=A, is not conditioned upon anything outside of it, its is *unconditioned*. Hence, it is the *subjective form of thought* that is properly unconditioned. Because such a proposition abstracts from the *reality* of A, it states that *whatever its content may be*, it must be self-identical. As an analytic judgment or judgment of identity, the certainty of the self-identical character of the thinking of the subject can be evaluated *without comparing it to a distinct object*. As Schelling puts it:

> The knowledge in this proposition is thus conditioned purely by my thinking (the subjective) that is, as explained above, it is unconditioned.[151]

The certainty of the proposition of identity—the form of thinking—is conditioned purely by subjectivity, or thinking itself—thus it is unconditioned. In the analytic judgement, the *subject corresponds with the subject itself*.

The second premise of the deduction appears to *contradict* Schelling's claim that the principles of logic are not unconditioned. Indeed, since A=A is true in virtue of thought alone, it is unconditioned, and yet in order to plausibly establish the first principle, the laws of logic cannot be unconditioned. Schelling recognizes this conflict and integrates it into the deduction. In the third step of the argument, Schelling re-iterates that knowledge always requires truth, namely the *correspondence* of the subjective with the objective. Since in the self-identity of A=A, the *objective is not present* (for we abstract from it in order to formulate the principle), the statement of identity cannot be a *principle of truth*. Rather, only in synthetic propositions are subject and predicate linked by something *alien to identity*, such that the *truth* of the predication in the judgment is established by comparing it with the object itself. Thus, Schelling argues that only in the *synthetic judgment* could we have a *principle of truth*, for the correspondence of the subject with a *distinct* object is only possible in the synthetic judgment. Thus, the first principle of knowledge cannot be analytic, since it fails to live up to the definition of truth (and thereby knowledge) specified at the very outset of the *STI*. In step three of the argument, Schelling re-iterates what we already know: one cannot *produce truth* by mere analysis.

Unfortunately, it appears that the first principle *cannot be synthetic* either. Because every synthetic judgment connects the predicate to the subject in virtue of a *mediating* principle, the truth of the synthetic judgment is conditioned upon something *outside* of the concepts themselves. Thus, every synthetic judgment is a result—it is *always* conditioned. Thus, the first principle cannot be synthetic, for the first principle must be unconditioned, and synthetic propositions are *not* unconditioned. Since there is nothing unconditioned in the synthetic judgment, and the identical proposition, A=A, is an unconditioned certainty, it follows that the first principle could only be an identical proposition.

Before drawing the *most profound conclusion* in the deduction—step five of the proof—Schelling explicitly recognizes that the first four steps have deduced a *contradiction*. Most simply put: the first principle must be unconditioned and synthetic, but this is impossible: either the first principle is *unconditionally* analytic or it is conditionally synthetic. The first principle appears to have *contradictory* characteristics: it must be both *certain* and *true*. In other words, although all truth appears to be conditioned the general criterion of truth must be the unconditioned truth in virtue of which there *is* truth. From this position in the argument, Schelling draws the conclusion that

> This conclusion would be soluble only if some point could be found in which the identical and the synthetic are one, or some proposition,

which, in being identical, is at once synthetic, and in being synthetic, is at once identical.[152]

Because the first principle must be certain and unconditioned, it must be analytic. Yet, it must also be true, indeed—the principle of truth. Thus, it must be synthetic. Hence, the first principle must consist in the *identity* of analysis and synthesis.

Throughout the argument, we have supposed that analytic and synthetic knowing must be mutually exclusive. Namely, if a proposition is synthetic, then it cannot be analytic, and if it is analytic, then it cannot be synthetic. Were this assumption true, then it would render the concept of a first principle totally impossible. As Schelling argues, since all relative knowing is knowing that is dependent upon and thereby relative to something else, and all knowing must be grounded in unconditioned knowledge, all relative knowing depends upon unconditioned knowledge. The unconditioned knowledge—the first principle—cannot be relative, for its truth is not relative to another—it can only be *true in virtue of itself*. Indeed, as the principle of truth, it is that *in virtue* of which any relative knowing is true. Thus, its truth is not relative to another, but it must be true in itself—or *absolutely* true.[153] As Schelling states:

> so if there is such a truth [*absolute truth*] there must also exist a point at which the synthetic springs directly from the identical cognition, and the identical from the synthetic.[154]

Because the Absolute Principle must be true, it must be synthetic, for all 'true knowing' is synthetic. But it must also be an 'identical piece of knowledge' because it's truth is *in virtue of itself*—a feature characteristic only of analytic propositions. Because relative truth would be impossible without the One Absolute Truth, the separation of analysis from synthesis is wholly contingent upon their identity in the Absolute. Simply put, without this identity, there would be *no truth* at all. Schelling's proof demonstrates that *without the identity of synthesis and analysis*, no truth is possible. This conclusion reflects Schelling's earlier claim in the text that there must be a point at which the *content and form of cognition are identical*.

Since synthetic propositions compare the thought with the object, while analytic propositions compare the thought *with the thought*, and the absolute truth identifies the synthetic with the analytic, it follows that in the first principle, *the object* that is compared with the thought must be *identical* to *the thought* itself. Thus, whatever the first principle may be, it must immediately *identify thought with its object*—thing with presentation.[155]

Schelling further analyzes this feature of the first principle by means of the following classification: in any synthetic judgment, 'A is B,' the predicate of the judgment, 'B,' the concept, represents the thought of thinking *subjectivity*. The subject term of the judgment, 'A,' stands for the *object* about which one is thinking. When I evaluate the truth of the synthetic judgment, I investigate whether the attribute signified by the concept 'B' agrees with the feature of the object, 'A.'[156] Since the analytic proposition compares *the concept* with itself, in the analytic proposition the subjective thinking is represented by *both* the subject and the predicate of the proposition. Thus, Schelling proceeds to step seven: the identity of the synthetic and the analytic entails the *identification* of subjectivity with objectivity. In the Absolute, the subjective and objective must be one.[157]

The results of Schelling's clear and brilliant demonstration of the necessary characteristics of the first principle can be summarized as follows: the first principle must be the *Absolute* Truth upon which all other truth and knowledge depends, in which synthesis and analysis, subjective and objective thinking, are *one*. Indeed—this conclusion repudiates his earlier claim in *Vom Ich als Prinizip der Philosophie*, in which he proclaims that

Also muß die Urform des Ichs reine Identität sein.[158]

Following the form of the proof, Schelling *compares* these necessary features of the first principle with all of the *candidates* that could possibility fulfill such conditions. The *only* candidate that can fulfill such conditions is self-consciousness. For only in self-consciousness is the subject that thinks immediately identical to the object that is thought. If the subject thinks itself, then the subject is both the subject and the object of its thought:

The concept of an original identity in duality, and vice versa, is thus to be found only in the concept of a subject-object, and only in self-consciousness does such a concept originally manifest itself.[159]

Only in self-thinking thought is the presenter identical to the presented, the One who intuits *identical* to the One intuited. Thus, the first principle of all truth, Truth itself, is *self-consciousness*.[160]

The Inconsistency of a Synthetic First Principle

Immediately upon the completion of his proof, Schelling embarks upon a series of *elucidations* of what self-consciousness *means*.[161] The first elucidation, (a), returns to the second impasse that Schelling raised against the possibility of a first principle of philosophy. To put it simply: any attempt to produce *truth* by means of thinking alone seems to be impossible, for the form of thought is purely formal. From pure identity, A=A, one cannot produce a synthetic proposition, for pure-identity abstracts from a necessary constituent of truth: the *objective* side of thinking. Schelling's solution to the impasse is to deny the unconditional dimension of logic. As he states:

> There is admittedly no seeing how one could pluck something real out of a proposition of logic purely as such.[162]

Accordingly, Schelling argues that the principles of logic must be *conditioned*. They must be *derivable* from a higher proposition. Of course, as we noted earlier, Schelling is careful to be clear that such a principle cannot conflict with the laws of logic—it could not be in conflict with it—otherwise it could not be true. The principle must be 'brought about in accordance with logical laws' without being *derivable* from them.

Given that the first principle of truth and knowledge is self-consciousness, the principles of logic must be *conditioned upon* self-consciousness. Since the analytic proposition, A=A, compares the thought *with itself*, the only way to evaluate the truth of an analytic proposition, or *establish* its truth, is by an act of self-consciousness. Only by means of an act of self-consciousness can one compare thought with itself and establish that its form is self-identical:

> In every identical proposition, so we claimed, a thought is compared with itself, which assuredly takes place by an act of thinking. The proposition A=A therefore presupposes a thinking which immediately becomes its own object; but an act of thinking that thus becomes an object to itself occurs only in self-consciousness.[163]

Only in a form of thought where the subject and object are the same, namely in self-consciousness, can the self-identical form of thought, A=A, be established as the *form* of thought that thinks itself. Of course, this is a re-iteration of Fichte's insight. Regarding A=A, Fichte writes that concerning

> which law must therefore be given to the self, and since it is posited absolutely and without any other ground, must be given to the self by itself alone.[164]

Given that the principles of logic must be derived from a *proposition* that is at once analytic and synthetic, and the first *principle* is self-consciousness, the principle of self-consciousness ought to be formulated as a *proposition*. Indeed, because the *principle of truth* is itself *one truth* among others, the principle of truth ought also be formulated as the *unconditionally* true proposition in the totality of propositions that constitutes the system. This proposition is posited in elucidation G.[165]

The highest proposition must be an *identity* of subjectivity and objectivity. Since the subjectivity of thought is represented by the predicate position, and the object of thought is represented by the subject of the proposition, and in self-consciousness the self is both the subjectivity that thinks and the objectivity that is thought, *the very same* self must occupy both the subject and the predicate positions. Thus, the first principle of truth and knowledge is 'the self is the self,' or *self=self*. The predicate, 'self,' is contained in the subject term, 'self' by identity. Thus, it is an identical or analytical proposition. But it is *not merely formal*, for it is also the *identity of a subject with an object*. The self *qua* subject is not identical to the self *qua* object. Thus, it is a synthetic proposition. 'Self=self' expresses the self-consciousness in propositional form, and is thereby both identical and synthetic.

> Hence that principle must be expressed in the proposition self=self, since this very proposition is the only one there can be that is simultaneously both identical and synthetic.[166]

'Self is self' is *true* in the sense that in this fundamental proposition the self as subject corresponds with itself as the object. Thus, the self is true, for it lives up to what it ought to be: *the unity of synthesis and analysis*. By raising synthesis into the first principle, it can become a *true* principle of truth.

The self that thinks itself is *self-identical*, for the very same self is identical to itself in the subject and predicate position. 'Self=self' is certainly *in agreement with* the principle of identity *without being derived* from it. As is obvious, 'A=A' is a merely *formal* expression of the self-identical relationship expressed in the non-formal proposition, 'the self is the self.'[167] The difference consists in the fact that the principle of identity, A=A, abstracts from the content of selfhood. Accordingly, Schelling infers the Fichtean insight that the laws of logic as such, namely as *separate* principles that constitute the content of the *Science of Logic*, come to be by means of *abstraction*:

> thus logic can only arise as such by abstraction from determinate propositions. If it arises in a scientific manner, it can do so only by abstraction from the highest principles of knowledge.[168]

Given that although the principle self=self does not contradict the law of identity, the laws of logic are nonetheless grounded on an act of self-reflection of self-consciousness in which it *abstracts from itself and its own self-identity*. As Schelling points out in elucidation K, the original principle self=self simultaneously grounds both the form and content of knowledge. Thus, it is the principle of identity that is conditioned upon self-consciousness, not the other way around:

> Thus, so far from the self=self falling under the principle of identity, it is rather the latter that is conditioned by the former. For did not self=self, then nor could A=A.[169]

Having transformed the merely analytical dimension of thinking into a synthetic principle that is also analytic, Schelling announces the solution to the original impasse that appeared to undermine the possibility of a first principle of knowledge:

> Thus the proposition self=self converts the proposition A=A into a synthetic proposition, and we have found the point at which identical knowledge springs immediately from synthetic, and synthetic from identical.[170]

Certainly these reflections follow Fichte's own arguments in the *Science of Knowledge* rather closely. But if the principle of identity, A=A expresses the abstract form of the first principle, and the first principle is an identity of *identity and difference*, then the abstract principle, A=A, ought to contain difference. Schelling affirms this: since A is A can only equate the A *with itself* if each A occupies a *different position* in the proposition, so that even in the form of identity difference is contained. Thus, 'A=A' actually expresses the identity of identity and difference, or what is the same, the self-identity of A with itself in its differentiation from itself.[171] Following Schelling, Hegel will proclaim that the laws of logic, such as the PNC, are 'not merely analytic but of synthetic nature.'[172]

Kant in his *Opus Postumum* returns to the language of positing that is characteristic of his early work. More specifically, the self *posits-itself* in the intuition and *knows itself in* the intuition as *that which has posited itself therein*.[173] From the late Kant through Fichte and early Schelling, self-consciousness is consistently described as *self-positing*. For Fichte and Schelling, the first principle of philosophy is self-positing (*Selbstsetzung*). The transformation wrought by Schelling (and which had been *percolating* in the thought of Fichte) raises the demand that the self-positing first principle be constituted as an *identity of synthesis and analysis*. Both Fichte and Schelling refuse to describe the first principle as a mere thing, as a something—that would be a dogmatic assertion. Rather, in *Transcendental Idealism* the first principle is a pure act. According to Fichte:

> The self is absolutely active, and merely active—that is our absolute presupposition.[174]

That the self is an activity of self-positing (*Selbstsetzung*)—this is the absolute presupposition in the sense of posited in advance—or *Voraussetzung*. Indeed—Schelling is not wrong that it is a false dichotomy to proclaim that either the beginning is a thing or it is nothing—for it could be an absolute act.

Upon closer scrutiny, we discover that Schelling's profound insight that the first principle must be an identity of synthesis and analysis not only undermines the very possibility of a first principle but also requires the philosopher to accept that one cannot think the Absolute without the acceptance of *true contradictions*. Rather than an absolute Voraussetzung philosophy must become radically Voraussetzungs*los*. Schwab points out the self-refuting character of Schelling's first principle in *STI*:

> Dieser gesuchte ‚Punkt' ist nun selbstverständlich das reine Selbstbe-wusstsein. Schellings eigene Formulierung zeigt aber das Problem bere-its an: Es soll nun bloß noch der Punkt ausgewiesen werden, an dem das Objekt und sein Begriff ‚**schlechthin und ohne alle Vermittlung**' eins sind. So aber war die Aufgabe nicht formuliert worden: Soll eine Einheit von Identität und Synthese gefunden werden, so müsste an diesem ‚Punkt' die unmittelbare Einheit und zugleich die Vermittlung gegeben sein: mit der Identität also auch die NichtIdentität. Schelling stellt also am entscheidenden Punkt den Aspekt der vermittelnden Synthese zurück. In der Tat würde auch dieser unmittelbare Eintrag der Vermittlung ins Prinzip die transzendentalphilosophische Evi-denz ‚ruinieren': Die Evidenz des ‚Ich bin' liegt allein in der Unmit-telbarkeit intellektueller Anschauung.[175]

As Schwab points out, Schelling formulates the identity of synthe-sis and analysis as an identity 'ohne alle Vermittlung'—namely as a purely *immediate* unity. But since this only expresses one side of the unity of synthesis and analysis—it does *not correspond to what it ought to be*. We will remember that analytic propositions connect subject and predicate by means of *identity*, and synthetic proposi-tions do *not* connect subject and predicate by identity. Instead, they connect subject and predicate by a *different*, mediating term. Were analysis and synthesis identified, this would entail that *the very iden-tity* by which subject is connected to predicate would necessarily *be different* from that very identity. Thus, identity would be identical to difference—or what is the same: *difference would not be different from identity*. The identity of synthesis and analysis entails the iden-tity of identity and difference. Because identity is not non-identity, the identification of identity with non-identity is a *contradiction*. To put it another way: the Absolute truth becomes a *contradiction* wherein the agreement of identity with itself is the agreement with what is not identical. What Fichte and (especially) Schelling have taught us (without intending to perhaps) is that conceiving the Absolute is to think an inescapable contradiction. Hegel puts the problem this way in his *The Difference Between Fichte's and Schelling's Systems of Philosophy:*

> Suppose that the Absolute is expressed in a fundamental proposition, validated by and for thinking, a proposition whose form and matter are the same. Then either mere sameness is posited, and the inequality of form and matter is excluded, so that the fundamental proposition is conditioned by this inequality. In this case the fundamental proposition is not absolute but defective; it expresses only a concept of the intellect, an abstraction. Or else the fundamental proposition also contains both form and matter as inequality, so that it is analytic and synthetic simultaneously. In that case the fundamental proposition is an antinomy, and therefore not a proposition. As a proposition it is subject to the law of the intellect, the law that it must not contradict itself, that it cannot suspend itself, that it must be something posited. As an antinomy, however, it does suspend itself.[176]

As Hegel makes clear, the identity of synthesis and analysis in the first principle is a contradiction and is thereby an *antinomy*. The first consequence of such an insight is the following: because the identity of synthesis and analysis is an identity of identity and difference, it must simultaneously be the *difference* between identity and difference. Indeed—it is this latter claim that is absent in Schelling's first principle. Following Fichte, he reverts back to an immediate principle—a mere thesis—when in his *Elucidations* he claims that the 'I am' has 'no real predicate.' Despite Schelling's profound insight that *intellectual intuition must become synthetic*, in the STI he nonetheless reverts back to Fichte's purely *thetic* understanding of intellectual intuition. Therewith he denies the presence of difference in the first principle and has failed to consistently think through what follows from the identity of synthesis and analysis—a fundamental re-thinking of Fichte's concept of intellectual intuition.[177] To put it simply, either the first principle is an identity of synthesis and analysis *and* is self-contradictory or it is a purely *thetic* principle completely *devoid* of synthetic content.

Notes

1. The following brief discussion of Aristotle's concept of self-consciousness is discussed within the systematic framework of Hegel's concept of rational self-consciousness in Gregory S. Moss, "The Synthetic Unity of Apperception in Hegel's Logic of the Concept," *Idealistic Studies* 45, no. 3 (2016): 279–306, 280–281.

2. See Aristotle, "On the Soul," in *The Philosophy of Aristotle*, trans. A. E. Wardman and J. L. Creed (New York: Penguin Books, 1963), 269–270, in which Aristotle argues that the human mind does not have a Form of its own, but is a potential that can be formed according to the Form of the Thing that it knows. Aristotle's philosophy of mind had a significant impact on the history of the philosophy mind especially in the medieval tradition. See, for example, Moses Maimonides, *Guide for the Perplexed*, trans. Michael Friedlander (Sagwan Press, 2015 [1903]), which adopts this account of the mind wholesale.

3. Aristotle, "On the Soul," 270.

4. "But when the mind thinks each of its objects in the way that the man who is knowledgeable in actuality is said to (and this happens when he is able to be active on his own), even then the mind is still in a way in a potential state, though not in the same way as it was before it learned or discovered what it did learn; the mind is now able to think on its own." Ibid, 270.

5. 'If thinking is like perceiving, it must be either a process of being acted upon by the object of thought or by something else of the same kind. Strictly, this part of the soul must not be capable of being acted upon, but capable of receiving the form of its object; and it must be potentially like its object, without ever being its object; and indeed the relation of the mind to the objects of thought must be like that of the faculty of sense to the objects of sense.' Ibid, 269–270.

6. Aristotle, "Posterior Analytics," in *Aristotle's Complete Works, Vol. 1*, trans. Jonathan Barnes, 114–167 (Princeton: Princeton University Press, 1984), Book II, Part 19.

7. Ibid, Part 166.

8. Gottlob Fichte, *Science of Knowledge*, trans. and ed. Peter Heath and John Lachs (Cambridge: Cambridge University Press, 1982), 32.

9. Ibid, Second Introduction 45.

10. For a more complete description of Kant's methodology and the results of the *Critique of Pure Reason*, see Gregory Moss, Ernst Cassirer and the Autonomy of Language (Lanham: Lexington Books November, 2014).

11. Correlated with this important distinction is Kant's thesis that the *a priori* form of intuition contains its instances, rather than subsumes them, whereas concepts subsume their instances rather than contain them.

12. See Anthony Bruno, "Determinacy, Indeterminacy, and Contingency in German Idealism," in *The Significance of Indeterminacy*, ed. Robert Scott and Gregory S. Moss (New York: Routledge, 2018), 67–84.

13. Ibid, 69.

14. Immanuel Kant, *Critique of Pure Reason*, trans. Paul Guyer and Allen Wood, ed. Paul Guyer and Allen Wood (Cambridge: Cambridge University Press, 1998), B145–B146.

15. Fichte, *SK*, 46.

16. Descartes had already attempted to ground philosophy upon *immediate* self-knowledge in his *Meditations*, except in his case the self-knowledge is thoroughly a psychological experience. In any act of doubting the existence of one's own thinking, one's thinking, that is, one's own doubting, becomes present to consciousness. The psychological inescapability of encountering thought is an experience in time, and is in this way a form of inner psychological experience. As such, although it abstracts from outer experience, it does not actually abstract from all experience, but is itself an experience. Any immediate attempt at self-knowledge also leads to paradox. See Moss, "The Synthetic Unity of Apperception in Hegel's Logic of the Concept," 281–283.

17. G. W. F. Hegel, *The Difference Between Fichte's and Schelling's System of Philosophy*, trans. H. S. Harris and Walter Cerf (Albany: SUNY, 1977), 111.
18. See Fichte, *SK*, 46.
19. Ibid, 35.
20. Fichte is adamant that without intellectual intuition one would be helpless to account for the possibility of being conscious of the moral law, for this constitutes an immediate self-consciousness that is not sensory.
21. Fichte, *SK*, 47.
22. Ibid, 46.
23. Ibid, 39.
24. Ibid, 30.
25. Ibid.
26. Ibid, 40.
27. Ibid, 69.
28. Ibid, 42.
29. Ibid, 46.
30. Ibid, 32.
31. Markus Gabriel, *Transcendental Ontology* (New York: Bloomsbury, 2013), ix.
32. Kant, *CPR* (A596/B624).
33. This critique of Kant's account of existence was originally published in Gregory Moss, "The Paradox of Representation in Nishitani's Critique of Kant," in *Kant on Intuition: Western and Asian Perspectives on Transcendental Idealism*, ed. Steve Palmquist (New York: Routledge, 2018), 275–283, ft. 6, 282.
34. Fichte, *SK*, 32.
35. Ibid.
36. This term 'Self-in-Itself' arises in the first introduction of Fichte, *SK*, 10.
37. Fichte re-iterates this very same identity in multiple places: 'Hence, there is in the Intelligence, to express myself figuratively a twofold—Being and Seeing, the Real and the Ideal; and in the inseparability of this twofold the nature of the Intelligence consists. . . .' See Gottlob Fichte, "First Introduction to the Science of Knowledge," trans. A. E. Kroeger. *Journal of Speculative Philosophy* 1, no. 1 (1867): 23–36. In contrast, dogmatic knowing fails to achieve this unity: 'You were to prove the connection between Being and Representation; but this you do not, nor can you do it; for your principle contains merely the ground of a Being, and not of a Representation, totally opposed to Being. You take an immense leap into a world, totally removed from your principle.' See Fichte, "First Introduction to the Science of Knowledge," 30.
38. For a brief history of the development from Reinhold to Fichte, see Dieter Henrich, *Between Kant to Hegel*, ed. David S. Pacini (Harvard: Harvard University Press, 2003).
39. Fichte, *SK*, 44.
40. Ibid, 41.
41. See Gottlob Fichte, *Concerning the Conception of the Science of Knowledge Generally (1794)*, trans. Adolph Ernst Kroeger (Witthorn: Andos Books, 2017 [1794]), 9.
42. Ibid, 19.
43. Hegel, *The Difference Between Fichte's and Schelling's System of Philosophy*, 94.
44. Fichte, *SK*, 50. Also see Hegel, *The Difference Between Fichte's and Schelling's System of Philosophy*, 119.
45. Fichte, *SK*, 41. Indeed, in his description of contemporary philosophy Hegel writes that 'one cannot philosophize without transcendental intuition.' See Hegel, *The Difference Between Fichte's and Schelling's System of Philosophy*,

110. Hegel's use of the term 'transcendental intuition' appears to be conceptually identical to Fichte's concept of intellectual intuition here.

46. Hegel, *The Difference Between Fichte's and Schelling's System of Philosophy*, 120.

47. Fichte himself appeals to this very metaphor: 'Let science be a building, and let the chief object of this building be firmness. The foundation is firm, and as soon as it is laid down, the object.' See Fichte, *Concerning the Conception of the Science of Knowledge Generally*, 3.

48. Ibid, 2–3.

49. F. W. J. Schelling, *System of Transcendental Idealism (1800)*, trans. Peter Heath (Charlottesville: University Press of Virginia, 2001), 14.

50. See G. W. F. Hegel, *Science of Logic*, trans. George Di Giovanni (Cambridge: Cambridge University Press, 2015), 122. Also see G. W. F. Hegel, *Science of Logic*, trans. A. V. Miller (Amherst: Humanity Books, 1969), 152.

51. G. W. F. Hegel, *Phenomenology of Spirit*, trans. A. V. Miller (Oxford: Oxford University Press, 1977), 100.

52. Hegel, *SL*, trans. Miller, 152.

53. See F. W. J. Schelling, *Outline for a System of the Philosophy of Nature*, trans. Keith R. Peterson (Albany: SUNY, 2004), 194. Here Schelling proclaims, for instance, that the 'ideal must arise out of the real and admit of explanation from it.' Here Schelling states that 'Now it is the task of transcendental philosophy to subordinate the real to the ideal, it is, on the other hand, the task of the philosophy of nature to explain the ideal by the real. The two sciences are therefore but one science, differentiated only in the opposite orientation of their tasks.'

54. Schelling, *STI*, 15.

55. Ibid, 19.

56. Hegel, *The Difference Between Fichte's and Schelling's System of Philosophy*, 155.

57. Schelling, *STI*, 19.

58. Ibid, 15.

59. Ibid, 20.

60. Ibid, 18.

61. Ibid.

62. Kant, *CPR*, A58–A62, B82–B87, 197–199.

63. Schelling, *STI*, 20.

64. The assumption that contradictions cannot be true rests upon the principle of explosion, which states that everything and nothing follows from a contradiction. Following explosion, everything and nothing would be true.

65. Schelling, *STI*, 7.

66. Ibid, 20.

67. Kant, *CPR*, 198.

68. Ibid, 197.

69. To put the critique in terms of truth makers, Kant is arguing that Schelling's one principle of truth would demand that the truth of any proposition be evaluated by the same principle, such that the truth maker of one proposition would be the same for others, which seems completely misguided since the truth makers for all claims cannot be the same.

70. Fichte, *SK*, 32.

71. Schelling, *STI*, 83–90. See his deduction of matter and the chemical process. Further, he gives a deduction of organic nature. See Schelling, *STI*, 120–129.

72. Schelling, *STI*, 207.

73. Ibid, 48.

74. Ibid, 24–30.

68   *The Problem of Absolute Knowledge*

75. I would qualify Kant's claim with the following: analytic judgments are true if the predicate is contained in the concept of the subject.
76. Kant, *CPR*, 142.
77. Schelling, *STI*, "Deduction of the Principle Itself," 23.
78. Hegel, *The Difference Between Fichte and Schelling's System of Philosophy*, 173.
79. Fichte, *SK*, 45.
80. Ibid.
81. Fichte formulates this as follows: 'How do we come to attribute objective validity to what is only subjective?' Fichte, *SK*, 31.
82. Schelling, *STI*, 22.
83. Ibid, 20.
84. Kant, *CPR*, B 134.
85. Ibid, B 135.
86. G. W. F. Hegel, *Hegel's Logic (Encyclopedia Logic)*, trans. William Wallace (Oxford: Clarendon Press, 1975), 52.
87. In the Kantian terminology, all intuition is directed to existence of some kind (a posited or permanent); intellectual intuition would thus be the immediate consciousness of a nonsensuous entity; the immediate consciousness of the thing-in-itself, and that by way of pure thought; hence a creation of the thing in itself, and that by way of pure thought; hence a creation of the thing-in-itself by means of the concept (much as those who prove the existence of God from the mere concept are obliged to regard God's existence as a mere consequence of their thinking). Fichte, *SK*, 45.
88. Fichte schreibt Dezember 1793 an Stephani: „Kant hat überhaupt die richtige Philosophie; aber nur in ihren Resultaten, nicht nach ihren Gründen"(GA III/2, S. 28). Parallel heißt es in einem Brief Schellings an Hegel vom Januar 1795: „Kant hat die Resultate gegeben: die Prämißen fehlen noch."See Philipp Schwab, "Die Aporie des Anfangs. Zur Bestimmung des Systemprinzips bei Fichte, Schelling und Hegel," 1. presented at the conference entitled *Das Problem des Anfangs*, 18–20 February, Odense, Denmark.
89. Fichte, *SK*, 73.
90. Ibid, 114 (See Paragraph 3, Section 7).
91. Ibid.
92. Ibid, 112–113 (See Section 5 of Part III).
93. Also see the following: 'All syntheses established must be rooted in the highest synthesis which we have just effected, and be derivable therefrom. In the self and not-self thus united, and to the extent that they are united thereby, we have therefore to seek out opposing characteristics that remain, and to unite them through a new ground of conjunction, which again must contained in the highest conjunctive ground of all.' Fichte notes that from this point in the inquiry, the whole of the method will be synthetic in nature. (See section 4: *The Foundation of Theoretical Knowledge*, which contains a number of different syntheses, A through E.) As he states, the whole of section 4 is deduced from the second and third principles: 'The theoretical portion of our Science of Knowledge, which will actually be evolved only from the two latter principles.' (Fichte, *SK*, 119)
94. Fichte, *SK*, paragraph 3: Section 7: (113–114).
95. Fichte, *SK*, 95–96 (See step 5 of the deduction of the first principle). 'Thus the self asserts, by means of X, that A exists absolutely for the judging self, and that simply in virtue of its being posited in the self as such; which is to say, it is asserted that within the self-whether it be specifically positing, or judging, or whatever it may be-there is something that is permanently uniform, forever one and the same; and hence the X that is absolutely posited can also be expressed as I= I; I am I.'

96. The third principle states that 'in the self I oppose a divisible not-self to the divisible self.' See Fichte, *SK,* 110.
97. See Fichte, *SK,* 96. In addition, Fichte does claim that A=A is *unconditionally true and absolute.* See Fichte, *SK,* 94. The proposition A is A (or A=A, since that is the meaning of the logical copula is accepted by everyone and that without a moment's thought: it is admitted to be perfectly certain and established. Yet if anyone were to demand a proof of this proposition, we should certainly not embark on anything of the kind, but would insist that it is absolutely certain, that is, without any other ground: and in so saying—doubtless with general approval—we should be ascribing to ourselves the power of asserting something absolutely. He adds that A=A is purely formal: see Fichte, *SK,* 94–95.
98. Ibid, 99.
99. Ibid, 114.
100. Fichte is clear that there is no opposition within the self. The self only gives rise to opposition to the self: Nothing is posited to begin with, except the self; and this alone is asserted absolutely (§I). Hence there can be an absolute opposition only to the self. But that which is opposed to the self = the not-self. Fichte, *SK,* 104.
101. Schwab, "Die Aporie des Anfangs. Zur Bestimmung des Systemprinzips bei Fichte, Schelling und Hegel," 5.
102. Cited in Philipp Schwab, "The Crisis of the Principle. Schelling's Ages of the World and Erlangen Lectures in Light of the Debate with Hegel," 9 Presented at the conference Schelling: Crisis and Critique, 21–25 of February, 2017 in Mexico City. See Gottlob Fichte, *Fichtes Idealismus und die Geschichte: Kleine Schriften Werke Band I,* ed. Emil Lask (Jena: Dietrich Schegelmann Reprintverlag, 2002), 69.
103. See Manfred Frank, *Philosophical Foundations of German Romanticism,* trans. Elizabeth Millan Zaibert (Albany: SUNY, 2004), Ch. 12, 207 (KA XII:39).
104. See Hegel, *SL,* trans. Giovanni, 122. Also see Hegel, *SL,* trans. Miller, 152.
105. Much of the following discussion of Jacobi (with the exception of the discussion of Jacobi's concept of intuitive Reason and ecstasy) can be found in my article "Annihilating the Nothing: Hegel and Nishitani on the Self-Overcoming of Nihilism." See Gregory S. Moss, "Annihilating the Nothing: Hegel and Nishitani on the Self-Overcoming of Nihilism," *Frontiers of Philosophy in China* 13, no. 4 (2018): 570–600.
106. As Gillespie points out, Jacobi is not the first person in the West to employ the term 'Nihilism.' F. L. Goetzius employed the term in 1733 and D. Jenisch employs the term in 1796. See Michael Allen Gillespie, *Nihilism Before Nietzsche* (Chicago: University of Chicago Press, 1995), 65.
107. By 'Nihilism' here he seems to mean that in Fichte's philosophy only the 'nothing in itself' is known. Fichte's Idealism is a 'philosophy of the nothing,' meaning that it only has nothingness as its *object.* For Jacobi, if we were to take up the project of speculative Idealism, we would lose the world entirely, and in its place we find, at worst, *mere nothingness,* and at best, a mere chimera. See Friedrich Heinrich Jacobi, *The Main Philosophical Writings and the Novel Allwill,* trans. George Di Giovanni (Montreal: McGill-Queen's University Press, 2016), 519.
108. Hegel, *EL,* 96–109.
109. G. W. F Hegel, *Faith and Knowledge,* trans. Walter Cerf and H. S. Harris (Albany: SUNY, 1977), 170.
110. '[My philosophy] restricts reason, considered by itself, to the mere faculty of perceiving relations clearly, i.e. to the power of formulating the principle of identity and judging in conformity with it. . .' Jacobi, *The Main Philosophical Writings and the Novel Allwill,* 255–256.
111. Fichte, *SK,* 32.

112. Fichte's philosophy begins from the self-intuiting of the I, and this requires abstracting away all other contents of the mind. Fichte himself claims that the original principle concerns the form of thinking, not its content. See Fichte, *SK*, 1982, 94–95/ I, 93. Schelling himself, in speaking about the methodological work of Transcendental Idealism, claims that *philosophy makes the real world disappear*. See Schelling, *STI*, 14.
113. Jacobi, *MPW*, 80.
114. Ibid, 255.
115. Since the *a priori* form of reason is never sufficient to derive the content of reason, the content of reason must be arrived at *a posteriori*.
116. Jacobi, *MPW*, 509.
117. Ibid, 507–508.
118. Ibid, 376.
119. Ibid.
120. Friedrich Heinrich Jacobi, *Ueber die Lehre des Spinoza in Briefen an den Herrn Moses Mendelssohn* (Berlin: Hofenberg, 2017), 20–21.
121. Jacobi, *MPW* (Giovanni's, Introduction, 79).
122. Jacobi, *MPW*, 78.
123. Ibid, 551.
124. Jacobi, *Spinoza Letters*, Supplement VII, 1789, 370.
125. Jacobi, *MPW*, 91.
126. Ibid, 255.
127. Jacobi, *MPW (Aus erlesener Briefwechsel)*, 88.
128. Jacobi, *MPW*, 97.
129. Ibid, 104–105.
130. See Isiah Berlin, *The Magus of the North*, ed. Henry Hardy (London: John Murray, 1993).
131. Jacobi, *MPW* (Preface to David Hume), 541.
132. Ibid, 563.
133. Ibid. Here the faculty of reason is identified with the faculty of feelings.
134. Hölderin's insistence that the *indivisibility* of Being is inaccessible to the *division* imposed by judgment in his fragment Judgment and Being, exemplifies this well. See Friedrich Hölderlin, "Über Urtheil und Seyn," *Hegel's Development: Toward the Sunlight 1770 — 1801*, trans. H. S. Harris (Oxford: Clarendon Press, 1972), 515–516.
135. F. W. J. Schelling, *The Grounding of Positive Philosophy*, trans. Bruce Matthews (Albany: SUNY, 2007), 174.
136. Schlegel and Novalis explicitly identify their thinking in these terms. See E. Behler, *Frühromantik* (Berlin: Walter de Gruyer, 1992), 265–266. The Romantic circle in Jena was primarily concerned with the mysticism of Jakob Böhme.
137. Gottlob Fichte, "Grundlage der Wissenschaft der Praktiken," in *Fichte's Sämmtliche Werke, Erster Band* (Berlin: Verlag von Veit und Comp., 1845), § 5, 272, [265] 256. Zweiter Lehrsatz. Many thanks to Philipp Schwab for pointing me to this passage.
138. See Ibid, 223, I 252. Also note the way that objectivity necessary implies finitude: the object fails to achieve Absolute status. The object always implies restriction. 'Hence it is no longer pure but objective activity (which posits an object for itself. The word object (*Gegenstand*) admirably designates what it is meant for. Every object of an activity, so far as it is so, is necessarily something opposed to the activity, which rejects or objects to the same. If no rejection or resistance occurs, then there is simply no object of the activity, and no objective activity either; on the contrary, the activity, it is indeed

to be such, is pure, and reverts into itself. It is implicit already in the mere concept of objective activity, that resistance is offered to it, and hence that it is restricted). Thus the self is finite, insofar as its activity is objective.' See Fichte, *Wissenschaftslehre*, 227: I, 257.

139. Fichte, *SK*, 115. Fichte continues to proclaim that the counter-positing of the not-self is a hypothesis (I 253) that cannot be proved on rational grounds and can only be known by means of one's own experience of the fact of the counter-positing. He writes: 'In addition to the self-positing of the self, there is also to be another positing. A priori, this is a mere hypothesis; that such a positing occurs, can demonstrated by nothing other than a fact of consciousness, and everyone must demonstrate it for himself by this fact; nobody can prove it to another on rational grounds' (Fichte, *SK*, 224).

140. Fichte, *SK*, 115.

141. 'What this formality comes down to basically is that either the pure concept, the empty thought, supervenes incomprehensively upon a content, a determination of the concept, or vice versa: the determination supervenes incomprehensively upon the indeterminateness (of the pure concept). In Jacobi's dogmatism the objective, the Given, is called the first upon which the concept supervenes later. Fichte, on the contrary, makes the empty knowing, the Ego, into the first, which is essentially one and the same as the empty intellect of the analyzing philosophy. . . . But this contrast between Jacobi and Fichte makes not the slightest difference to the matter at issue.' Hegel, *Faith and Knowledge*, 156.

142. Hegel, following Fichte, also takes the annihilation of the finite as a goal, which he believes to have achieved. As Zizek notes, Hegel's nihilism consists in the fact that 'all finite determinate forms of life reach their "truth" in their self-overcoming' where . . . negativity is limited to the obliteration of all finite/immediate determinations.' According to Zizek, "What Is Missing Here, from a Nietzchean Standpoint, Is The Affirmative *no* [. . .]" Slavoj Zizek, *Less than Nothing: Hegel and the Shadow of Dialectical Materialism* (London and New York: Verso, 2012), 199.

143. Hegel, *Faith and Knowledge*, 168.

144. Ibid, 190.

145. Schelling, *STI*, 14.

146. Ibid, 4, 21–22.

147. Fichte, *SK*, 102.

148. Schelling, *STI*, 2.

149. Ibid.

150. Ibid, 21.

151. Ibid, 22.

152. Ibid.

153. Ibid, 23.

154. Ibid.

155. Ibid.

156. Ibid, 22.

157. Ibid, 24.

158. F. W. J. Schelling, "Vom Ich als Prinzip der Philosophie," in *Werke. Auswahl in drei Bänden*, ed. Otto Weiß (Leipzig: Fritz Eckardt, 1907), § 7.

159. Schelling, *STI*, 30.

160. Ibid, 24.

161. Ibid, 24–31.

162. Ibid, 24.

163. Ibid.

164. Ibid, 95.
165. Ibid, 27–30.
166. Ibid, 30.
167. Fichte is clear that the science of knowledge cannot be proven from the formality of logic:

> 'The science of knowledge can not be proven from the science of logic, and no logical proposition, not even the proposition of contradiction, must be accepted in advance as valid by the science of knowledge; but, on the contrary, every logical proposition and the whole science of logic must be proven from the science of knowledge.' Also see the following: 'Again, the science of knowledge is not conditioned and determined by logic, but logic is conditioned and determined by the science of knowledge. The science of knowledge does not derive its form from logic, but has that form in itself.' Fichte, *Concerning the Conception of the Science of Knowledge Generally*, 21.

168. Schelling, *STI*, 20. Fichte makes a similar point: 'By abstraction from the content of the material proposition I am, we obtained the purely formal and logical proposition "A = A." By a similar abstraction from the assertions set forth in the preceding paragraphs, we obtain the logical proposition "Not A is not equal to A," which I should like to call the principle of opposition.' Fichte, *SK*, 105.
169. Schelling, *STI*, 30.
170. Ibid.
171. Ibid.
172. Hegel, *SL*, trans. Giovani, 360.
173. See Immanuel Kant, *Opus Postumum*, ed. Paul Guyer (Cambridge: Cambridge University Press, 1998), xlii.
174. Fichte, *SK* (I paragraph 250), 221.
175. See Schwab, "Die Aporie des Anfangs. Zur Bestimmung des Systemprinzips bei Fichte, Schelling und Hegel," 8.
176. Hegel, *The Difference Between Fichte's and Schelling's System of Philosophy*, 103–104.
177. As Hegel puts it in his difference essay, 'philosophical knowledge becomes impossible when reflection gets control of transcendental intuition.' See Hegel, *The Difference Between Fichte's and Schelling's System of Philosophy*, 121.

2 The Problem of Emanation in Neo-Platonism

One and Intellect in Plotinus

Despite the widely divergent nature of the Neo-Platonic and classical German approaches to thinking, the problem of the existence of the Absolute is an ancient problem that is already visible in the case of *Plotinus*, the greatest of the pagan Neo-Platonists. As is clear from a cursory review of the tradition, we discover that the problem concerning the possibility of the existence of the Absolute does not first arise with German Idealism. A close reading of Plotinus will show that the same vicious circularity that undermined the early efforts of German Idealism to account for the existence of the Absolute is clearly discernable in Plotinus' attempts to account for how the One creates the world through *emanation*. As our analysis will show, in Plotinus there is a conflict between infinitude and finitude. Most pointedly, this conflict arises in Plotinus' account of emanation, namely his account of how that which is infinite becomes finite. Like Fichte and Schelling, Plotinus' qualification of discursive thinking will severely hamper his ability to discursively and to understand how the first principle could in principle produce a second. Because Plotinus conceives of universals as finite, they can grasp neither the infinite by itself nor the way that the finite comes to be. In what follows it shall be instructive for us to investigate how the finite understanding of the universal undermines our capacity to understand the activity of creation. The problem of the disappearance of the Absolute is just as much problematic for a philosophy that takes *Knowledge* as first philosophy as well as that philosophy which take *Being* as the object of first philosophy.

As we have established in our preceding analysis, one of the leading questions of German Idealism is the question: how does the infinite go forth from itself and make itself finite? Indeed, the question may be formulated in theological terms that evoke the concepts of 'God' and 'creation.' As our theological formulation of the problem will illuminate, the problem confronting Fichte, Schelling, and Hegel is no less than the problem of making intelligible *the process by which God creates the world*.

Consider the following formulation: how is it possible for God to create the world? On the one hand, the classical dogma that God creates the world out of nothing or *ex nihilo* appears impossible. If God creates the world out of nothing, and nothing comes from nothing—*ex nihilo nihil fit*, then it follows that there ought not be any creation at all. Yet, there is a world. Thus, God cannot create the world *ex nihilo*. On the other hand, God cannot create the world out of himself. If God contains no plurality or differentiation, and the principle of pure identity cannot be a principle of differentiation, then all creation *ex Deo* would be equally impossible. In other words, if there is a first principle such as God, then it would be impossible for anything else to be. For this reason, the belief that *God creates a world* (either out of himself or out of nothing) has most consistently been treated (at least in medieval philosophy) as a *truth of faith*.[1]

We should note in advance that one cannot overemphasize the fact that for the ancient Greeks, universals are not concepts. A concept is inherently 'conceived.' The German term for concept, *Begriff*, implies that to universalize is to grasp, take hold, or seize something. The English term 'concept' stems from the term 'conceptum.' Originally arising in the 16th century, the term implies something belonging to the mind. For this reason (among others), the identification of truth as a unity of subjectivity and objectivity would be an anachronistic way of characterizing Greek thinking. What is more, a number of problems plaguing post-Kantian thinking, such as how to integrate freedom and nature into one system of knowing, is not thematic of Neo-Platonic thinking. Naturally, the characterization of the systems are widely divergent—historically and systematically, as it would be unfitting to describe the Neo-Platonic system as a self-unfolding of self-determining Subjectivity in the sense of the German Idealists. Because the same problem facing the Idealists also plagues Neo-Platonism, the problem with which we are concerned in this chapter can be formulated *independently* of the particular technical determinations coloring the early Idealist tradition.

For the classical Greeks, the fundamental question of philosophy was the very 'Being of Being.' For Plotinus too, like Plato and Aristotle before him, the question of first philosophy is a question concerning the first principles of Being. Since for both Plato and Aristotle Form is eternal, such a question lacks any philosophical impetus, for Form always was, is, and will be. For Ancient Greek philosophy, the infinite (*apeiron*) is primarily a negative term, signifying either *the indeterminate*, that which has no form or limit, or that which is *always outstanding*, such as a numerical series. We may deem the latter the *quantitative* infinite, since the 'always outstanding' is unlimited in number.[2] Aristotle appears mostly to limit the restriction of infinitude to the *quantitative* infinite. Since one cannot run through an infinite series, the infinite series cannot be grasped by enumerating each member of the series. For this reason, the infinite is not intelligible, and philosophy cannot help but reject the assumption in an argument that leads to an infinite regress. As scholars know, for Aristotle infinitude does not exist as an actuality or a being-at-work, for it only exists in potential.[3] For Aristotle the question 'how does the infinite go forth from itself and make itself finite?' would be absurd not only because the world is not created but also because the first principle—thought thinking itself—is finite. *Form never oversteps its limit.*

Like Fichte and Schelling, who will later reject Kant's claim that truth cannot be grounded on one principle alone, Plotinus also rejects the duality, and in some cases plurality, of principles characteristic of earlier Greek philosophy. In the *Philebus*, for example, Plato makes it clear that there are *four* principles: the unlimited, the limited, the compound, and the generation of the compound.[4] For Aristotle, the Form is the principle of organization for the material, neither of which is reducible to the other, for which reason one must state both the proximate genus (the material) and the differentia (the Form) in the definition of the nature of a thing. Accordingly, for both Plato and Aristotle the principles of unity and difference and universality and particularity are (at least logically if not metaphysically) *more than one*. Plotinus, perhaps the most sophisticated exemplar of Neo-Platonism, likewise rejects the duality of principles constitutive of Plato's so-called unwritten doctrine.

Of course, Plato and Plotinus accept the 'One over many' principle according to which the One governs all pluralities. Elizabeth Brient notes that what enables Plotinus to propose the infinitude of the One is the fact that for Plotinus the One is beyond Being, or the region of Forms.[5] In one respect this is true, for the One itself is beyond all determination. As such, it is infinite *qua* indeterminate. But this is not enough to bring us to an understanding of the infinite *power* of the One, for Plato also posits that the Good is beyond Being,[6] yet does not seem to attribute omnipotence to the Good.

Why attribute omnipotence to the One? Omnipotence is unlimited power. As long as there are a duality of principles, One and Indefinite Dyad, the One cannot be the source of plurality *per se*. Surely, for Plato the One is only the source of unity, not plurality. Thus, if the unwritten doctrine is true, the One *cannot be omnipotent*. It would appear absurd from a Platonic perspective if the One could be the source of that in virtue of which the many were many or failed to be one. Elizabeth Brient is right to correct a common tendency made by scholars in this regard: Plato has more than one principle, whereas Neo-Platonists such as Plotinus only recognize one.[7] Indeed, for Plato in his so-called middle dialogues the particular is false or an illusion of the real, insofar as it is particular, that is, insofar as it fails to measure up to the universal, which is the real, true being. If there were only one principle of both particularity and universality, then *the principles of truth and falsehood, or reality and illusion, would also be the same.*

The One cannot be omnipotent if a duality of principles is accepted. Since the One is no longer limited by a contrary principle, the One is no longer limited. Given the Platonic context in which the One is the principle of the many, since the One is the principle of plurality, yet cannot rely on its contrary for the individuation of what falls under it, the One must function not only as the principle of unity but also the principle of plurality. Since the One is that power by which all unity and plurality is produced, there is nothing left over to limit the power of the One.

As is evident, Plotinus' theory of *emanation* precludes a duality of principles. Emanation is the flowing of beings from the One as a source. The term is a *metaphor* for the production of beings from the One, for it invokes the *image* of 'flow.' The One 'overflows' out of itself, like the Sun's production of light. Although the One 'overflows,' it does not destroy itself or negate its own unity in virtue of its emanation.[8]

Since the One emanates all things, the One is omnipotent. The infinitude of the One, therefore, is a property of *the power* of the One.[9] Since the One never exhausts itself, its power is inexhaustible. As an inexhaustible power, the emanation of the world never ceases and continues without end. Moreover, the infinite power of the One engenders Omnipresence: 'Universal power, extending to infinity, and powerful to infinity . . . god is so great that his parts have become infinite. For what place can we speak of where he is not there before us?'[10] The power of the One is omnipresent, for all things emanate from God's power. Since nothing can be divorced from God's power, all things have *one* power source. In this sense, all are encompassed by that power. Since this power is without limit, it cannot be restricted to a *definite quantity*. It appears that we can say more than 'the One is indeterminate,' for the One's indeterminacy is nothing more than the lack of limit inherent in the infinitude of God's power and the ubiquitous presence of that power.

Since the One emanates all things *from itself*, all generated entities have, in some respect, the same 'being' as their generating source. As Plotinus states, 'God is so great that his parts have become infinite.' Unlike the process of making in which the maker is not the same kind of thing as her artifact, the process of emanation is modeled on generation, a process in which the generated entity is of the same kind as the principle of generation. By modeling the first principle on the soul, the concept of emanation is in keeping with the ancient account of Form, for the first principle is a living source *that generates particulars*. In this sense, Plotinus' account of emanation is not unique. The divergence lies in *how* this production of the many from the One proceeds.[11] Indeed, for Aristotle, Form becomes productive only upon the realization of its potential. For example, the Form of a man only becomes able to reproduce upon the maturation of his potential.[12] *Deformed* or immature *Form* cannot produce.[13] Or, in the spirit of Plotinus, *what is perfect produces*.[14] Since what is perfect produces, and the One is perfect, it must produce.[15] Since it is entailed in the perfection of the One to produce, the One's creation is *necessary*, not contingent. If the One did not produce, it would not be what it is. Not only is the Form undiminished by its generation of particulars, but it is also an expression of the perfection of Form that it generates them. Because the One is perfect, it remains what it is despite its emanation of the world.

One might wonder how the One could remain one if it had 'parts' or 'infinite parts.' If the One remains itself despite its emanation, it is not rendered plural by its emanation. Yet, the One emanates the multitude from itself, giving rise to the totality of what is. Thus, the first conclusion one should draw from this process must be the following: the One *as one* is *not* generated by its own emanation. Otherwise, it would cease to be just one, and would be many. What is emanated is *other* than the One, for the One is *not* included in what is emanated. Yet, the others emanate from the One itself, so they cannot be absolutely or unconditionally other to the One, as the One is omnipresent. What emanates from the One *is* the one, but it is the One *as other* to the One, as the plurality. In order to express this relation of the others to the One, I shall use the expression 'self-externalization,' for the others are the One in its self-externality. Accordingly, we may discuss the One *in itself* or the One in its self-externality as the sensible Form appears in Plato. The One in itself *appears* to be *finite* in the ancient sense, for it *keeps to itself*. Yet, the One in virtue of its emanation does not keep to itself, and *qua* self-externalized is infinite. Clearly, we cannot absolutely separate the finitude and infinitude of the One, for it is the very being of the One, and in keeping with itself, to become self-external in the act of emanation. In this sense, the One *in itself is infinite*.

The One, as the ultimate 'one over many' is the measure of the many, in virtue of which the many is known. Since the One is indeterminate, it is *not itself measurable*. Though the One is the measure of the many, it is not itself one *of* the many. Thus, it cannot be included in what is measured. Since it measures all things, it is the all-inclusive measure. Since it is not included in what is measured, it is *unmeasured*. Thus, the immeasurability of the One is another aspect of its indeterminacy. Armstrong says it best: the One is 'without limit as being all inclusive and so un-included, immeasurable as having nothing outside it to measure it and as being itself the absolute standard of the measurement.'[16] Since self-predication requires that the particular be predicated of the universal, and the One as one is *not a one*, it follows that the One *in itself* is not self-predicative.

Although the One in itself is not self-predicative, insofar as the One emanates, it *is* self-predicative. When the One thinks itself, it becomes *both* the subject and the object of the thinking. Thus, the self-thinking one is not the One, for by thinking itself, the One is not just one, but a plurality. Although the Intellect is many, it is not indefinitely many, for its thinking and the object of its thought are the same. In this respect it is an *undifferentiated unity*. Intellect (*nous*), the second hypostasis, is constituted as self-thinking thought. Plotinus identifies self-thinking thought as the very what-it-is-to-be of the Intellect. Though Intellect is no longer the first principle, as in Aristotle, Plotinus uses the Aristotelian term for Being to describe the Intellect: Being-at-work [ἐνέργεια].[17] Taking Plato as his master, Plotinus identifies 'Being' with the realm of Form. Since the One is not a Form and is beyond the region of Form, Being cannot be said of the One. Moreover, since the Forms are inherently intelligible beings, one can discover the categories of Forms by uncovering the very structure of the Intellect itself. For this reason, we shall embark upon Plotinus' derivation of the categories of Forms from the Intellect.

Plotinus points out that one cannot have a theory of categories if Being is one, for categories classify groups of entities into different genera. Without a plurality of entities to place into various genera, there would be no categories. Thus, Being must be inherently plural in order for categories to exist.[18] Plotinus thinks Plato advocates this view of Being in the *Sophist*. One can only apply Plato's method of division if what is being divided is plural. For example, since the sophist is constituted by a plurality of Forms A+B+C, and so on, the philosopher can divide the sophist into the Forms in which the sensible kind participates. It is unclear whether Plato means to apply the method of division to Forms themselves. But since Plotinus takes Forms to be the things that are, *categories are of Forms*, not sensible kinds.

Since Plotinus thinks categories apply most directly to Forms, not sensible kinds, he rejects Aristotle's categories, for Aristotle's categories apply to sensible kinds, for example, men, horses, colors. Moreover, in good Platonic fashion, he insists that there is no common genus to Being and Becoming.[19] Not only does he deny that there is one genus of Being,[20] but he also rejects the assumption that prior and posterior can belong in the same genus.[21] From this premise, he argues that Aristotle commits a category error in his application of categories. For example, since there cannot be a single genus for Being and Becoming, sensible (first Substance) and intelligible Substance (second Substance) cannot share the common genus 'Substance' as Aristotle insists in the *Categories*.[22] Or take Quantity: though numbers fall under quantity, countable sensibles, for example, cows, ought not be counted as quantities.[23] In the division of Forms from sensibles, we see Plotinus insisting on the categorial difference between universals and particulars.

The Intellect is the One in the Form of Thought, and as such it *is Being*. Since it *is Being*, we must say that *its very being is to be*. As thought thinking itself, the Intellect is not the One, to which neither being nor non-being can be predicated, but the *One Being*.[24] The 'Being' here attributed to the One is not external to the Intellect, but is inseparable from its 'being Intellect.' As Aristotle argued, from any entity we cannot separate the being of something, the what-it-is-to-be, from the kind of thing it is. So, for example, the 'being' in 'being a stone' is not separate from 'being a stone.'[25] It is not as though one has the stone and *in addition* there is Being. If this were the case, the stone would simply not exist. There would be nothing to add to 'Being,' such as 'stone,' in virtue of which one could derive the formula 'being a stone.' In other words, *Being is not a separate predicate*. Even more evident, since something has being in virtue of its intelligibility, the being of Intellect is inseparable from Intellect itself. The very first category of the Intellect, therefore, is *Being*.

Plotinus notes that it makes no difference whether you call the primary category of Intellect 'Being' or 'One,' since being is not more nor less than the One Being itself and since Being is the very being of the One Being and is inseparable from it. Moreover, we noted that self-thinking thought is an activity. Its only activity is thinking itself. Insofar as it is thinking itself, it exhibits *movement* from itself and back to itself. The activity of thinking is a movement, but this movement is never other to itself. At every stage of the motion the thinking is always only thinking itself. In other words, the thinking never ceases to just think thinking. As such, the thinking is at *rest*. Plotinus notes that rest is the very character of Being, as each of the Forms is at rest with itself, never becoming other to what they are. In sum, it appears that Intellect is determined by three categories: being, motion, and rest.[26] Plotinus notes that all the categories definitive of Intellect are the same as those identified by Plato in the *Sophist*.

In addition, Plotinus adds two more categories: same and other. Since thought thinking itself is *One Being*, each of the categories is the same as the other. The being of the thinking is its movement. The One Being is at rest only insofar as it is in motion, never ceasing to move away from itself and back to itself. Yet, each category is *other* to one another, for we only list them as separate because motion is not rest, and to be is not to be at rest or to be in motion, but something else. Thus, five categories constitute Intellect: *Being, Movement, Rest, Same*, and *Other*.[27] As categories, they are not themselves Forms, but the principles of Forms. Forms such as 'Quantity' and 'Quality' take these as their constitutive principles, as that 'out of which' Intellect is Intellect, and Form is Form. Categories are highest genera, and as such they are the constitutive principles of universals Aristotle mistook for categories.

Self-predication is the key unlocking the door to understanding Plotinus' categories. Indeed, we might wonder why we should characterize the activity of Intellect as motion, or why Being is listed as one of the most universal predicates when we have gone out of our way to argue that 'what it is to be' as such cannot be separate from the 'what it is to be of x'. By elucidating the categories in virtue of the activity of self-predication, we shall also illuminate the mystical aspect and discursive failure of reason in its attempts to grasp the emanation of the One.

Plotinus does not explicitly represent his account *as self-predicating*. But he clearly indicates that this is his strategy for developing his metaphysics.[28] The Intellect must be both *a* forming principle and *the sum* of the forming principles. Thought thinking itself takes itself as the object of its thinking. Within this thinking a thought abides. Since this thought is nothing but the thinking itself, *thinking is within thinking*. Or thinking in term of *mereology*, thinking would simultaneously be external to thinking, insofar as the whole is simultaneously what is contained by the whole. As I noted earlier, 'Being' is listed as one of the categories, but it cannot be treated as a separate category. Why do we find ourselves in this predicament? Treating the problem schematically again, *if thinking thinks thinking, then the particular thought that thinking thinks would be the activity of thinking itself*. So, thinking must be *a thought*, if thinking thinks thinking. If thinking is a thought, thinking is self-predicative, since the universal, 'thought as such,' is a particular thought attributed to thought itself.

What is most striking about Plotinus' formulation that it is *a forming principle and the sum of forming principles* is how close it is to Hegel's formulation of the concept for which I shall advocate later in Part II. Hegel's formulation entails the following: *the concept is both the whole concept and an element of the whole concept*. Self-referential predication is constitutive of both principles.

In Plotinus' terms, it is the very being of the *One Being* to be. Thus, Being is the whole of Intellect, its very Being. But as the object of thinking, Being must also be a particular category, separate from the whole as such, yet within the whole, since it is what is thought. Thus, we have a solution to our problem. Plotinus is not confused when he argues that Being *is and is not* a separate predicate.[29] We might still be at an impasse concerning the category of movement, since Aristotle treats motion as something, which because it is incomplete, is not a proper Being-at-work. Concerning the motion of Intellect, Plotinus connects self-contemplation with plurality.[30] Since thinking (T1) as such is a particular thought (t1), *the particular thought itself (t1) must contain thinking as such (T2) as a part (t2)*. This new part (t2), as the whole thought thinking itself (T2), must contain itself as a part (t3), *ad infinitum*. Thus, from the self-predicating process of thinking, an infinite plurality of particulars is generated. Of course, we expect this from any self-predicating process, so finding it here is no surprise. Let us now proceed to apply the infinite regress to Plotinus' account of categories. Self-predicating thought thinking itself is its own particular. For this reason, thought thinking itself is counted as a particular category, 'Being.' Thought thinking itself is a motion, since it is always moving beyond itself from particular to particular. This process never ends, and there is no particular at which the process terminates. In this sense, the Being-at-work is a motion since there is *always an outstanding particular and/or universal* lying beyond whatever particular/universal is posited. The motion is at rest in itself, for it never moves beyond this process, in its eternal self-repetition. Thus, we see how self-predication illuminates why Plotinus uses the term 'motion' to describe the activity of Intellect. Moreover, thought thinking itself is other to itself, since it is simultaneously the whole and the part. Yet, it is the same as itself in its process of self-othering, since this is its very activity.

The Problem of Circularity in Plotinus

Succinct as it may appear, Plotinus' account of categories is inherently problematic, yet instructive for our inquiry. As Aristotle before him, Plotinus rejects the notion that there is one genus of Being for the same reason Aristotle rejects it: in the epistemic aspect, *the principles of unity and difference are separate*. When we give an *account* of a species, we cannot rely on the genus alone for the difference, but we must appeal to an *external* difference.[31] For this reason, we must reject the concept that there is one genus of Being. If there were one genus over all genera, the prior difference of that genus would require a prior genus. Since there would be a prior difference and a prior genus, there would already be a plurality of genera prior to the differentiation of the single genus into genera. Hence, if there were one genus of Being, *Being would already be divided into genera* before the division of Being into genera. This conclusion is absurd, for it begs the question. In order to ensure that we do not beg the question in our account, we must reject the concept that there is one genus of Being.[32]

The principle that postulates the separation of the principles of unity and difference is integral to Plotinus' account of the categories, for instead of positing one category, as the Stoics do, he gives *five* instead. Moreover, like Aristotle before him, the separation of unity and difference gives us an account of genera in which *individuals per se* at the lowest rung of the genus structure cannot be grasped.[33] Particulars, what are one in number, as such cannot be grasped, since they preclude all Form. As Plato says, they 'march off into infinity.'[34] This is matter, the lowest level of the structure of Being. Unlike the One, its infinity is not due to its unity, but its *lack of unity*. For the One, nothing of itself is outstanding. But for the material, the residue of divine emanation, the *negative quantitative infinite* arises. The lack of unity engenders an infinitude of differences, impossible to enumerate, in which at every point in the enumeration, there is always some difference still outstanding. For later Christian thinkers, this difference in the Divine and material infinity becomes central to Christian dogma.

Perhaps at this point in the argument the problem is obvious, but it is important to state anyway. As I stated at the very beginning, the *metaphysical* position that the One emanates the totality of beings presumes that the principles of unity and difference are *not* separate, for the One is the source of the unity and plurality of all beings. Since every account always presumes a duality of principles, there cannot be any account of how the One emanates. Because we cannot provide any conceptual determination of the emanation of the One, we are forced to employ metaphors such as 'emanation' in order to elucidate the generation of particulars and universals. One should immediately recognize that if it is in the very being of the One to be One, and eschew all plurality, there can be no knowledge of the One.[35]

Earlier we noted that Plotinus appeared to appeal to self-referential predication in order to make emanation work. Yet, this requirement appears inconsistent with Plotinus' assumption that for conceptual determinacy the principles of universality and particularity are separate principles. For this reason, Plotinus must appeal to metaphor. In Part II, I will argue that Hegel recognizes what is needed in order to grasp the process of emanation. What is needed is nothing more than the rejection of the separation of the principles of universality and particularity. By rejecting the separation of these principles, Hegel thinks that he can also avoid the move to metaphor.

Moreover, since it is necessary to the very being of the One to emanate, the inability to grasp emanation necessitates the inherent unintelligibility of the One itself, and, what is the same, the intelligibility of the One as the infinite and ubiquitous, world-producing power. Since the process of emanation only works on the assumption of self-predication, yet self-predication necessitates the rejection of dual principles of unity and difference, it follows that self-predication violates the conditions for giving an account. Thus, though Plotinus writes as though self-predication were the case, he cannot accept it if he also holds to the duality of principles. Moreover, since self-predication is the means by which we could see the self-derivation of the categories from the Intellect, as their source of generation, *by relying on thought alone*, it also follows that we shall not be able to grasp the categories by relying on thought alone. Instead, we shall require metaphor and analogy in our thinking about Intellect as well. For sure, Plotinus himself admits as much, as it is central to the mystical aspects of Neo-Platonism.

Of course, none of this on its own should be surprising to Plotinus scholars or Neo-Platonists. One might first complain that there is a conflict between the metaphysical postulates and epistemic structure. The metaphysical claims cannot be justified on the epistemic assumptions, and the epistemic assumptions cannot be true if the metaphysical claims are true. Still, one might point out that Plotinus recognizes this objection via his employment of metaphor. But even so, we cannot but help to notice that Plotinus invokes the principle in order to reject the metaphysical position that there is one genus of being, yet allows it in again in the metaphysical emanation of Intellect from the One.

In light of this conflict, Plotinus points out that we cannot grasp the One Being as a whole.[36] Earlier in the Enneads, Plotinus argues that we should not identify the One Being as a *genus* of the categories because it generates them. For example, if a person generates walking, it does not follow that the person is the genus of walking.[37] But Plotinus quickly corrects himself, stating that one should not assert that the One Being is the cause of the categories. I have attempted to motivate this reasoning, since the process by which the One Being generates the categories would violate the conditions for giving an account. The power by which the One is divided into the all is a 'wonderful power' that exceeds our grasp. Since we cannot grasp the internal self-differentiation, we can only think the One Being externally, namely by *thinking about thought thinking itself.* The One Being is thereby divided into the categories or elements of the whole by *our conceptions.* What are our conceptions? Plotinus states that we know the categories in the One Being by knowing them in ourselves by analogy.[38] As Plotinus makes clear, one must first see the category in oneself before one may see it in Intellect. When we grasp the category with discursive reason, we grasp it in accordance with its governing principles. One basic assumption entailed by the commitment to separating principles of unity and difference is the *PNC.*

Since we cannot grasp how one, as One, becomes many, we can only grasp the *self-abiding* of a universal, not its self-externality. In accordance with this principle, we grasp each category as a category only when we think each as a separate, independent genus. Indeed, independence is one necessary condition of categorial being. Motion is motion, not rest, and rest is rest, not motion. Unfortunately for us, in Intellect motion is rest, and rest is motion. Accordingly, when we attempt to think the categories, we fail, for they fall back into each other, or in the words of Plotinus, 'hasten to themselves.'[39] Appearing for us as a contradiction, we cannot grasp them insofar as each is the whole. We only grasp them as separate elements.[40] Thus, we fail to grasp how each category is the whole, and for this reason, we fail to grasp the whole as such, since the elements constitute the whole. Or, what is the same, we grasp the whole Intellect as a contradiction. Notably, early German Idealism suffered a similar fate. Not only the first principle, but also the *second c*an only be thought as a pure contradiction—a difference that is no difference at all.

In itself, Intellect is an undivided whole, since no category may be separated from any other. Since the division in the Intellect is due to our external conceptions, the distinctions in Intellect themselves look to *be illusory.* The One Being *appears* many. Since the very independence of the categories is what cannot be true of them, the categories disappear from discursive reason. Ontologically, the categories are not distinct. Logically, we can only grasp them separately and thereby only *as external to Intellect.* The categorial nature of Being eludes us because Being violates the conditions of intelligibility prescribed by discursive reason. Ironically, it is Intellect that fails to be intelligible.

Let us briefly consider the categories in relation to species that fall under them. Plotinus points out that the species of a category cannot come to be from any one category, since the difference is external, but it also cannot come from non-being. If the categories exist, the species must come from a mingling of the categories, since the highest genera are the only source of differences from which to form species. Hence, it is by allowing the highest genera to mix that one may derive the lower species.[41] For example, Plotinus states that 'number consists altogether of a mixture of movement and rest.'[42] Of course, this is a problem, for the categories cannot be intelligible on their own if we acquire the content of the lower species by mixing the highest genera.

Plotinus suggests that we can grasp how the lower species fall under the highest genera by employing the notions of potentiality and Being-at-work. The lower species are potentially the whole genus, yet in respect to itself each is actual. Likewise, the whole genus is only potentially the species, but in respect to itself it is actual.[43] Unfortunately, this *fails to say how the potential becomes actual.* For this one requires some robust metaphors. Plotinus provides a host of metaphors to describe how the categories give rise to all things posterior to it. Consider the following:

> Then when you see existing in it in the way proper to Intellect this greatness, along with the beauty that there is in it of its Substance and the glory and the light around it, you see quality also, already in flower on it; and with continuity of its activity you see magnitude, quietly at rest, appearing to your gaze.[44]

'Glory,' 'light,' 'in flower,' 'quietly at rest' all substitute for the reason that is not present. Unfortunately, at each step in the process emanation seems to fall subject to question begging. We are only able to make the initial distinction between One and Intellect after we have admitted the distinction. Because the One just is one, it cannot produce any plurality from itself. On its own *the One is not a one*. By insisting that 'the One produces' we fail to even ask *how it is possible* that the One produce plurality. Plotinus tells us that it is in virtue of the One *thinking itself* that the One produces a plurality and becomes the One Being. Since the One itself does not think, it is not the self-thinking thought in virtue of which there is a plurality. Surely, the One cannot think, for if it could, it would cease to be the One. Still, somehow it is the One that is the source of all plurality, since it is the source of emanation. Indeed, the One itself *cannot begin to think* without ceasing to be the One. Thus, in order to achieve a plurality via thought thinking itself, there must *already be a plurality* in the beginning. In fact, even on Plotinus' terms, to give an *account of plurality requires a plurality*. In order to achieve a plurality in the One Being the plurality must already be given before it can be postulated, for it must already be present in the One. Since it cannot be given in the One, the plurality of being is not properly philosophically motivated, but simply posited.[45] Emanation seems to be a picture we insert between the various hypostases of One, One Being, and Soul in order to provide our reasoning with the continuity it sorely lacks.

Thus, as is evident, the very same circularity that plagues the early attempts of the German Idealists to account for the *second* principle also affects the Neo-Platonic account of emanation. Just as a purely *thetic* principle cannot account for a synthetic principle without already being synthetic, so the One cannot emanate a plurality without already being plural. Yet, this is viciously circular.

The criticism that the 'Plotinian' account begs the question may be extended to each stage of the emanating process. Since we require metaphor to grasp the categories of Intellect, we must assume the sensuous image in order to grasp what has no sensuous content. Since the former follows the latter, we must presuppose what is derived in order to derive it. Moreover, since Forms such as 'Quality' rest upon the categories, and the categories are *our conceptions* of Intellect, our conceptions become conditions of Forms, not the Forms conditions of our conceptions. Indeed, it appears that the metaphorical appeal makes any account of emanation question-begging.

The only recourse we possess is the same employed by the ancients when they encountered first principles that appeared contradictory to discursive reason: *intuition*. Plato's intuition appears to know nothing of emanation, yet Plotinus' intuition runs over with it. Still, one could attempt to make the case that, like Plato (or a very particular reading of Plato), one can only have a *mystical* encounter with the One and the Intellect. By attempting to grasp the categories, one has insight into the unity of the Intellect through the failure of discursive reason. Still, one might be at an impasse concerning whether Intellect exists and not a *mere nothing* given that one only encounters contradictions when one attempts to think it.

The emanating One implies a new sense of infinity: the intensive infinite—an infinitude signifying *total perfection* in which *nothing* is absent. Since the One *in respect to its emanation* is omnipresent and all encompassing, there is nothing outside the One. Nothing comparable to this all-encompassing unity shows up in Aristotle, and no properly philosophical term is invented for it.[46] The One is absolutely complete, for there is nothing at all external to the One. The *totality* of what is must, in this respect, be contained by the One. Yet, though the One is absolutely infinite, the One is other to all that emanates from it, as it is one and not many. Thus, in respect to itself it appears to lack intensive infinity and appears finite. This seems to constrain the One and negate its infinity. On closer inspection, this is not the case. For in respect to itself the One lacks nothing in order for it to be, since *its very being is to emanate*. Thus, it is also perfect in respect to itself. Since its very being is to emanate, the One, in respect to itself *as One*, must be absolutely infinite. This infinity is no longer understood as the absence of Being or Form, but the very condition for any Being at all, since it is entailed in the very concept of God's divine emanation.

The absolute intensive infinity of God requires that God be different from itself, since the One necessarily entails that the One be other to the One. In the intensive infinite we cannot distinguish the One from what is not the One. Insofar as this is not thinkable, for us all universality and difference vanishes, and we only grasp God's perfection as that which exceeds all differences and our conceptions. Since difference requires negation, for example 'x' as 'x' is not 'y,' one could also say that the One is that which excludes all negation. God's infinity here cannot signify that something is always outstanding, but the opposite: that which has nothing outstanding. God's Being-at-work, his completion and perfection, no longer signifies the absolute limit of finitude, but the intensive infinite. Indeed, this intensive infinity appears to be contradictory and thereby unknowable.

From these considerations it is clear that *the intensive infinite is inconsistent with the conditions governing universality*. The principle by which universals can be grasped undermines the very principle by which they exist. While Plotinus clings to a conception of universality in which *the universal is finite*, his transformation of the concept of God's infinitude radically undermines his account of universality. As long as the principles of universality, that is the PNC and the duality of principles of unity and plurality, are inconsistent with the principle by which the universal exists (emanation), our metaphysical nightmare shall not end. Indeed, it appears that we shall have no shelter from the metaphysical horror generated by *the indivisibility of the first principle*. Our only refuge to contemplate universality lies in the metaphor of the 'overflow,' a metaphor that, unfortunately, only reminds us that we are still laden with the problem we set out to solve.

Concluding Remarks: Analysis of the Problem

For both Plotinus and early German Idealism, the constraints they place upon the form of knowing undermine the possibility of accounting for the existence of any synthetic unity or plural existence. Indeed, whether the purported first principle of knowing and Being is the I or the One, synthetic being and knowing as well as the being and the knowing of the many appear impossible. Yet, this is patently absurd—for synthesis and plurality exist and are known to exist.

Without an account of any differentiation, neither Neo-Platonism nor early German Idealism could *account for any positional being*—any determination positioned vis-à-vis another. In his *Science of Logic*, according to Hegel, 'determinateness is a negation posited as affirmative.'[47] Moreover, determinate being is 'the sphere of difference, of dualism, the field of finitude.'[48] One of Hegel's many insights is that every determinate concept already contains both reality and negation. Each concept has its own conceptual content—this is its reality. This reality is determinate if it excludes or negates what is *other* to it. Accordingly, what is determinate negates what is other, and thereby maintains its own independence apart from the other. In this way, every determinate concept contains *negation*—the exclusion of the other. Accordingly, whenever it is true to say of something that it is 'something' or 'other,' one is operating within the sphere of determinacy, which requires invoking both concepts of reality and negation (among others). This dualism can be described in different ways as the dualism of being and nothing, reality and negation, or something and other. Accordingly, for as long as Idealism remained at an impasse regarding the possibility of difference and finitude, it remained at an impasse regarding the possibility of *determinacy and negation*.

Because the Absolute principle cannot create any opposition on its own, it stands by itself. What stands absolutely by itself—*auto kath auto*—cannot be determinate. Since the Absolute principle of identity (or the One) appears to stand alone, it would be *absolutely indeterminate*. Indeterminacy poses a significant philosophical problem: every time one attempts to *conceive* of the indeterminate, one renders indeterminacy an object of *determinate knowing*. As long as the absolute indeterminacy remains *separate* from positional knowing (or positional being), it *cannot remain indeterminate*. But this paradox illuminates a further feature of this absolute indetermination: since indeterminacy cannot stand *opposed* to determinate being without becoming determinate itself, indeterminacy can only remain indeterminate by no longer remaining opposed to it. Thus, what is non-positional can only remain non-positional by occupying *every* position.[49] In terms of the infinite, infinity *qua* indeterminacy appears to engender the intensive infinite. Hegel's logic too begins with total indeterminacy and finishes with the intensive infinite—an infinity lacking nothing, perfect and complete.

If the One or the I cannot in principle produce an other from which it can stand in a determinate relation, then there is no other—no All—by which it would be rendered determinate. Since the determinacy of the first principle requires an other to negate, the first principle is absolutely indeterminate. Thus, the One cannot have the determination of *being one*, the I cannot *be the I*. Accordingly, the problem of the origin of the world might be rephrased as follows: how is it possible for there to *be anything determinate at all?* As it turns out, the problem of the origin of determinate being is also a problem of the *origin of negation*. By failing to account for how negation is possible, the putative first principle *negates itself*. Without the All, there is no One, for the difference between them is a condition for their determinacy, and it is exactly this difference for which one cannot give an account. Accordingly, this very *self-negation* must itself become thematic for speculative thinking, as it does in the mature thinking of Schelling and Hegel. Whether one takes a pure thesis as one's principle or the One, the world disappears in either case.

Despite the analogical problem in each system of philosophy, early German Idealism nonetheless makes an important *advance* upon the earlier Neo-Platonic paradigm. As Hegel acknowledges:

> It is only in recent times that thinkers have become aware of the difficulty of finding a beginning in philosophy, and the reason for this difficulty and also the possibility of resolving it has been much discussed. What philosophy begins with must be either mediated or immediate, and it is easy to show that it can be neither the one nor the other; thus either way of beginning is refuted.[50]

Fichte, Schelling, and Hegel all recognize the need for a *rational* account of *how* the infinite becomes finite. They recognize that in order for there to be a *science* of the Absolute, the principle in virtue of which the infinite becomes finite cannot depend upon an *extra-rational* principle. Accordingly, the mysticism of Neo-Platonism cannot be adopted without undermining the possibility of philosophical science. Indeed, one of the pressing philosophical emergencies of early German Idealism consists in the recognition that in order for there to be a science of the Absolute we must be able to show how the infinite becomes finite in rational terms, but this is exactly what we cannot accomplish. Hegel recognizes that the source of the impasse lies in the assumption that conceptual determination is structured *a priori* by the *absolute separation* of principles of identity and difference. As long as the difference cannot be deduced from identity, from pure identity no further determination can be deduced.

Thus far the argument has *only* shown that the duality of the principles of identity and difference is a problem only because all knowledge and being ought to be grounded in *one single principle of absolute identity*. As our analysis has shown, any attempt to ground knowledge or being in a single foundational principle cannot succeed, as long as one insists that the domain of concepts is constituted by the separation of the principles of identity and difference.

Notes

1. Although Aquinas does convincingly show in his *Summa Contra Gentiles* that creation cannot be out of a pre-existing material, his alternative conception, creation ex nihilo, is no more intelligible than the alternatives he refutes. See Thomas Aquinas, *Summa Theologica*, ed. Anton C. Pegis (Indianapolis: Hackett, 1997), 426–457.
2. See Plato's so-called 'unwritten doctrine' as it appears in Aristotle. Aristotle, *Metaphysics*, trans. Joe Sachs (Santa Fe: Green Lion Press, 2002), 987 b. The One is beyond all determination, and thus indeterminate, while the Indefinite Dyad, *qua* indefinite, posits the indeterminate as a principle. I would hesitate

to identify the principles of the unwritten doctrine with the quantitative infinite, since quantity is derived from these principles, as the second deduction in *Parmenides* shows. See Plato, "Parmenides," in *Plato: Complete Works,* ed. John M. Cooper (Indianapolis: Hackett Publishing, 1997), 359–398, 142b. Ironically enough, each principle is limited by its contrary principle. Moreover, the quantitative infinite reveals itself as a problem in Plato's Third Man argument from Plato, "Parmenides," 132a–d, 366.

3. Aristotle, "Physics," in *Complete Works of Aristotle,* trans. R. P. Hardie and R. K. Gaye (Princeton: Princeton University Press,1984), 315–447, 351–353. Nonetheless, we ought not oversimplify Aristotle's position on the infinite—the existence of potentiality does not completely exclude activity. For Aristotle's concept of prime material invokes the concept of the infinite as indeterminate. Prime material is not determined by a Form and is thereby infinite as indeterminate. For this very reason, prime material cannot be. Likewise, his definition of motion, the Being-at-work of potential *qua* potential, implies that motion is complete or a Being-at-work (the end is not outstanding) so long as it is potential or incomplete (the end is still outstanding). So, motion's determinate being is indeterminate in virtue of being the 'always outstanding.'

4. Plato, "Philebus," in *Plato: Complete Works,* ed. John M. Cooper (Indianapolis: Hackett Publishing, 1997), 398–457, 27c, 415. 'As the first I count the unlimited, limit as the second, afterwards in third place comes the being which is mixed and generated out of those two. And no mistake is made if the cause of this mixture and generation is counted as number four.'

5. Elizabeth Brient, *The Immanence of the Infinite: Hans Blumenberg and the Threshold to Modernity* (Washington: Catholic University of America Press), 111.

6. Plato, "Republic," in *Plato: Complete Works*, ed. John M. Cooper (Indianapolis: Hackett Publishing, 1997), 971–1224, 509b8.

7. Brient, *The Immanence of the Infinite,* 57.

8. Hegel, *SL,* trans. Miller, 153.

9. Plotinus, *Enneads,* 7 Vols. Loeb Classical Library, trans. A. H. Armstrong (Cambridge: Harvard University Press, 1988), 6.9.6.1–13.

10. Ibid, 5.8.9.25–28.

11. In Plotinus the generation of the world is grounded on one principle, not two. Unlike the ancient account moreover, the process of emanation is one of *degradation,* or process by which unity is lost, so that the lowest rung of being is an utterly indefinite plurality.

12. The productivity of Aristotelian Form is well exhibited in his affirmation of the validity of inferring the existence of particulars from the universal. For Aristotle, from the truth of 'All A is B' one can validly infer the truth that 'Some A is B' (the subaltern).

13. This also explains why, for example, children are not fully human on Aristotle's account or why persons whose reason is deformed are not fully human. One can only write a dissertation on universality if one's rational faculties have come to maturation.

14. Plotinus, *Enneads,* 5.1.6 37–39.

15. Of course, it almost goes without saying that the One is not like the examples I posit in defense of the principle that what is perfect produces, for the One is not many.

16. Brient, *The Immanence of the Infinite,* 113.

17. Plotinus, *Enneads*, VI. II (6.2), 131, 133.

18. Ibid, VI. II, 111.

19. Ibid, 113.

20. Plotinus rejects the genus of Being on the same grounds as Aristotle, namely that there would be no source of difference.
21. The ordering of species within a genus only appears to be horizontal.
22. Plotinus, *Enneads*, VI. I, 13–17.
23. Ibid, VI. I, 21.
24. The first and second hypostasis seem to at least loosely correspond to the first and second hypotheses of Plato, "Parmenides," 'The One is one' (137c) and 'The One is' (142b).
25. Plotinus, *Enneads*, VI. II, 127–129.
26. Ibid, 133.
27. Ibid, 137.
28. Plotinus, *Enneads* VI. II, 127. In this passage Plotinus is primarily discussing the soul. But it is clear that here he does not make a very fine distinction between Soul and Intellect. Plotinus states that the soul is 'from the intelligible place' (125) and consistently attributes life to Intellect (129 and 133).
29. Plotinus, *Enneads*, VI. II, 163.
30. Ibid, 129.
31. See, for example, Plotinus, *Enneads* IV. II, 117: 'for how could the one become many, so as to generate species, unless there were something else besides itself? For it could not by its own means become many' and 163: 'Does being, for instance, already divide by itself without the others? No: since it must take its differentiations from outside the genus.'
32. Plotinus, *Enneads*, VI. II, 117.
33. Ibid, 175.
34. Plato, "Parmenides," 144B4–C1, 377.
35. 'We in our travail do not know what we ought to say, and are speaking of what cannot be spoken, and give it a name because we want to indicate it to ourselves as best we can. But perhaps this name "One" contains only a denial of multiplicity. . . . But if the One—name and reality expressed—was to be taken positively it would be less clear than if we did not give it a name at all: for perhaps this name [One] was given it in order that the seeker beginning from this which is completely indicative of simplicity, may finally negate this as well, because, though it was given as well as possible by its giver, not even this is worthy to manifest its nature.' Plotinus, *Enneads*, 5.5.6.26–35.
36. Plotinus, *Enneads*, VI.II, 121.
37. Ibid, 119.
38. Ibid, 135.
39. As Brient points out, the Intellect and the Soul are complete and simultaneous unities, infinite in the sense of *adiastaton*. In the sense of *adiastaton* they are continuous with themselves, not discrete. Brient, *The Immanence of the Infinite*, 112.
40. For example, see Plotinus, *Enneads*, VI. II, 131,133, and 135.
41. Ibid, 165.
42. Ibid, 153.
43. Ibid, 166–167.
44. Ibid, 169.
45. Put more simply, if one asks 'why is there Intellect?' one cannot be given an answer without begging the question. Plato requires no account of emanation, so I do not think this particular objection applies to him.
46. Although the term 'cosmos' implies totality and completion, it does not imply a totality in which there is one principle responsible for all differences. It is this latter principle from which the intensive infinite is derived.
47. Hegel, *SL*, trans. Miller, 113.

48. Ibid, 157.
49. Indeed—the non-positionality of the indeterminate appears to be the conceptual *source* (ἀρχή) of the Ancient insight that the indeterminate exceeds its own limits.
50. Hegel, *SL*, trans. Miller, 67.

3 Dual Principles of Truth and the Problem of Instantiation

Introduction: Towards a Duality of Principles

If identity ought to be the *sufficient* principle of differentiated and determinate being, then the creation of difference from pure identity becomes an insoluble *mystery* or a truth of faith. Still, one might suspect that the reason this question cannot be answered philosophically lies in the *false* assumption that content can be sufficiently derived from form alone or difference from identity alone. To put it simply, one could avoid the appeal to faith and mysticism by *abandoning the commitment to one first principle*.

In order to maintain a commitment to the absolute *rationality* of being and knowledge, one could abandon the commitment to a first principle of knowledge and being. The solution appears simple: by denying that that there is *only* one principle of identity and difference, one is no longer charged with explaining *how* difference arises from identity or how plurality arises out of unity. Such a solution would insist upon (at the very least) the *irreducibility* of *two* separate principles in philosophical knowing—a principle of identity and a principle of difference. Indeed, this solution to the problem is the most pervasive and recurring solution to the problem of the disappearance of the Absolute in the history of Western philosophy. Note that this solution to the problem affirms a *return* to *the duality* of principles characteristic of Plato and Kant's philosophy. Of course, Hegel *too* abandons the project of deducing all truth and being from one principle, but he denies the path of Plato, Aristotle, and Kant in his *absolute denial of all first principles*— whether they be one or many.

In systematic terms, the recognition of the *irreducibility* of the division of principles of identity and difference reverses the order of identity and difference in knowing and being. Rather than taking identity as the given from which difference ought to be derived, this solution, to put it ironically, *unknowingly* takes *the difference* between identity and difference as *the single principle*. Because difference is taken for granted as an absolute starting point, the opposing sides of the difference, for example form and content or identity and difference, can be posited as particular principles that enable the philosopher to give an account of knowing and being.

One might suppose that the mistake of both Neo-Platonism as well as the early tradition of early German Idealism seems to consist in the *conflation* of the principles of identity and difference in being and knowing. Despite wide-ranging differences in the historical conception of the concept, this generic solution leaves some fundamental structures of logical or conceptual determination unquestioned. Indeed, this generic solution maintains with the early German Idealists that *concepts (or universals) are governed by a duality of principles*: a principle of identity as well as a principle of difference. The most important change for our reflections concerns the *application* of that conceptual determinacy.

In what follows, I show that although the problem concerning the *origin* of the world (the problem of Nihilism) does not arise in the *same* form that it appeared in Neo-Platonism and early German Idealism, this *generic* solution to the problem nonetheless falls victim to a host of intractable problems, including the disappearance of the Absolute. Importantly, at a very meta-philosophical level, despite the great variety in the way that concepts have been conceived historically, this generic solution does not question the duality of principles endemic to the form of the concept—instead it revises the content of its metaphysical and epistemic theories and expectations in order that they *correspond with the form of logical thinking* constituted in a *dualistic* manner. Accordingly, the true account of knowing and Being means to avoid the disappearance of the Absolute in philosophical thought (as expressed in the problem of Nihilism) by making its metaphysical and epistemic propositions conform to the *dualistic* form of the concept. Following this dualistic structure of the concept, this generic solution to the problem denies a *single* principle of truth.[1] If a coherent concept of truth cannot be achieved by appealing to one principle alone, truth may only be coherently conceived on the supposition of a duality of principles. As scholars of Kant know, it is Kant, more than any other before him, who recognized that such an approach is doomed to fail. When *difference is absolutized*, the Absolute cannot be truly conceived.

As is evident enough, Plotinus' account of emanation as well as Schelling's argument for *one* principle of truth deviate significantly from their predecessors. As we have already discussed in some detail, Kant posits at least *two principles* for truth—concept and intuition. Similarly, the Neo-Platonic grounding of all underlying subjects (Intellect, Soul, etc.) as emanating from One principle is a significant deviation from earlier Greek philosophy—especially Aristotle, despite his integration of various Aristotelian concepts. In Chapter 1 we demonstrated that the problem of the origin of determinate being, and thereby a determinate conception of the Absolute, affects philosophical thinking whether one begins with metaphysics or epistemology as first philosophy. Given the indifference of the problem to the way first philosophy is conceived, we ought to be able to *illustrate* the generic form of this solution to the problem of the origin of determinate being and knowing in both its 'critical' and 'pre-critical' forms.[2] Accordingly, I will indicate the trajectory of this tentative solution by reconstructing the duality of category and intuition that lies at the ground of Kant's *Critique of Pure Reason* as well as the irreparable dichotomy between universal and particular in the thought of Plato's *Parmenides*. Further, we will uncover the form of *logical* duality of Form and material endemic to Aristotle. In the course of the analysis, however, we will discover that the uniqueness of Aristotle's thought, among other things, lies in his recognition that one must significantly qualify any appeal to a duality of principles in one's account of the Absolute.

Following the reconstruction of two varieties of this solution to the problem, we will see that those who employ a duality of principles themselves raise significant critiques of the capacity of philosophy to know the Absolute. In the following chapters, I show that any view that insists upon the irreducibility of conceptual principles of identity and difference engenders *five paradoxes*: the problem of instantiation, the problem of the missing difference, absolute empiricism, onto-theology, and the Third Man. Accordingly, just as difference goes missing in the accounts of knowing and Being in Neo-Platonism and early German Idealism, so it also goes missing in their dualistic predecessors.

The Duality of Principles in Kant

For Kant, concepts may be conceived either empirically or *a priori*. An empirical concept is a common mark of some set of empirical intuitions, for example 'bald.' An *a priori* concept, though not simply a common mark, is a unity under which a multiple is grasped as one, for example 'bodies are extended.' In this judgement, I grasp a multitude of bodies as one in the predicate 'extended.' If I think about what is entailed in the concept, I do not thereby discover the instances of that concept. For example, if I 'divide' the concept of 'body' into the conceptual features constitutive of it, I do not discover the particular bodies that fall under 'body.' Instead, I simply find the 'what it is to be' of a body. Indeed, as a common feature of a plurality, or a *one* over many, the concept by itself does not specify which particulars fall under the concept, nor does it tell me what other properties belong to the objects to which the concept applies. Given this limitation, in order to acquire an *instance* of the concept, one must appeal to a principle external to the concept. This is a basic principle of Kant's: Sensibility provides the objects that the Understanding thinks, but the Understanding, the faculty of concepts, cannot provide its own objects. As is evident, the very distinction between the faculties tracks the difference between the concept and its instantiation. Further, Kant's commitment to the thesis that the concept is not sufficient to differentiate its own particulars that fall under it can be illustrated in Kant's distinction between concepts and intuitions.

Space and time are each, according to Kant, single. For Kant, since particular spaces or times may be accessed via a *limitation* of space and time, the instance of space and time is located *within* space and time. The relation of space to a particular space, as well as time to a particular time, is *immediate*, for one must not appeal to anything *external* to space, or any other mediating factor, to derive the particular. Space and time are sufficient for a complete derivation of their particulars. Concepts, on the other hand, only give us mediated access to the objects, for they do *not* contain their own instances. Concepts only provide a *partial* determination of their objects and require *external* principles for the derivation of the particular. Therefore, for Kant space and time are a *priori* intuitions, not concepts, for they contain a *manifold in them a priori*. As *a priori* intuitions, space and time contain their own *a priori* content. Each is a 'manifold' (*Mannigfaltigkeit*) of contents. As is evident, whereas the intuitions may be sufficient principles of their own particularity (even if those particulars are indeterminate), for Kant concepts are *not* sufficient for deriving their instances.

By the time of Kant's *Critique of Pure Reason*, Aristotelian logic had already undergone some fundamental changes. Aristotle's logic is inherently a *logic of truth*, whose terms are inseparable from beings that exist. Precisely to the extent that logic is inseparable from truth, Aristotle's logic is *not formal*. Though the reception of Aristotelian syllogistic retained much of the central tents of Aristotelian logic, its ontological significance had long been shed. By the time of Kant the tradition had rendered logic *per se* an inherently formal discipline. Kant's term for the content-free system of logic he inherited from the tradition is 'formal logic.'

Formal logic is the science of thinking *per se*, without regard to what is thought. As a science of thinking that does not take into account the content of thinking, formal logic ultimately rests on the *PNC*, which in Kant's terms, states that contradictory predicates cannot be attributed to the same subject.[3] The PNC gives a criterion of *consistency*. Though a proposition may be consistent, it does not follow that it is true, since a proposition may be consistent with itself and other propositions, yet still be false. This possibility shows that the PNC does not allow us to determine what is true, but at best, which judgments are *candidates* for truth. A logic that only determines the candidates for truth possesses a greater domain of application than any logic of truth, since the universe of discourse concerns what is logically *possible*, not what exists or necessarily exists. For the system of formal logic (and unlike Aristotle's system), 'Essence' is no longer an essential moment in the logical system.

In contrast to formal logic, Kant introduces his *own* truth logic, which he calls *transcendental logic*. Unlike formal logic, transcendental logic does not abstract from all content whatsoever, and although in his affirmation of a logic of truth Kant does not deviate from the Aristotelian tradition, the form of his truth logic does, for his truth logic is *transcendental*: it comprehends the necessary conditions for the possibility of experience. More concretely, transcendental logic grasps the categories that are necessary for *any object of experience to be an object of experience*. Such a logic could not abstract from all content without ceasing to be what it is: *the logical form of object-hood as such*. Since transcendental logic thinks what is universal and necessary to being an *object* of experience, it does exclude all empirical cognition. For insofar as any empirical cognition is not universal and necessary to any object of experience as such, but contingently related thereto, no empirical concept is entailed in the concept of the object as an object. Transcendental logic determines the truth as such, or better, what is true in *every experience of an object* as such. The content of transcendental logic does specify what logical structures *in the Understanding* are necessary for the possibility of experience. In this way, transcendental logic specifies how logical structures of subjectivity constitute the object.

As we elucidated in Chapter 1, when faced with the question, 'what is truth?', the formal logician is at a loss for words. Since truth is the *correspondence* of the concept with the object, and formal logic abstracts from all content, no general mark may be found for the correspondence of the concept with the object within the *canon* of formal logic itself. Indeed, if the rationalist's aim is to grasp the truth as such through thinking alone, yet reason is merely a formal discipline, it appears that Truth itself cannot be grasped by thinking alone. Rationalism cannot conceive of truth as long as it considers reason to be a merely formal discipline. Thus, in order for transcendental logic to establish *a priori* truth, *a priori* categories must have *a priori* content that is *not* culled from the categories themselves. Kant is clear: *a priori* truth is only possible if there are a *duality of a priori principles* of form and content. *Truth requires two principles.*

It is in a judgment that *different representations are ordered under a common one*, for example different bodies are ordered under 'body.' Kant calls the unity of action that orders different representations *under* a common one a *function*. Since judgment is just the application of a concept, each distinct form of judgment contains its *own distinct concept*. Each form of judgment, simply as a form of judgment, is *formal*, for it abstracts from what is being judged, or the content of judgment. Given that concepts only apply to objects in the act of judgment, Kant postulates that the *a priori* concepts inherent in understanding, the categories or unifying functions in acts of judgment, can be discovered by enumerating *every* form of judgment *per se*.

If we follow Kant that concepts without intuitions are empty and intuitions without concepts are blind, then concepts as concepts do not provide their *own* manifold of intuition. Kant separates the principles of unity (universal) and difference (the particular), except here they are posited as *faculties*. Understanding is a faculty of concepts (what we have been calling universals), and Sensibility is the faculty of intuition (particulars). For Kant, *without connection to the particular the universal cannot be given any determinate intuitive content*. Any account of truth, the correspondence of the concept with the object, will also be an account of the intuitive content of the concept. This is also why Kant calls the transcendental logic a 'logic of truth.'

The *Transcendental Schema* provides the representation that makes possible the application of the category to the empirical intuition. All empirical intuitions are given in time, which is a condition for the possibility of the givenness of phenomena. Not only are all empirical intuitions given in time, but time itself is pure: it contains an *a priori* manifold. Thus, time fulfills the conditions required of the Schematism: it is both pure and contains a sensible manifold. As we stated earlier, the *a priori* categories, in order to acquire content, require a pure *a priori* manifold in order to fulfill them with content. Since each category is distinct, each category will require a *distinct* transcendental time-determination by which it applies to intuition.[4] Indeed, we have no concrete understanding of the categories, that is regarding their content and application, unless we grasp the transcendental time determination that gives them content. In order for transcendental logic to establish *a priori* truth, *a priori* categories must have *a priori* content that is not culled from the categories themselves.[5] Since *a priori* concepts are empty in themselves, in order for them to function transcendentally, and not merely formally, they must have a content that corresponds to their *a priori* character. Since the categories cannot be their own source of *intuitive* content, the only *a priori* content available for the categories is the *a priori* manifold given in the intuitions of space and time.

Categories do not categorize themselves, or in Kant's language, categories do not synthesize themselves. Rather, they synthesize content outside of themselves—intuitions. Accordingly, Kant is clear that categories are *not* self-predicating: quality itself is not a quality, quantity itself is not a quantity. Were the categories self-predicating, they would themselves function as the matter for their own synthetic activity. Indeed, were the categories self-predicating, the category would itself count as an instance of the category: quality would itself be *a* quality. Since categories are empty independently of intuitions, categories cannot account for their own particularity. Rather, particularity must be garnered from another source, for example intuition. For Kant, the absence of self-synthesis is systematically connected with the requirement that a second principle in addition to categories must be supplied in order for the category to fulfill its synthetic activity. Positing a duality of principles—one of form, the other of material—entails a rejection of self-predication.

The function of the *Transcendental Analytic* and the Schemata in the *Critique of Pure Reason* is to set the limits for the proper application of categories. Upon demarcating the proper sphere of application for the categories to the contents given in Sensibility, all application beyond Sensibility is *verboten*, a category error. When reason treats formal logic as an *organon*, instead of a canon for thinking, it assumes that it can determine what is true irrespective of any appeal to intuition. When formal reason treats itself this way, it fails to understand itself and its limits. *Thinking as such cannot determine what is true independently of intuition.* Kant deems any logic that treats itself as an organon for truth, what Kant terms 'dialectic,' a *logic of illusion*, since it treats formal principles as though they were sufficient for the determination of their own content or their own truth. Indeed, without the inability of the concept to sufficiently account for its own instantiation Kant could not successfully make this distinction between logic as an organon and logic as a canon, which is so central to his critique of pure reason. Kant's theses that (i) *formal logic is not an organon for truth* and (ii) *no category ought to be applied beyond the limits of Sensibility* can only be defended if concepts are *not* self-particularizing.

The limitation of the knowable to appearances has another important subjective correlate in the concept of intellectual intuition. Since the thinking of the concept does not ensure the existence of the concept, the Understanding cannot have the power of intellectual intuition. In contrast to the human Understanding, Kant introduces intellectual intuition as a limit concept, analogous to noumena, which is problematic in a similar way. Since our Understanding does not provide its own manifold of intuition, *thinking cannot produce its own objects.*[6] A divine Understanding would provide its own manifold of intuition simply in virtue of thinking alone. The mistake of Rationalism is to confuse our Understanding with that of God, that is to think that thinking alone is sufficient for the comprehension of objects. Instead, the empiricists were right to limit the thinkable to experience, but they did not understand how the *a priori* could have a role despite that restriction. By requiring an external source of content, Kant renders the power of the concept merely discursive and banishes intellectual intuition from realm of the concept, instead demoting its status to that of a problematic limit concept. 'Intellectual intuition' signifies the possibility of intuiting the object merely intellectually. If we were able to intuit objects intellectually, in this case we would have no need for Sensibility. Likewise, we would have no need for the categories, since their basic function is to bring the contents of intuition to the synthetic unity of apperception. Indeed, we would grasp the object independently of how the object appeared to us: our grasp would be *noumenal*. Here it becomes evident that the concept of the noumena and intellectual intuition have been wedded together: the noumena is the object of an Understanding that intuits what it thinks. We do not intuit in virtue of thinking; thus, we do not grasp noumena.

Modern Rationalism, as exhibited in the philosophy of Descartes, Spinoza, and Leibniz, preserves *existential implication*, the deduction of the existence of the particular from the universal, in the concept of God.[7] Namely, it is in the ontological argument that existential implication retains its appeal: If God is God, then God exists. With Kant's *Critique of Pure Reason*, the last vestige of existential implication characteristic of Modern Rationalism disappears, a logical consequence demanded by the transformation of logic into a merely formal system.[8] Kant's rejection of the ontological argument is a particular application of his more *general rejection of existential implication*: since no concepts are sufficient for the deduction of their own instances, this principle must also apply to the concept of God.

Were human Understanding existentially implicative, it could know the object of the Idea. Since conceptual determination is determined by two principles of universality and particularity, Kant can bar the human Understanding from knowing what exists and is true *in itself*.

Kant raises three objections to the ontological argument. A contradiction is a logical relation that obtains between propositions, for example 'every man is mortal,' 'not every man is mortal.' In order to have a contradiction in which contradictory predicates are attributed to the same subject, one must already presuppose a subject to exist. The question concerning the existence of God is a question concerning the existence of the subject 'God.' If, by hypothesis, there is no God, then there cannot be a contradiction, for there would be no subject possessing contradictory predicates. So, it appears that the ontological argument must assume the existence of the subject to generate the contradiction, which begs the question.

Kant notes that the proponent can easily respond by arguing that there is at least one subject that could not fail to be without a contradiction— God. Still, even this response cannot help but be circular. For, 'God exists' is either an analytic claim or a synthetic one. If 'God exists' were an analytic claim, then 'exists' would be a mere repetition of what is already stated in the subject 'God,' rendering the claim a 'miserable' tautology. If 'God exists' were a synthetic claim, which Kant thinks it must be, since it concerns existence, we could not establish that God 'exists' by the employment of a merely formal principle, since analysis cannot, by itself, produce a synthetic proposition.[9]

Despite these arguments, the proponent of the ontological argument could argue that 'God exists' is a synthetic claim that is established by analysis alone. In response, Kant makes a distinction that he thinks has gone long overlooked and allowed Reason to neglect the bounds of its proper application. 'Existence' (*Sein*) cannot be analyzed out of a subject as a predicate, since 'existence' is not a predicate. When one thinks the concept of something, for example $100, and one thinks $100 that exists, 'that it exists' does not add anything to *the content of the concept*, namely it adds nothing to 'what it is' that I think. Whether the concept of '$100' is or is not, the content of the concept contains the same content, that is '$100.' To state that a being exists is not to predicate existence to an existing being, but instead *it is to posit the subject as such*. This is the function of the existential quantifier 'there is some x.' Some subject must exist in order for it to have predicates. The copula 'is' is a necessary condition for predication, for example 'x is,' but it is not a predicate itself. Indeed, *the distinction between analysis and synthesis* implies that existence cannot be analyzed out of the subject. If Kant allowed existence to be a predicate, the distinction between analysis and synthesis would collapse, as would his ban on intellectual intuition and our capacity to know Noumena. Certainly, Kant's separation of the principles of universality and particularity engenders the non-predicative character of existence.

Most important in these considerations is how they pertain to the concept of truth. What the previous argument illuminates is that concepts, in themselves, contain merely what is *possible*. The *actual* $100 does not contain *any more conceptual content* than what is contained in the *mere possibility* of $100. The point is simply that existence cannot be analyzed out of concepts, whether they are instantiated in intuition or not, since the concept itself only contains what is possible, not what is actual. If we allowed existence to be a predicate, we would *undermine the very possibility of truth*. For if the actual object contained more conceptual content than the concept itself, the concept would not be able to correspond with the object. In order for a concept to correspond with the object, the concept must find itself in the object, that is be immanent in the object. If there were no concept immanent in the object, the concept would not have anything with which it could correspond, since the only content would be *non-conceptual*. In order for the conceptual to correspond with what is non-conceptual, the concept insofar as it obtains in intuition (the non-conceptual content) cannot contain *any more* conceptual content than the concept *by itself* (considered independently of intuition). Otherwise, *all* hope for truth is lost. This illuminates something about objective truth, namely that it is the correspondence of the concept with itself, or the *self-correspondence* of the concept in content foreign to the concept, in Kant's terminology, 'intuition.'[10] Although the coherence theory of truth is often introduced only once correspondence of the concept with the object is deemed impossible, In Kant's analysis coherence is already built into the concept of correspondence. Correspondence is a kind of *coherence of the concept with itself in another*.

For Kant, truth is only possible if we maintain a rigid distinction between the concept and its particularization, and we never allow that the concept be sufficient for its realization. In short, truth is only possible on the supposition of a duality of principles. Profoundly, Kant's concept of truth, and the duality of principles endemic to it, are deployed in order to bar access to our knowledge of the Idea of God. For Kant, the system of knowledge precludes the possibility of the cognition of any Idea, which has *the Absolute* as its object. The Absolute cannot appear as an object of cognition, and it is exactly the *conditioned nature of cognition* that makes such an appearance impossible. Since any concept that is true in virtue of intuition is not true in virtue of itself, all concepts that are made true by intuition are *relative* truths. Since divine Understanding constituted by intellectual intuition would intuit its object in virtue of thinking it, intellectual intuition would know the truth of the concept by thinking alone. Thus, intellectual intuition would be a knowing that is Absolute (or non-relative), for the concept would be *true in virtue of itself*, not in virtue of something else. The object known by intellectual intuition (*Nous*), the *Noumenon*, would be that which is true in virtue of itself—that which is *true in itself*. The Absolute truth, what is true 'itself by itself' cannot be known. What can be known is what is true relative to us.

It is true that Kant's Copernican revolution takes the knowing of Being as the primary object of philosophical knowing, thereby displacing the inquiry into Being *qua* being as first philosophy. Nonetheless, from within this transcendental framework, Kant continues an Aristotelian tradition—truth is a way of saying '*existence.*' As our analysis has shown, a concept is true when it obtains in existence, or what is the same—when it obtains in intuition. When the $100 *exists* in my bank account I can say that it is *true* that I have $100. In short, from an analysis of the concept alone one just as little discovers whether the concept is true or whether it exists.

In sum, not only does the duality of principles in Kant undergird Kant's account of the possibility of experience, but it also provides the ground for his critique of speculative metaphysics. Most importantly, Kant's conception of truth only maintains its coherence upon the supposition of such a duality. Kant's Copernican revolution means not only to overthrow the old regime but also to *preserve* the commitment to truth, which he finds compromised within the confines of dogmatic metaphysics. Indeed, this commitment to truth leads Kant to deny that philosophy can have knowledge of the Absolute. What is true in virtue of itself—itself by itself—cannot be known as long as we recognize the duality of principles that constitute cognition proper.

The Problem of Instantiation in Plato

The appeal to a duality of principles of universality and particularity as constitutive of philosophical knowing is not unique to Kant, as a brief history of Western philosophy will attest. Still, in order to demonstrate that the problem of positing a duality of principles is just as much problematic for a philosophy that takes *knolwedge* as first philosophy as well as that philosophy which take *Being* as the object of first philosophy, we ought to briefly consider the case of Plato's *Parmenides*, which illustrates in its own unique way how the separation of universality from particularity undermines the possibility of Absolute Knowledge.

Young Socrates' Theory of Forms posits that each Form (*eidos*) is itself by itself, (*auto kath auto*). So, if any Form admitted its opposite, it would cease to be itself. It would be opposed to itself. Plato adopts this commitment to the PNC from Parmenides' *Way of Truth*. Universals have Being and are called the things that are (*ta onta*) because they are the objects of thought and are thereby non-contradictory. To take an example from *Phaedo*, while the Form of Equality is never itself unequal, but is always equal to itself, sensible objects, for example the human hand, are both equal and unequal to themselves and to others. The sensibles, unlike the Forms, admit the back-turning, and have their being in their non-being. On the one hand, each Form is '*auto kath auto*,' itself by itself. In its isolation, the Form never admits what is other and thereby never admits what it is not. Accordingly, what is 'itself by itself' cannot be contradictory. From the outset of the *Parmenides*, Young Socrates is committed to the thesis that universals are governed by the PNC. What exists 'itself by itself' exists in its own right and, to use our language, constitutes Absolute Being.

Unlike the variegated hierarchy of Forms in *Republic*, the Theory of Forms, as young Socrates posits it, is quite simple: there are universals, for example 'Likeness,' and particulars, for example a human hand. The things we call 'many,' the particulars, acquire their determinate character by 'partaking' or taking a share in the universal that shares its name. The universal is a 'one over many,' a thing in virtue of which particulars have being. Accordingly, a particular finger is like other fingers through participation in Likeness itself and unlike other fingers through participation in Unlikeness. As Socrates suggests, there is nothing wondrous about a human hand partaking in opposing qualities, since it is like and unlike via participation in different Forms.

Although Plato considers many arguments against the concept of participation, in what follows we focus on one argument—*the problem of instantiation*:

> 'So does each thing that gets a share get as its share the form as a whole or a part of it? Or could there be some other means of getting a share apart from these two?'
> 'How could there be?' he said.
> 'Do you think, then, that the form as a whole—one thing—is in each of the many? Or what do you think?'
> 'What's to prevent its being one, Parmenides?' said Socrates.

'So, being one and the same, it will be at the same time, as a whole, in things that are many and separate; and thus it would be separate from itself.'

'No it wouldn't,' Socrates said. 'Not if it's like one and the same day. That is in many places at the same time and is none the less not separate from itself. If it's like that, each of the forms might be, at the same time, one and the same in all.'

'Socrates,' he said, 'how neatly you make one and the same thing be in many places at the same time! It's as if you were to cover many people with a sail, and then say that one thing as a whole is over many. Or isn't that the sort of thing you mean to say?'

'Perhaps,' he replied.

'In that case would the sail be, as a whole, over each person, or would a part of it be over one person and another part over another?'

'A part.'

'So the forms themselves are divisible, Socrates,' he said, 'and things that partake of them would partake of a part; no longer would a whole form, but only a part of it, be in each thing.'

'It does appear that way.'

'Then are you willing to say Socrates, that our one form is really divided? Will it still be one?'

'Not at all,' he replied.[11]

In short, instantiation is only successful if the particular gets a share of the whole universal or a part of the universal. On the one hand, if the participant gets a share of the *whole* universal, then the *whole* universal would be in each particular. If the *whole* universal were in each particular, then the very *same* universal would be more than one in number. This would be absurd, because the universal is *one* in number; it cannot be in more than one particular at the same time without being *more than one* in number and thereby separate from itself. For example, were the concept of number instantiated in many numbers, the concept of number, which is *one* concept, would be *re-duplicated* as many times as it is instantiated. The concept of the human being is *one* concept, but it would be *indefinitely many* insofar as it would be instantiated in each human.

On the other hand, if the particular were only to get a share of *part* of the universal, then the universal would be divided. Given that for Plato Forms are each *indivisibly one*, no particular can participate in the part of a universal. Yet even abstracting from the indivisibility of Forms, if a *different* part of the universal were instantiated in each particular, then each particular would *not* be an instance of the *same* universal, but a different universal. Thus, if 'animal' were instantiated in one particular, and 'animal' in another, 'rational animal' would not be instantiated in more than one particular, but each part would be instantiated in a different particular.

On the assumption of either disjunction a contradiction is generated: if the universal Form were in each particular as a whole, then each Form would be different from itself; if only part of the Form were in each particular, then the same Form would be divisible and would not be universal, for it would not be instantiated in multiple particulars. Since contradictions are absurd, so is the concept of participation. Since in this case 'participation' is instantiation, the instantiation relation is absurd.[12] On Plato's conception of instantiation in this argument, Socrates rightly recognizes that each universal is one in number, and what is one in number is particular. Accordingly, the argument supposes that the *universal is itself a particular*. Indeed, the whole argument already presumes that the universal *itself* is particular. Indeed, it appears that the whole argument moves on the assumption that *the universals are particulars*.

Plato raises a number of other arguments against his Theory of Forms by showing how other methods of conceiving participation fail. One of these is the famous 'Third Man' argument. As Vlastos has noted,[13] the premise that moves the Third Man argument into *aporia* is the assumption that the universal exhibits *self-reference* or self-predication.[14] Although this argument will be more explicitly treated in the discussion of the Third Man argument in a later chapter, it is enough to point out at this point that for Plato self-predication is a *problematic* concept. Rather than make participation possible, self-predication is *one of the many failed ways* of conceiving of the relationship of instantiation.

One solution attempted by the young Socrates is the soul. Since it is by reason that we grasp the universal and the senses by which we grasp the particular, the soul seems to be the region where universal and particular meet. Still, Parmenides refutes this straightaway.[15] Although the soul appears to be the meeting ground of both universal and particular, this appears to postpone the problem: what is the unity of the soul by which the particular participates in the universal? We seem to find ourselves laden with two ontological regions with two distinct principles. Since the universal and the particular only have power in respect to themselves, and not to each other, they cannot share the same principles.

Since no rational account of the relation of universal to particular can be conceived, in the dialogue Plato advocates for an *ontological dualism*: one principle for universality, another principle for particularity. From this argument and others, Parmenides infers that since the participation of the particular in the universal is absurd, universals must be *absolutely separate* from the particulars. Form has its power (δύναμις) in respect to itself, and particulars have their power in respect to themselves, but neither interacts with the other. Since we are particulars, as particulars, we never cognize universality, since they are absolutely divorced from us. Therefore, the most immediate lesson we may learn from the criticism of theory of the Forms is that *universality is transcendent*. Indeed, only a 'naturally gifted man' could learn that there is a certain kind and

Beinghood (οὐσίᾱ), in itself, for each thing.[16] We seem to find ourselves laden with two ontological regions with two distinct principles. Since the universal and the particular only have power in respect to themselves, and not to each other, they cannot share the same principles. Thus, Plato advocates an ontological *dualism*: one principle for universality, another principle for particularity.

Starting at 134c Parmenides tells us that it is only through knowledge itself that each of the kinds of knowledge, each Form, is thought. Indeed, here we are invited to think about the Forms as constituting one region in which the Forms reside. Knowledge of the Form of knowledge itself, the *universal Form*, would give us knowledge of each species of Knowledge, each *particular* Form. Here, we see that Plato conceives of universality in terms of a kind of *universal* genus that contains *particular* Forms as its species.[17] Because the particulars must be conceived as absolutely separate from the universals, the particular Forms must also be absolutely separate from Form as such. Accordingly, the same problem that affects the relation of Forms to sensible things also affects the relation of Form to Forms within the intelligible realm itself.[18] As the discussion of the Form of Knowledge indicates, the identification of universal with particular shows that the problem of instantiation also concerns the relationship of universals to universality itself, or Form itself to the Forms. Plato's objections to his Theory of Forms raise a systematic question concerning the relation of the universal to the particular that is quite independent of whether the particular is construed as a sensible or intelligible entity.

Parmenides and Socrates (the characters in the dialogue) appear to have reduced all knowledge to that of particularity. First, on Socrates' own assumptions, particulars admit of contrary opposites, while Forms *ought not*. Yet, if Forms are conceived as instantiated in their particulars, they contradict themselves—for each is different from itself insofar as the very same universal is realized in different particulars, each which excludes the other. This, of course, leads us to ask whether we can in principle speak or think of the instantiated universal without violating the PNC. Second, it is only because each universal is a *particular universal* that it cannot be instantiated. In fact, given that the universal cannot be an instantiation on account of the fact that it is a particular, and given that universals are only universals insofar as they are *able to be instantiated*, the ontological dualism hardly divides universals from particulars; rather it divides types of particulars—'Forms' and 'sensibles.' Instead of gaining knowledge of universals, Plato's *Parmenides* undermines any coherent conception of universality at all.

Plato makes it clear that such a division between the domains of universality and particularity is deeply problematic. As he writes,

'And yet,' said Parmenides, 'if someone, in turn, Socrates, after focusing on all these problems and others still, shall deny that there are forms of beings and will not distinguish a certain form of each single thing, wherever he turns he'll understand nothing, since he does not allow that there is an ever-same idea for each of the beings. *And so he will entirely destroy the power of dialogue.* [emphasis mine] But you seem to me only too aware of this.'[19]

What young Socrates lacks is proper training in dialectics. The excursion into the hypotheses, the second and longest part of *Parmenides*, offers to give young Socrates this training.

Why does the instantiation problem undermine the power of dialogue? If the argument has eliminated the universal, and the particular is an instance of the universal, the particular must also be eliminated. Or, insofar as instantiations of universals are preserved, universals must thereby be preserved along with them. But in this case, the universals can only be present in the form of a *contradiction*. Thus, either we can speak about nothing at all, or we can speak, but this speech will be contradictory. On the one hand, without universality, we cannot know that 'this' is truly an instance of a human being or an otter. We cannot speak truly about humans or otters without having universals by which we can measure the proper and improper application of universal terms to particular instances. On the one hand, the only universal measures that the *Parmenides* allows are contradictory ones—measures that are different from themselves. Philosophy aims at knowing what is absolute, itself by itself, which is *consistent with itself*. Rather than knowing what is itself by itself, the problem of instantiation leads the philosopher to think what is never by itself but *itself not itself*.

Perhaps most illuminating is how the problem of instantiation undermines the very *being of Truth itself*. Although the language of correspondence is arguably relatively foreign to the Platonic concept of truth, it is not completely absent in Plato's thought, as the Sophist contests:

False belief is believing things that are contrary to those which are.[20]

Although there is still a deeper concept of truth in Plato underlying correspondence, this concept of correspondence is helpful for illuminating the significance of the problem of the instantiation, especially for the modern reader. Since our aim is to know the being of universality, we desire to know what concept of universality we possess corresponds to universality itself. Truth concerning universality or any universal at all, as the correspondence of a concept with its object, seems impossible. What is essential to note here is that *our inability to grasp the relation of our own thoughts about the universal to the universal itself engenders an inability to grasp the content of universality itself*. Since no particular can be correlated with universality, since universals are transcendent, the very what it is to be of any universal, including universality itself, escapes us. Therefore, the problem of instantiation undermines any attempt to discover the truth of universality. Indeed, the problem indicates that there ought to be *some consistent relation* of the particular to universality in order for the *truth of universality* to be revealed.

When one says of a friend that he or she is a *true* friend, one means that the friend lives up to or corresponds with the concept of friendship. A *false* friend may *appear* to be a friend, but nonetheless fails to live up to the concept. What we find *in* the true friend is the indwelling concept of friendship. What the true friend reveals is that truth assumes that the concept corresponding to the particular must also exist on the side of the particular. By 'on the side of the particular' I mean that the universal is *immanent* in the particular. If the universal were not immanent in the particular, the concept would have nothing to which it could correspond. So, what truth as correspondence assumes is that truth is the *self-correspondence of the universal with itself*.[21] 'Self-correspondence' in this case means that the separate universal 'friendship' is correlated with the universal friendship in the particular friend, not merely the friend as a particular. If there were no correspondence of the universal by itself and the universal in the particular, there would be nothing in common between the universal and the particular upon which a correlation could in principle be grounded. But if we maintain an absolute separation of universal from particular, the particular is severed from truth, for truth, as the correlation of universal to particular, requires the universal. Although universals ought to be inherently intelligible—they ought to correspond with themselves, the problem of instantiation shows that they fail to correspond with themselves.

Indeed, for Plato the things that constitute the object of *Nous* are *true* entities. 'Truth' must first be said of things that are before it can be said of our knowledge of things that are. The unity of the universal and the thing that would constitute true correlation must already be there in the thing to which the universal correlates—there must be an identity of *universality and Thinghood in the thing itself*. In Parmenides, Plato speaks about the *Form of Knowledge*:

> what each of the kinds themselves is, is known by that very form, the form of Knowledge?[22]

Knowledge—which for Plato is *always true*, is not only constituted by our knowledge of things, but is itself a Form, or a thing to be known:

> None of the forms, then, is known by us, since we don't partake of Knowledge itself.[23]

Given this conception of truth, it would be completely reasonable to posit that the true things are universals—for universals are (or at least ought to be) *particulars that are also inherently intelligible*. Indeed, what remains itself—the Form of the thing—is *true to itself*, for it never admits what it is not, unlike sensible particulars.[24] In losing access to the Form of Knowledge, one loses access to that which remains *true to itself*. Indeed, without this concept of truth in hand, we would be without the resources to unpack the meaning of other passages such as those in *Phaedo* where Plato speaks not merely about true or false propositions about states of pleasure but about *true and false pleasures*.[25] This is one of the most difficult aspects of the Greek concept of truth, namely that it is said of things, not just our beliefs or propositions about things, as is the common way of understanding truth in modern philosophy. Naturally, this concept is already present in Heraclitus (as well as other Pre-Socratics), who posits the *logos* not as his own account, but as the *account of the things themselves*:

> Listening not to me but the account [logos], it is wise to agree that all things are one.[26]

This account, which does not have its origin in Heraclitus, is that in virtue of which all things have their origin.[27] The attack on the intelligibility of universals in the problem of instantiation is therefore an attack on the very *concept of Truth itself*.

In book five of the *Republic*, Plato draws a distinction among three levels of knowledge. Knowing has *what is* as its object, opinion has *what is and is not* as its object, and ignorance has *what is not* as its object.[28] The problem of instantiation has eliminated knowledge of what is, for *only the contradiction is present*: particulars that both are and are not. Opinion, which takes sensory particulars as its object, are sometimes understood as false imitations of the truth. Nonetheless have being as imitations, as *false things*. They are that which *appears* to be true, but are not true.[29] As such, they both are and are not. But given the problem of instantiation, one cannot even proclaim these things to be false, for one has lost all access to the true standard of knowledge (the true things) by which one could legitimize that claim. Thus, the problem of instantiation leaves us in the lowest level of knowledge: ignorance that has nothing at all as its object.

The problem of instantiation seems to establish that no *universal*, construed as separate from the particular, *lives up to universality itself*. Even the true entities, Forms, seem untrue. Every universal we think fails to be a *true* universal. We find ourselves indelibly foreign to one side of truth, and therefore to Truth itself. According to Parmenides in the dialogue, young Socrates has shown too much disregard for what is ignoble and therefore failed to understand what is noble.[30]

The Duality of Principles in Aristotle

Following Plato, and anticipating Kant, Aristotle too commits himself to a duality of principles. Nonetheless, Aristotle recognizes that in order to solve the various *aporias* raised by Plato, one must attempt to unify all plurality in one principle. As Aristotle proclaims: 'everyone makes all things come from contraries, but neither the "all things" nor the "from contraries" is right.'[31] Accordingly, although Aristotle follows his master's insight that universality and particularity require a separation of principles, he will significantly qualify this claim by subtle arguments that are rife with impasses.

One of the impasses governing Aristotle's *Metaphysics* concerns the nature of the first principles. Are the first principles particular or universal? *Aporia* nine from book Beta of Aristotle's *Metaphysics* illustrates the duality of principles endemic to Aristotle's philosophy:

> Further, one might also be at an impasse about the sources in this way: for if it is in kind that they are one, nothing will be one in number, not even one-itself or being-itself. And how will there be knowing, if there is not something that is one in all the particulars? But surely, if it is one in number, and each of the sources is one—and not, as with perceptible things, different ones for different things—if, then, the sources of things are one not in that way but in number, there would not be anything else besides the elements. For what is one in number means nothing different from what is particular; for we speak of the particular in that ways, as one in number, but the universal is what applies to these.[32]

In this passage, Aristotle raises the question concerning the character of the first principles: are they one in kind or one in number? On the one hand, to be one in kind is to be one in respect to the *universality* under which one falls. For example, Socrates and Aristotle are one in kind, since they are both human beings. As human beings there is no difference that obtains between them. On the other hand, each is *a* human being and is counted as a separate human being. Socrates and Aristotle are one in number, as each is counted as a separate one. What Aristotle makes explicit here is that *to be particular is to be one in number*.

This distinction obviously reflects the division Plato introduced between universal and particular. Given this distinction we come to an impasse. Given that the principles (of knowing and being) are one in kind, nothing is one in number. To know 'human being' does *not* give us a difference between Socrates and Aristotle, since *qua* one in kind they are indistinguishable. Given some universal, I cannot deduce instances, since the universal does not differentiate its own instances. So, if the principles are one in kind, there are no particulars. This *aporia* is only intelligible under the assumption that concepts are not their own principles of differentiation.

What is more, there will be nothing common or universal to know *in* the particulars since there are no particulars. But the problem is even worse. If there is absolutely nothing that is one in number, or what is the same, if there were absolutely no particulars, there could not be any universals or unities in kind, *for no universal would be one in number.* In other words, each universal is only *a* universal if each is a *this* and can be counted as a separate universal. No universal could be *a* universal were there no particulars. Thus, there could not be 'one-itself' or 'being-itself.' Likewise, there could be no 'unity in kind itself,' for 'itself' signifies that the kind is one in number.[33]

Take the other horn of the dilemma. Presume that the principles (of knowing and being) are one in number. If they are merely one in number, then each is a separate one, since each is particular. Since each is separate, each is unique, and there is nothing in common between any particulars. If there is nothing in common, then there are no universals, and nothing is one in kind. If there is no unity in kind, then there is no knowing, since knowing is of what is universal, and to know the particulars they could only be enumerated *ad infinitum.* If there is nothing one in kind, there cannot even be 'being-one-in number,' since this could be treated as a kind of unity. As it appears, from particularity no universality can be inferred, and from universality no particularity can be inferred. Yet, in order to know what the universal is, we need the principles of universality *and* particularity. Although the criticism does seem aimed at Plato's Forms, it *re-enforces the need for a duality of principles.* As Sachs argues in his recent translation of Aristotle's *Metaphysics,* Aristotle does advocate for his own Theory of Forms, albeit distinct from the Platonic account.[34]

From the impasse the need for two kinds of principles becomes evident. On the one hand, if the principles were only one in kind, there would not be anything that is one in number—not even what is one in kind. But what is one in number exists. On the other hand, if the principles were only one in number, then nothing would be one in kind, yet there are things one in kind. Thus, in order to account for what there is, at least *two* principles are needed: one in kind and one in number.

The duality of principles in Aristotle's account of Being is also evident in his account of genera and species. The genus (γένος)[35] is an *inherently divisible universal.* A genus is a universal that *contains* other universals, its own differentiations. As such, it is divisible into its differentiations. The universals contained by the genus are called *species* (εἶδος). These species share the common feature of the genus, but are not identical as differentiations. Since the genus itself is only a common term, the difference (διαφορά) by which the genus is divided into species must have its origin *outside* of the genus in some other genus. This difference is a *prior* difference, since it must already be given for the differentiation of the genus. Since the genus does *not* provide the difference on its own, one cannot think the species simply by thinking the genus. On the other hand, the genus is implied by the species, for it is a differentiation of the genus. Accordingly, the difference ought to imply the genus.[36] Because genera are not sufficient for their differentiation, the particular instances of the genus cannot be derived from the universal content of the genus itself. Like Kant after him, Aristotle does *not* allow that the universal, in this case a genus, is self-differentiating or self-particularizing. Unlike Kant, Aristotle's genera are *of things*, not our intuitions of them.

Since a universal can be contained by more general universals and contain fewer general universals, the same universal can be both a genus and a species in different respects. For example, although human being is a species of mammal, its genus, 'mammal,' is also a species of the genus 'animal.' If there were no highest genus or lowest species, the series of genera would be infinite in both directions. Since an infinite regress is impossible, Aristotle infers that there must be a finite number of genera and species in between the highest genera and lowest species. The 'highest' genera (if one exists) cannot be subsumed under any more general terms. Collectively, the highest genera are called *categories*. Although he provides a different number of categories in different places, the categories include Thinghood, quality, quantity, relation, position, state, time, space, activity, and passivity.[37] Since no category may be subsumed under any other, each is *independent* of the other. Likewise, presuming that all individuals fall under some genus, the categories contain all individuals under themselves, since all lower species fall under them as well. The 'lowest' species is a universal that cannot be divided into further species. So, the lowest species contains only individuals under itself, for example individual human beings fall under the species human being.

Clearly, Aristotle's theory of the *divisible* universal is a further development of (as well as deviation from) Plato's method of division introduced in the *Sophist*. This method takes as its object sensible kinds and divides them into their respective Forms in which they partake. Since Forms themselves are indivisible, a method of division for Forms as such would be absurd, since Forms are not composed of Forms. So, as Aristotle notes, if one were investigating the Essence of the human being, the divider may state 'animal, mortal, footed, biped, wingless.'[38] Aristotle argues that this method of division fails to make any inferences or arguments, for the questioner asks the interlocutor whether subject x is a or b, and assuming that x is a, the interlocutor places x in that category. Each definition is merely assumed from the beginning, for which no arguments are given.[39]

As Plato assumed before him, Aristotle investigates the Being of Being on the assumption that *Being is indivisible*. Given the indivisibility of Being, any inquiry into the being of something, for example the human being, could not ultimately be an inquiry into the genus of that being, since the genus is *divisible* into species. Not all universals are genera, however, as the lowest species makes evident. Since the lowest species is *not itself divisible into species*, the lowest species is indivisible. Given that

Being is indivisible, any proper inquiry into the being of something ought to inquire into the *species being*.

When we inquire into Being (τὸ ὄν) we inquire into the Thinghood[40] (οὐσία) of something. For example, when I ask *'what is* the human being?' I am not asking about some attribute of the human being, for example its state, position, qualities, or any other category. Instead, I am asking about *what it is* that has these attributes. By what measure ought we investigate the Thinghood? Conveniently, Aristotle provides us a measure by which our investigation may proceed. Thinghood is *separate* (χωριστόν) and a *this* (τόδε τι).[41]

Aristotle's inquiry into Being is an inquiry into the first principle(s) (ἀρχή) of what has Being. As the source of what has Being, a first principle is not derived from something else, but is *that in virtue of which* anything has Being. As that in virtue of which anything has Being, Thinghood is what has Being *in virtue of itself* not in virtue of something else. Because it has Being in virtue of itself, Thinghood is separate or independent. Given that Being is what is separate, Aristotle argues that Thinghood is what it is for something to be (τὸ τί ἦν εἶναι) or what goes by the more familiar term 'Essence.' The 'what it is for something to be' is what something is *in its own right* (καθ' αὑτό)[42]. In other words, it is what something is *in virtue of itself*. Clearly, Essence or 'what it is in *its own right*' is separate and thereby fulfills the condition for Being as Being. What has being 'in its own right' is not relative to something else—it has *absolute Being*—it has being *in virtue of itself*.

The 'what it is to be' cannot be distinguished from the thing itself. This is evident by *reductio ad absurdum*.[43] For assume that 'Being' and 'what it is to be being' or 'being-being' were separate. Then 'what it is to be being' would *not be*, and Being would not be what it is to be. Likewise, being-one would not be one. In these cases, what something needs in order to be, the what it is to be, would be absent from Being, and the same would hold for one. But this is absurd, for then the very Form of Being, the what it is to be, would cease to have being. In order to preserve knowledge of Forms, the 'what it is to be' must not be separable from the thing itself. Among other things, what these arguments illuminate is that Aristotle has not wrenched himself from the Platonic concept of Form (εἶδος),[44] for here Aristotle identifies the 'thing' with the 'what it is to be', and the 'what it is to be' is *universal*. The 'thing' appears to be 'universal,' namely a Form. The what it is to be of something is *universal* (καθόλου)—that which makes the pious-pious, being-being, the one-one. Complicating this issue is the fact that asking 'what is being?' is reflexive, since we are asking about the *Being of Being*.

Further, what something is in its own right is in a way indivisibly one with the thing itself. For example, 'reason' is the principle of what the human being is in its own right and cannot be subtracted from the thing without the subject ceasing to be what it is. I cannot remove 'reason' from

Socrates without him ceasing to be a man. Accordingly, the proper definition of a thing, *the* definition, the genus plus the difference, expresses the
Essence of the thing. If I can remove something from something without
its ceasing to be what it is, I have not uncovered its Being. Employing the
same example again, although Socrates may be white, I can remove the
whiteness from Socrates without him ceasing to be a human being. Such
properties are *accidental* (*kata sumbebikos*) to the being of the thing.
Metaphysics is not an inquiry into accidentals.[45] The accidental is not
separate or independent. Quite the opposite; the accidental is *inseparable*
from something, for example white always inheres in some subject and
is thereby *dependent* upon that subject for its being. To sum up, metaphysical inquiry is looking for the definition of an entity that expresses
the Essence of a thing, its species being, not the accidents belonging to
that species. Although the inquiry into the what it is to be searches for the
species, the genus-species distinction makes possible what in Plato was
not possible, namely *definition*. If we only have recourse to indivisible
universals, then we cannot apply universals to other universals in order
to say what they are.

In contrast to accidents, an *attribute* is something that is *unique* to one
species or *convertible* with the species, for example 'capable of laughter'
is an attribute of the human being that is not identical to the proper differentia or Essence of the thing. Since species have attributes, and these
belong to the species in its own right, it appears that one could define a
species simply by stating the attributes that belong to the thing. Aristotle
excludes this as a possibility, since defining a subject-attribute compound
such as 'snub nose' defines *by addition*. Since an attribute is an attribute
of something, for example nose, 'snub' already implicitly contains 'nose.'
As Aristotle states, 'Therefore, that articulation in which something is
not itself present, when one is articulating it, is the statement of what it
is for each thing to be.'[46] Thus, any attempt to define a subject-attribute
compound such as snub nose results in the infinite proliferation of subjects, for example 'snub nose nose', and so on. So although attributes
may belong to a subject in virtue of itself, the attribute is not the Essence
of the subject. Instead, the attribute assumes the very what it is to be of
the subject, but is not that very 'what it is to be' and belongs to the subject in virtue of what it is.

Given that Aristotle's search for the being of the thing terminates in
an investigation into the independence of the thing, the attributes of a
subject provide *the clue* to discovering the 'what it is to be' of something.
The what it is to be ought to give the cause of the unique aspects or
attributes of an entity. Accordingly, since the what it is to be is the cause
of the attributes and what is expressed in a definition, we know we have
the specific difference when we have the cause of the attributes.[47] Given
these parameters, to investigate the being of something one must discover
(i) the attributes and (ii) their cause. Aristotle's logic, that is his syllogistic

and theory of demonstrative reasoning, provides a structure reflecting this metaphysical feature.

The *per se* differentia of some subject is the *first* differentia at which the attributes of some subject disappear. By first differentia, I mean the differentia *from which* all the attributes of a thing may be deduced. If we desire to know the what it is to be of some triangle[48] (in *Euclidean* Geometry), we first investigate some attributes, including 'the sum of the angles are equal to two right angles.' Given some isosceles triangle, if you take away isosceles from the triangle, and you only have the triangle remaining, you do not thereby destroy the said attribute. If you take away 'limit' and 'figure' you *do* destroy the attribute. Still, it is not in virtue of limit or figure that the triangle's angles equal 180 degrees, as limit applies to all other figures, not just triangles. So, although the attributes of the triangle *per se* are annihilated, so are all other attributes of other figures. The first difference the removal of which annihilates the attributes is being a *three-sided* figure. The three-sided figure is the first difference the removal of which annihilates the attributes and is thereby the proper definition of the triangle.

Although we are not primarily concerned with forms of inference, since inference is posterior to concerns about universality,[49] it will be instructive to briefly discuss the syllogism in order to understand the relation of Essence to attribute. The *per se* difference is the middle term in virtue of which some subject is connected with its attributes. In the Aristotelian syllogism, consisting of *three terms*, the middle term is the Essence or 'the what it is to be.' As that in virtue of which the conclusion is drawn, middle terms are *not themselves demonstrable*, since to demonstrate a middle term one must presuppose the middle term.[50] How then, does one arrive at the middle term? As we can see with our example, the middle term is *revealed in and through the demonstration itself*. By seeing that this term, 'three-sided' is able to derive the attributes, that is by seeing that it does function as a middle term, we *see* or *immediately apprehend* that it is the middle term. No separate process of inference is involved. Although we know the attributes before and after we demonstrate, we know *why* a subject necessarily has those attributes only once we have discovered the middle term.[51] As Aristotle points out, it is the first figure[52] that is the paradigmatically scientific form of the syllogism. Consider *Barbara*: All A is B. All B is C. Hence, All A is C.[53] As scholars know, the Aristotelian definition, as well as the paradigmatic syllogism is *universal and categorical*.

For Aristotle, truth is a way of saying Being:

> And since being and not being are meant in one sense by reference to the various ways of attributing being, and in another by reference to the potency and being-at-work of these or their opposites, but *the most governing sense* [my emphasis] is the true or the false.[54]

Aristotle's discussion of truth in the *Metaphysics* reflects the difference between knowledge of the middle term and knowledge of the attributes that belong to a thing. In order to know whether a judgment is true, one must consult the things themselves:

> For it is necessary to examine in what way we mean this. For you are not pale because we think truly that you are pale, but rather it is because you are pale that we who say so speak the truth.[55]

Truth occurs when the judgment 'S is P' corresponds with the state of the thing, namely when the attribute connoted by P actually belongs to the subject, S. Accordingly, this concept of the true and the false is instantiated 'in thinking'[56] such that it is the *judgment* about the thing that is either true or false. Moreover, since the truth of the judgment brings together (or separates) predicates and subjects, attributes and things, this correspondence of thought with the thing requires the possibility of combining and separating such predicates with their respective subjects. Thus, this concept of truth that takes *plural complexes* as its object cannot account for the truth of what is *simple*[57] (what does not involve combination and separation.) Since the simple is a condition for the complex, the sense of truth that applies only to the complex cannot be 'the governing sense of being'; rather it is a *secondary* concept of truth. Accordingly, Aristotle first introduces us to the derivative concept of truth in his discussion of incidental predication in book *E*.[58] Concerning the *derivative* understanding of truth,

> one who thinks that what is separate is separated and what is combined is combined thinks truly (ὥστε ἀληθεύει μὲν ὁ τὸ διῃρημένον οἰόμενος διῃρῆσθαι καὶ τὸ συγκείμενον συγκεῖσθαι) but one who thinks these things to be opposite to the way the things are thinks falsely.[59]

To summarize, at the level of discursive thinking, truth is combining and separating in thought what is combined and separated in the thing itself. In accordance with this view, those predicates that are *always connected* to their subjects, for example 'human beings are able to laugh,' are always true, and cannot be false, whereas those subjects that are sometimes connected to their subjects, for example 'Socrates is white,' are sometimes true and sometimes false.

Truth is not itself a thing—truth does not introduce a new subject such as 'Truth itself.'[60] In the same way, the highest genera, the categories, *only exist separately from the entities they categorize in thought*, such that the 'intertwining and dividing are in thinking, but not in things.'[61] They are not themselves independent entities. Such categories are only possible in the first place because there are a plurality of entities admitting of categorization. Since the derivative concept of truth cannot account for the truth of what is neither combined nor separated, Aristotle introduces a more fundamental concept of truth to account for what is simple.

Truth concerning the simple is not the same as that of the compound:

> But now for things that are not compound, what is being or not being, and the true and the false? For the thing is not a compound, so that it would be when it is combined and not be if it is separated, like the white on a block of wood or the incommensurability of the diagonal; and the true and the false will not still be present in a way similar to those things.[62]

The difference is summarized in the following way:

> So being in the sense of the true, and not-being in the sense of the false, in one way is: if something is combined, it is true, and if it is not combined, it is false. But in one way it is: if something is, it is present in a certain way, and if it is not present in that way, it is not. The true is the contemplative knowing of these things, and there is no falsity, nor deception, but only ignorance (τὸ δὲ ἀληθὲς τὸ νοεῖν ταῦτα: τὸ δὲ ψεῦδος οὐκ ἔστιν, οὐδὲ ἀπάτη, ἀλλὰ ἄγνοια) ([1052α] [1]).[63]

In order for the attribute to be truly predicated of the thing, there must be a thing in virtue of which the attribute is possible in the first place. The statement of the Essence or Thinghood of the thing is articulated in the middle term of the syllogism or the definition of the thing itself. For example, 'human being is a rational animal' articulates the definition of the human being, which functions as the middle term of the syllogism in virtue of which attributes are connected to their subject. However, if we were simply to follow the subject-predicate structure of the judgment, it appears that analyzing truth in the case of such judgments would follow the derivative concept of truth rather than the primitive concept that has simplicity as its object.

Importantly, Aristotle does not account for Being by simply reading it off of the structure of Greek grammar. Instead, the subject-predicate relation is not the ultimate guide to the ontological structure. Indeed, 'the human being is a rational animal' does not connect a separate predicate with a separate subject. 'Human being' is not a separate entity in addition to 'rational animal.' Rather, 'rational animal' specifies the very meaning of the term 'human being'; it constitutes its very content. Thus, in the case that one knows the Thinghood of the thing, the knowledge of the thing does not entail a plurality of characteristics that are combined or separated as in the case of attribution. Instead, the knowing is of something simple and independent, or in Aristotle's language, that which is *separable* from other things.

As we mentioned earlier, the knowledge of the middle term is *immediate*: by seeing how the middle term accounts for the attributes, one intellectually intuits the middle term. This means that the Thinghood of the thing becomes present to the intellect in an immediate way. Accordingly, Aristotle uses the term *nous* to describe this kind of truth, in which truth is *the contemplative knowing of things* (τὸ δὲ ἀληθὲς τὸ νοεῖν ταῦτα: τὸ δὲ ψεῦδος οὐκ ἔστιν, οὐδὲ ἀπάτη, ἀλλὰ ἄγνοια). Nonetheless, even though 'human being' and 'rational animal' do not connote two different entities, 'rational animal' can only be articulated by *combining* two terms: 'rational' and 'animal.' Thus, although in human life 'rational' does not exist apart from 'animal,' its articulation as the middle term requires logically separating the genus from the difference and then combining them into one *articulation*. In this sense, *the logical formulation* of the Thinghood of the thing and its discursive representation still demands an adherence to two principles of combination and separation.

If we desire to speak of correspondence, we can say that the obtaining correspondence is that of the immediate intellectual intuition and the Thinghood of the thing, *not* the correspondence of a judgment with a thing and its attributes. Yet, this truth is deeper than correspondence, for it is an identity. On Aristotle's theory of mind, the mind takes on the form of the thing that it knows. Accordingly, in the intuition of the thing, the mind *takes on the Form of the thing that it knows*. If one's mind has not taken on the Form of the thing, one is simply ignorant—ἄγνοια—nous is simply *not present*, as the alpha-privative indicates.[64] The immediate knowing of the thing characteristic of *Nous* is an act in which the mind takes on the Form of what it knows—it conforms itself to its object such that in knowing the thing it is knowing its own mind in the Form of that thing. Note here that when Kant critiques our capacity to cognize the *Noumenon*, he is proclaiming that we are no longer (or never were) in possession of *Nous*. Even if truth cannot be separated from the concept of existence or being in both Kant and Aristotle, for Aristotle the truth of *Nous* is constituted by the conforming of the mind to the thing, whereas for Kant truth is the self-correspondence of the mind with itself. By making the object conform to the mind rather than the mind conform to the object, the critical philosophy makes warfare against the most fundamental concept of truth in Ancient Greek philosophy.

Since Thinghood is *separate* (χωριστόν) and a *this* (τόδε τι) Aristotle argues that Thinghood is the *underlying subject* (ὑποκείμενον). Let us first discuss why Thinghood must be a this (τόδε τι). Consider the proposition 'Socrates is white.' 'White' indicates that Socrates is *such and such* a thing, where 'white' is a modification of the subject. Indeed, universals, as predicates and modifications of subjects, belong to subjects, but are not themselves subjects. 'What is being?' is an inquiry into what the subject is, and not what belongs to it, for Thinghood is independent and separate, not dependent and inseparable as predicates are. Since the universal, as a predicate, is not itself separate, and dependent on the subject, Thinghood cannot be universal or *such and such*. Aristotle seems to confirm this: 'Again, Thinghood is what is not attributed to any underlying thing, but the universal is always attributed to some underlying thing.'[65] If the universal were a thing, then a thing would belong to a thing, yet this is impossible, since independent things are not composed of independent things.[66]

Instead, Thinghood must be that which is *the subject* of predication, yet not predicated of something else. The subject which itself cannot be a predicate is what all predicates depend on. As a *this*, one cannot predicate 'Socrates' of another subject. Unlike 'white,' Socrates is not a property shared by multifarious particulars. Thus, it is a *this*, or an *individual*, not a such and such. The underlying subject of predication is independent and a *this*. Hence, Aristotle has two candidates for Being: the underlying subject and the 'what it is to be' each of which corresponds respectively to what Aristotle, in his *Categories*, calls first and second Substance.[67]

Given what we have already said, it should already be amply clear what is problematic here: the 'what it is to be' is something *universal*. How should we interpret the proposition 'Socrates is a rational animal'? Rational animal is the 'what it is to be.' But the what it is to be appears to be universal and belongs to the subject. Hence, the what it is to be cannot be the Thinghood. But Aristotle argues that the 'what it is to be' is the Thinghood of the thing. On the other hand, if Thinghood is the what it is to be, it is not particular, for example 'Socrates.' The Form is one in *kind*, but the underlying subject is *particular*, or one in *number*. Aristotle clearly opposes universal to particular in an impasse about the sources:

> For if they [the sources[68]] are universals, they will not be independent things. (For none of the common predicates signifies a *this* but rather an of-this-sort, while an independent thing is a this; while if the thing predicated in common were a this and were to be set apart, Socrates would be many animals-himself as well as human being and animal- if each of them signifies somehow that is one and a this.) So if the sources are universal, these things follow; but if they *are* in the same way as particulars, there will be no knowledge, since of all things the knowledge is universal.[69]

This problem implies an opposition between Form (εἶδος) and the composite and why Form and material (ὕλη) for Aristotle are *un*-generated. The underlying thing, for example Socrates, appears to be the material, a technical term first introduced by Aristotle, though present, in some way, in Plato. The material, one of the four causes, is that *out of which* something is, for example the wood of a table. In the syllable 'ab' the letters 'a' and 'b,' as constitutive *elements*, are the material of the syllable. The material is not what is predicated of something else, as the other categories are, but is *that which is rendered determinate* by the property or predicate attributed. The wood *receives* the design of the artisan, the letters the ordering of the syllable. Although compelling, the individual receiving some determination cannot merely be material, for if one strips away all the predicates of the subject, and thereby all the determinacy, there is *nothing* left to receive the predicates. Indeed, there would be nothing at all to receive them. Without Form, the what-it-is-to-be, there would not be anything identifiable to which one could *point*, no 'this-here' as in τόδε τι. Clearly, the assumption at work here is that without universality and Form, no *determinacy* is possible—not even unity in number. As it appears, Aristotle denies that material is separate. 'Prime matter,' matter without Form, does not exist.

Indeed, some Form appears necessary in order for the material *to be something* identifiable. In the term 'Socrates' we do not merely mean the indeterminate material substrate, which is indistinguishable from anything else, as Locke's 'I know not what,' for we also mean 'this *man*.' Aristotle's term for the unity of Form and material is the *composite*. Accordingly, whatever the underlying subject is, it could not just be material.

If the Thinghood of all things is one, then every particular would be one being, which cannot be the case. But if the Thinghood is distributed among the particulars, it is no longer one Thinghood, which is also absurd. According to Aristotle:

> Will the thinghood of all things, say all human beings, be one? But that's absurd, for all things of which the thinghood is one are one being. But is the thinghood many and different? This too is illogical. And at the same time, how does the material become each of these things, and how is the composite both of the two?[70]

Thinghood is both universal and particular, since it is both the what it is to be, and the underlying subject, yet Thinghood is a *this* and cannot be universal. When Aristotle's position is caricatured as positing the universal in the particular, and not independent of the particular, what is usually meant is that the universal is neither a *this* nor independent.

Moreover, Form itself does not admit contrariety. For example, the Essence of human life, 'rationality' itself does not admit contrary properties such as white and black. It is, in good Platonic fashion, an indivisible unity, which does not cease to be itself. In contrast to this, the composite particular, for example Socrates, *admits contraries*, for example white and black. Because Socrates is material, he is capable of being affected and this allows opposing qualities to exist in the composite at different times. Yet Thinghood is somehow both Form and underlying subject. How can Thinghood both admit and not admit contrariety? At the heart of this issue is the opposition between Form and material. The Form as such is not itself material, yet the composite is both Form and material. How can the Thinghood be a composite of Form and material?

> And an impasse no lesser than any has been neglected by both present and earlier thinkers, as to whether the sources of destructible and indestructible things are the same or different.[71]

Perhaps most disturbing, Thinghood is both generated and un-generated, since separately Form and material cannot be generated or destroyed, yet the composite can be (and is) generated and destroyed. According to Aristotle:

> Now since the composite whole and its articulation are different kinds of thinghood (and I mean that one kind of thinghood in this sense is the articulation with the material taken in along with it, while the other is entirely the articulation), there is destruction of all those things that are called independent things in the former sense (since there is also coming into being), but of the articulation there is no destruction.[72]

Since the composite is the unity of material and Form, the composite comes to be when Form and material are united. For example, a bronze sphere comes into being when the material, the bronze, is shaped into a sphere. But neither the Form nor the material brought to the composite can be generated. For, if the Form were generated, then the Form would come to be out of some material. Since every coming to be requires a given Form and given material, the coming to be of the Form would presuppose another Form, *ad infinitum*. Since this is absurd, the Form is not generated. Indeed, a similar argument can be made for the material.[73] As Plato would also have it, Form is eternal and the condition of the particular, and for this reason the proper object of definition and knowledge. As is well known, for Aristotle the universe along with the Forms that are the principles of motion, are *eternal*. Because Aristotle maintains the eternity of the world, he does not need to account for the absolute *beginning* of all things as Neo-Platonic and theistic thinkers do—irrespective of whether that beginning is conceived of in a temporal or non-temporal manner.

Aristotle goes on to argue that Form not only is the source of things in demonstrations but, taking the activity of life as a paradigm, Form is also the *generative principle* of particulars. If Thinghood is Form, then it is un-generated. But since the Form in the particular can come to be and cease to be in the material, the Form also *seems* generable. Thus, if Thinghood is both the 'what it is to be' and the underlying subject, then Form admits contrary properties. Indeed, Form, it appears, is both the generative principle and the generated. Since they cannot be both, a march to infinity is in order, for every generated Form would suppose another Form, the generating principle, *ad infinitum*.

I do not mean to present these problems as though Aristotle were not aware of them. Let us consider one last impasse:

> But there is an impasse. For if no independent thing can be made out of universals, because the universal signifies an of-this-sort but not a this, and no independent thing admits of being composed of active independent things, every independent thing would not be composed of parts, so that there could not be an articulation in speech of any independent thing. But surely it seems to everyone and has been said since the earliest times that a definition belongs to an independent thing either solely or most of all; but now it seems not to belong to this either.[74]

If an of-this-sort, or a universal, were a constituent of an independent thing, then the of-this-sort would be more primary than the independent thing, which is absurd, since the of-this-sort belongs to the independent thing, on which it is dependent. Yet, the independent thing cannot be composed of independent things either, for in this case the independent thing would not be independent. Thus, no independent thing can be composed of parts, since Aristotle assumes that everything is either an independent thing or belongs to an independent thing. Indeed, this is consistent with Aristotle's claim that Being in its primary sense is *indivisible*. But if an independent thing is indivisible, or has no parts, and every definition has a genus and a difference as its parts, it follows that no independent thing can be defined. Likewise, no definition ought to count as an independent thing. Although the genus/species distinction appeared to render definition possible, it actually seems to have foundered on the assumption of the indivisibility of Being.

In order to respond to these many problems which Aristotle himself recognizes, one must first consider the fundamental relationship between Form and material. This dualism constitutes the fundamental duality, the elucidation of which will clarify these problems and indicate plausible solutions. Aristotle's inquiry into the Thinghood of things begins with a search for why one thing belongs to another, for example why 180 degrees belongs to the triangle. He argues that when we ask 'what is the human being?' we are asking *'why is the material something?'* At least for composites, we know that material cannot be on its own, as material is something only because of Form. So when we ask 'why is the material something?' we are asking for the Form. Of course, this unity of Form and material is exactly the source of our impasses concerning universality and particularity.

The composite is *one whole of parts*. If we return to our example of the syllable, we can see that the composite is not merely an aggregate or a *conjunction* of elements as in the formula 'a' plus 'b.' For although the syllable 'ab' is composed of 'a' and 'b,' 'ba' is also composed of 'a' and 'b.' One can vary the order of the syllables while keeping the material constituents the same. This shows that the order of the composite is not a mere collection or aggregation of the material elements. Likewise, a human being is not merely the collection of organs, the house not merely a collection of bricks. With any composite, for example a house, if you destroy the composite or watch it degenerate, for instance destroy the house into a heap of bricks, you would still have the material constituents, for example the bricks, leftover. Thus, the material constituents are not sufficient for accounting for the Form. The parts are *organized* and structured according to some principle of order, not merely some conjunction. The Form, therefore, must be some *separate organizing source* in virtue of which the material is something. Although the Form and the material are unified, *only* the Form is *the principle of activity*—the material is a *passive* principle. Thus, although each is unified with the other, even in their ontological unity they remain *separate* principles—the One an active, the other a passive principle.

Similarly to Kant's account, Aristotle denies that the principle of order, here the Form, is self-organizing. Form does not Form itself. Rather, Form organizes the material upon which it works—the principle of organization does not organize itself. Because the Form does not work upon itself *qua* Form, Form requires material upon which it can work. Form requires the material exactly because it is not self-forming. Because Form does not form itself, another principle is required in order for Form to do its work. To put the same point in the terms of judgment, since the Form is articulated in *universal* terms, the universal 'what it is to be' of Form *cannot be predicated of itself*, for example 'rationality' itself is not *a* rational being. 'Rationality' is applied to animal—not to itself. Thus, just as in Kant's case, *the duality of principles engenders an absence of self-predication.*

This argument also shows that the elements are only *potentially* separate from the Form. By 'potency' I mean what Aristotle means here: the source of change in something else or the same thing as something else.[75] For example, the sources of change by which bricks become a house lie in the something other than the bricks. The bricks are potentially a house and come to be a house when an external source of change initiates the change.[76]

Since the elements only exist potentially, they are that into which the whole can may be divided, and as the material exists as the Form in potentiality. Naturally, the elements are only potentially elements of the Form, for insofar as they are separate from the Form of which they are a part, they are not elements or material constituents of that Form. Given that the composite cannot be reduced to the elements, the Form cannot be reduced to any list of elements, for instance 'rational' plus 'animal' as Plato's method of division appears to treat it. Although the Form of the composite is not ontologically separate from the elements, since *the Form is inherently the Form of elements*, the source by which the elements have Form is not identical to the source by which the elements are material. The Form can be conceived as united with the material if we conceive the Form as the *unity of* the material.

Indeed, Aristotle thereby retains the *duality* of Platonic principles, yet he differs from the Platonic account insofar as material is never separate from Form, and in the composite Form is never separate from material. Still, neither is *reducible* to the other. The difference here is in *the way* the principles exist. In a way, since the material exists potentially, the articulation of what the material is may be distinguished from the articulation of Form, as wood can be distinguished from a table or animal from rational. In the definition of something, the difference is the Form and the genus the material.[77] These are *separable in articulation*, but in the thing itself, for example the human being, the difference is not separate from the genus, for Socrates is *not two* separate things, 'animal' and 'man.'

In the thing, *the genus is in the form of the differentia*, as in the human being the animal is formed and organized by a rational principle. Further, the genus only is because the difference gives it being. On this account, there is no 'animal itself' as a species of animals alongside 'human being' and 'groundhog.' If Aristotle had accepted self-predication, animal itself would be an animal. In such a case, 'animal' would appear as one of its own species. On Aristotle's teleological view, we would say that in human beings the animal functions are for the sake of rational functions. Logically, Aristotle treats the genus as the material which is the Form only potentially. The principles form *one undivided whole*, from which neither can be extracted from the other without destruction of the whole.[78] In sum, the 'what it is to be' remains indivisibly *one*, even if its components can be divided logically in the conceptual articulation of them. By rendering the Form the principle by which the material becomes something at all, Aristotle significantly raises the Form to the principle of principles and significantly qualifies his dependence upon two principles.

Aristotle's teleological account of being construes the organizing principle of the material as an *activity—not a motion*. Aristotle argues that Being is Being-at-work (ἐνέργειἄ). To be at work, an action must be an end-in-itself. An end-in-itself is complete, as the term ἐντελέχειἄ implies. Being at work is Being at work staying itself, or that which is always already at or in its end (τέλος). Seeing, contemplating, and living all exemplify Being-at-work. When one begins to see, contemplate, or live, there is no time interval interceding between the activity of seeing and the end of seeing. Likewise, if one contemplates one has contemplated, if one lives one has lived. Grammatically, the present tense implies the perfect tense in which the past action continues into the present. Why is no time interval present? The means by which one lives, for example the process of homeostasis, is also that for the sake of which the activity of living aims. Life processes are not only that for the sake of which living aims, but it is also the process by which life itself is sustained. For this reason, the end is not external to the activity, but internal to it. Hence, the end is not outstanding, and it is complete or perfect and no time intercedes between the means and the end.

Activities stand in strong contrast to motion (κίνησις). Motions are inherently incomplete. For example, consider learning or building. The very process of learning is distinct from the end for the sake of which one learns. One learns in order to know, as one builds for the sake of constructing a house, and so on. Unlike activities, the end for the sake of which one acts is external to the activity. Since there is some distinction between means and end, motions have time intervals. Since the end is outstanding, each motion is incomplete. The incompleteness appears in the fact that the end is external to the means. Once the end is achieved, the means ceases to be. With the case of the house, once the house is built, the house building ceases to be. For activities such as living, the end does not negate the means, but instead the achievement of the end sustains the means, as the end is the means. Unlike motions, activities are self-preserving, whose ends are located within themselves. Thinghood cannot be incomplete activity, for the being of incomplete activity is in virtue of something other than itself, namely the external end that guides the means. As such, it fails to be independent. Only complete activity is independent, since it is the only activity that is its own end, depending on itself for its own realization. For this reason, it is what it is in virtue of itself. Its activity does not lie outside itself in a separate product.

Form is Being at work staying itself, and it is prior to potency (and material) in articulation, Thinghood, and time. What is relevant for us to consider is how the priority of Being-at-work undermines the conflict between the destructible composites and eternal Form. The potency of some thing does not set itself in motion, as it is the capacity to be affected. As such, it is in need of some Being-at-work by which it may be set in motion. Whether the motion be growth, locomotion, qualitative, or quantitative change, Being-at-work is the activity by which potential gets put to work. Form works on potency and thereby gives it an end for which it can work. The material of a thing, as its potency, is the Form's means, taken up by the Form for the sake of itself. By analogy with the reproduction of living things, Form generates its own instances, its composites, by working on material with the potential for that Form. Although the soul is not itself the solution, since some beings are not ensouled but still at work, Being is nonetheless modeled on the soul.

Since the composites have material, the material is capable of being determined in contrary ways. But since the capacity to be determined in contrary ways is an accidental feature, and the properties could be removed without removing the what it is to be of the thing, the capacity of the material subject to take on contraries does *not contradict* the fact that the Form, the what it is to be of the thing, cannot take on contraries.

Although each composite or particular is generated and destroyed, the Form or the Being-at-work, as the generative principle of each composite, is not destroyed. The Being-at-work is universal across all of its particular composites. As we have already stated, the universal does not ontologically transcend the material, since the Form is of the material, as is evident in the fact that one states the genus in the definition. But as long as there are composites by which and through which Being at work generates more composites, Form is eternal. Because Aristotle denies self-predication, any specific Form is not one of the composites that Form generates. Still, although Form is not generated or destroyed, the Form sustains itself by sustaining the composites, its particulars. Although Being at work generates the composite which is its particular, the composite is the existential condition of the Being at work which generates it. The universal Form exists in and through the particulars it generates. Because the Form is the principle of the composite, and the composite is existential condition of the Form, *the Form determines itself* as the principle of the composite.

Since the Form is the generative principle of its particulars, there are no particulars that do not depend on the Form. *Form itself is separate and a this*. It is true that when we think the articulation of some Form, the Form is separated from the individuals in which they are at work. In this sense, the Form can be treated as an abstraction, a one over many. But Being at work itself is separate and it is a this (and not just in the mind), for it is *not* a such and such *belonging* to a subject. Rather, being-at-work (Form) is the ultimate subject of all predication of essential or *per se* attributes.[79] Whatever sense in which Socrates can be a thing depends ultimately upon the activity of the Form—the thing as the what it is to be—that enables him to function that way. For example, when we predicate 'grammatical' of Socrates, it is not in virtue of Socrates that Socrates is grammatical, but in virtue of his humanity. Ultimately, because Form has universal articulation, and the Form is the Thinghood of the thing, not everything with a universal articulation will be an attribute of something else. Rather, Aristotle ultimately reserves the right to proclaim that some things with universal articulation, such as the Form of the thing, are themselves things—a *such and such* (universal) that is also a *this* (underlying subject).[80] By working through the conceptual relation between Form and material in Aristotle, we have offered solutions to the impasses that affect Aristotle's philosophy and have laid the groundwork for better articulating the way in which Aristotle's philosophy of Form undergirds his *truth* logic.

Although Kant and Aristotle both propound non-formal logics of truth, Aristotle's truth logic has a fundamentally different structure from that of Kant. Neither Kant nor Aristotle attribute *self-predication* to their categories. For Aristotle, Form is not at work on Form itself, and 'Thing-hood' is not itself one of the things in the class of Thinghood. Likewise, for Kant, 'quality' does *not* synthesize itself—rather it synthesizes *intuitions*. For both systems of truth logic, the commitment to the *duality* of principles of truth engenders a denial of self-predication. Although this commonality is not insignificant, it nonetheless covers over a very significant difference between the *form* of their truth logics. Kant denies existential implication, the thesis which states that *the existence of the particular can be deduced from the universal.* Rather, Kant posited a separate faculty, Sensibility, in virtue of which particularizations of universals may be given. Although Aristotle appeals to two principles, Form and material, he nonetheless integrates *existential Implication* into his *truth* logic. According to *existential implication*, one can (to use terminology from the classical square of opposition) infer an 'I' proposition from an 'A' proposition. This means that one can *non-trivially* infer the truth of the *particular case*, 'there is an x,' from the universal case, 'for all x.'[81] Or in traditional language: from the truth of 'All S is P' one can deduce the truth that 'Some S is P.' For example, given that *all* humans are rational, it would be valid to infer, on Aristotle's terms, that there is *at least one rational animal.* Although one cannot infer *which* particular it is, one knows that there must be some one particular. In standard and contemporary formal logic this inference is usually viewed as *invalid.* Indeed, the presence of existential implication in Aristotle's truth logic is the logical articulation of his qualification of the duality of principles that plagued knowing in Plato's *Parmenides.* We will further pursue other dimensions of Aristotle's qualification of the duality of principles in his account of the *pros hen* structure of categories in the discussion of the problem of onto-theology.

Without some understanding of Aristotle's metaphysics, we cannot really appreciate the role of existential implication in Aristotle's thinking. The material on which the Form works allows us to distinguish the instances of the particular generated by the activity of the Form on the matter. What allows the use of the subaltern on the square of opposition, the inference from A to I? Underlying the inference is the metaphysical view we have just uncovered: Form is a *generative principle* of particulars. Aristotle's syllogism reflects and is *grounded upon* ontological structure. For this reason, *no empty terms* are allowed in the system, for that would render the scientific structure of his system a complete absurdity. Were one to allow empty terms, from 'all unicorns are horned' one could infer that 'there is at least one horned unicorn.' For Aristotle, one can only analyze Forms with real instances. There are no Forms of what has *no* instances, and any content stipulated of them is arbitrary. Logic is of *Being*, not of merely formal-logical possibilities. The universal that stands for the Form is a 'concrete universal' in Foster's sense, that is, a universal that 'determines its own particularization.'[82]

Aristotle's logic deserves to be called a *logic of truth*. In order to dis-cover whether it is true that there are *instantiations* of the universal, and the universal connotes some Form, on Aristotle's system of logic the truth of the universal claim would imply the truth of the particular claim. The correspondence of the universal with its instantiations can be deduced syllogistically from universal premises alone. Ontologically, this is guar-anteed by the fact that Forms are the eternal organizing principles of material that also generate the composites, their existential conditions. The logic can thereby be described as *self-determining*, insofar as the *universal realizes itself in the particulars*. Note that although the Form is a self-realizing principle, it nonetheless cannot be responsible for the material content itself. Aristotle still relies upon two principles: Form and material—although the material never exists apart from Form, it is none-theless an irreducible principle that always receives its *own articulation* as the *genus* in the definition of a thing. Aristotle's claim to know what things are in their own right is a claim to absolute knowledge. Only by reading existential implication into the Form of the thing, only by grant-ing it the power to generate particulars, can Aristotle claim to achieve Absolute knowledge of Absolute being. This is why Foster is correct to note that 'to claim Aristotle as an authority for the abstract universal argues a misunderstanding of his doctrine.'[83] Foster is right that for Aris-totle, the Form is active insofar as it is responsible for determining 'the particular being of the separate instances of the species' and the sensible thing is indebted to the Form for its existence.[84]

Aristotle's qualification of the duality of principles in his account of the power of Form to particularize itself unfortunately does not in any way diminish the problem of instantiation. Since Aristotle's Form must have the articulation of a *this such and such*, it too must fall victim to the problem of instantiation. Given that the Form is a this, it is one in number—it is *this* Form—and thereby not repeatable. Since it is articu-lated as a *such and such*, it is *repeated in all of its instances*. Thus, the non-repeatable is repeatable, or what is the same: what can only be one in number becomes indefinite in number.[85] Yet, denying that the *same* Form is multiply instantiated would undermine the possibility of science.

To draw a brief point of comparison between Aristotle and Kant, by denying that the human understanding is in possession of *Nous*, Kant denies the self-realizing power of the universal that was operative in Aris-totle's thinking. This is tantamount to a denial that human beings can have absolute knowledge of things as they are absolutely determined—namely, as they are 'in their own right.' Indeed, his denial of intellectual intui-tion is meant to deny that we have the power to know whether there is a particular instance of the universal from the universal itself. The denial of *Nous* in Kant is not separable from the denial of existential implica-tion in his thinking. This profound shift in thinking in Kant's Copernican revolution goes unnoticed when we pass over Aristotle's endorsement of existential implication. Kant's critique, however, does nothing to alleviate the problem of instantiation, since the problem can be articulated completely independently of the problem of existential implication.

For Kant, the duality of principles explicitly engenders the unknowability of Noumena. Plato already anticipated such restrictions in his *Parmenides*, where he demonstrated that the duality of universality and particularity undermines the knowability of what exists and is true in virtue of itself. While Aristotle could successfully qualify the duality of principles approach operative in Plato, even his account falters on the problem of instantiation. By instituting a fundamental difference between principles of identity and difference, these various thinkers and traditions do *not* attempt to derive all difference from one principle of identity. These thinkers structure the content of metaphysical and epistemic theories and expectations in order that they *correspond with the form of logical thinking* constituted in a *dualistic* manner. But the insistence on this fundamental difference does not, it appears, further enable the philosopher to achieve Absolute Knowledge. As Kant finally recognized, rather than aid in achieving Absolute Knowledge, the separation of the principles of identity and difference fundamentally undermines every effort to achieve Absolute Knowledge. By construing the concept in a dualistic manner, any such generic solution to the problem that denies a *single* principle of truth therewith also seems to forsake any possibility of Absolute Knowledge. In conclusion, our historical inquiry repeatedly indicates that the separation between principles of universality and particularity not only undermines the capacity to know the Absolute but also engenders the perpetual problem of instantiation. Simply put, whether one attempts to deduce the principle of difference from identity or to posit each as irreducibly separate from the other (and thereby to raise difference to the absolute position), Absolute Knowledge appears impossible.

Notes

1. Indeed, for this generic solution, because concepts (or universals) are conceived as principles of identity, not of differentiation, concepts cannot be sufficient to account for their own differentiation. This solution recognizes that difference cannot be derived from a principle of identity alone (such as concepts or universals) in any field of philosophical discourse, such as metaphysics, philosophy of nature, or philosophy of mind. Instead, philosophy conforms its reflection on fields of discourse that are not reducible to logic, such as philosophy of nature and philosophy of mind, to the structure of the concept. By conforming the ontological and epistemic requirements of philosophical thinking to the duality of principles governing conceptual determination, the problem of the origin of the Absolute is not supposed to arise.

2. Note that these are mere illustrations of the type of solution I am exploring here. They ought not be taken as *exhaustive* of the various ways this generic solution could be employed.
3. Note the epistemic, and non-ontological formulation of the principle. Kant leaves out the qualifiers 'in the same respect' and 'at the same time.'
4. For the full list of the time determinations, see Kant, *CPR*, B182–B187.
5. In his *CPR* Kant writes that space and time must also be thought as intuitions themselves, not merely as forms of sensible intuitions: 'But space and time are represented apriori not merely as forms of sensible intuition, but also as intuitions themselves (which contain a manifold).' Kant, *CPR*, paragraph 26, 261. Also relevant here is Kant's footnote in paragraph 26 of Section II: Transcendental Deduction of Pure Concepts of the Understanding. See Kant, *CPR*, 261. Here he notes that geometry demands that space be conceived as an object:

> Space represented as object (as is really required by geometry), contains more than the mere form of intuition, namely comprehension of the manifold given in accordance with the form of sensibility in an intuitive representation, so that the form of intuition merely gives the manifold.

Kant also speaks about 'pure shape in space.' See Kant, *CPR*, 273 (A 141/B180).
6. Note that in Immanuel Kant, *Grounding for the Metaphysics of Morals*, trans. James W. Ellington (Indianapolis: Hackett, 1981), Second Section, 19–48, willing does produce its own duties from itself alone, without regard to sensible content.
7. Arguably, Descartes' cogito can also be read as another example in early modern philosophy of existential implication insofar as the very thought of the I entails that the I must exist. See Rene Descartes, *Meditations on First Philosophy*, trans. John Cottingham (Cambridge: Cambridge University Press, 1999), Second Meditation, 18.
8. Here we ought to note two senses of 'possible': formal logic determines what is logically possible, that is what is consistent. Transcendental logic determines what is *really possible*, that is what could be an object. Kant would allow that 'God' is possible in the former, but not in the latter sense, since God is not a possible object of experience.
9. See Kant, *CPR*, B622–B625.
10. Ibid, 567 (B624–B628).
11. Plato, "Parmenides," 131a–d, 364–365.
12. In Socrates' rejection of the second disjunction, he admits that each universal, for example 'Greatness, Equality, and Smallness, admits of a *particular* measure. If particulars received a share of Greatness, the particular would have a share of Greatness *smaller than* Greatness itself. This implies that Greatness itself has a magnitude, great or small, with which one could compare the share of the participant.'
13. See Gregory Vlastos, "The Third Man Argument in Plato's Parmenides," *Philosophical Review* LXIII (1954): 319–349.
14. Self-predication is not only a feature of the early parts of *Parmenides*. This pattern of reasoning is also evident in the hypotheses. For example, in the second hypothesis, Parmenides argues that the One Being is both the whole and part of itself. The One Being is a whole of parts, as it has two parts, 'One' and 'Being'. But 'One' is, so it has Being, and Being is one of the two parts, and so Being is One. Therefore, each part 'One' and 'Being' is 'One Being'. Thus, the One Being includes itself, the whole, as a part. Likewise, the same, as the same, is other to the other, and the other, as other to the same, is the

same as itself. Here, in both these examples, we see the self-predication in virtue of which a term, in virtue of being itself is not itself. Plato, "Parmenides," 142b–c.

15. Plato, "Parmenides," 132b–d, 366–367.
16. As we know from Aristotle's writings, another way to understand Plato's dualistic doctrine is on the terms of the Unwritten Doctrine, namely the One and the Indefinite Dyad.

> Now since the Forms are the causes of everything else, he [i.e. Plato] supposed that their elements are the elements of all things. Accordingly, the material principle is the Great and Small [i.e. the Dyad], and the essence is the One, since the numbers are derived from the Great and Small by participation in the One.

See Aristotle, *Metaphysics,* 987b15–20. 'From this account it is clear that he only employed two causes: that of the essence, and the material cause; for the Forms are the cause of the essence in everything else, and the One is the cause of it in the Forms. He also tells us what the material substrate is of which the Forms are predicated in the case of sensible things, and the One in that of the Forms—that it is this the duality (the Dyad), the Great and Small (Further, he assigned to these two elements respectively the causation of good and of evil.' See Aristotle, *Metaphysics,* 988 a.
17. Still, we must be careful, for since each Form is itself by itself, there is no prior difference that could differentiate a Form.
18. What the problem of participation shows is that in Platonic thought the genus-species and whole-part determination is in conflict with the specification that the Form is indivisible and exists by itself. The Forms themselves also fail to be universal, since they cannot be common terms.
19. Plato, "Parmenides," 135b–c, 369.
20. Plato, "Sophist," in *Plato: Complete Works,* ed. John M. Cooper (Indianapolis: Hackett Publishing, 1997), 235–294, 240d, 261. Also see Plato, "Sophist," 241a–e, 262: 'we'll also regard false speaking the same way, as saying that those which are not and that those which are not, are.'
21. Hegel, *Hegel's Logic,* 52.
22. Plato, "Parmenides," 134b.
23. Ibid.
24. See Plato's example of the Form of Equality in *Phaedo.* Equality is never unequal to itself, for it never admits what it is not. It is 'that which is' and accordingly is never untrue to itself. Plato, *Phaedo,* trans. Eva Brann, Peter Kalkavage, and Eric Salem (Newburyport: Focus Philosophical Library, 1998), 74D–75C, 48–50.
25. See Plato, "Philebus," 62c–a. In the *Phaedo* Plato argues that the *true philosophers* take pleasure in that which remains true to itself, and in this way the pleasure will not become a pain, as is the case with 'false' pleasures.
26. Jonathan Barnes, *Early Greek Philosophy* (Suffolk: Penguin Books, 2002), Heraclitus, B50.
27. Ibid, Heraclitus, B1.
28. For this hierarchy see Plato, "Republic," V, 477–479, 1104–1106.
29. Note that in the *Parmenides* Plato also refutes the very common concept of participation present in other Platonic dialogues in which the Forms are conceived as the paradigms that are imitated by the sensory particulars. Plato, "Parmenides," 132d–a, 366–367.
30. 'Well, you are still young, Socrates,' said Parmenides, 'and philosophy has not yet grabbed you as it will, in my opinion. Then you will dishonor none

of these things; but as for now, you still look to the opinions of men, because of your age.' Plato, *Parmenides*, trans. Albert Keith Whitaker (Newburyport: Focus Philosophical Library, 1996), 130e, 28.

31. Aristotle, *Metaphysics*, 249, 1075a.
32. Ibid, 999a.
33. This conclusion can be applied to critique Plato's concept of Form: since Plato's Forms admit two kinds of unity, unity in kind and number, neither of which seem derivable from the other, Forms could not be indivisibly one as Plato conceived them.
34. Among others, see footnote 20 of Sachs' translation of Aristotle's *Metaphysics*, 21. Sachs is correct that 'Aristotle is among those who posit forms as causes and as beings, and for that reason he is at pain to criticize in detail the technical working out of that doctrine.'
35. See Porphyry, *Isagoge*, trans. Edward W. Warren (Toronto: Pontifical Institute of Mediaeval Studies, 1975) for an extensive treatment of this concept.
36. The difference ought to imply the genus even if not explicitly stated only if the difference is unique to the species. Otherwise, multiple genera could be implied. Though one might dispute the idea that the categories are genera, Aristotle treats them as such.
37. See Aristotle, "Categories," in *The Complete Works of Aristotle: Vol. 1*, ed. Jonathan Barnes (Princeton: Princeton University Press, 1984), 3–24, section Four, 4, 1b25–2a10.
38. Aristotle, "Posterior Analytics," Part 5, 119–120.
39. Ibid.
40. Here I am following Sach's translation. The standard translation 'Substance' is translated from the Latin, and as a principle, I think it the best practice to translate directly from the Greek into English. 'Thinghood' is the very 'what it is to be' of a being or thing, and for this reason, 'Thingood' is a proper rendering. This term also frees the reader from connotations regarding Substance from the way the term is used in modern philosophy.
41. Aristotle, *Metaphysics*, 1029a28.
42. Note that 'in its own right' is another formulation of Plato's formulation of the Form as 'itself by itself.'
43. Aristotle, *Metaphysics*, 1031a30–b.
44. 'For this would be sufficient if it were granted, even if there were no forms, and perhaps even more so if there are forms.' See Aristotle, *Metaphysics*, Ch. 6, 1031b14–15.
45. See Aristotle, *Metaphysics*, Book E.
46. Aristotle, *Metaphysics*, 1029b20.
47. Although each knowledge studies one genus, since genera are, for the most part, measured by one species, for example 'white' is the measure of color, each knowledge studies, in this way, one primary species of the genus. This might cause a problem, as it undermines the claim to independence of inferior species. Since one knowledge studies one genus, one cannot take conclusions derived from one genus and apply them to another. Since a proper definition of a species requires, as stated earlier, a genus and a difference, knowing the species is tantamount to knowing the difference, as the genus is implied by the difference.
48. This example is culled from Aristotle, "Posterior Analytics," Book I, Part 5, 119–120. Although Aristotle does not think that mathematicals are things, it nonetheless exemplifies the process of Aristotelian science. For Aristotle, we may treat the object as though it *were* a thing, for the sake of demonstration,

although it is not. This allows us to treat all accidentals scientifically and makes the sciences of arithmetic and optics, among others, possible.

49. In order to make an inference one must already assume some universal. The reason for this is simple. An inference is the act of drawing a conclusion from a series of premises. One cannot draw an inference without premises, and premises are judgments of the form 'S is P.' Since judgments apply concepts, in this case predicates, to subjects, we must already have a concept of the concept before we can deal with inference.

50. We should note that one cannot deduce one middle term from another, since properly speaking, the middle term is the articulation of the essence of something. To demonstrate one middle term from another would imply that essences are not independent, and would annihilate the essential being of the deduced essence.

51. See Aristotle, "Posterior Analytics," Book II, Part 8, 153–154.

52. Ibid, Book I, Part 14, 129.

53. Aristotle himself appeals to variables in the *Prior Analytics*. Moreover, because there is a generic way in which inferences are drawn in the scientific syllogism, it is not inappropriate to use variables here, for they exemplify the generic process of inference.

54. Aristotle, *Metaphysics*, 183 (1051b).

55. Ibid.

56. Ibid, 115 (1027b).

57. Ibid.

58. Ibid, 1025–1028.

59. Ibid, 1051b1–5.

60. Ibid, 115, 1028.

61. Ibid (1027b).

62. Ibid, 184 (1051b).

63. Ibid, Book Theta (1051–1052).

64. Accordingly, Aristotle emphasizes the fact that one either knows it or one does not. Since there are ultimately no terms to be combined, one cannot combine the terms wrongly. Accordingly, there is no possibility of *deception*. See Aristotle, *Metaphysics*, Theta, 184 1052. This does not mean that one cannot be ignorant, as he states.

65. Aristotle, *Metaphysics*, 1038b15.

66. For further detail, see Aristotle, *Metaphysics*, 1038b20–1039a.

67. See Aristotle, "Categories," Section 5, 4.

68. The bracket is my insertion.

69. Aristotle, *Metaphysics*, 1003a10.

70. Ibid, 999b15–22.

71. Ibid, 1000a5.

72. Ibid, 1039b20–30.

73. Ibid, 1033a30–b5.

74. Ibid, 1039a15–20.

75. Ibid, lvii.

76. One of the *aporia* of book Beta concerns the being of material elements: 'In the same area as these things is questioning whether the elements have being potentially or in some other way.' Aristotle, *Metaphysics*, 1002b31–1003a.

77. The genus is, in principle, the material. As the material, it cannot differentiate itself. Matter is what receives the activity of Form. It does not possess, just as matter, the activity of Form.

78. Independent things are not essentially divided beings as long as they exist—to divide the thing itself into its genus and difference would be the destruction

of the thing. In order for the thing to remain what it is, the genus and the difference must form an indivisible unity. In this way, the definition of independent things remains possible.

79. For example, 'human being' is the subject of the predicate 'able to laugh' which is predicated of Socrates in virtue of the fact that he is a human being.

80. This remains a problem, as we will see with the discussion of the problem of the missing difference. Although the universal is such and such, and thereby belongs to a subject, since Thinghood is articulated universally and is the underlying subject, the underlying subject must be articulated universally. But if the universal belongs to a subject, then Thinghood must belong to a thing, which would be absurd.

81. Note that for Aristotle the statement 'All S is P' is not a statement about a class concept. Rather, universals are understood on the model of genera and species, not class-membership.

82. M. B. Foster, "The Concrete Universal: Cook Wilson and Bosanquet," *Mind* 40 (1931): 1–22, 1.

83. Ibid, 22.

84. See Foster, "The Concrete Universal," 2 and Jaeger, *Aristoteles*, 360, 407 (cited in Foster).

85. One could further explicate this problem in terms of eternal and sensible Form.

4 The Logic of the Finite Concept

Given that the failed approaches to Absolute Knowledge conceive of the concept on the model of a duality of principles of identity and difference, in order to make any progress on the question of the possibility of Absolute Knowledge a systematic inquiry into the structure of conceptuality is required. In the early phases of our inquiry, the operative opposition generating our problem of the origin of the Absolute is the opposition between identity and difference. This opposition will remain important for our reflections, but must ultimately take second place to a more fundamental distinction, which is nonetheless inseparable from the concepts of identity and difference: *universal and particular*. As we elucidated in the previous chapter, truth, as the correspondence of the concept with its object, must already presuppose a correspondence of the concept with the object on *both sides* of the opposition. In order for the concept to correspond with the object, the object must already be conceptually determined. Otherwise, the object would fail to possess any identity with the concept, and correspondence would be impossible. Likewise, without a unity of the object and the concept within the structure of conceptual determination, nothing on the side of the object would correspond with conceptual determination.

As we noted, *coherence* is already built into both conceptions of correspondence. For correspondence to obtain, there must be a *coherence* of *the concept with itself*, just as much as there must be correspondence between *the object and itself*. Insofar as thinking is performed by a subject, or more strongly, *constitutes* the subject's being as a rational agent, the correspondence of the concept and the object can also be described in terms of subjectivity and objectivity. Ancient Greek philosophy recognizes the truth (the unity of universal and its object) to be on the side of the *object* and discovers truth when it can successfully correlate the universal in its own thinking with the true universal that is *already there in the thing*. Kant's critical philosophy moves in the opposite direction: the object can be declared to be a *true* object only if it corresponds with the unity of the concept and the object in the conceiving subjectivity. To use a more recent turn of phrase, the 'truth maker' in each case is different: in one case it is subjectivity, in the other objectivity.

On either conception of the *logic of truth*, the correspondence can only obtain because there are two sides, one of which is a universal or conceptual determination. Thus, in order to properly elucidate the structure of the logic of truth, one must be able to explicate the truth of *conceptual determination* as such. Whether we occupy Kant's position and take up the Copernican revolution in epistemology or return to the metaphysics of the Ancient Greeks, such as that of Aristotle, truth is contingent upon *the truth of the logic of the concept*.

For both Kant and Aristotle, the universal is a principle of *the identity* of the particulars, not a principle of their difference. As we have clarified, Aristotle's concept of the genus only provides the principle by which the particulars in the genus can be unified. 'Mammal' only determines what makes each particular a mammal, not what differentiates mammals from each other. Indeed, at the level of the infima species (such as 'human being'), for Aristotle *only material* can distinguish one composite of the same class from another. Likewise, for Kant the category is empty without the intuitive content. As Kant points out:

> In the mere concept of a thing no characteristic of its existence can be encountered at all.[1]

For Kant, concepts by themselves do not provide for their own instantiation. The existence of the concept must be supplied by another principle: intuition. In sum, for Kant as well as for Aristotle, the logic of the concept is such that the universal is the principle of identity of particulars, but (even if it is a necessary condition) cannot be a *sufficient principle* of the *differentiation of the particulars*. Thus, on either conception the concept is constituted by a duality of principles in which the universal is the principle of identity, while another principle must be introduced in order to differentiate the particulars. Since truth depends upon the truth of the concept, the logic of truth in Aristotle and Kant depends upon the truth of the *separation of the principles of universality and particularity*. Thus, in order to properly investigate the merits of such dominant truth logics in the Western tradition, an investigation into the *logic of the concept* itself is necessary.

In the preceding analysis, we have raised a number of philosophical concerns about the plausibility of modeling a plausible conception of the Absolute on a *logic of truth* that separates the universal as the principle of identity from the particular as the principle of difference. Since our systematic question concerns whether a dualistic conception of the principles of identity and difference is sufficient to achieve Absolute Knowledge, the question can be reformulated in the following way: can one achieve a *true conception* of the Absolute upon the presupposition that the principles of universality (identity) and particularity (difference) are *separate* principles? Or is it the case that the separation of such principles fundamentally undermines any attempt to truly know the Absolute?

To put this question concerning knowledge of the Absolute in terms of truth, can one know the *Absolute truth* if the principles of universality and particularity are separated? Being both absolute and true, 'Absolute Truth' would not only engender the correspondence of the concept with its object but would also require that the truth be *un*conditioned. A truth that is *un*conditioned would not be true in virtue of another, but would be *true in virtue of itself*. Given the separation of the principles of universality and particularity that is apparently endemic to conceptual determination, is the concept capable of knowing what is true in *virtue of itself* or to use Plato's and Aristotle's nomenclature, what is true *kath auto*?

Universality and Particularity in the Abstraction, the Genus, and the Class

Because our investigations were anchored there in the idiosyncratic reflections of different philosophers, one might be inclined to think that Absolute Knowledge can be achieved by re-thinking the *way* we model the Absolute on a duality of principles of universality and particularity, rather than completely giving up on the project of knowing the Absolute on the model of a duality of principles. In order to demonstrate that there is *no way* to salvage any *true* conception of Absolute Knowing or Being that conceives of conceptual determination in terms of a duality of principles, it will be necessary to systematically think through what is necessarily entailed in conceiving of *truth logic* in terms of a *duality* of principles, in addition to uncovering the principle that lies at the ground of this conception.

Before proceeding, it is important to note that although Kant and Aristotle developed *truth* logics, namely logics that *have content* or are *non-formal* in character, their accounts of the concept are nonetheless still committed to a division between the principles of universality and particularity. Simply put, it would be an error to suppose that only varieties of formal logic suffer from this division. Of course, it is not difficult to show that formal concepts of logic do in fact engender a division between the principle of identity and difference. As long as we only consider logic as containing the form of thinking, the content of thinking must be culled from elsewhere. Still, the division between principles of universality and particularity is nonetheless evident even in non-formal concepts of truth logic, as is evident from Aristotle's conception of the genus as insufficient for deducing its particulars, as well as Kant's division between the concept and the source of its truth in intuition. For this reason, the critique of the logic of the concept that follows does not just concern formal logic, but is much broader, for it concerns classical logics of truth as well, including Kant's transcendental logic and Aristotle's syllogism of Form in which the middle term connotes the 'what it is to be' of the thing.

In this chapter, I will demonstrate the uncontroversial proposition that the traditional senses of the concept understood as an abstraction, a genus, or a set entails that concepts are never sufficient for the differentiation of their particulars. From the assumption that concepts are not sufficient to differentiate their particulars, I will further demonstrate that these traditional ways of construing the concept invoke the following features: an appeal to *the Given*, the *finitude* of the concept, and the rejection of *self-predication* as well as *existential implication*. As our analysis will show, these features are characteristic of the concept construed as an abstraction, genus, or class even if one abstracts from the question of *apriority* or *a posteriori* determinations. Finally, in order to motivate the attractiveness of the thesis that conceptual determination is governed by a duality of principles, I will demonstrate (both systematically and historically) that it is none other than the *PNC* that grounds these features of the universal.

With these propositions in hand, I will proceed in the *next chapter* to demonstrate that the sense of the concept as constituted by a duality of principles of universality and particularity entails the paradox of the missing difference. From this, it will follow that the concept, insofar as it is constituted by a duality of principles, is self-contradictory. This feature of the domain of concepts has mostly gone unnoticed in contemporary philosophy.

David Armstrong, in his *Universals: An Opinionated Introduction*, claims that the distinction between type and token is a prevalent distinction in contemporary philosophy:

> A distinction that practically all contemporary philosophers accept was drawn by the great U.S. nineteenth century philosopher, C.S. Pierce. He originally used it in the context of semantics, but in fact it is a perfectly general distinction applicable to any subject whatever. It is the distinction between token and type.[2]

Although Armstrong here employs more contemporary nomenclature such as type and token, it is clear from the context of his text, namely his concern with the problem of universals,[3] that 'type' signifies 'universal' while 'token' signifies 'particular.' One classical and still widely prevalent sense of 'concept' is that the concept is a common character or universal. Correlated with this sense of the concept is the sense of the particular as the instance of the universal or common character.[4]

Prevalent throughout the history of Western thought, although not at all absent from ancient Greek thought, *the abstract universal* is perhaps the most common way of thinking about universality. The most traditional construal of this kind of universal is most minimally construed as the 'one over many.' The view that the concept is a universal or common character is a perennial concept that re-appears throughout the history of Western philosophy. Although the term 'concept' does not appear in Ancient Greek philosophy, 'idea' and 'universal' do. In the *Parmenides*, Plato explicitly characterizes his Forms as universals each of which is a *one over many*.[5] Although Aristotle rejects the identification of the Form with universality, he identifies the universal, καθόλου, as a general idea, as a one applied to many.[6] Both Plato and Aristotle are explicit that the universal does not differentiate itself. In the *Parmenides*, Plato states that universals only relate to themselves and particulars only relate to particulars.

For Kant, a concept, *Begriff*, is contrasted with intuition, *Anschauung*, by having its instances subsumed *under* it rather than within it.[7] Central to this idea here seems to be that concepts are functions that unite different representations *under* a *common* one.[8] Kant's admission that the instances of the concept fall 'under' the concept imply quite clearly that the concept does not contain the various particulars to which it applies within itself. This is entailed in his famous quip that concepts are *empty* without intuitions. Accordingly, Kant's definition of the universal discussed in the previous chapter fits the model of the abstract universal quite well. For Kant, In the universal function as a common feature of a plurality, or a *one* over many, such that the concept by itself does not specify which particulars fall under the concept, nor does it specify what other properties belong to the objects to which the concept applies.

At the dawn of Analytic philosophy, there is a linguistic turn to conceive of concepts primarily in terms of predication. Frege, for example, claims that the concept is predicative in nature.[9] He claims that 'the behavior of the concept is essentially predicative.'[10] Although Russell has a notion of concepts as sets, he follows Frege in conceiving of universals as predicates too. Russell writes that universals (unlike particulars) 'can occur as predicates or relations in complexes.'[11] Following in the tradition, Husserl also identifies concepts as exhibiting a non-psychological type of *generality*.[12] In more recent philosophy, E. J. Lowe has identified sorts and kinds as universals that *instantiate* particulars, whereas individuals instantiate sorts and kinds.[13] For Husserl, Frege, Russell, and Lowe, predicates are neither self-differentiating *nor* self-instantiating. To know, for example, if a particular predicate obtains one cannot attend to the predicate's content alone. From this short survey, it becomes clear that in the history of Western philosophy one can find many prominent examples of (i) the juxtaposition of the concept as a general characteristic and (ii) the assumption that concepts do not differentiate themselves.

Since the content must be culled from some given, the universal must be discovered in and abstracted out of multifarious individuals. This process requires either discovering a common feature shared by many things and separating it from the individuals in which it inheres or simply selecting a single content to stand for other contents. Whether one speaks of *selecting* a singular content or *discovering* a common feature, one is engaged in a process of removing content and giving it some kind of universal significance. In a simple abstraction, the concept is thought to be distinct from a mere collection of individuals, since it specifies what property individuals must have in order to be an instance of the universal. Having completed the process of separating the universals from the individuals and from each other, the most abstract universals will contain all of the individuals under them as instances. Since the abstraction is only a common feature, it fails to specify how many instances, or particulars, there are. Moreover, as a common feature, it fails to distinguish particular instances from one another. Hence, for the abstract universal there is no account of the differentiated particular or the singularity of the instances.

By defining the concept as a common character, one is not necessarily committing oneself to a specific metaphysical position regarding the existence of concepts. Even if such a definition of the concept requires the philosopher to hold some metaphysical position regarding the ontological status of concepts (which is itself already a subject of dispute), the philosopher can nonetheless agree that the concept is a common character while simultaneously disagreeing about its ontological status.[14] Accordingly, the following argument ought also to have consequences for a variety of metaphysical perspectives on concepts. Irrespective of one's particular metaphysical commitments, we must acknowledge that the sense of the term 'concept' is itself already a subject of dispute.

That concepts are not sufficient to differentiate the particulars that fall under them is not a controversial assumption and can be made obvious by considering some common examples. Consider, for example, the concept of QUALITY. The concept of QUALITY is not sufficient to determine what kinds of qualities there are. The concept of QUALITY is necessary for the sense of every kind of quality, but obviously not sufficient for the sense of the kinds of qualities. What is pertinent here is not the kind of example, namely that I have used a sortal term or a term whose instances are concepts; what is pertinent is just that the concept of QUALITY is a concept. One could instead appeal to concepts that have non-conceptual particulars as their instances, such as the concept of HUMAN BEING. The concept HUMAN BEING is never sufficient for differentiating particular human beings. What usually goes without saying is that the concept of HUMAN BEING does not distinguish Socrates from Aristotle. Likewise, being 'snub-nosed' does not distinguish the various instances of such noses from one another. The obviousness of this feature goes without saying, and it usually does.[15]

Imagine a dinner party at which (to the chagrin of the host) some of the invitees find themselves in a dispute about concepts. If one of the disputants were to insist that the concept ANIMAL were sufficient to distinguish mammals from fish or honey badgers from dolphins, it would not take a professional philosopher to identify the mistake and kindly direct the confused disputant to register for a course in logic. In order to distinguish the particulars within the same class, one must appeal to a different concept outside of the class that one intends to divide. If the concept ANIMAL were sufficient to elucidate the sense of the concepts MAMMAL and FISH, MAMMAL and FISH would have the same sense as the concept ANIMAL. Given that the particulars are differentiations of the class of animals, this must, of course, be impossible. In this case, what is important is not only the biological error but also the logical confusion about what one can and cannot accomplish with a concept. I employ this illustration merely to indicate what we usually take for granted regarding the structure and power of concepts, not to wield ordinary language as a philosophical principle.

As the common character, the concept only specifies a feature that all of the particulars share. Since it only specifies the shared feature, and the shared feature does not distinguish one particular from another, the concept is not sufficient for the differentiation of the particulars. What often goes without saying in philosophical inquires into concepts is the assumption that concepts are not sufficient for the differentiation of their particulars. Though I have here employed the concept of the abstract universal as my example for the sake of analysis, a brief overview of the history of other major conceptions of the concept in the Western tradition, such as the genus and the set, betrays the *same* assumption with its accompanying constraints.

As a very prominent feature of ancient Greek philosophical systems,[16] such as that of Aristotle, a 'genus' is a universal containing different species within itself, for example 'quantity' contains 'discrete' quantities and 'continuous' quantities. The 'differentia' differentiates these species from one another. The genus and the differentia together define the species. Genera, insofar as they contain species, have an internal relation to other universals and do not exhibit a merely external relation to other universals. Since each species is a differentiation of the genus, the genus contains its particulars within itself. Each species, insofar as it is a genus for another species, also contains species, its particulars, within itself.

Although the genus immediately contains its own differentiations, within itself, and is constituted by the totality of its species, the genus itself does not provide an account of the process by which the genus is differentiated. As we discussed in the previous chapter, Aristotle rightly acknowledges this limit in his account of definition and the categories. For Aristotle, a genus does not differentiate itself. Although the genus contains the differentia of its species without which the species would not be defined, the differentia are not themselves derived from the genus, since the genus is in common to all of it species. For example, 'animal' is a genus and 'ox' and 'man' are species. Both 'ox' and 'man' are animals, and 'being an animal' does not provide us the differences by which 'ox' and 'man' are defined. Hence, the genus is *not* a sufficient condition to *derive* the differentiation of the species, even though it contains them. Instead, a prior difference must be imported in order to differentiate the contents. Hence, *the principle of differentiation* is still missing from the genus.

Any species that is not a genus for other species, the *infima* species, will not have any conceptual means for differentiating the particulars falling within it, since there is no lower species to differentiate the particulars falling within the species. In this case, the species is constituted by individuals it cannot differentiate. Hence, at the *lowest* differentiation, the species is a *class* whose members are distinguished by a principle external to the genus and species. The genus, although providing some differentiation of the particular, fails to differentiate its own species without a prior difference and fails to differentiate is own particulars at the highest and lowest levels of universality.

Examples of philosophers who draw a distinction between principles of universality and particularity are also easy to come by in medieval philosophy. Take, for example, Duns Scotus. Scotus is a realist concerning universals and posits two principles: the *natura communis*, the common nature, and the *haecceitas*, the principle of particularization. The universals, or common natures, exist in particular things, but they do not differentiate the particulars. 'Human being' specifies what each human has in common—it is the *natura communis*. The universal is 'contracted by haeccity' in each person, for example 'Socrates' and 'Plato.'[17]

Of course, many philosophers reject the identification of the concept with the universal, such as the host of nominalists, empiricists, and others who identify the universal with a class or set of particulars. Although empiricism, nominalism (both medieval and modern), and other forms of trope theory may not characterize the concept as a universal, the view that (1) the concept is defined by class membership nonetheless entails the thesis that concepts are not sufficient to differentiate their particulars. This is evident enough if one considers the concept of the set.

The concept underpinning the structure of contemporary deductive systems, the class, consists of a collection of individuals. Unlike the abstract 'one over many,' each particular is one member of the class, and taken all together, the class is an *aggregate of individuals*. As an aggregate, the universal is not distinct from the totality of the particulars, as the abstract universal is, for it is neither itself a separate member of the class, nor is it distinct from the aggregate itself. The universal simply is the totality of the particulars. Since the class is not distinct from the totality of the particulars, the universality is not as divorced from particularity in class membership as it is in the abstract 'one over the many.' On the one hand, unlike abstract universals, in the class the particular members are set into relation to each other when they are brought into the class. Accordingly, 'membership' signifies a relation between particulars. On the other hand, unlike the abstract universal, the identification of the universal with the aggregate precludes providing any standard by which particular members belong to any particular class or are excluded from the class. Moreover, the individuals in the class may be universal, but *qua* members of the class the universals are thought merely in terms of their membership. Since the class only specifies that each is a member of the class, it does not specify that in virtue of which each member is different from the others. Hence, the class does not provide any means of differentiating the particulars within itself. Just as abstract universality fails to distinguish instances, class membership also fails to individuate members. Accordingly, even the most universal classes will also be unable to differentiate the particular members from one another. Although the class is united with the particulars, its form of unity precludes any account of what individuates the members and the condition upon which membership ought to be granted.[18] As our discussion of the set indicates, the concept of the universal as an abstract universal (such as in Kant) or as a genus (as in Aristotle) are *not* exhaustive of the ways one can construe conceptual determination. One can continue to maintain the thesis that the concept is *not sufficient* for the differentiation of the particular by advancing a concept of the universal as a class. We will follow up on this form of the concept in more detail in the next chapter in our discussion of absolute empiricism. In sum, we find three dominant forms of universality enumerated in the Western tradition: genus, abstraction, and class. Throughout the history of Western philosophy, a variety of different concepts of the universal have developed, each with its own unique characteristics and problems. Despite this great variety in the way the universal has been conceived, we nonetheless discover common characteristics that pervade them all, one of which is the fundamental *inability* to *sufficiently* account for the differentiation of the particular.

The Relativity of the Concept

Given that the universal is not sufficient for the differentiation of the particular, a *second* principle must be introduced in order to account for the *differentiated* content of the universal. Although the universal specifies the content in virtue of which the particulars are *identified* with each other, the universal in virtue of which those very particulars are identified with each other is not the same principle as that which differentiates them. Accordingly, even if another universal is appealed to in order to differentiate the various particulars, it must be a *different* universal, since the same universal does not function as *both* a principle of universality and particularity. Ultimately, this just re-iterates the problem, for it shows that the universal to which we appeal in order to differentiate the particulars is also only a principle of unity and thereby cannot differentiate the particulars that fall under it. Thus, another principle of difference is demanded and thus postponed. For example, 'human being' is not sufficient to differentiate its particulars, for example 'Socrates' and 'Aristotle.' At the level of universals we discover a similar principle. When I 'predicate' 'Being' of each thing that is, I specify that each *is*. Specifying that each is does not specify what differentiates each. Insofar as each thing is, we remain just as ignorant as ever concerning what it is that specifies *the kind of thing* that is.

Given this duality of principles, in order to discover what differentiates the particulars that fall under the universal and thereby specify the *content* of the universal, one must appeal to some *given* content that is *other* than the universal itself—some *non-universal content*. Even if that content is already imbued with universality, in order to uncover the principle of differentiation for both individuals and universals, some non-universal content must be given in order to sufficiently differentiate the particulars. If the universal is only a principle of identity, ultimately the principle by which particulars are identified must come from some content outside of the universal. I have referred to this as a 'given' content, since the universal cannot produce, generate, or create these differentiated particulars *on its own*. The thinker must search for these determinations—she must explore *what is there already*.

Both Kant and Aristotle were well aware of the systematic commitment that the separation of principles engenders an appeal to a given that is *not reducible* to conceptual content. Given that the universal is not sufficient for the differentiation of its particulars, in order to specify the content of the universal, both appealed to some non-universal content from which the content of their categories acquired content. Kant posited the *a priori* forms of intuition as the *a priori* source for the *a priori* intuitive content of the universal without which the categories would be *empty* determinations. Their *differentiated intuitive* content requires a second principle. Indeed, *without intuition, no concept would exist*. Intuition, even *a priori* intuition, is for Kant a Given and is explicitly *not a concept*, for it contains its instances. Aristotle too recognized that without appeal to sense-perception, one could not discover the content of the universal. Without 'particulars taking a stand' or without perceiving various men, such as Callias, one could never know the content of the repeatable universal and Form of the human being. So reliant is Aristotle on the empirical Given that even his categories of Being are discovered empirically. Whether we take up the metaphysical or epistemic project of Aristotle or Kant, each adopts a kind of Foundationalism: one must appeal to a nonconceptual intuitive foundation upon which to build one's system. In the former case, one begins with the thing as the absolute foundation; in the latter case one begins with subjectivity.

When *no* truth logic is recognized at all, that is, when conceptual form is specified as a *purely formal structure*, then the requirement to appeal to the Given is certainly not diminished. Rather, it is augmented. When, for example, the universal only provides the abstract form of conceptual thinking as such, specified in terms of the PNC or identity, in which A=A, in order to discover what A is one must appeal to some non-conceptual given content. As is evident enough, one cannot deduce the differentiated content of various categories, such as 'quality' and 'quantity' from the fact of mere self-identity of categories in general.

Having explicated these two systematic features of the concept, the *finitude of the concept* becomes hard to ignore. Although I introduce the concept here, the total sense of the finitude of the concept will not become fully evident until we have completely worked through the various problems and paradoxes that arise upon conceiving the concept as finite. Most minimally, the finitude of the concept means that the concept is *internally limited*. The concept cannot be the principle of the differentiation of its particulars, and for this reason the source of the difference must be some non-conceptual given content. Since the concept cannot be the principle of the differentiation of the particular, it is *not* unlimited. Most significantly, the concept does *not have the power to differentiate itself* into particular instantiations. I employ the term 'finitude' to signify Hegel's sense of term—for him the finite is not just that which is limited, but that which possesses an *internal limit*. This inability of the concept to *particularize itself* is an *internal* limitation. It could not achieve this feat even if there were no external obstacles, as it were. Or to use other language, in *no possible world* would it have this capacity for self-particularization.

The separation of the universal from the principle of its truth can be further explicated in terms of possibility and actuality. Under this conception, the universal is construed as a possibility—a way the world *could* be. This possibility to be is *not necessarily* actualized. Whether it is actualized or not (as something other than a mere possibility!) depends upon another principle. From the fact of the possibility—from the explication of the content of the concept itself—we cannot know *whether the possibility is actual*, whether it is realized. Actuality is determined from the outside. If there is any necessity to the realization of the possibility, this necessity must come from the outside, for on its own terms it is contingent. The concept as such appears to be a mere possibility to be; it may or may not be. On its own terms, or by itself, its existence is a *contingent possibility*. Accordingly, we are all familiar with the logical relation that if the concept is actual, one can know that it is possible, but *if it is possible, it does not follow that it is actual*.

The concept is *limited by the second principle*. Only with both principles together can we gain an understanding of universality *and* particularity. Indeed, insofar as universality is instantiated in the particulars, without an account of the origin of the differentiation of particulars we would also fail to have an account of the potential for universals to be *instantiated*. In the case of the class wherein the concept is constituted by the particulars, without an account of the particular, one would fail to have an account of *the constitution* of the universal itself.

Most pertinent to our further investigations is *the way* that the concept is internally limited. Insofar as universals *qua* universals are not always already instantiated or particularized, universals do not correspond to their particulars simply in virtue of being universal. Rather, *the correspondence* of the universal with its particularization cannot be known by knowing the universal alone. In other words, I cannot know that 'this' is an instance of the universal *in virtue of knowledge of the universal alone*. In order to know that there are particulars that truly instantiate the universal, one must consult a principle *outside of the universal*. Thus, whether the universal is true, whether there are particulars that instantiate the universal, cannot be known by knowing the universal alone. On any conception of the concept that imposes a strict division between the principle of universality and that of particularity, the truth of the concept can only be determined by appealing to an external principle. Thus, the finitude of the concept may be re-formulated in terms of *truth*: the concept *cannot be sufficient to determine its own truth*. The internal limitation, the finitude, of the concept consists in *the externality of its truth*. These three features of the concept are tightly bound up together: the separation of the principles of universality and particularity is also a separation of the concept from its truth. The consultation of the Given, which is motivated by the separation of principles, is an investigation into *the truth of the universal*.

Because the universal is not the principle of its own particularity or truth, and must discover its true instantiation outside of itself, the concept ought not exhibit *existential implication*. Existential implication is the thesis that the universal is sufficient for its own particularization, such that from the claim that 'all S is P' one can infer that 'there is some S such that S is P.' Because concepts are *not* sufficient principles of their own truth, whether the concepts *exist* as more than mere *possibilities to be instantiated* cannot be determined by the concepts alone. The *existence* of the concept, namely whether there *are* instances of the concept, cannot be deduced from its logical content *alone*. Of course, the concept itself might exist even if there are no instances of the concept. But one can accept *the existence of the concept* as such *without* endorsing existential implication, for existential implication explicitly draws *the existence of the particular* out of the *universal alone*.

Kant's rejection of existential implication is most obvious in his overt rejection of *intellectual intuition*, the kind of Understanding that would intuit what it thinks. Since existence is given by intuition, intellectual intuition is a kind of Understanding that would be existentially implicative. Kant most clearly sees that the duality of principles governing conceptual content engenders the complete rejection of existential implication.

Unlike Kant, Aristotle certainly advocates for a kind of existential implication in his truth logic. Aristotle's insight that the sovereignty of the duality of principles must be significantly qualified in order to achieve Absolute Knowledge of what exists *in itself*, or *kath auto*, offers further support for the thesis that existential implication is impossible on the assumption of a duality of principles. The integration of existential implication into the logical articulation of Being is strategically integral to Aristotle's efforts to overcome the absolute dualism of principles that undermines our efforts to know the Absolute. In order to bring the universal and the particular into a unified whole, Aristotle unifies both principles under the *generative power of Form*, which is articulated as a universal in its logical representation.

Still, even in Aristotle's case, one cannot know that the universal engenders its own particularization without *first* anchoring that claim in observation. Independently of the experience of things, one cannot know that any particular Form exists. Indeed, without observation of the fact that composites such as Socrates exist, one cannot know that the Form of the human being is a generative power. Thus, in Aristotle the universal is only represented as self-particularizing in virtue of something other than the universal—namely observation of the Given. For this reason, Aristotle does not draw the existence of the particulars from the universal alone. Otherwise, Aristotle's metaphysics would have an entirely different character, for his logic would no longer be anchored in an account of Being that conditions it. As Aristotle takes pains to make clear, the universal as such is not what exists independently. For these reasons, from an epistemic point of view, both Aristotle and Kant advance truth logics in which the source of the truth of the universal is external to the universal itself.

The term 'existence' here signifies the existence of the universal *insofar as it is particularized*. Insofar as the universal is construed as being constituted by *the capacity for repeatable instantiation in its particulars* (as is at least the case in generic and abstract conceptions of the universal), without the instantiation of the universal in the particular, it follows that the *universal would not exist* for it would not exhibit instantiation in the particular. It would certainly exist in another way, for it would itself be instantiated by another concept—the concept *of the concept*. In this way, the concept of the concept would exist, because it would be instantiated in at least one concept. But as the specific concept that it is, for example 'human being' or 'quality' it would only exist as an *un*realized possibility. As we have stated already, in the case of the class, without the particular, the universal would not exist at all, since it is constituted by them.

If we return to the problem of early German Idealism, we remember that the main stumbling block for accounting for Absolute Knowing concerned the impossibility of grounding all knowledge on a principle that is merely *analytic*. The demand of the project, as Schelling recognized, required building *synthetic activity* into the first principle. Any programmatic attempt to construe the concept in terms of two irreducible principles of universality and particularity inevitably places the concept on the side of *analyticity*. Indeed, the foregoing reflections systematically reinforce the division between synthesis and analysis. The concept cannot amplify itself into particularity—it cannot be a sufficient principle of its own truth or existence. The *amplification* of the concept cannot be successfully achieved by the concept alone. For the amplification of the concept into truth and existence one requires other principles.

Earlier in this chapter, we asked the following question: can one know the *Absolute Truth* if the principles of universality and particularity are separated? Being both absolute and true, 'Absolute Truth' would not only engender the correspondence of the concept with its object but also require that the truth be *un*conditioned. A truth that is *un*conditioned would not be true in virtue of another, but would be *true in virtue of itself*. Given the separation of the principles of universality and particularity that is apparently endemic to conceptual determination, is the concept capable of determining what is true in *virtue of itself* or to use Plato's and Aristotle's nomenclature, what is true *kath auto*? Given that *the truth* of the concept cannot be determined by means of the concept alone, concepts are not *true in themselves*. Instead, concepts are true *in virtue of something other than themselves*. Since they are true in virtue of something other than themselves, and Absolute Truth is true in virtue of itself, no universal can count as an Absolute Truth. Rather, whatever universal one posits can only have relative truth. It is true relative to something else—in virtue of something else—whether that be a thing or an experience, its truth can never be Absolute.

Because the duality of the principles of universality and particularity engender this result, we have uncovered the basic systematic ground for the inability of philosophy to achieve Absolute Truth whenever it commits itself to the insufficiency of the concept to particularize itself. Whereas the Absolute is true in virtue of itself, the concept is never true in virtue of itself. Because of this fundamental incongruity, conceptual structure cannot be endemic to Absolute Truth. Failing to find itself in the Absolute, the concept has nothing to which it can correspond in the Absolute. Thus, the concept *can never correspond to itself in the Absolute*. Whenever the concept is raised to an Absolute status, it violates the principle that its truth is external to it. Accordingly, the concept cannot cohere with itself, *it cannot be consistent with itself*, as long as it is treated as though it were true in virtue of itself. The paradoxes that form the subject matter of our discussion in the following chapters, for example the problem of the Missing Difference, Absolute Empiricism, the problem of Onto-theology and the Third Man regress, *particularize this incongruity* in different ways.

Given that the truth logics of Aristotle and Kant are contingent upon the separation of the principles of universality and particularity, their truth logics are ultimately *relative truth logics*. This is also evident from the way that truth is anchored in each theory. Where Kant anchors his account of truth of the object in the conceptualizing subjectivity, Aristotle anchors the truth of one's thoughts about the thing in the independent thing itself. In each case, *one side of an opposition* is granted priority over the other, and the truth of one side is *relative* to that of the other. Neither grants *equal weight* to both sides of the constituents of truth. What is more, Kant and Aristotle both reject *self-predication* in their theories of categories. On its face, this might appear to be an idiosyncratic dimension of their thinking, rather than evidence of an important systematic contention. Quite to the contrary, the affirmation of self-predication is intimately bound up with Absolute Thinking. The existentially implicative dimension of self-predication, as well as its positive relation to Absolute Thinking, can be best illustrated in an example.

When one asks the question 'what is Being?' the question implores one to specify the 'what it is to be' of Being. By stating *what* Being *is*, one would state the *Being* of Being. Hence, in order to answer the question, one must predicate the term 'Being' to 'Being'. The question 'what is Being' can only be answered in a *self-predicative* way. By predicating Being to the subject 'Being' one would place 'Being' in the genus or class of Beings. By placing Being in the set of beings, Being would no longer merely be the class of all beings but would also be *one particular being within the class* itself. Being itself is the One particular that is engendered by the self-predicative attribution of Being to itself. Further, 'Being' is a universal term, and the 'what it is to be' calls for an answer in the form of a *predicate* that has the form *such and such*. Thus, an answer that takes the question seriously would take the form of the following: 'Being is *such and such*.' Further, by predicting *such and such* of Being, one would set Being apart from what differentiates it from other things and concepts that *are*—such as the 'what it is to be' of quality, quantity, and so on. As *such and such*, it would be distinguished from other beings in virtue of the predicates attributed to it. 'Being' would be an *instantiation of itself*; it would be a kind of Being—such and such *a* being. The apparently self-predicative dimension of any answer to the question concerning the Absolute casts further doubt on any expectation that concepts governed by dualistic principles could in principle lay claim to Absolute Knowledge. In our discussion of the Third Man regress we will systematically explore the relation between self-predication and Absolute knowing in more extensive detail.

Since self-predication engenders existential implication, self-predication can only be coherently maintained on the condition that the universal is *sufficient* for the differentiation of at least one particular: itself. Given that on the dualistic model of conceptual constitution the principle of universality and particularity are separate principles, and self-predication would enable the universal to be a sufficient principle for the production of the particular, it would follow that self-predication would not be consistent with the dualistic model of conceptual constitution. To put it another way, were self-predication introduced into the account of the categories, the particular could be deduced by the universal alone. In this case, one would no longer require a second principle (the differentia) in addition to the genus, for the genus would be its *own* principle of differentiation. Aristotle was right to acknowledge that the externality of the differentia entails a rejection of self-predication.

Moreover, given that self-predication entails existential implication, the repudiation of existential implication in one's theory of the concept would be sufficient to reject self-predication. For this reason, Kant's rejection of self-predication in his categories is consistent with his rejection of existential implication. It is important to note that although self-predication engenders existential implication, self-predication is just one method of achieving existential implication. For this reason, simply rejecting self-predication does not necessarily entail that one must also reject existential implication, for the latter might be grounded in another principle, such as in Aristotle's case, whose account of existential implication is grounded in the power of Form.[19] Indeed, Aristotle's rejection of self-predication is consistent with the fact that it is not in virtue of the self-relation of the universal by itself that the universal exists, but it is rather the generative activity of the Form on the material that grounds the existentially implicative form of the articulation of the Form in the syllogism.

The Principle of Non-Contradiction

What lies at the ground of the separation of the principles of universality and particularity? Indeed, given that the principles endanger our capacity for Absolute thinking, one might simply abandon the framework of the division of principles without further ado. The perennial attractiveness of this conceptual framework can be accounted for, I would contest, by the grounding work of the *PNC*. I mean this claim to be both *systematic and historical*. The PNC can be coherently and systematically employed to ground the separation of these principles and it also explains, in large part, the perennial attractiveness of their separation.

In his *Critique of Pure Reason*, Kant proclaims that analytic judgments are governed by the *Satz von Widerspruch* (principle of contradiction). This principle specifies that 'no predicate pertains to a thing that contradicts it.'[20] Analytic judgments that connect predicate to subject *in virtue of identity* establish the connection between predicate and subject by appeal to non-contradiction, for which reason one does not need to appeal to experience in order to become aware of the *necessary* truth of the judgment.[21] Indeed, the PNC is 'sufficient for all analytic cognition.'[22]

For example, one can know that 'all bachelors are unmarried men' simply by appealing to the PNC. Since a bachelor is by definition 'unmarried,' were one to predicate 'being married' to 'bachelor' one would be predicating an attribute to a subject that stands in contradiction with a predicate contained in the subject, namely the predicate 'unmarried.' Thus, one can know that it is true that 'unmarried' does not belong to the subject 'bachelor' by appeal to the PNC alone. It is true that bachelors are unmarried *in virtue of its meaning alone.*

According to Kant, however, the PNC cannot be a sufficient condition for evaluating the truth of synthetic judgments. He claims that the PNC is a 'negative condition of all our judgments,' which requires that they 'do not contradict themselves.'[23] As regards synthetic judgments that connect subject to predicate in virtue of something other than identity, this negative criterion is a 'negative criterion *of all truth*' [my emphasis].[24] Synthetic truth requires adherence to the PNC, but the PNC is not sufficient to guarantee synthetic truth. The synthetic proposition 'all professors at the Chinese University of Hong Kong are progressives' is certainly consistent with itself, for it contains no contradictions. Still, this consistency is not sufficient to establish its truth.

The PNC is a necessary and universal condition of all thinking of an object. As such, it is a fundamental principle of logic. The principle 'no predicate pertains to a thing that contradicts it' cannot specify the content of any predicate. Rather, it only specifies *the form* of the predicate itself. Thus, the PNC is a formal principle. In Kantian terms, this means that the principle does not contain any objects. As a merely formal principle, it can be employed to determine whether one consistently employs one's terminology. Because it does not specify the content of what is thought, but only specifies that whatever is thought not contradict itself, it cannot be sufficient by itself to determine whether a concept corresponds with *an object.*

Were the PNC sufficient for determining the truth of a synthetic judgment, one would not need to consult the relation of thinking to its object in order to know whether the thought were true. Rather, one would only need to check the thought for consistency in order to establish its truth. Thus, were the PNC sufficient for determining the truth of the synthetic judgment, one would be able to provide an *abstract and general criterion of truth.* However, as we discussed in our opening reflections, Kant thinks that an abstract and general criterion of truth is impossible. Because a general criterion of truth abstract from the content of the thought, it could only specify a *common form of thinking* that would be held in common, such as that specified by the PNC: 'no predicate pertains to a thing that contradicts it.' Since truth concerns the *relation of thought to its object,* while a general criterion of truth abstracts from the content of thought (and could thereby *only* specify a *common form* of the thought about the object), a general criterion of truth abstracts from the relation of thought to the object. Such a criterion such as the PNC would only be able to evaluate the truth of a thought in virtue of its *form alone* by checking it for consistency, *independently* of its relation to the object. But if truth is the *agreement* of the thought with its object, then treating the PNC as a universal criterion of truth would be *contradictory*, for it would evaluate the *relation of the thought* to its object in a way that is *independent of the relation* to the object. Kant's insight is that were one to treat the PNC as though it were sufficient to determine the truth of synthetic propositions, then the PNC would be self-contradictory.

Concepts, independently of all intuitions, are governed by formal-logical principles that abstract from all content. They are only sufficient for establishing the truth of analytic judgments, and they cannot be sufficient for establishing the truth of synthetic judgments (whether they be *a priori* or *a posteriori*). Thus, the formality of the PNC entails that in order to discover *the truth of the synthetic judgment*, one must consult a *separate source of truth* beyond the domain of logic. For Kant, this non-conceptual domain is that of *a priori* intuition. As is evident, the formal structure of the PNC engenders the duality of principles of truth in Kant's thinking. Accordingly, any attempt to undermine the duality of principles constitutive of the concept runs the great risk of sacrificing the PNC.

Kant reformulates the traditional articulation of the PNC by removing the qualification 'at the same time.' Because Kant posits the PNC as a principle of analytic judgments that abstracts from all intuition, the formulation of the PNC ought not be qualified by an appeal to intuition.[25] For this reason, Kant removes the qualification by intuition 'at the same time' that is formulaic for Aristotle's definition of the PNC. For Kant, it is enough that 'it is impossible for something to be and not to be.'[26]

Although these reflections are already enough to establish how the PNC grounds the fundamental logical division between the concept and its truth, the PNC is nonetheless a 'negative condition of truth.' Accordingly, it has its own 'negative content' that ensures not only the consistency of propositions and concepts but also the *determinacy of conceptual determination*. Kant formulates one of two principles of determination: *Grundsatz der Bestimmbarkeit*, namely the principle of determinability:

> every concept, in regard to what is not contained in it, is indeterminate [*unbestimmt*], and stands under the principle of determinability: that of every two contradictorily opposed predicates only one can apply to it, which rests on the principle of contradiction.

This principle of determinability 'has nothing in view but the logical form of cognition [*Erkenntnis*].'[27] For Kant, the principle of determinability is governed by the PNC.

In respect to one pair of contradictory opposites, such as F and not-F, every concept (in regard to predicates that are not already contained in the concept) can be made determinate by applying only *one side* of the pair of opposition to the concept. If both predicates were applied to the same concept, then the concept would admit both F and not-F, which would be a contradiction. This principle is formal, since it abstracts from the content of each predicate. Accordingly, the principle of determinability stands *under* the law of non-contradiction and thereby restricts all predications of a concept to affirm at most only one side of any pair of opposites. By contrast, the concept remains indeterminate insofar as the concept is neither F nor not-F. To *determine* the concept, one side of the opposition must be negated. It would appear that the concept of negation is in some sense derivative,[28] for it requires that some affirmative content or predicate be given in advance of the negation.

On the one hand, were neither 'F' nor 'not-F' predicated of the same concept, then the concept would remain *indeterminate*. On the other hand, were *both* 'F' and 'not-F' predicated of the same concept, then 'these judgments in themselves (even without regard to the object) are nothing.'[29] Or what is the same, 'contradiction entirely annihilates and cancels them.'[30] The negative condition for truth that is constituted by the PNC is also a principle of the determinacy of concepts. Concepts are only determinate if there is some predicate attributed to the concept by which it can be *differentiated* from others. Since for Kant concepts must be determinate in order to be particular concepts, and contradictions render concepts indeterminate, concepts can only *be* concepts if they are not contradictory. Otherwise, as Kant says, concepts are 'annihilated' and 'cancelled.'

Because truth is the *self-correspondence* of the concept with the object, the concept can only correspond with the object if *the object itself embodies the consistency of the concept*. Concepts can only truly apply to intuition if they are consistent, or what is the same, only if they are determinate concepts. Only if a concept is determinate can it give form to formless intuition. Indeed, *indeterminate* concepts cannot *determine* intuition. In order to determine intuition they must themselves be determinate concepts, and this requires non-contradiction. Since the PNC is a principle governing the determinacy of concepts, and since concepts make experience possible by determining the intuition, the PNC ranges over all of experience. In other words, the logical determinacy of the concept must also apply to the determinacy of its *intuitive instantiation*.[31] Conceiving or intuiting an object is to conceive or experience this differentiated and determinate object, an object that is governed by the PNC.

Unlike in Kant, Aristotle argues that Being *qua* Being is governed by non-contradiction. The range of the principle in Aristotle extends beyond possible experience to the things themselves. Whereas for Kant this determinacy is constitutive for experience, for Aristotle the determinacy is both experiential and *ontological*. Despite this significant difference, in Aristotle's *Metaphysics* not only does non-contradiction appear as a principle of consistency and *determinacy* but Aristotle too applies the determinacy of the universal to the determinacy of its instantiation.

In his *Metaphysics* Aristotle gives many arguments that the PNC governs speech, thought, and being. Aristotle is unequivocal that

> It is impossible for anyone at all to conceive the same thing to be and not to be as some people think Heraclitus says.[32]

In the following I will focus on two main arguments. Aristotle proclaims that

> If contradictory things are true of the same things at the same time, it is obvious that all things will be one.[33]

If all things are one, then *the same thing* will be a human being a well, and a battleship. Naturally, this is absurd, for they are *not* the same things. As a result, were there true contradictions, then Anaxagoras would be right that 'all things are mixed together,' and 'nothing is truly one thing.'[34] For Aristotle, were there true contradictions, then 'all things would be one' and nothing would truly be 'one thing.' Aristotle goes on to proclaim that all things would be indeterminate, and while people who assert contradictions believe they are talking about 'what is' they are really speaking about 'what is not.'[35] The reasoning for this conclusion is quite straightforward. Aristotle distinguishes between contradictions and contraries. Unlike the latter, contradictions have *no middle*. Something is *either A or not A*. Thus, if something does not fall into A, then it belongs to not A. Since nothing falls in the middle, *all things* fall either into A or not A. Everything other than A is *not-A*. Something is either a human being or it is not a human being. Were A the same as not-A, then everything other than A would be identified with A. Since not-A includes all other things, 'A' would be the same as all things. Thus, all things would be the same. But since this is not the case, it cannot be true that 'A' is identical to 'not-A.' This is not the case because in order to be a thing, a thing must be *one* thing. To be *one* thing requires that it be distinct from other things; it must be *finite*. If it is all things, it cannot be distinct from other things and therefore cannot be one thing.

What is more, although all things would be one if contradictions were true, all things would also be *nothing*:

> It also follows that it is not necessary either to assert or to deny something. For if it is true that it is a human being and not a human being, it is clear that it will also be neither a human being nor not a nonhuman being.[36]

In sum, were there *true* contradictions, then all things would be predicated of the same thing, and all things would be denied of the same thing. Indeed, if 'A' were 'not-A' then 'A' would be all things. But since a thing only exists if it is one thing, and nothing would be one thing, it would follow that no thing would exist at all. In other words, to say of something that it is 'both A and not-A' is tantamount to 'neither A nor not-A.' To use a provocative term, contradictions *explode* determinacy into indeterminacy. Were a contradiction true, determinate being would *explode into everything and nothing simultaneously*. The affirmation of the possibility that there could be true contradictions is an 'anarchic argument'[37] for there would be no determinate principles governing anything. For this reason, it makes no difference whether one proclaims that everything is true, proclaims everything to be false, or remains completely silent. To be more precise, it is not just the PNC that undergirds the duality of principles, but the principle that contradictions *explode into everything and nothing*, that they express the form of *absolute indeterminacy*, that motivates the duality of principles. Kant follows Aristotle here as well, for he proclaims that contradictions which identify A and not-A 'annihilate concepts.'

Both Aristotle and Kant defend the PNC in order to preserve the *determinacy of what truly is and what can truly be thought*. Contradictions engender an absolute affirmation and denial of all things, thereby rendering it impossible for something to be *one* thing. Aristotle then proceeds to make the now famous remark that they are like plants, for plants make no assertions at all.[38] Likewise, if a person does not distinguish between a well and what is not a well, then why wouldn't he just walk right into a well?[39] Simply put, even those who make the argument do not really believe their own claims. Otherwise, they would walk off cliffs and into walls.

In order for metaphysics to be possible as the science of Being, the principles that govern scientific thinking must also govern Being itself. Were the principles governing universality, judgment, and their logical relations not the same principles that govern Being, it would not be possible for the philosopher to know Being by means of the universal. Accordingly, Aristotle rightly recognizes that the principles of demonstration, including that of non-contradiction, cannot only govern our thoughts about Being but must govern Being itself. Accordingly, when we ask 'what is x?' we answer with a predicate: 'x is such and such.' Thus, when we answer the question concerning the being of something, we answer with a universal. The 'what it is' of something has universal articulation, and the principles that govern the latter also govern the former. Indeed, without the principles of science about Being governing Being itself, we could not in principle have *true thoughts* about Being. Following this line of thinking, if the PNC governs the domain of science, that is, if it governs the domain of universality by means of which science knows the thing, it must also govern the domain of Being. Accordingly, one of Aristotle's strategies is to show first that the PNC governs the domain of science, from which he can then infer that the PNC also governs Being itself.

The concepts 'Being' and 'non-being' mean something *definite*. In order for concepts to have any meaning at all, they must have definite meaning. For Aristotle, a concept has definite meaning if it means *one thing*. To have definite meaning means that a term must mean *this* or *that*. For example, 'human being' means *this*: 'rational animal.' As Aristotle points out, if in the case that a term means *more than one thing*, a different term can in principle be assigned to each distinct meaning. If a concept were to have an *infinite* number of meanings, the concept would not mean anything definite, for it would mean all things, while all definite meaning *excludes* something. For Aristotle, 'all things' is not itself 'one' thing. Since 'not-A' includes all other possible meanings besides 'A,' the identity of A and not-A would entail that A would have *every* meaning. Thus, were there true contradictions, it would follow that *the very same term would have infinite meanings*. If 'A' has every meaning, then 'A' means nothing definite, for it would not pick *this* out in contrast with *that*, but would signify *everything*. Thus, since concepts only have meaning if they do not mean everything, and contradictions entail that the same term means everything, it follows that contradictions strip terms of the *definite character* of meaning.[40]

As Aristotle points out, however, the real concern is not with names of things but with *things themselves*.[41] Aristotle asserts that for two things to be one thing means that their definitions are the same, since the definition states *what something is*. Thus, if 'human' had the same definition as 'not human' then the *being* of the human being would be no different from *not-being* human. Since 'human' and 'not-human' mean different things, and the meaning of the concept itself maps onto the thing (for when we say 'what the thing is' we supply the predicate 'such and such'), Aristotle infers that *the things themselves must be different things*.

In short, if contradictions were true of our concepts of things, they would be true of things as well. Since they are not true of the former, they are not true of the latter. Without the PNC governing our concepts of things as well as the things themselves, no concept would have any *definite* meaning and no being would have any *definite* being.

Aristotle's arguments undergird his commitment to the finite character of universals and the division between the genus and its particular species at the level of categories. Because A can never be not-A, A is *limited*: it does not include the negation 'not-A' but *excludes* it. Aristotle conceives of this finitude as the *condition of the intelligibility* of the universal. Upon introducing the negation of A into A itself, the thing loses its definite limit and becomes an *indeterminate infinity*. What is more, since the *identity* of A cannot be identified with what is *different* from A, Aristotle's PNC requires a differentiation between identity and difference.

This separation at the level of genera is visible in Aristotle's demand that the genus cannot differentiate itself. The genus provides the *universal feature* of the beings that fall under it. The genus 'animal' can only determine what is held in common by all animals, but cannot differentiate human animals from non-human animals. The *difference* by which *particular* species are determined must come from another category. Were the principle of difference (the differentiae) by which particular species are determined the same as the principle of universality (the genus) by which they are identified, it would follow that human animals would be differentiated from non-human animals *in virtue of being animals*. Were this the case, it would follow that all animals would be different from each other in virtue of the fact that each is the same as the other, which would be a *contradiction*. In order to provide a consistent account of the genera of Being, one must derive the difference from outside the genus. Thus, Aristotle's division between the universal principle of identity (the genus) and the differentiating principle of the particularity of the species (the differentiae) is motivated by the PNC.

To summarize, the duality of principles of universality and particularity is motivated by the PNC. In the history of Western philosophy, this duality is conceived in a variety of ways (only some of which are enumerated here), as is the PNC that undergirds it. Nonetheless, these thinkers were not wrong in undergirding the duality of their principles by the PNC. In what follows, we investigate the problems that follow from the duality of principles. Accordingly, each of the following problems affects not only the plausibility of the duality of principles model of the concept but also the PNC which undergirds it.

In the following chapters, we explore four problems that arise from the presumption of the duality of principles of universality and particularity: (Chapter 5) The Problem of the Missing Difference and Absolute Empiricism, (Chapter 6) The Problem of Onto-theology, and (Chapter 7) the problem of the Third Man regress. Following the systematic and historical explication of each problem, we will demonstrate how the only possible solution to these problems (in addition to the problems of Nihilism and Instantiation) demands an endorsement of Absolute Dialetheism— the view that the Absolute can only exist as a *true contradiction*.

Notes

1. Kant, *CPR*, 325 (A225–A226/B272–B273).
2. D. M. Armstrong, *Universals: An Opinionated Introduction* (Boulder: Westview Press, 1989), 1.
3. One formulation of the problem of universals concerns how the very same universal can be instantiated by two different particulars.
4. Some of the following points are repetitions of earlier arguments. In particular, see Gregory Moss, "Four Paradoxes of Self-Reference," *Journal of Speculative Philosophy* 28, no. 2 (2014): 169–189, 170–172.

5. See Plato, *Parmenides*, trans. Whitaker, 23–36, 126a–137c.
6. See Aristotle, *Metaphysics*, lix, 150, 1040b20.
7. Kant, *CPR*, 175, B40.
8. Ibid, 205, B93.
9. Gottlob Frege, "On Concept and Object," in *Collected Papers on Mathematics, Logic, and Philosophy*, ed. Max Black et al, trans. Brian McGuinness, 187–194 (New York: Blackwell, 1984), 185.
10. Ibid, 189.
11. Bertrand Russell, "On the Relations of Universals and Particulars," *Proceedings of the Aristotelian Society*, New Series 12, no. 1–24 (1911–12): 24.
12. See Edmund Husserl, *Shorter Logical Investigations*, ed. Dermot Moran, trans. J. N. Findlay (London: Routledge. 2001), 149.
13. E. J. Lowe, *More Kinds of Being: A Further Study of Individuation, Identity, and the Logic of Sortal Terms* (Oxford: Wiley Blackwell, 2009), 8.
14. For example, one can both hold that concepts are common characters and exist as mental representations. Likewise, one can hold the incompatible thesis that concepts are Fregean senses, reject the ontological thesis that concepts are mental representations, and still accept that concepts are common characters. Or again, the view that concepts are common characters is compatible with the ontological view that some concepts are innate (or native to the mind) or that all concepts are derived from experience. To go further, one could employ my arguments against the consistency of the concept of the UNIVERSAL to advocate for either a realist or nominalist perspective on universals. On the one hand, one could deny that there are true contradictions and therewith advocate with Locke the position that there are *only* particulars. So although empirical nominalists do not accept that there is a strict identity of type in each token thereof, they could still attempt to employ my argument as a *reductio*. On the other hand, one could also employ my arguments to develop a realist stance on universals that is also dialetheic. One can vary such ontological perspectives on the concept without affecting the definition of the concept. This would not hold in all cases of course.
15. Although it usually goes *without* saying, sometimes it is said. For example, Spinoza states this principle quite succinctly in his *Ethics*. See Spinoza, "Ethics," in *Complete works*, ed. Michael L. Morgan, trans. Samuel Shirley, 213–383 (Indianapolis: Hackett Publishing, 2002), 221. The reader will note that in this chapter and those that follow it in Part I, concepts are in all capitals. This formatting was required by the publisher (SATS) of an earlier essay, "Dialetheism and the Problem of the Missing Difference" of which some of this text is a reproduction. I have kept this formatting for the sake of maintaining continuity with that essay.
16. The most obvious historical example of the concept of the 'genus' is Aristotle, as any cursory reading of his basic readings should illustrate. This concept of the genus is also evident in the medieval development of Aristotle's ideas, such as in the thought of St. Thomas Aquinas.
17. See Thomas Williams' entry on Duns Scotus in the *Stanford Encyclopedia* of *Philosophy*, 3.3, https://plato.stanford.edu/entries/duns-scotus/#UniInd. Or see Duns Scotus, "Ordinatio," in *Five Texts on the Medieval Problem of Universals*, trans. Paul Vincent Spade, 57–113 (Indianapolis: Hackett Publishing, 1994), 2, d 3, pars 1, 99. 1–6.
18. Because this conception is more amenable to formalization, many 19th- and 20th-century philosophers, for example Mill and Tarski, prefer this conception of universality to other conceptions.
19. This is clear from the case of Aristotle. Aristotle's categories are not self-predicative, but he nonetheless accepts a form of existential implication in his

logic. The existentially implicative dimension of his logic is not grounded in self-predication since he rejects self-predication as a structure of the categories. Rather, the existentially implicative dimension of his syllogism is enabled and grounded by the activity of the *Form* as the *generative principle of the particulars*.

20. Kant, CPR, A151.
21. Ibid, 142.
22. Ibid, B191.
23. Ibid, 279.
24. Ibid, A151.
25. Ibid, B193.
26. Kant, *CPR*, 280. Kant also adds that the term 'impossible' should already be understood and is also superfluous.
27. Kant, *CPR*, 553, 652.
28. Ibid, 555.
29. Ibid, 279.
30. Ibid, 280.
31. Naturally the issue with which we are here involved concerns the question of logical possibility, not *nomological* possibility. Many determinate concepts will be logically possible even if they are not nomologically possible.
32. *Aristotle, Metaphysics*, 1005b20.
33. Ibid, 63–64, 1007b20. According to Aristotle, this must be if something admits of being affirmed and denied of everything.
34. Ibid, 1007b20.
35. Ibid, 1007. Here Aristotle reminds us that for him indeterminacy only exists in potentiality.
36. Ibid, 1008a.
37. Ibid, 1009a.
38. Ibid, 65, 1008b10–20.
39. Ibid, 1008b10–20.
40. Ibid, 60–61, 1006a30–b20.
41. Ibid, 61, 1006b20–30.

5 The Problem of the Missing Difference and Absolute Empiricism

This chapter will show that even when we bracket the question concerning the relation of the concept to the Absolute, we discover that the finite conception of universality is susceptible to two problems: the Problems of the Missing Difference and Absolute Empiricism.[1] In *Beyond the Limits of Thought*, Priest is concerned with contradictions that arise when one attempts to conceive of totality. He is clear that in order to generate such contradictions, his method invokes self-reference:

> In each case, there is a totality . . . and an appropriate operation that generates an object that is both within and without the totality. I will call these situations closure and transcendence, respectively. In general, such arguments both for closure and transcendence use some form of self-reference, a method that is both venerable and powerful.[2]

In what follows, I am concerned first with a *non-absolute* domain: the complete totality of concepts and second its relationship with *the* absolute domain: the domain of all domains. Following Priest, I argue that a contradiction arises in the domain of concepts that is generated by a form of self-reference.[3] In what follows I will employ Priest's terms 'transcendence' and 'closure' to signify that an object is 'within' and 'without' the totality of concepts.

The logical problem of which I spoke in the introduction to this chapter becomes evident when one considers the higher-order relationship between particular concepts and the concept. The CONCEPT signifies what every particular concept has in common, namely that in virtue of which each particular concept is a concept.[4] Every particular concept is an instance of the CONCEPT.[5] To put this distinction in terms of classes, the CONCEPT is the domain that includes all concepts as its members, each of which is a particular member of the class of concepts. Since every concept is an instance of CONCEPT, and all instances of concepts are particulars, every concept is a particular. Though concepts are universals, since they are common characters and each is differentiated from the others, each is an instance of the CONCEPT, and thereby also a particular. Accordingly, although not all particulars are universals, all concepts, insofar as they are universals, are also particulars. Each concept is a universal and a particular, but in different respects: each universal is particular insofar as it instantiates a higher order universal, while each concept is a universal insofar as it is held in common and instantiated by other particulars. Though it may appear controversial to attribute particularity to universals, it is an assumption that we implicitly endorse in our philosophical speech. Anyone who wishes to think or speak about concepts must be able to identify and distinguish them from one another as well as those entities and terms that are not concepts, such as the proper names 'Socrates' and 'Pegasus.'[6] In order to be able to identify distinct concepts, one must be able to count them as distinct, namely as particulars, each of which is one in number. For example, NUMBER, HUMAN BEING, and TRIANGLE are all concepts. The concept of the CONCEPT simply connotes that which they all have in common. Each concept is one in number, and accordingly each is a particular, an instance of the CONCEPT. Though each concept is an instance of the CONCEPT, none are identical to the CONCEPT itself, for each is a particular concept that is differentiated from other concepts by its unique conceptual content. Certainly it goes without saying that all concepts are instances of the CONCEPT. Or what is the same: there is not one concept, c^*, such that c^* does not instantiate the concept of the CONCEPT. To put the same principle in terms of classes, there is no concept that is not a member of the class or the domain of concepts.

Following the classical perspective of a concept as a common character, we discover the paradox of the missing difference when we ask the following question: how it is possible to conceptually differentiate the class of concepts into particular concepts? By 'conceptual difference' I am piggybacking on what Aristotle meant by the term 'difference' in his classical formulation of a philosophical definition as the 'genus plus difference.' For example, the term 'three-sided' is the conceptual difference (or more traditionally called 'the differentia') by which the triangular figure is distinguished from other kinds of figures. Simply put, at the most general level, the concept of CONCEPTUAL DIFFERENCE is just a concept that divides a class of concepts. In our example, the term 'three-sided' divides the class of Euclidean figures. Though the question 'how is it possible to conceptually differentiate the class of concepts into particular concepts?' may appear innocuous, it leads to a paradox. Notice that our question is modal, for it asks about the possibility of dividing the class of concepts into particular concepts. As I see it, there are only two options: either the conceptual difference by which the class of concepts is divided is either internal or external to the class of concepts that it divides.

One cannot account for the principle of difference of the class of concepts by appealing to any particular conceptual difference that is internal to the class of concepts. We have established that in order to differentiate particulars within a class, one must appeal to a difference outside of that class. One cannot appeal to the CONCEPT itself, for the CONCEPT is not sufficient to differentiate particular concepts from one another. Indeed, the CONCEPT only specifies the common feature of each concept. Every concept belongs to the class of concepts, and the concept CONCEPT only specifies that each member of the class is a concept and nothing else. Moreover, one cannot employ any particular conceptual difference already given in the class of concepts. One can, of course, quite easily differentiate particular concepts. But what is at stake here is not the definition of a particular concept, but the very possibility of differentiating concepts into particulars in the first place. For if one were to appeal to some given concept in the class of conceptual differences in order to give an account of the possibility of conceptual differentiation, one would have already distinguished the particular concept from the domain of concepts in general and would have always already assumed the principle by which the class of concepts is divided. So, on this approach in order to determine that by which the class of concepts is divided, one would necessarily assume the principle by which concepts are divided, which begs the question. In other words, one cannot just assume that negation is primitive. Since this principle of conceptual difference is what we wish to derive, we cannot appeal to any particular concept or conceptual differentiation within the class to divide the class of concepts. Since the CONCEPT cannot differentiate its own particulars, one cannot locate any difference within the class of concepts itself. Accordingly, in order to discover the conceptual difference between particular concepts we must appeal to a class that is outside of the class of concepts.

Unfortunately, it would appear that there is also no conceptual difference outside of the class of concepts either. Because the CONCEPT cannot differentiate the particular concepts, the only recourse available to us would be a concept that is not an instance of the CONCEPT. Because the CONCEPT is the most universal category into which all concepts fall as concepts, all concepts are instances of the CONCEPT. Hence, as we just stated, there is not one concept, c^*, such that c^* does not instantiate the concept of the CONCEPT. Thus, there is no concept (and thereby no conceptual difference) outside of the class of concepts that could in principle differentiate the instances of the class of concepts from one another. In sum, given that (i) concepts are not sufficient to differentiate their own particulars, (ii) to differentiate a class one must appeal to a concept outside of that class, and (iii) all concepts are instances of the class of concepts,[7] it follows that it would be impossible to discover a concept (and thereby a conceptual difference) either external or internal to the class of concepts in virtue of which particular concepts could be differentiated from one another. This is the problem of the missing difference.

Priest has pointed out that this argument appears to follow his inclosure schema.[8] In order to conceptually differentiate the class of concepts, one must appeal to a concept within the domain of concepts to differentiate the class. This is the aspect of closure. But it is also the case that no concept can differentiate the class of concepts. Thus, what distinguishes the class of concepts cannot be a concept. This is the aspect of transcendence. To put it briefly: in order to conceptually differentiate the domain of concepts, the domain must differentiate itself, but it cannot, so it must be differentiated externally. By an act of self-reference, by attempting to conceptually conceive of the CONCEPT the principle of difference falls within the totally. Yet, since the structure of conceptual differentiation requires conceptually differentiating the class from outside of the class, the principle of difference must fall outside of the totality.[9]

Aristotle's categories exemplify the problem of the missing difference in its most characteristic form. For Aristotle, Thinghood is separate and a this. As the source of what has Being, a first principle is not derived from something else, but is that in virtue of which anything has Being. Aristotle argues that Thinghood is what it is for something to be. The 'what it is for something to be' is what something is in its own right. As we argued earlier, for Aristotle, 'what it is in its own right' is separate and thereby fulfills the condition for Being as Being.

For Aristotle Being is said in many ways, though all senses of Being refer to one primary sense: *Thinghood*. All other ways of saying being—Quality, Quantity, Relation, Passivity, Activity, Condition, Position, Time, and Place, are not themselves things but *depend upon things* for their existence. Taken all together, these are the categories, the *highest genera*. Although each other way of saying being depends upon Thinghood, the sense of each category is *independent* of (and non-reducible to) the others, and together they contain *everything that exists*. Although Thinghood exists in all of its instances (the same could be said of each category), no category exists separately from the things it categorizes *except* in the mind of the thinker. In the mind they can exist as a *community of Forms* separated from their material instantiation. Still, having been separated from the material substratum, they can no longer be actively at work, since to be at work *the Forms require some material* upon which to work. Thus, the Form in the mind is not at work, but an *abstraction of something else* that is at-work. The Form in the mind is Form *subtracted from its activity*. Indeed, because the categories are not at work, they cannot legitimately be classified as things.

Were Aristotle's conception of the universal self-predicating, then Thinghood would itself *be a thing* (just as in Plato's *Parmenides* 'Greatness itself' is *a* great thing). Since Aristotle rejects self-predication, for Aristotle Thinghood itself cannot be a thing and is therefore not sufficient for differentiating itself into a particular thing. No genus is sufficient to derive its own species. For instance, the genus 'animal' does not divide itself into the species 'human being.' By knowing what an animal is, I only know what all animals have in common, not what differentiates them. In order to know the essence of the human being, I must also know its *differentia*. In order to differentiate the genus, the difference must have its origin in *another* category. Universals as genera do *not* differentiate themselves. In other words, a genus is *not* the source of its own species. Because no category is the source of its own differences, the principle of difference for any category must come from outside of the category. Since the only categories external to any particular category are more categories, only categories can differentiate other categories. Of tantamount importance is the fact that the duality of logical structure reflects a fundamental duality in the thing itself. The absence of self-predication at the level of the categories reflects the duality of principles in the thing itself: the *Form does not work on the Form*; the Form works on the material. This procedure of differentiation leads to a paradox when applied to Aristotle's categories.

Edward Halper raises this problem in its clearest form:

> So the differentia must not belong to the genus it differentiates. Indeed, the differentia must belong to some entirely distinct category. But we then face the disastrous prospect that that entity by which A differs from other genera and by which A is what it is, that entity which is A most of all, is not A. Since, for example, the differentia of the human being, a particular type of rationality, seems to be a quality, the nature of a particular Substance, namely, us, is not to be a Substance, but to be a quality, rationality.[10]

Thinghood is divided into things, and the principle that differentiates Thinghood into things cannot come from Thinghood itself, since Thinghood is not the source of its own differences. Thus, in order for Thinghood to be differentiated into things, differentia from other categories must be imported into the category of Thinghood in order to differentiate Thinghood. But since no other categories contain things, but are *dependent upon things*, it follows that Thinghood would only be differentiated into things by that which is not a thing at all. Rather, since the other categories already depend upon things in order to be, they cannot provide the principle in virtue of which there are things. To put it most simply, Thinghood has its being *in virtue of itself*—it is independent, or itself by itself. But it cannot have its being in virtue of itself, for it must acquire its difference from another category that is *not a thing*, from that which depends upon things. In order to be what it is, Thinghood cannot be independent. Put another way, since the definition of the thing requires the difference, one can only define what exists in virtue of itself by appealing to what *cannot* exist in virtue of itself. As a result, Aristotle's doctrine of the categories results in the paradox that because things would be defined by that which belongs to a thing, *things would themselves belong to things*, which is impossible.[11]

Of course, Aristotle contends that the differentia of the definition is said *of* the thing, rather than existing *in* it (just as rationality is the definition of the human being but not an attribute of the human being). But as Halper points out, this does not answer the objection.[12] The problem concerns the origin of this distinction. Indeed, the *justification of this distinction* is exactly the problem. Thus, either Thinghood maintains its independence and there cannot be differentiations of things, or Thinghood is no longer independent and therefore cannot signify the primary meaning of Being, as Aristotle maintains. In order to illuminate the problem of the missing difference that is less specifically tied to Aristotle's terminology, we can also approach the problem by following Hegel's reconstruction, which formulates the paradox in terms of independence and *relationality*.

In his phenomenology of perception[13] in the *Phenomenology of Spirit*, Hegel formulates the problem of the missing difference in a very similar way. What is necessary for our purposes here is not the meaning of phenomenology in Hegel or a faithful reconstruction of the whole, but Hegel's *recognition* and *formulation* of the problem. Following the dialectic of sense-certainty, the object of consciousness is characterized as a *mediated universal*[14] or a unified manifold. Each 'now' of sense certainty showed itself to be constituted by (or a unity of) a plurality of nows, each of which is itself characterized by a plurality of nows. Hegel initially characterizes the object of perception as a *thing with properties*,[15] in the sense that the thing is the universal that functions as the unifying principle of other universals. At the outset, the thing is characterized as the unity of the various properties, each of which belongs to the thing. This unity is characterized by the relation of conjunction— what Hegel calls the 'also.' Insofar as the thing is 'x' and 'y' and 'z,' the conjunction does not specify what 'x,' 'y,' and 'z' are. The 'also' does not specify the specific difference in virtue of which each is distinct from the other. Thus, the properties are conceived to be universal determinations of the thing, each of which is *independent of the others*.[16] The 'one' and 'also' not only characterize the relation of the properties to the things but can also be deployed in order to characterize the relation of things to one another and the kinds of properties that characterize that relation.

In the final development of his phenomenology of perception, Hegel distributes these two features of the thing with its properties to *different* things.[17] In this phase of the dialectical process, Hegel posits that each thing is an independent 'one' that exists in relation to others constituted by the 'also.' Because the conjunction does not differentiate any thing, and it is the mode of relation of each thing to the other, what differentiates each thing from the other is not specified by the relation each thing has to the other. Each thing is *one thing*, each of which is independent of the other. Insofar as each is independent from the others, the thing has its principle of difference within itself. It is not differentiated from the others by its relation to them, for this is *inessential* to what it is. The 'also' cannot specify the essential difference of one thing to another. As a result, the thing finds itself with *two* kinds of 'properties': essential and inessential. On the one hand, its relation to the others is inessential to what it is. It can be what it is independently of the relation to the others, which is external to its essential being. Thus, relations to others are incidental, or inessential to what distinguishes it. On the other hand, what differentiates the thing is essential to it—it has it *in virtue of itself*, or *kath auto*. Of course although Aristotle would not characterize the essential difference as a 'property,' Hegel's characterization of the thing with properties is very close to Aristotle here: the thing is *kath auto* and is defined by an essential difference, while its relations to others belongs in an *incidental* category.[18]

Hegel's relatively simple characterization allows us to see the problem very clearly. Each thing is independent of the other, such that 'what it is' is *not* dependent upon the other or its *relation* to the other. Each thing, however, is *only* an independent thing insofar as it *totally excludes* the other. The opposition of each thing to the other constitutes *the relation* of each thing to the other. Put in terms of difference, the difference of each thing from the other constitutes the *relation* of each thing to the other. Given that the independence of each thing consists in its *exclusion* of the other, and this constitutes its *relationship* with the other, Hegel demonstrates that the independence of the thing consists in its relationship with the other. But the thing is independent just insofar as it does *not* stand in a relationship with the other. Thus, a contradiction arises: the thing is independent just insofar as it is not independent—or its independence from the other is constituted by its dependence on the other:

> It is just through the absolute character of the Thing and its opposi-
> tion that it relates itself to others, and is essentially only this relating.
> The relation, however, is the negation of its self-subsistence, and it is
> really the essential property of the Thing, that is its undoing.[19]

To put this in terms of essential properties, when the relation becomes the distinguishing feature, the essential feature of the thing becomes inessential (since the relation is inessential), or the inessential property becomes the essential property. The paradox of the missing difference consists in the fact that the essential difference that distinguishes one thing from another cannot be accounted for by appealing to what the thing is 'in virtue of itself.' Rather, the essential difference always requires an appeal to something other than the thing, such that it is the essential difference that is ultimately responsible for the self-contradiction:

> The Thing has its essential being in another Thing.[20]

In even starker terms, we remember that the relation of each 'one' to the other ought to be determined by the relation of the 'also.' Insofar as the independence of the 'one' is determined by its relation, and its relation is the 'also' which does not differentiate anything, the differentiating principle can only have its origin in a relation that is not differentiating—rather the 'also' is a principle of identity—it cannot distinguish one thing from the other. Accordingly, each 'one' becomes indistinguishable from the others, for each one is indistinguishable from the others when it is essentially determined by the 'also,' which cannot distinguish one from the other:

> the object is in one and the same respect the opposite of itself: it is for itself, so far as it is for another, and it is for another, so far as it is for itself.[21]

Kant's categories fare no better. Just as in the case of Aristotle, we begin with Halper's analysis:

> I want to return to my original question, what is it that characterizes or differentiates entities within a single category? For Kant the entities are intuitions and the differentiae are concepts or what he terms 'categories.' The concepts or differentiae are supposed to be just what the intuitions are, but they cannot be because they belong to a distinct faculty. The attempt to differentiate intuitions by means of concepts must fail because intuitions and concepts remain ontologically distinct. Even if we know A as a C, we recognize that A is not C and that C fails to characterize it. In speaking of A, we are conceptualizing it and thus treating it as something that is thought. Paradoxically, Kant maintains that we need to think through the nature of A to recognize it as something that cannot be thought. Something is terribly wrong with categories that both are what they apply to and cannot be what they apply to.[22]

Unlike in Aristotle's account of categories, Halper is right that Kant's categories 'have no differentiae; but they are the differentiae of intuited things.'[23] This means that categories—as principles of synthesis, do *not* categorize themselves. Just as Aristotle's problem of the missing difference, the thing is transformed into a non-thing, as well as the non-thing into the thing, in Kant the problem also has two possible formulations. Categories become *non-categorical* and intuitions *non-intuitive*.

Consider the problem first from the side of intuition—as Halper does. For Kant 'concepts without intuitions are empty, intuitions without concepts are blind.'[24] Given the *separation* of the principles of universality and particularity, Kant insists that independently of categorial determination, the manifold of intuition remains fundamentally *in*determinate. As such, intuition independently of the principle of universality is a *content without form*. Accordingly, 'what' the intuition is can only be stated by importing a category, such as quality, quantity, relation, or modality. Thus, since the determinate form of the intuition is not an intuition, but a concept, the determinate form of the intuition *is not itself intuitive*. Thus, when we state 'what' the intuitions are, we must acknowledge *that intuitions are not themselves intuitive*. Indeed, the intuition *in its own right* as intuition *remains indeterminate*—it cannot be thought. When intuition is thought it is no longer intuition. Of course, expressed in terms more congenial to Kant, this just means that the *truth* of the concept, namely the correspondence of the concept with the object, is *the correspondence of the concept with itself*. Truth must be self-correspondence exactly because the form in the intuition to which a concept could correspond is *conceptual* form—not intuitive form. The first consequence of this restriction of truth to the side of the concept is that *the intuition cannot be true*, namely the intuition 'cannot correspond with itself.' To put it in my own language—*intuition itself cannot be intuitive*. While truth is the correspondence of the empty concept with the presence of the intuitively given concept, intuition itself does *not* have a correlate on the side of the empty concept to which it could correspond. The expression 'intuitions are not intuitive' only expresses one side of the problem—the other side of which concerns the concept.

Consider the problem from the other side. Categories are synthetic activities by which representations are brought under a common one,[25] and categories do *not contain* their own intuitions. As principles of synthesis of the manifold of intuition, categories synthesize a manifold *outside* of themselves.[26] Categories do *not* synthesize themselves. What is more, categories can only synthesize the manifold on the condition that they do *not (and cannot) synthesize themselves*. Were the categories self-synthesizing, the categories themselves would constitute their *own intuitive* content. Yet, according to Kant, categories are empty of all intuitive content. What is the same, if categories were to synthesize themselves, there would be no necessity to posit a source of intuition *outside* the categories. Indeed, the kind of Understanding that intuits what it thinks is *intellectual intuition*, what Kant claims we do not possess. Thus, in respect *to themselves*, categories must be *non-synthetic*.

Since the lack of intuition in the concept implies that the concept cannot synthesize itself, the emptiness of the category means that it is not just empty of intuitive content, but it must also be *empty of its own categorial content* as a synthesizing activity. The 'non-synthesis' of the category is not a *separate act* performed by the category. As an absence it does not have any *separable* being. Instead, it only *is* insofar as it is inseparable from the synthetic activity of the category. Hence, the 'non-synthesis' or 'non-category' is *not* a *separate* condition for the possibility of the act of synthesis and the category. Instead, it would be more accurate to say that the category is *non-synthetic* in its very act of synthesis. Given that categories do not categorize themselves, *categories are not themselves categorical*. By itself the category it is not 'true to itself.' Categories as categories are *un*true, for they cannot correspond to what they *truly* are. What is missing in the case of both the concept and the intuition is the principle in virtue of which each is what it is—an *intuitive principle* of intuition, a *conceptual principle* of the concept.

Rather, categories can only become categorial—they can only *be categories*, in virtue of something *other* than categories. Most paradoxically, it is in virtue of something *other* than categories that categories can *be* categorial. Since categories are only true when they correspond with themselves in intuition, and categories contain no intuitive content on their own, considered *by themselves* categories cannot be true. The absence of truth internal to the category requires that the *truth* of the category can only be discovered *outside* of the category, namely in the intuition. When they are true, namely when they *correspond with themselves qua* categories, categories are *intuitive*. To re-iterate Halper's terse formulation, 'something is terribly wrong with categories that both are what they apply to and cannot be what they apply to.'

This very same problem can be transposed into terminology of 'existence.' If we take 'Being' in the sense of sein, we know from Kant's famous critique of the ontological argument that 'Being' is not a predicate.[27] When we say of some concept that it is (or has being), we mean that it is given in intuition. Accordingly, categories as categories cannot exist. That categories *qua* categories cannot be said to exist follows from the fact that 'exists,' 'possibly exists,' and 'necessarily exists' are all categories, and categories do not apply to themselves. Thus, categories as such do not exist—only insofar as they are non-categorial do categories exist. Just as much as the truth of categories is outside of the category, so the existence of the category can only be located outside of the category.

To put it simply, neither principle of truth, neither the category nor the intuition, is itself true (or true to itself): the intuition cannot be intuitive; the category cannot be categorial. As we indicated at the outset of Chapter 1 in our discussion of Schelling, a coherent account of truth requires that *the principles of truth themselves be true*. The category can only exist as a category when it is intuitive—that is, when it is no longer categorial. Likewise, the intuition can only exist intuitively when it is categorial—that is, when it is no longer intuitive. Such paradoxes engendered by the problem of the missing difference lead us straightaway into another impasse, namely the problem of absolute empiricism.

The Problem of Absolute Empiricism

If one cannot appeal to the class of concepts in order to differentiate the concepts, then the only recourse to differentiating concepts would be to appeal to what is not conceptual. If one were to appeal to what is not conceptual in order to differentiate concepts from one another, one would be forced to admit a contradiction. For if the conceptual content of each concept (the conceptual content that distinguishes different concepts from each other) were not conceptual, then the conceptual content would be non-conceptual, which is a contradiction, (C1).[28] Given the need to appeal to a non-conceptual foreign content in order to differentiate the class of concepts, if we do not reject the PNC, we could not in principle explain how it would be possible for conceptual differences to exist. This is the problem of the missing difference. If we abide by the PNC, then in principle it appears that it would be impossible to conceptually differentiate the class of concepts. However, if we allow for some true contradictions, we can in principle accommodate the identity of conceptual with non-conceptual content.

More precisely, (C1) states the following:

(C1): Every particular concept, as a concept, is also not a concept.

Accordingly, (C1) states that of every particular concept one must predicate of it that it is a concept and that it is not a concept in the same respect. In other words, it is conceptual just insofar as it is not conceptual. This contradiction is generated from the three principles, (i) through (iii).

As we noted earlier, the leading question of the investigation is the following: how is it possible to conceptually differentiate the class of concepts into particular concepts? Certainly, the concept BACHELOR can be defined by appealing to other universals, such as MAN and UNMARRIED. Likewise, we might also establish the identity of a concept by ostension. For example, one could point to unmarried men in order to show that the concept BACHELOR instantiated such particulars. Accordingly, we are certainly not arguing that concepts should be disconnected from members of the class of non-conceptual particulars. Rather, what is at issue in the argument is the very possibility of differentiating the class of concepts into particular concepts. Accordingly, what is at stake is the possibility of any particular concept whatever.[29]

The argument demonstrates that without this act of identifying the concept of the CONCEPT with the concept of the NON-CONCEPT, there would not be any particular concepts. Without the contradiction, there would be no concepts, and therefore no base of comparison with members of the class of non-concepts. Accordingly, the identity conditions of particular concepts by means of other concepts or by reference to various particulars is only possible because of the contradiction (C1). (C1) is necessary to the very identity of any concept whatever because it is that upon which any conceptual differentiation depends.

On any construal of universals in which (i) through (iii) hold, this contradiction follows. But since we have shown that (i) through (iii) are at least entailed in the concept of the CONCEPT as a universal or common character, we will use this example to concretely instantiate the contradiction. Earlier we distinguished between universals and particulars. Although universals are also particulars, we supposed at the outset that each universal is a universal and a particular in different respects. A universal is not universal because it instantiates a universal, but because it can be instantiated by particulars. In other words, common characters are not common characters because they are particular. Accordingly, let us substitute the term 'universal' for the term 'concept' and the term 'particular' for the term 'non-conceptual.' Since (C1) states that of every particular concept one must predicate of it that it is a concept and that it is not a concept in the same respect, on this instantiation (C1) would read as follows: of every particular concept one must predicate of it that it is a universal and that it is a particular in the same respect. On this instantiation, a particular concept 'a' would be both a universal and a particular in the same respect, which is a contradiction, since the concept of the UNIVERSAL and the PARTICULAR are not identical.[30] If one accepts (C1) as necessary, what is left is to re-think the sense of the concept on dialetheic grounds.

If we stand by the principle that contradictions cannot be true, then we have a further problem. Since we can locate neither any universal, conceptual difference by means of which to differentiate the class of concepts nor any non-conceptual difference that does not lead to a contradiction, the very sense of the concept as a common, universal term would entail a complete absence of any inherent conceptual or universal differences. In order to avoid (C1), the advocate of the PNC must deny that there are any particular concepts. What follows from this is clearly false: the class of concepts must be inherently and necessarily undifferentiated.

If we consider each particular concept, for example NUMBER, TRIANGULAR, HUMAN BEING, as instantiating the concept in addition to some difference, then each differentiated concept would be a particular concept.[31] If CONCEPT were inherently undifferentiated, then there could not be any particular concepts. But of course there are particular concepts, for we are in possession of a good plurality of them. If there could not be any particular concepts, then the very sense of the CONCEPT would undermine the possibility of any concepts whatever except the concept of the CONCEPT itself. Since it is obvious that there are concepts other than just the CONCEPT, refusing to admit true contradictions would lead to a patently false result.

In his *Phenomenology of Spirit*, Hegel recognized the profound problem of Absolute Empiricism in the chapter on *Reason*. As Hegel writes, *Phenomenology* is 'the path of the natural consciousness which presses forward to true knowledge' that aims at an 'awareness of what it really is in itself.'[32] Here I do not mean to distract the reader with a long reconstruction of *Phenomenology*, whose goal is absolute self-knowledge. Rather I only wish to illustrate Hegel's recognition of the problem in that text. Importantly, 'reason' in *Phenomenology* is not solipsism, for it does not assert that a single individual mind or person is all reality. Reason is the result of the self-development of the shapes of consciousness and self-consciousness, in which consciousness pursued self-knowledge. Self-knowledge requires the *recognition of oneself* in the other, for the self can only know itself if it takes itself *as an object*.

Initially, in the *Phenomenology*, consciousness understood itself as a mere particular, as *this* consciousness. The problem with this approach is manifest: by thinking of oneself as a mere particular, consciousness could not recognize itself in the other. In order to recognize itself in the other, consciousness would need to conceive of itself as a *universal*, such that the *very same being* could be present in both the subject and its object (such as another consciousness) as the common term between them. In universal consciousness, wherein consciousness recognizes itself in the other, the other presents *no threat* to the self, for the multiple instantiation of the universal does not in any way threaten to undermine the being of the universal. Here in *Reason*, the individual now recognizes itself to be unified with the universal.[33] When consciousness considers itself to be merely particular, it cannot exist both in the subject and the object, for it is *one in number*. The recognition of itself in the other is a problem, since it cannot be both. Accordingly, the particular consciousness finds itself in conflict with another consciousness. Because the stage of reason overcomes this conflict in *recognizing itself as the universal*, Hegel points out that it is 'at peace with itself':

> But, as Reason, assured of itself, it is at peace with them, and can endure them; for it is certain that it is itself reality, or that everything actual is none other than itself; its thinking is itself directly actuality and thus its relationship to the latter is that of idealism.[34]

'Reason' is not just universal, but unconditionally universal, and for this reason, Hegel asserts that *the category* is all reality, for the category is the all-encompassing universal:

> Reason is the certainty of being all reality. This in-itself or this reality is, however, a universal pure and simple, the pure abstraction of reality. It is the first positivity in which self-consciousness is in its own

self explicitly for itself, and 'I' is therefore only the pure essentiality of the existent, or is the simple category.[35]

The categorical consciousness characteristic of reason is a condition for truth. Only if the universal shares a form in common with the object is it possible for the universal to correspond with the object. Were the form not held in common, then correspondence of one with the other would not be possible. In order to be able to have truth-apt thoughts about all things (including oneself), the self must recognize that all things have its own form—the form of the universal. The Idealism Hegel speaks of here is just this thesis that *the universal* is the Absolute form of all things which is just as much instantiated in 'my' particular empirical consciousness as it can be instantiated in 'your' empirical consciousness.[36] Because the Idealist posits the universal as the absolute form of all things, by knowing the form of reason one can in principle know the form of all things. Hegel exemplifies this form of consciousness by employing an example from Fichte.

> 'I am I', in the sense that the 'I' which is an object for me is the sole object, is all reality, and all that is present.[37]

The contradiction of Absolute Empiricism follows from the abstract concept of reason:

> This Idealism is caught in this contradiction because it asserts the *abstract concept* of reason as the truth.[38]

Because the concept of reason asserts the identity of the subject and its object, or asserts the identity of the universal in its different particulars, among other things it cannot account for the *plurality* of categories:

> Since Idealism proclaims the simple unity of self-consciousness to be all reality, and immediately makes it the essence without having grasped it as the absolutely negative essence—only this has negation, determinateness, or difference within it—this second assertion is even more incomprehensible than the first, viz. that in the category there are differences or species of categories.[39]

Because the concept is grasped abstractly as the self-identical and universal form, it cannot account for the plurality or species of the category. Although it posits that everything is categorial, and there is a difference there in the categorial form, for example the difference between subject and object (which are both determined to be categorial), it cannot account for the categorial differences that are present within the category. As is evident, Hegel recognizes the problem of the missing difference: by asserting the categorial form to be the form of all knowing, and thinking this form as the self-identical one cannot account for the categorial differences. Profoundly, for Hegel this problem is *endemic to the conceptual content of reason* itself. In order to understand why this is necessary from a logical point of view, we must delve into a deeper investigation into Hegel's logic of the concept, which we will execute in Part II.

Given the emptiness of reason, Hegel infers that rational consciousness is forced to discover that principle in virtue of which the concept is differentiated *outside* of the concept *per se* in something other than the concept. As a result, conceptual differentiations (including the concept itself) becomes explicitly identified with non-conceptual content. This is the 'direct contradiction' Hegel referred to in the passage quoted here. Because it must seek its content outside of itself, Absolute Idealism becomes Absolute empiricism:

> Its first declaration is only this abstract empty phrase that everything is its own. For the certainty of being all reality is at first [only] the pure category. This Reason which first recognizes itself in the object finds expression in the empty idealism which grasps Reason only as it first comes on the scene; and fancies that by pointing out this pure 'mine' of consciousness in all being, and by declaring all things to be sensations or ideas, it has demonstrated this 'mine' of consciousness to be complete reality. It is bound, therefore, to be at the same time absolute empiricism, for in order to give filling to the empty 'mine', i.e. to get hold of *difference* with all its developed formations, its Reason requires an extraneous impulse, in which first is to be found multiplicity of sensations and ideas. This idealism therefore becomes the same kind of self-contradictory ambiguity as Skepticism, except that, while this expresses itself negatively, the former does so positively; but it fails equally with Skepticism to bring together its contradictory thoughts of pure consciousness being all reality, while the extraneous impulse of sensations and ideas are equally reality. Instead of bringing them together, it shifts from one to the other, and is caught up in the spurious, i.e. the sensuous, infinite.[40]

Because reason cannot discover any differentiated rational content within the content of the category 'category,' in order to discover the differentiated content of the category 'category' it must look outside of the category in some 'extraneous' impulse, such as 'sensations' and 'ideas' (such as images). As Hegel makes clear, this is a 'self-contradictory ambiguity' since the categorial differences are both categorial (since they exist in the category as such), and not categorial, since the differences of the category do not originate in the category.

Because the category cannot account for its own differences, this abstract idealism really fails to establish itself as 'all reality' and ends up affirming a bad infinitude:

> This Reason remains a restless searching and in its very searching declares that the satisfaction of finding is a sheer impossibility.[41]

Because whatever differences one discovers are not conceptual differences, the search for the conceptual difference continues to fail. Rational consciousness discovers some content, let us call it NC1, for 'non-conceptual content.' NC1 is not the principle of categorial content, since it is not categorial. Thus, one is pushed further to discover another content, NC2, *ad infinitum*. The infinite at work here is spurious, or incomplete. The spurious infinite begins with the truth of conceptual consciousness and searches for its content outside of the concept. Because the latter fails to correspond to conceptual consciousness, it returns to its search again, always without avail and never with success.

As Hegel states, rational consciousness states that reason is all reality, but it does not yet *conceive* this:

> Thus, it merely asserts that it is all reality, but does not itself comprehend this; for it is along that forgotten path that this immediately expressed assertion is comprehended.[42]

In sum, the general problem of reason in the *Phenomenology* is the fact that the concept is *not yet conceptually determined*. Only once *the concept is conceptually determined* can *the concept be true to what it is*—can the concept cohere with itself. In order to more fully exemplify this problem in the history of philosophy, we should consider examples not only of the mistake of absolute empiricism but also those Idealist critiques of that empiricism who do not seem to fully acknowledge that their own view undermines itself and establishes exactly what they mean to critique.

The problem of Absolute Empiricism has many manifestations—two of which are Psychologism and Naturalism. In order to better illustrate this problem I will reconstruct the historical appearance of the former in the empiricism of Berkeley and Mill, as well as their critics in the Neo-Kantian and Phenomenological schools. I will conclude by showing that neither the empiricists nor their detractors ultimately see the problem as clearly as Hegel. Hegel recognized that as long as the concept could *not* work as a principle of particularity, the critique of the empirical position would simply play back into the hands of the empiricists. In order to provide more detail concerning the empirical, psychological deduction of the concept, I will employ Ernst Cassirer's description of Berkeley's psychological deduction of the concept in *Substanz und Funktion*,[43] in order to express the psychological production of the concept in the most efficient terms. I shall give special focus to the function of *resemblance* in the development of concepts.

Taking the stream of consciousness as a given, what resources stand available for concept formation? Each presentation of consciousness is a distinct, unique content, temporally ordered in relation to the others. Since every presentation that appears in the present immediately ceases to appear into the past, no constant presentation is given from which a concept may be derived. In fact, the unique quality of every psychological appearance bars us from identifying common features of any of the sensuous qualities that are given to consciousness. Instead, some particular content must be *selected* and removed from the whole process of contents by an act of *memory*. Though each sensuous content is in itself irretrievable, it may be withheld in memory. Here it may be important to note that *attention* is required in order to select out a *part* of the whole. As new contents are experienced, we may begin to identify *resemblances* and *dissimilarities* between the selected content stored in memory and the novel contents being given in our inner and outer perception. Having assimilated the novel content to the past content, a class is formed. In this way, the resemblance of particulars to some selected content forms the foundation of concepts. Since some particular functions as the measure of the class of particulars, the classes which are formed may be said to possess some qualitative measure, unlike the bare quantitative concept that constitutes the meaning of the class concept.

In one respect, both the Aristotelian and British Empiricist traditions are quite similar, for the mind, in order to know the universal, must *select out some part* of a given sensuous manifold, and therewith represent a plurality of diverse contents. In this respect, *abstraction* is the primary mode by which we know the concept as such in each of these accounts. On the one hand, in both accounts some common aspect or resemblance is identified in various particulars. On the other hand, as I argue later, on the modern empiricist paradigm no universal is really discovered in the particulars, but is instead *constructed* out of them. In this respect, the act of selection and abstraction is not merely moved to a different region of being as Cassirer claims. Instead, a novel treatment of universality is underway in Locke, Berkeley, and Hume. What is perhaps most striking is the rejection of classical ontology: *classes replace Forms*. The replacement of Forms by classes does not just undermine an ontology but also affects the logical structure of cognition, for Form, as the universal, is *the principle of the particular*, whereas in the perspective of modern empiricism the particular becomes the principle of the universal.

The nominalist view that replaces Forms with classes offers an attractive solution to the problem of instantiation we initially raised in the discussion of Plato. Rather than privilege the Form, whose articulation is universal, as the principle of the particular, the nominalist solution to the problem of instantiation completely eliminates the universal as a common term that is one in number. Nominalism, similarly to Aristotle, attempts to qualify the traditional duality of principles of knowing by reducing the duality of principles to *one principle*. Through its empowering of particularity as the principle of universality, it achieves this reduction by turning Aristotle on his head. Such a radical solution solves the problem of instantiation by inverting the Aristotelian paradigm, but only at the cost of self-consistency as well as raising new problems concerning the being and meaning of Truth itself.

Abstracting from its original theological motivation in Ockham's philosophy, the modern secular nominalist conception of concepts appears to avoid the problem of instantiation that plagues the concept of the universal as an abstraction or a genus. The problem of instantiation only arises if there is a universal that is itself *one in number*, that is repeated in a number of different particulars. Because the self-same universal must exist in different particulars, the self-same universal could not be the same universal. Either the universal is different from itself (which is a contradiction) or it is not held in common, namely it is not a universal. However, on the nominalist conception there is no universal term. Since only the concept is reducible to the aggregation, there is no self-same concept to repeat itself in a variety of particulars. Thus, the nominalist turn in modern thinking can solve the problem of instantiation because it denies the basic premise upon which the whole problem turns. The universal no longer stands for a power that generates particularity; rather the particular becomes the principle of the concept and constitutes it completely, in all its color and diversity.

With the banishment of universals from the particulars encountered in experience, what kind of universal could be constructed from particulars bearing no universality?[44] It is here, at this juncture, that the concept of 'class membership' finds some metaphysical and epistemic motivation. Since all beings are particulars, if the universal is grasped as an aggregate of particulars, universals can be constructed. Since particulars can be aggregated together, aggregates of particulars may be formed. Indeed, since the universals are banished from the particulars, the aggregation itself does not appear to be a function of the particulars that are aggregated. For this reason, they must have their origin in some external principle, such as a psychological subject who aggregates them together. As we've already indicated, in modern philosophy, thinkers usually appeal to resemblance or analogy as the method by which the classes are constructed. One can aggregate particulars of *any* kind—colors, houses, horses, amoebas, and so on—into groups such that the principle of aggregation is not necessarily connected to any particular quality in what is aggregated. As is evident, insofar as the universal is an aggregation of particulars, in the aggregate the particulars stand *in relation* to one another. What is it in virtue of which these particulars belong in one class? On the one hand, since there is no universal identity in the objects themselves by which the particulars may be distinguished from each other, their relation to one another in the class appears to lack any inherent principle of *universal* identity. On the other hand, each particular is a particular, and for this reason there is the universal 'particularity' that all of them share. But this is like saying that each has 'being unique in common.' That each is one in number does in fact allow each of them to be aggregated in the first place, and in this sense, there is some universality that is already built into the particulars from the outset. What this implies is that although nominalism attempts to derive all universals from particulars, some universal must be assumed from the outset in order for any universal to be derived. Thus, the problem of instantiation must again rear its head, for *each particular is at least one in number*, and this is a common feature of them all. Given these considerations, the true nominalist must argue that either the particularity of the members is not a true universal or that even the *particularity of each is a product of the aggregate of particulars*. On the one hand, because one can only aggregate if there are *already particulars* to aggregate, the aggregation cannot in fact account for the particularity of each. On the other hand, though one ought to distinguish 'one in number' from 'one in kind,' 'one in number' is already nonetheless a kind of universality, for it appeals to 'being countable' as a criterion for inclusion in the class.

At the ground of the totality of particulars, an *a priori* universal is lurking which undermines the radically nominalistic inferences made by Ockham and those who follow him. The indifference of particularity to universality is itself the common feature of all particulars that contribute to the class of particulars. More simply, all particulars exist in *the class of particularity*, namely the totality of given particulars. On this basis, a *quantitative universal*, namely *'for all x,'* is immanent in particulars. That a kind of rationalism makes nominalism possible will not fully be drawn out until Kant develops his Transcendental Idealism in the *Critique of Pure Reason*. It appears that whatever given there may be, it must always already be conceptually mediated.

If we tarry a while with the psychological derivation of the concept, we discover that the process by which we produce universals leads us in the opposite direction we intend to travel. Ultimately, knowledge should illuminate experience, which is radically particular. Yet, we find that the further we pursue the universal, the further we proceed from the particular. Since no particular shares a common feature with another, any resemblance we identify is not a common feature. Instead, in order to build the concept, we must *forget* or at least *ignore* the differences in the particulars. Only in virtue of forgetting their uniqueness can we identify one presentation with another. Moreover, the act of identification by which we connect unrelated presentations forms a new presentation in which the originally independent presentations are unified. This act of identification requires that one *judge* that the various contents are identical. This newfound identity is not itself a member of the original stream of contents given to the theorizer. Instead, it is a creation of the mind to which nothing in the original flux of consciousness corresponds. Accordingly, what consciousness knows in the judgment of identification is something it has produced for itself, not a description of the original contents themselves. For this reason, the universality of the concept is a principle by which the thinker becomes more distanced from the original manifold she set out to know.

If it is a requirement of knowledge that the vehicle of knowledge be universal, then insofar as the universal fails to grasp the particular, no knowledge of the particular contents is possible. Indeed, *skepticism about the empiricist paradigm itself must necessarily arise*, since knowledge claims concerning empiricism must also come under scrutiny. The *global skepticism* engendered by Hume's account is the most fitting conclusion to the *tabula rasa* tradition in modern philosophy.

My description of the empiricist-psychological view of the concept has closely followed Cassirer's own account of that perspective. Still, I wish to stray a bit from Cassirer's analysis at this point, although it shall be pertinent to refer to it at another stage in the argument. Since admitting anything other than the particular generates a radical skepticism about the empirical-psychological paradigm itself, what is demanded of the psychological-empiricist account is an account of inference that never abandons the particular. For an account of the concept that reduces the concept and all logical inference to the particular, we should briefly investigate how J. S. Mill attempts to re-vitalize the empiricist concept of logic in the 19th century. Here, in J. S. Mill's *Logic: Ratiocinative and Inductive*, we arrive at a concept of the concept that illuminates what logic must be on the assumptions of psychological-empiricism.

As I have noted, what is of special import for us here is the way Mill conceives of inference. In order to contextualize this move, we shall briefly touch on the understanding of logic in which this view of inference is embedded. For Mill, logic investigates the *actual mental processes* at work in making inferences.[45] At the outset, Mill distinguishes two fundamental types of knowledge: immediate and mediated. For example, one can know that one feels hot immediately, whereas knowledge of mathematical and historical truths are mediated, that is one cannot know them with direct reference to some inner or outer perceptual content. All mediated knowledge, in the tradition of British Empiricism, may be ultimately reduced to some knowledge of immediate truths.[46] For example, we know that $2 + 3 = 5$ because we have repeatedly experienced the objects in spatial intuition to be capable of such relations. We may find five pebbles in the dirt and separate them into groups of two and three, which we later re-combine into a group of five. Repeated encounters with such experience brings us to knowledge of the proposition that $2 + 3 = 5$. Accordingly, all our mathematical knowledge, like all knowledge, is contingent. Though Hume separates matters of fact from relations of ideas, the latter must ultimately owe their content to the impressions of experience, or they have no source at all, even if they are hypothesized.

Regarding definition, Mill claims that definitions are not of things, but *of names only*.[47] Since all knowledge is derived from a given plurality of individuals, no universal or definition could exist in the individuals *a priori*. Moreover, definitions are not composed of a genus and a difference, for this logical structure undermines itself.[48] Mill points out that if we continue in the logical progression from genus to genus, we discover that Being cannot be a genus. Either the system of genera is absurd at its ground or there is no logical ground of the system. Given this criticism of the structure of generic categories, Mill offers his own set of categories.[49]

Within this empiricist paradigm, Mill criticizes Aristotle's account of the syllogism and the theory of the syllogism that was handed down via the tradition. Taking the following syllogism as paradigmatic, Mill shows why the theory of the syllogism gives no new knowledge: (i) all men are mortal and (ii) Socrates is a man. Thus, Socrates is mortal.

But what grounds the universal proposition that 'all men are mortal'? If all knowledge of universals must be grounded on particulars, then one must have already run through all the particular men in order to establish the proposition concerning all men. If this is the case, we must already know that Socrates is mortal in order to establish the universal proposition concerning the mortality of all men. But, since 'Socrates is mortal' is the conclusion of the syllogism, it follows that the syllogism must assume what it intends to prove.[50]

Like Berkeley, Mill also relies on resemblance to arrive at classes. His claim about the process of inference clarifies how thought dwells in the paradigm of class membership. If the universal expressed in 'all men are mortal' already presupposes the inference that 'Socrates is mortal,' what is the logic underlying the syllogism? According to Mill, all inference is *from particular to particular*. The most primitive instances of reasoning we perform seem to correspond to this formula. For instance, when the child burns his hand on the stove, he need not perform a syllogism or cognize any universal to know not to burn his hand on the stove again. He makes the inference without having to appeal to a universal. Still, we should be skeptical that all inferences work this way. If we return to our sample syllogism concerning mortality, we can, via a process of resemblance, build a class. Initially, prior to the development of the class, I may observe that a particular person dies. On closer inspection, I note that others have died and continue to die. From this process I infer that each person whom I have considered is similar in respect to his or her mortality. Upon consideration of persons in general, I collect these particulars into the class of mortals.[51] For sure, in every day practice I do not enumerate each person, nor could I. If I do not consider each person, what justifies the inference that all men are mortal? By 'all' here we need only mean the persons thus far enumerated or, perhaps better, something comparative such as 'to the best of our knowledge' or 'as far as I know.' Since all knowledge is contingent, at any point our classes may be reformed according to novel observations. To sum up, we may bluntly claim that the universal is nothing other than the totality of particulars gathered together into a class.

The universal is no longer an essential element of inferential reasoning. Though Mill continues to rely on resemblance, insofar as inference is from particular to particular, the process of knowledge does not bring us farther away from the sensuous manifold as we reason; to the contrary, the process of reasoning never abandons the particular. Instead, the classes formed by the mind appear to introduce no other quality than what is present in the sensuous manifold. Accordingly, the universal only functions as an *abbreviation* of an inferential process already performed. Because it is more efficient to say 'all men' than to enumerate each man considered in making the inference, we invent terms such as 'men' to signify the group of particulars we mean to express. Once the abbreviation is established, one can make inferences *from and to the abbreviation*. Inferring to and from the abbreviation is important, but only as a means of organizing one's own mental notes. As long as the judgment of identity implicit in the formation of classes only produces abbreviations, the empiricist paradigm may not undermine itself, for the abbreviation only supplants the particular in regards to its efficient use, but fails to introduce a new content. On the one hand, since all knowledge of what is the case is had via inductive logic, that is the inference from particular to particular, inductive logic is the only *truth* logic. Truth, it appears, lies in the domain of the empirical sciences. On the other hand, the system of the syllogism is nothing more than a way of checking one's own thoughts for consistency.

Unlike the truth logic of Aristotle or Kant, Mill's truth logic is completely inductive. With the rejection of the *a priori* universal, truth logic no longer requires seeking out an *a priori* intuition to which the *a priori* concept can correspond. Likewise, the universal articulation of the thing no longer represents the power of the Form to generate its instances. Rather, now it is the particular that performs the work previously performed by the universal—truth logic is now fundamentally re-conceived as an inferential process proceeding from *particular to particular*. The universal—once the proud articulation of the existentially implicative power of Form—has been reduced to an *abbreviation*.

Still, it is unclear whether the appeal to resemblance can be made without the assumption that particulars share some common feature in virtue of which they are similar. Without the identical feature, each particular would fail to share anything. This makes it appear that even if the generation of the classes may escape our criticism of Berkeley, it seems to evade this only by risking *relativism*. In other words, if we identify particulars with one another on account of our recognition of resemblance, yet this resemblance cannot have its ground in the identity of particulars, particulars seem only to resemble each other because of our *stipulation* that they do. Without any ability to appeal to the particulars themselves in order to determine what classes we should and should not form, it appears that which classes one adopts is relative to whatever particulars the thinker decides to place into relation. The diversity of universals in natural language appears to confirm this account of universals, since no two languages contain exactly the same classes.[52] Unfortunately though, if universals are themselves relative, then the claim holds that the concept of the concept, 'class membership,' is also a merely relative determination and ought not be privileged over any other conception of the universal. Indeed, by limiting class membership to an *empirical* concept, we run into the same problem we encounter in Hume—either our justification for identifying the concept of the concept with the empirical class begs the question or it is merely stipulated without argument.[53]

I think it is instructive to consider the argument advanced by both the Neo-Kantian and Transcendental-Phenomenological schools against the radically empiricist concept of the universal as a class, and in particular, as an empirical class. Let us consider Husserl's basic phenomenological argument[54] against the universal as an empirical class, since Cassirer's argument in *Substance and Function* is a condensed version of the same.

Let us first consider what *we mean* when we talk about a concept. Take, for example, the concept 'four.' When we think 'four,' and what belongs to the concept 'four,' we treat 'four' as *a subject* of predicates. What is 'four'? Four is a natural, whole number. When we think that 'four' is a natural, whole number, we do not mean that four pebbles are a natural whole number or four feelings are a natural whole number. No, instead, we mean that 'four *itself*' has the predicates, not the particulars that are thought under it. It is absurd to predicate 'natural whole number' to four pebbles, since the pebbles themselves do not have the properties in question, nor do we mean them to have them. If what I mean by a concept always signifies some particular presentation, then concepts are ultimately *proper names*. But, we do not mean some particular content or plurality of particular contents except the universal presentation of 'four itself' when we attribute 'whole number' to 'four.' 'Four itself' appears as a *this*. In my nominalization of 'four' I cannot help but treat it as an independent object. Note that in thinking about 'four' I am not referring to any class at all, empirical or otherwise, but some content containing, if you will, the *intensive* predicates 'whole' and 'number.'

If we wish to explain what universals are in a way that is consistent with what we mean when we think concepts, then we assume, as a starting point of our investigation, that there are what Husserl calls 'universal presentations' of concepts and not just particular presentations. Instead of taking the universal concept 'four' as given foundation from which to begin an inquiry into universals, modern empiricism attempts to explain away the concept we mean in our signification. The key complaint here is that modern nominalism fails to take the ideal signification of concepts as the starting point of the inquiry.

If we proceed to think about what universals are in light of this ideal signification, we come to see how absurd the empiricist rendering of the concept is. If the universal is merely some psychological appropriation of given individuals into classes, each of which is originally given separately from the others, the universal is something which only exists in the *particular mind* that makes the class. If the universal exists in the particular mind that makes the class, the universal only exists in those *temporal moments* when the thinker comprehends the particulars into a class. So, how many 'fours' are there? There are as many concepts of 'four' as there are minds that comprehend 'four.' Yet, when someone tells me that 'four' is a natural number, *this does not mean that 'her four' is a natural number*. It means that 'four' itself, irrespective of the thinker, is a natural number. If it were her four, she could not make a claim concerning its universal application to any four as such. Accordingly, she should give up making any claim to know what 'four' is. Instead, there are only particular contents for particulars, no universal contents. When the empiricist claims that every thinker has a different image of a table in her mind, and therefore has a different concept of the table in her mind, *the* concept has been eliminated; instead, there are diverse images denoted by the word 'table.' This kind of empiricists is only talking to herself.

Further, the concept itself is a particular psychological presentation in the mind of the thinker at *some time*, such that the universal cannot simultaneously exist at other times in the minds of the same thinker. Each universal would have a particular temporal duration, such that as a particular temporal content, it is a distinct universal from contents that appear at other times. Thus, there are in principle *no repeatable* terms. When I think what 'four' is, I determine it irrespective of what time it is thought or where I am when I think it. I am able to cognize the 'same four' irrespective of the time. Thus, the 'four' itself is not inherently connected to any particular temporal duration of my consciousness. I encounter 'four' as a *self-same* presentation whose content is not constituted by *who* thinks it or *when* they think it. Still, for the empiricist who posits the universal as an empirical class, there can only be a passing temporal flux which bars any further unification of the particulars that is not merely symbolic or itself particular. Again, when I say that 'four' is a natural number, I do not mean that 'four now' is a natural number, but may not be tomorrow. If we wish to revise our concepts such that we now mean by 'four' 'my four now,' there shall no longer be any discussion of 'four.' On such a perspective, there is nothing for us to speak about that is the same in any case either to ourselves or in the company of others. Indeed, we cannot even say 'my' or 'yours' without falling into the same trap. Instead, we bottom out in one in number, having entirely lost what is one in kind. Reducing one in kind to one in number seems indistinguishable from the annihilation of universality altogether.[55]

By rejecting what is one in kind we also undermine unity in number. Insofar as the universal is a *self-same* presentation, it cannot be temporal, without ceasing to be itself every time it is thought. In reducing the universal to a psychological class, each four is a four. What is 'four,' then, if 'four' is 'a four'?[56] There is no difference! Since we have no unity in kind, we cannot even talk about 'a four,' since there is no instance of a common term. As such, we have no identity by which we could identify resemblances and differences. We cannot form classes and instances of 'four' without some identity by which to identify the instances. It appears that resemblance can only do work if there is something *in virtue of which* they resemble each other, that is some *common* mark. This common mark cannot be a class, for it is that in virtue of which the class is formed.

We might attempt to ground the universal, not in any psychological content, but in a psychological *act*. The problem with the latter point of view is that it fails to escape the temporal limitations constraining the psychological contents. If we grasp universals as somehow constituted by psychological acts, then we fail to grasp the self-identity of the universal that persists irrespective of the temporal variations.

We might also point out, with Cassirer, that we cannot find psychological presentations with which many concepts can be correlated. Though we may be able to distinguish 10,000 from 9,999, we do not possess psychological presentations that correlate to 10,000 by which we distinguish it from 9,999. Likewise, any concept of the infinite cannot be grounded in any particular presentations, since we only ever consciously encounter finite presentations. With what presentation shall we correlate an *uncountable infinity*? It seems that we are not only better suited to render the difference without appeal to some psychological presentation but that reducing the difference to one pertaining to some private, temporal determination at least muddles, but at worst undermines, the very possibility of making the distinction in the first place.[57]

The main function of the preceding arguments is to show how the *empirical* class concept fails to do justice to what we mean when we think what is universal and when we make conceptual distinctions, since it entails the untenable commitment to psychologism. The non-psychological position, which we shall discuss later, does *not* commit itself to a psychological theory of the universal.

Still, we shall find that some of the previous criticisms should apply to any concept of the class concept *whatever*. First, since the universal does not primarily signify the mere extension, and class-membership is exhausted in the extension, it follows that class membership, empirical or not, fails to constitute what we mean by 'universal.' Second, some *common* terms appear necessary in order to provide the identity conditions of *any* class-membership. Thus, even non-empirical classes, whatever they may be, appear to stand in need of some prior conceptual factor that makes them possible. The abstract universal could in principle offer a way to make them possible, for it is able to provide a conceptual factor by which the identity conditions of membership are specified. Overall, class membership comprehends the universal wholly from the side of the particular. It is a mode of self-indifference, in which the universal is only conceived in the mode of self-negation.

We might also note that what is being rejected in these criticisms is a *cluster* of related ways of thinking about the universal. Insofar as modern nominalism entails psychologism, the rejection of psychologism also entails a rejection of modern nominalism. First, we may say that the critique of psychologism, that is, the rejection of the view that the concept has its being in some particular temporal presentation or act of consciousness, constitutes a rejection of modern empiricism. In sum, the critique of psychologism undermines the psychological context of the universal.

Should the universal be conceived as an abstract 'one' over many, or should the many themselves constitute the universal itself? It seems that this question may be asked independently of whether one is committed to an empirical or non-empirical theory of the universal. Yet, either answer is problematic. However you answer the question, you are taking one side of the *same* duality. If one in number is the essential factor, and one in kind unessential, you can remove unity in kind and still have one in number. But if unity in kind is absent, not only can there not be any common feature, for example not even 'one in number,' for 'number' seems to make an appeal to a universal that is not merely a class, but provides an *intensive difference* with other kinds of unity. We may say that all classes are *arbitrary*, including the concept 'class membership.' Without one in kind, there are *no instances* of the kind and thus no particulars. If one in kind is essential, and one in number unessential, there cannot be one in kind. For without particulars, there cannot be any term common to the particulars. Thus, without what is one in number there is no unity in kind. It appears that intensive unity requires extensive unity, and extensive unity requires the intensive. Each is a condition of the other. In other words, class membership is a condition for the abstract universal and the abstract universal is a condition for class membership. In this regard, the question, 'is the universal a class or an abstraction?' is misguided, as each is a one-sided emphasis of one opposition. Indeed, we have already been over this ground in our discussion of Aristotle's *aporia* concerning the derivation of one in kind from one in number and one in number from one in kind.

As we demonstrated earlier, the attempt to conceptualize the Absolute by positing one principle as the ultimate source of all particularity and differentiation fails because the concept of the concept undergirding that attempt is constituted by a duality of principles of universality and particularity. By modeling one's conceptualization of the Absolute on the duality of principles constitutive of the concept, the philosopher means to avoid the problem of the disappearance of the Absolute as expressed in the problem of Nihilism, that arises from the attempt to derive all differentiations of the Absolute from *one* principle. On its face, it initially appeared to be the case that appealing to dual principles of truth (as exemplified in Aristotle and Kant for instance) would avoid falling victim to similar systematic impossibilities as the early German Idealists or Plotinus did. However, we can already see that any conceptualization of the concept that construes the concept as constituted by a *duality* of principles of universality and particularity falls victim to at least these two *additional* problems—the missing difference and what I have called 'absolute empiricism.' Thus, were we to *bracket* any question about whether the Absolute can be truly conceived by modeling it on the dualistic structure of conceptual determinacy, any concept of the concept constituted by the duality of principles of universality and particularity is already (and on its own terms) inherently incoherent. Because it is incoherent on its own terms, it certainly cannot function as a plausible model for thinking the absolute.

Notes

1. The content of the article, "Dialetheism and the Problem of the Missing Difference," is distributed throughout Chapters 5 through 7. For a more streamlined and non-historical version of the arguments presented here, please see Gregory S. Moss, "Dialetheism and the Problem of the Missing Difference," *Northern European Journal of Philosophy* 19, no. 2 (August 2018): 1–22.
2. Graham Priest, *Beyond the Limits of Thought* (Oxford: Oxford University Press, 2003), 3–4.
3. This argument expands upon the arguments for Dialetheism in *Beyond the Limits of Thought*. Priest's enclosure schema provides a "precise characterization of the limits of thought." See Priest, *Beyond the Limits of Thought*, 3. For a more formal description of the enclosure schema, see Priest, *Beyond the Limits of Thought*, 133–135.
4. My concern with the concept of the CONCEPT mirrors Plato's reflection on the Form of Forms in *Parmenides*. See Graham Priest, *One: Being an Investigation into the Unity of Reality and of Its Parts, Including the Singular Object Which Is Nothingness* (Oxford: Oxford University Press, 2014), Part II, Ch. 7.
5. We are abstracting from the content of universals and particulars in order to reflect on the content of the terms 'universal' and 'particular' and their relationship.
6. Although one can use the term 'concept' in a way much more general way such that one can speak of 'a concept of Socrates,' I am using 'concept' in the restricted sense of a universal.

7. This principle is another formulation of the 'domain principle.'
8. Priest made this observation in personal conversation at the Chinese University of Hong Kong on June 8, 2017.
9. Although similar, note that the problem of the missing difference is not identical to Grelling's paradox, or what is known as the *heterological* paradox.
10. Edward Halper, "Hegel and the Problem of the Differentia," in *Form and Reason: Essays in Metaphysics* (Albany: SUNY, 1993), 197–209, 198.
11. See Aristotle, *Metaphysics*, Book Zeta, 123–125 (1030b–1031a).
12. According to Halper, this solution 'is scarcely more intelligible. The problem undermines the independence of the categories.' Halper, "Hegel and the Problem of the Missing Differentia," 199.
13. Hegel, *PS*, trans. Miller, Ch. 2, 67–79.
14. Ibid, 67, paragraph 112.
15. Ibid, paragraph 112.
16. See this initial characterization in Hegel, *PS*, trans. Miller, paragraph 113, 68–69.
17. Hegel, *PS*, trans. Miller, paragraph 74–75, 123.
18. This is a brief summary of key features of Hegel, *PS*, trans. Miller, paragraph 124.
19. Hegel, *PS*, trans. Miller, paragraph 75–76, 125.
20. Ibid, paragraph 76, 128.
21. Ibid.
22. Halper, "Hegel and the Problem of the Missing Differentia," 201.
23. Ibid, 200.
24. Kant, *CPR*, B75, 193.
25. Ibid, B93, 205.
26. Ibid, B146–B147, 254.
27. Ibid, A596, B624.
28. For a concrete example of this contradiction, consider the problem of Psychologism in the history of philosophy. Psychologism, the view that concepts are psychological contents, is often identified with an empiricist treatment of concepts, though transcendental philosophers such as Kant have been accused of identifying concepts as psychological contents. Some of the philosophers who reject Psychologism, for example Frege, in his *Foundations of Arithmetic*, Husserl, in his *Logical Investigations*, and Cassirer in *Substance and Function*, do so exactly because purely non-temporal and non-spatial logical concepts are identified with temporal mental representation(s) or relation(s). In the case of Psychologism, the accusation is that one appropriates what is not conceptual, such as sensory particulars, and treats them *as though they were* conceptual or universal. Rather than simply follow these thinkers here, my argument here implies that on the model of the concept as a common character, something like the Psychologistic account of the origin of particular concepts appears necessary.
29. Because what is at stake is the possibility of differentiations of the class of concepts in general, and particular concepts are differentiations of the class of concepts, what is at stake is the possibility of particular concepts.
30. For anyone who holds a Fregean view of concepts as senses, such as Peacocke, this specific instantiation of the contradiction, for example the identification of the universal with the non-conceptual particular, would entail (a presumably unacceptable) identification of sense and reference. See Christopher Peacocke, *A Study of Concepts* (Cambridge: MIT University Press, 1993), 3. Nonetheless, I do *not* mean to say that this is the only possible instantiation of the contradiction, for any concept of the CONCEPT which

adheres to principles (i–iii) would also lead to a contradiction. Thus, other instantiations are also possible. In addition, although various ontological perspectives would certainly be affected by the argument, any ontological perspective on the concept that accepts principles (i–iii) would also be lead to a contradiction. For this reason, the contradiction does not appear to be indebted to any extraneous ontological principles.

31. Here it is important to note that we are not identifying the terms 'difference' with 'instance.' Rather, difference is a necessary condition and ingredient for instantiating the concept CONCEPT in cases where the instantiations are not *identical* to the CONCEPT. Each particular concept is an instance of the CONCEPT on the conditions that (i) it is a concept and (ii) it is differentiated from other concepts (including the CONCEPT) by some difference. In this way, the conceptual content of a particular concept is constituted by a genus and a difference. Accordingly, they can be conceived as species of a genus. I take this term 'content' to signify the answer to the question 'what is the concept?' If I ask 'what is the concept number?' then the content of that concept is the predicate of the sentence 'Number is such and such' in which 'such and such' connotes one specific differentiation of the CONCEPT.
32. Hegel, *PS*, trans. Miller, 49.
33. Ibid, 139.
34. Ibid.
35. Ibid, 142.
36. Idealism has many forms. One can be an idealist if one argues that all things have categorial form. In addition, one can conceive of idealism in terms of the mind, namely that all things exist in the mind. One can also combine and separate these views in various ways.
37. Hegel, *PS*, trans. Miller, 140.
38. G. W. F. Hegel, *Phenomenology of Spirit*, ed. and trans. Terry Pinkard (Cambridge: Cambridge University Press, 2018), 142.
39. Ibid.
40. Ibid, 144.
41. Ibid, 145.
42. Ibid, 141.
43. See Ernst Cassirer, *Substance and Function,* trans. William Curtus Swaby and Marie Swaby (New York: Dover Publisher, 1953), Ch. I, Part 2, 9–18.
44. At this point in the argument I leave undetermined the way that the class may be constructed. In modern philosophy different theories of class construction are posited. In principle, though, since we are motivating class membership along nominalist lines, I tend to think of construction as a psychological activity that is to be distinguished from geometrical construction.
45. John Stuart Mill, *A System of Logic, Ratiocinative and Inductive, Definition and Province of Logic* (Charleston: Biblio Bazaar, 2009), 1–8.
46. Ibid.
47. Ibid, Ch. VIII, of Definition, 86–103.
48. Ibid, 89.
49. Unfortunately, Mill pays no heed to the problem of differentiating categories. I will make the argument that any system of class membership must necessarily fall victim to the problem of the categories.
50. Mill, *A System of Logic, Ratiocinative and Inductive*, Functions and Value of the Syllogism, 119–136.
51. Ibid, 133.
52. Take, for example, the various different color concepts in different languages. How the color spectrum is divided up is a matter of relativity.

53. For example how could one form the universal 'class membership' except by enumerating all classes?
54. See Husserl, *Shorter Logical Investigations*, Investigation II, Ch. 3, 145–160.
55. Cassirer, *Substance and Function*, Ch. 1, Part 2, 9–18.
56. See Husserl, *Shorter Logical Investigations*, Investigation II, Ch. 3, 145–160.
57. Again, see Cassirer, *Substance and Function*, Ch. 1, Part 2, 9–18.

6   The Problem of Onto-Theology

If commitment to the PNC is maintained, then the philosopher can no longer appeal to non-conceptual content in order to differentiate the domain of concepts. Thus, in order to be consistent, the defender of the PNC could neither appeal to the CONCEPT *per se* (since on its own terms it cannot be the principle of its own differences) nor to any non-conceptual content. Thus, the defender of the PNC would be required to maintain the thesis that the CONCEPT be truly *undifferentiated*, and there could not be any particular concepts whatever. If there cannot be true contradictions, then there cannot be any particular concepts. Thus, the philosopher would be forced to advocate for a conceptual *Monism* in which not only is the Concept the *only concept* there is but also that concept is internally one, for it would be *totally indivisible*. Were there no particular concepts, then even the concept of the CONCEPT would be impossible, since this would be *a* particular concept, namely that conceptual content which specifies whatever it is to be a concept. For this reason, the defender of the PNC can only avoid (C1) by running into another contradiction: if there cannot be any particular concepts, then there cannot even be the concept of the CONCEPT in general.

Aristotle raised this precise problem in his *Metaphysics*. If there is absolutely nothing that is one in number, or what is the same, if there were absolutely no particulars, there could not be any universals or unities in kind, *for no universal would be one in number*. In other words, each universal is only *a* universal if each is a *this* and can be counted as a separate universal. No universal could be *a* universal were there no particulars. Thus, there could not be 'one-itself' or 'being-itself.' Likewise, there could be no 'unity in kind itself,' for 'itself' signifies that the kind is *one in number*.[1]

If there were *no conceptual differences* whatever, there would be *no conceptual difference between the CONCEPT (the universal genus) and particular concepts* (the particular species of the genus) or the conceptual members of the domain of concepts. If there were no conceptual difference between the CONCEPT and the particular, the universal CONCEPT would be indistinguishable from the particular concept—which is

190 The Problem of Absolute Knowledge

absurd, since according to the duality of principles, the universal and the particular are necessarily non-identical. To put the contradiction another way, the universal, the concept of the CONCEPT, is also particular; it is *this* concept, even if it is also the *only* particular.

In order to differentiate the CONCEPT from instances of the concept and establish the conceptual identity of the CONCEPT, one must specify what differentiates the CONCEPT from particular concepts. If UNDIF-FERENTIATIED were predicated of the CONCEPT, the CONCEPT would be differentiated from the instances of the CONCEPT (for each of these is a differentiated concept) by the predicate UNDIFFERENTIATED. If the CONCEPT were differentiated from the particular concepts, then the CONCEPT would itself be a particular concept and would therefore be an instance of the CONCEPT. This is another formulation of con-tradiction (C2): the CONCEPT would be differentiated from particular concepts in virtue of its very lack of differentiation. Or what is the same: the CONCEPT would be a particular in virtue of its lack of particularity. Put more precisely, if one posits that there is only the undifferentiated CONCEPT as such, and no particular concepts, then there are no dif-ferentiated or particular concepts. Yet, in this scenario there must be at least one particular or differentiated concept: THE CONCEPT as such. We may articulate (C2) as follows:

(C2): There cannot be any particular concepts and there is at least one particular concept.

Since the defender of the PNC insists that there is at least the concept of the CONCEPT, if there is such a concept as the CONCEPT, then a con-tradiction, (C2), results. In order to avoid contradiction (C2), one might be forced to accept a form of *Conceptual Elimativism*: if there cannot be any true contradictions, then there cannot be any concepts. In short: *Monism entails Eliminativism.*

Given that its very lack of differentiation entails that the CONCEPT cannot be differentiated from particular concepts, the CONCEPT itself must be a particular concept. Because concepts are assumed not to be self-predicating, the concept could *not* be the source of its own instances. Accordingly, the philosopher is coerced to appeal to a *second* principle— a principle of differentiation by which particulars would be won. Indeed, by following this argument it is easy enough to grasp that a logically consistent rejection of self-predication entails conceptual monism. What is more difficult is to see how (C2) arises. In order to see this contradic-tion, one needs to be able to think *dialectically*. The monist takes herself to deny that the concept is the source of its own particularization. By doing so, however, the concept is transformed into *the only concept*. It becomes the *only* member of the class of concepts. In short, it denies there are members and posits one member—itself. Although this conceptual monism is engendered by the absence of self-predication, monism contradicts itself by *unknowingly* predicating conceptual content to itself. Accordingly, the contradiction lies in the underlying structure—*by denying self-predication it affirms it*. This contradiction is easier to see in an historical example and will provide us with a convenient point of transition to discuss the greater implications of this problem for thinking about the Absolute on a dualistic model of conceptual determinacy.

Parmenides and Heraclitus

In the *Way of Truth*, Parmenides states that there are only two roads of inquiry: the way of being and the way of non-being. The way of non-being is not a way of inquiry, because any attempt to inquire into non-being renders non-being to be some being. Therefore, inquiry cannot help but place one on the inquiry into Being, as there is no other path that is thinkable.[2] As the argument shows, Parmenides identifies Being (εἶναι) with thought (νοῦς).[3] Unlike the inquiry into non-being, the inquiry into being does not transform the object of inquiry into its opposite. What can be thought and can be stays itself, while that which cannot be, non-being, admits what it is not, being. There is no contradiction in 'Being is.' Being is, and non-being is not. As Parmenides writes:

> for it can be, and nothing cannot. This I bid you ponder. For from this first road of inquiry <I bar you> and then from the road along which mortals who know nothing wander, two-headed; for impotence in their breasts guides their erring thought. And they are carried along both deaf and blind, bewildered, undiscerning crowds, by whom to be and not to be are deemed the same and not the same; and the path of all turns back [παλίντροπος][4] on itself.[5]

Most notable here is the claim that it is an error to identify Being and non-being. This identification happens on the side of non-being. Non-being is not, but it also is, as Parmenides' inquiry into non-being exemplifies. Hence, it is both the same as itself and not the same as itself. Non-Being is opposed to itself. Here we find one of our earliest, if not our earliest commitments to the PNC. What turns back on itself (παλίντροπος) is not. Plato famously adopts this commitment from Parmenides' *Way of Truth*. Universals have Being and are called the things that are (ὄντα) because they are the objects of thought and are thereby non-contradictory. To take an example from *Phaedo*, while the Form of Equality is never itself unequal, but is always equal to itself, sensible objects, e.g., the human hand, are both equal and unequal to themselves and to others. Moreover, for Parmenides, Being is indivisible. If Being were divisible, it would be divisible into Being and non-being. Yet, there is no non-being into which Being could be divided. Thus, there is *only Being in Being*.

Hence, 'Being is' shows that Beings is indivisible. Being is Being and is not non-being. As such, Being is indivisible from itself. Non-contradiction insures that Being is indivisible. What is indivisible cannot cease to be, whereas what is divisible can be divided and thereby can cease to be. Conspicuously, Plato adopts this measure of Being in his Theory of Forms insofar as he establishes the eternal existence of Forms by appealing to the indivisibility of their being. Parmenides' influence cannot be overstated.[6]

For Parmenides, Being itself—the what it is to be—is the only being that is. Being is both that which is thought (*nous*) and the only being that is. *Being is a being*, and it is *the only being* there is. Parmenides does not see any contradiction in his proclamation that only Being is. Rather, he only sees contradiction in what is not. Parmenides' identification of non-being with sensible things can also be traced to Parmenides' *Way of Opinion*, for Parmenides' examples of 'back turning' are culled from nature.[7] To be is to be thinkable, and this requires the mutual exclusion of opposites. Sensible objects are not *qua* sensible thinkable, as their principles are contraries.

In order to know that non-being is not a road of inquiry, I need to think non-being, in order to see how it transforms into what it is not, namely Being. Thus, in order to see Parmenides' argument I need to be able to think what is not thinkable.[8] The very fact that Parmenides proposes the *Way of Opinion* is a problem, since this has no being. Parmenides' account famously turns back on itself (παλίντροπος) by contradicting itself in its very exclusion of non-being from what can be thought. Indeed, since the knowledge that Being is the only intelligible object of inquiry depends upon this contradiction, even the inquiry into Being itself appears paradoxical.

Though this is the most obvious contradiction, the contradiction most pertinent to our analysis comes into play when Parmenides' identification of Being with a being introduces *division* when he means to exclude it. Being is a being: it is *both* universal and particular: it is *the* being that is. There is no particular—there is *only* Being, yet there is at least *one* particular—Being *itself*. In other words, insofar as Being is universal, it ought *not* be particular, and *vice versa*—yet they are here identified. Or still in another formulation, difference becomes present exactly where it cannot be present—the contradiction arises precisely because difference arises where there is *no* difference at all. This logical problem is quite independent of the fact that Parmenides' position, were it consistent, is nonetheless false, for *beings exist* in addition to Being itself.

In the Western tradition, the claim that 'the universal is a particular' is a conceptual formulation of a *problem* that goes by the name 'ontotheology.' Of course, Parmenides does not recognize the identification of Being (the universal) with a being (the particular) as a problem. Quite the contrary—he considers it *the only consistent position*!

What for Parmenides is the way of opinion is for Heraclitus the way of truth. According to Heraclitus, 'They do not comprehend how, in differing [diaferomenon], it agrees with itself-a back turning harmony [παλίντροπος] like that of a bow and a lyre.'[9] Plato states in Cratylus 402A that 'Heraclitus says somewhere that everything moves and nothing rests; and comparing what exists to a river, he says that you would not step twice into the same river.' If what exists is like a river, then it is always changing. Since it is always changing, the change is constant. Therefore, the change itself is not changing but is itself constant. The 'back-turning harmony' is a self-referring harmony: change, insofar as it is change, is not changing.[10] In virtue of the river's differing, it agrees with itself, and in its self-agreement it is self-differing. Like Parmenides, Heraclitus' discussion of the back-turning harmony applies to nature: 'God is day and dusk, winter and summer, war and peace, satiety and famine.'[11]

The unity of opposition constituting what exists hides in thinking, for when we say or think that 'what exists is changing', our judgment implies that it is 'not constant.' If we say that 'what exists is constant' then we imply that that is 'not changing.'[12] So, as Plutarch states in "Why the Pythia No Longer Prophesies" in Verse 404 E, instead of speaking, we indicate: 'I think that you know Heraclitus' remark that the king whose is the oracle at Delphi neither speaks nor conceals but indicates.'[13] Heraclitus' aphorisms are obscure, not simply because we do not have the context of his writing, but because he violates non-contradiction in his own thought by predicating opposing predicates to the same subject in the same respect.

Heraclitus rightly recognizes the necessity of the *truth* of the identification of opposites, or the necessity of the truth of contradiction, while Parmenides fails to see that his own position turns back on itself. Parmenides misses the dialectical and thereby self-undermining aspect of his own thinking, as is *par for the course* in onto-theological thought. By insisting on the *univocity* of thought, thought becomes *equivocal*, or what is the same, *Monism eliminates itself* through its own back-turning procedure.

The Elimination of the Absolute

Already we can see that any conceptualization of the concept that insists that the concept is constituted by a *duality* of principles of universality and particularity falls victim to at least these *three* problems—the Missing Difference, Absolute Empiricism, and Onto-theology. Earlier I noted that even if we *bracket* any question about whether the Absolute can be truly conceived by modeling it on the dualistic structure of conceptual determinacy, any concept of the concept constituted by the duality of principles of universality and particularity is inherently incoherent. Because it is incoherent on its own terms, it certainly cannot function as a plausible model for thinking the Absolute. Now I propose that we un-bracket the question concerning the relationship between the concept and the Absolute and consider why modeling the Absolute on the dualistic conception of the concept engenders *the complete disappearance of the Absolute* or what in the modern literature one might more call—in the terms of Markus Gabriel—'the disappearance of the world.' In what follows I demonstrate that any attempt to *preserve* the being of the Absolute by modeling our understanding of it on the dualistic conception of the concept leads to its complete *annihilation*. Accordingly, the problem of onto-theology has a special place in our critique, far more than any other, it illuminates the impossibility of successfully grasping Absolute Being or Absolute Knowing by positing two principles of truth.

The Absolute is not just universal but unconditionally universal. As unconditioned, it excludes nothing and is thereby all-encompassing—it is the One and All, the Ἓν καὶ Πᾶν. Per the analyses in Chapters 1 and 2, the Absolute can be construed in terms of knowing or being. Either tendency in conceiving the Absolute must take the other into account, for the knowing would not be Absolute knowing were it to exclude Being, just as Absolute Being would not be Absolute were it to exclude knowing. In either case, the universal would be conditioned upon something that it excludes. Thus, whether the inquiry into the Absolute be primarily characterized as metaphysics or epistemology, the epistemic must be metaphysical and the metaphysical epistemic. Because of this mutual inclusivity, I will employ overtly metaphysical terminology. In addition, I will also use this language in order to simplify the terms of the argument and because it is in closer keeping with the terminology of the philosophers I will be discussing later in the chapter, most importantly Aristotle and Aquinas.

Indeed, in the discussion of the finite form of the concept, we demonstrated that because the dualistic conception of the concept is true in virtue of something other than itself, it cannot achieve truth in virtue of itself alone. Thus, we inferred that this construal of conceptual truth is incongruent with *Absolute truth*. Because the concept is incongruent with Absolute truth, any act of absolutizing what does not have absolute truth, what cannot be *auto kath auto*, ought to result in contradiction. In what follows we will demonstrate this by *reductio*: upon raising the concept to the status of the Absolute, the Absolute disappears. Or what is the same: by raising the concept to the status of the Absolute, the concept fails to abide by the principles of conceptual determinacy by which it is intelligible. Accordingly, the divorce between the dualistic construal of the concept and its *true existence* can be more vividly and precisely demonstrated by assuming that the Absolute is structured according to a separation of the principles of universality and particularity, and thereby reduce the claim to an absurdity on its own terms.

In his *Critique of Pure Reason*, Kant undertakes a radical new philosophical beginning by uncovering a latent dogmatism in traditional metaphysics. Any inquiry into the 'what it is to be' of Being must already assume that the subject, via its reason, has the capacity to know 'what it is to be.' Accordingly, in order to attain a critical relationship to our own question about the meaning of Being, the philosopher must interrogate her own reason. We can return to the question again: is *reason capable of knowing what it is to be*, or more simply: *to what extent is Being accessible to reason*?

Given the fact that the mode of conceptual thinking here operative demands an appeal to the given, irrespective of whether what it is to which we have access is present to us merely *phenomenologically*, what is given to philosophical reflection nonetheless *is*. Insofar as there is the fact of the givenness or presence of *some being* to philosophical reflection, we are justified to raise the question: 'what is it to be?' Being is that *in virtue of which* that which is given *is*. Perhaps ironically then, we follow Heidegger by asking the old question again and interrogate Being. What is it to be?

Since the Absolute is unconditioned, it is autonomous, for there is nothing limiting it by which it could be in relation to another. Thus, in order to raise the concept to an Absolute status, we must posit the structures of conceptual determinacy as though they were *autonomous*. Since Being is all-encompassing, and nothing lies outside of it, in order to know it one must think it *by itself*. Thus, our method consists in thinking Being *autonomously*. Following Heidegger, 'to think is to confine yourself to a single thought.'[14] As I will show, by isolating Being and attending to it *auto kath auto*,[15] the concept of Being shows itself to be both self-predicating and self-negating. Having witnessed the self-negation of Being, the dualistic model of conceptual determination that rejects self-predication must recognize its own *impotence* in the face of Being. The impotence of the concept in the face of Being discloses the impossibility of a dominant strain of traditional metaphysics and epistemology. On the model of the dualistic constitution of the concept, reason cannot know what it is to be. Nonetheless, through the failure of reason to think Being, a new path opens in the *Lichtung*. Though metaphysics appears to be impossible, the 'what it is to be' of Being cannot remain hidden: it is revealed as what *exceeds* the dualistic conception of the concept in the experience of the annihilation of conceptual determinacy.

In order to demonstrate that Being exceeds conceptual determination, I will proceed by assuming that Being has conceptual form (as specified on the dualistic model) and thereby reduce the assumption to an absurdity on its own terms.[16] What is Being? Being is that in virtue of which any being *is*. As Heidegger noted, the question 'what is Being?' is self-referential.[17] In asking 'what is it?' one must already implicitly appeal to Being. Being *appears* to be the most *universal* predicate. Indeed, there appears to be nothing more general and nothing more extensive to predicate of a subject. Everything is a *differentiation* of Being and accordingly belongs in the *genus* of Being. As the most universal predicate, one cannot posit anything *beyond* Being. Since Being is not only universal but also the most universal predicate, on this view Being would be unconditioned, for there is nothing outside of it that could condition it. As the unconditioned universal it is *the absolute*. Schelling, in his unpublished *Ages of the World*, foretells what we may expect from the unconditioned absolute.[18]

In order to evaluate Schelling's claim that thinking the Absolute results in contradiction, we must first consider the *generic* structure of concepts. After all, if Being is the most universal predicate or concept, one must first posit what a concept is *in advance*. To be brief, earlier we established that traditionally concepts have been conceived as governed by the *PNC*, whether they be construed as genera, abstractions, or classes. Despite their significant differences, each of these traditional perspectives shares a structure in common. In each case it is assumed that concepts are governed by the PNC and that *concepts are not sufficient to differentiate their particulars*.

Take, for example, the concept 'mammal.' As an abstract universal, 'mammal' only specifies the common feature of the particulars; it does not differentiate 'ox' from 'human being' or 'Socrates' from 'Aristotle.' If we conceive of the 'mammal' as a genus, the genus may contain other universals, namely species, but it cannot be the principle by which those species are differentiated. Again, 'mammal' may *contain* the species 'human being,' but specifying what a mammal is will not give sufficient conditions for differentiating 'human being' from 'ox.' Otherwise, being a mammal would be *sufficient* for being a human or an ox, which would engender a contradiction. In such a case, the genus would also be its own species—the universal its *own* particular. Given that concepts are governed by the PNC, 'mammal' cannot be sufficient for differentiating its particulars. Finally, even on the conception of the universal as a class, in which the particulars *constitute* the universal as the *members* of the set, neither the totality of the set nor the fact of membership in the set will be sufficient to differentiate each member. If we conceive of 'mammal' as the totality of mammals, we do not possess the resources to differentiate each of the particular members from each other. As long as concepts are governed by the PNC, universals cannot be sufficient principles for the differentiation of particulars.

Given that concepts are not sufficient for the differentiation of their own particulars, in order to differentiate the particulars that fall under any abstract universal (or within any class or genus), one must appeal to other concepts *outside* of the class or genus that one intends to differentiate. Accordingly, as we established earlier, it appears to be a classical principle of conceptual determinacy that the principles of universality and particularity are *separate* logical principles.[19] As long as concepts are governed by the PNC, the principles of universality and particularity must be separate. When we reflect on the Absolute or Being, we find that Being appears to stand in stark conflict with these features of conceptual determinacy.

The question 'what is Being?' looks toward what differentiates Being as such from beings. By differentiating Being, we are looking to think it *separately*, in order that we may get at Being as it is *autonomously* of that to which it is attributed. Since on the traditional view no concept can be self-differentiating, the difference by which a concept is differentiated must come from *outside* of that concept. Given that there is nothing more universal than Being, there is neither a concept (nor any*thing* else for that matter) by which Being could be differentiated. Since there is nothing external to Being by which it could be differentiated, Being must be *undifferentiated*. The claim that Being as such must be *undifferentiated* is not novel. Indeed, in the tradition thinkers as diverse as Philo and Meister Eckhart have posited Being as indivisible. Since Being as Being is utterly undifferentiated, Being as such is not only in fact undivided but is necessarily *indivisible*. Since unity in its most primary sense is indivisibility, Being is simply one and thereby has a *univocal* sense.

In the book of *Exodus*,[20] Moses asks God for his name. God's response is 'I am that I am.' The name of God is 'Being.' For medieval philosophy, the inquiry into Absolute Being can just as well be discussed as an inquiry into God. Duns Scotus famously argued that speaking of the 'Being' of God and the 'Being' of what is not-divine, such as a human being, is not a difference in *kind*, but in *degree*. Although God exists to a greater degree than other beings, 'Being' is *univocally predicated* of God and other beings. Indeed, Scotus has good reason to affirm univocal predication. By knowing our own perfections, we are able to know those of God—although of course the latter are superior in degree to the former. If the predicates applied in the case of creatures such as human beings are not the same in *kind* as those in the case of God, we will not be able to infer anything about God's perfections from knowledge of the creation. In order for us to be able to know the predicates that apply to God (among other reasons), the perfections we apply to God ought to be the same that apply to the creatures.[21] Simply put, the univocity of predication ensures the possibility of *kataphatic* theology pursued from a natural theological point of view. Still, as we will shortly see, the univocal view of the meaning of Being undermines itself and engenders an *equivocal* perspective.

Through thinking Being autonomously, we discover Being to be *autonomous*, for it is set *apart* from all differentiated beings. Insofar as it is set apart from all differentiated beings, it *transcends* all differentiated beings. As a result of taking up Being as the most universal predicate, we are easily led to posit Being as the transcendent, undifferentiated unity as distinct from all differentiated beings.[22] In Kantian terminology, taking up Being as a predicate engenders transforming the *regulative* principle of thoroughgoing determination into a singular entity that transcends beings.[23] In Heidegger's language, the philosopher who identifies Being as a predicate risks falling into the trap of *onto-theology*: the identification of Being with a being we discovered in the thought of Parmenides. On its face, the undifferentiated state of Being appears to correspond with the thesis that the domain of concepts is itself undifferentiated.

Of course, it is not the case that *only* Being is. Given that beings *exist*, what is the status of the various beings, the various differentiations of the highest genus? Since Being is undifferentiated, the differences cannot have their origin in Being. Indeed, they seem to *disappear* into nothing. Since the differentiation of Being must have its origin outside Being, and only nothing is outside Being, each differentiation of Being can only have its origin in *nothing*. Since the differences as such can only have their origin in nothing, there cannot be any absolute ground of the differentiation of beings *insofar* as they are. To the question: 'why is there anything at all?', there could not be a response that appeals to any *being*. To answer with 'nothing' in response to the question is tantamount to the impossibility of any 'why.' In this way, there is no necessity for the existence of the differentiation of entities. Given that their being is not necessary, their being is *contingent*. In respect to its being, each being could have been (and could be) *otherwise* than it is. In the absence of any ground for the being of particular differentiations in general, their being appears *spontaneous*: they appear *un*caused, for there is no being that could be responsible for the differentiations as such.[24] The contingency of the differentiation is grounded in its origin in the nothing out of which it comes.

The traditional perspective of the *creation ex nihilo* maintains that creation is *out of nothing*. Indeed, insofar as God is indivisibly one, it would be problematic to have all things come from God. On the other hand, since God is posited as the cause of all things, God cannot rely upon a pre-existent material out of which to make the world. As Aquinas points out, creation ex nihilo appears to be the only other plausible answer. Of course, as we discussed in Chapter 2, this thesis is not rationally coherent, for on the terms of the theologians themselves, *nothing comes from nothing*. Only something with the potential to be something can give something, and nothing as such has no potential. Thus, for traditional theology creation must be accepted as a truth of faith.

Nonetheless, the doctrine of *creation ex nihilo* can be employed to advocate for the view that predications of God and the creation are always *equivocal*. For Maimonides, because God is indivisible Being, God cannot have any attributes. If God had any attributes, God would be divisible, for each attribute would be distinguished from the others. 'Power' is not the same attribute as 'wisdom.' One necessary condition of each attribute is that each is distinct from the other—each has its *own articulation*. Thus, any attribute predicated of God would divide God. In order to preserve the indivisibility of God, God cannot have any attributes. According to his *Guide for the Perplexed:*

> If you have a desire . . . to hold the conviction that God is one and possesses true unity, without admitting plurality or divisibility in any sense whatever, you must understand that God has no essential attribute in any Form or any sense whatever.[25]

Of course, for Maimonides, God cannot have any incidental predicates either, for this would also engender divisibility. Indeed, any attempt to introduce attribution into God using human terminology is tantamount to an affirmation of *polytheism*.

Since God precludes all negation, and creation is created by God *out of nothing*, creatures are *divorced* from God by an inseparable gulf: they are constituted by negation, while God is *free* of all negation. Accordingly, whatever predicates one might ascribe to God would be completely different in kind than those attributed to creatures. Indeed, Maimonides famously proclaims that God and human beings have *no similarity*:

> Since the existence of a relation between God and man, or between Him and other beings has been denied, similarity must likewise be denied.[26]

Because God and creatures are neither related nor similar, when one speaks about the Being of God and the Being of creatures, the terms cannot have the same meaning. Although each term has the same sensory form expressed in the word 'Being' the meaning is completely different or *equivocal*. The terms have the outer form in common but completely non-commensurate meanings. Accordingly, the terms are *homonyms*:

> The term existence, when applied to God and to other beings, is perfectly homonymous. In like manner, the terms wisdom, power, will, and life are applied to God and to other beings by way of perfect homonymy, admitting of no comparison whatever.[27]

Naturally, this leads to paradoxical utterances, for the term 'existence' is uttered by the human being who only has access to predicates applicable to the creature. Accordingly, Maimonides informs us that God 'exists without the attribute of existence' and has 'life without the attribute of life.'[28] Ultimately, the non-relationality of God to the creatures engenders a radically *negative* theology. Having seen the true implication of the view, the theologian endorses silence as the only true posture towards the indivisible God.

Indeed, if we follow what is entailed by the *undifferentiated* characteristic of Being, we discover that there is no principle that necessitates the differentiation of Being from nothing. Beyond the undifferentiated character of Being, both Hegel and Heidegger recognized the necessary *identity* of Being and nothing.[29] As what has *no* difference at all, Being as such is nothing. Given that there are no differences *in* Being from which it could be differentiated from anything else, no difference between Being and nothing can be discovered. If Being were differentiated from nothing, then it would not be undifferentiated, and there would be something outside Being by which Being would be differentiated from nothing. Since this is impossible, Being is *in*distinguishable from nothing. If Being were *some-thing*, then it could in principle be differentiated from other *some-things*. Since Being does not stand opposed to other beings (for it is supposed to be the most universal genus), but only to nothingness, Being is not a being and does not have a difference. As identical to nothing, Being *not only is univocal* but must also be *equivocal* in meaning.

This fact is recognized in the Sufi saying that 'God is greater'; he is not greater than anything, since there is nothing with which to contrast God. He is simply 'greater.' Indeed, this shows the depth of the Sufi reading of the Muslim statement of faith 'there is no God but God.' This means not only that there is only one God but that there is no division in that one God. God is the only being and that being is indivisible. Still, if this were true, the problem of the origin of division and plurality would be radicalized. How in principle could there be plurality or division? If it this is simply denied, how is the illusion of plurality to be accounted for? Indeed, at least the illusion of plurality exists, and this is not the same as the reality that there is no plurality.

Indeed, to return to Scotus, if we acknowledge the univocity of Being, we cannot give an account of the difference between Being and nothing, for attributing 'Being' to a thing does not differentiate it from any other thing that 'is.' Accordingly, the univocity of Being enders not only that it is *undifferentiated* but also that it cannot be distinguished from nothing. Thus, insisting on the univocity of Being results in contradiction—in equivocation. To return to Maimonides, we might express ourselves by proclaiming that the very same gulf that supposedly separates creatures from divinity is that which connects them together. In the case of God, insisting on equivocal predication is not really distinct from univocal predication as Maimonides might insist, for the univocal sense of Being engenders an absolute equivocation. Indeed, the Being of God is univocal and equivocal—God's equivocity is the equivocity of univocity and equivocity—and *identity of opposition*.

Taking a clue from Meister Eckhart, although Being appears to transcend all beings, this cannot be the whole truth.[30] Insofar as Being is the undifferentiated *nothing*, it cannot be differentiated from any particular being whatever. Accordingly, Being as nothing cannot be distinguished from all differentiated beings. As Eckhart teaches:

> Therefore, God is free of all things, and therefore he is all things.[31]

Medieval mysticism—especially that of Meister Eckhart—draws the dialectical inference underplayed or not fully appreciated by Scotus and Maimonides. Being is not just univocally said of God and creatures—for this misses the difference in kind. Predication of God is not merely equivocal in relation to non-divine predication, for this misses their identity. It is rather that exactly in virtue of the divorce of Being from all beings that Being is indistinguishable from all beings.

Being as the undifferentiated nothing is necessarily *omnipresent* and *immanent* in all entities. Given that the nothing is omnipresent in all things, and there is *nothing beyond the nothing*, the nothing is *absolute*. 'Nothing' in this sense is not a particular negation of *this* or *that*, but Absolute Nothingness. Given that this nothing is omnipresent and immanent in all entities, and this nothing is absolute, Absolute Nothingness is omnipresent and immanent in all things. Our reflections have brought us to the doorstep of *Metaphysical Nihilism*, by which I mean the thesis that *Being is absolutely nothing* which necessarily pervades all things. But it is not just that Absolute Nothingness pervades all beings, for our discussion of the contingency of beings indicates that all beings also have their *origin* in nothingness. This is one reading of Heidegger's famous line that '*Das Nichts nichtet.*' This phrase 'Das Nichts nichtet' expresses both the creative and destructive side of nothingness: all beings *arise from* nothing, and all beings *return to* Nothing—for there is nothing else from which or to which the beings may arise or to which they may return.

From the preceding argument we can infer that Being does not have conceptual form according to the traditional determinations of the concept. Given that categories are differentiated externally, and Being cannot be externally differentiated, it follows that Being is inconsistent with the form of conceptual determination. Indeed, while concepts (on the traditional model conceived earlier) are governed by the PNC and ought not admit their negations, Being admits its own negation, nothing, and is *identical* with it. Accordingly, on this model *Being is not a predicate*. Still, our argument for falling in line behind Kant in this matter is different.[32] Being is a contradiction for on the model of finite conceptual determinacy it exceeds conceptual determination. Being and predication fall onto opposing sides: predication precludes Being, and Being precludes predication.

Each being, insofar as it is differentiated from others, *excludes* what is other to it, and in this way requires some particular negation(s) for the formulation of their differentiation. Given that nothingness is undifferentiated, if nothingness were conceived as a separate being, or a particular negation that stood opposed to others, it would fail to be undifferentiated. Thus, to be undifferentiated, Absolute Nothingness must be differentiated into particular, differentiated beings, which require particular negations for the formulation of their differentiation from each other. Thus, nothingness can only be undifferentiated insofar as it *differentiates itself from itself* into differentiated beings and their corresponding negations. In this way, the negating process of Absolute Nothingness is also a *self-negating* process. Only through its differentiation from its undifferentiated being (and thereby its identity with differentiated beings and their corresponding negations) can Absolute Nothingness (or Absolute Being) be truly absolute and undifferentiated. Accordingly, Absolute Nothingness (and Absolute Being) returns to itself out of its own negation, that is, it appears to be a *self-differentiating* process. Absolute Being, as well as Absolute Nothingness, *is* absolute in virtue of the identity of differentiation and its negation (identity).[33]

The process of self-differentiation mentioned earlier may also be described as a process of *self-creation* and *self-destruction*. If all differences and determinate beings are grounded in nothing, which is tantamount (under this conceptual scheme) to being utterly groundless or without reason, then the difference between Being and nothing must have its origin in nothing and must also be contingent. Since Absolute Nothingness has its origin in itself, all differentiations of Nothing have their origin in nothing. Or what is the same: all differentiation of Being have their origin in Being itself. Simply put: *Being is self-differentiating*. Since, on the model of finite conceptual determination, there is no reason for this creation, and no reason can be given, the differentiations of the Absolute are contingent.

What is posited or represented *as* Being or *as* nothing could be otherwise. Likewise, any difference posited between *Absolute* Nothingness and *relative* negations, or *Absolute* Being and *particular* beings, would also have its origin in nothing and would be contingent. Since any difference posited between Absolute and relative Nothingness (as well as Absolute and relative Being) has its origin in the Absolute Nothing, any determination or representation of Absolute Nothingness (as it might contrast with relative negations) has its origin in the Absolute itself.

What is more, any distinction that has being (and this includes conceptual differentiation) must ultimately be grounded in the non-conceptual form of Being as such, otherwise it would not *be*. The existence of conceptual differentiation, indeed, any differentiation whatever, must be grounded in Being's *non-conceptual* self-differentiation. In this way we make some headway in unraveling a cryptic aphorism of the great Romantic Novalis:[34]

Wir suchen überall das Unbedingte, und finden immer nur Dinge.

The preceding argument is a *reductio ad absurdum* on the assumption that Being is conceptually determined. If we assume that Being is determined conceptually, then we must always posit an external difference by which Being is differentiated, for concepts (on a variety of traditional perspectives) are not sufficient principles for the differentiation of their particulars. Following this requirement, if Being were conceptual in form, it would be externally differentiated, which would be impossible, given that *there is nothing* external to Being. Given that Being must be undifferentiated, it follows that Being could not be differentiated from nothing. Thus, if Being is posited as having conceptual form, then Being is contradictory. Now, if we were to attempt to escape this absurdity, we would be required to *reject the principle that led to the contradiction in the first place*. The principle that engendered the contradiction is the principle that a concept must be differentiated externally. Therefore, in order to avoid the contradiction (the identification of Being with nothing), we must reject the very assumption that Being has conceptual form and is governed by the PNC. So, our only hope to avoid the contradiction would be to reject the assumption that Being has conceptual form. But if we reject the assumption that Being has conceptual form, then we would have demonstrated the very conclusion we wish to avoid, namely that Being is non-conceptual.[35] Regarding those who hold that Being is conceptually determined, we might allow Heraclitus to speak on our behalf: 'They do not comprehend how, in differing, it agrees with itself-a back turning harmony [παλίντροπος] like that of a bow and a lyre.'[36]

These reflections demonstrate a deeper sense of *the finitude of the concept*. The concept is not only finite because it is true in virtue of an external principle, as we elucidated before. Rather, its finitude lies in the fact that because its truth is outside of itself, it is *in itself a falsehood*. Or what is the same, the finite is that which, because its limit is contained within itself, contains its own *non-being*. The finitude of the concept has here been thought through to its logical conclusion: the concept *negates itself* or ceases to be in virtue of what it is. Self-annihilation is the truth of finitude.

We read that Jacob wrestled with God. This old allegory continues to nourish us deeply, for we, every one of us, is Jacob, and we wrestle with and interrogate the first principle, whose secrets are only revealed when we cease to inquire after its name. Insofar as concepts *qua* concepts have no Being, is it not a wonder that we ever encounter them at all? Indeed, insofar as we do encounter concepts, we may make the same claim about concepts that we made about Being: in order to believe 'that the concept is,' we must also believe the impossible to be possible. But in this case, the only way the concept would have being would be *as* non-conceptual. As Heidegger succinctly states:

That a thinking is, ever and suddenly—
Whose amazement could fathom it?[37]

Given that Being eschews conceptual determination, the truth of Being cannot be understood in terms of the correspondence between a concept and an object. In this case, every conceptual correspondence fails, for Being is a necessary mystery. But given that Being is nonetheless uncovered as Being in the clearing away of conceptual determinacy, truth acquires a more fundamental significance as *non-conceptual disclosure*, or revelation to the subject. Accordingly, truth must be conceived as a relation of Being to the subject who receives it. Being is true or in its truth when it is no longer being concealed in the form of a matrix of concepts. In this case, any truth that is explicated in terms of the correspondence of a concept with an object is *contingent upon* the disclosure of what transcends concepts. The very existence of conceptual correspondence must itself be revealed in some non-conceptual act, without which it would not be possible. Truth becomes an act of recollection of what there is there before we ate of the Tree of Knowledge.

From these reflections we must conclude that it is in principle implausible that the Absolute can be *consistently* grasped on the model of conceptual determinacy in which the concept is constituted by a duality of principles of universality and particularity. To the contrary, any attempt to model the Absolute on a finite conception of the concept leads to the disappearance of the Absolute. Thought contradicts itself—Being becomes nothing. What is worse, traditional thought falls prey to this nihilism without knowing it. Indeed, it annihilates itself because it has the good intention of attempting to save itself from the nihilism that is engendered by attempting to deduce all difference and determination from one principle. Thus, on the finite model of conceptual determinacy, only *relative* determinations can be grasped, but even these relative determinations cannot be grasped as relative determinations *of the Absolute*, since the latter exceeds what can be consistently thought by the finite determination of the concept. For this reason, not even the relative determinations can be consistently grasped by the finite conception of the concept. Simply put, nothing at all should be, yet something is.

The world disappears whether we attempt to know the Absolute by modeling it on one principle of identity or a duality of principles of identity and difference. Because the Absolute cannot be conceived on the model of finite conceptual determinacy, a new opposition arises between the Absolute and conceptual determination. The Absolute appears to be *self-differentiating*, while concepts appear to be differentiated by *external principles*. The Absolute is infinite, and without conditions, while concepts are conditioned and finite. The PNC appears to extend over the latter, but does not appear to extend of the former. Any attempt to extend the PNC over the Absolute results in *self-contradiction*. In metaphysical parlance, by excluding the conceptual from the Absolute, the *very being* of the conceptual determinations are put into question. How in principle could conceptual determinations *exist*, if they can only exist in the Absolute as relative determinations of the Absolute?

Following the consequences of this reductio through to its final conclusions, we are reminded that both Aristotle and Kant introduce the PNC in order to *preserve the determinacy* of concepts, experience and, in Aristotle's case, things themselves. Following the specifications of Aristotle and Kant, contradiction engenders *total indeterminacy—each thing would be one thing and nothing at all*. Without the PNC, all conceiving of the object, as well as those objects conceived, would be radically indeterminate. Yet, our *reductio* has led to a startling conclusion: were the PNC treated as an Absolute principle, then the Absolute would itself be contradictory. Since contradictions engender absolute indeterminacy, it follows that when the PNC is absolutized, it cannot preserve determinacy, but rather *annihilates* it. But if we reject the PNC, or at least specify that there are exceptions, then the very same indeterminacy is realized. Accordingly, the depth of the paradox could be articulated as follows: were the PNC an Absolute principle, then it would engender an absolute indeterminacy. Yet, were the PNC not posited as an Absolute principle, then contradictions could still be true. Since contradiction engenders absolute indeterminacy, the denial of non-contradiction also leads right back into absolute indeterminacy. In sum, the self-destruction, or ceasing to be of the finitude of rational principles, leads to an impasse: how is *absolute conceptual determinacy* possible?

The problem of onto-theology manifests itself as the problem of the disappearance of the Absolute. More precisely, what has disappeared is any *determinate conception* of the Absolute. Absolute determinacy appears impossible. The PNC, if it has any application at all, appears to be a *relative* principle of knowing that can only govern the knowing of *relative* objects. The absolute principle and form of knowing has disappeared along with its object. Under the rule of non-contradiction, all conceptions become *relative conceptions of relative objects*.

Although it appears impossible for conceptual determinacy governed by non-contradiction to have Absolute status, as we indicated earlier, it appears just as impossible for it to have relative status. This absolute dichotomy between Absolute Being and the concept is problematic for many reasons, one of which is the fact that it ironically renders the indeterminate Absolute determinate. Indeed, this dichotomy places the Absolute—what has no conditions—on one side of an opposition and thereby *conditions the unconditioned*. This conditioning relativizes the Absolute, such that it stands in relation to something outside of it. This relativizing of the Absolute appears, ironically to *render the indeterminate Absolute determinate* and *relative to another*. If the Absolute is not governed by principles of conceptual determinacy, then it is not absolutely Absolute, but only relatively Absolute. Since the relative is not Absolute, the 'relative Absolute' is the *Absolute that is not Absolute*.

Ironically, the exclusion of the concept from the Absolute appears to make the *concept absolute*, for it preserves the self-identity of each as constituting two mutually exclusive sides of a contradictory opposition. Were the concept constituted by one side of an opposition, the Absolute would be rendered determinate and thereby conceivable. Thus, by relegating the PNC to one side of an opposition, the concept acquires Absolute Form, or what is the same: *the relative becomes absolutely non-relative*. By relegating the concept to relative status, it loses its relativity and acquires an absolute status, thereby becoming indeterminate and annihilating its determinate being. If the concept is merely determinate, then it cannot be determinate—it must be absolutely indeterminate. Simply put, the non-absolute character of the PNC is just as contradictory as its absolute character.

Because philosophical knowing proceeds by means of concepts, and raising the concept to an Absolute status, engenders a contradiction, philosophical knowing by means of concepts cannot achieve Absolute Knowledge. The externality of the truth of the concept *cannot be maintained* when the concept is rendered Absolute. Because the finite model of conceptual determination can never successfully conceptualize the Absolute, Absolute Knowing is just as much beyond its prospective scope as Absolute Being.

Without re-thinking the form and content of the concept of the concept, the Absolute *cannot be for conceptually thought* except *as a contradiction*. Absolute knowing *of* Absolute Being only exists for finite conceptual consciousness *as a contradiction*. Since the finite concept of the concept depends upon the Absolute in order to be (for it is a relative determination of Absolute Knowing and Being), conceptual thinking cannot remain satisfied with this opposition. Indeed, philosophical thinking cannot know itself if it does not know its condition, and its condition cannot help but appear to be a contradiction. If the condition for philosophical thinking were a contradiction, the true conception of philosophical thought would depend upon the truth of a contradiction. Yet, if philosophy proclaims that contradictions cannot be true, then the inability to think the Absolute consistently endangers the coherence of philosophy's own self-conception. In short, the Absolute (as well as a coherent concept of philosophical knowledge thereof) disappears *whenever* it is modelled on the finite determinacy of relative conceptuality.

The Pros Hen Account of the Absolute

In the historical reception of the problem of Onto-theology, Martin Heidegger stands out as the philosopher who most explicitly thematized this issue. Heidegger points out that the indefinable character of Being only means that Being cannot have the character of an entity.[38] In a famous passage, Heidegger claims that

> The Being of entities 'is' not itself an entity. If we are to understand the problem of Being, our first philosophical step consists in not muthon tina diegeisthai, in not 'telling a story'—that is to say, in not defining entities as entities by tracing them back in their origin to some other entities, as if Being had the character of some possible entity.[39]

Just as Being is always only the Being of beings, for Being is not a separate thing apart from beings, we are only ever on the way to Being, for it is just this absence of Being as a thing that sets us on a course without end. Long before Heidegger, Hegel and Kant recognized the significance of the problem.

Hegel's *Wissenschaft der Logik* begins with Being (*Sein*): 'Being is the indeterminate immediate.'[40] It is 'pure indeterminateness.'[41] As indeterminate, it cannot be posited vis-à-vis nothing and cannot be distinguished from it: 'each of them [Being and nothing] is in the same way indeterminate.'[42] Just as nothing is seen in pure darkness, so can nothing be seen in pure light. Hegel is careful not to fall into an onto-theological way of thinking, for he carefully distinguishes *Sein* from *Dasein*—the latter is *determinate* being, not mere Being. Hegel is clear that '*determinate being* is the first category to contain the real difference of being and nothing, namely, something and other.'[43] Since free science begins with indeterminate *Sein*, determinate being, *Dasein*, must develop out of the indeterminate.

Given that determinate being and knowing must arise out of indeterminate being and knowing, Hegel points out that philosophers have 'placed the essence of philosophy in the answering of the question: how does the infinite go forth from itself and make itself finite?'[44] Although Hegel discusses this question in respect to the infinite, the fact that the indeterminate has the infinite as one of its primary cognates is sufficient for us to introduce it here but in a new form: how does the *determinate* come to be out of the absolutely *indeterminate*? Indeed, it is only because of the recognition that philosophy cannot begin with determinacy that the problem of how the determinate arises in the first place becomes of central issue. Put in metaphysical terms, this is one of the most familiar questions: why is there something instead of nothing? *Ex nihilo nihil fit* stands as a testament to the hegemony of determinacy.

Before Hegel's dialectical treatment of the issue, Kant explicitly identified the problem of onto-theology in his *Critique of Pure Reason*. In his table of categories, 'negation' appears as the second category of three under *Quality*: reality, negation, and limitation.[45] The third category is a synthesis of the first two: limitation is *reality combined with negation*.[46] Indeed, as a category, it is not derivative, but *un*derived. For a concept to become determinate, the possible predicates that could apply to it must be *limited*. Accordingly, determination requires both the concepts of reality (in this case some affirmative conceptual content) and negation. Following the tradition, Kant ascribes the law of non-contradiction to the form of logical knowing, such that only *determinable concepts* can count as abiding by the form of logical knowing. In this vein, although contradictions are necessarily false, consistent propositions are not necessarily true, but are candidates for truth, for the concept could still fail to correspond with its object. Following the tradition, Kant restricts the form of logical cognition to *determinate knowing*, according to which determinacy has been privileged over indeterminacy as a necessary condition for entering into the domain of truth.

Long before Heidegger's famous critique of onto-theology, Kant offered his own critique of onto-theology grounded in the principle of thoroughgoing determination (*Grundsatze der durchgängingen Bestimmung*).[47] By positing a transcendental substratum under the sum of all possible predicates, one arrives at a concept of a being, namely God, which becomes the subject of the sum of all possible predicates.[48] If the thoroughgoing determination of things is grounded on a transcendental substratum, reason arrives at the concept of the All of Reality or the *omnitudo realitatis*.[49] The condition of the possibility of the complete determination of things, is thereby transformed into the Transcendental Ideal, a concept of a thing-in-itself (a thing independent of all possible experience), which has been variously described as an *ens realissimum* (the most real being), *ens orginarium* (the original being), *ens summum* (the highest being), and *ens entium* (the Being of beings).[50]

Although reason does presuppose the Idea of such a being,[51] and this Ideal represents a relationship between an Idea, a representation of the Absolute, with concepts,[52] the Ideal, the Being of beings, *cannot be given determinately*:

> Now if we pursue this idea of ours so far as to hypostatize it, then we will be able to determine the original being through the mere concept of the highest reality as a being . . . in a word, we will be able to determine it in tis unconditioned completeness through all predications.
>
> Meanwhile, this use of the transcendental ideal would already be over-stepping the boundaries of its vocation and its permissibility. For on it, as the concept of all reality, reason only grounded the thoroughgoing determinacy of things in general, without demanding that this reality should be given objectively, and itself constitute a thing. The latter is a mere fiction, through which we encompass and realize the manifold of our idea in an ideal, as a particular being; for this

we have no warrant, not even for directly assuming the possibility of such a hypothesis.[53]

Indeed, Kant's insight is profound: *the principle of all determinations cannot itself be a determination*. Kant is clear that there is no object congruent to this Ideal,[54] it can never be given in concreto.[55] Indeed, the Idea of the Absolute, the principle in virtue of which there are determinations, must remain indeterminate. Despite their very different philosophical approaches, just as for Kant the Being of beings, that is the Transcendental Ideal, is not itself a being, for Heidegger Being is not a being.[56]

In short, every attempt to conceive of the Absolute restricts the Absolute to a particular determination, a thing among things. Even conceptualizing the Absolute *as indeterminate* places it into a determinate relation with determinacy and thereby falls victim to onto-theology. The indeterminacy of the Absolute can only be appreciated if one recognizes that the Absolute exceeds every concept (even that of indeterminacy).

Since Heidegger's critique of onto-theology, Aristotle and the Aristotelian tradition, including Thomism, have been charged with peddling a form of onto-theology. But if we take a close look at the thinking of both Aristotle and Aquinas, it becomes evident that their account of the genus of Being as *pros hen* cannot be appreciated without acknowledging the fact that it is introduced (at least in the case of Aristotle) to *undermine* the naïve identification of Being with a being. Despite this nuance, the *pros hen* account of being inevitably falls victim to an onto-theological conception insofar as God, the being upon which all beings depend, is both *Being itself* and a particular being. This is most obvious in Thomas' appropriation of Aristotle's conception of *pros hen* in his *analogical* unity of Being.

As is well known, Aristotle is committed to the thesis that Being is not a genus.[57] A genus provides an account of what unities the members of the genus, but a genus does not provide for the differentiation of the species. To find some way to differentiate the genus, one must look outside the genus. This process poses a particular problem for the most universal genera, as we have already indicated. Since Being includes all beings, nothing external to Being could differentiate it. Hence, none of the species of Being could be differentiated. As the highest genus, one could only distinguish the genus of Being from others by knowing *how* it is distinct from its own species. Since the differentia for the species are unknown, Being is also unknown. So, if being were a genus, then Being could not be differentiated from Nothing, since there would be nothing external to Being to divide the genus.

If Being were a genus, then it would be nothing, and this is a contradiction. Hence, Being is not a genus. Since one science studies one genus, if Being is not a genus, there is no science of Being. Since for Aristotle one science knows one genus, a science of Being would study one genus of

Being. In order to establish that there is a science of Being, Aristotle must establish the generic unity of Being. But given the fact that *the generic structure of genera* precludes any science of Being, Aristotle must introduce another kind of genera in order to account for the possibility of a science of Being.

Spinoza famously argues that there is only one Substance. One major systematic problem for Spinoza, however, is how one ought to derive the attributes of God. The origin of the difference between the attributes could not be found in the concept of the one Substance. Instead, these attributes had to be posited from *outside the concept*. By positing one Substance, one fails to account for the differences that are necessary for the explication of the divine attributes. One of Spinoza's external sources is Descartes by re-thinking the Cartesian Substances of 'extension' and 'thought' as attributes. Aristotle avoids this problem in advance by rejecting the monism of Substance.

To avoid the conclusion that there cannot be a science of Being, Aristotle distinguishes between two kinds of genera: *kath hen* (according to one) and *pros hen* (pointing towards one) genera. Aristotle's argument against the generic structure of being is directed toward the former: Being cannot be a *kath hen* genus. We can correlate the argument in Gamma that being is governed by the PNC with Aristotle's argument that being is not a genus. Since Being would admit contradiction if it were a kath hen genus, Being can only be governed by the PNC if it is *not* a kath hen genus. The conclusion that Being is not a kath hen genus only follows if the meaning of Being is not contradictory. The arguments in Book Gamma for the thesis that Being is governed by the PNC ensures that being does not admit non-being. Aristotle's *Metaphysics* is an inquiry into Being *qua* Being, which can only be possible if the principles of thought extend over Being.[58] Although Aristotle first addresses the possibility of a science of metaphysics in book Beta, it is in book Gamma where Aristotle establishes the fact that there *is* a science of Being *qua* Being.[59]

Since for Aristotle contrariety is the *greatest difference* within one genus,[60] a genus cannot be divided further. Since one side of the contrariety is a privation, and is thereby the lack of some positive content, the unity *measuring the genus* cannot be the privation. Instead, the measure of the *kath hen* genus is the affirmative side of the contrary, for example for Aristotle white is the measure of the genus of color, and black is the privation.[61] Since each knowledge studies one genus and the affirmative side of a contrary measures the genus, for kath hen genera, each knowledge studies *one pair of contraries*.

Since the genus only provides the *unity* of the members, but not that which differentiates them into species, something external to the genus must divide the genus. The differentia is what differentiates the genus, and the genus is the matter for the differentiation. This difference is the prior difference which divides the genus into species. The genus together with the differentia is the measure of the genus, or the definition, which is the positive term in the contrary. For example, in the *kath hen* genus of color, 'white' is the measure of the genus of color and 'dilating' is the differentia of that genus. Each contrary has an opposite, and this is the absence of that measure. If there is a middle in between the contrary terms, this is a composite of the privation and the measure.

Aristotle recognizes that there are many different kinds of things. These different kinds of things are defined by their own differentia. Were Being one *kath hen* genus, then Being would be differentiated by a single difference. Since the difference specifies the what it is to be (or the Essence) of the thing, were Being differentiated by one single difference, then Being itself would have *one Essence*. Thus, all beings insofar as they are beings, would have the same Essence, and they would also thereby possess the same essential attributes as all other beings. But Aristotle is clear that this is not only logically impossible (as we have already demonstrated) but even if it were logically possible, it would still be *factually inaccurate*: what it is to be a human being is not the same thing as what it is to be a heavenly body, just as the *per se* attributes of the One are not the same as that of the other. There are many kinds of entities, each of which are in possession of their own essential attributes. Aristotle's argument against the generic structure of Being is a way of warding off *onto-theology*. Were Being defined by one genus and a difference, then all beings would be reduced to one thing. By rejecting the conception of Being as univocally measured by one principle (*kath hen*), Aristotle can successfully avoid the charge of onto-theology.

If Being is not said univocally, for each genus has its own measure, then one might raise the concern that the term 'Being' is simply equivocal, for it means something different in each case, and there is *not one thing* that is connoted in each case. The term 'Being' without further specification simply appears to equivocate on all the various measures of all the various genera: 'X,' 'W,' and 'R.' To put this worry in another language, it seems to be impossible to have a science of what is Absolute—there can only be science of *relative* determinations of the Absolute.

Since there is not one measure measuring all of the genera, each genus has its *own* measure. Because each has its own measure, and each is distinct, the structure of being is *not* the same for all beings. Instead, each genus is *analogous* to the other, since each shares the same *kind* of structure, yet each has a *different* measure. Thus, the structure of being is a kind of *analogy*. Such an analogous unity might be represented as a kind of proportionality: X/Y, W/Z, R/Q.[62] Here it is important to note that Aristotle draws a distinction between categories that belong to a thing, and the category of Thinghood. Although the measure of color can be defined by appealing to a difference and a proximate genus, and the human being is also defined by appeal to the difference and the proximate genus, *color is not an independent thing*. Aristotle is clear that insofar as each science studies one kind of thing, in order to treat the science of color as its own science, one must treat color as though it were an independent thing. Independent things, and what belongs to independent things (what falls in the categories of such as quantity, quality, relation, etc.), each have their own *analogous* measure.

Famously, Aristotle proclaims that *Being is said in many ways*. Being is not meant equivocally or univocally, but like the term 'health' all the various meanings of Being point toward one meaning (πρὸς ἕν):

> Being is meant in more than one way, but pointing toward one meaning and some one nature rather than ambiguously.[63]

This 'pointing to one' applies not only to the various meanings of Being, that is the ten categories, truth and falsehood, and potency and Being-at-work, but also to the beings themselves. Aquinas give a very excellent definition of the *pros hen* genus. In the *pros hen* genus:

> all are predicated through a relation to some one thing, and this one thing must be placed in the definition of them all.[64]

To exemplify the definition, consider the categories of accidentals, such as quality, quantity, and relation. Quality is *of some thing*. Likewise, quantities are of something, just as relations are the relations of things. When one speaks of something in the category of 'Thinghood' or 'quality,' one is certainly saying 'Being' but in different ways. The former is stating a thing, while the latter is stating that which belongs to a thing. Aquinas, like Aristotle before him, appeals to health as the primary example by which to illustrate this relation.[65] On the one hand, the *pros hen* genus acknowledges that there are many ways of saying Being, so it rejects an overtly univocal way of understanding the genus. On the other hand, it also rejects the overtly equivocal view, for there is *one unity* that pervades all of the senses of being: *Thinghood*. Whenever we speak about Being for Aristotle we are always speaking about things or what belongs to things. For this reason, Aquinas speaks of the *pros hen* solution to the problem of the unity of the Absolute as a kind of 'mean' in which the forms of determination are 'not totally diverse' though 'not one and the same' either.[66] For Aristotle and Aquinas all univocal names are grounded in the non-univocal meaning of Being:

> all univocal names are reduced to one first non-univocal analogical name, which is being.[67]

By appealing to the *pros hen* structure of the Absolute, one could argue that there is an Absolute Science. This solution nicely avoids the paradoxical results we deduced earlier by eschewing either a univocal or equivocal way of speaking about the Absolute. 'Thinghood' can be the one meaning of being without undermining the plurality of ways of speaking about Being.

Aristotle further denies that Being is governed by contrariety:

> For everyone makes all things come from contraries, but neither 'all things' nor 'from contraries' is right.[68]

Aristotle claims that although 'everyone makes all things come from contraries,' he does not equivocate when he proclaims that neither 'all things' nor 'from contraries' is correct. Interestingly, Aristotle does not exclude Plato from the class of 'everyone.'[69] Indeed, this might be the case because Aristotle seems to hold the view that Plato was committed to the so called 'unwritten doctrine' in which Being is governed by the contrary pair of the 'One' and the 'Dyad.'

First, let us consider the whole of Being—both things themselves and what belongs to them. Since contrariety is the greatest difference in a genus, were the whole *pros hen* genus of Being governed by one pair of contraries, then the contrariety in the genus of Being would be the greatest difference in the genus of Being. Given that 'Thinghood' is the measure of the class of beings, the greatest difference in the genus of being would be constituted by the opposition between Thinghood and its *privation*. If Thinghood is the Form, then the privation would be *material completely devoid of Form*. If there were a principle *contrary* to Being, it would be *prime material*, that is, that material utterly *devoid of Form*. Yet there is nothing that is utterly devoid of Form. All material is material of some kind. Only Form has *separate* ontological existence; Form is what exists separately, while material cannot exist separately, for it is always the *material of something*, for example the bricks of a house. As he states, 'Let there be one lord.'[70] Thus, there is nothing contrary to Being as such, no second principle.

Given that there is nothing contrary to Thinghood in the genus of Being, the genus of Being as such is not governed by contrary pairs. Just as much as nothing is contrary to Thinghood as such, nothing is contrary to particular things themselves, for example nothing is contrary to 'human being.' Thus, if anything, contrariety is a structural feature that belongs to *kath hen* genera and is structurally endemic to incidental modes of predication (quality, quantity, relation, etc.) but does not appear to be constitutive of things in the class of Thinghood (such as rational animals), the class of Thinghood itself (humans, plants, and animals, etc.) or the genus of Being as such taken as a whole.

Indeed, since Aristotle seems to hold the view that independent beings do not admit contrariety (except by accident), it would appear that contrariety applied only to accidental genera. Aristotle provides many arguments demonstrating that Being *qua* Being does not admit contrariety. If contrariety does not apply to Essences or things proper, and contrariety is the condition for the unity and intelligibility of a *kath hen* genus, Thinghood cannot be understood as a *kath hen* genus. Being is not a *kath hen* genus means that it is not governed by *one set of contraries* in the same way that 'white' measures the genus of color. Since being is not a *kath hen* genus, it cannot admit contrariety.

Although Aristotle employs *two principles for the logical articulation of truth*, Form and material, Aristotle rejects Plato's so-called unwritten doctrine of the One and the Indefinite Dyad. Aristotle explicitly rejects the view that all things come from contraries,[71] a view he attributes to most if not all thinkers, who came before him. Fascinatingly, in order to preserve the Being of Being, Aristotle's pros hen maneuver requires *the rejection* of the duality of principles. In other words, in order to preserve the Being of Being, one cannot posit two principles of the Absolute— one can only tolerate one. Unlike Neo-Platonism or early German Idealism, because Aristotle is committed to the eternal being of Form, he is not under the added obligation to show how *material comes to be from Form itself*. Rather, Form and material have *always existed* and *both* principles are irreducible and absolutely required for an account of the whole. Although material might be separable in thought, it is not fully separable in existence outside of thinking. Aristotle can thereby retain a dualism in the his categorial structure in which the genus, the material, always requires another principle, the difference, while still acknowledging the inseparability of material from Form in non-mental existence.

In book *Lambda*, Aristotle argues that all beings point toward one kind of being: *thought thinking itself*.[72] Thought thinking itself is the One (hen) to which *all beings* point (pros). This concludes Aristotle's inquiry into the central books of the *Metaphysics* into *Being qua Being*. The investigation proceeds by assuming that to be is indivisible and that which is indivisibly one is independent and a this. Being-at-work-staying-itself, *Energeia*, is what is independent and a this. Thought thinking itself, as that being which fully instantiates Being *qua* Being is fully Being-at-work-staying-itself. It is not only a *species* of Thinghood, but it is the perfect instantiation of Being. The opposite of mere Being-at-work would be a pure *potency* devoid of any activity. But pure potency—*itself by itself*—does not have any being. As Aristotle says:

> For there is no contrary to what is primary, since all contraries have material and such things have being by way of potency; but the ignorance that is contrary to wisdom would be directed to a contrary being, while to the primary being nothing is contrary.[73]

Thought thinking itself is the measure of all other beings insofar as they are being, and as such it does not admit of any non-being. While book

hen solution can only avoid the disappearance of the Absolute into nothing by falling into the problem of the missing difference elucidated in the previous chapter. Rather than defining Being as nothing, the *pros hen* solution finds itself defining the thing as that which is not a thing or defines the thing as that which belongs to another thing. Since things are defined by what belongs to things, the very category of Thinghood itself becomes empty—that which belongs to things appears to take its place. But 'what belongs to a thing' cannot exist if things do not exist. Thus, the *pros hen* account is just as feeble as the univocal or equivocal account of Being in its attempt to give an account of the science of the Absolute.

The Aristotelian account of Absolute Knowledge is also problematic on account of how it construes the *pros hen* approach. Still, when one turns one's mind's eye to pure intellect itself, one finds a contradiction. For both Aristotle and Thomas the *pros hen* account of Being ensures that the Absolute can be a proper subject matter of philosophical inquiry. Accordingly, the first being—that which establishes the unity of the whole genus, must exist *in* the genus of Being. Without all things existing in the one genus of Being, there cannot be one science of Being. Indeed, Aquinas' argument for God's existence, specifically the 'fourth way,' assumes that the 'maximum' *in* the genus of Being is the cause of all things in that genus, and it proclaims God (who is Being by definition) to be the maximum *in* the genus of Being. Since God is the maximum *in* the genus of Being, and the maximum in the genus is the cause of all things in that genus, God is the cause of all things.[84] Yet, Aquinas explicitly proclaims elsewhere that

> God is not related to creatures as though belonging to a different genus, but as transcending every genus, and as the principle of all genera.[85]

Were God in a genus, then God would be *differentiated by an external principle*. Thus, if God were in a genus, God would be divisible. Yet, God is not divisible. Thus, God cannot be in a genus. But Aquinas needs God to be in the genus of Being as the maximum in that genus; otherwise the fourth way cannot succeed. Thus, God both *is and is not* in a genus, which is a contradiction. Aristotle also falls victim to an objection similar in form.

Aristotle identifies pure intellect as the first cause of motion, *as a being whose being is what it is to be as such*. Indeed, scholastics such as Aquinas adopt this stance: God is 'pure act.' Any mediated knowing, inferential knowing, of pure intellect shows that God, or mere *Being at work as such*, though immediately one, must be at work *on itself*, since to be at work is to be at work on something. Since we cannot think of pure Being as a genus, we cannot think of Being at work as having material, since the genus is the material for the Form. For all beings with potency,

Being-at-work *works on material*. In the case of the divine, there is no material for Being-at-work to work on. Thus, pure Being-at-work is either not at work at all, which is absurd, or it is at *work on itself*. If the latter, then it is also *pure potency*, or pure material, since it is the material which receives the activity, not the Form. But since thought thinking itself is indivisible, that which receives the activity would be *identical* to the principle of activity. In other words, the Form would be *identical* to the material. But this is absurd, for Being-at-work as such is utterly devoid of potency and material. Hence, it is both Form and potency *in the same respect*. For it is not *qua Form* that something is acted on, and potency is *not* the activity.

According to Aristotle, our minds, unlike pure intellect, are essentially a potency to receive Form.[86] Since our minds, as potencies, are shaped into the Form of what we think, our minds preclude the grasp of what has no potency. Alas, our attempt to *conceptually determine the Form of Form fails*.

Since there is no genus, species, or difference without potency, pure intellect cannot be in a genus and cannot be a species, nor can it have an essential difference. In forcing Form to exist *by itself*, we are unable to know *what the Form is*. In order for one to logically articulate *what* the first principle is, one *contradicts oneself*, for one must provide an essential difference for the first principle. Since the first principle is not in a genus (for it is not material), there cannot be an essential difference for the first principle. Because of its indivisibility, the first principle cannot have a definition. Thus, at the ground of any non-contradictory articulation of *pros hen* Being lies either a *contradictory* articulation of Being, or one ceases to give an account of the *pros hen* structure all together. In the former case, the intelligibility of the Absolute is undermined. In the latter case, one fails to give an account of the Absolute. For the theologian who is satisfied with the incoherence of the Absolute this is not a problem, but for a theologian such as Aquinas the problem cannot just be chalked up to a 'truth of faith,' for the contradiction violates a basic principle of reason (the PNC), and no truth of faith ought to be inconsistent with truths of reason.

Because God is a being, but can only be defined as that being that is Being itself, at least in the case of the first principle, both Aristotle and Aquinas employ *self-predication*. God is both *Being* itself (which is universal) and *a* being (a particular). Although Aristotle's categories are not self-predicating, God transcends all of the genera and is *not* confined to the structure of categorial thought. Indeed, in order to ground the non-self-predicating categories in one *Absolute* Unity, the grounding principle must abide by the structure of the Absolute, which can only be articulated in a *self-predicating* way: expressing the 'what it is to be' of Being requires applying *'Being' to itself*. Because the categories are not self-predicating, and one must employ the categories in order to articulate the unifying principle of the Absolute, the real problem with the Thomistic-Aristotelian approach is that it attempts to employ *non-self-predicating* categories to that which can only be articulated by means of self-predication. Thus, the Aristotelian-Thomistic approach still falls victim to the pitfalls of onto-theology.

Aquinas states that this entails that 'we do not know what he is.'[87] Indeed, because Being is the Absolute Genus, there is no difference outside of Being by which Being could be defined. Accordingly, one might expect that if God is Being by definition, then God would be indefinable. Unlike all other beings, who have an Essence that might not be particularized because that particularization comes from the outside, God's very Essence, the 'what it is to be' of God, *is his very being*. The self-predicational structure of the articulation of the first principle comes into play exactly because God has no external principle of particularization. Because Being is not particularized in virtue of another principle, God is that being whose *very being is to particularize himself*. Or in more traditional language, God is that being whose *Essence is his existence*. God is self-caused—the being who *implicates his own existence*.

Rather than inferring that a God exists who cannot be thought or defined, the lack of definition could *also* imply that there is *nothing* there to define—since the definition is the logical articulation of the what-it-is-to-be or the Essence. Instead, one might infer that the Absolute has disappeared because it was *never there* in the first place. Indeed, as we have already demonstrated, the *pros hen* account, like the univocal and equivocal accounts, also makes the Absolute disappear. For this reason, the *pros hen* account finds itself in the same problematic position as those who attempt to derive all difference from one principle of identity—without a world, swimming in a void.

Notes

1. According to Aristotle, 'one might also be at an impasse about the sources in this way: for if it is in kind that they are one, nothing will be one in number, not even one-itself or being-itself.' Aristotle, *Metaphysics*, 999a.
2. 'For what is approaches what is' [B 8.25] and 'it is indifferent to me whence I begin, for there again I shall return.' Barnes, *Early Greek Philosophy*, B5.
3. 'What can be said and be thought of must be; for it can be, and nothing cannot be.'
   Barnes, *Early Greek Philosophy*, B6.1–2.
4. *Palintropos* is from *palin*, back and *h τρόπος*, turn.
5. Barnes, *Early Greek Philosophy*, B6.1–3, B6.4–9.
6. As we will see, not only for the history of metaphysics, but in the consideration of universality itself, the indivisibility of Being functioned as a basic premise for much of ancient and medieval philosophy.
7. For Parmenides, nature is ruled by contraries: 'And since all things have been named light and night and their powers assigned to these things and to those, everything is full of light and invisible night, both equal, since nothing falls to neither.' Barnes, *Early Greek Philosophy*, B9.

8. In the fifth hypothesis, Plato points out that 'So it looks, then, that the One that is not, is. For if it's not to be something that is not, and instead will somehow let go of being in order to give way to not-being, straight away it will be something that is.' Plato, *Parmenides*, 162a, 81. This contradiction, in an indirect way, supports Parmenides' point.

9. Barnes, *Early Greek Philosophy*, B51.

10. 'Combinations-wholes and not wholes, concurring differing, concordant discordant, from all things one and from one all things.' Barnes, *Early Greek Philosophy*, B10.

11. Barnes, *Early Greek Philosophy*, B67.

12. 'For nature, according to Heraclitus, loves to hide itself.' Barnes, *Early Greek Philosophy*, B123 See Themistius' Speeches, V 69B.

13. Ibid, B93.

14. Martin Heidegger, "The Thinker as Poet," in *Poetry, Language, Thought*, trans. Albert Hofstader (New York: Harper and Row, 1971), 4.

15. This phrase, *auto kath auto*, has its origin in Plato, who famously claims that each Form is 'itself by itself.' My own methodology is inspired by Plato's *Phaedo*, in which Plato argues that in order to know what is itself by itself, namely what truly is, reason must employ unadulterated thought which is 'itself all by itself.' Plato, *Phaedo*, 66A, 37.

16. It is important to distinguish between the thesis that Being is governed by the dualistic principles of conceptual determinacy and the thesis that Being is a predicate. If Being is a predicate, then it must be governed by principles of conceptual determinacy. If something is governed by principles of conceptual determinacy, it does not follow that it is necessarily a predicate. In what follows, I show that Being cannot be governed by dualistic principles of conceptual determinacy. Therefrom it follows that Being cannot be a predicate.

17. See the "Formal Structure of the Question of Being," in Martin Heidegger, *Being and Time*, trans. John Macquarrie and Edward Robinson (New York: Harper and Rowe, 1962), 25.

18. [...] 'in true science, each proposition has only a definite and, so to speak, local meaning, and that one who has withdrawn the determinate place and has made the proposition out to be something absolute (dogmatic), either loses sense and meaning, or gets tangled up in contradictions.' F. W. J. Schelling, *Ages of the World*, trans. Jason Wirth (Albany: SUNY, 2000), 4.

19. Although many thinkers such as Aristotle conceive of the principles of universality and particularity as unified in the thing itself, even such thinkers usually separate the principles in their logic, as Aristotle does in his account of categories. In contrast, Hegel (as we see in Part II) re-thinks the concept as a process of self-differentiation in which the universal particularizes itself. See Hegel, *SL*, trans. Giovanni, 530–534. Accordingly, Hegel rejects the separation of principles of universality and particularity as separate logical principles. Hegel's rejection of the separation of the principles of universality and particularity also entails a rejection of the PNC. Accordingly, Hegel's concrete universal does not fit the pattern ascribed here. Accordingly, the argument against the conceptual structure of being that I am advancing here does not apply to Hegel.

20. See "Exodus," in *Bible*, New International Version (Grand Rapids: Zondervan, 2017), 3:14.

21. See the *Stanford Encyclopedia of Philosophy*, entry on Duns Scotus. See https://plato.stanford.edu/entries/duns-scotus/

22. Although Aristotle famously claims that Being is said in many ways, in *Metaphysics* Lambda he argues that there is a being upon which all other beings

depend. This being is pure Being itself, pure *Being-at-work-staying-itself*. See Aristotle: *Metaphysics*, 231–253. In Aristotle, the various ways of Being still depend upon the identification of a being with Being itself. Although Aristotle conceives of the various ways of being as pointing to one meaning (and one being) as *pros hen*, he nonetheless identifies Being with a being. In this way, it is arguable that Aristotle too requires a kind of onto-theology as the groundwork for his *pros hen* account of Being.

23. See Kant, *CPR*, 553–559 (B600–B611).
24. Naturally, particular beings may have their cause in other particular beings. Here we are not inquiring after the cause of any particular being, but the origin of determinations in general, which cannot have their origin in any particular determination.
25. Moses Maimonides, *Guide for the Perplexed*, Part I, section 50.
26. Ibid, section 56.
27. Ibid.
28. Ibid, 57.
29. See Hegel, *SL*, trans. Giovanni, 59–83. See Martin Heidegger, "What Is Metaphysics?" in *Basic Writings*, ed. David Farrell Krell (New York: Harper Collins, 1993), 89–111, 108.
30. See Meister Eckhart, "Sermon 52," in *The Essential Sermons, Commentaries, Treatises, and Defense*, trans. Edmund Colledge, O.S.A. and Bernard McGinn (Mahwah: Paulist Press, 1981), 199–203, 201.
31. Ibid, 201.
32. Kant argues that Being cannot be a predicate by appealing to truth as correspondence. For Kant, if it is true that I have $100, and Being is a predicate, then the concept of $100 insofar as it obtains in the world would be different from the concept insofar as it is merely thought. But this would mean that even in the case where I have $100, it would be false that I have $100, which would be absurd. Interestingly, the argument I am presenting here is the inverse: Being cannot be a predicate because it can only be thought in a contradictory way. In order to discover the truth about Being one must abandon the view that truth is correspondence, at least as it pertains to the absolute. See Kant, *CPR*, 567 (B627).
33. Given the identity of Being and nothing, we could just as well have discussed the self-differentiating process of nothing as the self-differentiating process of Being. Here I discuss the process in terms of nothingness, since I think we are *less inclined* to slip into an onto-theological way of thinking when we substitute nothingness for Being. To see how these reflections relate to a traditional question of evil and its relation to the self-differentiating process of Being, see Gregory Moss, "The Problem of Evil in the Speculative Mysticism of Meister Eckhart," in *The Problem of Evil: New Philosophical Directions*, ed. Benjamin McCraw and Robert Arp (Lanham: Lexington Books, 2016), 35–51. In addition, to see how these issues connect with Heidegger's late philosophy of language, see chapter seven of Moss, *Ernst Cassirer and The Autonomy of Language*.
34. 'We search everywhere for the unconditioned, and find only things.' See Novalis, *Blütenstaub*, ed. Michael Brucker (1992), http://gutenberg.spiegel.de/buch/aphorismen-5232/1.
35. Like Kant, reason's metaphysical inquiry into what is results in contradiction.
36. Barnes, *Early Greek Philosophy*, 50 (B51).
37. Heidegger, "The Thinker as Poet," 4.
38. Heidegger, *Being and Time*, 23.
39. Ibid, 26.

40. Hegel, *SL*, trans. Miller, 81, and *EL*, 124.
41. Hegel, *SL*, trans. Miller, 87.
42. Ibid, 92.
43. Ibid, 88.
44. Ibid, 152.
45. Kant, *CPR*, 212, B106.
46. Ibid, 215, B111.
47. Immanuel Kant, *Kritik der reinen Vernunft* (Hamburg: Meiner Verlag, 1998), B600, 652.
48. Kant, *CPR*, 555.
49. Ibid.
50. Ibid, 556–557.
51. Ibid, 557.
52. Ibid.
53. Ibid, 558.
54. Ibid, 554.
55. Ibid.
56. Long before Kant, however, the Neo-Platonic mystic Meister Eckhart had already acknowledged the problem of onto-theology and was an important source for Martin Heidegger. As a number of scholars have noted, Heidegger himself draws upon Meister Eckhart to develop a non-onto-theological conception of Being. A brief look at Eckhart's distinction between 'God' and the Godhead shows that the problem of onto-theology already received extensive treatment in Eckhart's thought in the 14th century. One can arguably trace Eckhart's acknowledgement that the Godhead is not a being to Plato's insight that the Good is beyond Being.
57. See Aristotle, *Metaphysics*, 43, Book *Beta*, 998b20: 'But it is not possible for either oneness or being to be a single genus of things.'
58. See Aristotle, *Metaphysics*, Ch. 4–7 of Book *Gamma*, 1006a–1012a30.
59. 'There is a kind of knowledge that contemplates what is insofar as it is, and what belongs to it in its own right.' Aristotle, *Metaphysics*, Gamma, 1003a21, 53.
60. Aristotle, *Metaphysics, Iota*, 1055a1–10, Ch. 4, 192. It is important to note that for Aristotle contradictions have no middle, while contraries can have an in-between. Thus, there is no middle between 'white' and 'not-white,' but there is a middle between the contrary terms 'white' and 'black.' In this chapter on forms of unity, Aristotle also considers relative terms, which I will forgo for the sake of brevity.
61. For more on the privation or deprivation see Aristotle, *Metaphysics*, Iota, 194, 1055. Aristotle explicitly claims that 'the specific difference is a contrariety.' See Aristotle, *Metaphysics*, 1058a10–20, 200.
62. According to Aristotle: 'Accordingly, these perceptible things have the same elements and sources. . ., but it is not possible to say in this way that all things have the same elements and sources, *except by analogy*, [my emphasis] just as if one were to say that there are three kinds of sources: form, deprivation, and material. But each one of these is different as it concerns each class of things; for instance, among colors they are white, black, and surface, or light, darkness and air, out of which come day and night.' Aristotle, *Metaphysics*, Book Lambda, 1070b15–25, 235.
63. See Aristotle, *Metaphysics*, Book Gamma, 1003a3–b, 53.
64. Aquinas, *Summa Theologica*, Sixth Article, Question XIII, 122.
65. 'Healthy applied to animals come into the definition of healthy applied to medicine, which is called healthy as being the cause of health in the animals.' See Aquinas, *Summa Theologica*, 122.

66. As Aquinas puts it: 'the name which is used in a multiple sense signifies the various proportions to some one thing.' See Aquinas, *Summa Theologica*, 121.
67. Aquinas, *Summa Theologica*, 121.
68. Aristotle, *Metaphysics*, 244, 1075a20–30.
69. Ibid, 249, 1075a20–30.
70. Ibid, 1076a.
71. Ibid, 1075a20–30.
72. Aristotle establishes the existence of the first mover, thought thinking itself, by assuming the eternity of motion. Without the existence of an eternally moving body, motion would not be eternal. Further, Aristotle goes on to argue that even an eternally moving body is not sufficient to sustain the eternity of motion, for since they are composed of material, they still have potentiality, and could in principle cease to be. Thus, for Aristotle without the eternal existence of a non-material Form, motion could cease to be. Since motion is eternal, there must be a non-material Form, a pure Being-at-work without any material or potentiality that ensures the continued existence of the eternal world. Aristotle characterizes this Form as an Intellect that only thinks itself. Were it to think something else, it could potentially *not* think that object and could potentially cease to think. In this case, thought thinking itself could cease to be, which is absurd, since the first principle ought not have any potentiality I only briefly gloss this argument here, since it is not central to the task of evaluating the relative success of *the pros hen* account of Being. For more see Aristotle, *Metaphysics*, Lambda, 6–7.
73. Aristotle, *Metaphysics*, Lambda, 251.
74. See Ibid, 1075a10–30, 249.
75. In fact, this is how desire works. We desire something because we think it is good. We do not think it is good because we desire it.
76. Aquinas, *Summa Theologica*, Question XIII, 5th Article, pg. 118.
77. Ibid, 120.
78. Ibid, Question IV, 2nd Article, pg. 38–39.
79. Ibid, Question IV, 3rd Article, Reply to Objection 1.
80. Ibid, Question XIII, 5th Article, pg. 120.
81. Ibid.
82. Ibid, 122, Question XIII, 6th Article.
83. Ibid, 23, Question II.
84. Ibid.
85. Thomas Aquinas, *Summa Theologica*, Reply to Objection 2, 41, Question XII. Also see the 5th Article of Question III: 'God is not in any genus.' Aquinas appeals to Aristotle here, who argues that all genera have differentia outside themselves, and Being has nothing outside itself. See Aristotle, *Metaphysics*, 998b22.
86. See Aristotle, "On the Soul," 269–270.
87. Aquinas, *Summa Theologica*, 111, Reply to Objection 1, Question XII, 13th Article.

7 From the Third Man Regress to Absolute Dialetheism

The Third Man

The problem of Onto-theology showed that if commitment to the PNC is maintained, then the philosopher can no longer appeal to non-conceptual content in order to differentiate the domain of concepts. Thus, in order to be consistent, the defender of the PNC could neither appeal to the CONCEPT *per se* (since on its own terms it cannot be the principle of its own differences), nor to any non-conceptual content, for this would engender the problem of Absolute Empiricism. Thus, we showed that the defender of the PNC would be forced to hold that the CONCEPT is completely *undifferentiated*. On the assumption that the universal cannot be a sufficient principle of its own instances, we find ourselves saddled with the unpleasant result that beyond the concept of the CONCEPT, no other concept can be. The problem of onto-theology entails that if there cannot be true contradictions, then there cannot be *any* particular concepts. As we showed in the previous chapter, the philosopher would be forced to advocate for a conceptual *Monism* in which not only is the Concept the *only concept* there is, but also that concept is internally one, for it would be *totally indivisible*. In the preceding chapter, we also established the following: given that its very lack of differentiation entails that the CONCEPT cannot be differentiated from particular concepts, the CONCEPT itself must be a particular concept. We were thereby saddled with an unsettling contradiction: the concept is the only undifferentiated concept, and a particular(or differentiated) concept. To put it simply and formulaically: *conceptuality itself is a concept*. Out of the problem of onto-theology, an infinite regress follows, what since Plato has been known as the 'Third Man.'

In Priest's terms, the CONCEPT exhibits 'closure' because it is a particular *contained within* the domain of concepts. After all, the concept CONCEPT is a particular concept itself, for it is one in number and differentiated from the particular concepts that are its instances, such as NUMBER and TRIANGLE. Let us call this (UC1). Since (UC1) is a particular concept, and it is the CONCEPT itself, (UC1) would be an *instance of itself* or its own particular simply in virtue of what it is.[1] In other words, (UC1) would exhibit self-differentiation. (UC1) entails (C2), for it is both the undifferentiated CONCEPT, and a particular, differentiated concept.[2] For this reason, it is clear that the self-differentiating character of (UC1) is contradictory. Yet, it is impossible for the UNIVERSAL to exhibit self-differentiation, since concepts are universal characters and do not differentiate themselves into particulars. Thus, if (UC1) is a particular concept, then it cannot be the CONCEPT itself. Thus, what all concepts have in common cannot be (UC1), but some other common feature, (UC2). Given that (UC2) is undifferentiated, it cannot be differentiated from particular concepts and must thereby also be a particular concept. The content of (UC2) is no different from (UC1). It is only counted as a separate universal: in all other respects it re-iterates the contradiction in (UC1). Since (UC2) must also be a particular concept, it is also one concept among many and cannot be what all concepts have in common. Since any conceptual content that ought to hold for all concepts must be undifferentiated, an infinite regress is generated (UC1, UC2, n) in which an infinite number of contradictions would be generated.[3] Thus, it seems impossible to think the sense of the CONCEPT at all. Instead, only particular concepts are encountered. To appeal once again to *Beyond the Limits of Thought*, the CONCEPT has the property of transcendence, because it must be completely outside of the totality. Ironically, though the particular concepts were those concepts which were originally impossible, at this point in the argument it appears that only particular concepts can be thought. In sum, if the CONCEPT were undifferentiated (as discussed in the problem of onto-theology), there would be no way to describe the CONCEPT itself. If one were to describe it, one would be differentiating it and would thereby fail to describe the undifferentiated CONCEPT.[4] For this reason, any defense of the PNC must lead to the impossibility of thinking the CONCEPT as such.

Following the procedure from the previous chapter, were we to *model* our understanding of the Absolute on the dualistic form of conceptual structure, then any attempt to conceive the Absolute would only allow the Absolute to function as the principle of identity of what falls within it. Accordingly, the principle of difference could only be accessed by transcending the Absolute. But since there is nothing outside of the Absolute, there could be absolutely no differences in the Absolute. Thus, the Absolute would *be absolutely un-differentiated*. Given the lack of differentiation inherent in Absolute Being, any attempt to conceive of the Absolute would contradict itself. Were I to state 'what' Being is, then I would predicate 'such and such' to Being. By predicating 'such and such' to Being, I would differentiate Being from what is distinct from it. Indeed, by stating what the Absolute is, I differentiate it from what is *relative*. By conceiving the Absolute by means of a concept, I differentiate the Absolute and thereby fail to think the undifferentiated Absolute.

Rather, each conception of the Absolute differentiates what is undifferentiated and thereby fails to think the undifferentiated Being of Being. Accordingly, every conceptualization of the Absolute appears to limit the content of Being to a particular domain of Being or to one division within the whole of Being.

To put the problem another way, every attempt to differentiate the Absolute requires the transformation of *nothing into something* for the nothing must function as the source of difference. Accordingly, one never finds the limit of the Absolute, for every attempt to secure the limit only *extends the limit further*. Because one only ever knows some determination of the Absolute, rather than the Absolute itself, philosophical thinking finds on the way to Being, to use a phrase of Heidegger's. Or what is the same, God is always disappearing, and the only possible theology at our disposal is a radically negative, self-contradictory *apophaticism*. Simply put, were the Absolute modeled on the dualistic construal of the concept, it would be impossible to *truly think* the Absolute.

Very early in the history of Western philosophy, this problem was thoroughly explicated by Plato in his *Parmenides*. It goes by the name of the 'Third Man' and, like the problem of instantiation, it is a *variety* of the problem of participation in Plato's corpus. 'The Third Man' regress is an objection Plato raised against his own Theory of Forms.

> If then, someone shall try to show that for things such as stones and wood and the like, the same things are many and one, then we will say that he's demonstrated that some thing is many and one, not that the One is many or the Many's one. He's not even said anything wondrous, but only what in fact all of us should readily agree upon. But if someone, as I said, shall first distinguish the forms as separate in themselves, such as Likeness and Unlikeness and Multitude and the One and Rest and Motion and all the like, and then will show that in themselves these things can be mixed together and separated, I'd admire that with wonder, Zeno![5]

What does it take to make the young Socrates of Plato's *Parmenides* wonder? As the quote indicates, Zeno must not only show the mundane thesis that sensible things are many and one, for example a human hand, as Zeno's treatise demonstrates, but that Likeness itself is Unlike, and Unlikeness itself Like, and *likewise* for all other Forms. The reason is clear: young Socrates' Theory of Forms posits that each Form (*eidos*) is itself by itself, (*auto kath auto*). So, if any Form admitted its opposite, it would cease to be itself. It would be opposed to itself. Socrates challenges Zeno to show him that the Forms themselves admit their opposites. As is evident, from the outset of the *Parmenides*, Young Socrates is committed to the thesis that universals are governed by the PNC. Parmenides takes up the challenge and through the criticisms of the Forms and the hypotheses constituting the majority of the work systematically brings Socrates to the place of wonder.

The Third Man argument can be found in the *Parmenides* at 132a-b. As in the first objection we considered, in the Third Man argument we find Socrates again admitting that the *universal is particular*. Parmenides questions Socrates about the relation of universal to particular:

> 'I think that you think that each form is one because of this: when-ever many things seem to you to be great, it seems probable to you, as you look over them all, that there is one and the same idea. From this you conclude that the Great is one.'
>
> 'That's the truth,' I replied.
>
> 'But what about the Great itself and the different great things—if, in the same way, you look over them all with your soul, will there not appear, in turn, some great thing that makes all of them, by necessity, appear great?'
>
> 'It looks that way.'
>
> 'A different form of Greatness, then, will be revealed in addition to what was Greatness itself and the things that partake of it. And above all of these, in turn, another, that makes them all great. As so each of your forms will no longer be one, but will be boundless in multitude.'[6]

For every plurality, there is some one universal over that plurality in virtue of which that plurality is one. So in the case of great things, looking over all great things, we notice that all of them are great and draw the inference that there is some one universal of Greatness over the many great things in virtue of which the many great things are great. Moreover, we can form another plurality by including the universal of Greatness in the set of great things. Since we have a second plurality, and for every plurality there is some one universal over that plurality, a different and second universal of Greatness must be posited over the second plurality. Since this universal can be counted in the set of great things, a third universal will be a neces-sary condition for this third plurality, and so on. As Parmenides states, 'each form will no longer be one, but will be boundless in multitude,' a result quite similar to the One that follows from the first disjunction in the argument from parts and wholes. Either we *eternally approach* the universal of Greatness, yet never reach it, or the universal is not one, but indefinitely many. Since universals are indivisible in themselves, the uni-versal cannot be many by addition or division. Since this argument applies to any universal that stands over a plurality, the argument indicts all uni-versals, not just Greatness. Thus, no universal is ever cognized. Indeed, we find ourselves in a dilemma: either universals do not exist, or they exist but cannot be thought. The latter would be quite peculiar, since universals seem to be exactly that which is *inherently* thinkable and intelligible.

As Vlastos has noted, the premise that moves the argument into aporia is the assumption of *self-reference*. What is predicated of Greatness in the proposition 'Greatness is great'? If we look at the form of attribution, and momentarily shy away from considering the content of the predicate itself, we see that a universal, 'great' is predicated of the subject, 'Greatness.' When we say 'x is great' we do not mean that 'x is Greatness,' but an instance of Greatness. 'Greatness,' as the subject of the predicate, is necessarily one instance of Greatness, a great thing, or better, a particular. Among other examples that could be elucidated, consider the following proposition: 'The Universe is great.' Here 'the Universe' is also a particular subsumed under 'greatness.' But there's an important difference in the two propositions: unlike 'the Universe,' 'Greatness itself' is a *universal*, since Greatness contains the very 'what it is to be' of Greatness. The what-it-is-to-be of Greatness, the universal, is an instance of itself, the what-it-is-to-be of Greatness. Ironically, Greatness is in fact great, since it is infinite in number. Since this argument applies to all universals, each universal is both universal *in itself* and a particular. Hence, on either objection participation leads to a startling contradiction: *the universal is particular*. Since contradictions cannot be true, participation must be rejected. Socrates is brought to the place of wonder, for exactly that which ought not admit of its negation, the universal Form, admits of its negation.

Aristotle argues that his Theory of Forms does not fall victim to a Third Man style argument. Consider the following comment on participation from the *Metaphysics*:

> And to say that they [Forms][7] are patterns and the other things participate in them is to speak without content and in poetic metaphors. For what is the thing that is at work, looking off toward the Forms?[8]

As Aristotle notes, participation is a poetic metaphor. Lacking any conceptual determination of the unity of universal and particular, what participation is has been left for future generations of philosophers.[9] In another passage, Aristotle writes that participation is not helpful for knowing what is responsible for the appearances.[10]

For Aristotle it is in virtue of the separation of the sources of universality and particularity that self-predication cannot be true. Their unification in the composite, though, requires another distinction about which Aristotle writes in the following passage concerning participation, and in particular, the Third Man:

> On account of this impasse, some people talk about participation, and are at a loss about what is responsible for participation and what participating is; others talk about co-presence of knowing and a soul, while still others say life is a composition or conjunction of a soul

with a body. And yet the same formulation applies to everything: for being healthy will be a co-presence or conjunction or composition of a soul and health, and the bronze's being a triangle will be a composition of the bronze and triangle, and white will be a composition of surface and whiteness. And the reason they say these things is that they are looking for a formulation that unites potency and complete Being-at-work, plus a difference. But as we said, at the highest level of material and the Form are one and the same thing, the former potentially, the latter actively, so that looking for what is responsible for their being one is like looking for a cause of one thing; for each of them is a certain one, and what is in potency and what is in activity are in a certain way one thing.[11]

True, we cannot look for the differentia of Form and matter, since the difference just is the Form, and we would thereby be inquiring into the Form of Form, *ad infinitum*. As is evident, the solution hinges *not only* upon a rejection of self-predication but also on the distinction between potentiality and Being-at-work explicated earlier. The material is the unity of the composite only potentially, the Form 'actively.'

To appreciate how Aristotle has solved the Third Man regress, consider Aristotle's *reductio* against the claim that the *Form is an element of the whole*. After all, it seems reasonable to treat Form as an element, since together the Form and the material seem to be *parts of the composite*. If the Form, F1, were an *element alongside the material or a plurality of elements*, then instead of having a plurality of merely material constituents, 'a' and 'b,' one would have a new plurality of elements, for example 'a,' 'b,' and 'ab.' Since the Form is a new element, there would be a *new plurality*. Since the Form is hypothesized as one element among others, it excludes the others and would require a new source in virtue of which it could be conjoined to them. In other words, the element *as an element* cannot give the whole order. Since there would be a new plurality of elements, a new Form, F2, would be required in order to organize the new plurality of elements. Again, if this is an element, then a new plurality of elements would be generated, of which a new Form, F3, would be required, *ad infinitum*. On the face of it, Form and material remain separate principles: the former is the principle by which particulars are *one in kind*, as Aristotle and Socrates are both human beings, the latter, at least in one sense, is that by which those particulars are *one in number*.

Strikingly, Aristotle's argument against treating Form as material mirrors the Third Man argument. If we treat Form and material themselves as the elements of the composite whole, then both Form and material would march off into infinity. If the material *itself* were *a* material element, then an infinite regress of material would result. If Form were both *the whole* itself, the Form, and *a part* of the whole, a material element, or *the universal* structure and *a particular*, then Form would march out into infinity. If we accept *self-reference*, then we generate the Third Man argument, in which the universal, the Form, becomes a particular, and the particular a universal. If, for example, we allowed 'animal,' a genus, to be *an* animal, *a species of itself*, we would have an infinite regress. For another example, consider Plato's One Being in the second hypothesis of *Parmenides*. The One Being exhibits this self-referential structure, for the One Being is both *the whole and a part of itself*. Aristotle's brilliance lies in his diagnosis that *self-reference* is the source of the Third Man argument. By rejecting self-reference, Aristotle finds a suitable treatment and avoids the infinite regress.[12] Although Kant does not explicitly respond to the problem of participation, his construal of the categories prevents the problem from arising in the first place.

It is with the Schematism that Kant completes his project of setting the limits for the proper application of categories. Unfortunately, the Schematism not only brings to light the brilliance of Kant's system but also uncovers its greatest weakness. Kant's solution to the problem of participation follows Aristotle's model. Aristotle's solution requires a rejection of self-predication. Kant's solution is similar: because the concept is a condition for the possibility of objectivity, if we were to ask 'what makes the concept possible?' we would be forced to answer that the 'concept makes the concept possible.' This is absurd, for the concept would precede itself. Thus, though we hoped that Kant's transcendental investigation would provide a novel approach to the question 'what is the concept?', unfortunately, the transcendental question cannot be applied to the concept itself without absurdity. *The universal is not an instance of itself.* If the universal could be an instance of itself, we would be permitted to inquire into the condition for the possibility of the concept. Our inability to inquire into the condition for the possibility of the concept uncovers a basic feature of Kant's categories that he shares with Aristotle: categories are not self-predicative.

What does this restriction on the question illuminate? It informs us that there is an absolute, epistemic separation of the sources of the principles of universality and particularity. For Kant, with the rejection of self-predication comes the correlate position: since the universal is not an instance of itself, in order for particulars to be subsumed under universals, we must posit a separate source of particularity that is external to the universal itself. The universal, by itself, is empty of content and is a merely formal unity of synthesis, which has no specific content besides being a category. Like Aristotle, neither pure Form (categories) nor pure matter (pure intuition) is generable. Again, if the categories were objects, they would be made possible by an antecedent set of categories, *ad infinitum*, placing us squarely in the Third Man problem. Kant stops the regress the same way Aristotle does: he rejects self-predication and posits two logically separate, yet metaphysically co-operating principles by which objectivity is formed. Unlike Aristotle, Kant's rejection of self-referential predication entails a rejection of existential implication: 'thinking' is not an organon, but a mere canon for thought. Existential implication is banished along with the concept of intellectual understanding.[13] From the perspective of Kant's transcendental method, Aristotle only preserves existential implication because he, like Plato before him, still confuses the concept with intuition. For Kant, Aristotle's rejection of self-predication is not thorough enough. Indeed, for Kant, Aristotle's qualification of the fundamental division of cognition into a duality of principles is connected to his problematic affirmation of existential implication. By working out their absolute separation, the separation of the principles of universality and particularity, reflected in the difference between concepts and intuition, Kant ensures that Forms never propagate again.

If we learned our lesson from Aristotle, however, we would see that the strength of his solution is also its weakness. In the Third Man regress, only one possibility for grasping the unity of universal and particular is entertained: the universal itself must be a particular. Aristotle challenges this, showing that there is another way of grasping the unity of universal and particular as the Form of matter. Although, in Kant Thinghood has been metaphysically transformed into universal relation, *the category is still the form of the intuition*, whose content cannot be grasped independently from the intuition. Like Aristotle, we cannot say what Form (category) is without specifying the material (pure intuition). Still, just as in Aristotle's thought, this novel solution integral to Kant's thought generates *the problem of the differentia*. From the rejection of self-predication, and correlatively, the separation of principles of universality and particularity, we find Kant's transcendental system subject to the same problem of the differentia elucidated in Chapter 5.

The inquiry into the 'what it is to be of universality' or the Form of Forms, aims at what is common to every universal. Since we are asking about what is universal about each and every universal, our inquiry may be formulated reflexively: 'what is universal about universality?' Just as the thinking of thinking is reflexive, so is the inquiry into the universal character of universality. We do not mean to inquire into what is contingently universal, but what universality is *necessarily*. So we might phrase our question again more exactly: what is necessarily universal about universality? The question, 'what makes universality be what it is?' covers up a reflexivity folded within the question. As mentioned previously, the 'what-it-is-to-be' itself expresses universality. Plato teaches us in his Socratic dialogues that an inquiry searching for the 'what-it-is-to-be' always desires the universal. To take an example from *Euthyphro*, Socrates' question 'what is piety?' desires to know piety *qua* piety in all pious things. Accordingly, by substituting this universality for 'what it is to be' we find ourselves asking about the universality of universality, or, in another parlance, the concept of the concept. The self-referential activity attributed to the Forms in the Third Man argument appear to follow from the nature of the question concerning the 'what it is to be' of universality.

Given that universality cannot be kept separate from particularity, how in principle can universality and particularity be kept separate? If we must assume that the universal is not particular, and the particular not universal, universality itself must either be universal or particular. On the one hand, if I grasp it *qua* particular, then I am grasping *the universal as a particular*. On the other hand, if I grasp the Form *qua* universal, then it must be a particular instance of itself, since the universal necessarily admits self-reference. Both disjunctions lead to a contradiction: *the identity of universal and particular*. Just as Being cannot help be conceived as a being, so the concept cannot help to be conceived as a concept—*ad infinitum*.

Towards Dialetheism

During the past few decades, Graham Priest has advocated for dialetheism,[14] the controversial position that some contradictions are true.[15] In recent decades the philosophical community has begun to recognize the significant challenge posed by Priest's arguments.[16] Priest has primarily appealed to paradoxes of self-reference, such as the Liar Paradox[17] to support his position. Following Priest's approach, I have offered another argument for dialetheism, which appeals to a self-referential paradox that has been more or less ignored in the philosophical literature on the subject: the paradox of the missing difference.[18]

When we reflect on the question 'what is a concept?'[19] from the perspective of a classical model of conceptual analysis, we arrive at the paradox of the missing difference. In *In Contradiction*, Priest argues that

> Hegel was right: our concepts, or some of them anyway, are inconsistent, and produce dialetheias.[20]

Although contradictions may be improbable, when we reflect on the question 'how is the domain of concepts possible?', we are led to a startling principle: without dialetheia concepts (from a classical perspective) would be impossible. Or what is the same: Dialetheism is a necessary condition for articulation of the sense of a domain of concepts in general.[21] As a result, dialetheism may even be more central to philosophical reflection than even dialetheists themselves have recognized.[22] This thesis directly contradicts the dominant tradition of Western philosophy regarding the PNC, which is best exemplified by the Aristotelian and Kantian schools. Traditionally, the PNC is held to be an *inviolable* principle governing the domain of concepts as such the preservation of which is a necessary condition for the determinacy of concepts. As we have shown, however, this principle does not preserve the determinacy of conceptual determination, but undermines it.

My claim that the domain of conceptual determination is contradictory is conditioned upon the assumption that the concept is *not* sufficient for the differentiation of its particulars. Since this assumption is grounded in the PNC, by showing that the separation of principles leads to a contradiction, one can successfully show (see Chapter 6) that *the PNC itself leads to a contradiction*.

Since one cannot find a conceptual principle of differentiation, if we hold to the PNC then there can only be one concept at most: the concept of the concept. If there are no differences, then there is no necessity to introduce dialetheism, since dialetheism is introduced in order to account for the missing difference. Accordingly, dialetheism would only be a necessary condition for the possibility of more than one concept. But given that the concept of the concept is dialetheic (as we have just established), even this one concept would be dialetheic. What is more, we have just established that even if there were only one concept, then that concept would be undifferentiated, indescribable, and inconceivable. The PNC cannot range over the domain of concepts even if there were only one concept, for that one concept would be conceived as being inconceivable and described as indescribable. Since this is itself a contradiction, dialetheism is a necessary condition for the domain of concepts as such, whether the concepts are one or many. As a principle, Priest suggests that we should accept dialetheia only when it appears that there is no better way to go.[23]

In this case concerning the concept of the CONCEPT, there appears to be no better way to go, and for this reason, as Priest suggests, we ought to infer that the improbable is the case. To briefly re-cap: if one holds to the PNC, the assumption that the CONCEPT is a common character entails that the CONCEPT is undifferentiated. Further, the very attempt to specify what the undifferentiated CONCEPT is results in the identification of the CONCEPT with a particular concept. As a result, the CONCEPT would be an instance of itself. Yet, this is impossible, since concepts are universal terms and do not differentiate themselves into particulars. Accordingly, an infinite regress is generated in which the CONCEPT fails to appear. If one holds to the PNC, not only do concepts disappear but the CONCEPT as such also goes on holiday. The CONCEPT exhibits both closure and transcendence, because it must be both within and without the totality. These arguments lead us to dialetheism. Hence, the first principle established by these arguments is the following: the concept of the CONCEPT is dialetheic.

At first glance, it seems quite unlikely, to put it mildly, that the PNC would not govern the domain of concepts as a whole—whether that domain be construed in terms of genera, sets, or abstractions. Indeed, one might think that if the PNC applies anywhere, surely it applies to the domain of concepts. Despite this reasonable hesitation, the defender of the PNC cannot rest easy without first addressing the following arguments, which, by my lights, ought to put to rest any certainty that the PNC governs the domain of concepts.

Earlier we stated the principle that integral to every concept is the salient feature that 'all concepts are instances of the class of concepts.' Note that the principle that 'all concepts are instances of the class of concepts' is another formulation of what is perhaps better known as the domain principle. In Priest's words, the domain principle is 'a formulation of the Kantian insight that totalization is conceptually unavoidable.'[24] If we translate our discussion of concepts into the language of predication, principle (iii) entails that the predicate 'is a concept' is a necessary condition for every concept to be a concept and thereby attain membership in the class of concepts. If the predicate 'concept' is dialetheic, then it follows that every subject to which that predicate applies must also be dialetheic. This is the case even if in other respects particular concepts have consistent predicates. Since every particular concept in the domain of concepts is the subject of the predicate 'concept,' it follows that every concept contains a contradiction.[25] Accordingly, the second principle established by these arguments is the following: dialetheism is a necessary condition for the possibility of any concept whatever.

What is more, since there are, in fact, particular concepts, and it would be impossible to establish any conceptual differentiation without a contradiction, (C1) follows, namely that every particular concept, as a concept, is also not a concept. Thus, dialetheism is a necessary condition for establishing the conceptual content of any particular concept. Since the CONCEPT or the domain of concepts is just as much a particular concept as any other, dialetheism is also a necessary condition for recognizing the domain of concepts in general. Without a diatheleic logic, we cannot admit that there is such a thing as a concept or a domain of concepts. If the advocate of the PNC wishes to avoid (C1), she must deny that there are concepts. Besides being false, this leads to another contradiction, (C2), namely that there cannot be any particular concepts and there is at least one particular concept. No matter what way we turn we are forced back into dialetheia.

In the preceding, I have only attempted to establish a necessary condition for the possibility of concepts. What remains is to elucidate a theory of conceptual formation on dialetheic grounds. The principle that dialetheism is a necessary condition for the possibility of any concept whatever leaves us wondering how a dialetheic conception might appear, and this is one of the main tasks to which the second part of the investigation is dedicated.

One might object that the account of the CONCEPT I have proposed is self-referentially inconsistent. Naturally, this is exactly what one ought to expect, given that I am here arguing for a dialetheic conception of concepts. Ironically, rather than undermine the account, the self-referential inconsistency merely betrays the consistency of the dialetheic approach for which I am here advocating. One might instead proclaim our leading question to lack any meaning whatever, or that it is necessarily false, given that it leads to a contradiction.[26] Unfortunately, such an objection presumes that the only meaningful utterances are non-contradictory. Since this is exactly what is at stake in the arguments, the objection begs the question and is of no avail here.

One might go further and attempt to reject the assumption upon which the argument is grounded, namely that the CONCEPT is not sufficient for the differentiation of its particulars. First, such a response might appear to concede the argument that the concept of the CONCEPT is contradictory on the assumption that concepts are not self-differentiating. But note that if one were to reject the assumption that the CONCEPT is not sufficient for the differentiation of its particulars, then one would be saddled with the claim that the CONCEPT could in principle be sufficient to differentiate its particulars. If the CONCEPT not only was a common character but was also able to differentiate its particulars, then the CONCEPT would be self-differentiating.[27] If the domain of concepts were self-differentiating, in virtue of being a universal the CONCEPT would also be its own particular concept and would thereby be an instance of itself. Because the concept of SELF-DIFFERENTIATION engenders a contradiction (C2),[28] one cannot appeal to self-differentiation in order to defend the PNC. Since self-differentiating concepts are contradictory,[29] we could not defend the PNC in this way without falling again into contradiction once again.

In principle, it appears that dialetheism in the domain of concepts may be avoidable by adopting a form of Conceptual Eliminativism in which the CONCEPT is eliminated from one's logic, epistemology, and metaphysics. Likewise, a form of Conceptual Pluralism may also avoid such a result, in which conceptual structures are irreducibly plural. Neither of these approaches seems plausible. Each of them would require a rejection of the domain principle to be successful. But if there were no domain of concepts, then one could not in principle identify the concept CONCEPT in virtue of which each concept is distinguished from what is not a concept. Indeed, in order to distinguish concepts from what are not concepts, we must predicate of concepts that they are 'such and such.' By predicating of them that they are 'such and such,' we cannot help but presuppose a domain of concepts that has particular features.[30]

In both cases of Conceptual Eliminativism and certain forms of Conceptual Pluralism, the concept CONCEPT would be completely eliminated.[31] In *Beyond the Limits of Thought*, Priest has convincingly argued that such a move would be self-contradictory and so would not escape dialetheism. Although he does not address the case of the CONCEPT *per se* exactly in these terms, his arguments there apply in this case as well. To illustrate why this strategy is self-contradictory, we ought to first consider how such an objection might work. Consider Russell's VCP

(Vicious Circle Principle) for which 'whatever involves all of a collection must not be one of that collection.'[32] Indeed, this is one more example of the most persistent historical strategy, namely to deny the existence of ultimate totality. Priest calls this strategy 'denying inclosure' and it appears to be the standard strategy to avoid paradox and contradiction when attempting to coherently conceive of totality.[33] In our case, such a strategy might be employed to deny the existence of the totality of concepts. Another way of formulating this strategy is 'parameterization': 'the pertinent structure of statements of any discourse cannot be expressed by statements of that discourse.'[34]

Rather than avoid a contradiction, this strategy actually leads us right back to (C1). If we cannot conceive of the domain of concepts as a whole from within the domain of concepts, or from within the domain of conceptual discourse, then our only recourse to conceive of that domain would require an appeal to conceive of it from outside the domain of concepts, namely to conceive of the domain of concepts non-conceptually. But this is exactly the original contradiction, (C1).

What is more, as Priest points out, on a principle such as the VCP, since the whole collection cannot be treated as a member of the collection, some member of the totality would be outside of the collection. For this reason, one cannot 'quantify over all propositions' or in our case, make a universal claim about every member of the domain of concepts. But, the VCP in fact ranges over all propositions. Applied to our case, if one assumes that whatever involves every member of a collection of concepts must not be one member of that collection of concepts, then one has made a statement about every concept. So even if 'denying inclosure' eludes contradiction by ceasing to think the whole domain as a member of itself, it still generates a contradiction when that principle is expressed. For this reason, Priest is not wrong to emphasize that denying totality simply re-locates the contradiction elsewhere.[35]

Finally, in our case, it seems that the persistent historical attempt to deny that there is totality is tantamount to a denial of the domain principle, the principle that totalization is conceptually unavoidable. In the case of the concept, denying that there is a domain of concepts does not just result in a contradiction at the level of expression. Rather, if one conceives of all concepts as not falling within one domain of concepts, then one is still applying a concept to all concepts and thereby specifying the universal character of conceptual determination. Since one cannot help but construe all concepts in some conceptual way, the attempt to conceive of all concepts as not belonging to the domain of concepts cannot help but indirectly introduce a domain of concepts into one's thinking. For this reason, the attempt to 'deny inclosure' is especially problematic in the case of the domain of concepts and contradicts not only its expression but the very act of conceptualizing conceptual structure.

The paradox of the missing difference in addition to the dialetheic conception of the concept that follows from it appears to be motivated by the question 'what is the concept?' To this extent, it seems that the various paradoxes enumerated in Part I may apply to any attempt to answer the question at all that remains committed to the duality of principles and the PNC that undergirds it. To say 'the concept is such and such' would specify the sense of the term through itself, which would be circular. As we demonstrated earlier in the discussion of the Third Man, the circularity of the sense would entail an infinite regress. Yet, if we wish to avoid specifying the sense of the term through itself, and we refrain from predicating any concept to the concept, then we fail to answer the question, or what is the same, we say nothing at all. If we wish to speak, but speak in such a way in which our speech is not circular, then we will be forced to predicate what is not conceptual to the concept and thereby tempted to fall into absolute empiricism. However great our distaste may be at this sorry state of affairs, we find ourselves thrust once again into the arms of dialetheism.[36]

To briefly summarize, the duality of principles of truth—and the duality of the principles of universality and particularity underlying them—engender the four paradoxes enumerated in Chapters 5 through 7. Not only does the existence of any consistent conception of the Absolute disappear, but even any consistent concept of the Concept disappears as well. Because in every case we fall into contradiction, it is the contradiction itself that points the way out of the impasse.

Absolute Dialetheism

In the foregoing reflection, we have articulated a philosophical impasse that threatens to undermine the very possibility of philosophy: the disappearance of the Absolute—the One and All. Because philosophy distinguishes itself from the sciences as an inquiry into the Absolute, the disappearance of the Absolute threatens to rob philosophy of its proper object. In order to escape this impasse, it will be of import for us to briefly formulate the results of our inquiry thus far.

The attempt to ground truth on *one principle* alone undermined every attempt to give an account of the existence of particularity or difference. Accordingly, not even the difference between the One and the All could be established. As a result, the attempt to ground truth on one principle alone led to the complete disappearance of the Absolute. Since everything relative is a relative determination of what is Absolute, the disappearance of the Absolute counts for nothing less than the disappearance not only of all knowledge but also of any being at all. In Jacobi's terms, the attempt to ground all knowledge on one principle leads to *nihilism*: the affirmation that only nothing is. On the terms of the one-principle method, not only does Absolute Knowledge disappear, but Absolute Being goes

240 The Problem of Absolute Knowledge

missing as well. Importantly, the critique of the one-principle method is not restricted to transcendental idealism or the transcendental turn. Rather, we discovered analogous problems in metaphysical (and non-transcendental) thinkers antecedent to Kant, such as Plotinus, for whom the same problem arises. This shows that the problem of the disappearance of the Absolute is not limited to metaphysical or transcendental thinkers. Rather, it is a problem that arises independently of whether Being or knowledge of Being is adopted as the primary object of philosophical knowing.

Given the failure of any attempt to ground truth on one principle alone, in order to salvage the Being of the Absolute, we explored the possibility of thinking about truth in a *dualistic* way. Rather than attempt to deduce difference from pure identity, by positing two separate principles (one for universality, the other for particularity), Absolute Truth and Absolute Being might be salvaged. What is essential here is not the dyadic principles *per se*, but the appeal to a *plurality* of principles (more than one). Unfortunately, this model of thinking about truth suffered from the very same deficiency as the first method. Both Kant and Plato recognized, each in his own way and on his own terms, that such an approach to truth can only undermine our efforts to discursively cognize or articulate the universal content of the Absolute. Even more devastating, the two-principle approach to truth systematically led us into a host of problems: the problem of Instantiation, the problem of the Missing Difference, the problem of Absolute Empiricism, the Third Man regress, and complete disappearance of the Absolute in the problem of Onto-theology. Just as in the case of the one-principle approach, the two-principle approach led to the complete disappearance of the Absolute in knowing and Being. Just as in the first case, the failure of the pluralistic method can be articulated independently of whether Being or knowing is taken as the primary object of philosophical knowing.

Given that the Absolute disappears whether one conceives of philosophical truth as grounded on one principle or multiple principles, the problem of the disappearance of the Absolute arises independently of whether one attempts to derive particularity *out of* self-identical universality or whether one posits particularity as a given principle alongside universality. Since the problem is common to both approaches, in order to evaluate the reason for the impasse, we investigated the common commitments of these approaches. As our investigation showed, each method for accounting for a logic of truth presupposed a finite conception of conceptuality, whereby the concept, whether it be construed as a genus, abstraction, or a class, is insufficient to account for its own particularization.

The division of the principles of universality and particularity that characterized the conceptuality of the concept entailed a number of other features, such as the finitude of the concept, the denial of self-predication and existential implication, and the appeal to some kind of justifying non-conceptual foundation. The concept of truth characterizing these formulations of the concept engendered a *relative logic of truth* in which the concept is true in virtue of another principle. At bottom, the PNC, and the correlated principle of explosion, gave justification to this *relative* logic of truth. We discovered that all six problems—the problem of Nihilism, Instantiation, the Missing Difference, Absolute Empiricism, Onto-theology, and the Third Man—were all indebted to the division of principles of universality and particularity constituting the finite concept of the concept and the PNC that grounded it.

Given this diagnosis, we are in a position to systematically think through the possible solutions to the problem of the missing Absolute. Given that the PNC is the ultimate source of the relativity of truth, the only way the Absolute can be and can be known is by adopting *Absolute Dialetheism*. Most simply, this means that the Absolute can only be if it is contradictory. *If the Absolute exists it is a true contradiction. If there are no true contradictions, then the Absolute cannot be.* Likewise, if the Absolute is known, then there are true contradictions. *Were there no true contradictions, then the Absolute could not be known.*

Absolute Dialetheism may appear to be a *single* path, but it certainly is not. Because the concept can never have absolute truth if the PNC remains in force, *two* paths appear possible. Each of these paths are species of the same genus—they are species of the same generic solution to the problem of the disappearance of the Absolute—Absolute Dialetheism. (I) The Western tradition might have been fundamentally misguided in supposing that the PNC (and the correlated concept of explosive contradictions) is a necessary and essential feature of conceptual form. If this is the case, the Absolute could be salvaged by denying that the PNC governs conceptual determinacy. On certain sub-species of this solution, rather than discovering its truth outside of itself, the concept might be re-conceived to be *true in virtue of itself*. (II) Alternatively, if the PNC governs all conceptual determinacy, then the contradictory status of the Absolute would indicate that the Absolute is beyond all conceptual determination. This species of Absolute Dialetheism is what I call '*total absolute* mysticism.'

On the one hand, if rational knowing is constituted in a fundamentally determinate way, rational knowing would be insufficient for uncovering the truth of the indeterminate Absolute and its constitutive autonomy. We might designate this second species of Absolute Dialetheism, the non-discursive path to uncovering the indeterminate, as the *existential* variety, and it connotes one of the forks in the Western tradition. On the other hand, rather than give up on rational knowledge of the indeterminate Absolute, philosophy might instead *re-think* the very structure of conceptual knowing. We can re-think the domain of conceptual determinacy by denying that the PNC is a necessary structural condition of the truth of concepts or argue that the Absolute transcends conceptual form exactly because the PNC governs the domain of conceptual knowing. Indeed, in Hegel's own time, these were the two most plausible possibilities, which Hegel explicitly addresses in his famous preface to the *Phenomenology*. Rather than attempt to take refuge in one or more foundational principles, both species of Absolute Dialetheism recognize the need to *begin without any principles at all*. Because the Absolute disappears whenever one supposes any fundamental principles (whether they be one or many) in order to salvage the Being and knowledge of the Absolute, philosophy must *begin without any principles*. If philosophy endorses any principles, these must arise from a ground that is without any principle. To borrow a term from Schelling in his *Freedom Essay*, the principle must itself be an *Ungrund*.

The Absolute contradiction is a conceptual truth (I), or it transcends all conceptual truths (II). Within the former conception of the Absolute contradiction as a conceptual truth (I), there are generally two methods for proceeding. In *contemporary* philosophy, Graham Priest's paraconsistent logic and dialetheic theory of truth called into question dogmatic approaches to the PNC and its interpretation. On the one hand, Graham Priest has argued that one can move beyond the traditional logic with a *formal* paraconsistent logic. On the other hand, Hegel's dialectical logic in his *Science of Logic* develops a *non-formal truth logic* of the Absolute. Regarding logic, he says:

> This realm is truth unveiled, truth as it is in and for itself.[37]

And this realm of truth in and for itself is nothing other than the science of absolute form:

> Since logic is the science of the absolute form, this formal discipline, in order to be true, must have a content in it which is adequate to its form, all the more so, because logical form is pure form and logical truth, accordingly, the pure truth itself.[38]

Although Priest does not think that the existence of the world as such is a true contradiction, one could *extend* Priest's dialetheism to include the existence of the world as one instance of a true contradiction, or what I have called 'Absolute Dialetheism.'

Both Hegel and Graham Priest reject the *principle of explosion* and argue that there can be *true contradictions*. Since the non-positionality of the indeterminate certainly leads to a contradiction, namely both F and not-F, in order to affirm the truth of the indeterminate Absolute one might argue that contradictions can be true. Although the form of Graham Priest's logic (*paraconsistent* logic) by which he defends his theory of truth (*dialetheism*), is formal (while Hegel's dialectic is not), if the

Absolute *really is* contradictory as I have argued, both Hegel and Priest's conception of logic have the potential to give an account of the possibility of a *science* of the indeterminate Absolute. Although Hegel's version of Absolute Dialetheism commits him to an endorsement of a kind of 'onto-logical argument' for God's existence, affirming Absolute Dialetheism does not necessarily commit one to accepting a form of the ontological argument and all of the problems that arise with such an endorsement. The most common response to the problem of Absolute Knowledge, however, lies in a completely different direction than that of Hegel or Priest. Rather, in Western philosophy the most common solution to the problem in the tradition (and in Hegel's own time) is the second species of Absolute Dialetheism (II), namely some variety of mysticism which proclaims the Absolute to transcend conceptual determination.

The second species of Absolute Dialetheism—the view that the Abso-lute exists but transcends conceptual determination, cannot help but be profoundly *ironic*. If the being of the concept *as such* is contradictory, and the Absolute is contradictory, it would follow that the contradictory form of the concept as such would correspond to the contradictory form of the Absolute. Thus, the contradiction in concept would be true, for it would correspond to the contradiction in the Absolute. Given this result, mysticism would be forced to ironically proclaim the opposite of its own view, namely that *it can know the Absolute by means of the concept*. Although this might seem to refute mysticism, mysticism is the kind of view that can only succeed if it refutes itself. Given that all conceptual attempts to know the Absolute must fail, *the articulations of the mystic* too must fail. Thus, the mystic can demonstrate the truth of her position only via *the self-negation of all views*, including her own. By failing to conceptually articulate the concept, the mystic *experiences* the falling of the conceptual into the non-conceptual and thereby encounters the non-conceptual being that lies at the heart of the concept. The mystic must not necessarily proclaim that the concept does not exist, but rather that it exists in a form that negates conceptual truth, namely *as a contradiction*.

The most common solution to the problem in the tradition is to posit the Absolute as beyond conceptual knowing. Indeed, it is primarily in the *mystical* traditions of the various religions of the world, for example Sufism and Christian mysticism (Catholic, Eastern Orthodox, and Prot-estant), that we find exemplifications of such a view. In the 19th through 21st centuries, this position has been developed in various directions in philosophies as diverse as early German Romanticism, various strains of *Lebensphilosophie*, and most recently in the guise of the so-called theo-logical turn in French philosophy. In the 19th through 21st centuries the negative theological tendencies of the tradition were radicalized.

Philosophy in the so-called 'Continental tradition' has explored this possibility in a variety of ways. Traditions as diverse as the Kyoto School, Existentialism (e.g. Nietzsche and Kierkegaard), and Post-Structuralism (to take a few visible examples) acknowledge the existence of the indeterminate (and in some cases, *assert* that the indeterminate exists), but either problematize any complete scientific grasp thereof (such as in Deconstruction) or problematize any discursive account as violating some privileged logical form. If the form of knowledge is fundamentally positional and precludes the possibility of contradiction, in order to access the indeterminate condition for determinate knowledge claims, philosophy must *transcend the limits of conceptual knowing* and come to terms with the *insurmountable gap* between philosophical knowing and the indeterminate Absolute. In this sense, philosophy becomes a crisis in the sense of κρίσις—it is a crisis constituted by the *separation* between the Absolute indeterminacy and determinate philosophical knowing. Most recently, the work of William Desmond and William P. Franke has explored this direction of inquiry in their own very provocative ways.[39] The latter has not only argued for the plausibility of this view in his recent book *A Philosophy of the Unsayable* but has also encyclopedically documented varieties of this position in the history of philosophy in his two-volume set *On What Cannot Be Said*.[40]

Given the attraction of mysticism in Hegel's own time, Hegel directly addresses the mystical solution in his famous introduction to the *Phenomenology of Spirit*. Given the thorough treatment of this issue in the literature, we will focus on one main line of critique Hegel wields against this solution to the problem in that text. Naturally, Hegel's critique of the immediate non-conceptual approach to knowing the Absolute cannot address all of the various ways that conceptual knowing of the Absolute has been critiqued in the tradition after Hegel's own time.

If we assume that *philosophical* speech is governed by the parameters of conceptual determination and principles, how ought the philosopher relate to Being in regard to her speech? Clearly, the exceeding of the concept by Being points, without equivocation, to *silence*. It is in silence, not in the word, where Being directly reveals itself to philosophy. From this metaphysical nihilism we arrive at *total mysticism*. I call mysticism the thesis that *existence transcends conceptual determination and is accessible through non-conceptual or immediate means*. I add the term 'total' to signify that the object of the mystical insight is the absolute, the *totality*. Metaphysical nihilism entails a *total mysticism* in which Being can be, after the manner of Wittgenstein, only shown or pointed at with conceptual and philosophical language, rather than satisfactorily expressed in or by that language.[41] Rather than attempt to grasp Being in judgment, mysticism *employs the argument to transcend the argument* and thereby *experience* Being in a non-conceptual way. Indeed, this is the essence of Schleiermacher's *Rede* of 1799. Because the Absolute cannot be known conceptually, it can only be known in a way that transcends reason, which constitutes the meaning of religion. This appeal to an immediate knowledge that transcends reason was attractive not only to Catholic thinkers such as Jacobi but also to protestant thinkers such as Schleiermacher, for whom religion is *the intuition (Anschauung) of the universe.* As Hegel describes this mysticism:

> However much, that is to say, the true exists only in what, or rather exists only as what, is at one time called intuition and at another time called either the immediate knowing of the absolute, or religion, or being—not at the center of the divine love, but the being of divine love itself—still, if that is taken as the point of departure, what is at the same time demanded in the exposition of philosophy is going to be instead the very opposite of the form of the concept. The absolute is not supposed to be conceptually grasped but rather to be felt and intuited. It is not the concept but the feeling and intuition of the absolute which are supposed to govern what is said of it.[42]

This kind of mysticism is *mono*chromatic, for it posits the Absolute as accessed only in purely *immediate* knowledge, thereby *eschewing all mediation* and differentiation. Indeed, monochromatic mysticism 'craves for its refreshment only the bare feeling of the divine in general,' such that it is not the concept that is called for but ecstasy:

> The beautiful, the holy, the eternal, religion, and love itself are all the bait required to awaken the craving to bite. What is supposed to sustain and extend the wealth of that Substance is not the concept, but ecstasy, not the cold forward march of the necessity of the subject matter, but instead a kind of inflamed inspiration.[43]

In his *Phenomenology of Spirit* Hegel shows why monochromatic mysticism cannot succeed. Monochromatic mysticism fails to treat the Absolute *as Absolute.* Indeed, since speech about the Absolute is impossible, no principles of true and false speech can be invoked—therefore whatever speech the mystic employs becomes *radically contingent,*[44] and there is no necessity in what is said. Connected with this contingency, the monochromatic mystic reduces the Absolute to *finitude.*[45] Because the Absolute eschews all difference, determination, and conceptual structure, the Absolute excludes all difference, determination, and conceptual structure. Thus, the Absolute is *relative* to something that it excludes. The finitude of such a relation to the Absolute renders it *conditioned,* and thereby it cannot be Absolute. The monochromatic mystic reduces the Absolute to a relative feature of the Absolute. She replaces God with an idol and worships it as though it were God. What I have called 'monochromatic' mysticism is not the only kind of mysticism. There is another species of mysticism, *hermetic* mysticism, that affirms the possibility of mediated knowledge of the Absolute (e.g. via images) and for this reason does not fall prey to this objection.[46]

This very same argument is famously wielded against Schelling's *Identity* philosophy, for whom nature and spirit are grounded in a pure identity. This pure identity is 'indifferent' because it is held in common by both nature and spirit and does not differentiate between them. Mysticism is indeed motivated by the failure of all abstract approaches to the Absolute. Yet, by rejecting all mediated cognition and raising up immediacy as the truth of the Absolute (as Schelling does in the Identity philosophy) mysticism also falls victim to one-sided thinking and ironically relates to the Absolute in a *formal* way, for it treats the Absolute as one side of an opposition: the Absolute is 'A' and the non-Absolute, not-A, stands opposed to it. In the absolute identity of the Absolute immediacy, no difference can be discerned, nor can any difference be derived from what is not differentiated. To put it simply, monochromatic formalism falls victim to a version of the problem of the missing difference. Out of the immediate, no mediation can be derived. The night is black, and the cows are too:

> Nowadays we see all value ascribed to the universal Idea in this non-actual form, and the undoing all distinct, determinate entities (or rather the hurling of them all into the abyss of vacuity without further development or any justification) is allowed to pass muster as the speculative mode of treatment. Dealing with something from the perspective of the Absolute consists merely in declaring that, although one has been speaking of it just now as something definite, yet in the Absolute, the A=A, there is nothing of the kind, for there all is one. To pit this single insight, that in the Absolute everything is the same, against the full body of articulated cognition, which at least seeks and demands such fulfillment, to palm off the Absolute as the night in which, as the saying goes, all cows are black—this is cognition naively reduced to vacuity. This formalism which recent philosophy denounces and despises, only to see it reappear in its midst, will not vanish from Science, however much its inadequacy may be recognized and felt, till the cognizing of Absolute actuality has become entirely clear as to its own nature.[47]

Given the failure of monochromatic formalism, Hegel demonstrates that the first species of Absolute Dialetheism cannot succeed. Rather than preserving the Absolute, the mystical approach shrinks the Absolute to a relative and conditioned being. Indeed, because this form of mysticism undermines the Absolute status of the Absolute, it approaches the Absolute in the same way as the conceptual approach. Thus, in negating the conceptual, the mystic in fact adopts the same relativizing of the Absolute that characterized the traditional conceptual approach to Absolute Being and Knowing. Thus, the only species of Absolute Dialetheism left standing is the second method: re-think the conceptuality of the concept. In the following chapter, we will begin by turning to Hegel's solution to the problem of Absolute Knowledge, a solution that systematically develops a conceptual approach to Absolute Dialetheism.[48]

Notes

1. Priest points out that if a form were to instantiates itself, there would be no empty universals. Priest, *One* 111; note 21.
2. (C2) was introduced in the previous chapter. It states that there cannot be any particular concepts and there is at least one particular concept.
3. Because the undifferentiated character of universality leads to its own differentiation, it appears sufficient to sufficiently distinguish at least *one* of its particulars: itself. In addition, each of the particulars (U1-n) may be further distinguished by the order in which the particulars appear. Note also that at every stage of this regress, the same contradiction (C2) is repeated.
4. One might object that the infinite regress (UC1, UC2, n) is not vicious. For on non-well-founded set theory, sets can contain themselves. On this model, there would be nothing vicious about the universal containing itself as a particular. In response to this, one might be concerned that this argument would only apply to well-founded set theory such as ZFC in which sets cannot be members of themselves. Nonetheless, I think that this regress is arguably vicious for reasons independent of the mere *fact* that there is an infinite regress. In this regress the universal *sought after* is undifferentiated. Yet, the contradiction *thought* is differentiated. The undifferentiated universal becomes differentiated when it is posited a member of itself, for it is different from other members of the domain. Thus, the universal that is sought (the undifferentiated) is never thought. The viciousness of the regress lies in the semantic content of the concept that is posited here, namely the concept UNDIFFERENTIATED, not the mere fact of self-inclusion. Our concern here mirrors the *Third Man* argument in Plato's *Parmenides* concerning the Form of Forms. Priest correctly points out that in the *Parmenides* 'Socrates takes the Forms to be separate from the things that instantiate them. A form, then, cannot be identical to any of its instances.' Although Priest provides a different evaluation of this assumption, it nonetheless reflects the problem at hand. See Priest, *One: Being an Investigation into the Unity of Reality and of its Parts, Including the Singular Object which is Nothingness*, 111.
5. Plato, *Parmenides*, trans. Whitaker, 27, 129d–e.
6. Ibid, 30, 132a–b.
7. This is my insertion.
8. Aristotle, *Metaphysics*, 991a20.
9. Ibid, 987b11–15.
10. Ibid, 992a29–30.
11. Ibid, 1045b8–25.
12. 'But the most difficult thing of all to examine, as well as the most necessary for knowing the truth, is whether being and oneness are the principles of things,' Aristotle, *Metaphysics*, 1001a5 In a way, we see why they cannot be here. 'Form' itself is not a separate thing.
13. Note the correlation we established earlier in the modern section between the rejection of existential implication and the adoption of formal logic.
14. The term 'dialetheia' is a neologism, which means 'a true contradiction.' For more on the history of this term, see J. Norman, R. Routley, and Graham Priest, ed., *Paraconsistent Logic: Essays on the Inconsistent* (Analytica) (Oakland: University of California Press, 1989).

248 The Problem of Absolute Knowledge

15. Graham Priest, "What Is So Bad About Contradictions?" *The Journal of Philosophy* 95, no. 8 (1998): 410–426, 416. Also see Graham Priest, "Dialectic and Dialetheic," *Science & Society* 53, no. 4 (1989–90): 388–415, 388.
16. Recently work on Dialetheism connects the subject to a wide variety of philosophical issues. In Armour-Garb Bradley and J. C. Beall. "Further Remarks on Truth and Contradiction," *The Philosophical Quarterly* 52, no. 207 (2002): 217–225, the connection between Dialetheism and truth as correspondence is thematic. Also see their essay "Should Deflationists be Dialetheists?" *Noûs* 37, no. 2 (2003): 303–324. The relation between Dialetheism and Omniscience is discussed in Peter Milne's, "Omniscient Beings are Dialetheists," *Analysis* 67, no. 295 (2007): 250–251, and Jesper Kallestrup's, "If Omniscient Beings are Dialetheists, So Are Anti-Realists," *Analysis* 67, no. 3 (2007): 252–254. In comparative philosophy, Priest has worked together with Yasuo Deguchi and Jay L. Garfield, "The Way of the Dialetheist: Contradictions in Buddhism," *Philosophy East and West* 58, no. 3 (2008): 395–402. Moreover, the discussion of Dialetheism has made its way into a variety of textbooks; for example, see chapter seven (150–158) of the third edition of *Paradoxes*, by R. M. Sainsbury, who has devoted a chapter to discussing Dialetheism as a response to paradoxes of self-reference, such as the Liar and Russell's Paradox. See R. M. Sainsbury, *Paradoxes* (Cambridge: Cambridge University Press, 2015). The relation between Idealism and Dialetheism is discussed in Francesco Berto's, "Is Dialetheism an Idealism? The Russellian Fallacy and the Dialetheist's Dilemma," *Dialectica* 61, no. 2 (2007): 235–263. For further responses to Priest's work, as well as the connection between Dialetheism and Analetheism, Logical Inference, Consequence, and Triviality; see J. C Beall and David Ripley, "Analetheism and Dialetheism," *Analysis* 64, no. 1 (2004): 30–35; Nicholas Denyer, "Dialetheism and Trivialization." *Mind*, New Series 98, no. 390 (1989): 259–263; Bruno Whittle, "Dialetheism, Logical Consequence and Hierarchy," *Analysis* 54, no. 4 (2004): 318–326, Anthony Everett, "Absorbing Dialetheia?" *Mind* 103, no. 412 (1994): 413–419, Jürgen Dümont and Frank Mau, "Are There True Contradictions? A Critical Discussion of Graham Priest's 'Beyond the Limits of Thought'," *Journal for General Philosophy of Science* /Zeitschrift für allgemeine Wissenschaftstheorie 29, no. 2 (1998): 289–299, and Terence Parsons, "True contradictions," *Canadian Journal of Philosophy* 20, no. 3 (1990): 335–353.
17. Graham Priest, "Logic of Paradox," *Journal of Philosophical Logic*, 8, no. 1 (1979, 1986): 219–241. Also see Priest, "What Is So Bad About Contradictions?" 415.
18. This problem has been raised and discussed within the context of the history of philosophy, but has not been systematically investigated independently. See Halper, "Hegel and the Problem of the Differentia."
19. More specifically, in this text I will be employing the term 'concept' to mean the 'concept of being a concept.'
20. Graham Priest, *In Contradiction* (Oxford: Oxford University Press, 2006), 4.
21. Given the availability of competing 'non-classical' logics, such as Priest's Logic of *Paradox* which is wholly compatible with Dialetheism, it is neither responsible nor sufficient to reject Dialetheism out of hand by noting its incompatibility with traditional methods of formal analysis. At this juncture I wish to sideline the question about whether dialetheism requires paraconsistent logic, though we will return to these issues in our discussion of Hegel in Part II. One must also be careful not to conflate dialectical logic with Dialetheism. See Priest, "Dialectic and Dialetheic," 396. For more on the connection between dialectical logic, Dialetheism, and paraconsistent logic, see Priest's "The Logical Structure of Dialectic," (Draft).

22. Every philosophical theory or argument employs concepts. If it were true that any theory of concept formation must entail *true contradictions*, then the classical formal logic of Frege and Russell would fail to give sufficient articulation to such a theory. Accordingly, not only would dialetheic logic be more suitable for articulating a theory of concepts, but it would also be *more general* than the so-called classical formal logic, for the most general logic possible would be that logic by which the form and structure of concepts in general could be articulated. Priest states it succinctly: 'Thus we may stretch Hegel's claim a little as follows: (Frege/Russell) formal logic is perfectly valid in its domain, but dialectical (dialetheic) logic is more general.' See Priest, "Dialectic and Dialetheic," 395.

23. Priest, "What Is So Bad About Contradictions?" 424.

24. Priest, *Beyond the Limits of Thought*, 124. In 8.7 of the same text Priest provides a more precise formulation of the principle in respect to the infinite: 'for every potential infinity there is a corresponding actual infinity.' For Priest's defense of the principle, see 8.8. Since my concern in this text is not infinity *per se*, at this juncture it is only necessary to emphasize the necessity of totalization rather than the relation of potential to actual infinities. Cantor defends the principle in the following way: 'for a statement about some variable quantity to have determinate sense, the domain of variability must be determinate,' Priest, *Beyond the Limits of Thought*, 125.

25. Hegel, in his *Science of Logic*, says as much (though for different reasons perhaps): 'every determination, anything concrete, every concept, is essentially a unity of distinguished and distinguishable elements which, by virtue of the determinate essential difference, pass over into elements which are contradictory.' Hegel, *SL*, trans. Giovanni, 2015, 384.

26. Of course, as meaning goes, even if there were no true contradictions, it would not be obvious that contradictions could not be meaningful. For as Quine points out in "On What There Is," if we could not identify the meaning of the contradiction, then we would not know what we mean to reject. Willard L. Quine, "On What There Is," *Review of Metaphysics* 2, no. 5 (1948): 21–38.

27. This is the way Hegel construes the concept. Hegel rejects the PNC as an absolute principle of logic. See Hegel, *SL*, trans. Giovanni, 384.

28. C2 states that 'there cannot be any particular concepts and there is at least one particular concept.' See Chapter 6 for more details.

29. See Part II for Hegel's dialetheism. For Hegel's dialetheic account of the CONCEPT as self-differentiating, see Hegel, *SL*, trans. Giovanni, 529–549.

30. One might argue that to possess a particular concept is nothing more than to have *the ability* to differentiate instances of the CONCEPT from what do not count as proper instances. On this view, such a claim would not answer one very important question: *what* is it *in virtue of which* one is able to differentiate instances of some concept from non-instances of the same concept? In a case in which one is attempting to differentiate concepts from what are not concepts, being in possession of the predicate 'is a concept' appears necessary to embark on such a classification.

31. If conceptual pluralism entails that there is not one overarching domain of concepts, then conceptual pluralism would entail the elimination of such a domain.

32. Priest, *Beyond the Limits of Thought*, 136. The VCP is developed in response to Russell's paradox. Russell's paradox is the simplest contradiction to which one can appeal to show that the naïve conception of a set is inconsistent. See Priest, *In Contradiction*, 29–30.

33. Priest points out, I believe correctly, that Russell, Kant, and Aristotle all deny enclosure in different ways. See Priest, *Beyond the Limits of Thought*, 136.

Although this requires more space than I am allotted here, for Aristotle, 'Being' is not a univocal genus, for it is *'pros hen.'* See Aristotle, *Metaphysics*, 998b20. For Kant the sum of all possibilities cannot be transmuted into *a* 'highest being' or the 'being of all beings.' See Kant, *CPR*, B601–B606. Markus Gabriel's denial of the existence of the world also seems to deny enclosure.

34. Priest, *Beyond the Limits of Thought*, 223, fn 24.
35. Priest represents the re-location in the following way: the contradiction in the VCP is relocated from a paradox of thinking to a paradox of expression. For Priest, 'Russell's theory cannot be expressed [transcendence], but he does express it [closure]. Hence we have a contradiction at the limit of expression,' Priest, *Beyond the Limits of Thought*, 140. For Priest Russell's theory of orders involves universal quantification insofar as it explains that 'every propositional function has a determinate order.' See Priest, *Beyond the Limits of Thought*, 138, 140, 155, 10.7.
36. I am deeply indebted to Graham Priest for his comments on these issues.
37. Hegel, *SL*, trans. Giovanni, 29.
38. Ibid, 524.
39. See, for example, Desmond's provocative concept of 'over-determination.' William Desmond, "Overdeterminacy, Affirming Indeterminacy, and the Dearth of Ontological Astonishment," in *The Significance of Indeterminacy: Perspectives from Asian and Continental Philosophy*, ed. Robert Scott and Gregory S. Moss (New York: Routledge, 2018), 51–66.
40. For a more focused treatment of this tendency in the thought of Nietzsche, Kierkegaard, the early Heidegger, and Sartre, among others, see Gregory S. Moss, "The Emerging Philosophical Recognition of the Significance of Indeterminacy," in *Significance of Indeterminacy*, ed. Robert Scott and Gregory S. Moss (New York: Routledge, 2018), 1–47.
41. It is important to distinguish speech that is governed by the parameters of conceptual determination and speech that frees itself from such boundaries. For example, it is not evident that all speech, such as some forms of literary or poetic speech, must necessarily abide by the PNC and other limits imposed by formal logic. There may be other kinds of speech which are capable of successfully communicating some meaning other than that employed in conceptual and philosophical discourse.
42. Hegel, *PS*, trans. Pinkard, 6.
43. Ibid, 7.
44. Ibid, 6.
45. Ibid, 4.
46. My distinction between hermetic and non-hermetic mysticism tracks Muratori's distinction between two types of mysticism. See Cecelia Muratori, *The First German Philosopher: The Mysticism of Jakob Böhme as Interpreted by Hegel* (Dordrecht: Springer, 2016), 87. Glenn Magee, in *Hegel and the Hermetic Tradition*, convincingly shows that Hegel's metaphysics is a rationalization of the hermetic mysticism of Boehme and others. Hermetic mysticism is the view that (among other things) God is completed by means of the human knowledge of God. Unlike immediate monochromatic mysticism, hermetic mysticism does allow *mediated* knowledge of God, for example via images and representations. It is unclear whether hermetic mysticism can provide a plausible alternative to Hegel's system. See Glenn Magee, *Hegel and the Hermetic Tradition* (Ithaca: Cornell University Press, 2008). What can be said in advance of a more substantial discussion is that without the rationalization of hermetic mysticism, the knowing of God via the imagination remains bound to *contingent* determinations.

47. Hegel, *PS*, trans. Pinkard, 9.
48. Redding is right that the problem of contradiction in Hegel re-raises the question of Hegel's metaphysics. See Paul Redding, *Analytic Philosophy and the Return of Hegelian Thought* (Cambridge: Cambridge University Press, 2007), 219. As I understand it, the middle term here is the absolute, for true contradictions are necessary in order to conceive the Absolute.

Part II

Hegel's Absolute Dialetheism

8 Hegel's Logic of the Concept
The Concept of Self-Particularization

The Dialectic of Identity and Difference

In the previous chapter, we demonstrated that the separation between principles of identity and difference leads to *contradiction*. It is important to note that Hegel's *Logic* develops these logical relations as well, though according to his own *dialectical* logic. By briefly re-constructing Hegel's dialectic of identity and difference from his *Logic of Essence*, we can motivate Hegel's dialetheism while also illustrate the identity of synthesis and analysis (in its purely categorial sense). For Hegel, every concept in the Logic is a definition of the Absolute:

> Being itself and the special sub-categories of it which follow, as well as those of logic in general, may be looked upon as definitions of the Absolute.[1]

Since every concept in the *Logic* is a definition of the Absolute, and the categories of identity and difference are categories in the *Logic*, we can employ Hegel's elucidation of these categories as instances of what he considers to be Absolute concepts. Regarding the Absolute Difference (between identity and difference), Hegel writes that

> It is essential that we grasp absolute difference as simple. In the absolute difference of A and not-A from each other, it is the simple 'not' which, as such, constitutes the difference.[2]

The principle of identity that states that 'A' is necessarily 'A' entails that 'A' is not 'not-A.' The 'not' that separates 'A' and 'not-A' is the absolute difference. The PNC, as well as the principle of identity, require the elevation of an absolute difference between 'A' and 'not-A.'[3] This is evident in the principle of excluded middle. Absolute Difference, as *absolute*, is not itself opposed to anything else. Unlike 'something' and 'other' in the *logic of Being*, in which the 'other' is one side of an opposition, absolute difference is not one side of an opposition. It is the difference *simpliciter*, not difference opposed to some other. Absolute Difference is not itself immediately opposed to identity. Instead, absolute difference is *the Difference* itself between 'difference' and 'identity.' Accordingly, Absolute Difference is itself *not different from anything*—as absolute it is not conditioned by an '*other*'; it is not *relative* to an 'other.' To put it another way, absolute difference is the *whole* of the opposition: it is the Absolute. According to Hegel:

> Difference in itself is the difference that refers itself to itself; thus it is the negativity of itself, the difference not from another but *of itself from itself*; it is not itself but its other. What is different from difference, however is identity. Difference is, therefore, itself and identity. The two together constitute difference; difference is the whole and its moment.—One can also days that difference as simple difference, is no difference; it is such only with reference to identity; even better, that as difference it entails itself and this reference equally.[4]

Since difference is absolute, it neither stands in any relation to an other nor is it opposed to anything other to itself. Hence, difference is *not different* from anything. For something to count as a difference, and stand in a relation of difference, it must stand in a negative relation to something in virtue of which it is *not* that other. Absolute Difference, however, does not stand in any relation of difference to anything, for it is absolute. Thus, Absolute Difference, or difference *as such*, is *different from difference itself*. As Hegel comments here, difference turns back on itself, for it is *self-referring (sich beziehen)*. Its form of self-reference is a *self-negation*: it is 'the negativity of itself.' Insofar as 'difference is different' difference is *self-identical*. It is an analytic truth that 'difference is different'—the quality of 'being different' is engendered by difference itself. We find that the predicate 'different' is contained in the subject: 'difference.' But it is not just analytic. Given that difference as such is not just different, but *different from itself*, and what is different from difference is just identity, difference is *not different* from identity. Insofar as it is not different from identity, it is identical to identity. Thus, difference is synthetic, for it is connected to what is completely different from it. In addition, because difference is still *different* from difference, difference as such does stand in a relationship of difference—it stands in a difference *with itself*. Thus, difference *as difference* is both *difference and identity*. Its identity is to be *different from itself*. Or: its self-difference is its self-identity. That in virtue of which it is connected to another, identity, is that in virtue of which it is identical to itself: difference—through the self-referential application of the category to itself— it is a unity of synthesis and analysis.

This moment of Hegel's dialectic exemplifies the way that analysis and synthesis are integrated into purely conceptual relations. 'Difference is different' compares the concept with itself—yet through this analytic self-comparison, the concept *amplifies itself* into identity with its other: identity. Dialectic is the *self-amplification of thought* by means of the self-referential character of conceptual thinking. Through self-reference, the category synthetically connects itself to its negation: it is the *self-mediating determination* sought by Schelling in *STI* by which truth (the agreement of the concept with itself) can be attained by *thinking alone*.

As a result, difference as such *differentiates itself into two differences*: difference and identity. Difference cannot be distinguished from the elements which are opposed. As Hegel writes, 'it [difference][5] is the whole and its moment.' Put another way, the absolute difference is the *self-identity* of the whole opposition of A *or* not-A[6]: Concerning Absolute Difference, Hegel claims that it contains an *implicit* contradiction:

> Difference as such is already implicitly contradiction; for it is the unity of beings which are, only in so far as they are not one—and it is the separation of beings which are, only in so far as they are separated in the same reference connecting them.[7]

More exactly, the category of difference immediately gives rise to diversity, from which polar opposition arises. It is out of the concept of polar opposition (of the positive and negative) that the category of contradiction is posited *per se*.

Although my intention is to show the implicit contradiction in the concept of absolute difference, it may be of some use to briefly elucidate what Hegel calls the 'posited contradiction.' Each of the constituents of difference—identity and difference—are diverse. They can be compared to each other as *like* and *unlike*. Determinations of like and unlike however, do not affect the identity of each of the elements that are compared. Each could be what it is without the comparison—without being determined to be 'like' or 'unlike' something else. Since absolute difference gives rise to both identity and difference *as relative differences*, and each admits the other, identity contains difference and difference contains identity. The former is the *positive*, identity and difference in the form of identity, and the latter is the *negative*, identity and difference in the form of difference. The positive contains its other (the negative) as its negation—as what it is not, and is what it is through its negation of the negative. Likewise, the negative is what it is in virtue of its negation of the positive.[8] Unlike something and other, 'positive' and 'negative' are contraries, in the sense that the opposition here is one of *specific difference*. The negative is the specific other of the positive; the positive is the specific other of the negative. In other words, each is *its* other, *not* just *any* other.[9] The positive is the unity of identity and difference in the form of identity, while the negative is the unity of identity and difference in the form of difference. Since in the formulation of each, identity and difference are united, each is reducible to the formulation of the other: the positive is negative and the negative positive. Each contrary, though opposed to its other, has an identical formulation: *each is what it is through the negation of its negation*. Accordingly, the category of contradiction consists in just this: the positive is negative in virtue of itself and the negative positive in virtue of itself. From the identity of identity and difference, Hegel proceeds to further develop his concept of 'Ground.'[10] Contradiction as such is posited through the failure to distinguish identity from difference and difference from identity. Hegel sums it up neatly:

> Contradiction is the very moving principle of the world: and it is ridiculous to say that contradiction is unthinkable. The only thing correct about that statement is that contradiction is not the end of the matter, but cancels itself. But contradiction, when cancelled, does not leave abstract identity; for that is itself only one side of the contrariety. The proximate result of opposition (When realized as contradiction) is the Ground.[11]

Given that absolute difference necessarily gives rise to the polar opposites of negative and positive, one would be mistaken to claim that these principles have *separate* roots—as the tradition tends to maintain. Instead, their *common root* would be absolute difference. What is more, if absolute difference violates the PNC, and is an element of itself, then absolute difference would instantiate the very definition of the concept of the concept that is evident in Hegel. Following this reasoning, the absolute separation of the affirmative and negative cannot help but *turn back on itself [Rückkehr in sich]*[12]; the affirmation of the absolute separation of affirmation and negation is also the absolute negation of the separation of affirmation and negation.

Throughout this dialectical endeavor we are reminded of Aristotle in book Lambda of his *Metaphysics*. Aristotle tells us that Plato argued that 'all things come from contraries.' But neither 'all things' nor 'from contraries' is correct. Instead, in the vein of Aristotle, let us speak as one voice with him: 'Let there be one Lord.'

The Logic of the Concept: Truth Logic and Self-Particularization

In *The Concept in General*, Hegel begins by pointing out that it is difficult to discover what others have thought about the concept. In the history of philosophy the concept itself has rarely been treated as its own object of inquiry:

> And also, whereas the concept of the concept as deduced here should in principle be recognized in whatever else is otherwise adduced as such a concept, it is not easy to ascertain what others have said about

its nature. For in general they do not bother at all enquiring about it but presuppose that everyone already understands what the concept means when speaking of it. Of late especially one may indeed believe that it is not worth pursuing any such enquiry because, just as it was for a while the fashion to say all things bad about the imagination, then about memory, it became in philosophy the habit some time ago, and is still the habit now, to heap every kind of defamation on the concept, to hold it in contempt—the concept which is the highest form of thought—while the *incomprehensible* and the *non-comprehended* are regarded as the pinnacle of both science and morality.[13]

In this passage Hegel recognizes the attraction of mysticism in his own time and speculates that the attraction of mysticism has encouraged thinkers to ignore the issue altogether. In the history of philosophy, discussions of concepts in general are often bound up and conflated with other issues of greater import to philosophers, such as Form, God, or objectivity.[14] By attending to what the concept is, Hegel aims to thematize a question rarely asked in its own right[15] and hopes to thereby avoid the appeal to mysticism that is arguably already evident in the writings of the most noble Plato.

Hegel recognizes that the paradoxes governing the relation between universal and particular are not primarily about the relation between universals and sensual (temporal and spatial) particulars. Instead, the problem of participation of the particular in the universal (as it pertains to the problem of Instantiation and the Third Man) primarily concerns the relation of universals to particulars *simpliciter*, without further qualification. What is of primary concern is the logical status of their relationship. Hegel returns to the question 'what is universality?'

Hegel's definition of the concept is the power of self-differentiation or better: *self-particularization* in which each element of the whole is identical to the whole itself. As we have shown, the concept of absolute difference (as well as self-identity) must be an element of itself and accordingly has the form of a concept:

> Difference is the whole and its own moment, just as identity equally is its whole and its moment. This is to be regarded as the essential nature of reflection and as the *determined primordial origin of all activity* and *self-movement*.[16]

This definition is a re-working of Schelling's concept of the *self-mediating principle* of philosophy. In Hegel's words, 'each of these moments is no less the *whole* concept than it is a *determinate* concept and *a determination* of the concept.'[17] Hegel's definition of the concept reflects Schelling's insight that the truth must be an element of itself: the subjective pole (as well as the objective pole) of the subject-object unity must itself be a unity of the subject and the object. Or put in terms of *synthesis*: synthetic unity accounts *for itself*—synthesis makes itself possible.

The dialectic of identity and difference demonstrates that any attempt to posit an *absolute difference* between identity and difference necessarily engenders a self-particularizing structure. Indeed, although 'self-particularization' *itself* is not the category that follows from the dialectic of identity and difference, the dialectic of identity and difference nonetheless *instantiates* the structure of self-particularization endemic to all concepts of the Absolute. What is more, if we consider the question 'what is the concept?' on its own terms, we discover that the only legitimate answer to the question is one that is self-particularizing.

The collapse of the concept of the concept merely as a principle of identity invites us to return to a very basic question: *what is the concept?* Given that on the traditional conception of the concept as governed by duality of principles of universality and particularity no description of the concept seems possible, the concept itself is never actually thought at all. So, what is the sense of that about which one inquires into the sense of the concept? Having considered *six* distinct problems, namely the problem of Nihilism (Chapters 1 and 2), Instantiation (Chapter 3), the Missing Difference (Chapter 5), Absolute Empiricism (Chapter 5), Onto-theology (Chapter 6), and the Third Man regress (Chapter 7), we should take a moment to reflect on the very *sense* of the question: 'what is the concept?' in which the 'what' connotes some *sense*.

When we inquire into the conceptual character of some particular concept, such as the concept of number, we are interested in the extent to which a particular concept, such as number, exemplifies the characteristic that is constitutive of the concept. When we ask 'what is the concept?' we must answer that 'the concept is such and such.' To say of a subject that it is such and such is to attribute a concept, a universal, to the subject. Accordingly, we are not inquiring into how some particular concept exemplifies the characteristic of the concept, but how the concept itself exemplifies the concept, namely whatever it is to be conceptual. The concept, of course, is that in virtue of which any particular concept, such as number or quality, is universal. Naturally, then, it would appear that our question 'what is the concept?' must take for granted that the concept itself has that very characteristic 'being conceptual' in virtue of which it grants conceptual content to every concept. For this reason, the question 'what is the concept?' asks 'what is conceptual about the concept?' This formulation applies the term 'concept' *to that which is already inherently conceptual* or that which is conceptual *in virtue of itself*. Instead of applying 'the concept' to a particular concept, the question apparently implies that we must apply the term 'concept' to the term 'concept.' Accordingly, the question 'what is the concept?' requires a self-referential answer.

One might suppose that the question 'what is the concept?' is peculiar insofar as it requires a self-predicative answer. But in fact it shares a common feature with other related questions concerning the Absolute, such as 'what is Being?' and 'what is Knowledge?': Each of these questions asks about the Absolute. The former inquiries into Absolute *Being*, while the latter formulates the question of the Absolute in terms of Absolute *Knowledge*. When we answer the question 'what is Being' we must answer that 'Being is such and such.' This answer *predicates the concept of Being to itself*. When one specifies what Being is, or specifies what it is for Being *to be*, one has applied the concept back to itself. The self-referring reflexivity of the question demands a self-referring and reflexive answer. Likewise, the question 'what is knowledge?' can only be answered by proclaiming some *knowledge about what knowledge is*. Knowledge as such is *un*conditioned, for it contains all knowledge and is not conditioned externally by any form of knowledge. Likewise, Being is *un*conditioned, for it is not conditioned by any being that lies beyond it. Given that each is universal and unconditioned, each is *Absolute*. As Absolute, there is no knowledge outside of knowledge by which knowledge can be determined, no being outside of Being by which Being can be determined, and finally *no concept beyond the concept* by which the concept might be determined. Simply put: any question concerning the Absolute requires a self-predicative answer because each is Absolute.

Upon recognizing that the question is self-predicative, we may also immediately recognize why the question itself implies the infinite regress we encountered in the paradox of the Third Man regress. Because the question 'what is the concept?' covertly applies the concept to itself, the concept itself must also have some universal, conceptual content. Insofar as the concept has some conceptual content that is its own, that conceptual content will constitute the predicate in the following judgment: 'the concept is such and such.' Because the concept will then have its *own* conceptual, universal content, it cannot be identified with *other* particular concepts, such as the concepts of number or quality. Hence, the concept must therefore be a distinct concept that is different from others. As a distinct concept, it will be a particular concept that is *one in number*. As a particular concept, the concept appears to be its own particular, or its own instance. In sum, the self-referential aspect of the question 'what is the concept?' implies that it is an instance of itself. Thus, the self-predicative character of the question implies that the concept is *existentially implicative*. In order to answer the question 'what is the concept?' not only must the concept apply to itself in a self-referentially and self-predicative way but it must also be sufficient for the creation of a particular instance of that self-predicative concept, namely *itself*.[18]

The existentially implicative aspect of the concept of the concept is also evident in the questions concerning the Being of Being and the knowledge of knowledge. Since the question 'what is Being?' can only be answered in a *self-predicative* way, by predicating Being to the subject 'Being' one would place 'Being' in the genus or class of Beings. By placing Being in the set of beings, Being would no longer merely be the class of all beings, but would also be *one particular being within the class* itself. Likewise, knowing what knowing is introduced a special kind of knowledge: epistemology, which is a knowing that is *distinct* from other kinds of knowing.[19] Just as the inquiry into the absolute determination of the concept engenders existential implication, so do the inquiries into Being and Knowledge. Simply put: any inquiry into the Absolute will discover that its concepts cannot do without self-predication and existential implication.

Following the self-predicative and existentially implicative dimension of the question: 'what is the concept?' we immediately discover that the question 'what is the concept?' requires that the only legitimate answer to the question must establish an *internal* principle of truth. Because the universal must be particular in virtue of itself, the correspondence of *this* particular, namely, the particular concept 'universality itself' can be established by consulting *the concept of universality alone*. Thus, the only legitimate answer to the question 'what is the concept?' demands that the answer construe the concept as that which is true in virtue of itself. The truth of the concept, or the *existence of the concept in instantiated form*, can be achieved by means of the concept alone without having to refer to *other principles*. Since 'Absolute Truth' not only would engender the correspondence of the concept with its instantiation but also requires that the truth be *un*conditioned, a concept would be absolutely truth if it were not true in virtue of another, but would be *true in virtue of itself*.[20] Since the question 'what is the concept?' is *existentially implicative*, it follows that the concept is true in virtue of itself and is thereby *absolutely* true. Indeed, the concept of the concept that is self-predicative and thereby existentially implicative ought to also be absolutely true, true in virtue of itself, or *kath auto*. Thus, the question 'what is the concept?' invites us to answer the question *absolutely*.

Following this line of thinking, the question 'what is the concept?' leads us to re-think the finitude of the concept. Since the concept as such must be self-predicative, existentially implicative, and true in virtue of itself, it would no longer be finite in the sense that it would no longer depend upon another principle of truth that would lie outside of it. To put it in the language of early idealism, anyone who takes the logic of the question 'what is the concept?' seriously ought to recognize that the concept cannot just be *analytic*, but must be *synthetic* too. Since the question 'what is the concept?' demands an existentially implicative answer, the concept 'goes beyond itself' into particularity, or is *ampliative*. However, it would not be ampliative in virtue of another principle in addition to or beyond the concept. Rather, it would be synthetic in virtue of the *analyticity* of the concept (that which is true of the concept in terms of what is already *contained* within it). The universal would be connected to what is different from it, or not-identical to it, for example particularity, in virtue of its *own* universal content alone; it would be synthetic in virtue of its analyticity. Just the same, the concept would no longer be a mere possibility to be, but insofar as it is *possible*, it would *necessarily be actual*. In short, no absolute knowing is possible without self-particularizing concepts, and self-particularizing concepts are synthetic in virtue of their very analyticity, as is exemplified in the dialectic of identity and difference.

Because the universal is self-predicative and existentially implicative, it must also be contradictory. Because the PNC necessarily entails that the principles of universality and differentiation are separate, and the question 'what is the concept?' can only be legitimately answered by negating the separation of these principles, the question 'what is the concept' entails that any legitimate answer to the question will reject the PNC. Or to put it another way, since the universal is particular *in virtue* of being universal, its particularity consists *in* its universality. Since it is a contradiction for the universal to be particular *in virtue* of its universality, the question 'what is the concept?' implies a contradiction and calls for a dialetheic answer. One of Hegel's most profound insights is that *truth logic is dialetheic*.

Hegel's logic of the concept, which follows the logic of the question 'what is the concept?' recognizes that the concept must be self-predicative, existentially implicative (or self-particularizing), true in virtue of itself (absolutely true), simultaneously synthetic as well as analytic, infinite (not limited by an external principle), and contradictory. Given that *truly conceiving* the Absolute is only possible by integrating self-predicative and existentially implicative structure into conceptual determinacy, any conception of the concept that denies these features of conceptual determinacy cannot succeed in *truly* conceiving the Absolute. Having recognized this, Hegel no longer models his concept on the separation of the principles of universality and particularity. Rather, he acknowledges the self-predicative feature of the concept in order that the concept can achieve Absolute Knowledge.

The inability to successfully conceive the Absolute in thinkers as diverse as Plato, Aristotle, Kant, Fichte, and Schelling is fundamentally grounded in their insistence on a dualistic interpretation of *concepts* in which the principle of the particular and the universal are separated. Such a separation engenders a denial of self-predication and (in *most* cases but not all) existential implication and thereby the impossibility of Absolute Knowledge. Where self-predication is acknowledged as it is in Plato, it is present only as a *problem*. Naturally, Kant's thinking distinguishes itself insofar as he draws the inference that the Absolute cannot be known if we abide by the duality of principles of universality and particularity. The denial of self-predication as well as the tendency to split conceptual determinacy into a duality of principles continually introduces new paradoxes and problems concerning Absolute Knowledge that cannot be solved on merely conceptual grounds. Most baldly formulated, since there cannot be Absolute Knowledge without *true* contradictions, the tradition can only offer headway on the problem of Absolute Knowledge in those thinkers such as Hegel who have acknowledged the *truth of contradiction.*

Having explicated the question 'what is universality?', we have also elucidated the necessary features of any successful answer to the question. First, the universal is self-referring. Second, in virtue of its self-reference, the universal creates its own particulars. If we consider universality as a domain, each particular instance of the domain would be a differentiation of that domain. Accordingly, the particular instances of universality would be differentiations of the domain of universality. Third, the particular universal created by the self-referring universality is identical to universality itself. Since these three features follow necessarily from the question itself, any sufficient answer to the question 'what is universality?' must accommodate them. Indeed, Hegel's initial specification of universality in his *Doctrine of the Concept* incorporates each of these features into the construal of the universal. Having recognized that the universal, though its self-referential activity, creates its own particulars or differentiations, Hegel's universal is the power of self-particularization. Since the particular is universality in some differentiated form, the power of self-particularization is just as much the power of self-differentiation.[21] Self-differentiation is the way that universality acts on or refers to itself. Moreover, since universality is its own particular and differentiation, universality is the whole in which each element of the whole, or each differentiation of the whole, is the whole itself. We cannot do justice to the question 'what is universality?' while denying the identity of the whole with its elements or differentiations.[22]

The differentiations of the universal, as differentiations, are distinct from universality itself. Yet, the differentiations, or particulars of universality are nonetheless identical to universality. Thus, the universal *remains itself* even in that which is distinct from it, namely its particulars. This is another dimension of the Neo-Platonic legacy in Hegel, for Plotinus also conceives of thought thinking itself as staying the same as itself in its otherness.[23] It does *not* become or cease to be what it is in its differences or confront an 'other' in its differences in which it does not find itself. Moreover, it is only what it is, the self-differentiating universal, only insofar as the universal stays itself in virtue of differentiating itself into various contents distinct from it, which it nonetheless contains within itself. For Hegel, to be a universal is to admit what is *other* to itself and to *maintain its identity* in lieu of the self-differentiation. Hegel writes:

> The universal, on the contrary, even when it posits itself in a determination, remains therein what it is. It is the soul [Seele] of the concrete which it indwells, unimpeded and equal to itself in the manifoldness [Mannigfaltigkeit] and diversity [Verschiedenheit] of the concrete.

It is not dragged into the process of becoming, but continues itself through that process undisturbed and possesses the power of unalterable, undying self-preservation [Selbsterhaltung].[24]

Hegel claims that 'each of the moments is just as much the *whole* concept as it is *determinate* concept and *a determination* of the concept.'[25] Since the self-differentiating universal must be indistinguishable from its differences, each difference posited by the concept must be the whole concept. In other words, *each* differentiation of the universal is just the universal. Because all otherness has been transcended, all otherness between all differences posited by the universal must be overcome—it cannot help but find itself in each difference—in each moment of otherness. Accordingly, the universal is identical with its differentiations, or its particulars. The unity of the universal with the particular is what Hegel calls the *singular* (*Einzelheit*), or what has for a long time been translated and discussed as *the individual*. Each universal is 'such and such'—it is universal. Yet, each universal is particular, for it is a differentiation of universality or an *instance* of universality. Each is a *this*. Since the universal is both a 'this' and a 'such and such,' it is a *this such and such*, it is not just universal or particular, but it is *both*. The identity of each universal as *this such and such* is what Hegel captures with this term 'singularity': it is the unity of universality and particularity. Given that the universal is identical to the particulars, the universal is singular and particular, the particular is universal and singular, and the singular is universal and particular. Indeed, insofar as each of these is its own determinate concept that is opposed to the others, each of the moments is a *determinate* concept.[26] In other words, each is a particular. Insofar as each is a constituent *of* the concept as such, each is also a determination *of* the universal *per se*. In other words, each is a singular concept—this such and such. In sum, the whole concept has three elements each of which is the whole concept: the universal, particular, and singular.

The Absolute Determinacy of the Concept: Foundation Free Logic

At this point, two concerns might be justifiably raised. First, one might reasonably hypothesize that Hegel proceeds by modeling the features of the concept on a particular construal of the Absolute. Given that the Absolute is infinite and must be true in virtue of itself, it would be reasonable to model the construal of conceptual determination on the Absolute. On this understanding of the procedure, the Absolute would be a kind of given—a fact—which would provide a model for imbuing the concept with the very features acknowledged to exist in the Absolute. Second, one might reasonably ask *why*, despite our particular critiques of Kant (as we laid them out in Chapters 1 and 5), the transcendental turn cannot succeed. In other words, if we cannot think the Absolute by means of concepts, there may be good reason to prohibit any attempt to imbue the concept with the features of the Absolute.

Beside the more obvious fact that Hegel's philosophy ought to be without presupposition, in order to understand why Hegel does not model his concept on the givenness of the Absolute, as though it were given in advance, we must first appreciate why one cannot be satisfied with the transcendental turn. There are two problematic features of the transcendental turn I would like to highlight here, though there are certainly more. First, we must note that for Kant the *category of existence is not self-predicative*. This is immediately problematic. First, the existence of the category itself, namely the *category qua category*, cannot be established, for existence applies to what is other to the category. Since the category only applies to intuition, existence can only be predicated of that which is *instantiated in intuition*. But since transcendental subjectivity *itself* is not instantiated in intuition, we cannot say of *transcendental subjectivity* that it exists.[27] Since transcendental subjectivity cannot exist, neither can any of its intuitions. Indeed, without acknowledging *the self-predicative aspect of existence*, one cannot establish *the existence of the category itself*. This very specific problem exemplifies a broader problem of transcendental philosophy adeptly acknowledged by Wittgenstein in the preface to the *Tractatus*.[28] In order to draw a limit to what can be known, one must know what is included and excluded by the limit. Thus, in order to draw a limit to what can be known, one knows that which lies beyond the limit of knowledge. Indeed, Kant cannot help but predicate existence of a subjectivity that lies beyond all possible experience.

The foregoing reflections indicate why one cannot be satisfied with a transcendental prohibition on Absolute Knowledge. The impasse can also be construed in terms of the sublimity of the Absolute. Kant famously said that the world, as it exists 'by itself,' is 'not to be met with at all.' Every intuition we might have of the world, indeed every conceptualized intuition or image we have of it, always results in an incomplete cognition of the world. Kant is clear that 'the world does not exist at all' by which he means that one cannot in principle meet with it in experience. Rather, the best one can encounter is a 'regressive series of representations' such that the world can only be encountered in its *incompleteness*. The regulative function of the Idea of the world for the Understanding depends on the fact that 'it [the world] exists neither as an in itself infinite whole nor as an in itself finite whole.'[29] The sublime is that which is absolutely great beyond all comparison.[30] Because every object of cognition is finite, no object of cognition is great beyond all comparison. Rather, Kant claims that the sublime is 'found only in our ideas' and true sublimity can only be found in the mind of the judge such that the 'mind feels itself elevated in its own judging.'[31] Indeed, because the Idea of the world is too great to be realized in any cognition (for no cognition truly lives up to it) the judgment that the Idea of the world fails to be instantiated (and can nei-ther be sensibly intuited nor imagined) indicates that it is the *Idea of the world* that is absolutely great:

> But just because there is in our imagination a striving to advance to the infinite, while in our reason there lies a claim to absolute totality, as to a real idea, the very inadequacy of our faculty for estimating the magnitude of the things of the sensible world awakens the feeling of the supersensible in us.[32]

The sublime is the 'feeling that we have a pure self-sufficient reason' that cannot be rendered intuitable except by its very inadequate fulfillment in experience.

When the philosopher wonders about an object, he presumes that it is in principle *knowable*. Given the unknowability of the Absolute, wonder is transformed into *awe*. What is it before we stand in awe? It may appear that because the Absolute exceeds conceptual knowing, that we would stand in awe before the power of the Absolute to transcend our rational faculty. But since we do not encounter the Absolute at all, we do not find ourselves in awe before it. Rather, we stand before our very Idea of the Absolute—we are in awe of our own reason. Awe is the comportment (*Einstellung*) of the subject to the sublime, which is its object. As Kant says, every attempt to sensibly intuit or imagine the whole fails: 'bound-less imagination pales in comparison with the ideas of reason,' the latter of which is the 'supersensible' sublimity, the object of our awe.

Unfortunately, this leads to another impasse. If the Idea of the Abso-lute cannot be realized in intuition, then it is *not* absolutely great. Rather, it is conditioned by that in which it cannot be realized. Thus, the Idea of the Absolute fails to be sublime. Indeed—what is it but a mere Idea, and what is less, a *non-existent* one! Rather than elevate the Idea of the Absolute to the sublime, Kant has degraded the Absolute (as well as the Idea thereof) to a conditioned, *relative*, and profane reality that fails to correspond to what it ought to be. Not only does the Absolute itself find itself conditioned, and thereby relative, but the Idea of the Absolute also becomes *divorced from the Absolute*. Accordingly, the Idea of the Absolute is not sublime, but *false*, for it fails to correspond to what it is and *ought* to be. To put it polemically—the Absolute becomes *absolutely small*. The Absolute *ought* to be Absolute, but it is not what it ought to be.[33]

Once mysticism posits the Absolute as beyond the concept (and thereby sublime), it has relativized the Absolute and posited it as one side of an opposition. Accordingly, the Absolute itself becomes *conceptu-ally knowable*. Rather than deny the truth of conceptuality, mysticism ironically and indirectly affirms the capacity of the concept to think the Absolute. Instead of the absence of conceptual knowing, the Absolute becomes present to conceptual knowing only in the form of the contradiction. Accordingly, Hegel's rejection of mysticism is also an *integration*: it is the very self-destruction of mysticism that establishes the conceptual accessibility of the Absolute in the form of contradiction. Hence, Hegel's affirmation of a rational form of Absolute Dialetheism is not a simple rejection of the mystical alternative. If it were, Hegel's Absolute Dialetheism would not be absolute, but relative. Instead, it endorses the mystical relation to the Absolute as a true stage in the self-development of Absolute Knowing, albeit an insufficient and incomplete one that is perfected by his own conceptually mediated form of Absolute Dialetheism.

Most simply, by placing the Absolute and relative knowing in an opposition, each on one side of a limit, relative or limited knowledge is raised to an Absolute status. One cannot restrict conceptual knowing to one side of an opposition, without simultaneously negating that limit—by restricting it to one side of an opposition, one transforms the structures of relative and determinate conceptual knowing into the Absolute. The relativizing of the Absolute is at the same time *the absolutizing of what is relative*. This result ought not be a surprise, but is in fact what we discovered previously. The PNC that ensures the determinacy of relative knowing undermines itself: it engenders a self-contradiction and introduces the indeterminacy that it so dearly attempted to hold at bay. Or what is the same, even the denial of self-predication and existential implication turns out to implicitly result in the endorsement of both as is evident in the case of the problems of Onto-theology and the Third Man, though their appearance can only ever be understood as a problem to finite knowing.

As we established earlier, the finite conception of the concept relies upon the PNC: A is necessarily not-A, and the determinacy of A depends upon its exclusive relation to not-A. This conception of determinacy ensures that there is no coherent conception of *Absolute Determinacy*, for the determinacy of every determination depends upon excluding another with which it stands in relationship. Accordingly, the reign of non-contradiction ensures that only *conditioned* concepts can count as determinate concepts. Thus, any true conception of *Absolute Determinacy* requires a *true contradiction*; it requires a violation of the PNC.

Any attempt to proclaim that relative conceptual determinacy, and its principle, the PNC, only has relative application cannot help but negate its relative status and raise itself to an Absolute Position. The relative is 'A' and the Absolute is 'not-A'; each stands in a position of relative and determinate knowing governed by non-contradiction. Given that any attempt to raise the PNC to the position of an Absolute Principle results in contradiction, *the self-negation of relative knowing itself establishes the true character of Absolute determinacy*. Absolute Determinacy is constituted by the *self-exceeding* of relative determination—it is constituted by the *identity of relative and Absolute Being*—it is a true contradiction.

In order to arrive at his specification of the concept as *self-exceeding*, Hegel does not need to model his concept of the concept on a given and separate Absolute.[34] As Houlgate notes, Hegel does not begin with a given or presupposed idea of the Absolute.[35] We could put this another way: Hegel only needs to follow the *self-destruction* of relative knowing. By watching relative knowing destroy itself, Hegel witnesses the very birth of Absolute Knowledge. Hegel does not need to posit anything in advance. Rather, relative knowing construes itself as Absolute by negating its own relativity. As Hegel proclaims:

> We usually suppose that the Absolute must lie far beyond, but it is precisely what is wholly present, what we, as thinkers, always carry with us and employ even though we have no express consciousness of it.[36]

Indeed, by paying attention to the way Kant's own philosophy unknowingly compromises itself, Hegel simply begins with what is *left over*. What is left over is radical indeterminacy—the *absence* of any given determinate content. Hegel's *Phenomenology of Spirit* performs just this *reductio*. The *Phenomenology of Spirit* performs an internal reduction to the absurd on the assumption that knowing is constituted by finite structure, for example subject and object as constitutes the opposition of consciousness, form and material, truth and certainty. The result of that reduction to the absurd is the *Science of Logic*, which begins from pure indeterminacy. The *Science of Logic* must begin without presupposition because thinking with determinate presuppositions has *destroyed itself*.

The contradiction that follows from the identity of synthesis and analysis also illuminates another distinct feature of Hegel's system—the system as *Voraussetzungslos*. Unlike any before him, Hegel uncovers the incongruity between the *identity* of synthesis and analysis and the *very concept of a first principle*. The concept of the first principle requires the *presupposition* of some given determination—such as thing-hood or the activity of self-positing. As Schelling himself indicates with his formulation of the first principle as an 'immediate unity' of synthesis and analysis, the concept of the first principle is *one-sided*; in the case of Fichte and Schelling the one-sided emphasis is on identity (though one might also posit *difference as such* as a first principle). By positing the first principle as the identity of synthesis and analysis, the principle immediately undermines itself, for as the identity of both, it must be the difference between synthesis and analysis. Thus, because it is the identity it must also be the difference. Hence, the first principle *immediately negates itself*. The night is still black—and the cows are too. In this way, Schelling's reversal back to the absolute Identity in his *Presentation of My System* is already implicit in the *STI*.

Schelling seems to have learned from Hegel's critique, for in the *Erlangen Lectures* he argues that any determination of the Absolute negates itself. He calls this self-negating feature of the Absolute *Ecstasy*. In Erlangen, the Absolute *transcends* every determination imposed upon it, even *indefinability itself*. The Absolute shows itself to be indefinable by overcoming all definitions, including indefinability. Thus, although Schelling does not accept Hegel's system, I would suggest that he appears to have learned an important lesson from his critique: free thinking becomes ecstasy: *it is the experience of the overcoming of all first principles* in thought.

Because one must overcome all first principles, the foundation of science cannot begin from the postulate of self-consciousness. For in this case, self-consciousness has not determined itself to be self-consciousness. Arguably, Schelling had already realized that the foundation of science could not be self-consciousness in his move to the *Identity philosophy*, in which the highest principle is the pure identity that is not reducible to nature or mind. Still, Schelling had not transcended first philosophy or drawn the inference that the identity of synthesis and analysis demands the abolishing of all first principles.[37]

Philosophy ought to begin without any presuppositions—this means without any *Setzung* that is made *in advance*.[38] Houlgate is right that in philosophy

> We do not take for granted any particular conception of thought and its categories at the outset of philosophy.[39]

This of course is already implicit in Fichte's and Schelling's philosophy, for each argues that the first principle is freedom. As freedom, the first principle must *posit itself*—it must determine itself. Whatever determination with which one begins has not determined itself to be the beginning—but is posited 'in advance.' Thus, the very character of the methodology of the science as the identity of synthesis and analysis cannot be given at the outset. Rather—Hegel is correct that the identity of synthesis and analysis must be the result of the whole science. Accordingly, Hegel describes the Absolute Idea (the unity of theoretical and practical reason), the end of the *Science of Logic*, as an identity of synthesis and analysis:

> This is what Plato demanded of cognition, that it should consider things in and for themselves, that is, should consider them partly in their universality, but also that it should not stray away from them catching at circumstances, examples and comparisons, but should keep before it solely the things themselves, . . . but should keep before it solely the things themselves and bring before consciousness what is immanent in them. The method of absolute cognition is to this extent

analytic. . . . But the method is no less synthetic, since its subject matter, determined immediately by a simple universal . . . exhibits itself
as an other. This relation of differentiated elements which the subject
matter thus is within itself, is however no longer the same thing as is
meant by synthesis in finite cognition.[40]

What is more, the dialectic itself (the result of the whole *Science of Logic*)
can be described as an identity of synthesis and analysis:

> This is no less synthetic than analytic moment of the judgment, by
> which the universal of the beginning of its own accord determines
> itself as the other of itself, is to be named the dialectical moment.[41]

In order for science to begin it must destroy the appeal to presuppositions from within the presuppositional framework of science itself. Hegel
employs the same language of the *STI*:

> Hitherto, the concept of logic has rested on the separation, presup-
> posed once and for all in the ordinary consciousness, of the content
> of cognition and its *form*, or of *truth* and *certainty*.[42]

Although Schelling calls for the negation of the difference between truth
and certainty, his own formulation of the first principle *fails to embody
their identity*. Indeed, it is the goal of the *Phenomenology of Spirit* to
show the impossibility of separating truth and certainty:

> as the course of the *Phenomenology* showed, it is only in Absolute
> knowing that the separation of the object from the certainty of itself
> is completely eliminated; truth is not equated with certainty and this
> certainty with truth.[43]

Hegel shows that the attempt to hold truth and certainty apart from
one another leads to their identification. Accordingly, the *Phenomenology* might be best described as the self-determining process by which
presuppositional-knowing *collapses on itself*. Phenomenology clears the
way for a presuppositional science by allowing presuppositional knowing to self-destruct.[44]

To review, Schelling's identification of synthesis and analysis in
the *STI*—rather than preserve the possibility of the first principle—
completely annihilate it as a possibility. What is more, Hegel recognized
that it calls for a *revolution* in the *Science of Logic*. The traditional principles of logic, such as self-identity and non-contradiction, are not self-
developing and self-determining and are thereby the improper organs for
the self-determining science. The very need to appeal to such principles
in demonstrations of the first principle appear to betray a principle that

cannot move beyond itself, a principle that is *not truly synthetic*. Hegel's great insight is the development of logic as *dialectic*: a science that is simultaneously synthetic as well as analytic. By integrating contradiction into the structure of logic itself, the contradictory character of the Absolute is *no longer an obstacle to its conceivability*.

While Schelling's argument for the identity of synthesis and analysis does show that self-thinking thought must be the beginning of philosophy, self-thinking thought may be *purely categorial*, rather than the self-thinking thought of consciousness. Since Schelling's proof does not account for this other sense of self-thinking thought, his proof is not valid. Indeed—Hegel's *Science of Logic* is the domain of self-thinking thought, but one in which categories apply to themselves *without the intermediary of consciousness*. Philosophers may think the dialectical transitions, positings, and developments in the *Science of Logic*, but the philosophical thought of them by the philosopher is not the proof upon which they rest. Rather, the identity of synthesis and analysis can be exhibited in a purely categorial sense. The dialectic of identity and difference in the categorial domain makes self-consciousness (which is not reducible to logic) possible in the first place.

Hegel's self-refutation of the presumption that knowing is relative and finite not only constitutes the *Phenomenology* as the self-removing propaedeutic of the *Science of Logic* but also appears in the structure of the *Logic*. Indeed, the *Science of Logic* repeats (albeit in different ways) the self-overcoming of finite and relative oppositions throughout the course of the text: the difference between difference and identity negates itself within the logic of Essence, just as the opposition between finite and infinite negates itself in the course of the logic of Being.

Because the *Science of Logic*, the science of the purely logical content of the Absolute, begins without any determination posited in advance, it begins with the indeterminate. Indeed, for Hegel indeterminacy has the *positive significance* of constituting the *beginning* of philosophy. Perhaps more than any other, Hegel is profoundly sensitive to the dialectical features of indeterminacy. Since the whole science is the activity by which the indeterminate *exceeds itself* into various determinate forms, the whole of the science can be characterized as various determinations of indeterminacy. Again, since every category of the logic is a definition of the Absolute, or what is *by itself*, and the latter is indeterminate, the indeterminate is not maintained as *one* category alongside others, but is integral to the content of the other categories that are developed. Indeed, that the non-positionality of indeterminacy renders it indistinguishable from the various categorial positions in the logic can be gleaned from a brief gander at the text. The One is 'indeterminate but not, however, like being, its indeterminateness is the determinateness which is a relation to its own self, an absolute determinateness.'[45] Essence is '*indeterminate* simple unity from which what is determinate has been eliminated in an *external manner*.' Or more starkly: 'Absolute Essence . . . has no determinate being.'[46] In regard to mechanism, Hegel points out that 'the object is therefore in the first instance *indeterminate* insofar as there is no determinate opposition in it.'[47] As is evident, in Hegel indeterminacy acquires the enormously *positive* significance that the *various determinations* of the Absolute, such as One and Mechanism, are all forms of indeterminacy. Whether it be the development from indeterminacy to determinacy, and or from determinacy to Absolute Determinacy, dialectical logic constantly *exceeds itself*. On one 'side' of relative determination we discover indeterminacy, the condition for relative determinacy. On the other 'side,' we discover absolute determination—the self-negation of relative determinacy. The absolutely determinate content the concept possesses as an identity of universal and particular cannot be taken for granted from the outset; rather it must itself be the result of the development of the logic.

Integral to dialectic's self-exceeding is the correlate concept of *absolute determinacy*. In exceeding itself, the non-positional becomes positional and thereby excludes no determination. Every determination, including determinacy and indeterminacy, have been cancelled and preserved. Since this non-positional character is not devoid of determination, but includes them all, Hegel calls it absolute determinacy in which the negation that constitutes determinacy has been negated and is expressed in Hegel's famous expression of the *negation of negation*. Take two examples: 'Being for Self' is an *infinite determinateness*, because it has absorbed all distinction.[48] The concept is an Absolute Determinateness.[49] For Hegel, the negation of negation is a formula of the *logic* of freedom. Although initially absolute and indeterminate, freedom gives itself a relative and determinate form. Finally, freedom negates its own form of determination, thereby re-establishing its absolute character, though now in determinate form, as the negation of negation. Just as thinking governed by the PNC only possessed relative determinacy, thinking that exceeds such a principle, self-exceeding thought, possesses Absolute determinacy. Absolute Knowing is Absolutely determinate and can know its own Absolute Determinacy.

Hegel—more than any other—recognizes the profound implications of this impasse when he proclaims that the beginning 'may not presuppose anything.'[50] Philosophy cannot begin by presupposing any epistemic or metaphysical foundation. As is well known, for Hegel Absolute Knowing and Being can only be achieved if philosophy *frees itself of all foundations*. Note that this is not tantamount to a rejection of metaphysics or epistemology. Rather, it is a rejection of any *foundationalist* epistemology or metaphysics.[51]

As is well known, Hegel recognizes that as long as the principle of identity and difference are conceived as separate principles, no conception of the Absolute will be possible. He proclaims as much in his *Science of Logic*:

> The analysis of the beginning would thus yield the notion of the unity of being and nothing—or, in a more reflected form, the unity of differentiatedness and non-differentiatedness, or the identity of identity and non-identity. This concept could be regarded as the purest, that is, most abstract definition of the absolute—as it would in fact be if we were at all concerned with the form of definitions and with the name of the absolute. In this sense, that abstract concept would be the first definition no this absolute and all further determinations and developments only more specific and richer definitions of it.[52]

Schelling's insight in the *System of Transcendental Idealism* that synthesis is analysis and analysis is synthesis has profound implications for the history of German Idealism. Although it is Schelling who seems to first propose the identity of synthesis and analysis as a solution to an impasse that plagued Fichte's philosophy, it is Hegel who recognizes the true implications of this insight. Rather than make the first principle possible, Hegel recognized that the identity of synthesis and analysis in the Absolute requires the abolition of all first principles.

Hegel's Dialetheism

Since the identity of identity and difference is a contradiction, 'A=A' certainly does not reflect the *form* of the first principle. Rather—if one insists on formalizing the insight—the principle of thought would be that 'everything contradicts itself,' namely always *both A and not-A*:

> If now, the first determination of reflection, namely, identity, difference, and opposition, have been put in the form of a law, still more should the determination into which they pass as their truth, namely contradiction, be grasped and enunciated as a law: everything is inherently contradictory, and in the sense that this law in contrast to the others expresses rather the truth and the essential nature of things. The contradiction which makes its appearance in opposition, is only the developed nothing that is contained in identity and that appears in the expression that the law of identity says *nothing*.[53]

For Hegel 'Difference as such is already implicitly contradiction.'[54] Hegel is absolutely right that the law of identity and non-contradiction are not laws at all:

> What emerges from this consideration is therefore, first, that the law of identity or of contradiction which purports to express merely abstract identity in contrast to difference as a truth, is not a law of thought, but rather the opposite of it.[55]

Another way of describing the self-exceeding character of the logic is to invoke dialetheism, the thesis that there can be, and are, *true contradictions*. As Hegel makes explicit, *every* concept is contradictory:

> On the contrary, every determination, anything concrete, every concept, is essentially a unity of distinguished and distinguishable elements which, by virtue of the determinate, essential difference, pass over into elements which are contradictory.[56]

As Hegel makes explicitly clear, *every concept is contradictory*. Although we have already shown that the concept of absolute difference engenders contradiction, for Hegel contradiction is a category that applies to every concept in the *Logic*. Because each concept of the Logic is a concept *of the Absolute*, contradiction applies to every concept. Indeed, because contradiction is one of the Absolute concepts alongside all of the others, it is just as much a *true* conception of the Absolute as any other category in the *Logic*. Just as there is no need to explain away the presence of the concept of Being, there is just as little need to explain away the presence of contradiction in the *Logic*. Indeed, as a true concept of the Absolute that deserves its place in the logic alongside the other true conceptions, *contradiction itself is absolutely true*. Just as we speak of the Absolute as 'Being,' we can also safely speak of the Absolute as 'contradictory.' In the following, Hegel makes it clear that contradiction is the *moving principle of the world*:

> Contradiction is the very moving principle of the world: and it is ridiculous to say that contradiction is unthinkable. The only thing correct about that statement is that contradiction is not the end of the matter, but cancels itself. But contradiction, when cancelled, does not leave abstract identity; for that is itself only one side of the contrariety. The proximate result of opposition (When realized as contradiction) is the Ground.[57]

This passage is very important, for it indicates that without contradictions there would be no 'moving principle of the world' and denies that contradictions are not un-thinkable. Contradictions *are thinkable*, and without them we would not have an account of self-differentiation or self-particularization—the more precise terminology for 'moving principle.' First, note that the passage signifies that contradictions do not violate the principle of thought, but are *consistent* (ironically) with the concept of conceptual thinking propagating in the logic. Second, the concept of conceptual thinking requires contradiction, for without it one would not have a concept of the 'movement' of self-differentiation *characteristic of Absolute Thought*, to employ Hegel's metaphor again. Nonetheless, contradictions cancel themselves and resolve themselves in other concepts, just as Hegel argues that the concept of contradiction resolves itself in the concept of ground, or becoming resolves itself in determinate being. Indeed, Hegel's logic is such that the *self-particularizing* character of logic engenders a conception of contradiction wherein particular results follow from the self-contradiction of each particular concept:

> Speculative thought consists solely in *holding on to the contradiction*, and thus to itself. Unlike representational thought, it does not let itself be dominated by the contradiction, it does not allow the latter to dissolve its determinations into other ones or into nothing.[58]

The self-contradiction of *Becoming* gives rise to *determinate being*; the self-contradiction of difference gives rise to *opposition*. Self-particularizing logic entails that the contradiction of the concept does not engender everything and nothing (as in Aristotle and Kant), but rather *particular* results are engendered by the particular contradictions. Thus, Hegel's rejection of the PNC is at least a rejection of *the principle of explosion*. Contradictions do not explode into indeterminacy. Rather, contradictions are *productive* insofar as each contradiction in the self-differentiating process produces different concepts of different types.[59] This is the way that one can speak about contradiction as the 'moving principle of the world' rather than as a force of world annihilation, as it is usually conceived.

In the *Phenomenology* too, Hegel challenges us to confront contradiction with strength and honesty:

> We have to think pure change, or think antithesis within the antithesis itself, or contradiction. For in the difference which is an inner difference, the opposite is not merely one of two—if it were, it would simply be, without being an opposite—but it is the opposite of an opposite, or the other is itself immediately present in it.[60]

This contradiction that arises at the close of Force and Understanding would require its own exegesis. I merely invoke it here to make use of a helpful turn of phrase Hegel employs: the *inverted world*.[61] The dialetheic world is not our *consistent* world of 'super-sensible' laws (laws conceived though not directly perceived), but it is that *consistent world inverted*, such that it is a 'difference which is no difference' and constitutes its infinity.[62] The Absolute Concept[63] of which Hegel speaks in this chapter is a true contradiction. Or rather, the relative world of oppositions in which concepts remain what they are in excluding their negations is itself the *inversion of the inverted world*—the dialetheic world turned upside down.

Despite such proclamations, some scholars, for example Guido Kreis and Robert Brandom[64] *et alia*, defend the view that Hegel's logic does not admit true contradictions. Kreis' close analysis concludes that

> Hegels Lösung der schwerwiegenden Widersprüche im menschlichen Denken besteht ganz im Gegenteil darin, keine wahren Widersprüche zu akzeptieren, sondern die jeweiligen inkonsistenten Begriffe in ihrer bisherigen Verwendungsweise aufzugeben, zugleich aber ihre begrifflichen Gehalte konstruktiv in die Bildung höherstufiger Begriffe und letztlich in die Bildung eines Gesamtsystems von Kategorien zu integrieren, in der alle begrifflichen Gehalte aller Kategorien konsistent miteinander vereinbar sind.[65]

This view might be supported by the passages such as the one quoted here in which Hegel proclaims that contradictions are *cancelled*. Since contradictions cancel themselves, they prove themselves to be false and are resolved in more complex concepts that are not themselves contradictory, for example the contradiction of becoming resolves itself in determinate being, reality and negation, and the concepts of something and other. Contradictions are always arising, but always cancelling themselves. On this reading, contradictions are not true, but are *always shown to be false on their own terms*. Although there is good reason to read Hegel along these lines, I think it is problematic. As a method for proceeding, I think Kreis is right that the best method for adjudicating this issue is to focus on the development of particular categories.[66]

In order to make this evident, consider the case of the contradiction 'Being is nothing.' Since the logical development from Being to determinate being has been so thoroughly discussed in the literature, I do not mean to rehash them here in detail.[67] Since logic cannot begin with any given determinacy or positing-in-advance, it cannot begin with any determinate content. Rather, it must begin with that which is *indeterminate as such*, but *not* a *determinate indeterminate* which would already stand in contrast to determinacy. Only that which can be *indeterminately indeterminate* (or *absolutely* indeterminate) can function as the beginning of the *Science of Logic*. The beginning *is*, but without further qualification, for the predicate 'is' does not draw any differentiation between anything. 'Is' is completely void of all determinate differentiation. Accordingly, there are no determinations there to speak of. Because Being—the *absolutely* indeterminate itself—has no content at all, it is in virtue of having no content that it *becomes its opposite*: nothing—that which is completely empty of all determination. Likewise, Hegel points out that 'nothing' is just as much 'Being' as 'Being is nothing.' Because each immediately vanishes into the other, each is becoming: Being *ceases to be* Being, and nothing *comes to be* Being. Since each is immediately the other, each constitutes a unity of Being and nothing: Being is the unity of Being and nothing, and nothing is the unity of nothing and Being. Since each is immediately the other, what does *not vanish* is the very unity of Being and nothing—this is the 'stable' unity of Being and nothing constitutive of determinate being that Hegel characterizes as quality. Being becomes qualified being, but it can only become qualified being through the self-negation of becoming. Vanishing itself vanishes, for in every case we find always the self-same unity that never ceases to be: the unity of Being and nothing. Hegel proceeds to identity the stable (non-vanishing) unity of Being and nothing in the form of Being as reality, while the stable unity of Being and nothing on the side of nothing is negation. Note, of course, that 'negation' is not identical to 'nothing', but is rather a further development out of it (on the other side of Becoming if you will). In the logic of Determinate being (*Dasein*), 'reality' and 'negation' become the moments of the categories of 'Something' and 'Other.' Indeed, 'reality' is *not negation*, and thereby *admits negation*, while 'negation' has its *own reality* apart from reality itself, and thereby *admits reality*. 'Something is constituted as a unity of reality and negation in the form of reality, while the "other" is the unity of negation and reality' on the side of negation. Accordingly, Hegel rehearses how determinate being arises necessarily out of the indeterminately indeterminate: pure Being as such.[68]

The PNC demands that 'to be' and 'not to be' are not the same. But *in virtue of what it is*, Being is nothing. Since the *Science of Logic* is a science of categories that are *a*temporal, it cannot be the case that 'Being is nothing' is true at one time and false at another. Rather, 'Being is nothing' is an *eternal (and purely) logical truth* that is not all affected by what happens in time or space, nature or mind. Thus, the judgment 'Being is nothing' is *always true*. Even if this truth is resolved in a higher category whose *initial* formulation is not contradictory, this higher category does not undermine the truth that 'Being is nothing.' Being is still nothing—it is a contradiction, indeed a truth, that *always was and always will be*. One cannot proclaim it to be true at one time, but cancelled at a later time—since time has no application whatsoever. Even though 'nothing' becomes 'negation,' 'otherness,' and so on, it does not follow from this that 'nothing' itself at any point is not 'Being.' Because 'nothing' is a category that is *atemporal*, it is *always Being and* always progressing beyond Being. This, of course, is what enables us to return time and again to Hegel's categories and find the very same movement time and again.

'Being is nothing' must develop into more complex categories, for Being and nothing are not *sufficient* to account for the logical articulation of the Absolute. But the fact that they are insufficient for the logical articulation of the Absolute does not make it the case that the truth vanishes. In fact, what does vanish is the concept that 'Being is nothing' is the *complete articulation* of the Absolute, for another category takes its place. The vanishing of the sufficiency of the claim 'Being is nothing' *only exacerbates the contradiction*. Rather than showing that contradictions are not true, it only generates new contradictions. Even though it is the case that Being, nothing, and becoming resolve themselves into a consistent category, the inconsistency nonetheless *remains preserved*. Indeed, 'Being is nothing' must *remain* true, despite the fact that it is *cancelled* in the development of determinate being. For this reason, *it is true and false*. This is the meaning of dialectics as *'cancelling and preserving.'* Cancelled contradictions are *also* preserved. Since these developments do not happen in time, the truth and falsehood of the contradiction—before and after its cancelation, not only preserves the truth of contradiction but *grows* them. This is why Priest is exactly right to proclaim the Absolute to be the 'biggest contradiction of them all.'[69]

The moving principle of the world, the concept of self-particularization, is never completely cancelled, but it is always *preserved*. Indeed, insofar as the self-particularizing concept always preserves itself, and is internally contradictory (for it is both universal and particular in the same respect), the contradiction predicated of it cannot just be cancelled, but it must always be preserved. Indeed, the category 'contradiction' does not appear until the logic of Essence, such that one cannot proclaim that 'Being is nothing' is contradictory until after one has arrived at the logic of Essence, where the concept of contradiction arises. It is also true that the determination of the Absolute as contradiction is not the final determination of the Absolute—its truth lies in the concept of self-particularization and its various manifestations. But this does not mean that contradiction ever ceases to be true. Rather, showing that it is false (that it is cancelled), shows that *contradiction is both true and false*. Thus, by showing that contradiction is true and false, contradiction is revealed to be contradictory.

When contradiction itself is shown to be contradictory, contradiction itself becomes the subject of an act of self-referential predication. As such, *contradiction itself is contradictory*. Since contradiction is contradictory, *contradiction is consistent with itself*, for its predicate *corresponds* to what it is. Thus, the consistency into which the contradiction develops cannot be a complete cancellation of contradiction, but must rather be just the opposite: it is *the preservation* or *ossification* of the contradiction itself into a consistent form. Thus, one cannot affirm Coherentism as an adequate theory of absolute truth, if coherence requires the impossibility of true contradictions. Coherentism can be an adequate theory of Absolute Truth only if the coherence advocated is the *coherence of incoherence*. Simply put, *inconsistency is preserved in the self-referential predication of the contradiction to itself*. When the contradiction itself is contradictory, it is consistent (or coherent) with itself. By following the self-referential dimension of contradiction, we discover that consistency is the consistency of contradiction.

Since consistency is also the *negation* of contradiction, one could properly construe consistency as the self-externality or self-alienation of contradiction with itself. This self-alienation arises in virtue of the self-contradictory relation of contradiction to itself that ironically constitutes its consistency! This can also be properly described as a process in which the living and creative power of contradiction is stilled and negated in a dead, inert, and consistent form. The cancellation of the contradiction in the dialectical development is nothing less than the self-preservation of the power of contradiction that enables the consistent form to overcome itself in a further dialectical development. Finally, contradiction is constantly preserved in different conceptual transformations of increasing complexity. Indeed, the Absolute Contradiction prefigured in becoming is further *preserved* in a new form, namely that of *self-particularization* (in addition to others). The overcoming of otherness in ideality cannot be understand without *acknowledging the Absolute as a true contradiction*.

The reading of Hegel's philosophy as containing true contradictions is not my own alone. It is shared (although construed in different ways) by Richard Winfield, Stephen Houlgate, Elena Ficara, and Graham Priest, to name a few. Houlgate is exactly right:

> For Hegel, the concept of being is profoundly contradictory, but it is no less valid for that.[70]

Indeed, this school has the straightforward and most charitable reading, for it takes Hegel at his word without forsaking any of the content of his thinking, while refraining from making excuses for the master.[71]

Perhaps more controversial is my use of the term 'dialetheism' to describe the truth of contradiction in Hegel.[72] Michele Bordignon argues, for example, that although Hegel's logic contains true contradictions, he should not be described as a dialetheist, due to some significant differences between Hegel and Priest's view of contradiction.[73] Priest thinks that contradictions require incompatible statements, such that he has a syntactical view of the true contradiction, such that sentences are the kind of thing that can contradict each other.[74] In contrast, the contradictions in Hegel's logic are not just syntactical, but ontological. In contrast with Priest, however, Bordignon is exactly right that for Hegel what is contradictory is not just said of sentences, but of 'thought determinations' that are 'pure forms of thought and being.'[75] Likewise, in Hegel we find the 'self-contradiction of one and the same logical content' that is constituted by 'self-differentiation.'[76] Thus, we should heed Bordignon's words, when she writes that

> Rather, we need to consider the relation between the contradictory structures of reality, which are, at the same time, the structures of objective thought, and the linguistic expression of these contradictions.[77]

Finally, Bordignon is also right to insist that unlike in Priest's system, there is no 'external agent that assigns truth to logical determinations on the basis of some external criteria.'[78]

Although there is a 'formal parallel' between Hegel's and Priest's conception of the truth of contradiction,[79] Bordignon claims that each logical determination does not have a double truth value, but each logical determination is 'simply and radically true.'[80] Because dialetheism means that contradictions have a 'double truth value,' namely that they are *both true and false*, and Hegel's concepts are only true, Hegel is not a dialetheist in Priest's sense. Although I agree that 'the absolute truth of the absolute idea and the truth of each determination are one and the same truth,'[81] it seems to me that denying falsehood to any logical content in the *Science of Logic* would be problematic. First, it is hard to see how there can be any true contradictions if no category in the logic is *false*, for falsehood is a condition for there to be contradiction. There can only be a *true contradiction* in Hegel's thought if there is falsehood too. Since Hegel is clear that there *are* true contradictions, falsehood, as well as truth, must be predicated of the logical determinations. Hegel himself proclaims that 'judgment is one-sided on account of its form and to that extent false.'[82] Because judgment is a category of the logic (and thereby a true concept of the Absolute), on Hegel's own terms it cannot only be a true category—it must also be false.

What is more, were each determination only true, but never false, then the concept of truth would remain radically *one-sided*. In order to avoid a one-sided conception of truth, Hegel offers a dialetheic conception of truth. Indeed, the unity of opposition characteristic of Hegel's categories of finitude and infinitude, or Being and nothing, *achieve their truth* in the contradictory identification of each category with its negation. Since truth is *instantiated* in each of these contradictions, the concept of truth that is instantiated in each contradiction *cannot preclude falsehood*, for in this case truth would fail to be the unity of opposition that is instantiated in each of its instances, for example 'Being is nothing' and 'finite is infinite.' Simply put, Truth itself must *also* admit an identity with its negation, which is none other than falsehood, if the instances of truth (such as 'Being is nothing' or 'finitude is infinite') themselves truly instantiate an identity of opposition.

Finally, although it is true that 'the negation of a determination is nothing but the further-level articulation of the content of the determination itself,'[83] the very need for a 'further-level articulation' indicates that there is initially, at the *outset* of the development, a *lack* of *a truly Absolute* Determination, such that in the beginning the Absolute Truth is *not* true to itself or is not what it *ought* to be. In other words, the fact that truth *must* develop indicates that truth in its more undeveloped stage does not yet correspond with truth in its completion (as it truly is) or *the Absolute as it ought to be*. A developmental conception of Truth itself demands dialetheism, namely that truth can only be true to itself if it falsifies itself. As Priest states: 'dialectic is dialetheic.'[84] Only by *failing to be true to itself* can it ultimately be true to itself: without falsehood there is no truth either. For these reasons, Priest's claim that 'dialectics is dialetheic' still stands. In the following chapters, we will develop the meaning of this conception of truth in more detail.

Notes

1. See *EL*, paragraph 85.
2. Hegel, *SL*, trans. Giovanni, 361.
3. Hegel argues that identity or self-identity gives rise to difference. We achieve a small glimpse of that here, where the principle of identity necessarily entails absolute difference.
4. Hegel, *SL*, trans. Miller, 362.
5. The brackets are my insertion.
6. More exactly, the category of difference immediately gives rise to diversity, from which polar opposition arises. It is out of the concept of polar opposition (of the positive and negative) that the category of contradiction is posited *per se*. As we have shown, the concept of absolute difference (as well as self-identity) must be an element of itself and accordingly has the form of a concept.
7. Hegel, *SL*, trans. Miller, 375.
8. See *EL*, 173, paragraph 119.
9. Hegel distinguishes two senses of polar opposition. On the one sense of the term, either opposite may be viewed as positive or negative and it is a contingent and external signification to call one 'positive' and the other 'negative.' In another sense, one opposite is inherently positive and the other inherently negative.
10. Hegel, *EL*, 175.
11. Ibid, 174.
12. G. W. F. Hegel, *Wissenschaft der Logik II* (Frankfurt am Main: Suhrkamp, 1986), 35, 41.
13. Hegel, *SL*, trans. Giovanni, 514.
14. I do not wish to claim that the concept has no bearing on these issues but that the issues are separate and the systematic treatment of the concept can be investigated without appealing to these terms.
15. Hegel thematizes this issue again at the very end of *The Concept in General*. He points out that neither in the critical philosophy of Kant nor in the description of Aristotle were the forms of concept ever subject to philosophical criticism. Hegel, *SL*, trans. Giovanni, 525.

16. Hegel, *SL*, trans. Miller, 362.
17. Ibid, 600.
18. David Gray Carlson recognizes that the universal must be its own principle of particularity in his Commentary on Hegel's *Logic*, where he writes that 'particulars are produced out of the concept' and 'this process of thinking its own self into existence is what Hegel calls the proximate realization of the Notion.' See David Gray Carlson, *A Commentary to Hegel's Science of Logic* (New York: Palgrave Macmillan, 2007), 438. In regard to the self-containment of the Absolute concept, Carlton recognizes that one of the members of the universal set is the set itself. Carlson, *A Commentary to Hegel's Science of Logic*, 450. Rosen seems to miss this dimension of self-containment, however, for he states the exact opposite, namely that 'the set of all sets is not itself a set in the sense that it is a member of itself.' Stanley Rosen, *The Idea of Hegel's Science of Logic* (Chicago: University of Chicago Press, 2013), 398.
19. Indeed, having a particular kind of knowledge is not tantamount to being an expert in epistemology, as any Socratic dialogue establishes.
20. As David Gray Carlson notes, logic is 'on its own account truth, since its content is adequate to its form, or the reality to its notion.' See Carlson, *A Commentary to Hegel's Science of Logic*, 438 and Hegel, *SL*, trans. Miller, 593.
21. Numerous scholars, such as Kenley Dove, Richard Dien Winfield, Edward Halper, and Dieter Henrich, have recognized the importance of self-determination in Hegel's philosophy. For this reason, it is not unique to my account. Most recently, see Christian Georg Martin, *Ontologie der Selbstbestimmung, Eine operationale Rekonstruktion von Hegels "Wissenschaft der Logik"* (Tübingen: Mohr/Siebeck, 2012). What I believe is unique about my account is the way that I use Hegel to solve the problem of the disappearance of the Absolute as explicated in the first section. Although Trisokkas employs Hegel to solve different, yet related problems of skepticism that stem from the ancient skeptics, his approach is similar to mine insofar as he applies Hegel to solve problems that stem from Ancient philosophy. See Ioannis D. Trisokkas, *Pyrrhonian Skepticism and Hegel's Theory of Judgment: A Treatise on the Possibility of Scientific Inquiry* (Leiden: Brill, 2012).
22. See Hegel, *SL*, trans. Miller, 600. Also see paragraph 161 of the lesser logic where Hegel claims the following:

> For in the notion, the elements distinguished are without more ado at the same time, declared to be identical with one another and with the whole, and the specific character of each is a free being of the whole notion.

See Hegel, *EL*, 224.
23. See the analysis of the Plotinian categories in Ch. 2.
24. Hegel, *SL*, trans. Miller, 276, 602.
25. Hegel, *SL*, trans. Giovanni, 529.
26. At this point in the argument, we have not yet arrived at any determinate concept. But insofar as each is distinguishable from the other, each is a determinate concept.
27. See Gabriel, *Transcendental Ontology*, ix.
28. Ludwig Wittgenstein, *Tractatus*, trans. C. K. Ogden (Mineola: Dover, 1999), 27.
29. Kant, *CPR*, A644/B67.
30. Immanuel Kant, *Critique of the Power of Judgment*, trans. Paul Guyer and Eric Matthews, ed. Paul Guyer (Cambridge: Cambridge University Press, 2001), 131–132.
31. Ibid, 139.
32. Ibid, 138:5, 254.

33. This brief discussion of Kant's concept of the sublime and its connection to the world is originally discussed in connection with Romanticism in Gregory S. Moss, "Absolute Imagination: The Metaphysics of Romanticism," *Social Imaginaries* 5, no. 1 (2019): 57–80.
34. For this reason, I think Sellars is wrong that Hegel is still indebted to the myth of the given, as he claims in Wilfred Sellars, *Empiricism and the Philosophy of Mind*, ed. Andrew Chrucky, 127, http://selfpace.uconn.edu/class/percep/SellarsEmpPhilMind.pdf
35. Stephen Houlgate, *The Opening of Hegel's Logic* (West Lafayette: Purdue University Press, 2005), 57.
36. Hegel, *EL*, 24.
37. I am indebted to Philipp Schwabb for this insight that Schelling had already seen the need for transcending nature and mind in order to ground the system of philosophy.
38. See Houlgate's excellent reconstruction of Hegel's position in Houlgate, *The Opening of Hegel's Logic*, 29–30. Houlgate is clear that he is not offering a new interpretation here, but 'his concern is to join such commentators as Richard Winfield, William Maker, and Alan White.' See Houlgate, *The Opening of Hegel's Logic*, 57.
39. Houlgate, *The Opening of Hegel's Logic*, 30.
40. Hegel, *SL*, trans. Miller, 830–831.
41. Ibid, 831.
42. Ibid, 44.
43. Ibid, 49.
44. Maker describes the Phenomenology as a 'self-sublating mediation or pre-supposition.' See William Maker, *Philosophy Without Foundations* (Albany: SUNY, 1994), 76.
45. Hegel, *SL*, trans. Miller, 164–165.
46. Ibid, 389–390.
47. Ibid, 712.
48. Hegel, *EL*, 141; Hegel, *SL*, trans. Miller, 157.
49. Hegel, *SL*, trans. Miller, 603.
50. Ibid, 70.
51. As Kreines points out in his discussion of monism in Hegel, foundational-ist metaphysical monism 'clashes too badly with Hegel's commitments.' See James Kreines, "Fundamentality Without Metaphysical Monism," *Hegel Bulletin* 39, no. 1 (May 2018): 13, 138–156.
52. Hegel, *SL*, trans. Miller, 74.
53. Ibid, 439.
54. Ibid, 431.
55. Ibid, 416.
56. Hegel, *SL*, trans. Giovanni, 384.
57. Hegel, *EL*, 174.
58. Hegel, *SL*, trans. Miller, 440–441. Bordignon calls this principle the 'speculative self-contradiction.' See Michela Bordignon, "Contradiction or Not-Contradiction? This Is the Problem," ed. Andreas Arndt, Myriam Gerhard, and Jure Zovko, *Akademie Verlag* 163 (2013): 163–171, 165. Bordignon introduces another sense of contradiction in Hegel which she calls the 'meta-phorical sense' (164). In this analysis we will focus on the sense of contradic-tion as an error of the Understanding and the dialectical sense of contradiction as a non-explosive principle by which the categories of the logic develop into specific determinations.
59. Nahum Brown is right that 'destruction is also productive' in chapter two of "Hegel on Contradiction: From the Categories of Reflection to Ground,"

in Nahum Brown, *Hegel on Possibility* (New York: Bloomsbury, 2020), 102–103.

60. Hegel, *PS*, trans. Pinkard, 99.
61. See for example, the super-sensible world, which is the inverted world, has at the same time overarched the other world and has it within it; it is for itself the inverted world, that is the inversion of itself; it is itself and its opposite in one unity. Hegel, *PS*, trans. Pinkard, 99.
62. Hegel, *PS*, trans. Pinkard, 99.
63. Ibid, 100.
64. According to Brandom, 'In a conceptually deep sense, far from rejecting the law of non-contradiction, I want to claim that Hegel radicalizes it, placing it at the very center of his thought.' Robert Brandom, "Holism and Idealism in Hegel's Phenomenology," in *Tales of the Mighty Dead* (Harvard: Harvard University Press, 2002), 179. For a critique of Brandom's view, see Stephen Houlgate, "Phenomenology and De-Re Interpretation: A Critique of Brandom's Reading of Hegel," *Hegel Bulletin* 29, no. 1–2 (57–58) (2008): 40, where he rightly claims that 'almost all the basic concepts that Hegel associates with the Understanding exhibit the structure of contradiction.'
65. Guido Kreis, *Negative Dialektik des Unendlichen: Kant, Hegel, Cantor* (Berlin: Suhrkamp, 2015), 335–336. Also see Stefan Schick, *Contradicto est regula veri. Die Grundsaetze des Denkens in der formalen, transcendnetalken und spekulativen Logik* (Hamburg: Meiner Verlag, 2010).
66. See Kreis, *Negative Dialektik des Unendlichen*, 322–323.
67. For a thorough summary, explication, and critique of the various and more recent approaches to the dialectical development from Being to nothing, see Brown, *Hegel on Possibility*, 46–64.
68. Hegel, *SL*, trans. Miller, 109.
69. Priest, "Dialectic and Dialetheic," 402.
70. Houlgate, *The Opening of Hegel's Logic*, 43.
71. For a fuller categorization of the myriad ways of conceiving contradiction, for example in Hahn's *Contradiction in Motion*, De Boer's *On Hegel: The Sway of the Negative*, etc., see Brown, *Hegel on Possibility*, 73–81. Although on his classification, I take the 'non-qualifier approach' to contradiction, my own unqualified view is not as far away from his own 'substitutional' view as it might at first appear.
72. Hegel is not a trivialist who thinks that *all* contradictions are true.
73. Michela Bordignon, "Hegel: A Dialetheist? Truth and Contradiction in Hegel's Logic," *Hegel Bulletin* 40, no. 2 (2017): 198–214.
74. Ibid, 205. Priest claims that 'consistency is a property of sentences.' See Priest, *In Contradiction*, 159.
75. Ibid, 201.
76. Ibid, 205.
77. Ibid, 206.
78. Ibid, 209.
79. Ibid, 208.
80. Ibid, 209.
81. Ibid.
82. See Hegel, *EL*, 31R.
83. See Bordignon, "Hegel: A Dialetheist? Truth and Contradiction in Hegel's Logic," 209–210.
84. Priest, "Dialectic and Dialetheic," 388–389.

9 Relative Dialetheism
The No-World View

The No-World View

Part I concluded that the Absolute could only exist and be known as a true contradiction. Most recently, two notable philosophers, Badiou and Gabriel, have argued that an *un*restricted absolute totality *cannot exist*. These positions are worth investigating, for the simple fact that there is no longer any need to appeal to a true contradiction (to Absolute Dialetheism) if there is no world described by that contradiction. Badiou in his *Being and Event*[1] (1988) and his most recent *Logic of Worlds* (2009),[2] and Gabriel in his *Warum es Die Welt nicht Gibt* (2013) and, more notably, *Fields of Sense* (2015),[3] give different reasons for rejecting an absolutely unrestricted totality, or what I, for shorthand, will simply call the 'Absolute.' Badiou appeals both to Cantor's theorem and Russell's paradox to refute the existence of 'the One' in the sense of an all-inclusive *set of all sets*.[4] Gabriel is clear that although he agrees with Badiou's conclusion, he disagrees with his *reasons* for that conclusion.[5]

Gabriel argues that one problem with identifying the Absolute with a set is the fact that a set must abstract not only from the qualities of the objects but also from the way they are organized. Given that the concept of the set (what I have mostly discussed in terms of the concept of 'class membership') must abstract not only from the quality of the members of the set, the set-theoretical conception of the Absolute is *formal*. As formal, it supplies an incomplete concept of the Absolute, for it leaves the qualitative determinations of the members of the set unaccounted for. For this reason, Gabriel argues that whatever limits or problems befall set-theoretical constructs, they do not seem to immediately imply the non-existence of an absolutely unrestricted totality. Indeed, *the* limitations befalling the set already indicate that the *set is a restricted totality*. As Gabriel points out, Cantor himself distinguishes the concept of the set from the Absolute:

> Dagegen gebrauche ich das Wort "absolut" nur für das, was nicht mehr vergrößert, resp. vervollkommnet würden kann, in Analogie

des "Absoluten" in der Metaphysik. Meine eigentlich unendlichen oder, wenn Sie lieber wollen, transfiniten Zahlen w, w+1, . . . sind nicht "absolut", weil sie, obgleich nicht endlich, dennoch der Vergrößerung fähig sind. Das Absolute ist jedoch keiner Vergrößerung fähig und daher auch für uns inaccessible.[6]

Finally, since the concept of the Absolute at play is formal, it interprets the set in merely syntactical terms. Without semantics, however, no paradox or contradiction can arise.[7] Accordingly, in order for any *reductio* on the concept of the unrestricted totality to be successful, it must move beyond a formal conception of the Absolute. In *Fields of Sense* Gabriel means to supply this reductio against the existence of the world understood in a non-formal sense as *the unified totality*.[8]

Both Priest (2019) and Gabriel argue that whatever concept of the world we employ, it ought not be a *formal* conception. While Priest has advanced a view of the world as a *mereological fusion*, which he holds to be consistent, Gabriel claims that he is not committed to the view that the world is a whole of parts.[9] These disagreements (and others) aside, both reject the formal set-theoretical conception of the world. Unlike Priest, however, Gabriel has famously argued that even if one rejects a formal conception of the world, it is nonetheless impossible for the world to exist. Accordingly, we find that in contemporary European philosophy, we find arguments against the existence of the Absolute irrespective of whether one invokes a formal (in the case of Badiou) or a non-formal concept of the absolute (such as Gabriel's concept of the world as a *unified totality*).[10] In what follows, I will briefly sketch Gabriel's argument against the existence of the world and Priest's most recent set of replies to this argument. Gabriel's arguments are of special interest to us as well because of what I am calling his *relative* dialetheism. Finally, I will defend Absolute Dialetheism, the view that the world does exist, but that it can only exist as a *true contradiction*.

In an earlier chapter, we showed how the problem of onto-theology engenders the complete elimination of the Absolute, or in other words, the world. Although Gabriel offers his own language by which to discuss the issue of the non-existence of the Absolute, he also gives his argument in Heideggerian terms. Because we are approaching his text with Heidegger's problem of onto-theology as our starting point, it is a congenial starting point to motivate Gabriel's argument by starting from the problem of onto-theology. Gabriel writes:

> Heidegger does not claim to have discovered the ontological difference. Rather, the ontological difference is precisely the destiny of metaphysics; it is the metaphysical idea that being is not a being, where this means that there is a relation between being and beings.

> Yet, this turns being into a being, which is the basic move behind ontotheology.[11]

'Being' is not itself a being. Rather it is that *in virtue of which* a being *is*. As such, Being is *instantiated* in every being, but is not itself a being among the others. 'Being' does not differentiate among the various beings—it does not contain any differentiating feature by which it would be distinguished as 'this' in contrast to 'that.' As Gabriel notes, however, because 'Being' is not a being, it is in relation to beings insofar as it *excludes* them. This mutual exclusion is a kind of *relationship* constituted by negation. Insofar as it is constituted by negation, 'Being' itself is *positioned* vis-à-vis beings and thereby is transformed into a determinate being—a being with position. Thus, in an effort to eschew onto-theology by proclaiming 'Being is not a being,' one transforms Being into a being. Thus, 'Being' disappears. In its stead we discover *a being*; not Being itself. Since 'Being' can only exist if it is *not* a being, and it can only exist as a being, it follows that *Being just does not exist.*

Gabriel is also right that one cannot respond to these problems by reconceiving the world as 'horizon.'[12] Horizon stems from the ancient Greek ὁρίζων, which signifies to 'mark out a boundary.' Following our conceptual analysis, horizonality would signify some kind of *determinacy*, for the determinate is a limiting concept. Ordinarily horizon connotes *the line* where the sky meets the ocean. Nothing appears *beyond* the horizon. Accordingly, horizons limit and thereby *determine* what can and cannot appear in any particular experience. For this reason, the horizon is that which *enables* phenomena to appear. Although the horizon appears to be a principle of determinacy, it is itself *relative* and *indeterminate*. The horizon does not have an absolute position. Where the horizon appears depends upon the situation of the subject of experience. Wherever I happen to be, the horizon cannot be. It is always at the *fringe* of the field of experience (whether understood psychologically or phenomenologically). The relativity of the horizon indicates its indeterminacy: as I approach it, it *recedes*. Accordingly, it is a limit which cannot be *surpassed*; it is a line that cannot be crossed. As I approach the position of the horizon, its position changes: its absolute position is *indeterminate*. Whenever I arrive at the place of the horizon, the horizon has shifted.

Although the horizon is an *indeterminate limit*, in Husserlian terms, I can determine the horizon for an object and constitute it as a *determinate object of intentionality*. Nonetheless, since the horizon always again pivots to the fringe, I can never *exhaustively* determine the horizon. Although the horizon appears *determinable*, it cannot be *exhaustively* determined. Unlike Hegel's concept of *absolute determinacy*, in which philosophical thinking of the absolute can be completed, any phenomenology of *the Absolute Horizon* remains an *infinite* task.

This becomes most evident when we reflect on the concept of a *world-horizon* understood as the horizon of *all* horizons. As Absolute, it should be complete, with absolutely *no remainder*. Yet, whenever I attempt to take the horizon of all horizons, H1, as the object of my thematization, another horizon, H2, appears that enables my thematization of the H1. Since every horizon I thematize must always exclude some further horizon that makes that thematization possible, horizonality engenders a fundamental *relativity* and *incompleteness* that is incompatible with the Absolute. Thus, a 'world-horizon' understood as an 'Absolute Horizon' is a contradiction in terms, for it is only ever the appearance of an *incomplete horizon*. Since it always recedes upon approach, the *position* of the limit of phenomenological consciousness is irreducibly indeterminate. Because I cannot set the world-horizon into a *determinate relation* with other noema, for it encompasses them all, what makes any phenomenological field accessible and determinable is an absolutely indeterminate limit—an ὁρίζων. Whatever absolute limit there may be must be an indeterminate, *unsurpassable horizon*. Indeed, because horizons are incomplete, and the Absolute does not appear in experience, phenomenology cannot save the world by appealing to 'horizon.' The most one can encounter phenomenologically is a *horizon of some horizons*.[13] For Gabriel, horizons are horizons of beings—there is no *world* horizon.

Gabriel's thesis that the world does not exist is established by the self-refutation of onto-theology. As we have pointed out already, the problem of onto-theology has a long and distinguished tradition in the West that can be traced back to Ancient Greek thinking. Since onto-theology engenders the complete elimination of Absolute being, when Gabriel claims that onto-theology is the 'destiny of metaphysics' this also entails that the no world thesis is the destiny of metaphysics. As we have shown in our explication of the problem, onto-theology does in fact entail the elimination of the Absolute, *under the condition* that 'Being' cannot be and be 'a being.' To put it in the simplest of terms, Gabriel has simply inferred what no one wants to admit, but is entailed by the assumption that renders onto-theology problematic: the complete non-existence of the Absolute. Even if Gabriel's claim is false, it is nonetheless *historic* and deserves special attention for the simple fact that the whole history of some of the most significant metaphysical problems points towards the elimination of the Absolute.

The argument against the existence of the world can just as much be made employing Aristotelian terminology. In our discussion of Aristotle, we reconstructed Aristotle's argument that Being is not a genus. Gabriel agrees with this thesis

> There is no existence domain in the sense in which there could be a green domain. There really are the several domains, but they are not instances of a higher genus, the all-encompassing existence domain.[14]

To briefly re-iterate the problem of the missing difference, were Being a genus, then it would be predicated of all things and would only provide the identity of each being as a being. Because the principle of difference could not come from Being, the principle of difference could only come from the genus of non-being, or what is the same: there could not be any differences. Thus, because 'Being' could not be distinguished from anything else, it could not be distinguished from nothing at all. Thus, if Being were as a genus, we would be forced to identify it with nothing.[15] In order to avoid the inference that 'Being is nothing' Aristotle famously proposes that Being is *pros hen*—pointing to one, not *'kath hen.'* Unlike Aristotle, who (very problematically) attempts to salvage the unity of Being by re-thinking the structure of the genus of Being, Gabriel does not attempt to salvage the unity of Being. On the contrary, he simply accepts Aristotle's initial conclusion that 'Being is not a genus.'

In Part I, I have attempted to show that the problem of the elimination of the Absolute, which as Gabriel has pointed out, is just Hegelese for the problem of the elimination of the world,[16] has been a perennial problem in the history of Western philosophy. Rather than offering a new solution to a new problem, Gabriel is offering a new solution to a set of old problems, a solution to a host of problems endemic to the metaphysical tradition of the West. The problem of Nihilism (Chapters 1 and 2), the problem of the Missing Difference (Chapter 5), and the problem of Onto-theology and the Third Man (Chapters 6 and 7) can all be deployed to establish the nothingness of the world.

One reason thinkers have hesitated to infer this conclusion stems from the fact that thinkers have assumed that if the Absolute cannot exist, then neither can any *relative* being exist either. Accordingly, one deep anxiety stems from the worry that if the Absolute (or the world) does not exist, then *nothing* can. From this anxiety thinkers make every effort to salvage Being from non-existence, such as appealing to *pros hen* genera for example. But the problem of Onto-theology seems to show the opposite: what always disappears in the argument is 'Being' itself. What always appears in the place of Being is *some being* or being(s). Thus, Gabriel's no-world thesis does not deny all existence. On the contrary, it only denies the existence of the world. Beings do *not* disappear—only Being does.

Because Being does not exist, and metaphysics has Being as its object (or the Absolute more generally), metaphysics is a science that has *no object*. A science that has no object at all is not a science. For this reason, Gabriel is a 'meta-metaphysical nihilist.' This means that the critique of the existence of the Absolute 'leaves all other domains and their objects intact.'[17] In his own terms:

> The no-world defended in this book argues that metaphysics is, strictly speaking, impossible. It is ontologically impossible; the object of metaphysics, the world, cannot exist, and therefore no particular

claim regarding its nature (that it consists of sets, of elementary parti-
cles, of social facts, of solipsistic monads, or what have you) can ever
be substantiated. Metaphysics is the error of Parmenides, as well as
of some of his Asian contemporaries. It might have a longer prehistory and might be someone else's fault. It does not matter whom we
blame, the temptation of metaphysics is universal anyhow, though it
is not built into human nature, but is rather definitely the result of
a long prehistory of human attempts to make sense of things. Nevertheless, it is always as overgeneralized as the view that everything
is water, although its contemporary ramifications are much better
disguised.[18]

Because all other *relative* domains still exist, Gabriel's realism is an
ontology (indeed a 'new realist ontology')—it is a study of *beings*, not
of Being. 'negative ontology' proclaims the non-existence of the world,
whereas 'positive ontology' develops the science of the structure of beings
and the domains in which they exist on the basis of the non-existence of
the world.[19] Because Gabriel can preserve the existence of beings while
simultaneously denying the existence of Being, Gabriel avoids falling victim to the problem of total nihilism that problematized early German
Idealism. Gabriel has tamed and minimized the problem of metaphysical
nihilism, as it were.

Because the world does not exist, Gabriel further infers that the non-
existence of the world is not a truth about any object.[20] For Gabriel, a
concept can only be meaningful if it has truth-conditions. Since claims
about the world cannot refer to anything, and a claim can only have truth
conditions if it refers to something, Gabriel infers that claims about the
world do not have truth-conditions.[21] Given that a statement can only be
meaningful if it has truth-conditions, Gabriel infers that claims about the
world are meaningless:

> For me, saying anything about the world is plain nonsense, like say-
> ing the following: XCEANNRs12.[22]

Because Gabriel's argument against the existence of the Absolute is
formulated in his own terminology, it would be of some use to work
out the basic meaning of his terminology. As we have elucidated earlier,
although Gabriel's argument denies the existence of an absolute domain
of all domains, this does not undermine the existence of *relative domains*
of existence. Gabriel's fields of sense ontology is a variation on domain-
ontology, where to exist is to belong to a domain. Rather than use the term
'domain,' Gabriel will employ the term 'field.' The term 'field' indicates
that the domains in which entities exist are 'generally unconstructed' and
means to distinguish his view from anti-realist domain ontologies such
as those that endorse 'transcendental asymmetry,' whereby the subject

constructs or conditions the domains in which objects exist.[23] What is more, each field (or domain) is distinguished from others in virtue of what he calls 'sense.' 'Sense' is that in virtue of which fields are individuated from each other,[24] with the important qualification that there is no 'overall principle of individuation' that one can know 'in advance' of the investigation of particular fields.[25] Gabriel's appeal to 'sense' is important because it distinguishes his ontology from the more formal varieties of domain ontology, which think of domains as 'sense-less' extensions. Accordingly, Harman is right to classify Gabriel's view as a kind of *ontological descriptivism*.[26] 'Fields of sense' connotes both a realist and non-formal ontology.

Rather than employ the term 'belong to,' Gabriel prefers 'appearance' to describe the relationship between an entity and the domain in which it exists. In Gabriel's own language, to exist is to *appear* in a field of sense.[27] 'Appearance' here signifies that the object 'stands apart from a certain background' such that the field is the background and the object is the thing that stands out against it.[28] In layman's terms, 'appearing in a context' means that beings only exist 'in a context.'[29] The Absolute never 'appears' because it does not exist *in* a context. Ultimately, existence is a property of fields of sense,[30] a kind of *relation* between an object and the field of sense in which it exists:

> objects could not exist alone; they are not absolutes, but only exist as *relata*. Objects only exist relatively to their domain, as existence is the property of their domain to contain exactly them.[31]

Importantly, Gabriel is clear that 'being in a context' or 'appearing in a field of sense' is not reducible or identical to *falling under a concept*. The coffee appears in the cup. The cup is one field of sense in which the coffee exists, but the coffee is not an instance of the universal 'to be a cup.'[32] Here Gabriel also diverges from the tradition, which tends to think of existence as 'disclosed to some sort of most basic categorial judgment, thought, or proposition.'[33]

Because existence means to appear in a field of sense, or more colloquially, to be 'in a context,' in order for any field, F1, (or domain of entities) to exist, it must exist in some field, F2. For F2 to exist, it must exist in a field of sense, F3, and so on. As Gabriel summarizes:

> if there is anything whatsoever, there are at least indefinitely many fields. The basic argument goes roughly like this: if something exists, it has to appear in a field, which entails that there is a field. For this field to exist, there has to be another field within which it appears, and so on infinitely.[34]

Thus, one can never find the *Absolute Limit* to fields of sense. Because there is no field of all fields, there is always some object that is outstanding. In this sense, Gabriel's critique of the existence of the Absolute lands him in an affirmation of what Hegel would polemically call 'bad infinity' in the sense that no matter what field one considers, there is always some existent entity that remains 'outstanding.' This feature of Gabriel's ontology belongs to positive ontology and is worked out on the basis of the no-world view. When there is no absolute limit to existence, existence can only ever have a *relative limit*.

One of the more interesting applications of Gabriel's account is the case of *negative existentials*. For Gabriel, terms have meaning if they have truth conditions, and only terms that refer to objects can have truth conditions. Accordingly, for him a term can only be meaningfully employed (or conceived) if it *actually refers to an object*. Thus, Gabriel affirms a kind of Meinongianism:

> absolute non-existence is impossible. Everything exists, but in different fields of sense. It does not co-exist. There is no all-encompassing field in which surprisingly there somehow are unicorns and there are no unicorns. There are unicorns (for instance, in the Last Unicorn), and there are no unicorns (for instance, in Milwaukee).[35]

Gabriel calls his view 'formal Meinongianism,' which means that 'we cannot claim that something does not exist without thereby committing to its existence.'[36] This is tantamount to the view that *conceivability implies actuality*.[37] Because Gabriel has contextualized (or what is the same, *relativized*) all existence claims, things do not exist or not-exist absolutely, but rather, each thing exists only *in relation to some field of sense*. Although witches do not exist in Salem, Massachusetts, they do exist in Goethe's *Faust*. To claim that 'witches do not exist' is incomplete, for they do not exist in some field of sense, for example Salem. But they certainly do exist in other fields of sense, such as the epic poem *Faust*. 'The world,' by contrast, does not have meaning because there is no object to which the word could refer (in any field of sense), such that the witches in *Faust* are more real than 'the world.'

Gabriel's claim that 'everything exists, but in different fields of sense' commits him to dialetheism, the view that *some* contradictions are true.[38] Although this may seem surprising, after some reflection it should not be. If everything exists, so must contradictions. Indeed, Gabriel's concept of existence is such that 'absolute non-existence is impossible.'[39] Since absolute non-existence is impossible, *it is impossible for contradictions, or the states of affairs they describe, to be absolutely non-existent*. These contradictions do not absolutely exist, but they certainly exist *relative to some field of sense*. The 'round square' certainly does not exist in the field of sense investigated by geometry, but it certainly can exist in the domain of contradictory objects. The 'round square' refers to an object in this domain and successfully instantiates the form of the contradiction: 'a and not-a.' Even if we deny that it is true that round squares exist in the field of sense studied by geometry, we know what people *mean* when they claim that 'the square is round.' Since for Gabriel conceivability implies (some form of) actuality, the 'round square' must exist, but obviously in a field different from that studied by geometry. Simply put: *contradictions can be conceived, so they exist* (again not absolutely, since that is meaningless, but only relative to some field of sense).

Priest's Critiques of the No-World View

Gabriel and Priest disagree on the existence of the world (again, among other things too), but their disagreement is a *family dispute*, for they are both dialetheists, as am I. Gabriel's new realism is also a *new dialetheism*. What Gabriel denies, but I affirm, is *Absolute* Dialetheism, which is the view that the world exists and can only be articulated as a *true contradiction*. Gabriel's view is a *relative* dialetheism, which means that *every* contradiction exists *except* for the contradiction that constitutes the existence of the Absolute. Importantly, Gabriel's argument against the world does not proceed from the assumption that the PNC is an absolute principle of all being, by which one could determine what absolutely does not exist, for he denies any absolute principle by which one would determine what can and what cannot exist in fields of sense.

Gabriel remarks that because the world is meaningless, speaking about the world means nothing different from 'XCEANNRs12*.'[40] Since Gabriel writes about the world in *Fields of Sense*, Priest draws the following inference:

> Gabriel avers that, despite appearances, the noun phrase 'the world' is meaningless, as, then, is any statement about it. Not only does this seem implausible (we appear, after all, to understand the claims in question), but it makes Gabriel's own claim that the world does not exist meaningless.[41]

When Gabriel argues that the world does not exist, he is either saying something meaningful or he is not. Given that the noun phrase 'the world' is meaningless, it follows that he is not saying something meaningful. Saying 'the world does not exist' is like saying '"XCEANNRs12*" does not exist.' Since this is meaningless and has no truth conditions, Gabriel cannot claim *that it is true* that the world does not exist. As long as truth depends on meaning, Gabriel cannot affirm the truth of the claim. Gabriel does indeed claim that the no world view is 'like a declaration' about the end of an illusory era.[42] But what era is coming to an end? When Gabriel says that the era of world pictures is coming to an end, one probably does not understand that the era of XCEANNRs12* is coming to an end.

But why can Gabriel not claim that the world is meaningful? If we return to the point about negative existentials, we remember that Gabriel endorses a view under which conceivability *implies* actuality. If the word 'world' is meaningful, then it must have truth conditions. For Gabriel this is only possible if we acknowledge that there is some object to which we are referring when we speak about the world. Thus, if we can speak meaningfully about the world, then the world must exist. Since the world cannot exist, Gabriel must proclaim 'the world' to be a completely meaningless phrase. But this does seem to be problematic, for only if I understand the meaning of what Gabriel has written about the world can I know that the era of the world-picture has come to an end. But this would seem to imply that the world must exist. In other words, if Gabriel is speaking meaningfully when he claims that the world does not exist, then he must admit that it exists. Thus, Gabriel can only avoid admitting the existence of the world by talking nonsense like 'XCEANNRs12*.' But if this cannot be true, since it is not meaningful, then we seem stuck in a dichotomy: either the claim that 'the world does not exist' is meaningless (and cannot be said to be true or to be false for that matter), or it is meaningful and is false. However we spin it, our proclamation that the world does not exist is either meaningless or false. A further worry would be that 'negative ontology' would appear to contain many meaningless claims (like 'the world does not exist') that further function as the groundwork of meaningful claims in positive ontology that are true.

This dilemma places Gabriel very close to the mystical traditions, but he does not make use of them in the text. One traditional mystical view is that the world exists, but it transcends what can be said in a meaningful way. This type of mysticism defends itself against the criticism I have raised previously in the following way: given that no speech about the Absolute is meaningful, *the mystic's own speech about the world cannot be meaningful*. Were the mystic's speech meaningful, then it would be false. Thus, the only way for the mystic to succeed in the argument is to *speak meaninglessly*. By speaking meaninglessly, the mystic presents a coherent view, for she speaks in a way that *is consistent with her thesis*. The mystic cannot meaningfully say what she means. Instead, all she can do is point to, or show the meaninglessness of what she is saying, by speaking meaninglessly herself and by drawing all claims about the Absolute into meaninglessness. Only by drawing all claims about the Absolute into meaninglessness can the mystic *show* the truth of what she is saying, since she cannot say it meaningfully.

Gabriel is not a mystic, since although he denies that we can speak about the world meaningfully, unlike mysticism, he denies that it exists. Nonetheless, given his insistence on the meaninglessness of speaking about the world, he could also employ this very same tactic to defend himself against this objection. Were he to employ this tactic, I think he could successfully overcome the objection. For example, once one sees that Gabriel's own claims are meaningless (and that no claim about the world could be said in a meaningful way), the meaninglessness of the claims would *show* that there is nothing there to speak about. The truth of his claim is established in his own *performance of meaningless speech*. Once you see what he cannot mean, then you understand that the non-existence of the world is nonsense. But Gabriel does not seem to employ this tactic. To the contrary, he is quite hostile to mysticism (at least in *Fields of Sense*). Gabriel quotes Ramsey:

> As Frank Ramsey said in a similar context about Wittgensteinian nonsense: 'But what we can't say, we can't say, and we cannot whistle it either.'[43]

But one could say this about negative ontology too. One cannot meaningfully say that the world does not exist and one cannot whistle it either. But if we take the mystic seriously, we cannot simply dismiss him, and we would be forced to re-evaluate the plausibility of the mystic's argument.

As readers of *Fields of Sense* know, Gabriel's argument against the existence of the world *assumes* the truth of Gabriel's definition of existence and is formulated in his own terminology. The argument is quite succinct: since to exist is to appear in a field of sense, the world must appear in a field of sense in order to exist. Given that it must exist in a field of sense in order to exist, the world can *either* appear in another field, or it can appear in itself. Since the world can neither exist in another field, nor in itself, the world cannot exist in any fields of sense. Thus, the world does not exist at all.[44]

For the argument to succeed, Gabriel must demonstrate why the world cannot exist in another field of sense or in itself. If the world existed in *another field*, this field in which the world exists would encompass the world. Because Gabriel's definition of existence entails that 'for every domain there is something *not* [my emphasis] appearing in it,'[45] the world would necessarily appear as *one field alongside other fields*, which would contain other objects. Since the field in which the world exists would 'encompass more than the world,' the field in which the world exists would contain *more objects than exist in the world*. In this case, the world would not be the totality of all things, which is absurd, since it is by definition the unified totality of all things. It is easy enough to see, I think, that the world cannot exist if it must exist in another field of sense. Thus, the world, as the field of all fields, could only exist if it exists *in itself*. The world (as the object) must appear in the world (as the field of sense).

According to Gabriel, it is impossible for the world to appear in itself:

> Now that cannot mean that the world appears within the world alongside other fields, as this would repeat the problem of the world being a field among others (now within itself). The problem was that

the world appeared alongside other fields, and we cannot overcome the difficulties with this by adding that the world appears alongside other fields within itself. If the world itself (and not something like its Doppelgänger shadow) really appears within itself, it cannot do so alongside other fields. But then how does the world manage to appear within itself?[46]

It is important to note that Gabriel does *not* posit a universal rule precluding self-containment. Instead, Gabriel's argument is only that *totality cannot contain itself.*[47] Just as Gabriel never posits a universal rule for individuating fields of sense, there is no abstract rule for what exists in them *a priori*, such that there is *no a priori principle* excluding the possibility of self-containment.

If we read this passage carefully, we see that Gabriel invokes the *same assumption* as in the first disjunct. If the world exists within itself (rather than in another), Gabriel claims that it will still appear alongside other fields. The reason is the same: Gabriel's definition of existence, 'appearance in a field of sense,' entails that for every domain there must be something that does *not* appear in it, but appears in *another* field. For this reason, if the world appears in any field of sense at all, irrespective of whether this is itself or another, it will appear alongside other fields in which other objects appear that do *not* appear in it. Thus, since the world can only exist by excluding some objects from itself, it can only exist if it is *not the world*. Thus, in this case too, only the Doppelgänger shadow appears, not the real thing, and for this reason the world cannot exist in itself as its own field of sense.

In another passage, Gabriel gives the same argument against self-containment, but employs the language of genus and species:

> Now this straightforwardly entails that there cannot be a domain of all domains, or an all-encompassing domain, as this domain would have to belong to a domain in order to exist. The all-encompassing domain cannot belong to any of the domains it encompasses. It cannot belong to itself, as belonging to it is defined in such a way that whatever belongs to it appears alongside other domains. Imagine there were only three domains: Chemistry, sociology, and Indian studies. If the domain encompassing these three domains belonged to one of its sub-domains, it would either be a chemical object, a sociological object, or an object relating to India.[48]

In the language of genus and species, the world would be *the most universal genus*. Gabriel claims here that the genus could not belong to itself, since 'belonging to it is defined in such a way that whatever belongs to it appears alongside other domains.' Simply put, Gabriel has defined the appearance in a field of sense to mean that 'if there is anything whatsoever, there has to be some object that does not exist.'[49] For this reason, if the genus exists in itself, it could only exist in one of its *species*, such as that of chemistry, to use his example. But were it to exist in one of its species, it would not be the genus of all genera, for it would exclude other species in that genus, such as Indian studies or sociology.

One of the most important features of Gabriel's argument against the existence of the world is illuminated not only by his use of the problem of onto-theology but also by his use of the concept of the *genus*. When one argues from onto-theology, one supposes that Being could not exist if it were a being. This assumes that the universal, 'Being,' cannot be identified with a particular, 'a being.' It also assumes that the principle of identity of each being, 'Being itself,' cannot be that in virtue of which each being is differentiated from others—that in virtue of which it is *this* or that. Although Gabriel argues against the existence of the world *as a universal genus*, not a set, both the set and the genus have a common feature, which we analyzed in Part I: each assumes that the universal is not itself particular and not sufficient for the differentiation of the particular. Just as membership in a set cannot differentiate each member that falls within the set, so the genus is not sufficient for differentiating the species. Each form of unification assumes the duality of principles of identity and difference. Indeed, this assumption is clearly laid out by Gabriel in other terms, when he claims at the outset of his argument against the world that as the unified totality, 'this unified totality differs from each and every thing that is unified by it, and accordingly becomes an additional field of sense, the field of all fields.'[50] The assumption stated at the very outset is that the principle that *unifies* all fields is fundamentally different from the fields that are *unified* by it. What is precluded from the very beginning is *absolute self-unification*.

As we demonstrated in Part I, the elimination of the Absolute follows from the assumption of the irreducibility of the duality of principles of identity and difference. Accordingly, irrespective of whether one begins with the concept of the world as a set or a genus, in each case one can infer the non-existence of the world, but only because of the fundamental assumption shared by both. For this reason, since the division of principles of identity and difference transcends the distinction between formal and non-formal ontology, once we recognize this common assumption that motivates their arguments, each can be classified as two species of arguments that belong to the same genus. This becomes evident enough when one considers one objection raised by Graham Priest in his essay *Everything and Nothing*.

In a footnote, Priest argues that Gabriel's argument against Absolute self-containment assumes what it wants to establish:

> In (2015), p. 188, Gabriel does concede that it is possible for a field of sense to be a part of itself. The problem is specifically with the f(e).

This concession would seem to weaken his case. What is required, if f(e)'s being a proper part of itself cannot be ruled out on general grounds, is an independent justification for the claim that f(e) is different in this regard from any other field of sense. He says (p. 189) that if f(e) were part of itself it would 'differ from each and every single thing that is unified by it'—which would have unacceptable consequences. But this is precisely to claim that f(e) is not a proper part of itself, and so begs the question.

It is clear enough that if the world exists in another field of sense, then it is not the world—for in this case, it would not be the unified totality. So, if the world must appear in another field of sense in order to exist then the world could not exist. But Priest's argument here is directed against Gabriel's thesis that the world cannot exist in itself. Here Priest speaks about the world as a whole of parts, which is language that is foreign to Gabriel's ontology. But this difference in approach does not affect the effectiveness of Priest's argument here. Rather than 'proper part of itself' one can substitute 'Absolute self-containment' or 'exists such that it is both the object and the field of sense in which it exists.' Priest employs f(e) as a formal way of describing the world, the object e, that exists in a field of sense, signified by f(x). Clearly if the world exists, it must exist in itself, for this is the only way that it can exist *absolutely*.

In order to argue that the world does not appear in itself (as its own field of sense), Gabriel invokes his definition of existence, 'appearance in a field of sense,' which entails that for every domain there must be something that does *not* appear in it, but appears in *another* field. But this would be tantamount to stipulating that *nothing* can exist absolutely, for Absolute Existence means that it does not exist 'alongside' anything else but contains everything. Accordingly, the premise contains the stipulation of the impossibility of Absolute Existence. But we cannot assume the impossibility of Absolute Existence in the premise, since this is what we must establish in the conclusion. For this reason, Priest infers that Gabriel's argument against the possibility that the world exists as both the object and the field of sense in which it exists is circular. Rather than demonstrate that the world cannot exist absolutely (in itself), the argument appears to assume that existing in itself is impossible.

To put Priest's argument in other terms, Gabriel's argument here seems to assume from the beginning that the world can only exist if it exists *relatively*, such that 'this unified totality differs from each and every thing that is unified by it.' Once we have stipulated (in this argument anyway) that existence is contextual, and *relative to something else*, it follows straightaway that the world cannot exist. But this stipulates from the beginning, or is analytically entailed, if you wish, that the context of all contexts is impossible. 'Relative being' seems to be analytically entailed in Gabriel's concept of existence as 'appearing in a field of sense.' Because

Gabriel claims that existing in itself is generally possible on his concept of existence, it seems problematic to assume it to be impossible in the argument. Because for Gabriel it is generally possible for an object to be its own field of sense, the impossibility of self-containment cannot be read out of the definition of existence as such. Since the argument against the existence of the world neither assumes the impossibility of self-containment more generally and assumes (rather than proves) the impossibility of self-containment in the case of the world, Priest seems to be onto something when he argues that Gabriel has not yet shown that it is impossible for the world to exist in itself.[51]

In line with this critique, Priest has offered an alternative model for conceiving the existence of the world. He argues that Gabriel conceives of the world on an *anti-symmetrical* model, in the sense that if the world (as an object), e, exists in some field of sense, a, then the field of sense, a, cannot itself exist as an object, a, in the field of sense e. Since it has not *yet* been shown (on Gabriel's own terms) to be conceptually impossible for the world to exist in its own field of sense, Priest offers an alternative model that drops the assumption of anti-symmetry:

> The sort of parthood structure involved in Gabriel's situation can be illustrated by a simple model. Let us suppose, for the sake of illustration, that there are, as well as the objects, e and f(e), two other objects, a and b. Then if we write x → y to indicate that x is a proper part of y, the model can be depicted thus:
>
> f (e)
> ↑↓
> e
> a ↗↖ b
>
> Every object distinct from e is a proper part of it. And e, in turn, is a proper part of f(e).[22]

'a' and 'b' stand for objects appearing in the world, as the field of all fields, while 'e' is the world that exists *both* as the object (e) and the field of sense, e, in which it appears.

Now it is the case that for Priest the world is a mereological sum, and is consistent with itself, such that he conceives of the objects existing in the field of all fields as 'parts' of one 'whole.' He argues that recent work on mereology shows that such self-containment is not inconsistent and can be adopted by 'simply dropping' the anti-symmetry axiom:

> However, there is a perfectly good mereological theory which allows for loops of this kind. Cotnoir and Bacon give such a theory. Indeed, they show how one can be obtained by taking a standard

axiomatization of mereology, and simply dropping the anti-symmetry axiom.[52] And of course, since the standard mereological theory is consistent, the theory obtained by dropping this axiom is also consistent.[53]

Although Priest argues for the consistency of the world, he argues in the same text that nothing is dialetheic and is the ground of reality. Insofar as the ground of reality is not relative to anything else, it is Absolute (as the ultimate ground). For this reason, Priest's position could be described as an Absolute Dialetheism, not because he views the world as inconsistent, but because he takes the ground of all reality, nothingness, to be so.[54]

Hegel and the No-World View

Hegel, like Priest after him, rejects an absolute anti-symmetrical conception of the Absolute. Hegel claims that 'each of these moments is no less the *whole* concept than it is a *determinate* concept and *a determination* of the concept.'[55] For Hegel, universality, particularity, and singularity, are each the whole concept, a determinate concept, and a determination of the concept. Accordingly, there is a radical *symmetry* between the concept and its moments. Because Hegel's concept is the form of Absolute Knowing and Being, and denies the absolute anti-symmetry assumed in Gabriel's argument against the existence of the world, Hegel offers a concept of the Absolute that remains unaffected by Gabriel's objections.

For Hegel, the Absolute exists in itself. Rather than a merely unified totality, Hegel's concept of the world is the concept of a *self-unifying totality*. Because it is a self-unifying totality, it does not 'differ from each and every thing that is unified by it' and thereby does not fall victim to Gabriel's arguments. Rather than suppose that the universal 'Being' cannot be 'a being,' the concept of the *self-particularizing universal* undermines any absolute separation between universal and particular, thus enabling the identification of universal with particular. Because Hegel's logic of the concept is not a mereology (for the logic of wholes and parts is a constituent of the logic of Essence), one certainly cannot identity Hegel's logic of the concept with Priest's formal mereology.[56] But this difference does not seem to undermine the analogical solution to the problem of the existence of the world one can find in both Priest and Hegel.

Although Hegel clearly endorses a kind of symmetry that Gabriel denies at the level of the Absolute, Hegel acknowledges Gabriel's point that if the world were to exist, then it would need to *exist relatively*. Indeed, when Hegel conceives of the concept as self-particularizing, he is acknowledging that the Absolute can only exist if it *relativizes itself*. If the Absolute universal remained opposed to the particular (or the Absolute opposed to the relative), it would not be Absolute. But the relativizing that Gabriel

302   Hegel's Absolute Dialetheism

posits as an objection to the existence of the world Hegel would claim to be the solution to the problem, for the Absolute can only be Absolute if it exists in itself (namely as a *relative* determination of itself). However, for Hegel this must entail that the world (or the Absolute) is *inconsistent* because the self-particularizing concept transforms the universal into a particular. Because the particular *qua* particular is not universal, their identity in the concept must be formulated as a contradiction. Like Gabriel, Hegel must affirm that the world is contradictory, but unlike Gabriel, Hegel proclaims the world to be a *true contradiction*.

Hegel's construal of the concept as *self-particularizing* instantiates the very general feature of Hegel's logic, namely *the relativizing* of the Absolute. As self-particularizing, the concept relativizes itself, for it determines itself to be one differentiation of the concept *alongside others*. As a differentiation of the concept, or as particular, the absolute concept exists in a relative form, for it is one difference that excludes other differences, thereby standing in relation to them. In the language of onto-theology, the universal 'Being' stands as one determination (a being) among others. Because this difference is also the concept as such, or the universal, the particular is also not just relative to others, but it is the absolute whole in which the differences exist. Hegel's definition of the concept relativizes the Absolute as much as it absolutizes the relative.

The contradictory aspect of the concept also highlights the anti-symmetrical aspect of Hegel's account of the Absolute. Because the concept *absolutizes the relative*, Hegel's Absolute Concept also exhibits *asymmetry*. The relativizing of the Absolute signifies the moment of self-alienation in Hegel's thought. The Absolute can only exist if it exists 'outside itself' or is alienated from its being. One might think that this implies that Hegel conceives of the whole to be an illusion, but this, I think, would be a mistake.[57] Despite this necessary moment of self-loss, in the concept Hegel is unequivocal that the concept, which is the Absolute (or the world in this discourse) does not completely lose itself in that alienation, but continues to *preserve itself* in its otherness:

> It is not dragged into the process of becoming, but continues itself through that process undisturbed and possesses the power of unalterable, undying self-preservation [Selbsterhaltung].[58]

Because the concept *preserves* its Absolute Being even in its self-particularization, the relativizing of the Absolute does not undermine its Absolute Being. The concept is the whole, and it is in a constant state of self-negation, but it preserves itself in each act of self-negation such that the concept, or the totality, 'preserves itself' and remains 'undisturbed.' This structure is clearly visible in the structure of the universal which repeats itself in a number of different, independent particulars. Each particular is different, and the same universal exists in each. Accordingly, the universal is 'outside itself' insofar as each particular instantiates the whole universal. Although it is 'outside itself' in each case (and thereby replicates itself indefinitely as you would expect in a case of Absolute self-containment),[59] it preserves itself as the self-same universal. Here we can only briefly indicate the structure Hegel develops, which we will explore in more depth in the coming chapters.

In sum, for Hegel it is through the process of self-negation that the concept renders itself the totality in which each determination of the concept is the concept itself. Its symmetry lies in its anti-symmetry, as one might expect from an absolute dialetheist such as Hegel. Although he certainly could not have been aware of a position such as Gabriel's, his own concept of the concept was formulated in order to overcome the objections by Jacobi that philosophical Idealism leads to a total nihilism—a total elimination of the world. By re-thinking the form of the concept, Hegel means to rescue the world from its non-existence.

Curiously, Hegel's position seems to be something like the inverse of Gabriel's, for Hegel's dialectic attempts to show that the conceivability of the Absolute (such as God) is what engenders its existence, whereas merely relative concepts (such as empirical concepts like the concept of $100) do not imply their own existence. For Hegel, the existentially implicative aspect of the concept of the concept is also evident in the questions concerning the Being of Being and the knowledge of knowledge. Since the question 'what is Being?' can only be answered in a *self-predicative* way, by predicating Being to the subject 'Being' one would place 'Being' in the genus or class of Beings. By placing Being in the set of beings, Being would no longer merely be the class of all beings but would also be *one particular being within the class* itself. Likewise, knowing what Knowledge is introduces a special kind of knowledge: epistemology, which is a knowing that is *distinct* from other kinds of knowing.[60] Just as the inquiry into the Absolute determination of the concept engenders existential implication, so do the inquiries into Being and knowledge. Simply put: any inquiry into the Absolute will discover that its concepts cannot do without self-predication and existential implication.[61] Self-predication and existential implication are the conceptual structures by which Hegel's concept of *self-containment* are developed.

Gabriel does briefly comment on Hegel's philosophy in *Fields of Sense*. His main objection is that Hegel never establishes *the boundlessness* of the conceptual.[62] But I would contend, as I have already argued, that Hegel establishes this thesis in his *Phenomenology of Spirit*. Here he performs a reductio on the finitude of the concept and thereby shows that conceptual knowing is Absolute. By means of the self-negation of the finite conception of the concept, the *Phenomenology* prepares the way for a presuppositional logic. In what follows, I will argue that it is also the task of Hegel's ontological argument to work out the boundlessness of the concept in a *positive* way, only part of which we will be able to reconstruct here. Gabriel is therefore right that in order to do justice to Hegel's concept of the boundlessness of the conceptual, one must 'go through the entire *Encyclopedia*.'[63] Gabriel claims that his view is superior to Hegel's insofar as his view requires there to be thinkers in order for there to be concepts, but he does not *yet* confront Hegel's dialectic in detail. He claims that 'the relevant self-referentiality of concepts does not spread out over totality by itself' but he must show why Hegel is wrong to think this by a deep engagement with Hegel's corpus, such as Hegel's *Logic* and *Encyclopedia*. Because *Fields of Sense* only supposes Hegel to be wrong and does not establish that the Absolute does not appear in itself, Hegel's Absolute Dialetheism stands as a *plausible alternative* to the no-world view.[64] Because Hegel's logic of the concept, as a self-differentiating and self-unifying totality, is predicated upon the self-refutation of the division of principles of identity and difference that arguably underlies an essential premise in Gabriel's against the existence of the world in *Fields of Sense*, Hegel's logic provides a way to rescue the world from Gabriel's objections. Indeed, it is quite fitting that Gabriel's Neo-Schellingian ontology would be challenged by neo-Hegelian metaphysics. Hegel means to resuscitate the world and to save it from the critique of nihilism. Once we take up the position of *Reason*, Hegel provocatively suggests that 'it is as if the world had for it only now come into being':

> for it is certain that it is itself all reality, or that everything actual is none other than itself; its thinking is itself directly actuality and thus its relationship to the latter is that of idealism. Apprehending itself in this way it is as if the world had for it only now come into being; previously it did not understand the world; it desired it and worked on it, withdrew from it into itself and abolished it as an existence on its own account, and its own self qua consciousness—both as consciousness of the world as essence and as consciousness of its nothingness. In thus apprehending itself, after losing the grave of its truth, after the abolition of its actuality is itself abolished, and after the singleness of consciousness is for it in itself Absolute Essence, it discovers the world as *its* new real world, which in its permanence holds an interest for it which previously lay only in its transiency; for the existence of the world becomes for self-consciousness its own truth and presence; it is certain of experiencing only itself therein.[65]

Notes

1. See Alain Badiou, *Being and Event*, trans. Oliver Feltham (London and New York: Continuum, 2005), PT I, Section 3.
2. See Alain Badiou, *Logics of Worlds*, trans. Alberto Toscana (London and New York: Continuum, 2009), BK II, Section 3.1.
3. Markus Gabriel, *Fields of Sense* (Edinburgh: Edinburgh University Press, 2015), 7.

4. For Badiou . . . 'there is no Whole,' (180f).
5. Gabriel, *Fields of Sense*, 117.
6. Georg Cantor, *Briefe*, ed. Herbert Meschkowski and Winfried Nielsen (Berlin and Heidelberg: Springer, 1991), 139.
7. Gabriel, *Fields of Sense*, 117–118.
8. Gabriel also considers the case of an 'additive totality' which I will not consider here.
9. Gabriel, *Fields of Sense*, 191.
10. Ibid, 189.
11. Ibid, 205.
12. This maneuver cannot help and does not help bring the world back into existence. Let us say that the world as the field of all fields is not an object, but rather only a field within which all other fields appear. If in addition it is not an object, but rather only a field within which hall other fields appear. If in addition it is not an object, we have to come to the conclusion that it does not appear in a field of sense. Yet, this still implies that it cannot exist. Gabriel, *Fields of Sense*, 205.
13. For more on this concept in connection with indeterminacy in general, see Moss, "The Emerging Philosophical Recognition of the Significance of Indeterminacy," 1–47.
14. Gabriel, *Fields of Sense*, 60.
15. Both Hegel and Heidegger draw this exact inference that Being is nothing (though each understands something very different by this claim, and neither thinks that this entails the non-existence of the world).
16. 'In Hegel's language the problem of the world is the problem of the absolute.' See Gabriel, *Fields of Sense*, 227.
17. Ibid, 145.
18. Ibid, 123.
19. This division of ontology, which is the study of the meaning of existence (Gabriel, 318) is clearly indebted to Schelling, whose later philosophy is divided into negative and positive. Gabriel admits the importance of Schelling's *Freedom Essay* in the development of his Fields of Sense ontology. Unlike Schelling, however, Gabriel denies the existence of the *Ungrund*. See Gabriel, *Fields of Sense*, 167–168.
20. Gabriel, *Fields of Sense*, 174.
21. Ibid, 203.
22. Ibid, 200. See Gabriel's longer discussion of this issue in Gabriel, *Fields of Sense*, 200–205.
23. Ibid, 157.
24. Ibid, 139, 131.
25. See Gabriel, *Fields of Sense*, 243–244.
26. Gabriel, *Fields of Sense*, Editors Preface, vi–ix.
27. Gabriel, *Fields of Sense*, 158. 'I understand existence to be the fact that some object or objects appear in a field of sense.' Gabriel prefers 'appearance' to 'belonging' because the latter has connotations of set-theoretical ontology. See Gabriel, *Fields of Sense*, 158.
28. Ibid, 166.
29. Ibid, 158.
30. Gabriel, *Fields of Sense*, 65. His view is distinguished from other ways of conceiving of existence as a metaphysical, logical, non-discriminatory property, or not as a property at all. See 43–66 for a further discussion of this.
31. Ibid, 140.
32. Ibid, 160.

306 Hegel's Absolute Dialetheism

33. Ibid, 162.
34. Ibid, 159.
35. Gabriel, *Fields of Sense*, 178. Gabriel puts it more speculatively here: 'if there is anything whatsoever, there has to be some object that does not exist.' Gabriel, *Fields of Sense*, 60.
36. Ibid, 180.
37. Ibid, 185.
38. Gabriel announced this dialetheism in a seminar with Graham Priest in the summer semester in Bonn, 2019.
39. Ibid, 178.
40. Ibid, 200.
41. Graham Priest, "Everything and Nothing," presented at the University of Bonn on July 17, 2017.
42. Ibid, 206.
43. Ibid, 201.
44. Ibid, 189.
45. Ibid, 60.
46. Ibid, 189.
47. Ibid, 188.
48. Ibid, 140.
49. Ibid, 60.
50. Ibid, 189.
51. For Gabriel's most recent engagement with Priest's view, see his forthcoming book, *Fiktionen*.
52. A. Cotnoir, and A. Bacon, "Non-Well-Founded Mereology," *Review of Symbolic Logic* 5 (2012): 187–204, §4.1.
53. Priest, "Everything and Nothing," 10.
54. Interestingly, Hegel identifies the concept of nothing as a concept of the Absolute. Accordingly, from a Hegelian viewpoint, if nothingness is dialetheic, then so is the Absolute. The term 'Absolute' is my language (and Hegel's), not Priest's.
55. Hegel, *SL*, trans. Miller, 600.
56. This is made even more obvious by the fact that for Hegel (unlike for Priest) the world is contradictory.
57. See Gabriel's implicit endorsement of this reading in Gabriel, *Fields of Sense*, 209.
58. Hegel, *SL*, trans. Miller, 276, 602.
59. See Gabriel, *Fields of Sense*, 90.
60. Indeed, having a particular kind of knowledge is not tantamount to being an expert in epistemology, as any Socratic dialogue establishes.
61. As Sainsbury points out in his discussion of the liar paradox, self-reference by itself does not always engender paradoxes. For example, I can talk about this sentence without engendering any paradox. But as concerns absolute concepts, e.g., the concept, being, or knowledge itself, the self-referential character of the concept engenders its own instantiation. See Sainsbury, *Paradoxes*.
62. Gabriel, *Fields of Sense*, 288.
63. Ibid, 229.
64. 'The relevant self-referentiality of concepts does not spread out over totality by itself. It would, if we had reasons to think of totality as encompassed by a given actual thought no thinker we are acquainted with holds. But if such a form of idealism is the only way of solving the puzzles of the no-world view, the no-world view has the advantage of not being committed to the idea that totality is always already encompassed by some actual thought or concept.' Gabriel, *Fields of Sense*, 228.
65. Hegel, *PS*, trans. Miller, 140.

10 Hegel's Solution to the Problem of Absolute Knowledge

Why the World Exists

In *The Concept*[1] of Hegel's *Science of Logic*, Hegel provides one solution to all *six* paradoxes and provides us a place to begin searching for a way to solve these classic problems. Here Hegel presents the reader with a novel answer to these classic questions. If the universal is self-particularizing and thereby self-differentiating, then all of the features of the finite concept are undermined.[2] As self-differentiating, the universal can escape the traditional construal of the finite concept and thereby escape the problems associated therewith. Moreover, because the difference is not external to the universal, the universal is no longer finite. Accordingly, it is *infinite*.[3] Thus, if the universal is self-differentiating, universality is no longer beholden to any of the features of the finite concept, or the features that follow from the separation of the principles of universality and particularity and the PNC that undergird it. Since the universal escapes this division, it also escapes *all* of the problems that follow from them.[4]

In the introduction to the *Doctrine of the Concept*, Hegel writes that goal of his *Doctrine of the Concept* is not to produce new materials, but to enliven and ignite dead material. For Hegel, the task of logic is not to build a city out of nothing or from new materials, but to re-construct an ancient city. The materials for successfully defining the concept are there, but there is nothing to dwell in. There are bricks, lumber, nails, and so on, but they fail to form anything in which one can dwell philosophically. By giving the dead materials the organizing principle of self-differentiation, the difference of the principles of universality and particularity becomes enlivened with the power and life of the concept.[5] Hegel enlivens the concept with various features of Ancient Greek thinking, such as his appropriation of the Greek concept of the Presocratic 'back-turning' and the development of self-predication and existential implication. In Hegel's logic, palintropos becomes *Rückkehre*.

The self-differentiating universal only stays itself *in virtue of differentiating itself* into various contents distinct from it, but which it nonetheless contains within itself. *To be a universal is to admit what is other* to itself and to *maintain its identity* in lieu of the self-differentiation. Because this is the definition of the concept, the concept can be instantiated in many particulars. Because the concept is that which maintains its identity in what is other to itself, the self-same universal can be multiply instantiated in different particulars without ceasing to be what it is. Note that this would not be possible if the universal were not contradictory. Only because the universal is a true contradiction can the self-same universal remain itself while *simultaneously being present in more than one particular*. Hegel has no problem of instantiation, because his *truth logic is dialetheic*.

The concept as self-differentiation is both the determiner and the determined. Insofar as self-differentiation negates any difference between determiner and determined, self-differentiation determines what it is, for it is not differentiated by any other principle external to it. Since it determines for itself what it is, it must be the source of its own content and is rightfully called 'self-determining.' Since the concept *qua* self-particularizing contains what is different from itself, the concept is *absolutely determinate* only in lieu of *the contradiction* it contains. Since the universal contains its own difference, it is not simply a self-identical 'one.' Since it is not simply self-identical, but contains its own differentiating principle, it is *not* beholden to the PNC as the finite universal may be. Because it is not beholden to this principle, it is no longer beholden to those principles that the PNC makes possible.

As self-particularizing and self-differentiating, the concept is both the principle of its unity *and* the principle of its difference. Hence, construing the concept as the *self-particularizing determinacy* does not presume the separation of the principles of universality and particularity, for it has no need to appeal to an external principle of differentiation to account for its content. Because the universal is not only unconditioned but also the source of its own differentiation, the problem of Nihilism raised by Jacobi against Fichte is no longer legitimate. As Bowman points out, although for Jacobi, 'on the point of Nihilism, there can be no self-grounding science,'[6] Hegel's logic of the concept is designed to overcome such objections. Jacobi's refutation of Fichte is contingent upon the inability of Fichte's first principle, which is a pure thesis, to account for the existence of difference, for which a synthetic principle is required. As a purely *thetic* principle devoid of any plurality or difference, it could not even account for the difference between itself and synthetic knowledge. Indeed, because the principle of difference is nothing other than the principle of identity, the concept can amplify itself into differentiated existence by itself. Thus, because of *the identity of the analytic and synthetic* features of the concept, the Absolute *can be* and *can be known*. In the following chapters, we will further explore Hegel's response to Jacobi's accusation of nihilism by showing how Hegel develops his logic of the concept as an ontological 'argument' for God's existence. Bowman has it exactly right when he claims that 'absolute negativity is made to do important metaphysical work' and 'denotes the source of the fundamental structure of reality by virtue of which atheism, fatalism, and nihilism prove to be false.'[7]

Because it is *the principle of its own difference*, the problem of the missing difference does not arise. Indeed, the problem of the missing difference followed from the necessity to discover the principle of the difference outside of the universal itself, a requirement demanded by the limited construal of the universal as a principle of identity of its particulars. To avoid this problem, Hegel posits that universals must provide for their own differentiations. If the universal self-differentiates, it is also self-particularizing, for the particular is the principle of differentiation. Because the universal is *self-particularizing*, universals must exhibit *existential implication*. Thus, without existential implication Hegel cannot solve the problems plaguing the finite conception of the concept. Moreover, the universal achieves existential implication through *self-reference*. The self-referential aspect of the universal is already evident: when we think the self-identity of self-identity, we cannot help but encounter non-self-identity. The universals, in virtue of self-reference, imply their own particularity and thereby their own content. This implication is 'existential,' for *the existence of the particular instance of the category* is created by the category itself.

In addition, because it is its own principle of difference, there is no *non-conceptual content* to which the concept must appeal in differentiating its various aspects. On the traditional model, an appeal to the given seems necessary since the content of a category is determined by something other than the category, such as an external category, an appeal to a given content in experience or to beings. Since universals posit their own content, foundationalism can be avoided, since there is no need to look outside of the universals for their content or for the differentiation of the particulars. Thus, it also avoids the need to appeal to non-conceptual foundations and avoids having to conceive of itself along non-conceptual lines, as we illustrated in the psychologistic and naturalistic conceptions of the concept that arise in absolute empiricism that follow from such appeals. Once we have overcome the separation of the principles of universality and particularity, the problem of the Missing Difference and Absolute Empiricism are solved.

The problem of onto-theology is only generated because conceptual determination precludes any identification of the universal with the particular, and onto-theology identifies the universal, Being, with a being, a particular. Given that the separation of the principles of universality and particularity is no longer a legitimate principle, the *identification* of universal with particular is no longer a problem. In fact, the self-particularizing universal requires that the particular be universal! Thus, onto-theology can only be viewed as a problem for a view of the concept that demands the duality of principles.

The problem of the Third Man arises because of the same supposition of the absolute *non-identity* of universal and particular. Because (i) the particular is an instance of the universal (for which reason it is not universal) and every attempt to think the universal results in the identification of the universal with the particular, an *infinite regress* is generated without end. Given that the problem of the Third Man is only generated by the separation of the principles of universality and particularity (just as in the case of the problem of onto-theology) and the self-particularizing universal eschews any appeal to a second principle of difference, the universal as self-particularizing completely eschews the Third Man regress. For Hegel, the universal is neither merely an abstraction nor a class nor a genus, for each of these fails to be existentially implicative and self-predicative. By existential implication, the universal establishes for itself what its content is. For this reason, existential implication establishes the *true* content of the universal, or the content to which the universal corresponds. The concept must, by itself, give itself its own 'truth.' Only on a concept of the universal as *true in itself* do these problems cease to arise.

Each of the classic answers to the question concerning the constitution of universality precludes any derivation of the differentiated particular from universality itself. If the universal is self-differentiating, it must contain not only particularity but also the differentiated particular or singularity. By removing the dualistic constraints on conceptual determination, the universal as self-differentiating must individuate its own instances. Since the universal as self-differentiating generates its own content, and must be its own particular, it must also *determine itself to be self-determining*. It must include *self-differentiation as such* in the forms of its own self-differentiations. In other words, insofar as self-determination can account for its own differences, and these differences specify the 'what it is' of its own content, the concept of self-particularization must account for its own content. Unlike other forms of universality, the universal as self-determining *individuates itself*. Although the text indicates that the universal individuates itself into many distinct forms of universality, it seems that Hegel introduces the concrete universal, or self-differentiation, as *the particular form of universality as such*.

As every reader of Hegel knows, because the text is a systematic unity, any reconstruction of a portion of Hegel's text cannot be achieved in total isolation from the other sections. Thus, I do not have the luxury to ignore other portions of Hegel's text entirely. The reason for this is the fact that Hegel appeals to other categories in his *Logic* such as 'Being in Itself' and 'illusion' in his description of the features of the concept. Accordingly, in order to properly relay the dialectical process to the reader, I will take the liberty to discuss these concepts to the extent to which they illuminates Hegel's claims. Perhaps unsurprisingly, our analysis of the concept will lay bare not only the conceptual character of the other categories in Hegel's *Logic* but the motivation for the *overall division* of the *Logic* into three sections. We shall make a special effort to note the differences between the concept and other categories with which the concept has traditionally been identified.

In sum, my reconstruction of Hegel's solution to these problems is, in one way, admittedly *hypothetical*. If we adopt the *assumption* that the concept is self-particularizing, then we *can* solve all of these aforementioned philosophical problems that have compromised the possibility of metaphysics and epistemology since the dawn of the tradition. Indeed, although Hegel's *Logic* is not presented as a hypothetical argument, *my* argument in this work cannot help but appear to be hypothetical. At one level, the hypothetical nature of my argument is simply a function of the narrow limit of this project, namely to show how Hegel's *Doctrine of the Concept* is designed to solve a host of perennial philosophical problems, including *the possibility of the existence of the Absolute*. Indeed, one could easily build upon this project by offering a thoroughly internal motivation of the concept of the concept by re-constructing the development of the concept of the concept from mere 'Being' at the outset of the *Science of Logic*.[8]

On the other hand, although I do not reconstruct the previous categories in the *Science of Logic*, my argument still offers a different type of *internal* motivation for adopting Hegel's concept of the concept. So long as we accept the truth of the self-identity of the concept, we cannot help but *think the truth of contradiction*. What is self-identical cannot help but be what it is not. When we think what is self-identical, we think what is not self-identical in virtue of self-identity. The self-negation of self-identity itself cannot help but posit the universal as self-differentiation *on its own terms* and as the unity of opposition that is characteristic of Hegel's concept of the concept. Thus, Hegel's claim that the universal is self-differentiating is in fact not hypothetical at all. Instead, it is necessarily what the self-identity of self-identity *gives*. In this respect, all that is needed in order to provide an internal motivation for the posit that universality is self-differentiation is the analysis of the absolute difference between difference and self-identity and the dialectical results thereof, which we have already demonstrated.

The differentiations of the universal, *as differentiations*, are distinct from universality itself. Yet, the differentiations, or particulars of universality are nonetheless identical to universality. Thus, the universal *remains itself* even in that which is distinct from it, namely its particulars. It does not become or cease to be what it is in its differences or confront an 'other' in its differences in which it does not find itself. Moreover, it is only what it is, the self-differentiating universal, only insofar as the universal *stays itself* in virtue of differentiating itself into various contents distinct from it, which it nonetheless contains within itself. Since the whole concept is *present in each particular*, the concept must be completely *outside itself*, or *exceed itself*. Insofar as the universal is particular, the whole must be outside itself and it is thereby *alienated from itself.* Thus, self-alienation or 'self-externality' is a central feature of the universal insofar as it is instantiated in particularity. Indeed, this is in fact how Hegel construes the universal in its particularity and is one of the more obvious moments of his Neo-Platonic heritage. In particularity, universality is self-negating. In the reflections on empirical concepts, judgments, and inference I will show how the structure of *empirical concepts, judgment, and inference* all exemplify this self-alienation.

Indeed, this inevitable self-alienation is clear enough from what self-differentiation and self-particularization require: since the universal *differentiates itself from itself*, it must negate itself. As a result, the universal *differentiates itself into that which is not self-differentiating.* Because abstractions, classes, and genera do *not* differentiate their own particulars or generate their own content, one might rightly wonder how the self-differentiating universal could account for these, since they are *not* self-differentiating. Because the self-differentiating universal *must* undergo this process of self-alienation, it can in principle accommodate forms of conceptual determination that do not exhibit the self-differentiating features of Hegel's concrete universal. As a principle of unification and differentiation, the universal construed as self-determining must be both a universal and a particular and should thereby be able to function as the universal that puts forward the traditional forms of universality: abstraction, class membership, and genera. On the one hand, this can only succeed if the other forms of universality, that is abstraction, class membership, and the genus, could be viewed as distinct forms of universality. As we will see, Hegel argues that abstraction, class membership, and the genus are all particular instances of universality. If these are forms of the self-differentiating universal, they will embody the form of the self-particularizing universal in its *self-alienated form.* Indeed, it is important to note that this would mean that each form of universality, for example abstraction, class membership, and genus, could not each be treated as the *sole* form of universality as they have been traditionally viewed. Instead, they have a principle that undergirds them which makes them possible in the first place. To use the worn phrases of Kant, the concept is reason, *Vernunft*, that contains within it the moments of the Understanding, *Verstand*. *Verstand* does not stand beside reason, but it is reason's self-expression.

Still, the self-differentiating universal does not remain in a state of mere self-negation, for the very concept of 'self-negation' undermines itself and turns back upon itself. If self-negation is really self-negating, the concept of 'self-negation' will apply to itself. Through the self-predicative structure of self-negation, *self-negation must negate itself.* Accordingly, one could just as well describe the self-differentiating universal as Bowman does, namely as *absolute negativity*.[9] Accordingly, through the self-negation of the universal in its self-external form, the universal is no longer outside of itself. Rather, the universal coheres with itself and is consistent with itself, but it can only achieve this internal self-coherence *by means of self-negation and self-return*. This final return of the universal to itself, or the self-negation of self-negation is what Hegel will call *singularity*. Without the aspect of self-alienation, the concept would not have any content. Indeed, it is important to note that this aspect of self-alienation is *necessary*—not a contingent feature of Hegel's thinking. Without the inversion of the self-particularizing universal, neither would there be any differentiated content there in the universal (since its content is to be that which is self-differentiating), but no return to the origin either, and thereby *no singularity*. This process of self-negation and self-return happens in different ways throughout the logic and is endemic to the *concept of method*, which only arises *as method* at the very end of the logic in the Absolute Idea.

The logic of finitude in the *logic of Being* prefigures the inevitable self-undermining of finite forms of universality within the logic itself. The *Science of Logic* begins with the purely indeterminate, which is indeed 'infinite' in the sense that the indeterminate has no limits or differentiations. Hegel does not classify the indeterminate as a kind of infinity, but it certainly has been grasped this way in the history of philosophy, and it is not hard to see why. This infinitude of pure indeterminacy ultimately gives way to *finitude*. As the logic of being develops, something is finite if it has its limit within itself. Finitude is that which comes to an end, or *ceases to be*. Because it contains its limit within itself, or has its own ceasing to be within itself, it contains its *own negation* within itself. When finitude is posited as Absolute, it is no longer in a relationship of *limitation* but is without limit. Insofar as it is without limit, *that which ceases to be* does *not* cease to be. When finitude no longer ceases to be, it can no longer be finite. Instead, finitude itself becomes *non-finite*. Hegel develops this dialectic further to show how the bad infinite and the true infinite develop therefrom.[10]

As is well known, the bad infinite arises from the non-finite. Given that the non-finite is not finitude, it stands in opposition to finitude. This opposition to finitude renders the non-finite finite. With the disappearance of the non-finite, only finitude remains. Because finitude cannot help but refute its own finitude, it inevitably gives rise once again to non-finitude, *ad infinitum*. This infinitude is 'bad' in the sense that it is *incomplete*, for there is always one more. Because the infinite *qua* non-finite is always in opposition to another that it excludes, it is not truly infinite, but a *false infinitude*. The *true* infinite cannot be opposed to an *external* finitude, but cancels and preserves finitude as a moment within itself. Indeed, just as the self-overcoming of the separation between difference and identity are overcome in the course of the logic, so is the opposition of the finite and the infinite.

As Hegel points out, all that is necessary to appreciate the development of true infinity is to grasp what is already there in the false infinite. In each alternation of finitude to infinitude, each side of the opposition is transformed into its opposite. In the finite the infinite is uncovered; in the infinite the finite is uncovered. The finite is not just finite, for it is also infinite. Likewise, the infinite is not just infinite, for it is also finite. Thus, *both* sides of the opposition themselves constitute the unity of finitude and infinitude. Because each side always already is either the *finitized infinite* or the *infinitized finite*, the development is a *circle*: whenever one begins in infinitude, one falls into finitude, but this falling into finitude is just a rising again into infinity. This circle is closed in the sense that it ends in the exact place from which it began: the infinite. But this return indicates a change in significance. Rather than being an infinitude that is other to finitude, infinitude now is the very self-enclosed circle that *includes* both finitude and infinitude as poles—each which constitutes the whole totality—each constituting its beginning and end. Because finitude is cancelled and preserved in the infinite development, it no longer stands opposed to the infinitude. Infinitude only becomes true when *finitude itself is the true infinite*.

This contradiction of finitude and infinitude *anticipates* the contradiction of the concept and its identity of universal and particular. Because the cancelling and preserving of these forms of universality cannot proceed in the exact same fashion as the dialectic of finitude, conceptualizing the development and demise of these forms of universality requires investigation into the logic of the concept per se. Although the *infinitude* of the concept is the true infinity, not the false infinity, it would be a mistake to think that the true infinite were merely *opposed* to false infinity. Were this the case, then the true infinite would be limited by another. Similarly, one might falsely imagine that the self-differentiating universal were simply opposed to non-self-differentiating universality—which would be a mistake, for it would transform the self-differentiating universal into just one more concept among others. Indeed, it would cease to be properly Absolute. The false infinite is not independent of the true one. Rather, false infinity is the process of continually circling the true infinite expecting it to come to an end. False infinity is the continual motion around the circle—infinitely proceeding in a circular way towards the infinite and infinitely proceeding in a circle towards the finite. Never to proceed to true infinity is failing to grasp that you are moving in a circle. But having recognized you are on a circle, this does not prevent one from moving around it without end, such that there is *always* the potential to move around it again, *always once more*.

Because the self-particularizing concept does not *lose itself in its negation*, its contradictory character makes it possible for philosophy to attain knowledge of the whole itself—it no longer need rest content with 'infinite approximation' or a *bad infinity* as is the case in the problem of the Third Man regress. When the concept, the universal, meets its other, that which is its very self-negation—the particular—it only meets itself. To put it simply: the Absolute Truth corresponds to itself *as* the contradiction that maintains itself. Even when it is outside itself in particularity, it is still itself—the universal. As Hegel makes explicit, *every* concept is contradictory:

> On the contrary, every determination, anything concrete, every concept, is essentially a unity of distinguished and distinguishable elements which, by virtue of the determinate, essential difference, pass over into elements which are contradictory.[11]

Hegel treats singularity as the truth of particularity and universality. The return of the category to itself, what in Greek was called the *palintropos*, is what Hegel will often describe as the truth of the category. What does it mean to say that singularity is the 'truth' of the universal? The idea is simple: universality, insofar as it is self-differentiation, is not itself insofar as it has not differentiated itself. In other words, it is not truly universal if it does not differentiate itself. Only in the act of self-differentiation is self-differentiation itself. Since self-differentiation necessarily particularizes itself as the self-alienated universal (the particular), without particularity the self-particularizing universal could not be what it is. Accordingly to Hegel, if we simply think the universal, or self-particularization, as such, we shall arrive at particularity and finally singularity. By isolating the universal, that which is *itself by itself*, the universal connects itself to particularity and singularity. For Hegel singularity just is the complete consequence of the self-differentiation of self-differentiation: the correspondence of universality with itself in particularity. Singularity is the 'truth' of the universal for it is what the universal determines itself to be: it is the universal that negates itself and negates that negation.

When Hegel uses the term truth in this way, he means something like what people say when they tell others to 'be true to themselves.'[12] The universal, in virtue of what it is, is singular. The universal is only being 'true to itself' when it is singular. This is Hegel's sense of the term in this context. Because singularity is the truth of the concept, the truth of any concept as a concept is its singularity. Indeed, since our main concern here is what the concept is, it naturally concerns us to also elucidate what 'the truth of the concept is.'

Edward Halper, in his "Hegel and the Problem of the Differentia," rightly points out that Hegel's *dynamism* is inseparable from his concept of *self-reference*.[13] For Hegel, the universal achieves self-particularization through self-reference. Self-reference is implied in the very concept of self-differentiation. Because self-differentiation differentiates itself, its activity is not directed at anything other than itself. Its activity is only directed at itself. 'Self-reference' expresses the self-directed activity of self-differentiation. Self-reference does not exhaust the concept of self-differentiation, but self-differentiation is necessarily self-referring.[14] The term 'self-reference' does not necessarily imply any connection to the structures of judgment. Indeed, judgment is the attribution of a predicate to a subject, and 'self-reference' invokes neither the term 'subject' nor 'predicate.' In addition, the reference involved in 'self-reference' does not appeal to a mind or another principle in virtue of which something is pointed out, for it is the universal that refers itself to itself. Finally, because Hegel himself uses this term throughout his analysis of the concept (the original German is '*Beziehung auf sich*' or '*sich beziehen*'), I find it a relatively uncontroversial way of communicating the overall structure of the *Doctrine of the Concept*.[15]

Hegel has many ways of expressing the logical structure constitutive of self-reference. In the *Encyclopedia Logic* Hegel employs various terms such as 'having turned back into itself' (*Züruckgekehrtsein in sich selbst*),[16] 'withdrawing inwards' (*Insichgehen*), 'sinking deeper into itself' (*ein Vertiefen desselben in sich selbst*),[17] 'return into themselves,' 'back turning into themselves,' or 'return-into-self' (*ihrer Rückkehr in sich*).[18] In the concept of the *Rückkehre*, we find the German correlate of the Greek *palintropos*.

What is more, I will employ the phrase 'self-prediction' first for continuity with our previous analysis, in addition to the fact that the self-referential application of the concept cannot help but be expressed in self-predicative judgments. Although this term invokes the concepts of 'subject' and 'predicate' while 'self-reference' does not, the self-predicative mode of *expression*, which is inevitable, by no means entails that the concept of judgment is already operative in the dialectical development of the concept, which only develops *after* the logic of the concept.

Given that self-differentiation includes its differences, and is infinite, it is not opposed to any differences or determinacies external to it. Accordingly, self-differentiation transcends all otherness or negates all external differences. The concept of ideality connotes *the transcending of all otherness or differentiation*. Thus, self-differentiation is an ideality exactly in Hegel' sense of the term.[19] The way the universal concept achieves ideality has already been stated: through its self-referential activity, the universal creates its own particulars or differentiations. Since these particulars are identical to the universal, the universal admits its own opposite or negation through its self-referential activity. Accordingly, the ideality of the concept entails that the universal is united with its negation, the particular. If the particular were external or other to the universal, if the universal and particular remained separate principles, the concept would not be an ideality and would certainly not be self-differentiating. In short, it is the back-turning of the concept in virtue of which the self-differentiating universal is an ideality. Without the concept of the back-turning, Hegel's concept of ideality would not be complete.

From Palintropos to Rückkehre: Hegel's Appropriation of Greek Philosophy

Hegel's resurrection of the Presocratic *palintropos* into the life of the self-differentiating concept is not surprising given his ringing endorsement of Heraclitus, who, according to Hegel, initially put philosophy on its road to the speculative Idea. Hegel writes that

> The advance requisite and made by Heraclitus is the progression from Being as the first immediate thought, to the category of Becoming as the second. This is the first concrete, the Absolute, as in it the unity of opposites. Thus with Heraclitus the philosophic Idea is to be met with in its speculative form; the reasoning of Parmenides and Zeno is abstract understanding. Heraclitus was thus universally esteemed a deep philosopher and even was decried as such. Here we see land; there is no proposition of Heraclitus which I have not adopted in my Logic.[20]

In Heraclitus, what differs, insofar as it differs, remains the same. Accordingly, it is in virtue of the back-turning of difference that what differs becomes unified with its opposite.

Hegel's appropriation of the *palintropos* is reflected in his affirmation of Heraclitus' concept of becoming. As is evident, Hegel sees neither the activity of back-turning nor the resulting unity of opposition in the philosopher Parmenides, though in other places he does recognize what he calls an 'external dialectic' which corresponds to our exegesis of the dialectic of Parmenides and Plato.[21] Given that Hegel fails to locate the back-turning concept in Parmenides, we will see that Hegel also underestimates, to some extent, the influence of Parmenides (and the back-turning therein) on Plato's thought. Instead, in the thought of Parmenides he finds mere 'abstract understanding.' Further, Hegel claims that the idea of philosophy in Plato and Aristotle has its origins in Heraclitus:

> In Heraclitus we see the perfection of knowledge so far as it has gone, a perfecting of the Idea into a totality, which is the beginning of philosophy, since it expresses the essence of the Idea, the Notion of the infinite, the potentially and actively existent, as that which it is, i.e. as the unity of opposites. From Heraclitus dates the ever-remaining Idea which is the same in all philosophers to the present day, as it was the Idea of Plato and Aristotle.[22]

What is missing in Heraclitus, according to Hegel, is that the cycle of becoming should be recognized as the universal concept. With the development of the *Doctrine of the Concept*, and finally the Absolute Idea, Hegel takes himself to have completed what Heraclitus initiated.

Given that Hegel understands Plato to belong to the distinguished lineage of Heraclitus, we will now turn to Plato to inquire to what extent Hegel's concept of universality may be read out of, and perhaps into, the dialogue *Parmenides*.[23] Having uncovered the resurrected back-turning as the self-differentiating universal, we may now apply Hegel's definition of the concept to the problem of the Third Man at 131a–e and the argument from wholes and parts at 132a–b in Plato's *Parmenides*.

Hegel roundly rejects the reading of Plato as a mystic, who elevates the ineffable as the principle of philosophy:

> However much, therefore, Plato's mythical presentation of Philosophy is praised, and however attractive it is in his Dialogues, it yet proves a source of misapprehensions; and it is one of these misapprehensions, if Plato's myths are held to be what is most excellent in his philosophy.[24]

Instead, Hegel discovers his own self-differentiating, back-turning concept in Plato's *Parmenides*:

> On the one hand, this reflection into itself, the spiritual, the Concept, is present in the speculation of Plato; for the unity of the one and many, &c., is just this singularity in difference, this being-turned-back-within-itself in its opposite, this opposite which is implicit; the essential reality of the world is really this movement returning into itself of that which is turned back within itself.[25]

Plato's positive legacy, for Hegel, is the extent to which speculative dialectics makes an appearance in his dialogues. Not only does Hegel discover his own self-reflected concept in Plato's Parmenides, he also claims that it is the true revelation of all the mysteries of the divine Essence:

> Nevertheless, the Neo-platonists, and more especially Proclus, regard the result arrived at in the Parmenides as the true theology, as the true revelation of all the mysteries of the divine essence. And it cannot be regarded as anything else, however little this may at first appear.[26]

I do not mean to comment on the extent to which Hegel agrees with the Neo-Platonic reading of the Parmenides, but it is important to note that Hegel uncovered a primitive vision of his concept of the concept in that dialogue, for this provides a hint about how to apply Hegel's concept of the concept towards a solution to the problems of participation in

Plato raised at 131a–e and 132a–b. Although for Hegel (and the Neo-Platonists) the Parmenides contains the true theology, Hegel thinks that it is nonetheless a flawed presentation:

> The dialectic of Plato is, however, not to be regarded as complete in every regard. Though his main endeavor is to show that in every determination the opposite is contained, it can still not be said that this is strictly carried out in all his dialectic movements, for there are often external considerations which exercise an influence in his dialectic.[27]

As an example of the unity of opposition that is based on an 'external consideration' Hegel provides the second hypothesis as an example, in which the One Being infinitely contains its whole self. The Platonic reflects are still only hypothetical, rely upon given stipulations, and proceed by way of the comparison of different concepts.

As a result of this limitation, Plato stumbled upon the truth of the concept, but it ultimately appears in *the form of a problem*. Let us begin by turning back to the argument from wholes and parts at 131a–e, what I have called 'the problem of instantiation.' In the argument from wholes and parts, participation is only successful if the particular gets a share of the whole universal or a part of the universal. On the one hand, if the participant gets a share of the whole universal, then the whole universal would be in each particular.

On Hegel's conception of the universal, the universal must necessarily be in each particular as a whole, for 'the elements distinguished are without more ado at the same time, declared to be identical with one another and with the whole, and the specific character of each is a free being of the whole notion.'[28] Here what Plato takes as a problem Hegel sees as the *solution*. For Plato the universal cannot be one in number and simultaneously present in a variety of different particulars, while for Hegel that is *exactly* what is entailed in the concept of the concept. For Hegel, that the self-same universal is multiply instantiated and thereby 'outside itself' in each particular is no longer seen as a problem once we have denied the separation of the universal and the particular. Indeed, it is what the question itself demands. The universal is exactly that which *maintains itself* in its identity with what it is *not*. In sum, Hegel's concept of the concept is defined in such a way that they may be straightforwardly applied to answer the objections raised in Plato's *Parmenides*.

If the whole concept is present in each particular, then the concept must be completely outside itself, or exceed itself. Insofar as the universal is particular, the whole must be outside itself and it is thereby alienated from itself. Indeed, this is just how Hegel construes the universal in its particularity. In particularity, universality is *self-negating*. This is evident from what self-differentiation requires: since the universal differentiates itself from itself, it must negate itself. As a result, the universal differentiates itself into that which is not self-differentiating. Still, the self-differentiating universal does not remain in a state of self-negation, for the very concept of 'self-negation' undermines itself and turns back upon itself.

As we briefly noted earlier, the concept of self-negation is itself self-negating. Since self-negation negates itself, it remains itself and *is consistent with itself*, for its own qualitative determinacy, 'self-negation' constitutes what it is. Simply put, were self-negation not self-negating, then it would not be what it is. *It can only be what it is if it negates itself*. Because the term 'self-negation' necessitates that it negate itself, the negation of self-negation is self-preservation. Indeed, insofar as the self-negating content negates itself, it simply *preserves* its own form of self-negation and must thereby be identified with that which *preserves itself*. The self-negation of self-negation is also *self-preservation*. As self-preservation it is not self-negation but an *activity that remains itself even in its identity with what is other to it*.

Insofar as the particular is the universal in the form of negation, the negation of the particular resurrects the universal from its bondage in the particular. Thus, with the negation of self-differentiation removed, what is present is the *self-preserving* self-differentiation. Thus, the self-identity and self-relation that comes to be upon the self-removal of autonomous particularity is nothing other than that with which the process of the concept began, namely the universal. But the *return* of self-differentiation from its exile is not the same determination as the universal aspect, for the universal moment did not itself arise out of exile, that is out of the particular. Hence, we have a novel content: the return of the universal, or what Hegel calls 'the singular.'

For Hegel, the logic of the concept is specifically suited to solve the problem of instantiation. The self-same universal, which is one in number, is present in each particular. Insofar as it is present in each particular, the self-same universal is 'other to itself,' since each particular is different and excludes the others. Nonetheless, the same universal is present in each different particular, for it is that which *remains itself* (and can only remain itself) insofar as it is identical to what is other to it. The obvious consequence is that without the contradiction in such a formula, no comprehension of instantiation would be possible. Dialetheism is a condition for the possibility of instantiation.

In addition, Hegel's self-differentiating concept is also implicitly at work in the Third Man argument at 132a–b, though it is not recognized as such. Just as in the problem of instantiation, the Third Man argument presents Hegel's logic of the concept, but only *in the form of a problem*.

Earlier we derived three necessary features of any successful answer to the question 'what is universality?' First, the universal is self-referring. Second, in virtue of its self-reference, the universal creates its own particulars. If we consider universality as a domain, each particular instance of the domain would be a differentiation of that domain. Accordingly, the particular instances of universality would be differentiations of the domain of universality. Third, the particular universal created by the self-referring universality is identical to universality itself. Since these three features follow necessarily from the question itself, any sufficient answer to the question 'what is universality?' must accommodate them.

In Plato's Third Man argument, each of these three features appears. First, in the argument each Form is self-referential, for the quality to which it is applied to its instances applies to itself. For example, Plato has young Socrates accept that Greatness is itself great. The palintropos of the Pre-Socratics is evident in the self-referential activity of the Forms. Second, in virtue of the self-referential attribution of the Form to itself, the Form itself is sufficient for creating its own particulars. From 'Greatness is great,' Parmenides infers that there must be a 'boundless multitude' of particular Forms of Greatness. What is more, the third condition is immediately fulfilled upon the completion of the second condition: each particular Form of Greatness is identical to the universal Form of Greatness. Thus, within the Third Man argument, we discover the self-differentiating universal. Each universal, in virtue of its self-referential and self-differentiating activity gives rise to its particulars. These particulars are themselves indistinguishable from each other and from the universal under which they fall. As we noted earlier, in the Third Man argument, the universal is particular. It is in this unity of universal with particular that Hegel sees the primitive formulation of his concept of the concept. Through the back-turning of the Third Man argument, the universal admits its opposite, the particular, thereby giving birth to the concept of singularity. Each Form is universal and *this universal*; thus each Form is *singular*. Hegel's concept of the concept lies waiting in the surface grammar of the argument.

Of course, Plato does not take the Third Man argument as a confirmation of his definition of the universal, but a problem for the theory of participation. Most simply put, Hegel takes what Plato viewed as the problem, namely the self-referential activity of the universal, and posits it as *the solution*. There is no mystery to participation, for the universal is connected to the particular in virtue of its own self-referential and self-differentiating activity. Since the universal is not absolutely separate from particularity in the concept of self-differentiation, Hegel's definition of the universal is not susceptible to the problem of instantiation or the Third Man regress. Although one can read Hegel's account of the universal out of the problem of the Third Man argument, Hegel's account of the self-referring and existentially implicative features of conceptual determination in his *Doctrine of the Concept* is not yet applied to all concepts, but rather only the concept of the concept. In order for these features to be applied to other concepts beyond the concept of the concept and its constituents (universality, particularity, and singularity), other logical developments are necessary.

Plato repeatedly emphasizes that the Forms are principles of becoming,[29] yet Aristotle complains that the Platonic Forms do not account for motion.[30] Indeed, one of Aristotle's motivating problems in re-thinking Form as a Being-at-work is to demonstrate how Form could be a principle of motion. In a way, the self-reference of a Form does account for some logical 'motion,' if you will excuse the metaphor, since self-reference produces an infinite number of particular universals. This is evident from the Third Man argument: the Form, in virtue of being Form, is a particular form, and for this very reason another Form must be posited, *ad infinitum*. The paradoxical result is a number of 'particular' forms. The self-reference of Forms expresses not only their status as principles of motion but also their own becoming, for the Form is always ceasing to be Form and coming to be a particular. As a result, we cannot properly delineate the difference between universal and particular.

Plato seems to reject the possibility of the self-differentiating universal because he is committed to the absolute separation of the universal from the particular. Given Plato's ontological dualism, the universal and the particular cannot be identified. Since the self-differentiating universal identifies universal with particular, for Plato the self-differentiating universal appears inherently problematic. Each Form, according to Plato is itself by itself, *auto kath auto*. This seems to entail that each Form is by itself and is indivisible, having no intrinsic relations to other Forms or to particulars. Any connection, it appears, must come from outside, and such connections would not be accidental to the what it is to be of the Form.

Hegel, perhaps surprisingly, appropriates Plato's concept of '*auto kath auto*' and re-thinks its significance. Instead of positing the universal as an inert being independent of other universals and particulars, what is 'itself by itself' is just the very process of self-differentiation. What appears as itself by itself in the Third Man argument is not the Form that is beyond all language. Indeed, it does not appear at all. In fact, it shows itself to be nothing at all. What appears as *itself by itself* is the self-differentiating, Heraclitean *palintropos*. What Hegel sees in Heraclitus he also discovers in Plato: the independence of process by which concepts admit their negations. The self-development of universality into particularity and singularity is presented with the force of necessity. As long as the philosopher is not committed to the absolute separation of universal from particular, there is no longer any philosophical quandary concerning the relation of universal to particular at least as it regards their purely logical relations. For Hegel, through the back-turning of the 'itself by itself,' the universal becomes a power (*Dunamis*), for it gives rise to particulars. Through the re-appropriation of the *palintropos* in the Third Man argument,

Hegel means to revitalize an 'ancient city.' Hegel re-invigorates the concept, which in modern philosophy is often conceived to be an inert and powerless representation with the implicit power that it possessed in the Ancient concept of Form. This power, of course, is even more robust, for it is a *creative* power. Wonder becomes knowledge, and knowledge is power. The real meaning of Idealism lies in the recognition that universality is a power, such as the power of Aristotle's Form, by which particulars are generated.

As we have seen, Hegel's definition of the concept not only unravels two specific arguments against the Forms in *Parmenides*, but it is already at work there in the form of a *problem*. There is also a significant connection between Hegel's solution to the problem of participation and Aristotle's *Metaphysics*, as recent scholarship has indicated.[31] As we demonstrated earlier, at the level of the *syllogism*, Aristotle's concept of Form is articulated in an existentially implicative form. This logical relation of universal to particular is grounded in the ontological relation of Form to its composite, whereby the former is the generative principle of the latter. Aristotle, like Hegel after him, introduces an existentially implicative logic. Unlike Aristotle, however, Hegel does not appeal to any non-logical content, such as experience, in order to ground the system of existential implication. Rather for Hegel the concept alone is sufficient for its own particularization, and this is made possible by a feature completely missing in Aristotle: the self-referential application of the concept to itself.

Both Aristotle and Hegel recognize the need for the *this such and such*, though their solutions to the problem of the Third Man move in opposite directions. Aristotle denies self-reference, for he posits it as *the source of the problem* (not as its solution!), and he does so in order to preserve consistency. Hegel moves in the exact *opposite direction*, for he endorses the self-referential application of the category to itself, which can only have a contradictory formulation. This fundamental opposition between their solutions to the problems of participation finally highlights one of the more striking similarities (and differences) between their concepts of the power of Form. For Aristotle in his *Metaphysics*, the 'what it is to be' is constituted by the 'Being-at-work-staying-itself.' Hegel's account of the concept is close to Aristotle's, insofar as the concept is *the self-preserving power by which particulars exist*. As Ferrarin correctly points out:

> Aristotle is never a thinker of the understanding for Hegel—his concept is vitality, entelechy.[32]

In this respect, Ferrarin is right that Hegel treats Aristotle 'at the level of the concept.'[33] Hegel's rendering of Aristotle's concept of Energeia means 'the process of thought's self-actualization in finite reality.'[34]

Unlike Aristotle, however, for Hegel not only is it the concept itself that is that self-preserving power, but Hegel modifies Aristotle's formulation of being-at-work. The Being-at-work-staying-itself of Hegel's universal is not only self-preserving, but it is self-preserving only insofar as it must 'pass over into elements which are contradictory.' The concept is certainly a 'being-at-work-staying-itself' that is the source of its own particulars, but only on the condition that it preserve itself in virtue of its own self-negation, and is identical with what it is not. Otherwise, there is no way to conceive of the *this such and such* and its power of instantiation and existential implication.

Perhaps there is no better illustration of Hegel's divergence from Aristotle by comparing their perspectives on the freedom of thought, the concept of the limit, and its relation to completeness. Consider the πέρας in peripatetic thought in Aristotle's concept of ἐντελέχεια: Being-at-work-staying-itself. *Nous* is one of Aristotle's primary examples of ἐντελέχεια. It is an activity in which the end (purpose) is *not distinct* from the means. As Aristotle states: 'one sees and at the same time in a state of having seen, . . . one thinks contemplatively, and is at the same time in a state of having thought contemplatively.'[35] This is different from house building, for example, where in the act of building the house one is *not* in the state of having built the house. Unlike in house building, when one achieves the end or purpose of *Nous*, namely when one knows the first principle, the means by which one knows does not cease to be. Because the end is the means, the means continues to be with the achievement of the end. *Nous* is an *end-in-itself*. Aristotle is clear that what exists in virtue of itself (καθ'αὐτὸ) is *self-sufficient* and complete. For Aristotle, what has nothing outside it is complete, and 'nothing is complete which has no end (τέλος), and the end is a limit.'[36] In order to be complete something must have a limit (πέρας) *within itself*. In the case of ἐντελέχεια, the activity is complete because the end or the limit is identical with the means and is not outside it: there is *no* instance where the means is present and the end is not. In *Nous* the *limit* is present at every instance of the activity: it is an act in which the limit is one with (ἐν) the purposive activitiy (τελέχεια). For Aristotle, philosophical knowing of first principles is a knowing that is not ἄπειρον, for it *never oversteps* its own limit; rather it *maintains itself at its limit* (πέρας). It is the (πέρας) or determinate which is perfect and complete in knowing and Being.

Aristotle famously argued that philosophy is the freest of the sciences.[37] A person is free who is an end in himself and philosophy is the only science that seeks knowledge as an end in itself. Thus, philosophy is free. In the practice of Nous, the philosopher practices a kind of knowing in which means and ends are identified. Accordingly, *Nous is free knowing.* In sum, autonomous knowing means knowing what is autonomos or καθ'αὐτὸ and knowing it in an autonomous way: free knowing in Aristotle may appear ironic to us, for it is *bound* and determinate. Free knowing never exceeds its own limits.

For Aristotle, free thinking is constituted by νοῦς, in which thinking *never* oversteps its own limit, but rather remains at the place of its own limit: ἐντελέχεια. Following Hegel, if free science must integrate the indeterminate, and thereby become non-positional, free thinking can no longer remain at its limit as with ἐντελέχεια. Rather, it must do the very opposite: *overstep its own limit*. For the non-positional Absolute is that which exceeds its own limit: *in virtue of standing opposed* to positionality it *ceases to stand opposed* to determinate being and thereby becomes what it is not. *Aufhebung* is constitutive of free thought, for it is the activity by which thought exceeds its own limit. *Sein*, the indeterminate, *exceeds its non-positionality* in order to become determinate or positional in *Dasein*. Indeed, non-positionality does not have a position in the system of knowledge until it is brought into relation in *Dasein*.[38] In other words, the indeterminate can only acquire the position as the *first* category once it has exceeded itself and given rise to a *second* with which it can stand in contrast as its beginning.

Indeed, the self-exceeding power of the indeterminate has immensely positive significance for philosophical method. For Aristotle, the Noumena or first principles are thought by means of *Nous*, each of which is conceived as determinate. Kant, having brilliantly recognized that what is properly *autonomous* cannot be rendered determinate by cognition, relegated the Noumena to the unknown. Having banished the Noumenon to the indeterminate beyond, Kant banishes Nous[39] as well from the purview of human knowing. By introducing the indeterminate into the content of philosophical science, Hegel means to develop a science of Noumena. But Hegel recognizes that this science of Things in Themselves requires a radical transformation of both Nous and *Noumena*. To think the indeterminate Noumenon, Nous must be constituted by indeterminacy—what exceeds its own limit—and become *Aufhebung*. Hegel recognizes that in order for knowledge to be possible, the indefinite must be introduced into the *body* of knowledge *per se*. In other words, the indeterminate cannot be known as a condition of knowledge without being constitutive of knowledge in some way. Because the *Science of Logic* begins with the indeterminate, for Hegel indeterminacy has the *positive significance* of constituting the *beginning* of philosophy. Perhaps more than any other, Hegel is profoundly sensitive to the dialectical features of indeterminacy. Since the whole science is the activity by which the indeterminate *exceeds itself* into various determinate forms, the whole of the science can be characterized as various determinations of indeterminacy. Of course, for Hegel these forms of indeterminacy transform themselves into relatively determinate and finally absolutely determinate forms.

Just as Aristotle conceived of free thought as the contemplation of thought thinking itself, νοησις νοησεως νοησις, so Hegel conceives of the freedom of logical science as consisting in *self-thinking thought*. Whereas for Aristotle self-thinking thought is radically finite and eschews indeterminacy, for Hegel it contains indeterminacy, exceeds itself, and thereby constitutes itself as *in*finite. Unlike Aristotle, what is at work and *preserving itself* in free-thinking is the *self-exceeding* itself—the contradiction constitutive of dialectical thought. Despite these subtle and yet important differences, Hegel is clear that the 'older metaphysics' (by which I understand Aristotle, among others) had a higher conception of thought:

> The older metaphysics had in this respect a higher conception of thinking than now passes as the accepted opinion. For it presupposed as its principle that only what is known of things and in things by thought is really true in them, that is, what is known in them not in their immediacy but as first elevated to the form of thinking, as the things of thought. This metaphysics thus held that thinking and the determination of thinking are not something alien to the subject matters, but are rather their essence, or that the things and the thinking of them agree in and for themselves (also our language expresses a kinship between them); that thinking in its immanent determinations, and the true nature of things, are one and the same content.[40]

It is this higher conception of thought upon which Hegel re-builds the logic. Rather than start with completely new materials, Hegel infuses new life into ancient material.

Notes

1. See Hegel, *SL*, 600–622, or Hegel, *Wissenschaft der Logik* II, 273–301.
2. Findlay fails to recognize that the concept is a sufficient source of the specific species within it, or the individuals that instantiate it, when he writes that 'there is no trance in his practice, despite some use of general metaphors, of any attempt to beget what is specific or individual out of the mere universality of the notion.' J. N. Findlay, *Hegel, A Re-Examination* (New York: The Macmillan Company, 1958), 226. For his full account of the concept, see 221–228.
3. The precise senses of the infinite that are relevant here will be discussed at greater length in our discussion of Hegel's *Ontological Argument* in Chapter 12.
4. Oddly, Julie Maybee, in her book *Picturing Hegel*, does not list the self-differentiating universal as one of the senses of the concept. She has all the senses of the concept qua particular represented: abstraction, class, and set, yet leaves out the principle from which they follow. See Julie E. Maybee, *Picturing Hegel: An Illustrated Guide to Hegel's Encyclopaedia Logic* (Plymouth, UK: Lexington Books, 2009), 16–18.
5. In Hegel's remark on *Universality, particularity, and singularity* in his *Science of Logic*, trans. Miller, 612–618, Hegel points out that the self-differentiating concept is not psychological. It does not concern itself with psychological distinctions such as 'obscure,' 'clear,' or 'distinct.' Hegel, *SL*, trans. Miller, 613. Naturally, Hegel avoids having to identify the concept with psychological content because he takes himself as having eschewed various paradoxes

that are engendered by finite universality. As long as one insists on the difference between universal and particular, as is the case in mathematics, Hegel
points out that we will be unable to understand the relations of universal,
particular, and singular. For instance, the universal is not just *more extensive*
than the particular. In this representation of the concept, the concept cannot
refer to itself, or particularize itself, because it cannot quantify over itself.
Universality is not a merely quantitative determination. For Hegel, to hold
on to this perspective is to treat the universals as fixed concepts that are
externally related to each other. Naturally, the universal cannot be reduced
to a mathematical determination as long as the separation of universality and
particularity has been undermined. See Hegel, *SL*, trans. Miller, 617.

6. Brady Bowman, *Hegel and the Metaphysics of Absolute Negativity* (Cambridge: Cambridge University Press, 2013), 26–27. For another account of
Hegel's response to Nihilism see Zizek's *Less than Nothing: Hegel and the
Shadow of Dialectical Materialism*. Here Zizek is right that Hegel's 'nihilism' is the fact that 'all finite determinate forms of life reach their "truth" in
their self-overcoming.' Zizek, *Less than Nothing: Hegel and the Shadow of
Dialectical Materialism*, 199.

7. See Bowman, *Hegel and the Metaphysics of Absolute Negativity*, 57.

8. There are a number of excellent commentaries on the whole of the Logic,
and too many excursions into other categories would distract from my main
purpose here.

9. See Bowman, *Hegel and the Metaphysics of Absolute Negativity*, 27.

10. For the full transition, see Hegel, *SL*, trans. Miller, 136–137.

11. Hegel, *SL*, trans. Miller, 384.

12. When one is not being oneself, and one is told 'to be oneself' the implication
is that it is possible for me *not* to be myself and that when I fulfill this possibility of not being myself I am not corresponding to what I am. In this case,
my being is a false being. Of course, here there is also a *normative* element.
Truth, in general, is a normative concept. When I am not being myself, I am
being someone other than who I ought to be. Here, who I *truly* am, and who
I *ought* to be, are identical. In truth there is a fulfillment of the normative
'ought.' Although in the *Doctrine of the Concept* Hegel does not discuss the
normative element in truth, we can still make normative judgments about
the concept and treatments of the concept. We can say this account of this
concept 'x' does not live up to the concept of the concept proper. Likewise,
we can say of moments of Hegel's development, when they are isolated from
one another, such as the element of particularity, that they do not *live up* the
concept of the concept. Although the normative aspect of truth as such is not
yet worked out, we may still make normative judgments that take the full
development of the concept as the measure.

13. See Halper, "Hegel and the Problem of the Missing Difference," 202.

14. Because one claims that 'self-differentiation' is self-referring, it does not follow
that 'self-differentiation' is just self-reference or reducible to it self-reference.

15. There are numerous passages in which self-reference arises. Miller sometimes
translates them as 'self-relation,' sometimes as 'self-reference.' See for example, 'diese reine Beziehung des Begriffs auf sich' (pure relation of the concept
to itself) (Hegel, *Science of Logic*, trans. Miller, 274, 601), 'die einfache Beziehung auf sich selbst' (simply relation to itself) (275, 602), 'self-relating' (*sich
auf sich beziehende*) (601), and 'self-reference' (*Beziehung auf sich*) (619).
Note that 'sich beziehen auf' can mean relation and reference. Miller has
taken the nominal form 'Beziehung' as 'self-reference' and the participle as
'self-relation,' but he could have taken the participle as 'self-referring.'

16. See Hegel, *EL*, 121, paragraph 83.

17. Ibid, paragraph 84.
18. Ibid, paragraph 162, 225. Also see Hegel, *SL*, trans. Miller, 274, 601.
19. See Hegel's *SL*, trans. Miller, 119.
20. G. W. F. Hegel, *Lectures on the History of Philosophy: Greek Philosophy to Plato*, trans. E. S. Haldane (Lincoln: University of Nebraska Press, 1995), 279.
21. On the role of the Eleatic dialectic see the following:

> he further now took into the objective dialectic of Heraclitus the Eleatic dialectic, which is the external endeavour of the subject to show forth contradiction, so that in place of an external changing of things, their inward transition in themselves, that is in their Ideas, or, as they are here, in their categories, has come to pass out of and through themselves. Plato finally set forth the belief of Socrates, which the latter put forward in regard to the moral self-reflection of the subject only, as objective, as the Idea, which is both universal thought, and the existent. The previous philosophies thus do not disappear because refuted by Plato, being absorbed in him.

Hegel, *Lectures on the History of Philosophy: Greek Philosophy to Plato*, 279.
22. Hegel, *Lectures on the History of Philosophy: Greek Philosophy to Plato*, 282.
23. Regarding the extent to which Hegel deemed Heraclitus the teacher of Plato, we need only read Hegel's comments regarding the matter:

> The obscurity of this philosophy, however, chiefly consists in there being profound speculative thought contained in it; the Notion, the Idea, is foreign to the understanding and cannot be grasped by it, though it may find mathematics quite simple. Plato studied the philosophy of Heraclitus with special diligence; we find much of it quoted in his works, and he got his earlier philosophic education most indubitably from this source, so that Heraclitus may be called Plato's teacher.

Hegel, *Lectures on the History of Philosophy: Greek Philosophy to Plato*, 281.
24. G. W. F. Hegel, *Lectures on the History of Philosophy: Plato and the Platonists*, trans. E. S. Haldane and Frances H. Simpson (Lincoln: University of Nebraska Press, 1995), 19.
25. Ibid, 61.
26. Ibid, 60.
27. Ibid, 58.
28. Hegel, *EL*, 224.
29. See the so-called 'second sailing' in Plato, *Phaedo*, 95A–102A, 74–82.
30. See Aristotle, *Metaphysics*, 231–252.
31. See Alfredo Ferrarin, *Hegel and Aristotle* (Cambridge: Cambridge University Press, 2004).
32. See Ibid, 196. Ferrarin also notes that Hegel reads Aristotle through Neo-Platonism.
33. Ferrarin, *Hegel and Aristotle*, 195.
34. Ibid, 196.
35. Aristotle, *Metaphysics*, 174 (1048b).
36. Aristotle, "Physics," 351–353 (Book 3, Ch. 6).
37. Aristotle, *Metaphysics*, 982b.
38. Hegel, *SL*, trans. Miller, 81.
39. Of course, Kant's construal of *Nous* is his own and is quite different from Aristotle's definition. For Kant *Nous* is intellectual intuition, in which the conceiving of the object would be sufficient to give the existence of the object in intuition. The Noumenon is that object which humans would know were they to be in possession of such a power.
40. Hegel, *SL*, trans. Giovanni, 25.

11 Hegel's Ontological Argument

The Existence of the Absolute

How the Infinite Becomes Finite

Jacobi's criticism of Fichte discussed in our opening reflections called into question the very existence of the Absolute. The problem of Nihilism raised by Jacobi plagued every attempt of the early Idealists to demonstrate that the Absolute exists. Without a demonstration of the existence of the Absolute, the Idealists were also unable to demonstrate the existence of anything possessing relative being. The main question of German Idealism, we will remember, is the following:

> The essence of philosophy has often been located by those already adept in the things of thought in the task of answering the question: *how does the infinite go forth out of itself and come to finitude?*— This, as opinion would have it, escapes *conceptual comprehension.* In the course of this exposition, the infinite at whose concept we have arrived will *further determine* itself, and the desideratum—*how the infinite* (if one can so express oneself) *comes to finitude*—will be manifested in it in the full manifold of forms.[1]

Hegel's answer to this problem *is rendered explicit at the outset of Section II, Objectivity.* The concept, as the self-particularizing power, overcomes all otherness and thereby constitutes *ideality.* Having overcome all otherness, the concept is the sole principle of its own particularization. As such, the concept is not true in virtue of another, but is only true in virtue of itself. Because it is true in virtue of itself, it is absolutely true, for its truth is not relative to another or in virtue of another. Hegel does not establish the Absolute character of the concept by modeling the concept on a given Absolute form. Rather, the concept has *determined itself* to be Absolute. Because the concept has determined itself to be Absolute, Hegel's proclamation of the Absolute character of the concept is not a presupposition, but a result of the self-development of foundation free science. Thus, given the ideality of the concept, namely its Absolute being, *the concept is the source of its own existence.*[2]

In the *Doctrine of the Concept*, the universal, which is infinite, becomes finite and particular through the act of self-particularization. In order to overcome the impasse, concepts must be imbued with the power to *particularize themselves*. According to Hegel:

> Of the concept, we have now first shown that it determines itself as objectivity. It should be obvious that this latter transition is essentially the same as the *proof* form the *concept*, that is to say, from the *concept of God* to his existence, that was formerly found in *Metaphysics*, or the so-called *ontological proof*.[3]

Hegel is clear that *the concept must objectify itself* and that this process of self-objectification is identical in character with ontological proof. In the ontological proof the concept of God is *sufficient* for the realization of that concept. By re-thinking the concept as self-particularizing, Hegel identifies the concept with God:

> The concept of God realizes itself most fully as this universal that determines and particularizes itself—it is this activity of dividing, of particularizing and determining itself, or positing a finitude, negating this—its own finitude and being identical with itself through its negation of this finitude. This is the concept as such, the concept of God.[4]

'God' is synonymous with 'Absolute.' Hegel's qualification of God as the Idea is significant, for this means nothing less than the fact that *God is the true concept*. Or in more sober terms, the concept now plays the same role that God plays in pictorial consciousness. For Hegel the term 'God' adds *no additional conceptual content* to the Concept or the Idea. It certainly does not signify the 'sum of all possible predicates.' God or the Absolute is not just a 'sum,' but *the power of self-particularization*. Because the concept of the Absolute concept is sufficient for the realization of the concept, the self-particularization of the concept in the *Doctrine of the Concept* is what formerly appeared as the 'so-called ontological proof.' As Hegel writes in his lectures on religion, the ontological proof is the only authentic one.[5] Hegel's concept is not only a principle of identity, but also a principle of difference—although the concept constitutes the subjective character of his logic, *it differentiates itself into objectivity*. The concept must be a synthetic principle that *amplifies itself* into existence and objectivity. The concept of the Absolute, or to use theological language, the concept of God, must *particularize itself*.

Although the tradition will speak about the existence of the concept, Hegel is clear that rather than 'existence' the proper term to employ is 'objectivity':

> But the essential subject matter of the treatment of the proof, the connectedness of concept and existence, is the concern of the treatment

of the concept just concluded and of the entire course that the latter traverses in determining itself to objectivity.[6]

Objectivity signifies what is 'existing in and for itself':[7]

> At the present standpoint of our treatise, objectivity has the meaning first of all of the being in and for itself of the concept.[8]

Objectivity signifies self-subsistent totality. As such it is different from 'existence' or 'being':

> We have previously called attention to the several forms of immediacy that have already come on the scene, but in different determinations. In the sphere of being, immediacy is being itself, and existence [Dasein]; in the sphere of essence, it is concrete existence [Existenz] and then actuality and substantiality; in the sphere of the concept, besides being immediacy as abstract universality, it is now objectivity.—These expressions, when the exactitude of philosophical conceptual distinctions is not at stake, may be used as synonymous; but the determinations are derived from the necessity of the concept. Being is as such the first immediacy, and existence is the same immediacy with a first determinateness. Concrete Existence [Existenz], along with the thing, is the immediacy that proceeds from the ground, from the self-sublating mediation of the simple reflection of essence. . . . Finally, objectivity is the immediacy as which the concept has determined itself by the sublation of its abstraction and mediation.[9]

'Sein' and 'Dasein' belong in the logic of Being. Neither connotes self-determination. The former is purely *indeterminate* being, while the latter is the concept of *determinate* being. The concept is not just being or determinate being, for it is *self-determined* being. Existenz, unlike *Sein* and *Dasein*, is a category of the logic of Essence, which is structured according to a distinction between determiner and determined. In particular, the category of *Existenz* connotes the distinction between ground and grounded. What exists is what 'proceeds from the ground' or is *grounded*. But the concept does not proceed from any ground. Rather, it is its own ground, or what is the same, it is that which is no longer in need of a ground. As self-determining being, the being of the *Begriff* is more complex than the concepts of *Sein, Dasein, or Existenz*. For this reason, Hegel reserves the term 'objectivity' for the *overcoming of the mediated existence* that is constituted by relations of determiner and determined. Objectivity connotes the *self-determined being* of the concept or that being that the concept acquires by overcoming the mediation of determiner and determined.[10] The potentiality of the concept to objectify itself is already evident in the initial specification of the concept as that which is *self-sufficient* as regards its own particularization. As Winfield writes:

> Precisely because conceptual determination is self-determining, the objectivity of thought cannot be given as something underlying reason. Rather, it must be the result of conceptual determination, which has no given content but must produce through its own activity all known content that counts as rational.[11]

It is true that the concept of objectivity only arises after the conceptual development of concept, judgment, and syllogism. Accordingly, in order to completely work out the logical form of the ontological 'argument' in Hegel one must work through all of these categorial developments. Despite this qualification, because the concept *particularizes itself*, already in the concept of singularity we discover the first instance of the ontological argument:

> The concept, as absolutely self-identical negativity, is self-determining; it was noted that the concept, in resolving itself into *judgment* in singularity, already posits itself as *something real, an existent*; this still abstract reality completes itself in *objectivity*.[12]

As is evident, Hegel is clear that the solution to the impasse concerning the existence of the Absolute has already begun in the *Doctrine of the Concept*. As Hegel makes clear, before the category of objectivity arises, the concept had already 'posited itself as something real, an existent.' For Hegel, the concept as such, considered by itself, is *not* devoid of being:

> The concept, even as formal, already immediately contains being in a truer and richer form, in that, as self-referring negativity, it is *singularity*.[13]

Accordingly, in order to fully understand how the ontological argument is fully realized in the transition from concept to objectivity, we first must understand how it is that the concept develops into the Absolute totality signified by the concept of *singularity*. Because the conceptual developments from universal to singular (i) are already successful instances of the ontological 'argument,' (ii) are necessary for the further development into objectivity, and (iii) have been neglected in ways that Hegel's discussion of judgment and inference have not, I will focus on the development of the universal, particular, and singular in my reconstruction of Hegel's position.

Having learned from the failures of his predecessors, Hegel recognizes that the only way to secure the existence of the Absolute is by transforming the concept into a principle of *intellectual intuition*, certainly not in Fichte's sense, but Kant's, whereby the concept becomes *the synthetic principle responsible for its own instantiation.* Although Fichte and Schelling both recognized the need for intellectual intuition, neither fully acknowledged that thought could only be the *sole principle* of its own existence by affirming the ontological argument. Unlike his predecessors, however, Hegel does not conceive of the concept itself as a mind. Although mind is needed for the philosopher to think the concept, the concept realizes itself without the assistance of the mind that thinks it. Although it is a conceiving that creates its object in virtue of conceiving it, and in this sense fulfills Kant's criterion of an 'intellectual intuition,' it is *not* a mind with intuitions. Given the possibility of confusion, it is more precise to say that Hegel's logic of the concept provides *the logical conditions* for the possibility of any act of intellectual intuition. In the concept of God we discover a concept that is both analytic and synthetic, for *it amplifies itself into existence in virtue of what it is.*

Jacobi's charge of nihilism against Idealism followed from the apparent inability of reason to discover the principle of the difference within the concept itself. By re-thinking logic as the identity (and difference) of synthesis and analysis, Hegel means to fulfill the dream of Idealism: to transform freedom into intellectual intuition and thereby account for *the existence of the world by thought alone.* For Hegel, speculative Idealism can avoid the annihilation of the world if it integrates the power of *self-synthesis* into the concept of logic. Although Hegel clearly comes to the rescue of speculative Idealism, and does so through Schelling and his *STI* as his springboard and inspiration, he can only rescue it in its hour of greatest need by fundamentally transforming it. For it is no longer *the I* which posits the world, but *the concept itself,* of which the I is but one of its realizations. If the absolute cannot be thought except by identifying synthesis and analysis, then thought must develop without any presuppositions, by means of *true contradictions.* Indeed, Hegel recognized that the ontological argument can only succeed if there are true contradictions. Without Absolute Dialetheism, the ontological argument cannot succeed.

Hegel's Metaphysics

In recent scholarship, a debate concerning the metaphysical status of Hegel's thought has been initiated due to non-metaphysical readings of Hegel's thought. See, for example, Hartman (76), Kolb (86), Pinkard (86, 94/96), and most famously Pippin (89). Pippin, for example, claims that Hegel is still following the paradigm of philosophy laid out by Kant:

> Hegel is still adhering, roughly, to the Kantian strategy on how to establish basic or fundamental components of any conceptual scheme or rules for any objective judgment about determinate objects, one

that makes essential reference to the possibly self-conscious nature of all judgment.[14]

Pippin, in his *The Satisfaction of Self-Consciousness*, is well known for claiming that the metaphysical Hegel is a 'pre-modern anachronism.'[15] Pippin argues 'if the metaphysical view attributes to Hegel a pre-critical monism' that is 'indefensible in itself' and 'at odds with much of what Hegel actually says about his project' then there is good reason to abandon the metaphysical view of Hegel's philosophy.[16] McDowell also claims to follow Pippin in respect to Hegel's Kantianism:[17]

> Conceptuality as such is categorial, in a more or less Kantian sense that we can gloss in terms of apperceptive spontaneity.[18]

I do not mean to fully reconstruct the debate concerning Hegel as a metaphysician here, since this is thoroughly trodden ground. Instead, I wish to point out that Pippin's early dismissal of Hegelian metaphysics, and his construal of Hegel as a kind of transcendental epistemologist[19] has come under serious examination and critique by excellent Hegel scholars, such as Bowman[20] and Houlgate.[21] Ultimately, Bowman is right that the 'logic has metaphysical significance'[22] or as Houlgate puts it 'Hegel's logic is metaphysics.'[23] Hegel is explicit that the subject matter of logic is the concept, which is nothing less than 'the absolute, self-subsistent object, the logos, the reason of that which is, the truth of what we call things.'[24]

Magee is right that this critique of the metaphysical reading of Hegel tends to identify metaphysics with special metaphysics, understood as an inquiry into transcendent entities, such as the soul, world, or God.[25] Certainly, Hegel does not suppose *the givenness* of any transcendent entity, as a given subject matter for philosophical investigation. Because Hegel does not philosophize about any given transcendent entities, Hegel is not a metaphysician in this sense. Metaphysical dimensions to Hegel's thought are often acknowledged, but they are minimized or reconceived in a deflationary way.[26] In such a deflationary model, metaphysics is conceived as a kind of *general metaphysics*, in the sense that metaphysical inquiry is here conceived as an ontological inquiry into the categories of beings. Such a deflationary perspective is evident in Hartman, for instance, who would allow that Hegel is a metaphysician in the sense that he offers a categorial ontology. Bungay also echoes Hartman, insofar as the 'categorial philosopher' 'is worth hearing.'[27] Or as Lau puts it, Hegel's logic is a 'second order theory of categories' that does not directly describe the world but develops concepts necessary for understanding it.[28]

It is impossible to provide a coherent reading of Hegel without acknowledging that he understood his own work as a kind of metaphysics. Beiser is not wrong when he argues that Hegel's claim to Absolute Knowledge (which Hegel already proclaimed to be the goal of philosophical knowing in his *Differenzschrift*) certainly counts as metaphysics.[29] Just as in *Phenomenology* Hegel proclaims the goal of philosophy to be 'actual knowledge of what truly is',[30] in Hegel's *preface* to the first edition of the *Science of Logic*, Hegel heralds a revival of metaphysics.[31] For these textual reasons alone, it is clear that if there is any relevant question about the status of Hegel as a metaphysician, the question can only concern *what kind of metaphysics* Hegel propounds. As Kreines puts it, the question is not whether he is a metaphysician, but *how*.[32] Hegel certainly rejects dogmatic metaphysics, and we do well to steer away from any attempt to portray Hegel as a philosopher who takes Being itself as privileged and presupposed object of philosophical inquiry. Indeed, Hegel is clear that the critical philosophy had already overcome the dogmatic metaphysics he describes as the first relation to objectivity in the *Encyclopedia Logic*. Whatever metaphysics it may be, it is not dogmatic, but *critical*.

Hegel is a metaphysician, but his metaphysics is by no means merely deflationary insofar as this requires a separation of general from special metaphysics. First, as Magee and De Boer point out, Hegel undermines any attempt to separate special from general metaphysics.[33] This is obvious enough from Hegel's understanding of the categories of the *Logic*, which are not only categories that apply to non-logical beings, but also constitute the 'metaphysical definition of God':

> Being itself and the special sub-categories of it which follow, as well as those of logic in general, may be looked upon as definitions of the Absolute, or metaphysical definitions of God: at least the first and third category in every triad may—the first, where the thought-form of the triad is formulated in its simplicity, and the third, being the return from differentiation to a simple self-reference. For a metaphysical definition of God is the expression of his nature in thoughts as such.[34]

Each category of the logic is a category of the Absolute—each is a metaphysical definition of God. Logic, Hegel informs us, constitutes 'God's thoughts before the creation.'[35] If special metaphysics takes God as its object, and general metaphysics takes the categories of being as its object, the *Science of Logic* most certainly collapses the difference between the two. Any inquiry into the categories necessary for describing the world or any inquiry into the categories of Being is also an inquiry into the being of God, or in less theological terms, the Absolute.

Although De Boer is not wrong that Hegel's objective logic replaces former metaphysics, in addition to Kant's transcendental logic,[36] because 'logic in general' can be viewed as the 'metaphysical definition of God' we should not only look to the logic of Being and Essence to understand Hegel's metaphysics (though certainly we should), but we should also look to his logic of Subjectivity, where we discover Hegel's endorsement of a kind of ontological argument. By looking to the logic of subjectivity, we discover that Hegel's categories are *self-objectifying*. Because the concept 'posits itself as *something real, an existent*',[37] we cannot understand Hegel if we insist upon any absolute separation between the categorial content and its instantiation or existence. Instead, because 'the concept of God realizes itself' and this concept is nothing other than 'the concept' itself,[38] the categories of the logic should not be read in a deflationary way whereby the concept is treated in a way such that it is divorced from existence or the world to which it applies. Instead, the ontological argument that characterizes Hegel's logic of subjectivity shows that the concept (and its forms) is everything, and it is *in virtue of itself* that it is everything:

> The concept is all and that its movement is the universal absolute activity, the self-determining and self-realizing movement.[39]

Or as Hegel puts it in the third volume of the *Encyclopedia*:

> Philosophy certainly has to do with unity in general . . . but with the concrete unity (the concept), and that in its whole course has to do with nothing else; each step is a phase of this concrete unity.[40]

Hegel makes it abundantly clear that philosophy has to do *with nothing else* except for the concept. Magee points out that the greatest weakness of the deflationary view of Hegel's metaphysics certainly consists in their difficulty in making sense of the role of God in Hegel's system.[41] Hegel proclaims that

> God is the one and only object of philosophy.[42]

Magee's critique, however, can be easily expanded. Because the concept of God is identical with the concept of the concept, the inability to account for the role of God is tantamount to the inability to account for the concept of the concept. Even if the term 'God' is a metaphor, and we speak instead of the concept, or the Absolute, the same problem remains, because it is the concept that is *existentially implicative*. Certainly, there are many dimensions to Hegel's metaphysics that cannot be completely circumscribed by a short essay on Hegel's ontological argument, many of which have been helpfully uncovered by recent Hegel scholarship. Nonetheless, one necessary dimension to his metaphysics is the ontological argument, and we can attain neither a clear nor a complete concept of what Hegelian metaphysics involves without reconstructing the various developments in the logic of the concept (that constitute the beginning of that 'argument') and connecting those developments to the metaphysical problems Hegel solves by means of that logic. Pippin is right that the 'textbook formulation of Hegel's position' invokes the 'self-actualization of the concept.'[43] The 'textbook formulation' is not wrong, for it captures the way in which Hegel's logic of the concept functions as a kind of ontological argument.

In his most recent book, *Hegel's Realm of Shadows: Logic as Metaphysics in The Science of Logic*, Pippin himself has made it clear that he has never actually advanced a reading of Hegel that denies all metaphysical significance to Hegel's work.[44] He makes it clear that one must acknowledge that we cannot understand Hegel's *Science of Logic* without recognizing its contribution to metaphysics. Pippin's view is that Hegel's critique of *dogmatic* metaphysics gives rise to a new *critical* conception of metaphysics:

> The claim (which I also defended in Pippin 1989) is that Hegel opposes the modern dogmatic metaphysics that Kant opposes as well: rational psychology, cosmology, and natural theology. But that Hegel does so by an exposition of the 'logic' of these projects is also a critique (what he calls the 'objective logic'), all of which culminates in a positive metaphysics of an unprecedented sort, the subjective logic, in which we see how metaphysics is 'now' to be understood as 'logic.'[45]

Pippin, I believe, is right that Hegel does oppose dogmatic metaphysics, but he does not thereby abandon all metaphysics. Rather, he replaces the old metaphysics with an unprecedented metaphysics in his logic of subjectivity, which begins in the *Doctrine of the Concept*. Pippin argues that even if Hegel opposes the metaphysics of modern rationalism, he is nonetheless a metaphysician in the Aristotelian sense, such that what Hegel calls the concept, Aristotle calls 'substantial form.'[46] Further, Pippin identifies the new Hegelian metaphysics as a synthesis of Kantian and Aristotelian ideas,

> Put in terms of the history of philosophy, what all of this will amount to is an attempt by Hegel at a highly unusual synthesis of the Kantian revolution in philosophy, especially the anti-empiricism self-grounding character of reason (aka 'the Concept'), and the most important Kantian innovation, the spontaneity of thinking, together with essential elements of Aristotle's understanding of metaphysics, especially the Aristotelian notions of Energeia, which Hegel translates as Wirklichkeit, actuality, the proper object of first philosophy, and, as we have already seen, the core of the classical view that 'nous' rules the world, all in contrast to the rationalist metaphysics of nonsensible objects accessible to pure reason alone. Hegel is no metaphysician in this rationalist sense, but he is most certainly a metaphysician in the Aristotelian sense.[47]

I too have emphasized Pippin's point that Hegel's metaphysics does indeed integrate Aristotelian elements. However, at times, Pippin's reading of this integration diverges significantly from my own. For example, he claims that Aristotle is for the most part not interested in nonsensible objects that Kant and Plato took as the object of metaphysics.[48]

Admittedly, in many ways this is accurate, but in other ways it is highly misleading. In book Lambda, Aristotle argues that the unity of Being must be ordered by *thought thinking itself*, which he defines as an unembodied, *non-sensible Energeia*. All 'standard' and sensible beings depend upon it for their being. What is more telling is the fact that the final quote in Hegel's third installment of the Encyclopedia quotes Aristotle's description of non-sensible Energeia in book Lambda as a way of communicating the meaning of philosophical knowing. Finally, Pippin does not seem to notice the affinity between Hegel and Aristotle on the issue of existential implication: just as the concept is the principle of its own particulars, Aristotle's Form is the principle of its own particularization in composite beings.

Although Pippin locates Hegel's new metaphysics in the subjective logic, he hardly discusses the ontological argument, for it only appears in three footnotes.[49] Indeed, already in Kant, metaphysics was re-cast as logic, but for Hegel this engenders a *critical return* and affirmation of the ontological argument. Hegel's development of a new metaphysics in the logic of subjectivity cannot be fully re-constructed or appreciated without confronting Hegel's understanding of subjectivity in terms of self-objectifying conceptuality. Pippin acknowledges that in order to fully address the relation of Hegel to special metaphysics (metaphysical inquiry into God, the soul, and the world), one must deal with Hegel's reading of the ontological argument (which Pippin rightly reads as a logical issue), which he identifies as 'the most difficult issue' that 'makes everything much more difficult.' Pippin says that he does not see any evidence that Hegel is trying to resolve or answer traditional questions concerning God, the soul, or the world.[50] In other places, Pippin claims that although the concept is the condition for the intelligibility of being, it does not follow from this that one could 'derive' existence from the concept alone.[51] When Hegel describes the concept as self-objectifying, and describes this process as a kind of ontological argument, Pippin says that 'Hegel's alternate way of making this point can be quite confusing.' According to Pippin:

> But he quickly makes clear that his transition to 'objectivity' is quite a different matter, and that the concept of empirical existence ('sensible, perishable and temporal existence') at issue in the ontological proof is a crude misapprehension of the nature of the problem. We get a further, fuller sense of the metaphorical nature of Hegel's theological language when he tells us that what we have been reading

about pure thinking's movement, the 'exposition of the pure concept' is the 'absolute divine concept itself,' 'the logical course of God's self-determination as being' (21.29). He then hastens to note that he means by God what takes up as 'the Idea.'[52]

Pippin is right that Hegel's use of the term 'God' is metaphorical. In technical language, we can use terms such as 'Idea' instead. But one cannot simply explain away Hegel's critical re-thinking and *affirmation* of the ontological argument as simply metaphorical, for he expresses the very same content in non-metaphorical terms when he proclaims that the concept *objectifies itself*. And even if, as Pippin rightly indicates, readers should not mis-understand Hegel's use of the ontological argument, this does not entail that Hegel does not endorse the central concept in that argument, namely that the concept is *sufficient* to give itself existence. Hegel's critical *affirmation* of the ontological argument, which one can re-formulate without metaphors, is enough to indicate to us that Hegel does, in fact, believe one can derive existence from the concept alone. Of course, in the logic we are only concerned with *logical* existence, so the affirmation of the ontological argument in the logic is not yet a transition to non-logical existence. But this in *no way* implies that the concept is not sufficient for its own existence, for the concepts of the logic exist in a purely logical modality if you will, without reference to space or time. All that is necessary to appreciate this is to give up on the prejudice that by 'existence' somehow precludes logical being as such. Indeed, the autonomy of the logic can only be fully appreciated by recognizing how the presupposition-less autonomy of the *Science of Logic* requires that logical categories constitute the source of their own *logical existence*.

For Hegel, philosophy must not only begin without any presupposition, but the concept must be imbued with the power to determine and realize itself. Hegel's foundation free philosophy is a foundation free *metaphysics* in the sense that *the concept must be a principle of its own existence*, in a manner 'identical in character' to the ontological argument for God's existence. Otherwise, the infinite cannot 'go forth from itself and make itself finite.' By endorsing the ontological argument and imbuing the concept with the power of intellectual intuition, Hegel undermines the *separation* of knowing and being that lies at the ground of the transcendental turn: knowing cannot be separated from being—rather it must be the sufficient ground of its own existence. As De Boer has pointed out, for Kant, 'ontology purported to achieve knowledge of reality by means of pure concepts alone.'[53] With his *critical reformation* of the ontological argument, Hegel returns to the very ontology Kant spurned. This conception of metaphysics implied by the endorsement of intellectual intuition (or at least its logical principle) requires *collapsing* any absolute difference between epistemology and metaphysics. Hegel's logic is the metaphysics of the Absolute. If such a philosophy truly has the Absolute as its object, it must itself be Absolute and cannot take any determination for granted. Accordingly, Hegel's foundation free logic is a foundation free *metaphysics*. Insofar as our thinking remains within the confines of the logic, the only existence to which the concept gives rise is *logical in character*. Simply put, as long as we remain *in logic* the metaphysics of the logic does not exceed logical being. Not until the advent of the Absolute Idea does logic *particularize itself into non-logical being in nature*. Whether Hegel is successful in applying the logic of the ontological argument to the transition from logic of nature, which he appears to do, must be taken up as the object of a separate query. That Hegel understands his own system this way, however, seems evident enough from the texts themselves.

Just as much as each category of the self-mediating dialectic transcends its own categorial form, as difference transcends itself into identity, Hegel means to overcome Jacobi's charge of nihilism by arguing that the categorial form of thinking as such amplifies itself into *non-categorial being, namely into nature and spirit*. As Ferrarin points out, nature and spirit are 'moments of the Ideas self-actualization as free and self-determining spirit.'[54] This question 'how does the infinite go forth from itself and come to finitude?' can be raised in regard to many different categories. For example, one can ask a theological question such as 'how does God create nature?'

In virtue of the capacity of the universal's capacity to *refer to itself*[55] and to thereby *make itself particular*, it is able to create its own *synthetic content* (and thereby its own *truth*) from nothing but itself. The activity by which the concept gives itself its own content is an act of *self-particularization*. Rather than describe the act of self-mediation as a 'construction,' which Schelling was wont to do, and which draws on the metaphor of making in which form and material are separate principles, Hegel describes this act of self-particularization as the 'creative power' of the concept.[56] In Hegel's conception of universality, it is in virtue of self-particularization that the universal establishes for itself its own content and particularization. For this reason, self-particularization establishes the *true* content of the universal, or the content to which the universal corresponds. Since Hegel argues that universals must exhibit *self-particularization* and existential implication is that process whereby the universal gives rise to its particulars *by itself*, the concept is existential implicative because it is a process of *self-particularization*.

In his logic, Hegel claims that the concept is responsible for its own *logical* being. In the philosophy of nature, philosophy of mind, and the philosophy of history, Hegel goes further to insist the concept is also the creative power responsible for the other dimensions of the Absolute which are not reducible to logic, such as nature, mind, and history.

The presence of the self-realizing and autonomous reason in Hegel's own words is present throughout his entire mature corpus. According to Hegel, reason is *the material* for its own realization:

> Reason is for itself the *infinite material* of all natural and spiritual life, as well as the *infinite form*, and that its actualization of itself is its content. . . . That this Idea[57] is the True, Eternal, simply the Power—that it reveals itself in the world, and that nothing else is revealed in the world but the Idea itself.[58]

Kreines is right that Hegel's monism is epistemological.[59] Having acknowledged the central role of the ontological argument in Hegel's thought, however, we learn that *nothing else is revealed* except the true concept, or the Idea. Accordingly, because only the Idea is revealed, we must also endorse a kind of metaphysical monism, if by this term, however, we mean that what exists is *the singular agency of the concept*. Because the singular agency of the concept must be without presupposition, ultimately the concept (in its logical being) must *create itself*.

Jacobi charged that the Speculative Idealist destroys the world, including nature, by requiring it to be deduced from the concept. But given Hegel's abandonment of formal logic and his revision of the concept as a creative power, in the *Philosophy of Nature*, Hegel insists that nature too is created by reason:

> The world is created, is now being created, and has eternally been created; this presents itself in the form of the preservation of the world. Creating is the activity of the absolute Idea.[60]

Hegel states as much in his *Philosophy of Mind* in his discussion of revealed religion:

> Under the 'moment' of universality—the sphere of pure thought—. . . it is therefore the absolute spirit . . . (as underlying and essential power under the reflective category of causality) creator of heaven and earth.[61]

Nature is the manifestation of the concept in a form of otherness or self-alienation, out of which mind and *Geist* arises.[62] Reason becomes *Geist* only by giving rise to nature:

> The divine Idea is just this: to disclose itself, to posit this Other outside itself and to take it back again into itself, in order to be subjectivity and Spirit.[63]

In his discussion of revealed religion, Hegel claims that the Absolute Spirit is a 'self-determining principle,' an 'infinite, self-realizing form' which is 'manifestation out and out.'[64] Finally, in the philosophy of history, Hegel is unequivocal about history as the self-realization of the concept:

> And the time must finally come when we comprehend the rich product of creative Reason that is world history.[65]

Because the concept gives itself existence, Hegel identifies the development from concept to *truth and objectivity* in the *Science of Logic*, the process by which the concept determines itself to be objective, and thereby *true*, as a revised version of the ontological argument or 'proof from the concept,' wherein the concept of God is sufficient to justify the existence of God.[66] In Hegel's case it is the *divine* concept that gives itself existence:

> But in the exposition of the pure concept it was indicated that the latter is the absolute divine concept itself.[67]

Schelling already recognized that Hegel's project aimed at enlivening an older ontology in his Munich lectures. Regarding Hegel's attempt to make concepts principles of existence he writes that 'The attempt to make concepts the principles of existence and movement is an attempt to give life to an old ontology.'[68] The reading of Hegel I offer here is indeed identical to Schelling's reading of Hegel's philosophy. Of course, there Schelling employs this interpretative schema in order to critique Hegel for making God *co-extensive* with all things and for imbuing a power to thought which he thinks it cannot possess. Magee is exactly right when he points out that the Absolute is not something that transcends the world, but is *this world* (which naturally includes categorial determinations).[69]

Were the existence of the concept indebted to a principle *other* than the concept itself, the concept would *not* be true in virtue of itself. Rather, it would be true in virtue of something else and would thereby fail to be *absolute* or have being 'in and for itself.'[70] In addition, by introducing a *second* principle responsible for the existence of the concept, the philosopher would re-introduce the duality of principles that Hegel's philosophy categorically rejects. Indeed, by refusing to acknowledge that the concept is sufficient for its own existence, one would re-introduce an *absolute division* between form and content into the concept. With such a Manichean structure in place, the problem of the existence of the Absolute would rear its head again, and Jacobi's problem of Nihilism would remain unanswered. It is not just the 'determination of nature' or the 'determination of spirit' into which the concept particularizes itself. It must be nature and spirit themselves. Otherwise, an untenable dualism of thought and world arises that further re-instates the question of their relationship. Because the logical concept does its work *without* the help of the human mind, it would be an obvious and foolish mistake to claim that the human being is the cause of nature. Of course, whether the concept is *truly* conceived in the knowing of the Absolute in space and time depends upon the work of philosophy, which is the work of rational animals.

It is true that the non-metaphysical tendency of the non-foundation school has at times obscured Hegel's proclamation that the concept is the 'creator of heaven and earth.' As Clark and Fritzman state:

> It is only because his construction of space . . . refers back to experience—to outer space, that is, physical space in the external world—that he has provided a construction of space. Without such a reference his construction would be nothing more than, as meaningless as, the mental equivalent of manipulating marks on paper.[71]

Rather than prove that the non-foundational reading of Hegel is wrong, this argument only shows that the non-foundational reading of Hegel must be thoroughly metaphysical. Hegel proclaims the concept to be true in virtue of itself; it is an ontological 'argument' such that the concept exists (in nature and spirit) *in virtue of itself*. Thus, the concept gives rise not only to the concept of space but to *space itself*. For this reason, the philosophy of nature cannot be chalked up to meaningless marks on paper. As a result, their critique does not undermine the non-foundational view, but shows that it must be completed with a recognition of Hegel's ontological argument. The disciple of Hegel must seriously ask whether Hegel successfully shows that the concept gives rise to nature itself (and not just the concept thereof). It is not a question that can be simply brushed off as a bad reading of the master or a precritical perspective. Instead, the success of the system depends upon the successfully implementation of the ontological 'argument' at each stage of development—from logic to nature, and nature to spirit (not just the concept of spirit). In this book, I do not mean to answer this question. Instead, I mean only to show that it is a question that readers of Hegel ought to confront. If Hegel cannot successfully show how nature itself is created by self-thinking thought, it would not follow that Absolute Dialetheism as such is false. It would only imply that Hegel's construal of Absolute Dialetheism is problematic, and another formulation of Absolute Dialetheism would be required.

Kant could only refute the ontological argument on the supposition that concepts in isolation are merely analytic in character. Indeed, Kant's critique of the ontological argument first presumes that while concepts are content determinations, 'being is not a content determination.'[72] This fundamental opposition of Being to the concept is integral for Kant to uphold that *Being is not a predicate*. For Hegel, Kant does not clearly distinguish between different ways being is said—in particular between *Being (Sein) and determinate being (Dasein)*. Although Hegel acknowledges that existence is a matter of indifference for Being and nothing (since their content is indeterminate), existence is already no longer a matter of indifference for determinate being and nothing, for example *being something* or other.[73] Not only is 'Being' a content determination when it reaches the stage of determinate being, but even pure and 'indeterminate' Being is retroactively determined to be a determinate content, for it stands in determinate contrast with determinate being. For Hegel, Being is a content determination, for it negates its own indeterminacy and *gives itself determinate being* (what Giovanni has translated as 'existence.')

Kant's opposition between the concept and Being is a commitment to *the finitude of concepts*. The finitude of concepts entails that concepts are not true in virtue of themselves. Finite concepts have their existence granted to them by an exterior principle. Unlike concepts whose existence lies outside of them, such as empirical determinations, the concept as such is the source of its own being. Certainly, the concept of '$100' does not entail its own existence, for it is a finite thought-determination. Hegel proclaims the 'concept' of $100 to be a false concept,[74] for

> the form of simple self-reference does not belong to such a limited, finite content itself.[75]

Hegel is clear that the very definition of a finite concept is that in it concept and Being are different.[76] As we have already explicated earlier, finite concepts are empty possibilities whose being lies outside them.[77]

However, Hegel is clear that Kant's critique of the proof fails in the case of the concept of the infinite.[78] As Hegel writes:

> this antithesis that is found in finitude can in no wise occur in what is infinite, God.[79]

By showing that the concept of the concept does not follow the mold of the finite concept, Hegel means to rescue the ontological argument from Kant's critique. First, Hegel remarks that one cannot find Being in the concept if we suppose the concept to be finite:

> But of course the difficulty of finding being in the concept in general, and equally so in the concept of God, becomes insuperable if we expect being to be something that we find in the context of external experience or in the form of sense-perception, like the one hundred dollars in the context of my finances, as something graspable only

by hand, not by spirit, essentially visible to the external and not the internal eye; . . . such thought stands opposed to being.[80]

Since Hegel is clear that the abstract concept of God entails that the concept and Being are *inseparable* from one another,[81] the concept of God is infinite, not finite. Hegel proclaims that the 'true critique of the categories' really consists in an effort to 'prevent applying finite categories to God.'[82] Simply put, Hegel understands the true critique of pure reason as an effort to salvage the ontological argument against its critics.[83] As Collingwood remarked, logic must remain committed to the ontological proof:

> Logic, therefore, stands committed to the principle of the ontological proof. Its subject-matter, namely thought, afford an instance of something which cannot be conceived except as actual, something whose essence involves existence.[84]

Here it is clear that Hegel invokes self-reference as a condition for being a *true* concept, and the 'concept' of the $100 does not exhibit this self-reference.[85] For this reason, it cannot be a true concept. The concept of the concept, on the other hand, is a true concept, for it does imply its own existence by means of its self-referential activity. Put in less theological terms, 'the true critique of the categories' requires recognizing the self-referential structure of the categories, and this requires rejecting any concept of the concept that models its understanding on empirical representations (such as the representation of $100). Kant fails to recognize the self-referential and existentially implicative aspect of the concept, namely what makes a concept infinite, because he continues to think about concepts on the model of finite determinations, which do not possess this structure. Accordingly, one of the problems Hegel must address is how to account for empirical concepts, since they do not seem to abide by the formal specifications of what a concept is. Indeed, if the 'what it is to be' of the concept entails that it is self-particularizing, and empirical concepts are not self-particularizing, then it is not clear how one could classify empirical thought-determinations as concepts proper. For this reason, McDowell fails to recognize an important problem in Hegel when he claims that

> Hegelian talk of 'the Notion' does not allude to special non-empirical concepts about which an issue would arise about how they relate to ordinary empirical concepts.[86]

In fact, not only is the concept of the concept not an empirical concept, but its self-predicative and existentially implicative character places it squarely at odds with empirical determinations. At the close of our

reconstruction of Hegel's logic of the concept, we will return to this problem in our chapter 'Relativizing the Absolute: Empiricism, Judgment, and
Inference.'

That the critique of pure reason requires us to 'prevent applying finite
categories to God' could be re-formulated to say that the critique of pure
reason requires us to prevent applying finite categories to the *Absolute*.
Fascinatingly, Hegel considers the fulfilment of the critique of pure reason to consist in a vindication of the power of the concept in the ontological argument. This is no less obvious in Hegel's discussion of synthetic
a priori judgments in his discussion *Of the Concept in General* at the
outset of the Logic of Subjectivity.

Pippin famously invokes these passages in his reading of Hegel in starkly
Kantian terms. Hegel does indeed proclaim self-consciousness to be a
concrete instance of the concept.[87] Naturally, Hegel reads the unity of
self-consciousness in terms of Kant's synthetic unity of apperception:

> It is one of the profoundest and truest insights to be found in the Cri-
> tique of Pure Reason that the unity which constitutes the essence of
> the concept is recognized as the original synthetic unity of appercep-
> tion, the unity of the 'I think,' or of self-consciousness.[88]

What is most impressive for Hegel is Kant's recognition of synthetic
a priori judgments, which for him constitute a recognition of the necessary (but often neglected) element of differentiation in conceptual
determination:

> differentiation is an equally essential moment of the concept. Kant
> introduced this line of reflection with the very important thought
> that there are synthetic judgments *apriori*. His originally synthesis of
> apperception is one of the most profound principles for speculative
> development; it contains the beginning of a true apprehension of the
> nature of the concept and is fully opposed to any empty identity or
> abstract universality which is not internally a synthesis.[89]

In short, for Hegel, Kant's profound insight is that the concept itself
contains not only analytic truth (or truth of identity), but also *synthetic truth*. Hegel sees in Kant's concept of the synthetic *a priori* the
identity of synthesis and analysis that constitutes his own dialectical
method, which he explicates more fully in the chapter on the Absolute
Idea. Pippin is exactly right that Hegel's metaphysics, and in particular his insight into the unity of synthesis and analysis (the spontaneity
of thought), is indebted to Kant. What Pippin does not acknowledge,
however, is that Hegel's critique of the shortcomings of Kant lead him
to infuse the concept with the power endowed to it in the ontological
argument.

Famously, however, Hegel proclaims that 'the further development, however, did not live up the beginning.'[90] One of the significant problems, according to Hegel, is the fact that Kant posits the synthetic unity as being *external to* the concept, such that the concept remained an empty analytic unity that must seek its truth outside of itself in the manifold of intuition.[91] As Hegel writes, for Kant,

> we are not allowed to extract reality from it, for by reality objectivity is to be understood, since reality is contrasted with subjectivity. Moreover, the concept and anything logical are declared to be something purely formal which, since it abstract from content, does not contain truth.[92]

In order for the further development to fulfill the promise of Kant's beginning, the concept must be re-conceived to be true in virtue of itself. The concept ought to be the principle of its own existence, such that *the unity of the concept with reality* ought to follow *from the concept itself*:

> Now it must certainly be conceded that the concept is as such not yet complete, that it must rather be raised to the idea which alone is the unity of the concept and reality; and this is a result which will have to emerge in what follows from the nature of the concept alone.[93]

Accordingly, for Hegel unity of the concept with reality must follow 'from the nature of the concept alone'—only then can the concept truly be said to be *synthetic and a priori* (analytic). By failing to allow the concept to be its own autonomous principle of reality, the concept was denied its independence, such that in Kant the concept must acquire its reality from an external principle, namely in the material of intuition:

> In both operations, the concept is not the one which is independent, is not what is essential and true about that presupposed material; this material is the reality in and for itself, a reality that cannot be extracted from the concept.[94]

Rather than acquire its *Mannifaltigkeit* outside of itself in intuition, the *Mannigfaltigkeit* ought to have its *source* in the concept itself:

> And because this determinateness is the determinateness of the concept, and hence the absolute determinateness, singularity, the concept is the ground and the source of all finite determinateness and manifoldness.[95]

In short, Hegel integrates Kant's concept of the spontaneity of thought into his metaphysics. But the spontaneity of thought for Hegel consists in the power of the concept to *objectify itself*—only if we endow this concept with this power of self-objectification can we fulfill the critique of pure reason. By building synthetic power into the self-identity of analysis, Hegel imbues the concept itself with the power to *amplify itself into existence*. By drawing the identity of synthesis and analysis into the structure of the concept itself, Hegel gives *the concept the power of intellectual intuition*, whereby *the concept conceptualizes itself* and brings itself into existence *first as logic*, then as nature and spirit. Dialectics—the synthesizing (and analyzing) of synthesis and analysis—is the ampliative and synthetic knowing by which the concept amplifies itself beyond merely conceptual determinations into the worlds of nature and spirit. Without the identity of analysis and synthesis, Hegel cannot rescue the ontological argument from Kant's critique. Hegel's comments on Kant's critique of pure reason demonstrate that Hegel's Kantianism led him back to the ontological argument. Rather than eschewing all forms of modern rationalism, Hegel implores us to return to the very argument that underpinned modern rationalist (and in some cases medieval thought)[96] if we so desire to complete the critique of pure reason.

This return to the ontological argument, however, is *not* a return to dogmatic metaphysics, for Hegel makes it quite clear that the development of the real out of the concept is the result of *the self-destruction all finite thinking*, namely all conceptualizing that is true in virtue of another, or has its reality outside of itself:

> The derivation of the real from the concept, if 'derivation' is what we want to call it, consists at first essentially in this, that the concept in its formal abstraction reveals itself to be incomplete and through a dialectic immanently grounded in it passes over into reality: it passes over into it, however, as into something which it generates out of itself, not as it if were falling back again onto a ready-made reality which it finds opposite it, or as if it were taking refuge, because it sought for something better but found none, into something that has already been proven to be the unessential element of appearance.[97]

Hegel's endorsement of the ontological argument is not merely postulated as an *ad hoc* solution to the problem of the existence of the Absolute. Rather, the relative concept that has its truth outside itself, undergoes self-destruction in virtue of what it is, thereby giving rise to the self-particularizing concept. Thus, Hegel's affirmation of the power of the concept to objectify itself is not a dogmatic reflection. Instead, it comes on the heels of the self-criticism of all finite reason. Indeed, it is the truth of the *self-critique of pure reason*.

Hegel's twofold insight that the problem of the existence of the Absolute can only be solved if (i) the concept is the *sole principle* for its own existence and (ii) philosophy must be free of all foundations appears to entail a fundamental incongruity. The ontological argument for God's existence begins from a presupposition: *the concept of God*. If philosophy must begin without any foundation at all, and the Absolute is the self-realizing concept understood on the model of an ontological argument, then it would appear that the first condition conflicts with the second. In other words, how can the concept particularize itself if it cannot be taken for granted? In order to fully appreciate Hegel's answer to the question: 'how does the infinite go forth from itself and make itself finite?' Hegel must show how his endorsement of the ontological argument and Kant's concept of intellectual intuition does not conflict with the foundation free character of his system of knowledge.

Because the concept absolutizes itself, the concept is *not* a presupposition:

> But there is the following circumstance in this case, which makes the proof unsatisfactory. That most perfect and most real of all things is a presupposition, and being and the concept, on their own account, are one-sided when measured against it. Descartes and Spinoza define God as self-caused, *causa sui*. God's concept and existence are identical, or in other words God cannot be grasped as concept apart from being. What is unsatisfactory is that this is a presupposition, so that when measured against it the concept must of necessity be something subjective.[98]

Rather, the concept arises within the logic from pure Being, which is itself without any determinations posited in advance. Being transforms itself into Essence, and Essence transforms into the *Doctrine of the Concept*. For this reason, Hegel's identification of the logic of the concept as an 'ontological argument' does not problematize his commitment to foundation free logic. Rather, it is necessary for it. Were the concept not responsible for its own being, then some given external principle would be required in order for it to exist. It is without any foundation only because it is responsible for its own existence. As Hegel states:

> When we look closely at the nature of the concept, we see that its identity with being is not a presupposition but a result.[99]

Hegel's words here also shed light upon the problematic assertions of Wendy Lynn Clark and M. Fritzman, when they proclaim that while Hegel (like Sellars after him) rejects the concept of an immediate, non-conceptual given, *he affirms the given insofar as it is conceptually mediated*.[100] This is deeply problematic, for conceptually mediated reality is always a *result*, not an absolute beginning. As Hegel states, the unity of the concept with being is a result, *not* a presupposition. For scientific knowing, conceptually mediated reality can just as little be taken as a given as any purported non-conceptual immediacy. Finally, by no means does the rejection of the conceptually mediated given imply that conceptually mediated reality cannot be known. To the contrary, conceptually mediated reality is truly known only once it is established as the result of the free self-particularization of the concept.

This peculiarity of Hegel's system highlights a very important way in which Hegel's 'ontological argument' diverges from the traditional argument. The traditional ways of formulating the argument take for granted certain principles of inference, which are then applied to a particular definition of God. Because Hegel rejects the dualism of form and content, he does not proceed by applying principles of inference to a given conceptual content. Such a maneuver would introduce a division of form and content and would rob the content of its own self-development. Instead, for Hegel the concept particularizes itself and thereby demonstrates its own truth. Because Hegel takes nothing for granted, and premises are taken for granted, Hegel's 'ontological argument' is *not an argument* at all.[101] For this reason, it is no surprise that commentators have a hard time finding an ontological argument. Paul Redding and Paulo Diego Bubbio are exactly right when they point out how difficult it is to locate an argument in Hegel's text.[102] Oppy also points out that 'he gives no argumentative support for his assertions.'[103] The lack of an argument cannot be taken as a fault, however, since the way the concept exhibits existential implication is not by means of an argument, but the *dialectical development and progression* from concept to objectivity. For Hegel, this progression is not a return to an idealism that excludes the real, or a realism that denies the reality of the concept, but a unity of realism and idealism.[104]

Despite the wide-ranging variety in the way the ontological argument is formulated in Anselm, Descartes, Leibniz, and Spinoza, they all proceed by means of *presuppositional arguments*. Although it is not my intention to compare these thinkers in detail, as this has already been achieved elsewhere,[105] because Hegel's appropriation of the ontological argument undermines both its presuppositional and argumentative character, Hegel's version of the ontological 'argument' is to be distinguished from all others in the history of medieval and modern philosophy. Hegel's appropriation of the ontological argument is also *the destruction of its argumentative form*. By endowing the content with the power to establish its own truth, there is no longer any need for an argument to prove the truth of the concept. Rather, the concept can do all the work *by itself*.

Heinrich Heine provides a famous anecdote concerning Hegel's claim that 'what is rational is actual; and what is actual is rational':[106]

> At times I saw Hegel looking around anxiously as if in fear he might
> be understood. He was very fond of me, for he was sure I would
> never betray him. At that time I actually thought that he was very
> obsequious. Once when I complained about the phrase 'all that
> is, is rational,' he smiled strangely and remarked, 'It could also be

formulated, as all that is rational must be.' Then he looked about him hastily; but he was quickly assured, for only Heinrich Beer had heard his words.[107]

Of course, in order to do proper justice to this phrase, lots of exegetical work would be required. First note that this lovely anecdote is consistent with the ontological reading of Hegel offered here. First, 'Wirklichkeit' (or 'actuality') here belongs in the logic of Essence and can at least be read to mean that the truth of actuality is the *concept*, since the latter is the dialectical consequence of the former. But one can also read the anecdote as indicating something further, for 'all that is rational must be' indicates that *the existence* of *reason* is not continent. Its existence is necessary, and what is more, 'all that is, is rational' also means that reason is not other to what is actual or to be distinguished from it. Rather, it indicates that reason is co-extensive with what is *actual*. Hegel appears to be affirming both that what is actual is reason (albeit in various forms), and reason's existence is necessary. Put together, it is clear that reason's existence is necessary, and it cannot owe that existence to another, for reason is co-extensive with the actual. Thus, reason necessarily owes its (necessary) existence to itself alone. Indeed, Hegel's appropriation of the language of the ontological argument expresses exactly this point. Reason is Wirklichkeit in the sense that it has a 'Wirkung'—a 'Wirkung' it owes to no other but itself by itself (*auto kath auto*).[108] Or in terms of possibility, reason is not a mere possibility divorced from actuality, but it is *necessarily self-actualizing*.[109] As Hegel proclaims in his Introduction to the *Philosophy of History*:

> The insight to which philosophy ought to lead . . . is that the real world is as it ought to be, that the truly good, the universal divine Reason is also the power capable of actualizing itself.[110]

Accordingly, in *Speculation and the Hermeneutics of Effectual Reality* Maurizio Pagano and Hager Weslati rightly characterize 'Wirklichkeit' as 'reality in motion,' such that actuality would be better rendered as 'reality actualizing itself.'[111]

As is evident, Hegel's description of the concept as the creative power of the system explains his identity of the concept with God. What is more, like the Holy Trinity, each determination of the concept is itself the whole concept. Further, Hegel correlates each determination of the concept—universality, particularity, and singularity—with one moment of the Holy Trinity and one domain of the Absolute:

> Gott in seiner Allgemeinheit ist das Logische, Gott in seiner Besonderheit ist die Natur, Gott in seiner Einzelheit ist der Geist. In dieser Festhaltung, steht der Begriff.[112]

Patricia Marie Calton is quite right when she notes that for Hegel 'the world is God's concrete articulation.'[113] The Absolute, or God, is the self-realizing and self-creating concept by which the differentiations of the world are created and revealed. Indeed, Hegel's lectures on the logic in Berlin indicate that Hegel never hesitated to use Christian images and metaphors to teach logic. Although religion is a form of 'world spirit' it fails to think the Absolute conceptually. Nonetheless, this does not entail that there is no truth in religion whatsoever. Hegel's logic of the concept conceptualizes what exists pictorially in the Christian religion.[114] In the *Gospel of John*, we read that 'in the beginning was the word' and that 'the word became flesh.' Hegel re-thinks the imagistic world of the Christian logos with the self-particularizing concept. Jesus Christ is Immanuel, *God among us*. For Hegel Jesus Christ is, to use his language, *the universal in its particularized form*. Hegel conceptualizes this relationship of God the father to God the son which only exists in pictorial form in Christian belief.[115]

This concept determines itself to be the principle of all things and makes itself flesh by means of its existentially implicative content. Indeed, Neo-Platonism suffered a similar deficiency as Christian dogma, for it could not give an account of emanation without appealing to *metaphor*. As is evident here, Hegel draws from the deep well of Christian and Neo-Platonic conceptions of creation. At the same time, Hegel circumvents the appeal to metaphor by re-thinking the concept as its own principle of difference. By re-thinking the concept as the power of self-differentiation, Hegel does not suffer from the same problem under which both the Neo-Platonists as well as the early German Idealists suffered.

Although the Ancient Greeks tend to think about the relation of universal to particular more in terms of life than creation, they nonetheless have a concept of the universal as a principle in virtue of which particulars have existence. For this reason, Hegel's account of the concept appropriates this concept of *the universal as power* from the Greeks and integrates it into his concept of the concept, albeit by radically re-thinking the principle in virtue of which the universal creates particulars. Indeed, Hegel never tires of proclaiming the living character of his logic. Hegel's concept is the living and creative power by which the worlds of nature and spirit exist. Accordingly, despite the revolutionary dimension of his thinking, he is very obviously indebted to the Christian and Greek traditions that he has surpassed and into which he has breathed new life. Bowman points out that for Hegel the concept is a non-abstract and unique being 'whose various modifications and degrees of manifestation constitute the whole of reality.'[116] Still, Bowman is right that this gives us little insight into the actual content of the universal:

> Yet beyond specifying that a non-abstract concept would be one whose determinacy was at the same time the 'principle' of its

content—distinctions, the remark does not go very far in providing us with a notion of what the concept is supposed to be and how far it is different from ordinary concepts.[117]

One of the goals of this book is to do just that—to explicate in close detail, following Hegel's logic of the concept, exactly what the concept is supposed to be, and how it is different from so-called 'ordinary' concepts. In order to achieve this, we must embark upon a close reconstruction of Hegel's text, such as to lay bare the content and structure of universality, particularity, and singularity, each of which are integral to the being of the concept.

On the whole, the concept differentiates itself into three forms: logic, nature, and spirit, each of which comes to be by the self-creating and self-realizing activity of the concept. The Absolute, which certainly is a *totality*, is a unity of all three of these domains. Because the concept is the power of self-particularization, the self-differentiation of the concept into the three domains of logic, nature, and spirit is nothing less than the self-particularization of the concept.[118] Each domain of the concept is *one particular instantiation* of the concept. Each is *one in number*. Because each is constituted by the universal concept, each is also a *such and such*. Accordingly, each domain of the self-differentiating concept is a *'this such and such'* or what is the same: singularity.

Because the whole system of philosophy constituted by the threefold Encyclopedia constitutes the totality of the self-particularizing concept, Hegel's 'ontological argument' cannot be fully explicated without reconstructing his whole system of philosophy. Accordingly, our reconstruction of the logic of the concept cannot claim to be complete. Whether Hegel's ontological 'argument' is successful requires the Herculean task of reconstructing the creative power of the logic to amplify itself into nature and spirit—a task beyond the scope of this book, but demanded by a close reading of Hegel's text. At most, by reconstructing the self-predicative and existentially implicative dialectics constitutive of the concept as such, we can here successfully gain insight into the *logical structure* of Hegel's 'ontological argument.' By showing how the universal absolutizes itself, or singularizes itself, we can at least show how Hegel's ontological argument can successfully work at the level of *logic* alone.

Notes

1. See Hegel, *SL*, trans. Giovanni, 122; Also see Hegel, *SL*, trans. Miller, 152.
2. For this reason, Rockmore seems to be on the wrong path when he writes that 'the best we can do is to compare our views of the real with what is given in experience in continually adjusting the former in light of the latter. On this view, which I take to be Hegelian, concepts or theories arise within the effort to come to grips with the contents of experience.' Tom Rockmore, "The Pittsburgh School, the Given, and Knowledge," *Social Epistemology, Review and*

Reply Collective 2, no. I (2012): 8, 29–38. Such a description cannot make sense of Hegel's development and appropriation of the ontological argument and cannot be a true description of how the logic of the categories works in the *SL*.

3. Hegel, *SL*, trans. Giovanni, 625.
4. G. W. F. Hegel, *Lectures on the Philosophy of Religion*, trans. R. F. Brown, P. C. Hodgson, and J. M. Stewart (Berkley: University of California Press, 1984), 324.
5. G. W. F. Hegel, *Lectures on the Proofs of the Existence of God*, ed. and trans. Peter C. Hodgson (Oxford: Oxford University Press, 2007), 188.
6. Hegel, *SL*, trans. Giovanni, 626.
7. Ibid, 629.
8. Ibid, 630.
9. Ibid, 628.
10. Objectivity is most immediately the overcoming of the distinction between the middle and the end terms in the syllogism at the close of the logic of the concept. In the overcoming of this syllogistic structure, objectivity overcomes the difference between determiner and determined that arises within the logic of the concept itself.
11. Richard Winfield, "Hegel's Overcoming of the Overcoming of Metaphysics," in H*egel and Metaphysics: On Logic and Ontology in the System*, ed. Allegra de Laurentiis (Berlin: De Gruyter, 2016), 59–71, 67–68.
12. Hegel, *SL*, trans. Giovanni, 626.
13. Ibid, 627.
14. Robert Pippin, "Hegel and Category Theory," *Review of Metaphysics* 43 (June 1990): 839–848, 843.
15. Robert Pippin, *Hegel's Idealism: The Satisfaction of Self-Consciousness* (Cambridge: Cambridge University Press, 1989), 5.
16. Ibid, 178.
17. John McDowell, "Hegel's Idealism as a Radicalization of Kant," in *Having the World in View* (Harvard: Harvard University Press, 2009), 69.
18. Ibid, 86.
19. See Terry Pinkard, "How Kantian Was Hegel?" *Review of Metaphysics* 43, no. 4 (June 7, 1990): 831–838.
20. See Bowman, *Hegel and the Metaphysics of Absolute Negativity*, 124–125.
21. See Houlgate, *The Opening of the Logic*, 137–143.
22. See Bowman, *Hegel and the Metaphysics of Absolute Negativity*, 109.
23. Houlgate, *The Opening of Hegel's Logic*, 115. Or as he puts elsewhere, 'the concept is the true nature of being itself.' See Stephen Houlgate, "Why Hegel's Concept Is not the Essence of Things," in *Hegel's Theory of the Subject*, ed. David Gray Carlson (New York: Palgrave Macmillan, 2005), 19–29, 28.
24. Hegel, *SL*, trans. Miller, 39.
25. Glenn Magee, "Hegel as Metaphysician," in *Hegel and Metaphysics: On Logic and Ontology in the System*, ed. Allegra de Laurentiis (Berlin: De Gruyter, 2016), 43–57, 42.
26. See, for example, the recent paper by Chong-Fuk Lau, "A Deflationary Approach to Hegel's Metaphysics," in H*egel and Metaphysics: On Logic and Ontology in the System*, ed. Allegra de Laurentiis (Berlin: De Gruyter, 2016), 27–41.
27. Stephen Bungay, "The Hegelian Project," in *Hegel Reconsidered: Beyond Metaphysics and the Authoritarian State* (Dordrecht: Kluwer, 1994), 19–43, 38.
28. See Lau, "A Deflationary Approach to Hegel's Metaphysics," 29. For another account of the Absolute as a deflationary concept, see Gabriel, *Transcendental*

Ontology, 113, where he argues that Hegel's concept of the Absolute is 'deflationary.'

29. See Frederick Beiser, "Hegel, a Non-Metaphysician? A Polemic Review of H T Engelhardt and Terry Pinkard (eds), *Hegel Reconsidered*," *Hegel Bulletin* 16, no. 2(32) (1995): 1–13, 3–4.
30. Hegel, *PS*, trans. Pinkard, 46.
31. See Hegel, *SL*, trans. Miller, 25.
32. Kreines, "Hegel's Metaphysics: Changing the Debate," *Philosophy Compass* 1, no. 5 (September 2006): 466–480, 466. Rosen also acknowledges the ontological aspect of Hegel's categories. See Rosen, *The Idea of Hegel's Science of Logic*, 412.
33. See Magee, "Hegel as Metaphysician," 42. See Karin De Boer, *On Hegel: The Sway of the Negative* (New York: Palgrave, 2010), 39.
34. Hegel, *EL*, paragraph 85.
35. See Hegel, *SL*, trans. Miller, 50.
36. De Boar, *The Sway of the Negative*, 36.
37. Hegel, *SL*, trans. Giovanni, 626.
38. Hegel, *Lectures on the Philosophy of Religion*, 324.
39. Hegel, *SL*, trans. Giovanni, 737 (12.238).
40. G. W. F. Hegel, *Hegel's Philosophy of Mind*, trans. William Wallace and A. V. Miller (Oxford: Clarendon Press, 1971), 311, paragraph 573.
41. See Magee's discussion in Magee, "Hegel as Metaphysician," 52. Also see Kevin Harrelson, whose motivation for reconstructing Hegel's ontological argument is to 'combat the non-metaphysical readings of Hegel.' Kevin J. Harrelson, *The Ontological Argument from Descartes to Hegel* (New York: Humanity Books, 2009), 343.
42. Hegel, *Lectures on the Philosophy of Religion*, 84.
43. Pippin, *Hegel's Idealism: The Satisfaction of Self-Consciousness*, 3.
44. Robert Pippin, *Hegel's Realm of Shadows: Logic as Metaphysics in the Science of Logic* (Chicago: University of Chicago Press, 2019), 136.
45. Ibid, 4.
46. Ibid, 59.
47. Ibid, 35.
48. Ibid, 94.
49. See Pippin, *Hegel's Realm of Shadows*, 124n52, 188n4, 278n9.
50. Ibid, 124.
51. Ibid, 188.
52. Ibid, 278.
53. De Boar, *The Sway of the Negative*, 36.
54. Ferrarin, *Hegel and Aristotle*, 197.
55. For further explication of self-reference, see Dieter Henrich's "Hegels Grundoperation. Eine Einleitung in die Wissenschaft der Logik" in *Der Idealismus und der Gegenwart* (Hamburg: Meiner, 1976) and Anton Koch's "Die Selbstbeziehung der Negation in Hegels Logik," *Zeitschrift fuer Philosophische Forschung* 53, no. 1 (January 1999): 1–29, which further develops Henrich's model. Koch is right that in Hegel „die Negation in Hegel's Wissenschafter der Logik selbstreferentiell und autonomatisiert vorkommt." See Koch, „Die Selbstbeziehung der Negation in Hegels Logik," 1.
56. Hegel, *SL*, trans. Miller, 695.
57. Although the Idea is not identical to the concept, the concept is nonetheless a necessary constituent of the Idea. For Hegel, the Idea is the *truth*, or the concept insofar as it is *true*, the unity of the concept (subjectivity) and its object. The Absolute Idea is the self-knowing truth.

58. G. W. F. Hegel, *Introduction to the Philosophy of History*, trans. Leo Rauch (Cambridge: Hackett Publishing Company, 1998), 12–13.
59. Kreines, "Fundamentality Without Metaphysical Monism," 17.
60. G. W. F. Hegel, *Hegel's Philosophy of Nature*, trans. A. V. Miller (Oxford: Oxford University Press, 2004), 15. In his phenomenology, Hegel claims that eternal spirit creates a world. See G. W. F. Hegel, *The Phenomenology of Mind, Vol II* (New York: Routledge, 2013), 769.
61. Hegel, *Hegel's Philosophy of Mind*, 299.
62. Hegel, *Hegel's Philosophy of Nature*, 14–15.
63. Ibid, 14.
64. Hegel, *Hegel's Philosophy of Mind*, 297–298.
65. G. W. F. Hegel, *Introduction to the Philosophy of History*, trans. Leo Rauch (Cambridge: Hackett Publishing Company, 1998), 18.
66. Hegel, *SL*, trans. Giovanni, 625–626.
67. Ibid, 627.
68. F. W. J. Schelling, *On the History of Philosophy*, trans. Andrew Bowie (Cambridge: Cambridge University Press, 1994), 143–144.
69. Magee, "Hegel as Metaphysician," 43–57, 52.
70. Hegel, *SL*, trans. Giovanni, 630.
71. Wendy Lynn Clark and M. Fritzman, "The Nonfoundational Hegelianism of Dove, Maker, and Winfield," *The Philosophical Forum* 34, no. 1 (Spring 2013): 29.
72. Hegel, *SL*, trans. Giovanni, 62.
73. Ibid, Remark, 64.
74. Hegel, *SL*, trans. Giovanni, 64–65.
75. Ibid, Remark I (Being-Nothing-Becoming), 64–65.
76. Hegel, *SL*, trans. Giovanni, 66.
77. Ibid.
78. See Ibid, Remark I in the logic of Being, 62–66.
79. Hegel, *Lectures on the Proofs of the Existence of God*, 190.
80. Hegel, *SL*, trans. Giovanni, 627.
81. Ibid, 66.
82. Ibid.
83. As Rosen notes, in Kantian terms, Hegel does not distinguish between existence and predication. Rosen, *The Idea of Hegel's Science of Logic*, 418.
84. R. G. Collingwood, *An Essay on Philosophical Methodology*, ed. James Connelly and Guiseppina D'oro (Oxford: Oxford University Press, 2005), 131.
85. Hegel, *SL*, trans. Giovanni, 64–65.
86. McDowell, "Hegel's Idealism as a Radicalization of Kant," 86.
87. Hegel, *SL*, trans. Giovanni, 514.
88. Ibid, 515.
89. Ibid, 520.
90. Ibid.
91. Ibid.
92. Ibid, 516.
93. Ibid, 518.
94. Ibid.
95. Ibid, 520.
96. See the usual suspects, for example Descartes' *Meditations*, Spinoza's *Ethics*, and Anselm's *Proslogion*.
97. Hegel, *SL*, trans. Giovanni, 522.
98. Hegel, *Lectures on the Proofs of the Existence of God*, 190.
99. Ibid, 191.

100. Clark and Fritzman, "The Nonfoundational Hegelianism of Dove, Maker, and Winfield," 9.

101. If the argument fails, as Harrelson indicates, then this is not a particular problem for Hegel, since it is not an argument in the first place. See Harrelson, *The Ontological Argument from Descartes to Hegel*, 220.

102. See Paul Redding and Paulo Diego Bubblio, "Ontological Argument: Hegel and the Ontological Argument for the Existence of God," *Religious Studies* 50, no. 4 (December 2014): 465–486.

103. Graham Oppy, "Ontological Arguments," *Stanford Encyclopedia of Philosophy*, https://plato.stanford.edu/entries/ontological-arguments/.

104. Hegel, *Philosophische Encyclopedia*, Nuernberg 1812/13 (Hamburg: Meiner Verlag, 1992), paragraph 13, 58.

105. For an in-depth comparison and history of the ontological argument in early modern philosophy, see Harrelson's *The Ontological Argument from Descartes to Hegel*.

106. G. W. F. Hegel, *Elements of the Philosophy of Right*, ed. Allen W. Wood, trans. H. B. Nisbet (Cambridge: Cambridge University Press, 1991), 20.

107. See Robert Stern, *Hegelian Metaphysics* (Oxford: Oxford University Press, 2009), 111. Stern cites this passage from *Hegel in Berichten seiner Zeitgenossen*, ed. Guenter Nicolin, paragraph 383, 254–255.

108. Because the concept is the power of self-objectification, and existence or objectivity (self-sufficient existence) to be more precise, is its *Wirkung*, I cannot agree with McCumber's reading that Hegel's concept of philosophy concerns keeping 'company with words, rather than with extralinguistic realities.' It certainly keeps company with both, since the latter is just as much inundated with the concept as the former. See John McCumber, *Company of Words: Hegel, Language, and Systematic Philosophy* (Evanston: Northwestern Press, 1993), 20.

109. In order to fully work out the connections between the ontological argument in Hegel's logic and issues concerning possibility, actuality, and necessity, a thorough explication of the logic of possibility, actuality, and necessity would be necessary (no pun intended). For a recent and stimulating reading and reconstruction of these categories, see Brown, *Hegel on Possibility*, 105–134.

110. Hegel, *Philosophy of History*, 39.

111. See Paolo Diego Bubbio, Allessandro De Cesaris, Maurizio Pagano, and Hager Weslati, eds., *Hegel, Logic, and Speculation* (London: Bloomsbury, 2019).

112. G. W. F. Hegel, "Vorlesung Über Logik und Metaphysik: Heidelberg 1817," in *Ausgewaelte Vorlesungenund Manuskripten, Vol. 11* (Hamburg: Meiner Verlag, 1992), 145–146.

113. Patricia Marie Carlton, *Hegel's Metaphysics of God: The Ontological Proof as the Development of a Trinitarian Ontology* (Burlington: Ashgate, 2001), 82.

114. See Hegel's *Philosophy of Mind*, 303: 'Nothing easier therefore for the "Rationalist" than to point out contradictions in the exposition of the faith, and then to prepare triumphs for its principle of formal identity. If the spirit yields to this finite reflection, which has usurped the title of reason and philosophy—("Rationalism")—it strips religious truth of its infinity and makes it in reality nought. Religion in that case is completely in the right in guarding herself against such reason and philosophy and treating them as enemies. But it is another thing when religion sets herself against comprehending reason, and against philosophy in general, and specially against a philosophy

of which the doctrine is speculative, and so religious. Such an opposition proceeds from failure to appreciate the difference indicated and the value of spiritual form in general, and particularity of the logical form; or to be more precise still, from failure to note the distinction of the content—*which may be in both the same*—from these forms' [my emphasis].

115. Hegel is clear that 'there is divine providence presiding over the events of the world.' See Hegel, *Introduction to the Philosophy of History*, 15.
116. Bowman, *Hegel and the Metaphysics of Absolute Negativity*, 32.
117. Ibid, 33.
118. Also see Richard Winfield, *From Concept to Objectivity: Thinking Through Hegel's Subjective Logic* (Burlington: Ashgate, 2006), 141. There is a well-known debate about to grasp the relation between logic and nature. See Maker and Halper on this issue.

12 Forms of Ideality in Hegel's Logic
Being, Essence, and Concept

Having *externally* motivated the need for the concept of self-particularization by appealing to a set of metaphysical and epistemic problems plaguing the Western tradition, I now mean to provide an *internal* motivation for the concept of self-particularization by placing it in the context of the *Science of Logic*. Although self-differentiation is an ideality in virtue of the way that it turns back on itself, there are other forms of ideality distinct from the concept. Each division of Hegel's *Wissenschaft der Logik*, the logic of Being, Essence, and the *Doctrine of the Concept*, expounds a *distinct kind* of ideality with a distinct form of *back-turning*. So although the concept of the concept is an ideality, not every ideality is the concept of the concept.

The Logic of Being

In order to properly demarcate the structure of the universal against other categories of the logic, Hegel makes an effort to compare the concept with categories from the logic of Being and Essence. Let us begin with Being and proceed therefrom to consider his comparison of the concept with Essence. Because the comparisons between the various forms of logic are very abstract, if you will, I will give an example of the kind of logical process from each of the divisions of the logic, in order that the reader might have a concrete reference with which to compare the logic of the concept. On the difference between the logic of Being and the *Doctrine of the Concept*, Hegel writes the following:

> Accordingly, because of this original unity, the first negative, or the *determination*, is not, to begin with, a restriction for the universal; rather, the latter *maintains itself in it* and its self-identity is positive. The categories of being were, as concepts, essentially these identities of the determinations with themselves in their restriction or their otherness; but this identity was only *implicitly* the concept, was not yet made manifest. Consequently, the qualitative determination perished as such in its other and had as its truth a determination *diverse*

from it. The universal, on the contrary, even when it posits itself in a determination, *remains* in it what it is. It is the soul of the concrete which it inhabits, unhindered and equal to itself in its manifoldness and diversity. It is not swept away in the becoming but persists undisturbed through it, endowed with the power of unalterable, undying self-preservation.[1]

Hegel writes that in the logic of Being 'this identity was only implicitly [*an sich*] the Concept' for it 'was not yet made manifest.' Hegel's meaning is simple. In the logic of Being there is a process of self-differentiation, for this is evident in the immediate self-othering of categories of the categories of Being. By 'immediate self-othering' I mean that immediately upon being what it is, the category is what it is not. For example, Being, in virtue of what it is, is immediately nothing. There is no process intervening here: Being is immediately nothing, and nothing Being. Still, this process of self-differentiation in the logic of Being is not explicitly a process of self-differentiation. Self-differentiation as such does not appear in the Logic of Being. Only in the *Doctrine of the Concept* does self-differentiation as such appear. In the logic of Being the concept is not yet manifested. Instead, the categories of Being are only 'in themselves' conceptual. This means that each of the categories of Being are indeed concepts, although their conceptual content fails to be the very what it is to be of the concept *per se*. Although ideality makes its first appearance in the logic of Being, it does not make its last appearance there. The logic of Essence is also constituted by a process of ideality, although the way that otherness is overcome in that logic is quite different from the process in the logic of Being. In the logic of Essence, a process of reflection and mediation is at work there that is absent in the logic of Being. What counts as a transition in the logic of Being becomes a reflection in the logic of Essence.

Ideality in the logic of Being, such as in the transition of the category of the one to the void, renders the negation of the other an internal absence of the other in what negates the other. In the logic of Being each content loses itself in its transition to the other. It is only preserved in its negation, or as its other. It only exists as its other, or that into which it has transitioned. It does not maintain itself in its othering, in its transition, as the concept does. There is a return to self in the transition, but this return self-negates the beginning and gives rise to a new determination.

For some, the comparison between Being and the *Doctrine of the Concept* may appear to be a pedantic comparison that only serves those already familiar with the logic. Still, I think Hegel's comparison of the contents is helpful, exactly because it sheds light on how *not* to think about the development of particularity and singularity out of universality. It is particularly pertinent to our discourse, for it illuminates Hegel's criticism of the history of philosophy without having to name philosophers by name. In the history of philosophy, from Plato onwards, the universal is quite often, and without much resistance, defined as the 'one over many.' For Hegel, the concept of the 'one' belongs to the logic of Being, not the logic of the concept. As long as philosophers conflate concepts such as 'one' with 'concept,' we shall never get any clarity on the problems that plague our attempts to know *what* the concept *is*. In order to better illuminate Hegel's comparison between the logic of Being and *Doctrine of the Concept*, I have included a short explication of the transition from one to void in Hegel's logic of Being. What should become most evident here is the way that the transition from one to void happens. One, in virtue of the very *absence of otherness* within itself, *becomes* the void. It is not in virtue of the self-differentiating *content* and *activity* of the one that it is the void, but in virtue of the lack of all content whatever that leads it to the void. Let us take a brief look at the transition to illuminate the difference.[2]

Here in the logic of Being there is not yet a distinction between determiner and determined. The immediate content, the determiner, of itself becomes the void, and being-for-self now only is as the void, until the void of itself becomes what it is not. The movement of one into void is representative of the logic of Being as a development of *Ideality*. Although Ideality makes its *first* appearance in the logic of Being, it does not make its last appearance there. As we shall see, the logic of Essence is *also* constituted by a process of ideality, although the way that otherness is overcome in that logic will be quite different from the process in the logic of Being. In the logic of Essence, a process of reflection and mediation is at work there that is absent in the logic of Being. What counts as a transition in the logic of Being becomes a reflection in the logic of Essence.

Ideality in the logic of Being, for example in being-for-self, Being-for-one, and the one, renders the negation of the other an internal absence of the other in what negates the other. This ensures the immediate unity of determiner and determined in this move to the void, as the immediate being of the one. This shows that ideality in the logic of Being is integral to transition and the immediate self-determination of the thought-determinations here at hand. Indeed, each content loses itself in its transition. It is only preserved in its negation, or *as its other*. It only exists as its other, or that into which it has transitioned. It does not maintain itself in its othering, in its transition, as the concept does. There is a return to self in the transition, but this return to self negates the beginning and gives rise to a *new* determination.

One of the big mistakes of the tradition, for Hegel, is the mistake to universal for the one, which is a category in the logic of Being. The universal incorporates the determinacy of the one, but is not merely the one, for it has a richer content. Unlike the mere one and being-for-self, the immediate unity of self-differentiation is the immediate identity of all of its differences, not the absence of any difference whatever. In the logic of Being, it is the *very absence of any difference* whatever that characterizes the form of ideality. At the very outset of the *Doctrine of the Concept*, Hegel points out that the logic of Being and Essence are *unified* in the concept.[3] Hegel claims that the concept, the fulfillment of ideality as such, is constituted by the interpenetration of categories in the logic of Being and Essence. Self-differentiation as such is constituted by the interpenetration of two forms of ideality: one that is present in the categories of Being, and one that is present in the categories of Essence. In this way, self-differentiation is ideality fulfilled, or ideality perfected. In order to fully grasp the Logic of the Concept, therefore, one must have a basic grasp of the form of the logic of Essence.

At the very outset of the, Hegel points out that the logics are unified in the concept:

> The concept is the mutual penetration of these moments, namely the qualitative and the originative existent is only as positing and as immanent turning back, and this pure immanent reflection simply is the *becoming-other* of *determinateness* which is, consequently, no less infinite, self-referring *determinateness*.[4]

Because the concept is the interfusion of the logics of Being and Essence, in order to lay bare the concept as such, we must have a firm grasp of the *form* of the logic of Essence as well as the logic of Being. As I mentioned earlier, in his explication of the concept Hegel will constantly refer to terms that have their origin in the logic of Essence, and he will give special status to the term 'illusion.' In order to lay bare the meaning of the term 'illusion,' as well as explicate the form of the logic of Essence in general, I shall reconstruct the opening moves in the dialectic of Essence from *Essence* to *determining reflection* in which the term 'illusion' first makes its systematic appearance.

The Logic of Essence

Essence is that which posits or mediates that which is mediated. It is that first thought-determination of the logic of Essence, which arises from measure and the regress of measures in the logic of Being. Essence is the outcome of the determinations in the logic of Being. Still, Essence is not merely immediate, for its determination is *that which posits*. As that which posits, Essence is not that which is posited. That which is posited is not Essence. Since Essence is not what is posited, or is not that which is not positing, that which is not the positing is the unessential. Essence is present, or arises from Being as that which posits Being. As that which posits Being, the determinations of Being become present as that which Essence immediately is not, and Essence thereby excludes the unessential from itself as the positer of the determinations of Being. According to the very content of Essence, the very first determination of Essence is the *opposition* of Essence to the unessential. The unessential appears to be the *other* to Essence and Essence *appears* to be the other to the unessential.

If each were *a* something opposed to *an* other, then both would be self-subsistent, or independent determinations. This cannot be the case, for the unessential is exactly that which is posited by Essence, and for this reason it cannot be independent of Essence. If it were independent, then it would be that which mediates, not that which is itself mediated. Whatever is mediated is dependent upon that which mediates. The unessential, in itself, is that which is *not* self-subsistent, but is, according to its own content, dependent. It is that which *only appears to be the other to Essence*, but is not. Accordingly, it is *illusory being*. The *unessential is the illusion of self-subsistence*, or that which is but is *not* self-subsistent. The determinations of Being, as posited, are only illusory in Essence, and in this sense the *formula* of illusory being may be stated as *the non-self-subsistent that shows as self-subsistent*. Thus, the unessential is not the other to Essence, but is only the mere illusion of being an other to Essence, for it only has being *in* the positing of Essence. In sum, the unessential is illusory being, and illusory being is the *remainder* of Being, or what is left over. Since Essence is that which is self-subsistent, and illusory being is the illusion of the self-subsistent, illusory being is *the illusion of Essence*.

Since the illusory being is posited, and what is posited requires something that posits it, illusory being *points* to the positer, Essence, as its origin. To use Hegel's terms, as the illusion of Essence, illusory being *reflects*, or shows forth Essence as its illusion or posited being. Reflection is a return of Essence to itself through what it posits. This 'return to self' is not a negation of the difference between that which posits and the posited. Here in Essence, the reflection of one in the other preserves the difference between determiner and determined. Essence is *first* reflected in the positing of illusory being.[5]

Since Essence, as the mediator, does not determine the content of that which it puts forth in the positing, it must *presuppose* some content to mediate and posit. In Hegel's terms, Essence is *indifferent* to the determinations of the content which it posits. As we noted earlier, if one thing mediates another, one only knows that one thing is posited by another, but one does not know *why the content which is posited has the determinations which it does*. For instance, the fact that Being, as quantity and quality, is posited by that which posits, the Essence, does not itself specify why the contents posited are quantitative and qualitative contents. These contents were developed earlier in the logic of Being. Since the positing is indifferent to the determinations of the content, it must take up such contents *as given* or presuppose them.

Once Essence takes up these given contents, which were developed earlier, and takes them up as posited, their *mode of being changes* from being immediate categories of Being to being posited contents of Essence, or that which is the illusion of Essence. In the sense that the contents are posited contents, the contents *as* posited only come to be once they are determinations of Essence. In this sense, Essence determines the contents of what it posits insofar as the contents have the determination of positedness. In this sense, what is posited is not external to Essence, but internal. Accordingly, the positing and reflection of Essence are internal to the very activity of Essence itself.

What is posited is what is presupposed by Essence in *its act* of positing. Since there is nothing posited until Essence posits, there is nothing presupposed until Essence presupposes the posit. In the act of presupposing the posit, Essence *transforms* the content of what it posits from something external to Essence *into* something posited. In the act of presupposing the external content, the content ceases to be an external content. Instead, its content is now wholly determined as that which is posited, or more simply, *as the posited*. Naturally, this means that there cannot be a presupposition external to Essence. No presupposition exists *except in the positing* of Essence. This means that what is external to Essence is *only external* to Essence once Essence gives itself the given as a posit. In other words, only once the content it is rendered internal to Essence is there any 'external content' to speak of. Thus, the external posit must be internal to Essence itself, as that which belongs to the positing of Essence. From this it follows that *there is only that which is external to Essence within Essence itself*.

Reflecting upon the process of determining reflection further, we notice that it is not simply the external content of the presupposition that is transformed but it is also the very content of the positer itself. Initially, Essence appeared to be laden with the given content 'that which posits.' But in the act of positing, the character of Essence is also transformed. At the outset, Essence is simply that which posits. Until the act of positing however, Essence is not yet a positer, and cannot reflect itself in what it posits. Because it is in virtue of positing that *the positer exists as a positer*, Essence achieves its character as that which posits only in virtue of the act of positing. Thus, the act of positing negates the given character of Essence and posits Essence itself as one element of the positing relation. For this reason, Essence gives itself its own character as the reflecting relation. Essence is now no longer just the positer, for it is now constituted by a relation of reflection that has two sides: positer and posited. Each side is a function and result of the activity of positing. Accordingly, both the givenness of the positer as well as the externality of what is posited are negated. Now both become moments of one content: *the process of reflection*. To put it another way, Essence, in virtue of the activity of positing, is not just the positer, but the activity of reflection itself, which has swallowed up its own assumptions, namely the external character of itself and the content of what it originally posited. Essence 'returns to itself' in the case of *determining* reflection by transforming its own character.

Because Essence has posited its own character as that which posits, Essence has posited it own positing, or what is the same, it has reflected its own reflection. Hence, Essence is not mediated by any externality, but is *only self-mediated.* Insofar as the presupposition belongs to Essence itself, Essence is *reflected reflection,* or *mediated mediation.* External reflection is reflected in determining reflection, rendering Essence an internal mediated reflection in self. Essence is therefore not merely an immediate mediation, an external reflection, or a development out of the logic of Being. On the contrary, as self-mediating, it has its own determination. Since the positedness is itself reflected, Essence is *self-mediated [Mediation].* Essence's reflection in self is not merely an immediate reflection in self as in Illusory being, or a merely external reflection, but it is a *mediated reflection in self.* As self-mediated its positing is its self-relation and *reflects its reflection.* Essence as self-mediated has its *own internal content* and is self-identical. Internally it owes its own difference to itself, since it gives itself its own difference. Hegel goes on to explicate how Identity and difference develop out of the self-mediating and determining reflective character of Essence.[6]

Although the logic of Essence is an ideality, it is an ideality in which determiner and determined are nonetheless opposed to each other. Given our analysis, we have the resources to interpret the following passage:

> The *universal* is posited, on the contrary, as the *essence* of its determination, as this determination's *own positive nature.* For the determination that constitutes the negative of the universal is in the concept simply and solely a *positedness;* essentially, in other words, it is at the same time the negative of the negative, and only is as this self-identity of the negative which is the universal. To this extent the universal is also the *Substance* of its determinations, but in such a way that for the Substance as such was an *accident,* is the concept's own self-*mediation,* its own *immanent* reflection. But this mediation, which first raises the accidental to *necessity,* is the *manifested* reference; the concept is not the abyss of formless Substance, or the necessity which is the *inner* identity of things or circumstances different from each other and reciprocally constricting; rather, as absolute negativity, it is the informing and creative principle, and since the determination is not as limitation but is just as much simply sublated as determination, is positedness, so is the reflective shine the appearance as appearance of *the identical.*[7]

In the first instance of the logic of Essence, Essence only *shows* in the other, and it has the form of an 'external act.' The concept does not merely 'show' in its other or have 'illusory being.' The determinations of the universal, for example the universal, particular, and singular, do not relate to the universal as unessential moments of a relationship of positing. Instead, the determinations of the universal constitute 'its own positive nature.' If the moments of the concept did relate to the concept as the Essential relates to the unessential, each moment of the concept could not be the whole concept. Nonetheless, Hegel claims that 'the concept is the essential being of its determination.' Here Hegel seems to mean that the determinations of the concept result from the *activity* or the 'positing' of the concept *per se*. Still, because the universal is self-differentiating, the identity of the universal cannot be separated from the identity of its determinations or what it determines itself to be. Hegel claims that the universal is 'simply and solely a positedness' and that this is no other than 'the negative of the negative.' Here Hegel seems to mean that, unlike the character of Essence, in the negation of negation that which posits and that which is posited are *wholly identical*. The universal, by 'positing itself,' if we insist on that terminology, is just a pure positing, or what is the same, the *transcending* of the relation of positing altogether.

In contradistinction to transition, which is characteristic of the logic of Being, in the logic of Essence there can only be a reflection if difference is maintained. Essence cannot reflect if there is not something posited which reflects it. In the act of positing, Essence indeed negates any external mediation, and it thusly transcends all otherness. For this reason, in the category of determining reflection Essence also achieves ideality. But the transcending of otherness in the logic of Essence preserves a difference and mediation within itself, for its way of transcending otherness is a positing. A positing is such that it maintains the distinction between determiner and determined. In this way, reflection transcends otherness while maintaining the distinction between that which reflects and that which is reflected within its own self. Ideality in the logic of Being transcends otherness by rendering it absent within its own self, while the logic of Essence and its categories preserves some internal difference. In unifying itself to what it is not, Essence does not abolish the other or become identical in content with the other, but preserves what it is not within itself as different from itself. This tension is maintained until the development of the concept in which the distinction between determiner and determined is abolished.[8]

Just as the universal is not 'the one,' it is also not to be identified with the category of 'substance' which belongs to the logic of Essence, not the *Doctrine of the Concept*. Substance in Hegel's logic is a self-identical being. For Hegel, any alteration or alterable determinacies of substance is not a result of the substance itself, for as substance it is a mere self-identity and is not the principle of its differences. Accordingly, such alterations or alterable determinacies are accidents of the substance, which are contingent to its *a priori* identity. Because substance is not sufficient to account for its own alterations, substances cannot be self-determining or self-differentiating. The accidents are a 'contingency' for substance, because the relation of attribute to substance is external to what the substance is. Given that the substance is not the cause of its own accidents, the accidents and alterations must have their origin in some other substance or substances. When we consider the logic of substance, we immediately discover why it would be erroneous to identify the concept with the concept of substance. Because the cause of the accident is not in the substance that bears it, in substance there cannot be any self-determination. Instead, every alteration of substance is due to a factor that is external to it. Hegel spells out this relationship in terms of cause and effect. What is absent in substance is the identity of the substance and its determinations, namely its attributes and alterations. In order to discover the determinate states of the substance and distinguish self-identical substances from one another, we must appeal to other substances.

The Logic of the Concept

Having illuminated the basic forms of Ideality in the logic of Being and the logic of Essence, we are in a position to return to the very first paragraph of the chapter on universality, in which Hegel analyzes the concept in terms of its origin in the logic of Being and the logic of Essence:

> It is here, as the *content* of our treatise begins to be the concept itself that we must look back once more at its genesis. *Essence came to be out of being*, and the concept out of essence, therefore also from being. But this becoming has the meaning of a self-*repulsion*, so that *what becomes* is rather the *unconditional* and the *originative*. In passing over into essence, *being* became a *reflective shine* or a *positedness*, and *becoming* or the passing over into an *other* became a *positing*; conversely, the *positing* or the reflection of essence sublated itself and restored itself to a *non-posited*, an *original being*. The concept is the mutual penetration of these moments, namely the qualitative and the originative existent is only as positing and as immanent turning back, and this pure immanent reflection simply is the *becoming-other* of *determinateness* which is, consequently, no less infinite, self-referring *determinateness*.[9]

At the outset of this paragraph, Hegel recites the basic moves that have given rise to the *Doctrine of the Concept* in the *Science of Logic*. Essence arises out of Being, and *Doctrine of the Concept* in turn arises out of Essence. What is of interest to us is not the details of the whole development, but how the development of the concept sheds light on what the concept is. Hegel points out that the development of the concept is a 'self-repulsion,' in which the outcome of the process is the 'unconditioned and original.' Hegel continues to emphasize the outcome of 'originality'. Being became positedness, and transition became a positing. So far Hegel is simply rehearsing the system and pointing out the different structures of the logics of Being and Essence. What is striking is what comes next: positing has 'restored itself to a *non-posited* [*Nichtgesetztsein*], an *original being*.'[10] In what sense can the concept as such be the 'original being'? This question becomes especially urgent given the fact that it is the outcome of previous processes. In order to grasp the overall structure of the development of the concept, we must have some sense of where the concept falls in the *Logic* and how it both relates to other categories and ought to be differentiated from them. In doing so, we shall narrow the scope of our concern and avoid equivocation. Having elucidated the basic senses in which the categories of Essence and Being are idealities, we have the resources to illuminate this claim.[11]

The most obvious response to the question: 'in what sense is the concept the original being?' is quite simple. Given that the concept is self-differentiation, it is wholly self-determining. As self-determining, it is wholly original. What is original is not a copy or imitation of something else. The original is the beginning, and as the beginning it is novel. Naturally, self-differentiation appears to fit the bill. Yet, Hegel does not begin with self-differentiation in the *Logic*. Instead, the *Logic* begins with Being. We shall have the opportunity to discuss why Hegel begins the *Logic* with Being in a later section of this chapter, and we shall motivate that beginning only after having dissected the being of the concept. Still, why not claim that 'Being is the original being'? It is, after all, what comes first. Notoriously, Hegel thinks that the beginning is the end. But again, such dictums do not solve the problem; they only worsen it. After all, 'how can the beginning be the end?' is structurally analogous to 'how could the original being be an outcome of a previous process?' Upon elucidating the structure of the concept, we shall have reconstructed the whole of the Logic in the *microcosm* of the concept. By doing so, we shall have insight into the meaning of the phrase: 'the beginning is the end.' Nevertheless, I do not wish to fully postpone this discussion, for we already have the resources to grasp a basic sense in which the concept is the original being despite being an outcome.

The transition from the logic of Essence to the *Doctrine of the Concept* may provide some headway regarding this question.[12] The result of the concept of substance is cause and effect. It is the self-negation of the categories of cause and effect that gives rise to the concept. The cause, as a cause, gives rise to an effect. The effect is that which is produced by the cause, and the cause is that which produces the effect. When we think about the relationship, we usually immediately think about examples of particular causes, especially natural ones. But to see how the concept of cause and effect give rise to the concept, we must consider the concepts themselves, not our favorite examples. The effect, we know, would not be the effect without the cause. But it is equally the case that there would not be any cause if there were no effect. The condition for the existence of causation is the existence of the effect, and the condition for the existence of the effect is the existence of the cause. Because the effect is a condition of the cause, the effect itself is the cause of the effect. Likewise, the cause, as an effect of the effect, is no longer simply a cause but also an effect. Thus, the cause is both cause and effect, and the effect is both cause and effect. reciprocal causation gives rise to the self-cause, or what is the same: the concept. As is evident, the transition from cause and effect to the concept is analogous to the process by which the logic of Essence developed. The cause, in virtue of causation, gives rise not only to the effect, but more importantly, gives rise to itself. As the cause of causation, the concept of cause develops into the concept of the concept. Although there is an authentic opposition among substance, cause and effect, and freedom, in the *Logic* these oppositions are overcome.

Given that the logic of the concept ought not be identified with Essence or Being, it is deeply problematic to identify the universal with thing-hood, relation, or the one. Hegel's liberation of the absolute concept from the confines of the logical relations constitutive of the logic of Being and Essence signifies a break from the tradition that is primarily con-cerned with thinking the form of *things*, as is the case with Aristotle, or *relations*, as is the case with Kant. As long as philosophy privileges things or relations as fundamental to the structure of Being and know-ing, it will miss the central aspect of the Absolute, namely that it is *the self-particularizing concept*. Far from completely disappearing however, relationality and Thinghood are cancelled and preserved in the concept, as is the case with all the previous categories.

In the previous discussion I have, albeit very briefly, reconstructed the process in the *Logic* whereby what is original and unconditioned arises out of categories in the logic of Essence. As is evident, the original being is *initially* the result of *the self-negation* of the categories of cause and effect. Earlier we motivated the positing of 'self-differentiation' from *the self-negation* of the separation of the principles of universal-ity and particularity. Indeed, as long as one's concept of the concept remains tied to the logic of Essence, one must insist on the separation of the principles of universality and particularity. What we also noted earlier was that the self-negation of the separation of the principles of universality and particularity do *not* give rise to just *nothing*. If the self-negation of the logic of Essence were to give rise to just nothing, then the logic of Essence would not have negated itself. Instead, it would be re-instated, for the assumption that self-negation, or contra-diction, results in utter nothingness is itself one of the central theses of formal thinking. Instead, the result of the self-negation of the logic of Essence is the identity of determiner and determined. Or, as we formu-lated it in our initial discussion of Hegel, the result of the self-negation of separation of universality and particularity is the self-differentiating concept.

The concept is the 'mutual penetration' of Being and Essence:

> The concept is the mutual penetration of these moments, namely the qualitative and the originative existent is only as positing and as immanent turning back, and this pure immanent reflection simply is the *becoming-other* of *determinateness* which is, consequently, no less infinite, self-referring *determinateness*.[13]

'Mutual penetration' is the translation of *Durchdringung*, which more literally translated, is the 'pushing through' or 'pressing through.' The qualitative being of the concept is the unity of reflection into self (positing) and the sheer becoming other (transition). On the one hand, in the logic of Essence, the difference between determiner and determined places categories in terms of pure *mediation*. On the other hand, the logic of Being the absence of difference places categories in terms of pure immediacy. In the former, all immediacy is on the side of mediation. In the latter, all mediation is on the side of immediacy. For example, the transition from Being to determinate being is an *immediate transition*, in which Being undergoes a transition into nothing, a process of mediation, yet that transition is immediate. On the other hand, in the positing of Essence, the immediate content of Being is a function of the process of mediation (*Setzen*). In each case there is a unity of immediacy and mediation that is constitutive of different forms of ideality. Still, the unity of immediacy and mediation is only ever one-sided: in other words, the unity of immediacy and mediation is only ever given in the form of *either* immediacy or mediation, but *not both*.

In self-differentiation or pure ideality, there is the *unification* of both types of ideality in ideality itself: self-differentiation. The consequence of this unity is the 'infinite, self-relating, determinateness.' Fittingly, ideality in Being and ideality in Essence is preserved in the concept of ideality as such, as that which unifies Being to Essence and Essence to Being. Self-differentiation insofar as it differentiates itself, must immediately be what it is not, and in this respect, it is a 'sheer becoming other' and expresses ideality in the form of Being. Yet, it is also a 'reflection into itself' insofar as it is the self-identical being that posits or puts forward its own determinations. Nonetheless, because self-differentiation posits differences with which it is *identical*, its 'reflection into self' really is nothing other than its 'sheer becoming other,' and its 'sheer becoming other' is nothing more than its 'reflection into self.'[14] In the concept, the determinations of Being and Essence are raised into conceptual determinations.

In the logic of Being there is transition. Each returns to itself out of its other. The returning to itself out of its other is characteristic of ideality. In the category of the one otherness is simply absent. The one just is the void. It is the very absence of any difference whatever that gives the new differences. The very content of the one transforms into the content of the void. In this process, the content is lost in its new other, and by losing itself in its transformation, it returns to itself. The self-differentiating universal is distinguished from both. Unlike the logic of Being, the self-differentiating concept does not lose itself in its self-othering. In the process of ideality the self-differentiating universal remains the self-differentiating universal. Unlike the logic of Essence, in the self-differentiating concept all differences between determiner and determined vanish.

When we look over the logic of Being and Essence we encounter different forms of ideality and corresponding forms of back-turning. All are idealities, but different forms of ideality and back-turning. Hegel himself points out that the determinations of the Logic are categories insofar as they unite themselves with their opposites.[15] In the concept we encounter ideality as self-differentiation as such. Prior to the concept of the concept, every determination 'was only *implicitly* [an sich] the concept, was not yet made manifest.'[16] Ideality and back-turning are at work in Being and Essence as transition, and as positing but have not yet appeared *as self-differentiation*, as the principle of ideality or development.

Finally, in the concept as such, we just have the 'what it is to be the concept.' The concept is original for exactly this reason: the concept is the process of conceptual development that has always been at work in *the Logic*, both in the logic of Being as transition and the logic of Essence as positing, yet never as itself, as self-differentiating development. For this reason, the *Doctrine of the Concept* is a 'turning back into itself,' or a 'return-into-itself' [*Rückkehr-in-sich*]. The development of the *Doctrine of the Concept* is a result of the back-turning or *palintropos* of the whole of the logic of Being and Essence into the form of conceptual determination as such. Self-differentiation is the fulfillment and perfection of the *palintropos* of ideality as transition and positing.

For example, the categorial difference between 'identity' and 'difference' dialectically undermines itself, but its result is ultimately *another form of the distinction between determiner and determined*, namely 'ground' and 'grounded.' Although the logic is particularizing itself in this series of categories in the logic of Essence, not only is the category 'self-particularization' itself not yet at hand, but the application of the category of 'self-particularization' to 'difference' can only occur *after* the development of self-particularization as such. Upon the *complete* development of self-particularization in the logic of the concept, namely in the *Absolute Idea*, we discover that *positing* and *transition* were forms of the self-particularization of categories all along. Thus, by proceeding from transition to positing, and finally to self-particularization and its forms, positing and transition are not just left behind, but 'return to themselves,' or what is the same, they become *instances of conceptual development* themselves. Accordingly, they do not remain 'separate thought determinations' that are determinate beings other than conceptual development. Because the concept of 'self-particularization' has not yet arisen in the logic of Being or the *Doctrine of the Concept*, merely as transition or as positing they are not yet explicitly determined to be *instances* of conceptual determination. To put this in Hegelian terms, the categories of Being and Essence are in fact categories, but they are not yet determined to be categories—they are 'external to themselves' or alienated from their categorial character. Naturally, one can only know that this is the case from the standpoint of the *Doctrine of the Concept*.

In order to understand how the process of self-differentiation works in Being or Essence as transition and positing, we must understand the process of self-differentiation as such, or what Hegel calls 'development,' since the latter is the 'truth' of the former. In transition self-differentiation works through the absence of difference, and in positing self-differentiation works through the internalization of difference and the transformation of the two opposing sides of that internal difference. In the concept the process of self-differentiation is no longer in a form that is *alien to itself*: transition or positing. To the contrary, in the concept, ideality actually corresponds with the form of its very development: self-differentiation. Accordingly, it is in the concept of self-differentiation where the process of ideality is true to itself. At the stage of the concept, self-differentiation differentiates itself into self-differentiation. Indeed, by following the self-differentiation of self-differentiation the determinacy of the concept reveals itself to us. In its self-revelation, the concept is revealing not only what it is, but *what it is for any concept to be a concept*. For this reason, if we understand the revelation of the concept, we shall be grasping the form of the conceptual development as such in the *Science of Logic*.

In his commentary on the *Doctrine of the Concept*, McTaggart admits that he is unable to follow the development of the concept out of the previous categories and fails to understand how the universal or the singular could follow from the dialectical development. McTaggart goes on to provide his own account of the transition. Unfortunately, McTaggart appears to have forced a foreign notion of universality onto Hegel's text. He defines the universal as the 'common quality found in two or more things,'[17] which only expresses the self-identity of the universal, but fails to distinguish it from the universality that is *merely* abstract in form. Moreover, McTaggart also seems to insist upon a distinction between the singular and the universal: 'The universal must be common to many individuals, while the individual has to be determined by many universals.'[18] For Hegel, the universal just *is* the singular. The 'individual' or singular is not merely that which is determined by many universals. I would suggest that part of McTaggart's confusion regarding the transition is grounded on misconceptions of Hegel's concepts of universality and particularity which have their origin in traditional ways of thinking about universality.

Expressed positively, what is absent from McTaggart's position is the self-determining and self-differentiating character of the universal that provides the bridge from the *Essence* to the concepts of particularity and singularity.

Looking Ahead: The Formality of the Concept, Truth, and the Absolute Idea

Since the main objective of my reconstruction of Hegel's position is to demonstrate how Hegel solves these traditional and difficult metaphysical problems, I will not lose myself in a detailed commentary on the *Science of Logic*. Nonetheless, in order to clarify the scope and limit of my analysis, it would be prudent to *delineate the difference* between a number of important and relevant concepts that can only arise after (and rely upon) Hegel's elucidation of the concept, such as objectivity, truth, and the Absolute Idea. Accordingly, in the following I briefly delineate the meaning of the concept in connection to what categories arise after the development of universality, particularity, and singularity. In the spirit of Hegel's dictum that the truth is the whole, in the following we will carve out important aspects of the context in which the concept appears and give a sense of the importance of the concept of the concept for further developments in the logic.

What arises out of the self-negation of the category of causation is the *concept* or *ideality as such*. The only content that we aim to explicate is the content of conceptual determination *per se*. Since we are only explicating the content of the concept *per se*, we shall not be elucidating how or why each content of the *Logic* is a concept. The logic of the concept only specifies the concept of the concept *per se*—namely what is entailed in the concept *alone*. Accordingly, although the concept is not empty, for the determinations of universality, particularity, and singularity constitute the threefold content of the concept, the analysis of the concept into these determinations does not specify what categories are universals, particulars, or singulars. Thus, the concept of the concept is still formal in an important sense, for it does not yet specify what concepts there are.

Because the concept is a power of self-particularization, and this inevitably involves processes of self-negation and self-alienation, Hegel's elucidation of conceptual determination does not end with the specification of universality, particularity, and singularity. Instead, the concept finds itself subject to a host of self-externalities, including judgment and the syllogism. Importantly, Hegel elucidates the threefold constituents of the concept without ever appealing to judgment. Thus, for him it appears that the concept of the concept can be elucidated without ever appealing to judgment, even if it is the case that the concept develops into judgment as its 'truth' in the course of the logic. Judgment has the form of 'S is P,' in which the subject and predicate are connected *immediately* by means of the copula. In judgment, the contradictory form of speculative thinking remains hidden. Because 'S is P is true' implies that 'S is not-P' is false, the form of the judgment hides the unity of opposition that is constitutive of Hegel's dialetheic truth logic.[19] In the syllogism each term is no longer connected to the others by means of the immediate copula. Rather, terms are connected to one another in virtue of a *middle term*. Because syllogism is just as much a form of self-alienation as judgment, in which propositions are connected by means of middle terms, Hegel never provides a form of the syllogism for the concept as such. There are forms of syllogism for abstract universals, genera, and classes, but *no syllogism* is provided for the concept proper.[20] Naturally, this indicates that for Hegel both judgment and syllogism function as forms in which the concept is alienated from itself.

These categories—concept, judgment, and syllogism—are all instances of 'subjectivity' in the sense that they connote *agency*. The concept is the *free* agent that not only determines itself to be universal, particular, and singular. Because the concept is the principle of its own realization, *the agency is not anything other than the concept per se*. In addition, 'subjectivity' also has another sense that corresponds with the moment of its self-alienation. This is the sense of subjectivity as 'externality' and 'contingency.'[21] The agency is not a person that speaks or a mind that thinks the concept; rather it is the concept that conceptualizes *by itself*. As Winfield points out, at the level of pure logic we are dealing with a 'logical "selfhood."' [22] *The concept is the absolute free agency*. The free agency or subjectivity, in virtue of *determining itself*, particularizes itself, or creates its own determinate existence.

Because the concept does not require another distinct conceptualizing agent to think it, Hegel's system of philosophy does not fall victim to Meillassoux's objections to correlationism and idealism in *After Infinitude*. Meillassoux defines correlationism as 'the idea according to which we only ever have access to the correlation between thinking and being, and never to either term considered apart from the other.'[23] Meillassoux's objection against the correlationism consists in the charge that the correlationist can neither account for the *sense* or truth of *ancestral* statements, statements whose referents are *anterior to givenness itself*. The 'ancestral' signifies any reality anterior to the emergence of the human species—or even anterior to every recognized form of life on earth.[24] Without further specification, Hegel would be rightly considered a 'correlationist,' for thinking is infinite and no being exceeds it and all truth is the *self-correspondence* of *the being of thought with itself*. Still, Hegel falls outside Meillassoux's classification of correlationism, since for Hegel the correlation of thought and being at the level of the logic requires no reference to human thought, while according to Meillassoux, 'we do not know of any correlation that would be given elsewhere than in human beings.'[25] Because the concept (as it is 'given' in the logic) is its own agency and does not presuppose a human subject or any real entity in time and space, the correlation of thought and being at the level of the logic escapes Meillassoux's objection. Rather, in quite another sense, for Hegel the concept is itself *ancestral*—it is anterior to all givenness to human subjectivity. The concept is eventually given to human thought and thereby acquires a place in the *Science of Logic*, but this comes at the end of a long story about logic and nature that does not require reference to human beings.

As the principle of its own existence, the existence of the free agency of conceptual thinking is not indebted to another. Indeed, its very being is to be *self-subsistent*. Insofar as this particular is *the totality* of the agency of the concept, it stands *by itself* as a self-sufficient object. 'Objectivity' is a term Hegel employs for the *self-subsistent totality* that arises as a result of the self-particularization of the concept, and in the *Science of Logic* this arises most immediately by means of the collapse of the difference between the middle and end terms in the syllogism.[26]

In the development of objectivity, each term of the syllogism (the universal, particular, and singular) exchanges roles as the end and middle terms. Thereby, each becomes the whole *self-mediating totality*. The act of self-particularization of the logic of subjectivity as a whole (namely concept, judgment, and syllogism) posits an object that is the totality (just as the particular in the logic of the concept is the totality of universality, particularity, and singularity). Insofar as each object is the totality, *the being of the object is outside of itself* in another object, whose being is also outside of itself, *ad infinitum* in a bad infinite. Each object communicates itself to the others, such that there is a thoroughgoing *indifference toward the differentiating features of the various objects*. Thus, objectivity finds itself initially in an ordered series of determinations in which the unifying determination is indifferent to the qualitative differentiation among the objects. Rather than self-determination, objectivity initially appears as a process of mechanical determination, in which the principle of determination is external to the qualitative determination of each thing. From this initial specification of mechanism, the object develops into chemism, external teleology, and life.

Objectivity—like the subjective forms of judgment and syllogism, undergoes the very same process of self-alienation and self-return as the subjective agency of the concept and thereby possesses the same duality of meanings that constitutes the concept.[27] In the chain of mechanical determination, each being communicates itself to the other insofar as each has the same determination. The development of the categories of objectivity—from mechanism, chemism, and finally to external teleology, tell a story of how the concept, originally alienated from itself in the initial form of the mechanical object, resurrects itself in the object, such that it *overcomes its indifference* to qualitative determination that is characteristic of its initial mechanistic specifications.

Naturally, this process of the self-resurrection of the concept can only be one of *internal self-transformation*, since the concept must be responsible for its own objectification. The Idea is the true object—or *the object insofar as it is truly self-particularizing*. Without the object, the subject *cannot be true*. Thus, the process of objectification is the process whereby the subjective conceptual agency, in virtue of its act of self-determination, *creates* another self outside of itself, in order that it can find itself there again. Truth is, after all, the correspondence of the concept with itself. This means nothing less than the *self-correspondence* of the concept as subject with the very same concept as object. In truth, the concept maintains its identity in what is other to it—the object.

Insofar as the concept conceptualizes an object, this object cannot be given independently of the concept in virtue of another principle, for then the concept would not be responsible for its own object. Rather, in a way that mirrors the description of intellectual intuition in Kant, the concept is responsible for creating its own object by means of conceptualizing alone. Accordingly, the logic of objectivity follows directly from the logic of subjectivity, or the logic of the free agency of the concept. The path from concept to objectivity does not take a detour through experience, psychology, or nature. The free agency of the concept *objectifies itself* by itself in the sense that it *determines itself to be a self-subsistent totality*.

The concept of the concept is not identical to the concept of *truth* or what Hegel calls the *Idea*. Truth, or the Idea, is the correspondence of the subject (the concept) with the object; it is the true concept of the Absolute, which Hegel immediately characterizes as life, a category that for Hegel nicely illustrates the capacity of *self-particularization* in nature, as is evident enough in reproduction and homeostasis. In the concept of life the organs determine the whole and the whole determines each of the organs, such that the determinacy of life is not indifferent to the qualitative determinations of the organism as is the case in mechanical objectivity. Instead, in the concept of life the whole is self-determining. The true concept is alive.[28]

Since the concept as such is not yet an object and does not require the concept of the object, the concept as such is not to be confused with the concept of *truth*, which ultimately requires categories that are not yet in play in the explication of the concept. The fact that the category of truth is a further development of the concept is another dimension of the abstract dimension of the concept. Despite this restriction, for Hegel the self-determining concept develops into *truth* by itself. Of course, the path from the concept to truth is *long*, for it must pass through the other forms of conceptual determination, which I have very briefly enumerated, such as judgment, syllogism, and the forms of objectivity to which it also gives rise, namely mechanism, chemism, and external teleology. Nonetheless, the concept is already *implicitly true*, for its abstract content specifies that it must *particularize itself*, such that it alone is responsible for the *correspondence* of the concept with its own particular instantiation. Since the particular instances of the concept are the concept itself, the successful correspondence of the concept with its particular is the correspondence of the concept with itself. This self-correspondence is the coherence of the concept, for the very same concept is discovered in the universal and the particular. It coheres with itself in virtue of distributing itself into different particulars. Simply put, the abstract content of the concept of the concept is that *self-particularizing power that is true in virtue of itself*. Truth is the category that expresses the realization of the power of self-particularization that constitutes the concept.

Finally, there is a final distinction that should be made, in order that we do not make the error of identifying the concept or the Idea with the Absolute Idea. Because the concept has the Absolute as its object,[29] it is only fitting that it ends with the Absolute Idea. The Absolute Idea is *the unity of theoretical and practical reason*. In the former, truth is in the object, and subjective cognition seeks the truth that is already given in the object. Practical reason moves in the other direction, for it possess the truth in its subjectivity, for example the good, and aims to realize that truth in the object. The Absolute Idea is the realization of the unity of theoretical and practical reason, such that truth is not only the correspondence of subject to object, but that correspondence is already there in each element of truth, in both the subject and the object. By ensuring the truth of the elements of truth, Hegel is careful not to undermine truth by failing to account for the truth of the constituents thereof.

Because the self-differentiation of the concept only gives us the moments of universality, particularity, and singularity, the concept *per se* does not, on its own, explain why all of the other categories of the *Logic* ought to count *as categories*. Likewise, the Idea only specified the content of truth *per se*, but did not specify any further that the various categories of the logic were *true categories*. Indeed, because all of the determinacies of the logic have their truth in the *method*, which is the form of the whole, it is only with the concept of the *Absolute Idea* that all of the various contents in the *Logic become concepts per se*, or receive the predicate 'concept.' By granting truth to the elements or 'moments' of absolute truth, the Absolute Idea *retrospectively* determines each content to be a *true concept* of the same method—the Absolute Idea. Thus, the form of the whole also determines the content of each category, for it determines that each category *is a category of logic*.[30] Each category of the logic is *cancelled and preserved* as categories of the Absolute Idea. Only here do we achieve the 'concrete totality' of the logic[31] that contains 'all determinateness within it.'[32] In the Absolute Idea, each content in the *Logic* acquires the predicate that it is a *category of* the *Logic* as a whole. Because the various categories can only be said to belong to the whole once they have their truth in the *method* of logic, the logic only comes to be at the very end, thereby justifying Hegel's metaphor of the circular structure of the logic. Accordingly, even the determination of the concept only becomes a category, or a *concept of the logic*, in the Absolute Idea, or the *method*.[33]

Accordingly, it is the Absolute Idea that *particularizes itself into each category*. Each category is not only universal, but unconditionally universal, for each concept in the logic is an Absolute concept. Moreover, each concept is this Absolute concept, for it is differentiated from others—some instances of the logic of Being, others the logic of Essence, while still others the *Doctrine of the Concept*. Each is singular, for each is *this such and such*—the unity of particular and universal. The Absolute Idea, by retrospectively determining each content of the logic to be a true category of Absolute self-conceptualizing thought, *particularizes itself* into the various categories of the logic. The concept does not lose itself in its self-particularization, but maintains itself in that process. Accordingly, although the Absolute Idea, the method, divides itself into multifarious categories, it remains the very *same* self-particularizing concept in each instance of its particularization. That it remains the same universal method in its particularizations is exactly what constitutes its singularity as the *singular method of the totality*. In this sense, singularity comes to signify the 'one and only' or the singular method that also constitutes the singular totality. This method is *synthetic* for it transcends itself (indeed amplifies itself) in every new determination, but this is nothing less than its very analyticity: *to be that which transcends itself*. Beyond the Idea, the Absolute Idea is not only the *true self-particularizing concept*, for it also *conceives itself* to be the true self-particularizing concept. The Absolute Ideas is the absolute self-knowing concept.[34] Here the method knows itself as *the true method of logic*.

Given that our analysis requires the separation of the concept *per se*, namely the universal, particular and the singular, from the particular concepts of the logic, at this level of generality our inquiry requires a *separation of form from content* or the universal from the particular. Although in respect to the concept itself we shall show how the universal, particular, and singular are *inseparable*, our account shall leave undetermined exactly what concepts *manifest* these moments of the concept. In order to apply the concept of 'concept' to other concepts, the content of 'concept' itself must first be elucidated. Hegel's complaint that the concept itself cannot merely be formal comes down to this: the concept 'concept' must have some content *on its own* without which there cannot be any conceptual determinacy whatever. Of course, the Absolute Idea remedies this omission at the most general level by unifying *the form* of the concept, the concept *per se*, with the particular concepts of the logic—*the content* of the logic. Altogether the unification of the universal, the concept *per se*, and the particular concepts constitute the singularity of the *Logic*. As is evident from this brief overview of the categories that appear in the post-conceptual landscape of the logic, our inquiry is in *medias res*.

The Absolute Idea is the last category to arise in the *Science of Logic*. As we mentioned earlier, it is in virtue of the Absolute Idea that all the preceding thought determinations acquire their status *as categories* of the one logical system. Upon completion of the Absolute Idea, logic is complete, and the result is the simple proposition that 'logic is.' Insofar as logic is, logic is in the form of being, or immediacy. This immediacy can be clarified in terms of the particularity of the Absolute Idea. Because the Absolute Idea is one of the categories, it excludes all of the categories of the logic. As such, the method of logic *falls outside* of the categories of the logic itself. In sum, the completion of the logic also gives rise to the self-alienation of the logic from itself, or in Hegel's terms it 'discharges itself [*entlässt*]'.[35] 'That the logic is' leaves the whole of the logic undetermined by any logical determination—*no logical predicate* is ascribed to the logic as a whole. Thus, because logic is complete, and nothing can be added to the logic, this *immediacy* of the logical being is *external* to the logic. 'Nature' is the term Hegel employs for the initial status of the logic after it has fully created and completed itself. Because logic is in a form that is external to the logic, and it is logic that has given itself this form, in nature logic is 'outside itself' or inverted. Space and time constitute the initial determinations of the philosophy of nature.

Notes

1. Hegel, *SL*, trans. Giovanni, 531, 276 (Suhrkamp).
2. In what follows, I only provide a sketch of the transition from one to void in order to give the reader a more concrete sense of the comparison that Hegel is making. It would distract from my purposes in the book to provide a full-length detailed account of the transition, which requires more categories than I enumerate.
3. See Hegel, *SL*, trans. Miller, 601, 274.
4. Hegel, *SL*, trans. Giovanni, 530.
5. Hegel, *SL*, trans. Miller, 395–402.
6. Ibid, 405–408.
7. Hegel, *SL*, trans. Giovanni, 276–277, 531–532 (Suhrkamp).
8. In the logic of Essence the change in contents is a change in the relation between the positing and the posited. Although the relationships are defined by the opposition of positer and posited, the dialectical changes occur in respect to the content of the relata. The relation between determiner and determined acquires various forms, such as essence and illusion, ground and grounded, and cause and effect. In each new act of positing, one opposition is overcome and replaced by another, until the very content of the opposition can no longer sustain the difference between determiner and determined.
9. Hegel, *SL*, trans. Giovanni, 530, 274.
10. My emphasis.
11. Indeed, one might wonder why we ought not begin the *Doctrine of the Concept* as such. We will tackle this issue again later.

12. Longuenesse is exactly right that the credibility of the entire Hegelian system hangs on the transition to the concept from the logic of Essence:

> In another sense, however, the back and forth movement of reflection is still there, but it is internalized in the concept. Whether the concept actually overcomes the differences that predominate in essence is a key question for any evaluation of Hegel's claims in the *Science of Logic*. Indeed, on the answer to this question might well depend the credibility of the entire Hegelian system.

See Beatrice Longuenesse, *Hegel's Critique of Metaphysics* (Cambridge: Cambridge University Press, 2007), 35.

13. Hegel, *SL*, trans. Giovanni, 530.
14. As we shall see at the end of the development of the concept, the result of the development of the concept will be a pure immediacy. This will be constitutive of all conceptual developments.
15. Hegel, *SL*, trans. Miller, 607.
16. Hegel, *SL*, trans. Giovanni, 531, 276 (Suhrkamp).
17. John McTaggart and Ellis McTaggart, *A Commentary on Hegel' Logic* (Cambridge: Cambridge University Press, 1910), [London Fetter Lange], 194.
18. Ibid.
19. Hegel, *SL*, trans. Miller, 67.
20. See Hegel's account of syllogism in *SL*, for which no syllogism of the concept itself is given.
21. See Hegel, *SL*, trans. Giovanni, 629.
22. Winfield, *From Concept to Objectivity*, 134.
23. Quentin Meillassoux, *After Infinitude*, trans. Ray Brassier (London: Bloomsbury, 2015), 5.
24. Ibid, 10.
25. Ibid, 11.
26. For Hegel's initial specification of the form of objectivity see Hegel's discussion of Mechanism in Hegel, *SL*, trans. Miller, 711–714.
27. Objectivity is both that which stands *opposed to the self-sufficient subject* and that which is self-sufficient. See Hegel, *SL*, trans. Giovanni, 629.
28. For an depth discussion of life in Hegel's philosophy, see Karen Ng, *Hegel's Concept of Life: Self-Consciousness, Freedom, Logic* (Oxford: Oxford University Press, 2019).
29. Hegel, *SL*, trans. Miller, 737.
30. In the Absolute Idea, the concept is the 'fulfilled concept, the concept that comprehends itself conceptually' which constitutes an 'intensive totality.' Hegel, *SL*, trans. Miller, 752.
31. Hegel, *SL*, trans. Miller, 739.
32. Ibid, 735.
33. Ibid, 752.
34. Ibid, 737.
35. Ibid, 753.

13 The Logic of Singularity

Universality

In what follows, I shall reproduce an English translation[1] of many paragraphs of Hegel's text from *Chapter 1: the Concept*. In order to stay close to the original German, I shall insert the German[2] into the text where I see fit, in the case that it may be of some assistance in reading the text. Following the presentation of every paragraph, or every few paragraphs, depending on the content, I shall provide elucidation and commentary on that section of text.

> The faculty of concepts [Begriffe] is normally associated with the *understanding* [Verstand], and the latter is accordingly distinguished from the *faculty of judgment* [Urteilskraft] and from the faculty of syllogistic inferences [Vermögen der Schlüsse] which is formal *reason*. But it is particularly with *reason* that the understanding is contrasted, and it signified then, not the faculty of concepts in general, but the faculty of *determinate* concepts [bestimmten Begriffe], as if, as the prevailing opinion [Vorstellung] has it, the concept were *only a determinate*. When distinguished in this meaning from the formal faculty of judgment and from formal reason [formellen Vernunft], the understanding is accordingly to be taken as the faculty of the single determinate concept. [Vermögen des einzelnen bestimmten Begriffs] For the judgment and the syllogism or reason, as formal, are themselves only *a thing of the understanding*, since they are subsumed under the form of the abstract determinateness of the concept [abstrakten Begriffsbestimmtheit]. Here, however, we are definitely not taking the concept as just abstractly determined; the understanding is therefore to be distinguished from reason only in that it is the faculty of the concept as such.[3]

In the opening passage of *'Doctrine of the Concept'* Hegel is explicit that in his explication, 'the concept' does not rank as something merely 'abstractly determinate.' In contrast to Hegel's meaning, the faculty of concepts, the

Understanding, is *usually* thought to stand in contrast with the faculty of *Reason*, not as the faculty of the concept in general, but as the faculty of *determinate* concepts. In this case, the concept *itself* is grasped as *a single* determinate concept. In contrast, Hegel points out that the understanding is just *the faculty of the concept in general*. In sum, Hegel distinguishes the usual treatment of the concept as an abstract determinacy that is contrasted with formal reason, and his own account in which the understanding is *not limited* to abstract determinacy, and merely signifies the faculty of the concept in general.

Without some clarification of 'determinacy' and 'understanding,' this comparison, at first glance, helps very little with clarifying Hegel's position. The term 'Understanding' is Kant's term for the faculty of *a priori* concepts or *categories*. Accordingly, Hegel's comparison of the way the concept is usually understood with his own account is meant, at least in part, to distinguish himself from Kant. Hegel will nonetheless appropriate the term 'understanding,' but with the proviso that it has the general signification of the 'faculty of the concept in general.'

Hegel writes that as 'the prevailing opinion [Vorstellung] has it, the concept were *only a determinate*.' Note that Hegel does not write that 'the concept prevails that the concept is only a determinate concept,' but instead uses 'Vorstellung.' 'Vorstellung' in Hegel is diminutive. A 'Vorstellung' is not a proper concept. Instead, it is a *'before-putting,'* if you will, or what is a more usual translation, a 'representation.' As such, it is a psychological phenomenon, one that has a temporal existence in the consciousness of a subject. Any theory of concepts that reduces concepts to this state falls victim to what we have called 'psychologism.' Here in this passage Hegel implicitly connects the proposition that the concept is merely determinate with a mere 'idea,' with something less than conceptual. Though it may only be a representation that the concept is *only* a determinate concept, Hegel is obviously not here claiming that the concept is merely indeterminate.

Another conspicuous aspect of this passage is Hegel's claim that the idea prevails that the concept is only *the single* determinate concept. More directly to the point, Hegel writes that the concept is the '*Vermögen des einzelnen bestimmten Begriffs*.' What is curious here is Hegel's emphasis on the *singularity* of the determinate concept. Clearly, here Hegel is pointing out a relationship between two concepts that arise together in the usual understanding of understanding: determinacy and singularity. If we take a moment to dwell on Hegel's own specification of determinacy, we shall achieve some insight into why this identification is made.

As Aristotle argued, what is determinate must be in principle *distinguishable* from what it is not. Naturally, if the PNC is what preserves determinacy, it only makes sense to protect her reign. Unfortunately, the story cannot be so simple. Earlier we pointed out the basic problem with the assumption that the PNC is the principle of conceptual determination *per se*: the very determinacy *of* the PNC cannot be preserved by the PNC. If we hold fast to the PNC as the absolute principle of conceptual determination, the principle undermines its *own* determinacy. In fact, the result can only be atrocious for she who has adopted the PNC as her guide: the principle, when taken as absolute, turns out to render all determinations *indeterminate*. As it turns out, in order to protect the determinacy of the concept, we cannot begin with the PNC as the absolute principle of the concept.

Let us make an important distinction that will be determinative for our reconstruction of Hegel. On the one hand, our previous chapters show that insofar as contradictions are *explosive*[4] the principle cannot be absolute. As long as the PNC is interpreted on the traditional model as explosive, then we must reject it as an absolute principle. On the other hand, Hegel will show that some contradictions, in virtue of the particular character of the contradiction, are not explosive, but *create new* categories. On the whole, we may distinguish between two senses of the PNC. On the one model, anything follows. On the other model, from particular contradictions particular results follow. Hegel re-works the PNC such that the latter interpretation acquires dominance over the former. In our reconstruction of Hegel we must pay close attention to how the latter sense of the principle is developed. Indeed, if Hegel accepts that determinacy is generally non-contradictory in the traditional sense, then we would expect him to treat the determinate concept as a relative concept. In so doing, Hegel would not reduce the concept as such to a determinate concept and could integrate the traditional concept of non-contradiction into his account of the concept in general.[5]

Systematic philosophers tend to put Hegel's move another way: determinacy cannot *initially* be accounted for by positing anything determinate. Indeed, that would beg the question. Determinacy can only arise from what is not determinate. Notoriously, Hegel's *Science of Logic* does just this insofar as determinate being *(Dasein)* arises out of Being, nothing, and becoming, each of which are in themselves indeterminate. Of course, what is of central interest to us is not the way these give rise to determinate being, but exactly how Hegel characterizes determinacy. Indeed, one of Hegel's basic concerns with limiting the concept to the determinate concept is the very issue concerning the origin of the determinate concept. Without giving due countenance to the indeterminate, no account of the determinate concept can be given.

When Hegel employs the word 'determinate,' he has something very specific in mind. Indeed, the concept 'determinacy' is developed very early in the *logic of Being*. Hegel's specification of determinacy is not far afield from Aristotle's sense. Unlike becoming, determinacy, in Hegel's initial characterization, is the *stable unity* of Being and nothing. For Hegel, determinate being *qua* determinate is something. Something is the unity of reality and negation, but understood *as a reality*. Every determinate being is a something. As a something, it is opposed to some other. The other to which something is opposed is the inverse of something: the unity of reality and negation understood *as a negation*.

When Hegel claims that the understanding is usually grasped as the single determinate concept, he is pointing out that the concept is taken up as a generic 'something.' When the concept is grasped as a something, it is posited as having its own reality, apart from what is other to it. This independent qualitative being, to which the other is opposed, is what Hegel calls 'being in itself.' Insofar as the something is not the other because of its own independent reality, it is 'being for another' in virtue of its being in itself. Likewise, the other, in itself, is not the something, and is 'being for another.' Yet, insofar as it is in itself not the other, the other also has its own 'being in itself' in virtue of its being for the other.[6] When we grasp conceptual relations in this way, the only relation of the categories to one another is one of *exclusion*. Indeed, *the exclusion of each by the other is what constitutes their determinacy*. Of course, Hegel argues that the categories 'something' and 'other' are not mutually exclusive, and in fact each is something and other. The something is the other to the other, and the other as the other is something. Although here 'determinacy' signifies something relative, in his account of singularity, determinacy will acquire an *absolute* significance.

On this view of the singularity of the determinate concept, the PNC, on which the contradiction is explosive, is adopted in order to preserve the content of every reality against its negation. The PNC ensures that the well is never the battleship and that the battleship is never the well. Each is its own something and other to one another. Formal logical principles and the concept of determinacy are wedded: the relativity of non-contradiction is reflected in the relativity of something-other. Their unity is expressed in the concept of the abstract. The abstract universal is what it is and is not what it is not. Its relation to what it is not is defined by negation: it relates to its other by failing to be the other. It is an other to other abstract universals, each of which are also somethings.

As we can see from Hegel's terminology, to overcome the abstract universal means to overcome the view that the universal is only the single determinate universal. Accordingly, it falls on us to investigate how Hegel can introduce the determinacy of the concept and the PNC while at the same time rejecting the view that the concept is merely a determinate concept and the PNC is an absolute principle.

> The universal concept that we now have to consider contains the three moments of *universality* [Allgemeinheit], *particularity* [Besonderheit], and *singularity* [Einzelheit]. The difference [Unterschied] and the determinations which the concept gives itself in its process of distinguishing [Unterscheiden] constitute the sides formally called *positedness* [Gesetztsein]. Since this positedness is in the concept

identical with being-in-and-for-itself [Anundfürsichsein], each of the moments is just as much the *whole* concept as it is *determinate concept* and *a determination* of the concept.[7]

Here in the second paragraph, Hegel offers the first succinct description of what he takes the concept of the concept to be. Hegel writes that the concept gives itself its own difference and determinations. Accordingly, the concept is that which *self-differentiates*.

In the following paragraphs that precede *A. The Universal Concept*, Hegel introduces those various characteristics into which the concept differentiates itself. In these sections Hegel is *preparing* us for what is to come. We are told that the 'universal' concept contains three 'moments': universality, particularity, and singularity. By 'universal concept' Hegel means the concept as such, or the 'what it is to be' of a concept. In this signification, 'universal concept' identifies that which makes any concept a concept. The universal concept, we are told, is not just universal; it is particular and singular. What is striking here is the fact that Hegel does not exclude the particular and the singular from the universal concept, as is commonplace in the tradition. Moreover, Hegel is careful to *distinguish* the particular from the singular.

In Hegel, the term 'moment' is a very general term. Within the *Science of Logic*, 'moment' does not show up as one of the categories.[8] The term appears to signify 'element' or 'constituent' without further specification. Hegel himself employs the verb 'ausmachen' to describe the moments that the universal concept gives itself, a term which signifies *constitution*. Accordingly, the universal concept is constituted by three elements: universality, particularity, and singularity. Indeed, Hegel elucidates the being of the universal, particular, and the singular in the subsequent sections: *A. The Universal Concept* (530–534), *B. The Particular Concept* (534–546), and *C. The Singular* (546–549). Interestingly, Hegel has more to write about particularity than each of the others.

Hegel states that 'The difference [Unterschied] and the determinations which the concept gives itself in its process of distinguishing [Unterscheiden] constitute the sides formally called *positedness* [Gesetztsein].' Moreover, Hegel goes on to say 'this positedness is in the concept identical with being-in-and-for-itself [Anundfürsichsein].' To understand what he means here, we must say something about the term 'positedness' and 'being in and for itself.' As is characteristic of Hegel, much of his descriptions of the categories in the *Doctrine of the Concept* employ terms and categories from the *logic of Being* and the *logic of Essence*. Because Hegel continually contrasts the *Doctrine of the Concept* with these other sections of *the Logic*, we will shall have the opportunity to continually return to these categories.

Gesetztsein, literally 'being set down,' is the logical relation constitutive of *Essence*. Allow me to illustrate the relation of positing with an example from Aristotle. Aristotelian Essences posit their *per se* attributes. For example, the form of the human being, though not itself posited, posits the capacity of laughter. Moreover, in another weaker sense, insofar as every attribute, for example qualities and quantities, depends on the existence of an underlying thing for its existence, the form of the human being posits those attributes. The capacity to laugh is that which is posited by the form, the positer. Indeed, every positing is a relation between a positer and what is posited. Still, the relation has a particular structure, which distinguishes it from others. Although the form posits qualities, and is that in virtue of which the qualities exist, the very content of quality, or the what it is to be of quality, is not itself accounted for by the act of positing. In other words, though the quality is 'put forward' by the thing, and *exists in virtue* of its positing, the thing does not account for *what* it is positing. Accordingly, we may indeed know that qualities and quantities depend on things for their being, but that is very different from accounting for the qualitative or quantitative content of the qualities and quantities themselves. Colors, for example, have their own independent being, their own 'what it is to be' white and black, and so on, and this is perfectly compatible with their being posited by things.

In what respect is 'positing' relevant here? Hegel points out that the self-differentiation of the concept constitutes what was previously called positedness. Indeed, Hegel is explicitly not claiming that the concept is an act of positing. Instead, he is claiming that the act of self-differentiation has an *analogous* function to positing. Positing is responsible for *the difference*, by putting forward and setting down *the difference* between what posits and what is posited. Without the positing of the thing, there would be no difference between the essential (the positer) and the unessential (the posited). The act of positing posits that what posits and what is posited are different and it characterizes the way in which each is distinguished from the other, namely that one posits and the other is posited. Though positing accounts for the difference, wherever there is positing, *a difference* between positing and posited *remains*. In the act of positing, the relation between the determiner and the determined is *not equal*: the latter reflects the activity of the former but is not identical to the former. The posited is not what posits and what posits is not what is posited. Hegel's claim is that despite the differences between positing and self-differentiation, just as positing accounts for the difference constitutive of its relationship, so the self-differentiating universal accounts for its differences: universality, particularity, and singularity.

Hegel goes on to point out that the self-differentiation of the universal, what constitutes what was called 'positing,' is identical to being-in-and-for-self (*Anundfürsichsein*). We have already discussed what being in itself (*ansichsein*) signifies. What remains to be clarified here is what being for itself (*fürsichsein*) means. *Un*like positing, being for itself is a category from the *logic of Being*. Being for itself develops out of the true infinite, a category that arises from the self-negation of finitude. Our main concern here is the meaning of the term. Being for itself signifies *the transcending of otherness*. In this respect, what has 'being for itself' is what Hegel calls an *ideality*. Being for itself is not being for another, as is the case with something and other. If we reflect on self-differentiation, it becomes immediately clear why Hegel uses Being for itself as a description of the self-differentiating universal. What is self-differentiating must not appeal to any external category in order to possess its differences. Insofar as it differentiates itself, that which is other to the self-differentiating universal does not fall outside of the self-differentiating universal. Indeed, it is its *own other*, if you will. As its own other, there is no way to differentiate it from what it is not. Since what it is not cannot fall outside of it, there is no other external to the self-differentiating. Thus, in this respect *self-differentiation is being for itself*.[9] All differences fall *within* the self-differentiating universal. Accordingly, the independent being of the self-differentiating universal, its 'being in itself,' is nothing other than its 'being for itself.' The concept is *Anundfürsichsein*.

What is self-differentiating *cannot posit* any difference, for that would imply that there would be a difference between what posits and what is posited. Instead, self-differentiation is a process of *development* (*Entwicklung*), in which the determinations it creates are no different from itself. Insofar as it transcends all otherness in being for itself, it cannot maintain any separation between determiner and determined. In self-differentiation, there cannot be any difference between what differentiates and what is differentiated. The transcending of otherness in self-differentiation means that 'each of the moments is just as much the *whole* concept as it is *determinate concept* and *a determination* of the concept.' Hegel briefly indicates how we ought to interpret this in the following paragraph. This formulation of the concept is common throughout Hegel's lecture throughout his career. Consider for example, his *Vorlesung Über Logik* in Berlin from 1831:

> Jedes der Momente im Begriff ist aber zugleich das Ganze, der ganze Begriff. . . . Hier ist [der] Begriff an und für sich, jedes ist Totalität.[10]

We may begin to make sense of what Hegel means when he claims that the unity of the self-differentiation of the universal (what was called positing) and the being in and for itself of the universal implies that each of the moments is just as much the *whole* concept as it is *determinate concept* and *a determination* of the concept. Since the self-differentiating universal must be indistinguishable from its differences, each difference posited by the concept must be the *whole* concept. In other words, each is the pure universal. Because all otherness has been transcended, all otherness between all differences posited by the universal must be overcome: the universal is singular and particular, the particular is universal and singular, and the singular is universal and particular. Indeed, insofar as each of these is its own determinate concept that is opposed to the others, each of the moments is a determinate concept. In other words, each is a *particular*. Insofar as each is a constituent of the concept as such, each is also *a determination of* the universal *per se*. In other words, each is a singularity. In the following three paragraphs, Hegel provides a *preview* of the dialectical development in which each of the moments is no less the whole concept, a determinate concept, and a determination of the concept.

It is a peculiarity of the passage given earlier that Hegel includes universality as a moment of the universal concept. Accordingly, the universal concept is a *moment of itself* and is thereby particular:

> It is at first *pure concept*, or the determination of *universality*. But the pure or universal concept is also only a *determinate* or *particular* concept that takes its place alongside the other concepts. Because the concept is a totality, and therefore in its universality or pure identical self-reference is essentially a determining and a distinguishing [Unterschieden], it possesses in itself the norm by which this form of its self-identity, in pervading all the moments and comprehending them within, equally determines itself immediately as being *only the universal* as against the distinctness [Unterschiedenheit] of the moments.[11]

In this passage Hegel re-iterates what he says earlier: the universal concept is not only universal but also a determinate concept or particular concept. Here Hegel uses 'determinate' and 'particular' interchangeably. The identification provides us with a clue for interpreting the previous passage: when Hegel claims that 'each of the moments is just as much the *whole* concept as it is *determinate concept*' we must interpret the 'determinate' as the moment of *the particular*.

Initially, Hegel points out that the universal is just the *pure* concept, or universality itself. As such, we would initially expect the universal not simply to count as one more universal among others, since it is the very what it is to be of universality. But Hegel goes on to say that it is also the particular or determinate concept. Immediately this indicates to us that the pure concept, or mere universality, is *not in itself determinate*. Indeed, because self-differentiation as such has no other with which it can be contrasted, it would be *im*proper to attribute determinacy to self-differentiation as such. This fits well with Hegel's concern that the concept has been wrongly identified as the determinate concept. Moreover, what this indicates is that for Hegel, the tradition has had the tendency to uncritically identify the universal concept with the particular concept, or what is the same, *not* to recognize the purely universal concept at all.

Let us note that if the universal concept, the concept *per se*, is *also* a particular concept, then it is just another universal among many. First, we already noted the meaning of determinacy in Hegel, in which the determinate concept is a self-identity that is its own something and stands as an *other* to another self-identity. Accordingly, the determinate concept would be a self-identical concept opposed to other concepts. From the traditional perspective, it is also clear why the particular or determinate concept would stand among other concepts. Traditionally, to be a particular is to be *one in number*. Accordingly, each particular concept *qua* one in number can be *counted* as one concept.

At the end of this paragraph, Hegel gives a very brief *summary* of the transition from universality to particularity that he elucidates in greater detail at the end of his discussion of universality. Let us analyze our starting point: *the universal is self-differentiation*. When we say that the universal is self-differentiation we do *not* initially have two concepts. Before the predicate 'self-differentiation' is predicated to the universal, we do not know *what* the subject 'universal' *is*. Already in the *Phenomenology*, Hegel points out that before the predicate is attributed to the subject, the subject remains *indeterminate*. Thus, in this case too, the subject, 'universal,' is an empty term insofar as it is by itself. The universal just *is* the predicate: self-differentiation. Naturally, the 'is' establishes the identity of the universal with the self-differentiation, or what is the same, the identity of self-differentiation with itself. Accordingly, we only have one concept here: self-differentiation. If we wish to be precise, we can simply say that 'self-differentiation *is*' or 'the universal *is*' *without further qualification*. That 'the universal is' signifies a fundamental indeterminacy—it has not yet acquired its predicate.

When Hegel writes about concepts in their 'immediacy' or 'in the form of being' this is what he means. The form of mediation is one in which we understand one concept *through another*. Propositions such as 'self-differentiation is' do not yet achieve this, since it only posits the one content 'self-differentiation' by itself. The very absence of the predicate indicates the indeterminacy of self-differentiation. What is it? When we see that what we have given at the outset is just self-differentiation, we see that *all we have* at the outset is a simple self-identity:[12] *the self-identical content 'self-differentiation.'* Implied here is that what is not self-differentiating is *not given*. That we posited the universal as self-differentiation in the first place, in contradistinction to what is not self-differentiating, already implies this: insofar as we take self-differentiation for granted in distinction from what is not self-differentiating, we assume the simple self-identity of self-differentiation from the outset. Still, this does not mean that we know what we are saying when we claim that self-differentiation is. It is, at the outset, indeterminate.

We might also illuminate the initial status of self-differentiation as the pure universal by reminding ourselves that self-differentiation is 'Being in and for self.' As being in and for itself, it transcends all otherness. Insofar as it transcends all otherness, there is no other but self-differentiation. Self-differentiation is the *only one* there is. As the only one there is, there is no other to which self-differentiation may be contrasted. For this reason, it is easy to see the connection between self-differentiation as one and its indeterminacy. One of the big mistakes of the tradition, for Hegel, is to mistake the universal for the one. The pure universal incorporates the determinacy of the one, but is not merely the One, for it has a richer content. Unlike the mere one and being for self, the immediate unity of self-differentiation is the *immediate identity* of *all of its differences*, not the *absence* of any difference whatever. In the logic of Being, it is the very absence of any difference whatever that characterizes the one and being for self.

From this claim that 'self-differentiation is' we may immediately infer that it is the totality of differences and, in this sense, universal. *The universal is self-differentiation.* The sense of universality that we expect from the term is immediately acquired when we think about self-differentiation as such. As self-differentiation, the universal is the *totality*, for it contains differences that it gives itself, and none of these differences may subsist externally to self-differentiation. Thus, self-differentiation is *universal as totality*, for it is what pervades every difference.

But insofar as self-differentiation is, in its identity, a *differentiation* of itself, the pure universal, what is self-differentiating, *must differentiate itself* from what it is not. If the self-differentiating universal did not differentiate itself from what it is not, it would not be what it is, namely self-differentiation. So just in virtue of existing in and including all of the moments, it also determines itself solely to be the universal. By differentiating itself from what it is not, the universal stands opposed to what it is not, fully determinate in its opposition to what it is not and countable insofar as it is one in number. Here Hegel already specifies the concepts from which the self-differentiating universal distinguishes itself: the other moments of particularity and singularity. Thus, Hegel informs us that

> *Second*, the concept is thereby posited as this *particular* or *determinate* concept, distinct from others.[13]

When the universal is grasped just *as* universal, *itself by itself*, it is just the self-identical one. As the particular, it differentiates itself from its own differences. Here Hegel has given us a mere *glimpse* into why the universal, as self-differentiation, must be a particular concept. But it is merely a glimpse and the details remain missing. For instance, why are particularity and singularity the concepts from which the universal distinguishes itself? Also, why *must* the universal differentiate itself? Indeed, why is it not possible for the universal to just remain universal? Further, if the universal is one of its *own* particulars, then the universal is a member of itself. If the universal is a member of itself, then it seems that Hegel might fall victim to a *new* Third Man regress.

In the following section Hegel indicates the third stage of the argument in *the Concept*:

> *Third, singularity* is the concept reflecting itself out of difference into absolute negativity [absolute Negativität]. This is at the same time the moment at which it has stepped out of its identity into its *otherness* [Anderssein] *and becomes judgment* [Urteil].[14]

Here, in this paragraph concerning singularity, Hegel describes the last stage of the development of the concept. In singularity the concept is 'reflecting itself out of difference into absolute negativity.' At the stage of the determinate universal, or the particular universal, the universal is defined by its negative relation to the other. The determinate universal is not what is other to it. Accordingly, at the stage of particularity, the self-differentiating universal is divided from what it is not, and *negation* constitutes the relation of self-differentiation to its other. The stage of singularity, the last moment of the pure universal, is an 'absolute negation.' 'Absolute' signifies not only what is universal, but what is *unconditioned*. In order to achieve the absolute negation, *negation itself must be negated*. At the stage of singularity, the negation constituting the difference between universal and particular must be negated. This is what is signified by 'absolute negation.' Accordingly, the stage of singularity *unites* what is separated at the stage of particularity: the self-differentiating universal and what is other to it. The singular is *the unity* of the self-differentiating universal and that from which it differentiates itself, namely the other moments of the universal. This is why Hegel writes that the concept is reflected 'out of the difference' and into Absolute Negativity. Absolute Negativity is also absolute determinacy: it is constituted by *the self-negation of relative determinacy*.

In sum, in these initial paragraphs Hegel outlines *three* stages of development that the universal as such undergoes. First, as the pure universal, it is merely the self-identity of self-differentiation. As such, it is the immediate unity of all of its differences. This is the stage of the whole. In virtue of its self-differentiation, it differentiates itself into various differences or moments. This is the stage of particularity, or the determinate concept. Given the way that this stage develops, the specter of the Third Man regress arises. Without indicating how this singularity arises, Hegel claims that *out* of particularity, singularity arises, in which the self-differentiating universal is united with its differences. Let us note that in good Hegelian fashion *the end of the process is identical with the beginning*, for we have a unity of the self-differentiating universal with all of its differences. But there is a fundamental difference between the end and the beginning. Unlike pure universality, singularity is not just the immediate unity of the various differences posited by the self-differentiating universal. To the contrary, it is the *mediated* unity of these differences—a unity that results from the differentiation of self-differentiation in the process of particularity.[15]

It is important for us to discuss, in some detail, the connection between truth and singularity, since Hegel treats singularity as the *truth* of particularity and universality. The *return of the category to itself*, what in Greek was called the *palintropos*, is what Hegel will often describe as the *truth* of the category. What does it mean to say that singularity is the 'truth' of the universal? The idea is simple: universality, insofar as it is self-differentiation, *is not itself* insofar as it has not differentiated itself. In other words, it is not truly universal if it does not differentiate itself. Only in the *act* of self-differentiation is self-differentiation itself. Indeed, Hegel calls us to simply think the universal by itself or what is the same, the universality *of* universality, and see what follows.[16] Accordingly to Hegel, if we simply think the universal, or self-differentiation, as such, we shall arrive at particularity and singularity. The isolation of the universal is exactly what connects it to the other moments of particularity and singularity. Hegel will argue that singularity just is *the self-differentiation of self-differentiation*: the correspondence of universality with itself. It is our task to elucidate why this is the case.

The universal is only being 'true to itself' when it is singular. Because singularity is the truth of the concept, the truth of *any* concept *as* a concept is its singularity. Indeed, since our main concern here is what the concept is, it naturally concerns us also to elucidate what 'the *truth* of the concept is.' As Aristotle pointed out, 'truth' is another way of saying 'being.' When we ask 'what is the *true* universal?' our answer should correspond to *what* the universal *is*.

As is evident from these reflections, and Hegel's comments elsewhere, by 'truth' Hegel means the *self-correspondence* of the category with itself.[17] If we remember our formulation of the problem of instantiation in Plato and Kant, the problem of instantiation concerns *the possibility of truth*. For this reason, insofar as singularity is that moment of the concept which overcomes the Third Man argument, it is with the concept that the possibility of conceptual truth can be solved. Without an account of how the particular connects to the universal, we fail to have an account of truth, for truth relies upon the correspondence of the universal with the particular. Indeed, we discovered that the universal, in order to be a true universal, required that it itself already be a unity of universal and particular. Likewise, the particular, in order to be true, required the unity of the universal and the particular—singularity.

At the outset of this general outline of the dialectical development, Hegel notes that judgment and syllogism are *products of the understanding (Verständiges)* since they are determined abstractly. In one sense, we may read this as Hegel's admission that formal logic, namely the theory of judgment and the theory of syllogism, simply follow from the development of the understanding, or the concept *per se*. Since the theory of judgment and syllogism stand under the abstract determination of the concept, the outcome of Hegel's account of the concept must be *the abstract* aspect of the concept. Insofar as the concept is not in itself merely abstract, the fulfillment of the concept, namely singularity, gives rise to what is *other* to the concept. The concept 'passed out of its identity into its *otherness [Anderssein]*, and becomes the *judgment [Urteil]*.'[18]

In the opening paragraph of his analysis of universality, Hegel claims that we must 'look back once more at its genesis.'[19] In what follows, Hegel imports terms from the logic of Being and the logic of Essence to illuminate the determinacy of the universal. Regarding Being and Essence, he claims that the concept is the *Durchdringung*[20] of these moments. Nonetheless, Hegel offers a more detailed characterization of the universal in terms of categories that belong to the logic of Being and Essence.[21] First, the universal is the *interfusion* of the logic of Being and Essence, and second it has its *own* content *independent* of Being and Essence.

Though Hegel employs previous categories to describe the universal, Hegel himself nonetheless strives to explicate the what it is to be of the universal independently of such categories. Our main emphasis should not be so much on the origin of the universal as the initial content of universality as such that Hegel posits, and this can be achieved with some clarity without having to bog down the reader with technical terms.

> The pure concept is the absolutely infinite [Unendliche], unconditioned [Unbedingte] and free [freie].[22]

Insofar as the universal differentiates itself, it is its *own other*. As that which transcends the other, as *ideality*, there is no way to differentiate it from what it is not. Since what it is not cannot fall outside of it, there is no other external to the self-differentiating. Or what is the same, every attempt to find the 'outer boundary' of self-differentiation fails. To be sure, every attempt you make to abandon the universal places you right back in it. Because all differences fall *within* the self-differentiating universal, the universal is not finite, for there is no limit to the universal. Thus, the universal is *infinite*.

Even though Hegel does not explicitly name the kind of universality he is referring to here, if we simply follow the argument it should be clear. Earlier we laid out three kinds of infinity: indeterminateness, the quantitative infinite, and the intensive, or qualitative, infinite. Since the self-differentiating universal immediately contains all differences, it cannot be reducible to the quantitatively infinite, for the quantitative infinite is that for which something is *always outstanding*. Thus, we might expect that Hegel means either the indeterminate or the intensive infinite.

Earlier we noted that what we have given at the stage of mere universality is *just* self-differentiation. Because *all we have* at the outset is *the self-identical content 'self-differentiation'* the universal as such is indeterminate. The content 'self-differentiation' stands in no contrast with another content and has no predicate. As such, the given content self-differentiation appears to be infinite as the indeterminate. But the self-differentiating universal, at the stage of universality, is only indeterminate in virtue of the self-identical content that it is, namely self-differentiation. Indeed, the self-differentiating universal as the self-differentiating is complete insofar as there is nothing outstanding. It is only in virtue of its completeness that it is indeterminate, that it stands in no relation to an other as self-differentiating. For this reason, it appears that we would be justified in attributing the intensive infinite to the concept *qua* universal. Because the self-differentiating universal just as self-differentiating excludes nothing, it appears to lack no difference, and thereby no content, whatever.

Yet it would be premature to attribute the intensive infinite to the universal as such. At the stage of universality we only encounter self-differentiation as such, or the immediate identity of the differences contained therein. What we do not yet possess in any meaningful sense is the distinction between self-differentiation and what is *not* self-differentiation. This difference is not yet at hand. What is more, the indeterminacy of self-differentiation precludes it from being complete. At the stage of universality, self-differentiation has not yet differentiated itself into its various moments, for example 'particularity' and 'singularity.' Indeed, the immediate identity of self-differentiation as being-in-and-for-itself, as the immediate totality, excludes this as a possibility. To put it simply, at the stage of universality, self-differentiation stands alone, *itself by itself*.

Our analysis of the infinity of the universal provides an opportunity to discuss Hegel's initial description of the concept:

> Thus the concept is *absolute self-identity* [absolute Identität mit sich] by being first just this, the negation of negation or the infinite unity of negativity [unendliche Einheit der Negativität] with itself. This *pure* self-*reference* of the concept, which is such by positing itself through the negativity, is the *universality* of the concept.[23]

Hegel identifies the 'negation of negation' with the 'infinite unity of negativity with itself' and the 'absolute self-identity.' Earlier we noted that the singular is the negation of negation. But here, Hegel claims that the universal is the negation of negation. The difference is that the universal has not yet differentiated itself. The singular is the result of a process and therefore involves some form of mediation. The universal is not yet a result of its own process, whereas the singular is the result of the activity of concept. The universal *per se* is just self-differentiation *in the form of being*. This means that we are looking at self-differentiation *insofar as it is*, not insofar as it is determining itself.

Self-differentiation differentiates itself. As that which gives differences, it is the principle of its own determinacy. Each of the differences that result from the differentiating process is constituted by a negation. Each difference has its own being in itself and is contrastable with another. Each difference is itself and *not* the other. Yet, each of the differences *is self-differentiation itself*. Since self-differentiation is that into which it differentiates itself, it is itself insofar as it is different from itself, which is a contradiction. For this reason, the negation that constitutes the differences must necessarily be negated. Accordingly, the conceptual content of 'self-differentiation' is nothing other than the *negation of negation*.[24]

What follows from the universal as negation of negation? First, the negation of negation excludes no negation whatever—it is itself whatever negation that it creates, or what is the same, it negates the difference between itself and any negation that it creates. Because no negation is excluded, it is infinite. It is an *unending* unity of negation with itself. In this sense, the universal just is the unity of negation with itself. Moreover, the negation of negation, insofar as it is the unity of negation with itself, is *self-identical*. The negation of negation is an *absolute* self-identity, for there is no negation conditioning its unity as a negation of negation. It is the self-identity of negation with itself, and as such it is unconditioned, or absolute.

In the last sentence of the paragraph, Hegel gives us a brief formula for the universal: 'This *pure* self-*reference* of the concept, which is such by positing itself through the negativity, is the *universality* of the concept.' The universal is that which gives itself its own content, 'negation of negation,' in virtue of its differentiating activity, or its negativity. In this sense, it is a pure self-relation, *a relation of negation-to-negation*, and nothing else. Hegel further distinguishes the concept from categories in the logic of Being, such as 'becoming':

> The universal, on the contrary, even when it posits itself in a determination, *remains* in it what it is. It is the soul [Seele] of the concrete which it inhabits, unhindered and equal to itself in its manifoldness [Mannigfaltigkeit] and diversity [Verschiedenheit]. It is not

swept away in the becoming but persists undisturbed through it, endowed with the power of unalterable, undying self-preservation [Selbsterhaltung].[25]

Hegel illuminates the 'soul' or indwelling principle of the universal by contrasting it with becoming (*Werden*). Becoming is the ceasing to be of Being into nothing and nothing into Being. When one thing becomes another, what becomes ceases to be what it is and comes to be something else. For example, when wood is removed from the living tree and used as lumber, it ceases to be an organ in an organic unity and comes to be something else: a non-organic natural kind with a particular chemical composition. In the process of becoming, the wood does not maintain itself in its becoming. As becoming it ceases to be what it is and becomes something else: lumber.

In contrast to becoming, the concept maintains what it is in its differences. In other words, it does *not lose itself* in the process of differentiation, as the wood loses its being as an organ of a living being in the process of becoming. Instead, it 'holds itself' to itself (*Selbsterhaltung*) and remains 'equal to itself' in the many-foldedness (*Mannigfaltigkeit*) and diversity (*Verschiedenheit*)[26] of its differentiations. That Hegel attributes this feature to the concept ought not be too surprising, given what we have already uncovered. Insofar as self-differentiation is itself only insofar as it is united with what it is different from, self-differentiation can only be itself insofar as it maintains itself in what is different from it. Indeed, it is the very being of self-differentiation to be its other and to maintain itself in what is other to it. To use the language of genus and species, the self-differentiating universal *is* the difference and the genus, what is differentiated.

Hegel hints at this feature earlier when he writes that the universal is an 'Absolute Self-Reference.' Indeed, the concept of self-differentiation entails what Hegel claims. As self-differentiating, the concept must differentiate itself. As we noted earlier, in order to be self-differentiating, self-differentiation must differentiate itself from itself. Thus, it must differentiate itself into what is self-differentiating and what is not self-differentiating. In these differentiations, it might appear that self-differentiation has lost itself in its differences. Indeed, empirical concepts such as 'bald' and 'leaf' all involve non-self-differentiating differences. In the manifold differences into which self-differentiation differentiates itself, even the content 'non-self-differentiating' is nonetheless a differentiation of self-differentiation. Because it is one of the differentiations of self-differentiation, every difference that is not self-differentiation is nonetheless united with self-differentiation and inseparable from it.

This feature of the universal, that it remains itself in its differentiations, enriches our grasp of the infinity of the universal. Until now

I have been treating the universal as infinite because it has no limit, but the universal is also infinite because it does *not* cease to be what it is. Indeed, it is what it is irrespective of the changes—this makes it infinite. In contrast, the finite is that which has an internal limit—namely that which, in virtue of what it is, ceases to be. The mortality of the human being is the finitude of the human being. Unlike the human being, the concept does not cease to be what it is when it is differentiated into what it is not. Instead, the concept is infinite exactly because it maintains its identity in its self-loss. For this reason, we can see that the concept of the 'undying' and 'unchanging' are attributes of the infinity of the concept and provide contrast to the finite as something that can die and change. The finite concept, for example, that we investigated earlier, insofar as it is governed by the PNC, contains its own ceasing to be. Self-differentiation amends the concept by freeing it of its finitude and by doing so frees it of the possibility of its non-being.

The universal is self-determining and thereby free:

> The universal is therefore *free* power [freie Macht]; it is itself while reaching out to its other and embracing it, but without *doing violence* [Gewaltsames] to it; on the contrary it is at rest in its other as *in its own*. Just as it has been called free power, it could also be called *free love* [freie Liebe] and *boundless blessedness* [schranklose Seligkeit], for it relates to *that which is distinct from it* as *to itself*; in it, it has returned to itself.[27]

The universal is free power. It is a power because it is *the source of change*—the source of differentiations. Yet, it is free, for it is determined by itself, differentiated by itself. Accordingly, it is *free power*. Whatever it is, it is in virtue of itself.

To begin, let us not just say that the universal is free but that the universal is *freedom itself*. It is freedom itself, because it is self-determination, the very definition of freedom. If the universal were not free, it would be determined by something other than itself. In this case, the differentiating principle would be distinct from the universal. If the differentiating principle were distinct from the universal, the universal would not be that which self-differentiates. Thus, insofar as the universal is what it is, self-differentiation, the universal must be free.

When Hegel claims that the universal is free, he does not mean to claim that the universal has free will. Free will introduces more content than mere freedom *per se*, for the concept of the 'will' adds something over and beyond mere freedom or self-determination. In particular, the will is usually understood as a faculty of the mind. At this stage of the logical analysis, we have not yet reached the stage of 'mind,' though Hegel does appropriate the understanding as the 'faculty' of concepts. Still, in the concept of free will, freedom as such is obviously an integral and necessary element of the concept.

When Hegel identifies the universal with freedom, he also does not mean mere indeterminacy. Sometimes freedom is identified with simple indeterminacy or as something that is indeterminate. But Hegel means more than mere indeterminacy. Instead, *ultimately* freedom is determinate, for it gives itself its *own content*. But of course, in order to do this, it cannot already possess this content in a determinate way at the outset. If it did, it could hardly be said to give itself its own content; instead it would merely *repeat itself*. It makes itself what it is. Indeed, it becomes what it determines itself to be. It is not merely indeterminate. At the stage of universality, however, we are considering the universal *independently of its activity upon itself*, namely independently of its self-differentiation.

The concept is not only free and infinite, but it is also *unconditioned*. In order to illuminate the unconditioned, let us consider the following excerpt:

> *Universality* seems incapable of explanation [Erklärung], because it is the *simplest* of determinations; explanations must rely on determinations and differentiations and must apply predicates to its subject matter, and this would alter rather than explain the simple. But it is precisely of the nature of the universal to be a simple that, by virtue of absolute negativity, contains difference and determinateness *in itself* in the highest degree. *Being* is simple as an *immediate*; for this reason we can only *intend* it [Gemeintes] without being able to say what it is; therefore, it is immediately one with its other, *non-being*. The concept of being is just this, that it is so simple as to vanish into its opposite immediately; it is *becoming*. The *universal* is, on the contrary, a *simple* that is at the same time *all the richer in itself*, for it is the concept.[28]

Hegel claims that universality is a *simple* determination. Its simplicity is evident from its character as self-differentiation. As we have stated, self-differentiation, *in virtue* of being self-differentiation, is just one. Self-differentiation just *is* and stands *by itself*. Insofar as it stands by itself as the self-differentiating one, there is *no other* besides the One. Insofar as there is no other, there is *no difference* given at all. Thus, as the mere universal, the self-differentiating one is simple. The simplicity of the One is necessarily connected to its indeterminacy. The absence of the other, that in virtue of which it is simple, is the *same reason*, if you will, for its indeterminacy. So again, the ideality of the universal in virtue of which it is one and simple is also the reason for its indeterminacy. In sum, there is just *this one*: self-determination. To put the point another way, all that we have is the following claim: *self-differentiation is*. The universal is not the indeterminate itself. If it were, the universal would be identical to

Being. If it were identical to Being, it would not be the self-determining, since Being as such does not have that content. If the universal were identical to Being, it would be becoming. The universal is not at all identical to becoming, for it maintains itself in its differences; it does not lose itself in them. Being, as the indeterminate itself, has no content at all. It is in virtue of having no content that it becomes its opposite: Nothing. Unlike Being, the universal is not absent of all content: its content is self-differentiation. It is simple, indeterminate, and one *on account of its content*: self-determination. Hegel says as much at the end of the paragraph: 'The *universal* is, on the contrary, a *simple* that is at the same time *all the richer in itself*, for it is the concept.'[29] What is more: 'the simplicity which constitutes the very nature of the universal is such that, through absolute negativity, it contains within itself difference *[Unterschied]* and determinateness *[Bestimmtheit]* in the highest degree *[höchst]*.'[30] To put it ironically, it is because the universal is differentiated by itself that it has no differences. When we say that 'self-differentiation is' that is not the same as 'Being is.'

> The universal, on the contrary, even when it posits itself in a determination, *remains* in it what it is. It is the soul [Seele] of the concrete which it inhabits, unhindered and equal to itself in its manifoldness and diversity. It is not swept away in the becoming but persists undisturbed through it, endowed with the power of unalterable, undying self-preservation.[31]

Earlier we pointed out that Being, as the indeterminate itself, has no content, and it is only in virtue of having *no* content that it becomes its opposite: nothing. Unlike Being, the universal is not absent of all content, for its very content is self-differentiation. Although it has the content 'self-differentiation,' it is still simple, indeterminate, on account of that content.

Hegel is clear that in the logic of Being categories *transition* into their otherness. The qualitative determination by which a category is identified 'loses itself' in its other or, better, *becomes* the other. In transitioning into the other, the category does *not* maintain itself in its other, but is now the very determinacy of the other. As the determinacy of its other, the category is no longer the determinacy that it once was. For this reason, the new determination is a 'distinct determination.' The distinct determination into which the category has transitioned is not simply another aspect, side, or moment of the original category prior to the transition. Because the category in the logic of Being becomes a new categorical content in virtue of its transition, Hegel claims that such categories have their being 'in their limitation or otherness.'

Because the universal is simple, Hegel points out that the universal is *not capable of any explanation*. When we consider the simplicity of the one, its character as that which transcends otherness, the inability to explain the one is most evident. When we explain something, we posit some condition for it to be or to be known. Every condition conditions something else, the conditioned, and stands as a requirement for the existence or the knowledge of the conditioned thing. Because self-differentiation differentiates itself, and is the immediate unity of all of its differences, there is nothing external to self-differentiation that could in principle condition it. If self-differentiation had conditions, it would be determined by something else and would not be self-determining. Thus, self-differentiation cannot have conditions and is thereby *un*conditioned. Because it has no conditions to speak of, it cannot be explained. The universal is unconditioned, simple, and beyond explanation. Instead of claiming that the universal is explained by something else, one might claim that it *explains itself*. If this is the approach towards explanation, we must revise our understanding of conditions, in which there is a difference between determiner and determined.

The inability to explain the universal raises another interesting point regarding philosophical methodology. For the same reason that self-differentiation cannot be explained, it also cannot be the *conclusion* of an argument. As we have already indicated, the *truth* of the self-differentiating universal, as well as its justification, could not in principle depend upon premises. Premises are a type of foundation. Self-differentiation, insofar as it determines itself, cannot have its truth or justification dependent upon premises. For this reason, *we cannot argue for self-differentiation*. Instead, it establishes its own truth and justifies itself. We do not justify or secure the truth of the universal. Instead, our role is to merely dictate to ourselves and other minds what the universal is and its activity. In this respect, the philosopher writing about the universal is much like the prophet Muhammad receiving God's command: *dictate*!

Unlike the categories of Being, the concept 'preserves itself' and 'continues itself' in the 'manifoldness' and the 'diversity of the concrete.' In the moment of particularity, the concept determines itself into what is and what is not self-differentiating. These are the concrete moments, or what is the same, the particular elements of the universal as particular. Hegel's point is that even when the universal has differentiated itself into what is and what is not self-differentiating (the concrete diversity), it has not thereby ceased to be itself. Each element of the differentiation is a further *enrichment*, if you will, of the universal concept of self-differentiation. Instead of simply becoming a new category in the act of determining itself, as would be the case if the concept belonged to the category of Being, the concept has *more* content and a qualitatively *enhanced* content. The new elements, that into which the universal concept differentiates itself, are new elements of the concept *per se*. For this reason, it is better to think about the differentiating of the concept in terms of the *development of one content*, in contrast to a *transition into another content*.

Hegel writes that in the logic of Being 'this identity was only *implicitly* [an sich] the concept, was not yet made manifest.' Hegel's meaning is simple. In the logic of Being there is a process of self-differentiation, for this is evident in the *immediate* self-othering of categories. By 'immediate self-othering' I mean that immediately upon being what it is, the category is what it is not. For example, Being, in virtue of what it is, is immediately nothing. There is no process intervening here: Being is immediately nothing, and nothing Being. Still, this process of self-differentiation in the logic of Being is not *explicitly* a process of self-differentiation. Self-differentiation *as such* does not appear in the logic of Being. Only in the *Doctrine of the Concept* does self-differentiation *as such* appear. If self-differentiation as such were to appear in the logic of Being, the very logic of Being itself would be undermined. Instead of *transition*, there would be *development*. For this reason, in the logic of Being the concept is not yet manifested. Instead, the categories of being are only 'in themselves' conceptual. This means that each of the categories of Being are indeed concepts, although their conceptual content fails to be the very what it is to be of the concept *per se*.

Hegel employs 'absolute mediation' (*absolute Vermittlung*) as another way of expressing the universal *per se* as the negation of negation, or absolute negativity. Though it is an absolute mediation, it is not yet mediated (*Vermitteltes*).[32] The latter qualification expresses what we have already said: the universal is absolute mediation, or the negation of negation, as immediately given. It is not yet the result of any process. The mediated universal is the abstract universal. Hegel informs us that the abstract universal is opposed to the particular and the singular and will be addressed later. The abstract universal is not only the mediated concept but also the *determinate* concept.

At the outset of the *Doctrine of the Concept*, Hegel made it clear that the concept ought not be identified with the determinate concept. As we already suspected, he means the abstract, mediated concept. Indeed, our very move to identify the concept with self-differentiation is motivated by the inherent problems that follow from positing the universal as inherently abstract. For this reason, it is not at all surprising that Hegel opposes the abstract universal to the moments of the concept. What is perhaps more surprising is his insistence that *even* the abstract universal is a negation of negation.

In this paragraph Hegel establishes two theses: first, the abstract universal is a negation of negation, and second, the process of negating negation is posited as external to the content of the abstract universal itself. The opposition between the universal proper and the abstract universal is clear: the universal proper has for its content that very negation of negation that the abstract universal precludes from itself. The abstract universal is formed by a process of *subtraction* or omission. The thinker purviews a plurality of properties (*Eigenschaften*)[33] that subsist in some entity. By thinking one by itself, one property is separated from the others in thought. As Hegel states, this process involves two separate negations. First, each of the given properties is a negation, for each of them has its own determinate content, and negation is necessary for any determinate content. Second, in the act of omitting the various contents, the given negations or properties are negated. Thus, the act of abstracting some content from a manifold of contents is an act by which one negates negations.

Given that the act of abstracting is a negation of negation, let us proceed to the second thesis: in the abstract universal the content of the universal is separate from the negation of negation. This thesis is also evident from the process itself. First, the abstrac*ted* universal is just one content distinct from others. Second, the content that is removed from the manifold of contents is not itself the negation of negation. It is some given content, or *negation*, just as the other contents are. The negation of negation in regard to the abstract universal is not determined by that content. To the contrary, we discovered the negation of negation in *the act of omission* by some thinker, not in what is raised into the mind of the thinker. Indeed, upon the completion of the act of abstraction, what is left is not the negation of negation, but some specific or determinate negation. Thus, in the abstract universal, the negation of negation is posited as *external* to the content of the universal itself. In this scenario, the abstract universal does not develop itself or determinate itself. Its content is simply given. Thought gives some content to think about by omitting others, but it does not account for the content of the universal that it thinks.

Much of the time, Hegel employs the word 'abstract' in this derogatory way, to signify the process of omission that proceeds from a given. Though we must be sure to preclude this sense of the abstract from the concept, Hegel uses 'abstract' in another way. For example, certain passages show that Hegel has another, 'higher' and 'richer' understanding of universality than the derogatory sense: 'In this universality, the concept is *outside itself*, and because *it is it, the concept*, which is there outside itself, the abstract-universal contains all the moments of the concept.'[34] What I would like to point out here is that Hegel has multiple senses of abstract universality and that the abstract universal is not merely external to the concept. By retaining another sense of the abstract universal, Hegel holds the right to bring some determinacy to the universal that is not grounded on foundationalism and the other paradoxes that have plagued philosophy for millennia. Indeed, because Hegel identifies the abstract universal with the determinate universal, Hegel must reserve another sense for abstraction that he may legitimately employ, for otherwise he cannot introduce any determinate content to the universal.

At the very outset of the *Doctrine of the Concept* Hegel points out that the logic of Being and Essence are unified in the concept:

> The concept is the mutual penetration [Durchdringung] of these moments, namely the qualitative and the originative existent [ursprüngliche Seinende] is only as positing and as immanent turning back [Rückkehr-in-sich], and this pure immanent reflection simply is the *becoming-other* [Anderswerden] of *determinateness* which is, consequently, no less infinite, self-referring [sich auf sich beziehende] *determinateness*.[35]

Although Essence is an Ideality, it is an Ideality in which determiner and determined are nonetheless opposed to each other.[36] Hegel goes on to illuminate the difference between the *Doctrine of the Concept* and the logic of Essence by comparing the concept to substance. Through examining the comparison between substance and concept, we may glean a basic insight regarding the structure of the logic of Essence. Hegel writes: 'To this extent the universal is also the *substance* [Substanz] of its determinations, but in such a way that for the Substance as such was an *accident* [Zufälliges], is the concept's own self-*mediation*, its own *immanent* reflection.'[37]

Substance in Hegel's logic is a *self-identical* being that has attributes. As a self-identity, it excludes everything that it is not, and therefore cannot be the source of its attributes. Though the attributes belong to substance, it is not in virtue of the substance that the attributes exist. For this reason, the attributes of the substance are contingent. In other words, the substance could exist even if the attributes were not present in the substance. The attributes are a 'contingency' for substance, because the relation of attribute to substance is *external*. Accordingly, we might call these attributes 'accidents,' for the term expresses both the contingency and externality of the attributes. In Hegel's language, the substance is not 'self-mediated.' Given that the substance is not the source of its own attributes, the attributes must have their origin in some *other* substance. Accordingly, substances *cause* alterations, the *effects*, in other substances. For this reason, the substances are *mediated by another*. As mere self-identities, the substances themselves do not alter. Instead, the attributes of the substances alter in a causal change initiated by substances.

For these reasons, it may seem odd that Hegel would claim that the concept is the substance of its determinations. Indeed, Hegel himself points out that although the concept is the substance of its determinations, what was a contingency for substance is now the concepts own 'self-mediation' and 'immanent reflection.' At the outset of our analysis of universality we emphasized the *self-identity* of the universal. Because the universal is indeed self-identical, it is not completely unwarranted for Hegel to compare the universal with substance. Nevertheless, what sets the concept apart from substance is the content of the concept's self-identity. The concept is self-differentiation and is self-identical *as* the self-differentiating principle. As self-differentiating, whatever differentiations or determinations that belong to it are a result of the activity of the concept itself. What is distinctive about the universal concept is that it remains itself in its own differentiation of itself. Accordingly, the determinations of the universal are no longer external to the universal itself. As Hegel states, *each moment of the concept is the concept itself.* Because the relationship between the universal and its determinations are not external, the determinations of the universal are *not* contingently related to the universal. As Hegel claims, 'what was a contingency for substance becomes the concepts own *self-mediation.*' Thus, although the universal is the substance of its determinations insofar as it is the self-identical principle of self-differentiation, those differentiations of which it is the 'substance' are identical and necessary to its being.[38] Instead of the relations of reflection, positing, or causation, Hegel claims, as we have already seen, that the universal is the *creator* of its determinations.[39]

In his seminal *Freedom's Embrace*, Melvin Woody analyzes the opposition between concept and Substance in terms of freedom and substance. We might do the same. As noted, what is self-differentiating is nothing more nor less than what is self-determining or free. In his comparison between the concept and substance, Hegel is also pointing out that freedom cannot be reduced to substance. In the case of freedom, there is no need to appeal to cause and effect, for there is no external attribute that requires an explanation. Accordingly, the opposition between cause and effect and freedom is indeed an *authentic* opposition. On the one hand, Hegel's comparison between substance and freedom appears to shed light on the distinction between the logic of Essence and the *Doctrine of the Concept.* For the former, what determines, for example the cause, and what is determined, for example the effect, are not identical. Categories of Essence are defined by the opposition of determiner and determined.

The concept 'concept' is the truth of the concept 'cause and effect.' Though the pragmatists took this in a different direction, Hegel means, on the one hand, that the content of cause and effect is not complete by itself. The concept of cause and effect is negated, and it is negated not by any external act, but by itself. Because it necessarily self-negates, it is not true *by itself.* On the other hand, it is only true *as* the concept. This means that the content of cause and effect, though negated, is *preserved* only as the concept. Naturally, the *Aufhebung*, the negation and preservation of the concept is, in some sense, simultaneously a *transformation* of the concept. We have witnessed this process in the examples of transition and positing that I have reconstructed for illustration in the transition of the one to the void, the positing of determining reflection, and the positing of the concept. In each of these categorical processes, the initial determination, for example 'one,' and 'cause' all become elements of another category. The one becomes a moment of repulsion and attraction, and causation becomes a moment of reciprocal causation.

Given that the self-negation of the categories of Being and Essence give rise to the *Doctrine of the Concept*, once we arrive at the *Doctrine of the Concept* there is no longer any process that stands apart from the concept from which the concept derives its being. Instead, whatever it is that gave rise to the concept only exists in the form of the concept or *as* the concept. For this reason, once we arrive at the stage of the concept of the concept in the *Logic*, the only content that is present is the concept. Everything else has vanished into it. At this stage in the development, it is all that there is.[40]

In the concept of the concept Hegel explicates one *common* feature of both Being and Essence. In this sense, ideality is more general, if you will, than either, for it is *the common form* of both. The loss of the category in its other and the return to the category out of its otherness is one of the central features of Hegel's dialectic. In both transition and positing categories are engaged in conceptual self-differentiation, but as we noted earlier, they are not yet posited as concepts.

Towards the end of his discussion of universality, Hegel reminds us that so long as we consider the *universal by itself* we have not yet progressed to consider the *determinacy* of the concept.[41] The universal moment by itself is not yet determinate, for determinateness refers to the universal as particular and singular, not merely the universal moment. At the stage of the universal, the concept has not yet 'progressed to it' (*fortgegangen*) and created particularity. Still, Hegel is clear that when we think the universal, we cannot help but also think the universal in its determinacy, namely as particular and finally as *absolutely determinate*, or singular.

At the outset of the discussion of the concept, we pointed out that the concept itself is *indistinguishable* from each of its moments.[42] Accordingly, the moment of universality, the self-identity that is the negation of negation, must itself be grasped as the *totality* of its moments: 'As negativity in general, that is, according to the *first immediate* negation, the universal has determinateness *in it* above all *as particularity*; as *a second universal*, as the negation of negation, it is *absolute determinateness*, that is, *singularity* and *concreteness*.' In this passage, Hegel parses out the content of the universal as totality in terms of *two* negations. The first negation, he claims, is particularity, while the second is singularity. While particularity is the *determinacy* of the concept, singularity is the *absolute determinacy* of the concept. In our analysis of particularity and singularity, we must be careful to parse out the sense in which particularity is the determinacy of the concept and singularity the absolute determinacy.

Particularity

As the absolute negativity, Hegel writes that the negation of negation 'differentiates itself internally, and this is a *determining*, because the differentiating is one with the universality.'[43]

The universal is just self-differentiation as such. What is self-differentiation? It is that which differentiates itself. As a self-differentiation, it does not relate to an other; it only relates to itself, and this self-relation is one of self-differentiation. For this reason, the differentiation is 'internal.' The differentiation that it gives itself is 'one with the universality' exactly because the differentiation is *of* the universal *by* the universal itself.

What is it into which self-differentiation differentiates itself? If self-differentiation were not itself self-differentiated, then it would not be the identity that it is: self-differentiation. Thus, self-differentiation *must* differentiate itself. Into what differences can self-differentiation differentiate itself? The universal has no access to anything other than itself, namely that which is self-differentiating. Its contents cannot be derived from anything but self-differentiation, for otherwise it would not differentiate itself internally and would not be what it is. So, the differentiations of self-differentiation follow from the self-differentiation of self-differentiation and nothing else. Upon differentiating itself, self-differentiation immediately acquires a *predicate*: self-differentiation. Self-differentiation *is self-differentiating*.

Universality by itself is the simple subject 'self-differentiation.' Nonetheless, in virtue of its very content as a mere subject, it cannot help but immediately give rise to its predicate. Immediately upon grasping the subject term, the predicate immediately follows. Accordingly, the universal, in virtue of what it is, is *self-predicative*. By giving itself its own predicate, the universal renders itself *determinate*. By differentiating itself, the universal makes itself determinate. But what are the characteristics of that determination?

An act of *differentiation* is simultaneously an act of *negation*. Earlier we pointed out the connection among difference, negation, and determinacy. Determinate contents stand in a negative relationship with an other. They are differentiated from that which they are not. The determinate content, insofar as it is differentiated from that which it is not, excludes that which it is not. Insofar as it excludes that which it is not, the determinate content *negates* what it is not, what is other to it. The determinacy of the content is only determinate so long as the negation is active. Accordingly, whatever is differentiated is *also* negated. What is negated in the act of differentiating some content is the *unity* of the content that is negated. Differentiation takes what is whole and separates it from itself, thereby placing it in relationship with an other to which it is opposed.

In the case of self-differentiation, what is differentiated is self-differentiation, and what differentiates is self-differentiation. For this reason, no other outcome is possible than the following: in the act of self-differentiation, self-differentiation must *negate* itself. To differentiate oneself is *to negate oneself*. The negation of self-differentiation is that which is *not* self-differentiating. *Thus, self-differentiation differentiates itself into what is not self-differentiating.*[44] In terms of contradiction, it is in virtue of contradicting itself that it particularizes itself.

Of course, this is easier to see if one considers self-differentiation as the negation of negation. 'Negation of negation' is *explicitly* an act of self-negation. If the negation of negation as such were not to negate itself, then it would not be the negation of negation. Naturally, the negation of negation is, in itself, not a negation of anything other than itself. Negation of negation must negate itself if it is to remain what it is. Thus, the negation of negation negates itself. What is it into which the negation of negation must negate itself? It must be differentiated into *that which is not the negation of negation*. Thus, universality itself gives rise to that which is *not* the negation of negation, or that which is *not* self-differentiating. When considered in both of these ways, which are really two ways of expressing the same content, the moment of the universal, the negation of negation *per se*, is now 'in the form of negation' as Hegel likes to say. Particularity is the universal in the 'form of negation' and this is neither more nor less than the determinacy of the concept.

Clearly, particularity is not determinacy as such, but the determinacy *of* the concept. As we have already clarified, determinacy as such belongs to the logic of Being. In addition, unlike the logic of Being, particularity does not arrive out of universality by way of *transition*, but as a *development* of universality as such. In particularity, the universal is not in the presence of anything other than itself, for the particularity is *the universal* in *the form* of negation.[45] We have expressed this above by pointing out that it is self-differentiation that differentiates itself into what is not self-differentiation; it is the negation of negation that is in the form of negation. For this reason, the determinateness of the universal as particularity is not a limit, for there is no other to which the universal may be compared. The universal is by itself in its self-differentiation.

There is yet another way to understand how the universal becomes the particular. The concept in the form of mere universality is fully contained in the proposition 'the universal is.' But insofar as there is just universality given as the subject, and no predicate, there is not yet any predication. Accordingly, the first development we *witness* is that 'the universal is not universal.' But this is exactly what particularity is, namely the universal in its self-negation. Because of what it is, the universal immediately negates itself. As such, the universal is now in the form of its negation.

Hegel proclaims that it freely determines itself and renders itself finite. Here I think it is especially important to pay attention to the use of Hegel's language. Hegel uses the term '*Verendlichung*' here. This term means 'to bring to an end' or 'to render finite.' The act of self-negation brings the universal as universal to an end. By bringing it to an end, it renders the universal *finite*. How does it render the universal finite? *Prima facie*, one might think that Hegel has undermined his own claim. First he claims that in particularity the universal is only in the presence of itself, and no other is present. Second, he claims that there is an other present. Indeed, in the concept of the 'finite' there is the concept of the 'limit.' If the particular is not a limit, and the finite is that which has an internal limit, how can the particular be the universal in its finitude?

> The particular is the universal itself, but it is its difference or reference to an *other*, its *outwardly reflecting shine* [sein scheinen nach außen]; but there is no other at hand from which the particular would be differentiated than the universal itself. The universal determines *itself*, and so is itself the particular; the determinateness is *its* difference; it is only differentiated from itself. Its species are therefore only the (a) universal itself and (b) the particular. The universal is as concept itself and its opposite, and this opposite is in turn the universal itself as its posited determinateness; the universal overreaches it and, in it, it is with itself. Thus it is the totality and the principle of its diversity, which is determined wholly and solely through itself.[46]

In the act of self-negation, the universal creates that which is not the universal out of itself. Accordingly, the universal opposes itself to what it is not in virtue of its negation of itself. On the one hand, the result is that the universal itself exists *as* particularity, or as that which is not self-differentiating. This is what Hegel means when he considers the universal *as* particularity and what he means when he claims that in particularity the universal is in the presence of itself and that 'Thus it is the totality and the principle of its diversity.' Indeed, the universal is the unity of itself with its opposite, and in particularity the universal is that which it is not, what is not self-differentiating. On the other hand, the negation of self-differentiation creates *a new opposition* between self-differentiation and its negation. If the universal were merely that which is not-self-differentiating, it would not stand in opposition to itself, or what is the same, it would not be self-negating. Yet, the self-differentiation of self-differentiation is nothing more than the *self-negation* of the universal, the negation of negation. Thus, the self-negation of self-differentiation results in a duality: self-differentiation must be *different from itself*. Insofar as it is different from itself, *two* terms must be present: self-differentiation (the universal), and that which is not self-differentiating (the particular). Or what is the same: the negation *of* the negation of negation creates an opposition *within itself* between the negation of negation and the negation *of* the negation of negation. For this reason, there are only *two species or types of universality*: the universal *qua* universal, and the universal *qua* particular. No other differentiation of the universal is possible without appealing to an external difference. The limit of the universal is a limit that *it gives itself*. For this reason, although the finite differences are present within the universal, because the finite is the self-opposition of the universal, or results from the self-opposition of the universal, the finitude of the types of universality do not necessitate an appeal to an external difference.

Each term *limits* the other and comes to an end. The universal moment, as that which is self-differentiating, has *rendered itself finite* by opposing itself to that which is not self-differentiating, what Hegel calls 'the particular.' The results of the self-negation of universality are *fixed isolated differences*. In terms of contradiction, it is in virtue of the *self-contradiction* of universality that the universal gives rise to consistent, other-exclusive particulars. Since each term excludes the other, each term is isolated from the other. Insofar as each is isolated from the other, neither do they become each other nor are they to be identified with each other. The universal is what it is and is opposed to the particular. The particular is what it is and is opposed to the universal. Insofar as the particular moment is not the absolute determinacy of the universal and identifies the particular as the finite moment, the particular itself must 'come to an end.' The particular as such is not 'absolute determinacy' for exactly this reason: it is the finite moment and must thereby come to an end. Notice that particularity is consistent, for each species is itself and denies identity with its negation. On the other hand, this consistency is an *inconsistency*, in the sense that the consistency of the particular is the universal insofar as it is not universal, or the self-differentiating universal insofar as it is not self-differentiating.

One might wonder why Hegel employs the term 'particular' (*Besonderheit*). One could replace the term 'particular' with 'determinate universal,' 'differentiate universal,' or 'universal in the form of negation' if one preferred. But the term 'particularity' (*Besonderheit*) is well chosen for several reasons. The phrases 'Das besondere Begriff,' 'the particular concept,' and 'die Besonderheit,' particularity, are well-chosen phrases. 'Besonderheit' means *specificity*. In German, I might use the term colloquially to say '*Insbesondere* konzentriere ich mich auf den Film,' which means 'in particular or *specifically*, I am concentrating on the movie.' What is particular is specific. When one specifies something, the act of *specification* narrows what it is to which I am referring so that it may be picked out. In my example above, I said I was concentrating on the movie, not other topics. What is specific is 'this' and not 'that.' Without the act of exclusion or negation, an act of specification cannot be successful. For this reason, the term 'particular' is a proper term for this moment of the concept, for in *Besonderheit* the universal and particular exist as specific types of universality. The particular is 'this' and not 'that.' In the moment of particularity the universal becomes a specific, finite content that is opposed to another specific, finite content, the particular.

In the passage we have been analyzing, Hegel identifies the particular as an 'illusory reference outwards.' Earlier in his discussion of universality, Hegel claims that the determinate concept is constituted by two illusory references, one inward and one outward:

> More precisely, the universal shows itself to be this totality as follows. In so far as the universal possesses determinateness, this determinateness is not only the *first* negation but also the reflection of this negation into itself. Accordingly, to that first negation, taken by itself, the universal is a *particular*, and in this guise, we shall consider it in a moment. In the other determinateness, however, the universal is still essentially universal, and this side we have here still to consider.—For the determinateness, as it is in the concept, is the total reflection—a *doubly reflective shine* [Doppelschein], both *outwards*, [der Schein nach außen]as reflection into the other, and *inwards*, as reflection into itself. The outward shining establishes a distinction with respect to an *other;* the universal accordingly takes on a particularity which is resolved [Auflösung] in a higher universality.[47]

As is evident from this passage, the illusory reference outwards constitutes just one side of the determinacy of particularity. Particularity as such is constituted by two illusory references. The illusory reference involves a 'distinction with respect to an *other*,' and the universal has its resolution in a higher universal. This description is consistent with what Hegel has told us in the section on particularity, in which the illusory reference outwards is described as the universal insofar as it involves difference and a relationship to another.

One might wonder why Hegel would insist on introducing the term 'illusion' at this stage of the development. One concern is that the term 'illusion' implies that there must be a *mind* to which that illusion appears. Let us first remind ourselves that the term 'illusion' first arises in the logic of Essence. Here, as in the logic of Essence, 'illusion' does not necessitate a mind. Instead, the term signifies a *direction of determination* that is constitutive of particularity. In our discussion of universality we spent some energy towards its explication. Illusion, as we discovered, signifies *the non-self-subsistent that shows (Scheinen) as self-subsistent.* What is illusory *reflects* the self-subsistent, but is *not itself* self-subsistent. At the stage of particularity, the illusory is not yet known as illusory. Instead, it is simply illusory. In the stage of singularity the illusory will be shown to be illusory.

In the literature, there is some debate concerning the status of the illusory reference. Trisokkas in 'The Speculative Logical Theory of Universality' takes the illusory references to be constitutive of universality.[48] Against Friedrich Schick and Christian Iber, Trisokkas defends the view that the illusory reference is twofold and cannot be reduced to the illusory reference outward. Though Trisokkas is correct to argue against Schick and Iber that the illusory references are twofold, I am inclined to think of the illusory references as characteristic of the moment of particularity. It is tempting to view the illusory references under the heading of universality, for Hegel first introduces the concepts when he is discussing universality. Still, Hegel is clear that the illusory references are constitutive of the universal as determinate, and the determinate universal is the particular. For this reason, I take Hegel's comments here to be anticipatory of what he shall develop in the section on particularity.

In virtue of differentiating itself, the universal creates two *mutually exclusive* universals: particularity and universality. One dimension of the illusion is the fact that *the self-contradictory concept presents itself as consistent*, such that the illusion arises that the universal is not particular and the particular not universal. In virtue of the self-contradiction of universality, the illusion of the consistency and mutual exclusion of the universal and the particular arises. As we have already mentioned, each of these universals excludes the other. Moreover, they are fixed, isolated differences that do not unify themselves with the other in virtue of what they are. Indeed, in particularity the universal has negated itself. Accordingly, it is in the form of what is not self-determining. Thus, neither of the universals that results from the self-negation of the universal admits what it is not, and neither is the source of its own differentiation.

Because the universals 'universal' and 'particular' do *not* admit what they are not, the very differentiation of each of the universals must have an *external* source. Each of the differentiations in particularity can only be what it is if it is differentiated from what it is not. Indeed, this is a basic requirement of the relative determinacy of any content, namely that it exclude what it is not. For this reason, the determination of the contents 'universal' and 'particular' must have their origin in an external source. Moreover, any *relation* of universal to particular cannot be initiated by either term, for each is what it is and does not relate itself to the other. For this reason, any relation of universal to particular may only be achieved through an external factor, a third term. Indeed, because their relationship consists just in their differentiation from each other, the relationship of the one to the other must have its source in nothing other than that principle by which they are differentiated. Naturally, the self-differentiating universal (as the principle of unity and difference of the moments) is the one source of both moments. Indeed, for this reason, the unity and differentiation of universality and particularity, as moments of the universal, appear to have their origin in an external difference.

Each of the moments asserts themselves as independent of the other, as though they were not moments of one concept. Together, their mutual exclusion and difference from each other constitutes *the illusory reference outwards*. On the one hand, each of the moments shows itself as independent of the other, when *in reality*, neither is independent of the other. Or what is the same, each encounters *an other that is not really an other*, since each of the moments 'particularity' and 'universality' are moments of the one self-negating concept. In this sense, the illusory reference is *that there is an other*. Indeed, as moments of one universal, they cannot be independent of one another. The illusory reference is outward exactly because of the appearance of the self-subsistence of the moments. Because of the insistence on their separation, the unification and differentiation of each requires *a reference to a third term*, namely to an external factor in virtue of which their unity and difference may be grasped. Because the emphasis here lies in the *difference* between the universal and the particular, the illusory reference outwards may also be described as the *absence* of the unconditioned, absolute, and free universal. The illusion is that there is no unconditioned, absolute, universal. In this sense, the illusory reference outwards places all the emphasis on the side of the particular, or the division of the particular from the universal.

Hegel informs us that the particulars have their resolution in a 'higher universal.' The word for resolution is *Auflösung*, which can signify a 'loosening up' or 'dissolving.' As we shall see, there are two senses of 'higher universal' that are at work here. As long as we remain at the stage of particularity, we shall not properly resolve or dissolve the distinction between universality and particularity. The truly higher universal that undermines the difference between universal and particular, and weds them to each other, is the third moment of the concept: singularity. Still, there is another sense of 'higher universal' *as that external term* that unites the mutually external moments of 'particularity' and 'universality.' Since the illusory reference outwards is only one side of particularity, a complete explication of the category also requires a consideration of the illusory reference *inwards*.

Earlier in the *Logic*, when Hegel is discussing the relation between the infinite and the finite in the logic of Being, he asks a question that is pertinent to our discussion:

how does the infinite go forth out of itself and come to finitude?[49]

In this passage, Hegel is discussing the relationship between the infinite and the finite in the context of the infinite and finite *per se*, not the concept and the relation between two of its moments. Yet, the question is just as valid for our discussion of the concept as it is for the infinite and the finite *per se*. The concept, as the universal, is infinite, yet as a particular moment of itself, it is finite. Thus, the question regarding how the concept goes forth from itself and makes itself finite is just as relevant for our inquiry into the being of the concept as it is for an inquiry into the relation of the infinite to the finite.

The question is: 'how does the infinite go forth from itself and make itself finite?' The *answer* is: self-predication and existential implication.

In the particular, the universal has not only become finite, but it is now determinate. The universal is determinate because it stands in contrast to the other, the particular. In the act of self-predication, the universal gives itself its own determinacy by setting itself 'to the side' or making itself finite. Indeed, the universal itself has universality as one of its moments, for the universal, self-differentiation, has differentiated itself into self-differentiation and what is not self-differentiating. Indeed, the term 'self-predication' expresses the general form of the whole movement we have been tracing thus far. The universal, in virtue of an act of self-predication, gives rise to its own particulars. Insofar as the universal is the sole principle of its particular specificities, the universal is existentially implicating. In the *Doctrine of the Concept*, *self-predication* is the *principle* of *existential implication*. Particulars, in this system, do not have their origin in any principle outside of the universal. The universal itself creates the particulars on its own through an act of self-predication.

The issue of self-predication and existential implication is connected to Hegel's use of the term 'creation.' Indeed, Hegel's question regarding the way the infinite makes itself finite is nothing more nor less than the question concerning *the form of creation*. In German Hegel uses two phrases: '*schöpferische Macht*' and '*das Schaffen.*' The former literally means 'creative power,' while the latter means 'the creating.' Hegel's use of language naturally conjures up theological connotations. On the one hand, Hegel's use of 'creation' indicates that the process by which the particular develops from the universal ought not be grasped as a process of making, generation, or contingent spontaneity. Hegel, as is evident, rejects modeling the concept on any of these relations. Making, as it turns out, assumes form and matter from the outset, but cannot account for the form or the matter itself. Indeed, the concept cannot proceed as an act of making, or on analogy with it, for the concept cannot rely on any foundations. Moreover, there is no contingent spontaneity in the concept. It is true that the concept is free, because it is self-determining, but that freedom is not contingent. As we have shown, self-differentiation is not an act of caprice or a choice. Instead, self-differentiation *necessarily* gives the particulars in virtue of what it is.

In the case of freedom or the concept *per se*, although there is necessity, the necessity is not mechanical or blind, for the determination of the concept is not external, as is the case in a chain of efficient causation. If we insist on a metaphor, we could follow Hegel's lead and call the free necessity of the concept a 'living necessity' or 'organic necessity.' But if we employ this metaphor, we might wonder why Hegel does not use the term 'generation' in his explication of the moments of the concept. The concept *per se* is not literally *alive*, for it is *not* a living organism. Life, as Hegel argues further in the *Logic*, requires the concept for its possibility, and exemplifies the concept in nature, but the concept *per se* does *not require* the category 'life' for its possibility, but the concept is, however, retro-actively determined to be living' only after the development of the concept of life. Hegel argues that other categories beyond the concept are necessary for explicating the concept of life, namely 'teleology,' 'chemism,' and 'mechanism.'

Why ought we think about the relationship between the universal and the particular as an inherently creative one? In the first place, unlike life, the concept must completely *give itself* its own being. Its own being is dependent on what it determines itself to be. Insofar as the concept must give itself its own determinacy, or its own being, it cannot rely on any foundations for what it determines itself to be. Life, as is evident, depends on a multitude of foundations and given determinations, such as those that constitute its environment. Creation is that act of grant-ing existence to determinate beings without any appeal to *antecedent* principles. On the one hand, because the concept does not rely on any foundations, and is initially indeterminate, the concept appears to cre-ate itself *ex nihilo*. After all, it is the concept that is the 'original.' On the other hand, because the concept creates *itself out of its own self*, its creation cannot be out of nothing. Still, we must be careful to note that these two oppositions are unified, for although the determinations that the concept gives itself arise out of itself, the content that it is before it determines itself is an initially *indeterminate* content, and as such it is not initially a determinate 'something.'[50] The concept is that which brings itself out of its own indeterminacy and gives itself its own deter-minate being. In this way, the creative act of the concept is an act of *self-creation*. Or as David Gray Carlson has put it, the concept is its own origin, or the 'shaper and creator' of its own self.[51] Hegel also articulates the point theologically:

> The unity in question is to be grasped as an absolute process, as the living activity of God, . . . so that it is the absolute activity of eter-nally producing itself.[52]

The particular, though it is a separate moment from the universal moment, is also the determinacy of the concept itself. 'Creation,' unlike 'life,' 'making,' or 'caprice,' corresponds most closely to the activity of the concept. In the self-differentiating concept, Hegel thinks that he has the key to (i) grasping *why* creation is necessary and (ii) rendering the act of creation *intelligible*.

What is most striking about the creation of the particular from the universal is that finitude is *restored* to conceptual determinacy. Earlier we demonstrated that the concept could not be finite without engendering some fundamental paradoxes. For this reason, the concept was redefined as self-differentiation. Yet, Hegel argues that we cannot simply leave fini-tude behind. Instead, the concept, though it is infinite, *makes itself finite*.

The dogma of finitude is no longer a dogma, for we have discovered the *principle* from which it follows. Hegel writes that '

> The isolated *subsistence* [Bestehen] of the finite that was earlier determined as its being-for-itself, also as thinghood, as Substance, is in its truth universality, the form with which the infinite concept clothes its differences—a form which is equally itself one of its differences.

The isolated subsistence of finite determinations is one of the concept's differences. Indeed, without the finite opposition of universal to particular, the concept would fail to possess any determinate or specific content. According to Hegel, the mistake that led us to take finitude as a dogma of universality was to think of the universal as merely finite. Instead, finitude develops out of the free, infinite, and unconditioned concept as one of its elements.

Given that finite determinations develop out of the infinite concept, we are now in a position to begin to address some of our most basic questions. How can the various forms of finite universality, namely the abstraction, the set, and the genus, be elements or moments of the concept, given that the concept is infinite? Because the concept entails finite determinations within itself in the form of particularity, the genus, set, and abstraction may exist *as forms of particularity*.

Self-predication and existential implication, both features of the concept as such, cannot be limited to the moments of the universal. Hegel is clear that both the moments of universality and particularity exhibit self-predication and existential implication. Hegel expresses this by pointing out that the self-differentiation of the concept renders the moment of universality particular, and particularity universal:

> There is, therefore, no other true logical division than this, that the concept sets itself on one side as the *immediate*, indeterminate universality [unmittelbare unbestimmte Algemeinheit]; it is this very indeterminateness that makes its determinateness, or that it is a *particular*. The two are both a particular and are therefore *coordinated*. Both, as particular, are also *determinate as against* the universal, and in this sense they are *subordinated* to it. But even this universal, as against which the particular is determined, is for that reason itself also *just one* of the opposing sides. When we speak of *two opposing sides*, we must repeat that the two constitute the particular, not just *together*, as if they were *alike* in being particular only for external reflection, but because their determinateness *over against each other* is at the same time essentially only one determinateness; it is the negativity which in the universal is *simple* [einfach].[53]

It is here, in this small paragraph, that Hegel unveils the dialectical content of the concept, and it is also the clue to interpreting his claim that particularity is constituted by an illusory reference inwards and outwards. Hegel makes the bold claim that there is no other true logical classification than the division of the concept as such into the moments of universality and particularity. By differentiating itself, the concept 'sets itself on one side as the *immediate*, indeterminate universality.' In this first sentence, Hegel is distinguishing the universal as one separate moment of the concept. The universal, insofar as it is just the self-identity 'self-differentiation,' but is not yet self-differentiating, is immediately what it is, and not yet determinate. But upon differentiating itself, the universal is no longer just immediate and indeterminate. Now it is determinate and *mediated by its own activity*. By determining itself, the universal concept as such has divided itself into two moments: self-differentiation and the self-differentiation of self-differentiation. Accordingly, the concept has distinguished itself from the mere universality that is the self-identical, immediate, indeterminate universal. Now, the immediate, indeterminate concept is just one moment of the universal. The universal, insofar as it is just one of the specific moments of the universal concept as such, is now to be differentiated from the self-differentiated universal. Because the indeterminate, immediate universal is now set in opposition to the determinate, self-differentiating universal, the immediate, indeterminate universal now stands *opposed* to the determinate universal and thereby stands in a *determinate relation* to the self-differentiating universal. Thus, it is exactly the *indeterminate* character of the universal that constitutes its determinateness of the universal. When Hegel here speaks of the indeterminate universal as determinate he means the universal that is a moment of the universal concept as such. The universal concept has 'set itself' to the side. In other words, the universal is *existentially implicating*, for it is its *own* particular.

Given that the universal moment is now determinate as the indeterminate, immediate universal, and the determinate moment of the universal concept is the particular, the immediate, indeterminate universal is also particular. So, we can with confidence say that the universal moment is *a* particular. But Hegel says more, namely that *each* of them *is the particular* and is *co-ordinate* with the other. But we might wonder why this is necessary. Why is each *the* particular and not just *a* particular?

This is easy enough to see: when self-differentiation differentiates itself, it negates itself and gives rise to two opposite determinations: self-differentiation as such (the universal moment) and the self-differentiation of self-differentiation (the particular moment). Because *both* the former and the latter are now differentiated forms of self-differentiation, the immediate, indeterminate universal, as immediate and indeterminate, is no longer given. Instead, there is *only the particular moment*, the universal as determinate. In other words, because both the universal and particular are differentiated, only the universal as *differentiated*, or as particular, is given. This is why Hegel claims that their determinateness over and against one another is not a result of external determination or reflection, but is just *one* determination. Each is the same content, for each is the content *over against one another*, to use Hegel's words. The one determination is 'the negativity', or the universal *in the form of negation*. This is *simple*, because there is only *one* content present: particularity. Having taken the place of the universal, instead of 'universality is' we have 'particularity is.'

Insofar as there is only the particular, *the concept itself is the particular*. To see that the concept itself is the particular shows us that *the particular itself has particularity as one of its moments*. Because all that is given is particularity, particularity itself is not just a moment of the concept, but the concept itself. Hence, *the particular itself just is the universal*. Because the concept is divided into two moments: the universal and the particular, and the universal concept itself is the particular, it follows that the particular has particularity as its own moment. For this reason, we cannot limit existential implication to the universal moment. This is expressed in the judgment 'particularity is particular.' In the self-predicative judgment, the subject falls under itself as the predicate and is a moment of itself.

Another way to see how the particular itself is the universal is to remember that the universal, insofar as it negates itself, is the universal in the form of negation, or particularity. Already upon reaching this conclusion, we have the identity of the universal and the particular. Insofar as the universal exists in the form of negation, in particularity the universal is not in the presence of an other, but only in the presence of itself. Insofar as both the moment of immediate, indeterminate universality and mediated, determinate universality are differentiated from each other, and stand in opposition to each other, the whole concept no longer stands in the form of the mere unity of self-differentiation, but of *pure difference*. Each moment is differentiated from the other. In particularity, what is *absolute, unconditioned*, and *free* is the differentiation. Indeed, the free, unconditioned, and absolute *universal* is now the free, unconditioned, and absolute *particular*. Thus, one may proclaim that it is *not* just the particular that is particular and the universal that is universal, but it is *the universal that is the particular* and *the particular that is the universal*.

The *return* of particularity to universality out of the posited difference between the moments 'universality' and 'particularity' is what Miller translates as *the illusory reference inwards* (der Schein nach innen). Together, the illusory reference inwards and the illusory reference outwards (der Schein nach außen) constitute *the total determinacy* of particularity.[54] In my commentary I have been using Miller's translation of 'Schein' in this section as 'illusion' since it captures the concept that *the difference* between particularity and universality *is* the Absolute insofar as it only *seems* to be absolute, *but is not*. Giovanni himself indicates that

418   *Hegel's Absolute Dialetheism*

translating 'Schein' as 'shine' does 'not sit well in a procession of logical categories.'[55] As Giovanni points, out 'seem' and 'semblance' might also work as good translations, and here in the analysis of particularity, any absolute difference between particularity and universality must eventually show itself to be a *seeming-to-be*. At the close of his discussion of universality, Hegel indicates the basic structure of the illusory reference inwards (what Giovanni translates as the *reflective inward shining*).[56]

The illusory reference outward is necessary for the illusory reference inward. Hegel points out that although particularity is a *relative* universal, it does not lose its character of universality. The universality that applies to particularity is not one that is garnered from the outside, but he claims that particularity is universal because it is 'bent back into itself' out of its externality. Upon differentiating itself, universality becomes divided into two mutually exclusive moments. This is the 'externality' of the universal. It is 'bent back into itself' exactly at the moment one has posited the difference between the particular and universal moments. Immediately upon differentiating the particular and universal moments, *only* the differentiated universal, the particular, is given. Because the particular moment now stands alone, the particular is *positive*, and not merely a limitation as it must be in the illusion outward. The particular is now standing in 'free relation to itself' as the absolute content. For this reason, 'even the determinate concept remains in itself infinitely free concept.'

Given our analysis above, the illusory reference inwards is nothing other than *particularity as universality*. Universality has returned or 'bent back into itself.' In the illusory reference inwards, universality is particularity as such, not just self-identical universality. This is the meaning of the phrase 'bent back into itself.' In the illusory reference inwards, we discover the *relative* moment 'particularity' taking on the *significance of the absolute*. Although it is a relative universal, it is also still universal and exactly in virtue of that relativity. With the term 'Umfange' Hegel indicates that the particular now is just as *extensive* and *all-inclusive* as the universal. What makes the identity of particular and universal an *illusory reference* is the fact that it *shuts out and excludes* the very distinction between the moments of universality and particularity that is constitutive of the illusion outwards. At this stage of the concept's development, the particular asserts itself *as the universal*. The illusion is that *only the particular is independent*, unconditioned, and free. Indeed, the particular appears *as the self-subsistent universal*. Here the illusion is the opposite of the illusion in the illusion outwards. In the illusion inwards, the particular presents itself as though there were *no other* at all. This illusion is the illusion, for example, that the PNC is an *absolute principle*. This is the meaning of the 'reference *inwards*.' Ironically, the self-assertion of particularity as universality also entails the rejection of differentiation. The illusory reference inwards moves in the opposite direction of the illusory reference outwards (or what Giovanni translates as *reflective shining outwards*). Ironically, the universal *loses* the particular by becoming identical with it. When all that is given is 'particularity is,' particularity cannot be particular.

Insofar as the particular is the universal, the particular entails the absence of differentiation. All that is given is particularity. Yet, the very content of particularity is just pure differentiation, namely the differentiation of the universal from the particular moment. Hence, particularity is the pure absence and presence of the differentiation of its moments. In other words, particularity posits that which is not absolute as Absolute. Because it is the self-contradiction of universality that has been ossified into fixed and opposing differentiations, the contradiction of particularity consists in the *positing of the self-contradiction as a consistent determination*. Particularity is that which *excludes itself from itself*. Hegel claims that

> The isolated *subsistence* [Bestehen] of the finite that was earlier determined as its being-for-itself, also as thinghood, as Substance, is in its truth universality, the form with which the infinite concept clothes its differences—a form which is equally itself one of its differences.

This favorite metaphor of Hegel to which he shall appeal again and again in the chapter on particularity invokes the concept of appearance. The particular is not only the 'illusory being' but it is also that which 'clothes' the concept. The particular is the moment in which each moment of the concept is separate from the others. Although the concept is the totality of its moments: universality, particularity, and singularity, the concept always already appears as one of its moments: as universality, particularity, or singularity. In this sense, the concept, as the totality of the moments, is hidden by its own singular determinations. Yet, for those who can penetrate the content of each moment, the various determinations of the concept show themselves as appearances of the once self-determining concept.

In the history of philosophy, those who have taken particularity as the concept have taken the illusion to be the reality, such that for example the PNC has perennially been raised to an absolute principle. One of the basic errors that philosophers have made in the history of philosophy is the mistaken judgment that particularity, or some form of the particular universal, such as the genus, the set, or the abstract universal, is exhaustive of universality *per se*. Each form of universality we find in the tradition, the abstraction, the class, and the genus, engenders the division of the universal from the particular and as such belongs to the moment of particularity. This demonstrates that it would be a profound error to banish these forms of conceptual determinacy from Hegel's system.[57] On the one hand, the commitment to the universal as that which only exists in the form of particularity entails that no contradiction ought to be allowed, for particularity engenders the absolute separation of universal from particular. This is the side of the illusion outward. On the other hand, because particularity, or the absolute difference between universal and particular, must itself be universal, it must be identical with what it is not and therefore embody a profound contradiction.

Hegel promises us a third division of the concept, *singularity*, in which the division of the particular from the universal may be overcome. He writes:

> The truly higher universal is the one in which this outwardly directed side is redirected inwardly; this is the second negation in which the determinateness is present simply and solely *as* something posited, or as reflective shine. Life [Leben], the 'I' [Ich], spirit [Geist], absolute concept [absoluter Begriff], are not universals only as higher genera, but are rather *concretes* whose determinacies are also not mere species or lower genera but determinacies which, in their reality, are self-contained and self-complete. Of course, life, the 'I,' finite spirit, are also only determinate concepts. To this extent, however, their resolution is in a universal which, as the truly absolute concept, is to be grasped as the idea [Idee] of infinite spirit—the spirit whose *posited being* is the infinite, transparent reality in which hit contemplates its *creation* [Schöpfung] and, in the creation, itself.[58]

In this passage Hegel speaks of the 'second negation.' Earlier we identified the first negation as particularity and the second negation as singularity. The truly higher universal is the second negation, or singularity. Unlike the higher or lower genera that only push on the regress, singularity unifies the outward going side of the universal with the universal, that is, with the inward going side. In singularity we can expect that the illusory references will be posited as illusory. Or in other words, we will see the consistent mutual exclusion of each species *as illusory*. In particularity *per se*, they are illusory, but not posited *as* illusory. Or what is the same, the particular is the determinate universal not yet posited *as determinate*.

As the reader moves through Hegel's text, she naturally desires an example. In some sense, it is quite fitting for the reader to desire a particular concept in the case of particularity. Hegel notes a few examples of singularity: life, the I (*das Ich*), spirit, and the absolute concept. Each of these examples of singularity are self-contained and self-fulfilled. Thus, we ought to expect that singularity will be the concept *as self-contained and self-fulfilled*.[59]

One simple way to draw the contrast between properly logical and empirical concepts is the way that each related to the PNC. Indeed, the difference in their relationship to that principle provides us a clue to clarifying the role of non-contradiction in Hegel's logic. On the one hand, for empirical thinking, the classical PNC is the principle. Because empirical notions rely on the difference between universal and particular, the PNC must remain in place. For this reason, when empirical knowing contradicts itself, the result is an error.[60] When the understanding is separated out from the self-differentiating process of the concept, the contradiction in the understanding does not lead to a new concept. Instead, the contradiction is a road that is closed and leads nowhere.

On the other hand, the PNC is also at work in the logic of the concept *per se*. Because particularity is the concept in the form of the difference between universal and particular, the PNC is also applicable in the moment of particularity. Indeed, insofar as we have already identified the abstract universal as the particular, it clearly follows that the principle of abstract universality, the PNC, would also apply here as well. Unlike empirical knowing, however, which is divorced from the self-development of the concept, neither can the particular concept be held back from the universal nor the universal from the particular. For this reason, a contradiction arises within the moment of particularity. Instead of leading to nothing, however, the contradiction in the heart of particularity leads to singularity. The reason is clear: unlike the abstract universal that is divorced from the process of the concept, particularity is *self-differentiation as that which is not self-differentiated*. Because it is nestled in the concept, the particular *qua* abstract universal *per se* is only the 'clothing' and 'illusion' of the universal, as it were, and does not express the fact that it is *the self-differentiation* that is outside itself. The particular is a moment of the self-differentiating universal, and as such, its contradiction leads to a particular result, not merely to a nullity. Because it is a moment of the self-differentiating concept, the PNC is *that principle which contradicts itself*. This is what De Boer calls the principle of self-contradiction:[61]

> Speculative thought consists solely in holding on to the contradiction, and thus to itself. Unlike representational thought, it does not let itself be dominated by the contradiction, it does not allow the latter to dissolve its determinations into other ones or into nothing.[62]

Singularity

In Singularity[63] the universal concept frees itself from the imprisonment that it experienced in particularity. In his first remarks on singularity, Hegel lays bare some basic features of singularity:

> Singularity [*Die Einzelheit*], as we have seen, is already posited by particularity; this is determinate universality and hence self-referring determinateness, the determinate determinate [*das bestimmte Bestimmte*].[64]

Right away two features of singularity strike us. First, singularity has its origin in particularity. Particularity 'posits' singularity. Second, singularity is self-related, and the 'determinate determinate.' What could Hegel mean by 'determinate determinate'? Clearly, he is not simply stating a tautology. Earlier we discovered that particularity is the determinate concept, and singularity is the *absolutely* determinate concept. The simplest way to address the origin of singularity is in terms of self-predication. Particularity is the determinate concept. Singularity arises from particularity by predicating *determinateness* of the determinate concept *itself*. Particularity gives rise to singularity by *predicating its determination of itself*. Upon predicating its determination to itself, it ceases to be particular and is singular. Determinate universality becomes the fully self-relating universal, or singularity, by *truly corresponding to itself as determinate*.

First we will delineate the rise of singularity and its status as the completion of the development of the universal. Second, we will show how abstraction arises again in the form of singularity and how judgment arises from this revived abstraction. In the second paragraph discussing singularity, Hegel points out the two basic directions of determination that follow from particularity and provides a hint concerning how the development of particularity into singularity ought to proceed.

As Hegel points out, two directions of conceptual determination follow from the particular.[65] One direction is the *Abweg*, the straying path of abstraction. We have already discussed this false path in some depth. The false path of abstraction ossifies the difference between universal and particular. As one abstracts from the particulars, the universal content of each abstraction becomes more and more empty. For this sense of abstraction, the highest universals, such as Being, are the emptiest, and the particulars from which the abstraction originally arises are the richest. In this turn of fate, it is the non-conceptual particulars that are rich in content, and the thoughts that are empty. In this universe, what is not conceptual possesses the richest of contents. The false path of abstraction does not return to the concept. Instead, it has *abandoned* it and forsaken its beginning as the self-determining universal. For examples of these false paths, we always have nature and intuition as our witnesses. To use an analogy from Kierkegaard, the *Abweg* of abstraction is like an addict who attempts to escape the recognition of the nullity of his aesthetic self by abusing drugs. He abuses drugs in order that he may not have to think about the nullity of himself, all the while the drug abuse encloses and ossifies that nullity.

The second path is singularity. Hegel explicitly points out that the particular is constituted by the twofold illusory being. Singularity is the return, or 'back-turning' (*Rückkehr*) of the universal to itself. Hegel is clear that the particular *as determinate* returns to *the universal*: 'singularity appears as *the reflection* of the concept out of its determinateness *into itself*.'[66] Accordingly, singularity is the *unification* of the determinate concept, particularity, with universality. The return of the universal to itself is its self-enclosed or self-relating determination: *the universal returns to itself through the determinacy of the particular*. Indeed, this is what we anticipated the singular to be: *the unification* of the particular with the universal. This process is self-mediation, for the whole process begins and ends with the concept: the concept as universal gives rise to the particular, and the particular *in turn* gives rise to the singular. The singular is the same content as the universal, for as Hegel states above, the concept has re-instated itself in the form of absolute negativity, or the negation of negation. The difference, of course, is that now the concept is not immediately the negation of negation. Now, the negation of negation has been mediated *by particularity*. The concept re-instates the original determination of the universal in and through one of its own particular moments, particularity. For this reason, the beginning is the end: *the negation of negation*. But how does the particular giver rise to the singular?

Regarding the development of singularity, Hegel is quite brief. He only tells us that *the otherness* of the concept has 'once more been made into an *other*.' In the briefest of terms, the otherness of the concept is other to itself. Here again Hegel presses the self-predicative and *absolute determinacy* character of the singular: singularity is determined as the determinateness posited as determinateness, or *the determinate determinateness*.[67] Nevertheless, Hegel augments our understanding of the development with the following sentence: '*Die Bestimmtheit in der Form der Allgemeinheit ist zum Einfachen mit derselben verbunden.*'[68] The simplicity of singularity arises by *linking* (i) the universal and (ii) determinateness in the form of universality. Determinateness in the form of universality is particularity in the form of universality. Particularity in the form of universality is *the abstract universal* that is constituted by the twofold illusory references. Thus, in order to break the code of singularity, we must investigate the unification of universality proper, namely *self-differentiation, with the abstract universal*.

In a passage at the end of his discussion of particularity, Hegel further elucidates the development of singularity by connecting the fixity of the abstract universal with the development of singularity.[69] Hegel adds to our understanding of the development of singularity here by pointing out that it is only at the highest stage where its downfall begins. For particularity, the highest stage of its development is *the abstract universal*, which is *fixed* and does not admit its opposite. Exactly here, where the concept is most fixed, does it negate itself and unify itself with its opposite. Accordingly, abstract universality really is just a transitory stage and is not the absolute end of the development of the concept. In this dialectical maneuver, the finite universal is shown not to measure up (*unangemessen*) to the universal. This is the 'dissolution of the finite' and, as we shall see, parallels the self-negation of the finite that gives rise to ideality in the *logic of Being*. Hegel speaks of the 'spiritual impregnation' (*Begeisten*), or the 'spiritualization' of the abstract universal by the understanding. Hegel points out that if reason is unable to move beyond the abstract universal, this is not an inherent defect in Reason, but in its *subjective* use by some external agency. Indeed, Hegel hints that the abstract universal, insofar as it is an imperishable self-relation, fails to be distinguished from universality, for the determination of the latter is also that of the imperishable self-relation.

At the close of particularity, we discovered that particularity as such is *the* abstract universal, whose content is 'self-negation' as such. This content is the universal self-differentiation in *the form of negation*, or what is the same, *the self-negation* of the immediate, indeterminate content, 'self-differentiation.' At the stage of particularity the universal content 'self-negation' does *not* negate itself. Instead, it is just what it is and does not admit its negation. Since the universal is that which admits its own negation, we said that the stage of particularity is the universal insofar as it is 'external to itself.' In particularity, the universal is separate from the particular. Since the universal is that unity of universal and particular, the particular is the universal insofar as it has negated itself, or is 'other to itself.' In other words, particularity is *the pure difference* between universal and particular. The pure difference has two sides, 'universal' and 'particular,' each of which constitutes one side of the twofold illusory reference. At the stage of self-negation, self-negation is not yet negated. Insofar as it is not self-negating, the particular remains abstract and does not differentiate itself. The abstract universal as such ensures that the universal is separate from the particular. It is at this point where the dialectical fire begins.

The content 'self-negation' cannot help but negate itself. Self-negation, in order to remain what it is, must negate itself. If self-negation failed to negate itself, then it would not be what it is, namely 'self-negation.' And more than anything else, the abstract universal, self-negation, *must remain what it is*. The abstract universal must remain what it is, for its very form lies in its *fixed self-identity*. Hence, *self-negation is self-negating*.

Immediately we see that this phrase 'self-negation is self-negating' is another way of expressing how otherness becomes an other to itself. The concept as particular is the concept *as other to itself*. In the particular or the form of negation, the universal is not what it is, but it is what it is not. For this reason, we may reconstruct the transition in terms of the 'otherness of the concept to itself' or 'the self-negation of the concept.' We should remind ourselves that we are not rehashing the same development from universality to particularity. In the development of particularity, the universal negated itself as an immediate, indeterminate self-identity and gave rise to particularity as such. Now we have universality in the form of self-negation, or what is the same 'conceptual self-negation' as such. The transition to singularity takes *the universal in the form of the absolute difference* as the starting point, not the absolute immediate unity. Now we must consider what follows from the self-negation of conceptual self-negation.

Given that self-negation must negate itself, particularity is *self-predicative*. Particularity, as the determinate concept, must itself be determinate. Instead of just having 'particularity is,' we have 'particularity is particular.' If one wishes to emphasize the essential role of difference here, one might also express this by saying that 'the difference of the concept is different' or 'otherness of the concept is other.'

Self-negation *is self-negating*. Since self-negation negates itself, *it corresponds to itself*, for its *own* qualitative determinacy, 'self-negation' constitutes *what it is* and takes the place of the indeterminate predicate. Ironically, because self-negation is self-negating, self-negation cannot remain self-negation. If self-negation were to remain just what it is, then it would not in fact have negated itself. Because the predicate 'self-negation' necessitates that the subject negate what it is, the subject 'self-negation' cannot remain that which is self-negating. Instead, the self-negating content must *vanish*. Thus, the predication of self-negation to itself results in (i) *the self-identity* of the universal as such and (ii) the negation of particularity.

The result is simple, yet astounding. The self-negation of self-negation is *the negation* of particularity. Insofar as the particular is the universal in the form of negation, the negation of the particular resurrects the universal from its bondage in the particular. Indeed, by negating self-negation, *the negation* of universality *is negated*. Thus, what is present is just *the conceptual negation of negation*. Thus, the self-identity and self-relation that come to be upon the self-removal of particularity is nothing other than that with which the process of the concept began, namely the universal, since its content is exhausted by the negation of negation. But the return of the negation of negation from its *exile* is not the same determination as the universal moment, for the universal moment did not itself arise out of exile, that is out of the particular. Hence, we have a novel content: *the return of the universal*, or what Hegel calls the one and only—the singular.

That in virtue of which the particular truly *comes to be itself*, namely the predication of self-negation to itself, is that in virtue of which it *ceases to be itself*. The universal is just that which is what it is not. Since the particular admits what it is not in virtue of being itself, the particular necessarily develops into universality merely in virtue of what it is. Thus, the particular as particular admits its opposite, the universal, or the negation of negation. The universal returns to itself, or resurrects itself, out of its own self-negation, otherness, and difference. As it turns out, the universal never really abandoned the particular, though it may have appeared this way. This very process of negating itself and returning to itself is the very being of the concept; it is singularity.[70]

Earlier in our analysis of particularity, we already arrived at the self-negation of particularity. Still, because we insisted on the distinction between universal and particular, we were not able to admit to ourselves that each must be identified with the other. Singularity is the fulfillment of particularity, and it is opposed to that infinite regress, or quantitative infinite, that insists on the division. Given the result above, Hegel reminds us that understanding ought not be separated from reason.[71] The determinate and abstract concept is a condition of reason insofar as it gives rise to singularity *per se*. But it is not just a condition of reason but also one of the moments of the concept as such. Here again he employs the term '*begeisten*,' meaning 'to give spirit to something.' The finite form is 'pregnant' with the concept and gives birth to singularity.

The way in which the particular develops into the singular parallels the way the finite transitions into the infinite. The finite, in containing its own limit, contains what it is not, its own ceasing to be. In containing its own ceasing to be, the finite ceases to be. But in ceasing to be, the finite itself *preserves* itself, for the finite is just that which of itself ceases to be. Since it preserves itself, the finite does not cease to be and hence is no longer finite, for it never ceases to be. In not ceasing to be, the finite is, of its own accord, the non-finite. The parallel with the concept is clear: the finite gives rise to the infinite by staying itself. Insofar as it remains itself, it negates itself. Likewise, in virtue of remaining what it is, the particular negates itself. The analogy nicely illuminates how the particular is the *finite* moment of the infinite concept.[72]

Looking back over all three moments of the concept, we encounter three senses of the infinite, each of which correlating to one moment of the concept. In the universal moment, the concept is the infinite *qua indeterminate*. In the universal there is not yet a predicate, nor are there any specific differences yet posited. In the particular moment, the concept achieves a finite determination and thereby is only capable of *the quantitative infinite*, in which there is always an outlying determination. Finally, in singularity, the concept is recognized as *perfect*, as *that which has nothing outstanding*. In singularity, all the determinations of the concept are present: universality, particularity, and singularity. The *true infinite* is constitutive of the final stage of the concept, and it is that which moves beyond the infinite regress. Though the infinite regress indeed never ceases to produce more universals, the concept, as the true infinite, is that creative principle that underlies that regress and sustains it. The qualitative infinite constitutive of singularity is the relentless process by which finite particularity is rendered infinite universality, and infinite universality is rendered finite particularity.[73]

Just as the self-differentiation of self-differentiation rendered universality an element of the concept, so the self-negation of self-negation renders particularity an element of the concept. In each act of self-predication, the element is shown to be one element of the concept, and a new moment of the concept usurps the place of the concept as such. What is evident is that the necessary act of self-predication does not just entail existential implication but also initiates a new determination. In the case of universality, it is particularity. In the case of particularity, it is *singularity*. Having set itself to the side, particularity posits itself as a mere moment of the totality, and recognizes the rule of *singularity* as the true monarch. Let us briefly discuss how singularity is the totality of universality and particularity, as well as why Hegel chose the word *'Einzelheit.'*

The term *'Einzelheit,'* 'singularity,' signifies *totality*—the One and *only*.[74] It stands in stark contrast to *'Besonderheit,'* which implies a splitting difference. Singularity is *the totality* of the determinations of universality and particularity. Unlike *the moment* of particularity, in singularity universality is neither a merely immediate unity of particular and universal, nor is particularity the mere mediated difference of the two. Instead, immediacy and mediated determinacy are wedded. Hegel describes the transition of particularity into singularity as the connection between the abstract universal or particular and the universal. Indeed, this is what we have already witnessed. The particular, in virtue of being itself, *immediately* is the self-differentiating universal. Singularity is the self-relation of particular to universal and universal to particular. Neither universality nor particularity *by themselves as mere moments* could possibly be the totality, for in neither are the differences between the two (i) posited and (ii) unified together. In singularity the differences constitutive of particularity are unified in the concept of the negation of negation. In the initial appearance of universality there were no differences yet given. In the initial appearance of particularity, the absolute difference between the moments ruled supreme. In singularity, the differences are recognized as differences, yet are nonetheless brought together as differences *of* the one concept 'singularity.' For this reason, singularity is the true totality, and each concept of the concept, universality, particularity, and singularity are true totalities only *as singular totalities*.

In particularity, the particular and the universal are *one-sided* determinations. The universal and the particular, as particulars, are negations that exclude their opposites. Yet, insofar as the particular as such negates itself and gives rise to the negation of negation, neither the universal nor the particular may remain separate: the particular is given over to the universal and the universal is given over to the particular. The particular, as we showed above, cannot help but give the universal. Yet, the universal also ceases to be a separate determination. For this reason, singularity posits *the illusory being as illusory*. In particularity as such we had not yet arrived at singularity. Having arrived at singularity, we see that the illusory references inward and outward are *not really independent*. Instead, they were merely *reflections* of independence. The universal no longer has its content as a separate 'other' to the particular—

only if particularity as such were maintained could the separation of the universal from the particular be maintained. Thus, *each* becomes the negation of negation and is *in itself* singularity, and as such they are *indistinguishable*. That they are indistinguishable in singularity means that the illusory separation of universal and particular has been realized and overcome.

In singularity the universal and the particular are united.[75] But we must specify the sense in which they are united. In particularity the universal was the immediate unity of universal and particular, while the particular was the absolute difference of each. The separation of universal from particular in particularity placed both distinctions on one of its own sides: the latter side of the absolute difference. On the other hand, in universality the particular is immediately united with the universal, and the mediation fails to appear. In singularity, the immediate is not swallowed up by the mediation, nor is the mediation swallowed up by the immediacy. By giving the universal to the particular, and the particular to the universal, a *true* totality is granted in which universality and particularity exist *as absolute determinacy* or *singularity*. Insofar as singularity unites universality (the immediate unity of universal and particular) with particularity (the mediated unity of particular and universal) in *the negation of negation*, singularity gives a unity of opposites in which there is *the unity* of the immediate unity of the particular and universal and the mediated unity of particular and universal. In other words, instead of grasping universality just as a universal, or just as a particular, universality is grasped as *the universal-particular*. Likewise, instead of grasping the particular merely as a particular or as a universal, the particular is grasped as *the particular-universal*. Though earlier the unity of these was implied, it was *not posited as such*. Singularity posits the unity of universal and particular *as such*.[76]

Though we have abandoned the particular and the universal as *mere* moments of the concept, the particular that appears in singularity is the *true* particular, the universal the *true* universal. In other words, the true particular, as well as the true universal, corresponds to itself in singularity. In the moment of particularity, the abstraction 'self-negation' was separated from the self-negating particulars themselves. Because 'negation' and 'difference' may be used interchangeably here, the separation of self-negation from the particular negations is the same as the separation of 'self-differentiation' from the particular differentiations. The negation of the difference between universal and particular brings the abstraction 'self-differentiation' to the self-negating particulars and *vice versa*. Accordingly, self-negation itself, or self-differentiation itself, the universal, must be *a* self-negating, self-differentiating particular. Likewise, each self-differentiating particular must be *the* universal. Once again, the result is exactly that with which we began: the universal 'self-differentiation' is that which constitutes its own particular moments, and the moments of the concept constitute the concept as such. Or what is the same: particularity as such must be recognized as both the moment of the concept and the whole concept as such: it cannot merely remain particular but must also be singular. Universality as such must be recognized as both the moment of the concept and the whole concept as such: it cannot merely be universal but must also be singular. Because the universal and the particular are, in themselves, singularity as such, we ought to be able to elucidate how each is singularity from the very concept of singularity as such.

As we have shown above, there is no way to hold any of the differences 'universal,' 'particular,' or 'singular' separate, without confounding them. This is indeed the very concept of the concept, namely that *each distinction is confounded* with what it is not. Hegel points out that representational thinking, accompanied by quantitative analysis, attempts to hold these distinctions apart, and for that very reason they are both unsuitable for embodying the concept of the concept. Importantly, we ought to point out that *singularity is determinate* exactly because *the particular is the whole of singularity*. The particular, *qua determinate*, is *absolute* however, for the singular contains all of its differences within itself—there are no other distinctions to which the concept could be *relative*. Singularity is the Absolute Determination of the concept. Singularity may be grasped as the particular rendered *absolute*. For this reason, we cannot restrict the concept of determinacy to relativity, for its self-negation constitutes an Absolute Determinacy.

If we return to the beginning of our exposition of Hegel, we will remember that the most basic determination of the concept is that the concept as such is *indistinguishable from the moments of the concept*. Indeed, the self-negation of self-negation brings us directly to this result Since singularity is the negation of negation, though now considered as a result, every moment of singularity must not only be one moment of singularity but also singularity as such. This is also clear if one considers the singular as the self-differentiation of self-differentiation. As the self-differentiation of self-differentiation, singularity *differentiates itself into self-differentiated moments*. Each moment of singularity, namely 'universality,' 'particularity,' and 'singularity,' *is self-particularization*, or *singularity*, as such. Already we have noted that particularity and universality are each the particular-universal and universal-particular. Since singularity is nothing but the unity of these, and the particular and universal are each unified with the other, particularity *is* singularity and universality *is* singularity. Not only are each of these identified with singularity, but each is also a moment of singularity, for each is a moment of the concept. Thus, singularity is the content that is constitutive of the whole concept and the elements.

Hegel first identifies universality as singularity. He writes:

> *Universality* and *particularity* appeared, on the one hand, as moments of the *becoming* of singularity. But it has already been shown that the two are in themselves the total concept; consequently, that in *singularity* they do not pass over into an *other* but that, on the contrary, what is posited in it is what they are in and for themselves. The *universal* is *for itself* because it is absolute mediation in itself, self-reference [Beziehung auf sich] only as absolute negativity.[77]

The singular is *the concept as such*. Only in the singular is the concept truly self-differentiated. The singular is not just the assumption of the negation of negation, or self-differentiation, but *the self-differentiation of self-differentiation*. In singularity the self-differentiating concept has fulfilled one of its basic tasks: *to determine itself to be self-differentiating*. Having posited itself to be self-differentiating, the concept has given to itself what it originally took on as a *given* content. Singularity is universality exactly for the reason we have already mentioned: universality is the negation and negation, and singularity is the negation of negation. In singularity universality is not merely one moment of the concept. As the merely immediate unity it is one moment of the concept, and in this sense, it has been overcome in singularity. Yet, because the singular is the negation of negation, the universal has been resurrected. Here the universal, as the negation of negation, is unconditioned, free, infinite, and only in relation to itself. There is no other to which it could relate. It is, as Hegel states, *self-referring* and as such only 'for itself.'

Unlike the first appearance of universality, universality is now both particular and singular. Universality as singularity takes up all of the differences of universality, namely universality, particularity, and singularity, and posits them as differentiations of itself, the self-identical negation of negation. In this sense of universality, universality is the process by which it differentiates *each* one of its moments, universality, particularity, and singularity and simultaneously posits them as the *whole* negation of negation and as *moments* or elements of the negation of negation. In other words, true universality (singularity) just is *the whole dialectical process of self-predication and existential implication* that has wrought the three determinations of the concept. As is evident, if we had remained in the separation of the universal and particular, the whole process of self-predication and existential implication, in virtue of which that separation is initially posited, would not have been possible. The return to the universal out of the particular in singularity is that which makes particularity possible.

Perhaps the identity of singularity and universality is the most evident result of the dialectical process that particularity underwent. Indeed, because particularity had to negate itself in order to give rise to singularity, one might expect that particularity could not be identical to singularity. Though we have grasped the unity of universal and particular in terms of the universal, to see how singularity is also particular we must also grasp singularity concretely as particularity. Indeed, singularity just is the unification of universality and particularity, and so it cannot help but be both *universal and particular*. Before concretely exposing the identity of particularity and singularity, Hegel first reflects on the sense in which the particular universal as the abstraction has been left behind in the development of singularity.[78]

Hegel already points out the insufficiency of abstraction for achieving the negation of negation in his discussion of universality.[79] What is distinct is that here Hegel is comparing abstraction and singularity. Abstraction, as a process of removing content from a set of particulars in order to derive a common term, is not truly singular, for the process of abstraction is separate from the abstraction itself. Indeed, the abstract universal is the singular as it is *outside of itself*. In particularity, the *abstract* form of the 'this such and such,' the formula of singularity, is divorced from the *singular development* of the 'this such and such.' Indeed, this is the main determination of particularity. Hegel hints that even abstract universals, despite their abstract character, are nonetheless singularities.[80] Earlier we noted *two* senses of abstraction. One sense of abstraction connotes the act of deriving universals from a set of givens. The other connotes one moment of the universal: the particular. In this passage, Hegel points out that even in respect to the former sense of abstraction, there is a sense in which each of the results of abstraction are still singular.

The result of the abstractive activity is the abstract product, namely 'the unity of singular content and of abstract universality.' Hegel points out that the result is the 'opposite of what it is supposed to be.' Each abstraction is a determinate universal, and the determinate universal, like every moment of the concept, is singular. For this reason, even the abstract universals, insofar as each is a determinate 'this such and such,' are singular. Still, they are nonetheless still to be distinguished from the concept insofar as the process by which they come to be is external to them. Abstractions are *inverted* singularities, if you will. They are singulars that are *individuated by failing to have the form of singularity*.

To see this another way, consider that each abstract universal is universal, for it has the form of abstract universality, but also has some content by which it is distinguished from others. The abstract form in each and every universal is not separate from the content that is present in that form: the form is the form of some content. Or, as Hegel put it, each abstract universal is 'the unity of singular content and of abstract universality.' For this reason, every abstract universal is a synthesis of form and content, of *universality and particularity*. Singularity is just this: the unity of form and content or universality and particularity: *this such and such*.

For this reason, abstract universality as such fails to give an account of just what it is: singularity. It is the clothes or covering for something that it is not sufficient to explain. It is important that we recognize this, for it was initially the unity of universality and particularity in each universal that lead us to various paradoxes concerning the universal. It was the very singularity of the abstract universals that lead us to Hegel, and for this reason we cannot deny that singularity lies even at the heart of abstract universality. Abstract universality is posited by the concept, and abstract universality is only possible if we grasp the form of its singularity.

Earlier we showed how abstract universality contradicted itself. By my lights, the contradiction at the heart of abstract universality reveals that abstract universality is not just abstract—but that it is *singularity*, in whom each determination of the concept contradicts itself by admitting to being its other. Indeed, Hegel's method, at bottom, is quite simple. He solves the problem of the differentia by *allowing the abstract universal to simply be itself*. In virtue of being itself, the abstract universal negates itself. In that self-negation, what arises is nothing other than singularity, namely that universal in which universality is particularity, and particularity is universality. By getting out of the way and allowing concepts to be what they are, they admit what they are not and thereby show their contradictory character.

Having discussed the way that abstract universals, in whatever sense of the term, may be understood as singularities, Hegel goes on to explicate exactly how particularity as such is singularity. We have discussed this abstractly, as it were, as well as pointed out how universality is singularity. Hegel proceeds to show exactly how singularity may be grasped specifically under the determination of the determinate universal, or particularity.[81] We might at first be inclined to think of singularity as the whole concept whose elements or moments are the determinations of universality and particularity. Still, we must be careful to see why singularity belongs *among these as a moment of itself*, as well as why particularity encompasses the totality. Without grasping how singularity may be counted *alongside* the moments 'universality' and 'particularity,' we shall also fail to grasp the development of *judgment*.

Singularity offers a new determination: the negation of negation *qua* totality, or what is the same, the unity of the universal and the particular. Insofar as singularity is constituted by this determination, it is *different* from the moments of universality and particularity in which either self-differentiation was an immediate, undifferentiated content, or self-differentiation was differentiated from its differentiations. In singularity, self-differentiation is simultaneously itself and its differentiations in which the differences are posited and unified with each other. Because singularity offers a *new distinct content* from these other moments, it *excludes* the other moments from itself as distinct from it. The others, *insofar as they are not singular*, are not the totality of the concept. Since the particular is that universal which excludes what it is not, namely the determinate universal, and singularity excludes those universals that are not totalities, singularity is a determinate universal. Therefore, *singularity itself is a determinate universal.* In accordance with this result, we ought to list singularity or the unity of universality and particularity as *one moment* of the concept alongside and over and against the other moments 'universality' and 'particularity.'

As a determinate universal, singularity falls under the general determination of particularity. Particularity, or the determinate universal, now includes every moment of the concept within itself: universal, particular, and singular. Because each moment is a distinct content differentiated from the others (indeed, each has its own dialectical origin), each is a particular moment of the concept. Since the concept is fully constituted by the three elements of universality, particularity, and singularity, particularity itself must be the totality. As the totality, particularity is *singularity* as such. This also means that the PNC that ensures the mutual exclusion of universal and particular is also singular and absolute. This means both that the Absolute is consistent and inconsistent or *consistently inconsistent* (particular *qua* not-particular), for every application of the PNC to the Absolute produces an inconsistency. If we begin from the concept of the determinate universal we shall arrive at singularity. In addition, if we think about the content 'singularity' it appears that we shall also arrive at determinate universality. In the concept of determinate universality, singularity, particularity, and universality are unified.

The dialectical procedure that we initiated above is quite simple. If one grasps singularity as singularity, then it follows that singularity must be a moment of itself. By predicating singularity to singularity, *singularity implies itself existentially.* As a result, singularity is not only one moment of singularity but it is also grasped as a totality in the form of particularity. In sum, singularity is not just singularity, but it is also universality and particularity.

Heretofore our analysis has shown that self-predication not only gives rise to existential implication, but it also negates the very category that underwent that act of predication. In the case of singularity it is exactly the same. The key to grasping the development of judgment out of singularity is the particularity of singularity. Indeed, Hegel himself appeals to the syllogism to communicate this transition to judgment. As the principle of the totality, particularity is the middle term by which universality and singularity are connected.

Earlier we noted that the return of the concept to itself in singularity is also its *loss.* Though it may appear that particularity has simply reinstated itself, the re-emergence of particularity as the form of singularity gives rise to an altogether novel category, *judgment.* In section two of his treatment of singularity, Hegel addresses the transition of singularity to judgment.[82] For a Hegel scholar, there may perhaps be nothing more surprising than the following sentence: '*Abstraction*, which is the soul of singularity and so the self-reference of the negative, is, as we have seen, nothing external to the universal and the particular but is immanent in them, and these are concreted through it, they become a content, a singular.'[83] Though we have shown that singularity, the negation of negation, is immanent in universality and particularity, abstraction is what singularity *overcomes*. Insofar as abstractions do not unify themselves with their opposites, in Hegel's language, Hegel often calls abstractions 'dead.' The soul in this metaphor is the principle of life, or the internal principle of motion. Thus, we might ask, how could abstraction be the 'soul of singularity'?

If we reflect on the identity of particularity with singularity we arrive at the *abstract* character of singularity. Singularity is the totality of its determinations, *the negation of negation*. As such, we pointed out that singularity must be differentiated from the other elements of the concept, for the other elements of the concept, *qua* elements, are not the totality. Though in the moment of singularity each moment is identical to singularity, singularity as such is different from the other moments. Accordingly, singularity excludes the other moments and is listed alongside the others. Insofar as it is itself, yet excludes the other moments, we pointed out that singularity is a determinate universal. Because the determinate moment is nothing other than particularity, and particularity is constituted by the abstract universal, singularity as the separate content 'negation of negation' or 'totality' must be *an abstract universal*. That the negation of negation is inherently abstract is evidenced by its relationship to universality and particularity. Insofar as universality and particularity are differentiations of the concept, and singularity as the negation of negation excludes these moments from itself, singularity *excludes its own differentiations from itself*. Insofar as singularity excludes its own differentiations from its universality, singularity *qua* singularity initiates a *distinction* between its own universality and its particulars. As is evident, by identifying singularity with particularity, *singularity is shown to be an abstract universal* that is separate from its particulars or its moments. Thus, singularity as singularity is, as Hegel points out, 'posited abstraction.'[84]

In the passage above, Hegel points out that singularity, as the determinate determinateness, is now *difference as such* which is nothing other than singularity understood as *a determinate universal*. The difference, Hegel points out, is now *fixed*: negation of negation is negation of negation and not that which is not the negation of negation. Singularity, in virtue of what it is, has become a content that is just what it is and fails to admit what it is not. After all, singularity, as the negation of negation is that which it is not. Thus, it must admit to being what it is not: *the abstract universal*. As Hegel claims, insofar as the concept is 'internal to itself' it must be 'external to itself.' Since abstract universality is constituted by the separation of universality and particularity, and singularity just is their unification, singularity has become external to itself. Upon predicating singularity to singularity, singularity becomes the self-identical content 'singularity,' or 'negation of negation,' and nothing more. In the content 'negation of negation' negation is *unified with itself and nothing else*.

One might raise the concern that the concept has simply reverted back to the stage of particularity and is therefore doomed to re-iterate a vicious cycle from particularity to singularity and back again. Thankfully, we cannot return to the previous stage of particularity. For at that stage singularity had not yet developed. Indeed, particu-larity itself, as well as every other moment of the universal, has been transformed into singularity. The new content at hand is *singularity as abstract*, which is a novel determination. Hegel further illustrates the novel content that is the abstract universality of singularity as an act of self-repulsion.[85]

The dialectical situation is quickly sharpened when we consider abstract singularity in conjunction with the development of singular-ity itself out of particularity. Singularity, as it arose from particularity, could not in principle be separated from its moments. Both universality and particularity, as separate moments, were nonetheless identified with singularity. Evidently, it is the identification of singularity with particu-larity that leads to abstract singularity. In addition, the very universal content 'that which is the unity of particularity and universality' is the specific content that constitutes singularity as the abstract universal. Although it may appear that the abstraction 'singularity' posited itself as separate from something other than itself, the development of itself as an abstraction, is nothing other than its positing of itself as other than itself.

Particularity is singularity, and singularity must be separate from par-ticularity. Likewise, universality is singularity and singularity must be separate from universality. Given our earlier result that *both* universal-ity and particularity *are singularity*, and given that *as abstract*, singular-ity must be separate from both universality and particularity, it follows that singularity must be *separate from itself*. In other words, singularity *divides itself* into three separate singular totalities, each of which is *singu-larity as such*. Singularity, *as one content*, 'repulses itself' from itself, and puts forward *three* singular totalities. Indeed, singularity as that content in which the concept is its moments must divide itself.

Each moment of singularity is singularity itself. Singularity has given itself 'actuality' in the sense that it existentially implies its own particulars and singularities, though it has done so at the cost of transforming itself into an utterly abstract universal. Thus, singularity must exceed itself, or exclude itself from itself. This is the meaning of *'ausschließend'* or 'exclusive' in this context. The singular acquires an exclusive relationship towards itself. This is judgment or the original partitioning of the one concept into self-subsistent unities:[86]

> The concept, as this connection of its *self-subsistent* [Selbständigen] determinations, has lost itself, for the concept itself is no longer the *posited unity* of these determinations, and these no longer are *moments*, the *reflective shining* of the concept, but subsist rather in and for themselves.—As singularity, the concept returns in determinateness into itself, and therewith the determinate has itself become totality. The concept's turning back into itself is thus the absolute, originative *partition of itself*, that is, as singularity it is posited as judgment.[87]

Because each moment of the concept is now utterly independent of the others, they are no longer moments or elements of one concept. For this reason, it is fitting to claim that through the abstract determination of singularity *the concept has ceased to be the concept* and for this reason has 'lost itself.' Earlier in the domain of particularity, each moment was conceived in terms of an *illusory reference*. The illusion at that stage consisted in the illusion of their independence. Now, the illusion of their independence has ceased to be an illusion, for *it has become the reality*. The return to particularity in abstract singularity is the shattering of the unity of the concept, as well as the illusory references that constituted particularity. The determinate moment has truly become the totality, not merely the illusion of the totality. Instead of the concept, what is present is the judgment that *the singular is universal*. In the form of judgment the predicate excludes its negation: 'the singular is universal' does not mean 'the singular is not universal.' In the judgment 'the singular is universal,' the subject does not admit the negation of the predicate. Instead, we are in the presence of what Hegel is fond of calling a 'one-sided' determination.

Given that the singular is the abstract universal, all the features of the abstract universal come to bear upon the singular. Because singularity is the totality of its moments, each singular is *self-subsistent*. Each singular is the negation of negation and as the totality *excludes all the others*. Each of the others is given or presupposed as another singularity, but it is a singular that is *by itself*. This is what Hegel means by 'being for self.' As the totality each *transcends all otherness*. For this reason, Hegel uses the term 'indifferent.' Each singular has *no relation* to the others, or in anthropomorphic terms, 'no concern' for the others. Another way to put it would be the following: each singular takes itself to be *the totality*, all there is.[88]

As a self-identical negation of negation that excludes the other singularities, there is no differentiation that may be found in each singularity. Because universality, particularity, and singularity each fail to have any relation to an other, they undermine any internal contrast or determinacy that might be attributed to them. For this reason, although they are totalities, they are *simple* totalities. As simply there, in which each just is all there is, each is 'being for self.' As the simple totality, the singular is simply a 'one' or a 'this.' It is just singularity *as* 'being' or 'immediately there' without any further qualification. 'This,' in contrast to 'such and such,' denotes an indexical singularity.

The concept of the singular as a mere 'this' is *the abstract rendering* of the singular. As a result, when I say 'this' in reference to a singular, the only conceptual content that is there is *'being* a this' or 'being a singularity.' As the *Phenomenology of Spirit* teaches in Sense Certainty, even here in the bare 'this' there is some 'such and such.' Indeed, each has been reduced to the common content 'singularity.' Because each is a singularity, they have nothing in common except *that they are each singularities.* This is as if one were to point to a plurality of unique singularities and say 'they are all unique.' Indeed, it is *the relation of exclusion* that constitutes their universality. In the common term 'singularity' what individuates them cannot be determined. All that is certain is that each singular is *an instance* of singularity *per se.* Each has the 'this' in common, for as a 'this' each is *indistinguishable* from the others and cannot be separated from them. This, if you will, is the moment of 'attraction.' Yet, each is not the other, for each is 'the this itself,' and so each is its *own* 'this.' As Hegel points out, because the singular is *in the form of particularity*, the universal is excluded, yet must in virtue of that exclusion, nonetheless be related to the various particulars.[89]

Key here is the connection between the illusion of each separate determination in the other and the universality that is constitutive of each singularity. Each singularity, as a separate determination, excludes the universal from itself. For this reason, one might exclaim that there is nothing universal here at all, only particulars. After all, as abstract the singularity is in the form of one of its differences, namely particularity. Yet, insofar as each is separate, each has this in common, namely being separate, or being a *this.* Each appears as the other, or presents itself as the other. This is the 'illusory being of one in the other.' The separation of each determination from the other presents each singular as inseparable from the others in that very content 'separateness.' For this reason, Hegel points out that the contents are not inert. They are actively unifying and separating themselves from each other in virtue of what they are. The universal 'singularity' *appears in the exclusion of universality.* The singular, *as singular*, is universal. Because each singular is indistinguishable from the universal content 'singularity' the various singulars themselves are *abstract universals.* The self-negation of the concept does not give sensible particulars, but abstract universal ones.

We should note, as Hegel does, that in contrast to the *Phenomenology*, in the *Science of Logic* no singular is ultimately a singular in virtue of someone pointing it out. When the singular is a 'this' in virtue of some external act, the singular is posited as abstract *in virtue of something other than the activity of singularity per se*. When singulars are merely pointed out, the immediate existence that is denoted is separate from the act of mediation, or the act by which they are posited as immediate, namely the pointing.[90]

Each singular is a 'this,' in virtue of the self-negation of singularity.[91] Indeed, the meaning of 'posited abstraction' is just this: *singularity divides itself into a plurality of abstract singularities*. Because it is singularity that gives the plurality of abstract universals, it is only through singularity that, as Hegel says, 'the particular is determined.' The act by which the abstractions are differentiated and determined is not separate from or external to singularity per se. For this reason, even in the self-subsistence of universality where singularity posits itself as abstract, the abstract singular is still 'outside itself,' for as abstract it cannot express, and indeed actively *suppresses*, the act of differentiation in virtue of which it is posited. Judgment cannot fully contain the concept, for it determines the singular through one self-identical predicate.

In review, when the self-differentiating universal is grasped just as the self-differentiating universal, *itself by itself*, it is just the self-identical one. As the particular, when it differentiates itself, it differentiates itself from its own content. At this stage of particularity, the self-identical one is divided into various particular differences. At the stage of the determinate universal the universal is defined by its negative relation to the other. The determinate universal is not what is other to it. Accordingly, at the stage of particularity, the self-differentiating universal is divided from what it is not, and *negation* constitutes the relation of self-differentiation to its other. The stage of singularity, the last moment of the pure universal, is an absolute negation. In order to achieve the absolute negation, *negation itself must be negated*. At the stage of singularity, the negation constituting the difference between universal and particular must be negated. Accordingly, the stage of singularity *unites* what is separated at the stage of particularity: the self-differentiating universal and what is other to it. The singular is the unity of the self-differentiating universal and that from which it differentiates itself, namely the other moments of the universal. In singularity the concept has returned to itself and corresponds to what it is: the negation of negation. *The end of the process is identical with the beginning*, insofar as we have a unity of the self-differentiating universal with all of its differences. But there is, as always, a fundamental difference between the end and the beginning. Singularity is a unity that is *mediated* by the process of self-differentiation and the stage of particularity. Unlike pure universality, singularity is not just the immediate unity of the various differences posited by the self-differentiating universal. To the contrary, it is the mediated unity of these differences—a unity that results from the differentiation of self-differentiation in the process of particularity. Upon being taken up as its own independent determination, singularity negates itself and gives rise to judgment.[92]

Notes

1. Because Giovanni's more recent translation of 'Begriff' as 'concept' and 'Einzelhet' as 'singularity' is much closer to the original German sense of the terms, in this chapter, I will draw heavily upon Giovanni's translation. See Hegel, *SL*, trans. Giovanni, 529–549. Periodically, however, I will also refer to the Miller translation. See Hegel, *SL*, trans. Miller, 600–622.
2. See Hegel, *Wissenschaft der Logik II*, Werke 6 (Suhrkamp Taschenbuch Wissenschaft).
3. Hegel, *SL*, trans. Giovanni, 529.
4. An explosive contradiction is one from which everything follows. Such a contradiction does not produce specific results, but every result.
5. If this is Hegel's approach, a natural question arises concerning the determinacy of universality itself, which is not merely a determinate concept.
6. Plato already developed the relation of these categories in the *Parmenides*, especially the second deduction. See Plato, "Parmenides," beginning at 142b, 136.
7. Hegel, *SL*, trans. Giovanni, 601, 273 (Suhrkamp).
8. Nonetheless, I tend to think that although it may not appear as an explicit category, the category 'moment' does develop within the system—at the stage of the Absolute Idea. Here each of the thought determinations becomes categories or 'moments' of the logical system itself.
9. Again, there are other respects in which self-differentiation is distinct from Being for itself as such. Hegel points out these differences in section *A. The Universal Concept*.
10. G. W. F. Hegel, "Vorlesungen 10," in *Vorlesung Ueber die Logik*, Berlin 1831 (Hamburg: Felix Meiner Verlag, 2001), 177, 160.
11. Hegel, *SL*, trans. Giovanni, 530.
12. Note that I do not mean that we have 'self-identity' itself given at the outset but the self-identity that is 'self-differentiation.'
13. Hegel, *SL*, trans. Giovanni, 530, 274 (Suhrkamp).
14. Ibid.
15. Naturally, this signifies that both the universal and the singular are 'negations of negations.' The difference lies in the fact that the former is an immediate 'negation of negation,' whereas the latter is mediated by the process of particularity.
16. In order to elucidate Hegel's concept of the 'truth of a category,' we must distinguish truth from *tautology*. If truth is just the self-correspondence of the category with itself, how is the 'truth of the category' to be distinguished from the tautology? In addition, insofar as the self-differentiating universal is contradictory, we must also investigate the connection between the 'truth of a concept' and contradiction. Indeed, we shall see that tautology and contradiction are ingredients in formulating the concept of the 'truth of a concept.' Here, our reflections come close to Heidegger as well, who in his late phenomenological metaphysics recognized the intimate connection between tautology and truth.
17. Hegel, *EL*, 52.
18. Hegel, *SL*, trans. Miller, 601, 274 (Suhrkamp).
19. Ibid.

20. 'Durchdringung' might also be translated as the 'pushing through' or what 'thoroughly penetrates.' 'Dringung' has a connotation of force. Giovanni takes this as 'mutual penetration.'
21. See the last full paragraph on 602, as well as the first paragraph of 603 in Hegel, *SL*, trans. Miller.
22. Hegel, *SL*, trans. Giovanni, 530, 274 (Suhrkamp).
23. Ibid.
24. As Burbidge points out, 'the universal itself acts negatively, and this introduces particularity.' John Burbidge, *On Hegel's Logic, Fragments of a Commentary* (New Jersey: Humanities Press, 1995), 113–114.
25. Hegel, *SL*, trans. Giovanni, 531, 276 (Suhrkamp).
26. In passing I would like to point the reader to the etymological connection between 'difference' and 'diversity' in German. 'Diversity' is 'verschiedenheit' and 'difference' 'unterschied.' What varies here are the prefixes: 'unter' and 'ver.' The prefix 'ver' often has a negative connotation. In the case of 'verschiedenheit,' the prefix indicates a loss of unity to the differences, in the sense that they are merely scattered.
27. Hegel, *SL*, trans. Giovanni, 532, 277 (Suhrkamp).
28. Ibid, 530, 275 (Suhrkamp).
29. Ibid.
30. Ibid, 601–602, 275 (Suhrkamp).
31. Ibid, 531, 276 (Suhrkamp).
32. Ibid, 531, 275–276 (Suhrkamp).
33. 'Eigen' means 'own.' The properties are the things 'own.'
34. Hegel, *SL*, trans. Giovanni, 537, 608.
35. Ibid, 530.
36. Ibid, 276–277, 531–532 (Suhrkamp).
37. Ibid, 531, 275–276 (Suhrkamp).
38. For more on this opposition, see Melvin Woody, *Freedom's Embrace* (University Park: Penn State University Press, 1998); (University Park: Penn State University Press, 2007), 191.
39. As Rosen points out, "the concept produces its own content." Rosen, *The Idea of Hegel's Science of Logic*, 413–414.
40. Burbidge explicitly defends the *non*-temporality of the concept against Kojeve in his essay "Concept and Time in Hegel." See John Burbidge, "Concept and Time in Hegel," *Dialogue: Canadian Philosophical Review* 12 (1973): 403–422, 20. Here he points out that despite other interconnections between the concept and time, the concept is not identical with time.
41. Hegel, *SL*, trans. Giovanni, 277–278, 532–533 (Surhkamp).
42. In this connection see also Alexander Schubert, *Der Strukturgedanke in Hegels "Wissenschaft der Logik*, Band 232 (Meisenheim: Glan Hain Verlag bei Athenaeum Monographien zur philosophischen Forschung, 1985).
43. Hegel, *SL*, trans. Giovanni, 533, 279 (Suhrkamp).
44. I disagree with Alfred Schaefer when he argues that 'Hegel tries in vain to derive the particular and singular from the universal. He fails in this. The concept is empty and formal. The empty external reflection of empirical concepts also applies to the concept of the concept.' See Alfred Schaefer, *Der Nihilismus in Hegel's Logik: Kommentar und Kritik zu Hegel's Wissenschaft der Logik* (Berlin: Verlag Arno Spitz GmbH, 1992), 139. The concept gives rise to particularity exactly in virtue of its self-identity as that which differentiates itself. Unlike empirical kinds, the universal is self-referring. It is exactly in virtue of its self-referential character that it differentiates itself. Unlike empirical concepts, whose identities do not differentiate themselves, the self-identity of self-differentiation is exactly to differentiate itself.

45. Hegel, *SL*, trans. Giovanni, 534, 280 (Suhrkamp).
46. Ibid, 534–535, 281 (Suhrkamp).
47. Ibid, 532–533, 278 (Suhrkamp).
48. See Ioannis D. Trisokkas, "The Speculative Logical Theory of Universality," *Owl of Minerva* 40, no. 2 (2009): 141–172.
49. See Hegel, *SL*, trans. Giovanni, 122; Also see Hegel, *SL*, trans. Miller, 152.
50. The naïve objection to the possibility of self-creation relies of a false premise. The objection states that in order for self-creation to be possible, what self-creates must already exist in order for it to create itself. Unfortunately, this argument assumes that what self-creates must already be a determinate something, which we need not admit at the outset.
51. Carlson, *A Commentary to Hegel's Science of Logic*, 447.
52. Hegel, *Lectures on the Proofs of the Existence of God*, 192.
53. Hegel, *SL*, trans. Giovanni, 535, 281 (Suhrkamp).
54. See Miller's translation of these terms in Hegel, *SL*, 604.
55. Hegel, *SL*, Giovanni translation, translator's note, lxxii.
56. Hegel, *SL*, trans. Giovanni, 532, 278 (Suhrkamp).
57. Hegel is explicit that the genus, the class, and the abstract universal are all instantiations of the universal *qua* particular. See, for example, Hegel, *SL*, trans. Miller, 280, 606 (Suhrkamp), where Hegel identifies the genus and the class as differentiations of the universal qua particular. In addition, see the following passages for in-depth discussions of the abstract universal as an instantiation of particular universality: Hegel, *SL*, trans. Giovanni, 536–538, 283–285 (Suhrkamp). Here a further problem arises: while the abstract universal appears to arise for the first time in the section on judgment, Hegel already speaks as if the abstract universal had already arisen in particularity. This textual issue deserves further treatment and discussion.
58. Hegel, *SL*, trans. Giovanni, 533.
59. Among these examples, Hegel makes a distinction: life, the I, and finite spirit are all *determinate* concepts or particular concepts that have their resolution in the absolute concept, *the Idea of Infinite Spirit*. Here Hegel gives us a brief glimpse into the outcome of his system as a whole, something we can only briefly mention here.
60. As Bordignon point out, one sense of contradiction in Hegel is the 'error of the understanding.' Bordignon, "Contradiction or Not-Contradiction? This Is the Problem," 163.
61. De Boer points out that self-contradiction is the principle of development in Hegel. 'The contradiction . . . is the root of all movement and vitality; it is only insofar as something contains a contradiction within itself that it moves, has an urge and activity' (LII 75/439). See Karin De Boer, "Hegel's Account of Contradiction in the Science of Logic Reconsidered," *Journal of the History of Philosophy* 48, no. 3 (2010): 345–374, 366.
62. (LII/76/440–441) De Boer, "Hegel's Account of Contradiction in the Science of Logic Reconsidered," 366.
63. Robert Berman is exactly right that not only does Einzelheit evoke connotations of being a 'countable referent of a single term' but it also evokes connotations of exclusivity, virtuosity, and novelty. See Robert Berman, "Ways of Being Singular: The Logic of Individuality," in *Hegel's Theory of the Subject*, ed. David Gray Carlson (New York: Palgrave Macmillan, 2005), 85–98, 85–87.
64. Hegel, *SL*, trans. Giovanni, 546, 296 (Surhkamp).
65. Ibid, 546, 296–297 (Suhrkamp).
66. Ibid.
67. Ibid, 288, 540 (Suhrkamp).

68. Ibid.
69. Ibid, 539–540, 287 (Suhrkamp).
70. Haas points out that Hegel's commitment to the singularity of reason remains consistent throughout his career, from the *Differenzschrift* (1801) to the *Logic* (1832). In the *Differenzschrift* Hegel writes the following: 'the true characteristic of a philosophy is the interesting singularity in which reason, from the building-material of a particular age, has organized a form for itself; the particularity of speculative reason finds therein spirit from its spirit, flesh from its flesh, it looks at itself in it as one and the same, and as an other living being. Each philosophy is in itself complete and has, like a real artwork, totality in itself.' See Hegel, *The Difference Between Fichte's and Schelling's Systems of Philosophy*, 12. We should note that here singularity is Individualitaet, not 'Einzelheit.' See Andrew Haas, *Hegel and the Problem of Multiplicity*, SPEP Studies in Historical Philosophy (Evanston: Northwestern University Press, 2000), 170.
71. Hegel, *SL*, trans. Giovanni, 287–288, 540 (Suhrkamp).
72. Hegel, *SL*, trans. Miller, 129–156. What is more, the presence of the non-finite immediately brings forth that which is negated by the non-finite, for the non-finite is immediately that which is not the finite. Hence, the finite itself arises as the absence of the non-finite. Now there is an opposition between finite and non-finite. But the non-finite, as opposed to the finite, is finite, for it is limited by the non-finite. In becoming finite, the non-finite is no longer infinite, but finite. As finite, it immediately is not the infinite, or the non-finite. Hence, that which was opposed to the non-finite and was the return of the finite is now non-finite. This alternation of the finite and the infinite can be repeated *ad infinitum*. This continual disappearance and re-appearance of the non-finite and the finite to which it is opposed is the bad infinite, a second category to the non-finite. The bad infinite is the correlate to the infinite regress constitutive of *the illusory reference outwards*, as well as the false path from particularity, the *Abweg*, or the path of *errant abstraction*. But insofar as the non-finite, in negating the finite, negates its other, it becomes a finite-infinite or that which has brought the other into itself. On the other hand, the finite as negating the non-finite, is the infinite finite, or that which has brought its other into itself. Hence, the process of the bad infinite itself shows forth a process which is the removal of all external limitation and otherness. This is the true infinite, or that process by which each term in the negation of what is external, negates its other, thereby removing all external otherness, and in so doing it reforms its own content through the negation of its other. Negating the other brings the other into itself, thereby reforming those determinations, for they were external negations, and now they are of the same content. This is a determinate process, which although having an internal determinacy, is not limited by any external determination. Each term in the process, through negating its other, achieves a new content, namely ideality, or the transcending of otherness. The ideality of the true infinite has its correlate in singularity. The immediate result of this process is the negation of negation, since the negation that limited the non-finite is negated in the true infinite, that which results from negating the negation is itself the negation of negation.
73. As Lakebrink points out, singularity is freedom: 'So praesentieren sich in der spekulativen Einzelheit des Logos das Phaenomen der Freiheit und ihre ontologische Grundverfassung auf ueberraschende Weise. Denn in der Einzelheit wird es offenbar, was metaphysisch Freiheit ist.' See Bernard Lakebrink, "Der Begriff des Einzelnen und die Hegelsche Metaphysik," in *Studien zur Metaphysik Hegels* (Freiburg: Verlag Rombach, 1969), 89–120, 107.

74. Already in Nürnberg, Hegel refers to singularity as an absolute self-determination (absolute Selbstbestimmung). See G. W. F. Hegel, *Nürnberger Schriften*, Werke 4 (Frankfurt am Main: Suhrkamp Verlag, 1970).
75. Vittorio Hoesle describes singularity in terms of the synthetic unity of universality and particularity: Die Synthetische Bestimmung zur Allgemeinheit und Besonderheit ist nach Hegel Einzelheit. See Vittorio Hoesle, *Hegels System Der Idealismus der Subjektivitaet und das Problem der Intersubjektivitaet* (Hamburg: Felix Meiner Verlag, 1987), 233.
76. Hegel, *SL*, trans. Giovanni, 548, 298–299 (Suhrkamp). In his adept book *Hegel Im Kontext* Dieter Henrich drives this point home quite well: Dieter Henrich points this out in the following way: the universal and particular are not opposites that disappear into one another. Instead, it is that each from the beginning is inseparable from each other. Each is a different perspective of the whole concept. The goal is the complete structure. Here the idea is that the concept is immediately all three—the whole is in the form of the immediate—this distinguishes it from judgment. To speak with the utmost precision, we must agree with Henrich that in the concept each of the moments immediately is the other. None can be differentiated from the other. In judgment, on the other hand, the concept ceases to be in the form of identity, but is now swallowed up in the difference of particularity. See Dieter Henrich, *Hegel Im Kontext* (Frankfurt: Suhrkamp Verlag, 1971), 99. Following Henrich here, when Haas point out, for example, that the universal is 'abstract' (Haas, *Hegel and the Problem of Multiplicity*, 171, 184), he is correct just in the sense that the abstract universal constitutive of particularity is immediately identifiable with each of the other moments. For this reason, it appears that mediation or difference is excluded and reappears in judgment as distinct from that immediacy or identity of moments. The opposition of judgment and concept constitutes another side of the opposition of identity and difference and expresses an aspect of the 'subjectivity' of the concept.
77. Hegel, *SL*, trans. Giovanni, 546, 297 (Suhrkamp).
78. Ibid, 297, 546–547 (Suhrkamp).
79. Hegel, *SL*, trans. Miller, 602.
80. Hegel, *SL*, trans. Giovanni, 547, 298 (Suhrkamp).
81. Ibid, 547.
82. Ibid, 548, 299 (Suhrkamp).
83. Ibid.
84. Hegel claims that singularity 'enters into actuality.' Actuality is a category from the logic of Essence, in which determiner and determined are separate. What is clear here in this passage is that singularity has receded back into a form of reflection.
85. Hegel, *SL*, trans. Giovanni, 300, 548–549 (Suhrkamp).
86. Judgment in German is 'Urteil,' which can playfully be understood as 'the original separation or partition.'
87. Hegel, *SL*, trans. Giovanni, 549, 301 (Suhrkamp).
88. Gottfried Mann, is correct that 'man hat den Charakter von Hegels Logik dahin bestimmt, dass es ihre Hauptfunktion sei, das Einzelne mit dem Allgemeinen zu vermitteln, aus ihm zu entwickeln'; see Gottfried Mann, "Zum Begriff des Einzelnen, des Ich, und des Individuellen bei Hegel," (Dissertation Heidelberg, 1935), 39. Mann fills this in: 'Es ist allgemein, indem es sich auf sich bezieht, und einzeln, indem es sich negative-ausschliessend-auf sich bezieht'; Mann, *Zum Begriff des Einzelnen, des Ich, und des Individuellen bei Hegel*, 40.
89. Hegel, *SL*, trans. Giovanni, 300–301, 549 (Suhrkamp).

444   *Hegel's Absolute Dialetheism*

90. Ibid, 549, 300 (Suhrkamp).
91. As Schick points out, 'Das Einzelne ist nicht laenger nur das vorausgesetzte Jenseits des Begriffes, sondern-in seiner Jenseitigkeit- Moment der Bewegung des Begriffes selbst. Darin leistet die Subjektive Begriffslogik mehr als man, erkenntnistheoretisch vorgeprägt, von ihr erwarten könnte.' See Frederike Schick, *Hegels Wissenschaft der Logik-metaphysische Letztbegruendung oder Theorie logischer Formen?* (München: Verlag Karl Aber, 1994), 228.
92. Redding points out that the division of universality, particularity, and singularity corresponds to a threefold division in judgment: 'All S is P,' 'Some S is P,' and 'this S is P.' On the relation of this division to Aristotle's division, see Redding, *Analytic Philosophy and the Return of Hegelian Thought*, 89–90.

14 Relativizing the Absolute
Empiricism, Judgment, and Inference

Empirical Concepts

Are empirical determinations concepts? Hegel's answer can be gleaned from the following passage:

> With respect to completeness [Vollständigkeit], we have just seen that the determinate moment of particularity is *complete* in the difference of the *universal* and the *particular*, and that only these two make up the particular species. To be sure, there are more than two species to be found in any genus in nature, and these many species cannot stand in the same relation to each other as we have shown. This is the impotence of nature [Ohnmacht der Natur], that it cannot abide by and exhibit the rigor [Strenge] of the concept and loses itself in a blind manifoldness void of concept. We can *wonder* at nature, at the manifoldness of its genera and species, in the infinite diversity of its shapes, for wonder is *without* concept and its object is the irrational. It is allowed to nature, since nature is the self-externality of the concept, to indulge in this diversity [Verschiedenheit], just as spirit, even though it possesses the concept in the shape of concept, lets itself go into pictorial representation and runs wild in the infinite manifoldness of the latter. The manifold genera and species of nature must not be esteemed to be anything more than arbitrary notions of spirit engaged in pictorial representations [Vorstellen]. Both indeed show traces and intimations of the concept, but they do not exhibit it in trustworthy copy, for they are the sides of its free self-externality; the concept is the absolute power precisely because it can let its difference go free in the shape of self-subsistent diversity, external necessity, accidentality, arbitrariness, opinion [selbständiger Verschiedenheit, äußerlicher Notwendigkeit, Zufälligkeit, Willkür, Meinung],—all of which however, must not be taken as anything more than the abstract side of *nothingness*.[1]

In this passage Hegel elucidates the connection between nature and the concept. Whereas the concept as such is only constituted by three moments (universal, particular, and singular) Hegel admits that in nature there are more species in a genus and that the specific relations between the species of the concept cannot obtain between the species in nature. As long as we assume that the universal and the particular are separate, we shall not be able to derive the universal from the particular or the particular from the universal. The concept is that which, as the concept as such, is indistinguishable from its moments: universality, particularity, and singularity. Since the self-externality of the concept would be nothing more than the concept in the form of its negation, nature is the negation of this unity, in which the universal is identified with its particular moments. Since the concept is defined by the structures of self-predication and existential implication, we would expect that the concepts of nature would fail to exhibit these structures.

If we consider some examples of *empirical kinds* we shall see right away how nature fails to exhibit the 'strictness of the concept' and 'runs wild into the blind irrational.' Nature is 'impotent' to the extent that the powers of self-predication and existential implication are absent. Consider the concepts 'proton,' 'water,' and 'animal.' Whether we investigate matters from the point of view of physics, chemistry, or biology, the result is the same. The concept 'proton' is not *a proton*, water itself is not an instance of water, and the animal itself is not *an animal*. Indeed, we do not encounter 'the animal itself' out there in the zoo, only particular animals. As the Buddhist tradition teaches us, 'water does not wash water' and 'fire does not burn fire.'[2] The lesson, of course, is that empirical determinations are not reflexive or *self-predicative*. Since self-predication entails existential implication, the empirical universal by itself never implies the existence of the particular. Thus, no empirical concept exhibits existential implication. Indeed, we know this not from the example, but from the general principle that empirical kinds or empirical concepts are necessarily constrained by the opposition of the universal from the particular. Indeed, because they are not *of the Absolute*, empirical determinations are not concepts *proper*.

On the one hand, since empirical kinds are structured by the absolute separation of universal from particular, they are *not concepts proper*. On the other hand, Hegel claims that they are *the self-externality of the concept*. Why use this turn of phrase? First, the formula indicates that empirical determinations can be raised to have universal significance. For example, 'water' signifies what all instances of water have in common. Thus, it is a *universal*. What is more, it is also particular, since it is one in number. Thus, it is also singular, for it is *this such and such* or *this concept*. But unlike concepts that have the Absolute as their object, the concept of water is *not* self-predicating or existentially implicative. The concept of water is not itself water, and this concept does *not* imply its own existence. Thus, the concept of water is a concept that is *separated* from the process constitutive of conceptual development. For this reason, it is not incorrect to speak about empirical concepts as both concepts but also self-external or 'alienated' from the conceptual structures endemic to *the concept as such*. As these reflections also make evident, Hegel's logic is not an empirical logic, nor is it a logic *of the empirical*. Rather, the logic is a text that lays bare the *a priori* conditions for the possibility of the constituents of the empirical concept: universality, particularity, and singularity.

One simple way to draw the contrast between properly logical and empirical concepts is the way that each related to the PNC. Indeed, the difference in their relationship to that principle provides us a clue to clarifying the role of non-contradiction in Hegel's logic. On the one hand, for empirical thinking, the classical PNC is the principle. Because empirical notions rely on the difference between universal and particular, the PNC must remain in place. For this reason, when empirical knowing contradicts itself, the result is an error. When the understanding is separated out from the self-differentiating process of the concept, the contradiction in the understanding does not lead to a new concept. Instead, the contradiction is a road that is closed and leads nowhere. The indebtedness of the empirical concept to the PNC is a consequence of their separation from the self-predicative and existentially implicative character of the concept. In terms of the formula of self-externality, the consistency insisted upon by empirical thinking is a thinking that does not grasp the inconsistency of a priori conceptual determinations of the Absolute. The rule of non-contradiction in the case of empirical concepts is *the negation* of the concept's necessarily inconsistent self-predicative structure. Insofar as the abstract determination is the concept in the form of 'self-negation,' the non-foundationalist reading must not leave empirical determinations unknown and unaccounted for, as Clark and Fritzman have implied.[3]

For Hegel, empirical determinations are not just the self-externality of the concept, for the 'self-externality of the concept' is also an integral aspect of the determination of particularity as such. The empirical determination is indeed also to be grasped as *the wayward offspring* of the concept. The concept's infinite power is exhibited by its ability to abandon itself to 'self-subsistent diversity.' The division of the universal and the particular is essential to the *a priori* determination of particularity and hence of the concept. Still, it is nestled *within* a principle of self-determination and is only one moment of that self-determining principle. In the empirical determination, the difference between universal and particular is rendered *absolute*. The separation of the particular from the concept as a whole undermines its status as a proper particular and its capacity to be unified with the other moments of the concept. In the empirical determination, the determinations of universality, particularity, and singularity have broken away from the concept's self-development and is thereby *free-floating*. In Hegel's words, it is the 'abstract side of nothingness.' Here we can speak of the concept because the empirical determinations exhibit the structure of determinate particularity, but we must qualify it with the terms 'free floating' or 'self-external' because this structure is not integrated within the *a priori* development of the concept. No proper copy of the concept can be made exactly because the particulars are the self-externality of the self-external moment of the concept.

Naturally, when the concept is modeled on such empirical distinctions, we get the results that we enumerated in the dualistic and finite construal of the concept: the absolute rule of the PNC, the separation of universality from particularity, purely finite concepts, and appeal to foundations. Such finite thinking by its very nature loses itself and negates itself. From the formal logical point of view, nothing follows from a contradiction. For this reason, Hegel has chosen his words with some precision. The empirical determinations of nature constitute *the abstract aspect of nothingness*. Note that there is a concrete aspect to 'nothingness,' namely one that is nestled within the system of categories in the *Science of Logic*.

The nothingness that results from the formal logical system is also an infinite abundance, for according to the formal system, both nothing and everything follows from a contradiction. The contradiction engendered by the self-negation of the formal system must result in an infinite diversity that has no *a priori* principle of order. For this reason, Hegel has also chosen the word 'Mannigfaltigkeit' or *many-foldedness* with care. *A priori*, according to the formal worldview, we only know that from a contradiction everything exists. But of course this might just as well mean nothing. Categories have no *a priori* content. Whatever content we wish to posit appears *arbitrary*. Here in the categories of nature the PNC is quite applicable. As Karin De Boer points out, 'Thus, Hegel by no means wishes to reject the logical rules constitutive of empirical judgments. On his view, the Understanding is perfectly justified in avoiding contradiction as long as it is involved in the production of empirical knowledge.'[4] Here everything and nothing follows from a contradiction. Unlike the categories of nature, the concepts of the concept, namely universality, particularity, and singularity are not governed by the classical PNC. For these concepts, *particular* results follow from particular contradictions: particularity follows from universality and singularity from particularity.

Since for formal thinking categories have no *a priori* content, in order to know the content of what we are thinking, that is in order to discover the content of concepts, we must re-produce empirical givens or create new empirical determinations from those re-productions. In fact, we have already pointed out that this results in our discussion of *Absolute Empiricism*. Our concepts cease to be merely conceptual and become *natural* or *psychological*. The result, of course, is an utter lack of normativity, which is an expected consequence of the fallacy of *psychologism*, for example. In other words, our concepts become pictures or '*Vorstellungen*,' 'what is put before the mind.' This is exactly what Hegel points out: 'The manifold genera and species of nature must not be esteemed to be anything more than arbitrary notions of spirit engaged in pictorial representations.' These representations as empirical are *contingent*. Because they are separated from the concept, and a basic principle of reason, they are subject matters for *opinion*, not knowledge.

Since the finite determination of the concept renders all conceptual content empirical in kind, those contents for which we have no direct empirical presentation, such as most categories in the logic, will require the invention of a metaphor. Not every representation on this view will be a metaphor. We can, for example, discuss the representation of the tree as a tree. Yet, to discuss the concept as such, for which no representation is possible, we shall need to adopt empirical contents as representatives, or symbolic ambassadors of what cannot in principle show itself.

Although we have no concepts by which such empirical representations may be grasped, and thus no way to have knowledge of nature in this sense, we can *wonder* at it. To wonder why something is the case, or that something is the case, is not a state of knowing. Indeed, knowing is the resolution of the wonder. When I know why it is that the earth revolves around the sun, I am no longer *wondering why* it revolves. For the wonderer, what is wondered at is unknown. For this reason, we can *wonder* at the endless empirical diversity and acquire *a posteriori* knowledge of it. Because of the infinite variety of this diversity, this wonder really is *insatiable*. The wonder may be directed either at the empirical content as the object or at our own representations thereof. We can, in this respect, wonder at ourselves just as much as we can wonder at the object of nature.

In this rich passage on nature, the nuance of Hegel's account really presents itself. Hegel's account of singularity is not intended to provide knowledge of all individuals. If it were, then his account would require knowledge of *every natural singular thing* such as the famous case of *Krug's pen*, which as Ferrarin has pointed out, is not at all Hegel's aim.[5] Obviously, it is important to know which singulars are inherently knowable (*a priori*) and which can only be known *a posteriori* and as a totality can constitute an insatiable object of wonder. Still, the singularity that is knowable (the concept) is itself the pre-condition for the *a posteriori* knowledge of any natural singular being. Because empirical concepts are not properly concepts, Hegel refers to them as empirical representations. Much confusion regarding what the concept is results from the *over-estimation* of the importance of such representations. When the empirical determination is rendered absolute, the nullity of the *empirical concept* allows us to say whatever we want, as well as nothing at all. In terms of modality, Hegel can show the necessity of the empirical contingency, while it is beneath philosophy and methodologically problematic to expect it to deduce *a priori* every empirical contingency.[6]

Because the concept is true in virtue of itself, we must agree with McDowell that the conceptual is completely *unbounded*. This is the thesis of Absolute Idealism, namely that the conceptual realm has no outer boundary.[7] Because the conceptual is externally unbounded, McDowell places the 'empirical restraint' on reason within reason.[8] For McDowell, the idea of the Given that he rejects is that the 'space of reasons' is wider than the conceptual space.[9] As concerns the *correspondence* of logical categories to natural and spiritual determinations, such correspondence could not be possible without the existence of non-logical determinations such as nature and spirit. The correspondence of the logical category with natural and spiritual objectivities is, of course, not constituted by the correspondence of a category with something that is completely devoid of categorial content. Rather, as we have strained to point out, for Hegel truth is 'self-correspondence' such that the correspondence of the category with the natural or spiritual object is *the correspondence of the concept with itself* in nature or spirit. Whatever empirical determinations there are in the domains of nature and spirit (which are not themselves reducible to empirical determinations), they are constituted as the 'self-externality' of the concept, such that the empirical content does *appear* to be 'outside' of reason. Indeed, this is the strength of Hegel's account of empirical content: Hegel can account for the *appearance* of the complete independence of the empirical from the concept, exactly because the empirical has the *conceptual determination* to be the concept in its inverted and external form.

However, since the concept is self-objectifying, for Hegel it is clear that whatever role the empirical restraint plays in the truth claims of the philosopher in natural and spiritual philosophy, the empirical content (and thereby the restraint) itself would never be possible without the self-objectifying concept, which for Hegel makes nature and spirit possible in the first place. For this reason, if we are to properly appreciate the unbounded aspect of the concept, and the internality of the empirical restraint, we must first work out the self-objectifying aspect of the concept and only from this standpoint begin to raise questions concerning the relation of the logic to the empirical.

For Hegel, the internality of the empirical restraint could never mean, of course, that the empirical restraint is contained *within* pure logic, since the latter is completely *devoid* of any empirical content. The 'empirical constraint' can only be located within reason 'writ large'—in reason insofar as it is realized in nature and spirit. Since the dialectical character of Hegel's concept entails that the concept is *true in virtue of itself*, logical concepts are not made true in virtue of some other principle—external or internal. The concepts of logic, which have the Absolute as their object, do not have empirical determinations as their objects, and for this reason the 'empirical restraint' that appears within reason itself does not have any impact on the *logical truth* of the logical concepts themselves.

Simply put, Hegel's Absolute Idealism *radicalizes* the unbounded nature of the conceptual by rendering 'the empirical restraint' irrelevant for the truth of the logical concept. For example, in the *Science of Logic*, the objectivity of the concept (in its *purely logical objectivity*) is established by an ontological 'argument,' and ontological arguments make no reference to empirical content in order to establish the *logical objectivity* of the concept.

Of course, this cannot and does not mean that for Hegel empirical representations are true in virtue of themselves. Because empirical representations are not true in virtue of themselves alone, certainly the empirical restraint that is located within reason is relevant for truth claims concerning such determinations. But as concerns self-predicative and existentially implicative logical categories, such as those in the *Science of Logic*, which have the Absolute as their object, the 'empirical restraint' is without relevance for their truth *qua* logical categories.

In the second *Encyclopedia*, Hegel is clear that it is the necessity of the concept that is the foundation of science:

> However, the course of a science's origin, and the preliminaries of its construction is one thing, while the science itself is another. In the latter, the former can no longer appear as the foundation of the science; the foundation must be the necessity of the concept.[10]

We are reminded that for Hegel truth is constituted by the concept *alone*:

> To lay down the true shape of truth is scientific—or what is the same thing, to maintain that truth has only the concept as the element of its existence, seems I know, to contradict a view which is in our time as prevalent as it is pretentious, and to go against what that view implies.[11]

Because Hegel is clear that the concept is the only principle of truth, any correspondence between the concept and object in nature or spirit, namely any natural or spiritual truth, must itself not only be *due* to the necessity of the concept but must also have the concept as its *only* element. Indeed, Hegel is clear that the concept is the 'creator of heaven and earth'[12] and is the material for its own formative activity:

> Reason is for itself the *infinite material* of all natural and spiritual life.

Given that truth only has the concept for its element of existence, and natural and spiritual truths can only have the concept as their element of existence, whatever truth there is in nature and spirit have their origin in (and are constituted by) the concept alone. Although nature and spirit are not merely logical domains (for they contain non-logical determinations that are *not reducible* to merely conceptual contents, such as 'time' and 'space'), they are nonetheless thoroughly saturated with and insepara-ble from conceptual determinations. For this reason, the 'non-logical' domains of nature and spirit are not non-conceptual, rather, the 'non-logical' aspect of the 'non-logical' domain only signifies that its contents *cannot be reduced* to merely logical determinations.

Indeed, the unity of the form and material in nature and spirit is a func-tion of reason, and reason alone, such that it does not measure its truth by a principle external to it. As Houlgate points out, the concept determines itself *to be nature*.[13] Accordingly, whatever truth (self-correspondence of the concept with its object) there is even in the domains of the non-logical (namely, nature and spirit), they are themselves constituted and determined by the concept alone and do *not* rely upon any external or *empirical* principles; the unity of the concept and its nature or spiritual object is the unity of the concept with itself by means of itself. Because Hegel's ontological argument extends to nature and spirit too (since the *material* of nature and spirit is nothing other than reason), in order to provide a complete account of the relation of the concept to empirical content, a more specific investigation into how the ontological argument is extended from the logic into the domains of nature and spirit would be required, and I leave the details of Hegel's account of this process to another inquiry. Here I mean to provide the outline of an itinerary for such an inquiry by reconstructing how, for Hegel, the purely logical objectivity of the category depends upon *the category alone*.

We should note that Hegel also points out that intuitive contents, the psychological correlate to natural kinds, are just as empty of the concept as natural kinds are.

> But if by intuition we understand not merely a sensuous material but the *objective totality*, then the intuition is an *intellectual* [intelle-ktuelle] *one*, that is, in existence which is unalterable reality and truth—the reality only in so far as it is essentially in the concept and is *determined* by it; the *idea*, of whose more precise nature more will be said later. What intuition as such is supposed to have over the con-cept is external reality, the reality that lacks the concept and receives value only through the concept.[14]

The totality of the intuitions of space and time, in Kant's sense, exists in an indifferent and external sense. This means that the manifold of intui-tion is not *inherently* unified. The manifold of intuition as such is simply a *mani-foldedness*. As such, it corresponds to one side of the abstract universal, namely to the mutable side of particularity. Every particular intuition of space points to another space on the horizon. Likewise, each intuitive moment of time points to other moments of time, such as the future and the past. In experience the intuition of space and time always points us away from our own position towards further possible positions. At every possible spatio-temporal location we encounter another horizon that points to further points in an infinite quantitative sequence. Indeed, every experience of space and time is an experience of *incompleteness*. Instead of the universal appearing in the intuition, we only encounter 'the same thing again,' namely more mutually external particulars. Each is 'indifferent' to its own universal content. Instead of pointing to the universal which they embody, they point to particulars. Insofar as the sensible contents as sensible lack the concept, it is not to the advantage of any science to be grounded upon it.

In this passage Hegel contrasts the intuition of sensible manifold with the intuition of what is *imperishable* in the sensible manifold, namely reality as the objective totality or the sensible manifold insofar as it is determined by the concept: 'the reality only in so far as it is essentially in the concept and is *determined* by it; the *idea*.' In order to analyze this passage with any justice, let us briefly re-cap our discussion of intellectual intuition and discuss how Hegel's account of the concept plays a role in making it possible.[15]

Kant banished intellectual intuition from knowing. Categories, by themselves, are empty. For Kant, the very content of the category is not in the category, but in the intuition. Intuition is the source of particulars. For this reason, in Kant the content of the universal lies in the particulars given in intuition. (As we pointed out in our discussion of Kant, this is the source of many inner conflicts in Kant.) We have quite often come to this result: the content of the universal does in fact lie in *particularity*. Although Kant places the content of universality in particularity, he renders the particular *completely intuitive*. For this reason, no conceptual content may be elucidated independently of the separate faculty of intuition. The ban on intellectual intuition means that (i) we cannot read off the character of concepts without appeal to intuition and (ii) no particular may be derived from the concept without appeal to intuition. This is the ultimate meaning of the concept as a 'logical function of judgment.' Intellectual intuition would allow us not only to know particulars as they are irrespective of any appeal to intuition (*noumena*) but also to distinguish the contents of categories in sensible intuition purely *a priori*, that is without any appeal to the sensible manifold.

Kant's separation of intellectual intuition from knowing undermined Descartes' *cogito* in which intellectual intuition is employed to establish the existence of the self as well as any pretense of Aristotle's philosophy that the universally articulated Form might be sufficient for generating particular entities. The cogito shows that so long as I am thinking I cannot deny that thinking exists. The cogito is an intellectual intuition, for in virtue of thinking the universal 'thinking,' the particular thought,

454 Hegel's Absolute Dialetheism

'thinking' as such, exists. Of course, the content of the cogito is fully *psychological*. In other words, the content of the term 'thinking' is reduced to the psychological presence in the thought experiment. Descartes' 'proof' actually places all of the conceptual content for the 'I' in intuitive psychological content.

Unlike in Kant, there is a clean separation between the particular instance of the universal in nature or intuition and the particular concepts themselves. Kant claims that Intellectual intuition is a function of a divine Understanding but is beyond our understanding. Indeed, for Kant, we cannot establish the contents of categories by simply thinking them! Kant denied that the allocation of intellectual intuition to the human mind was possible. Instead, it is a problematic concept that belongs properly to a divine intellect.

In the tradition of German Idealism, the term 'intellectual intuition' has its origins in Kant. The term 'intuition' refers to the immediate relation to an object, while 'intellectual' qualifies the kind of immediacy. Kant limits human cognition to discursive Understanding. Discursive Understanding is a mediated relation to an object. On the one hand, for discursive understanding, concepts do not give us immediate access to objects. Intellectual intuition, on the other hand, signifies the immediate relation to objects *via* concepts alone. Accordingly, intellectual intuition, like discursive Understanding, signifies a *capacity*. In this passage Hegel is pointing out an *alternative way* to relate to the sensible manifold. Instead of simply following the horizontal reference of particular to particular, one can also take the whole totality of the serial determinations of particulars as the object of one's thinking. In the latter case, the intellect has *the concept in the sensible manifold*, or the concept *in virtue of which* the sensible manifold is a unified totality, as one's object.

Note that here the conceptual terms at play involve subject and object, two terms which are not directly thematic for this inquiry into the concept per se, though are indispensable for any thorough investigation into Hegel's philosophy. Moreover, since intellectual intuition is an *act of consciousness*, it is not strictly speaking a subject matter for logic. For this reason, the logic of the concept is *not itself* an intellectual intuition. Thus, it would be a category error to identify Hegel's logic of the concept with Kant's intellectual intuition in *CPR*, Schelling's first principle in *STI* or Fichte's first principle in the *Science of Knowledge*. Although Hegel's logic of the concept is existentially implicative (as Aristotle's Forms), and makes possible intellectual intuition, the categorial contents are not yet acts of mind.

Realphilosophie is a result of the activity of the Idea's unification with what is not logical, and this unity only results upon the completion of the logic. Despite the deficiency of the logical structure and merely conceptual determination for sufficiently circumscribing intellectual intuition, the concept as such is a *necessary condition* for its existence. Intellectual intuition is the immediate thinking of the object in virtue of thinking alone. This means that intuiting an object intellectually allows one to think the particular instance of the universal in the object through the universal *by itself*. Accordingly, in order for intellectual intuition to be possible, the concept by which we think must itself be capable of thinking the particular in virtue of the universal alone. The concept, according to Hegel, *creates the particular in virtue of its own universality*. Without the concept, there is no way to grasp the particular object in virtue of thinking alone. In short, the self-predicative and existentially implicative determination of the concept makes possible the intellectual intuition of consciousness.

The concept gives us a *purely logical template* for the structure of intellectual intuition in conscious activity. If we think back to our historical inquiries into intellectual intuition, we discover that none of the thinkers we have considered up through this point developed a *logical template* for the possibility of intellectual intuition. While Kant precluded it as a real possibility for human Understanding, both Fichte and Schelling's transcendental philosophy (despite their arguably diverse construal of intellectual intuition) begin with the self-thinking thought of *self-consciousness*. By providing a purely logical structure for intellectual intuition, Hegel makes logically possible what in all earlier forms of idealism is impossible: the intelligible rendering of the process by which the infinite makes itself finite. In Hegel, *creation itself* acquires a logic.

In the *Doctrine of the Concept* Hegel provides a ground upon which the conceptual content of categories that are manifest in the sensible manifold may be realized *a priori*. In the *Science of Logic*, the thinking of the concept generates the conceptual content of the concept without any appeal to intuition. Still, the logic itself is not yet a *mind*. For this reason, even at the stage of the *Logic* we do not yet have intellectual intuition, though we do have the condition for it.

In the logic of the concept, it is true that Hegel identifies the self-objectifying concept with *intellectual intuition*:

> But if by intuition we understand not merely a sensuous material but the *objective totality*, then then the intuition is an *intellectual one* . . . the reality, only in so far as it is essentially in the concept and is determined by it, the Idea.[16]

Indeed, Hegel gives us a logic by which we may restore intellectual intuition to human rational self-consciousness that Kant banished to the divine mind. Still, Hegel avoids Descartes' error of psychologizing the content of thinking, by securing the purely logical structure of universality, particularity, and singularity. Hegel provides a *logical backdrop* that *makes possible* the cognition of those logical forms by the philosopher, whose contemplation for him constitutes the *divine* knowing of the logical forms. Although the *Logic* constitutes 'God's thoughts before the creation' before the creation *no mind* is posited that could think those thoughts—unless we *metaphorically* consider *the self-categorizing of categories as mental activity*. In the *Doctrine of the Concept*, Hegel shows that the concept is constituted by a process of self-predication and existential implication. Self-predication and existential implication constitute the logical template for intellectual intuition.[17]

Just as the manifold of intuition points to the concept, so must nature. For this reason, Hegel's somewhat Platonic lambasting of nature cannot be the whole story regarding natural concepts. When we consider how nature arises from the logic as a whole, and remember the whole Hegelian song and dance, we quickly remember that there is another sense in which nature, although it is the externality of the concept, cannot be fully cut off from the clutches of the concept. Hegel writes that

> Of course, life, the 'I', finite spirit, are also only determinate concepts. To this extent, however, their resolution is in a universal which, as the truly absolute concept, is to be grasped as the idea of infinite spirit—the spirit whose *posited being* is the infinite, transparent reality in which hit contemplates its *creation* and, in the creation, itself.[18]

Indeed, life is not only a category of the logic, but it is a form of existence that belongs to nature. Beyond life, in this passage Hegel gives a brief summary of the upshot of his whole system of philosophy. The logic creates nature, and nature creates spirit. The whole procession of Logic into the *Realphilosophie* shows that it is absolute, or universal and unconditional mind that is the creative principle of the whole development of logic and the non-logical spheres. In the *Realphilosophie* the purely logical forms resurrect themselves with non-logical contents. The philosopher (in this case Hegel), as the real vehicle by which the absolute mind knows itself, contemplates the whole system and his own contemplation of the system. Accordingly, spirit, logic and nature are grasped as *moments of the absolute mind* that contemplates its creations. Surely, Hegel cannot accept that nature itself cannot recover from the self-abandonment of the concept. If this were his view, he could not complete his system or present such summaries of the *Realphilosophie*.

Hegel identifies space and time as functions of self-externality, or the particular concept. Though it is self-external, it is a result of the self-negation of the Absolute Idea. Because it is the Idea that is in the form of self-negation, time itself cannot be merely cut off from the other determinations of the concept. Instead, time integrates the other determinations of the concept, such as particularity and singularity. By making this distinction regarding the ways in which nature is said, we may allay concerns that Hegel's comments here concerning nature might undermine his project on the whole.

The Impasse of Judgment

Throughout the *Science of Logic*, Hegel continually points out that judgment is a defective means to express the concept.[19] For example, consider Hegel's comments about the insufficiency of judgments to express the identity and non-identity of Being and nothing:

> In this connection we must, at the outset, make this general observation, namely that the proposition in the form of a judgment is not suited to express speculative truths; a familiarity with this fact is likely to remove many misunderstandings of speculative truths. Judgment is an identical relation between subject and predicate; in it we abstract from the fact that the subject has a number of determinatenesses other than that of the predicate, and also that the predicate is more extensive than the subject. Now if the content is speculative, the nonidentical aspect of subject and predicate is also an essential moment, but in the judgment this is not expressed. It is the form of the simple judgment, when it is used to express speculative results, which is very often responsible for the paradoxical and bizarre light in which much of recent philosophy appears to those who are not familiar with speculative thought.[20]

For Hegel, the concept hides in the judgment. Speculative content expresses the identity and non-identity of categories. In the judgment 'S is P,' the predicate only expresses the identity of itself with the subject, but fails to express the non-identity of itself with the subject, namely that 'S is not P.' 'Being is nothing' only expresses the identity of Being with nothing, but fails to express that 'Being is *not* nothing,' which is *also* true. One could also state it the other way. The judgment, 'Being is not nothing' fails to express the unity of subject and predicate, for it presents the one-sided truth of their non-identity.[21] In this case, both 'S is P' and 'S is not P' are true: Being *qua Being* is nothing and Being *qua Being* is not nothing. For this reason, Hegel infers that judgments do not properly express speculative content. When we state these together, we have 'Being is nothing' and 'Being is not nothing.' Now we have a contradiction (mutually exclusive judgments). But this contradiction, although *true*, still fails to express the *developmental* aspect of the concept, for it is an *ossified* contradiction. What is worse, rather than facilitate further development, the contradiction will *stymie* any attempt to proceed by means of judgments and inferences.

Heraclitus said that 'nature loves to hide.' For Hegel, the unity of opposition, which is constitutive of Heraclitus' account of nature, also hides, though for Hegel it hides in judgment. In a judgment, the predicate only determines the subject in *one* respect, and implies that the negation of predicate, the opposite determination, does not determine the subject.[22] The back-turning that is constitutive of the concept remains hidden as long as the form of judgment is adopted as the *sole* form of conceptual determination. Judgment of course is necessary, for in order to recognize a contradiction between two judgments, there must be judgment. In order to have a true contradiction that is expressed in judgment, judgment cannot be completely erased from the science. Rather, it must be integrated and overcome from within.

Indeed, Hegel does claim that there is a form of judgment that expresses the truth of the concept: the apodictic judgment. The apodictic judgment is that judgment in which

> the universal that is itself and continues through its opposite, and is a universal only in unity with the latter.[23]

Only in the apodictic judgment do the subject and predicate 'correspond to each other' and thereby become a 'singularized universal.'[24] Here the subject loses its determinate being as something opposed to a predicate[25] for each has *the same conceptual content*. In self-predicative judgment, the subject *is truly itself*, for it is what it *ought to be*. The self-predicative judgment, insofar as it collapses subject into predicate, expresses the form of the apodictic judgment in which the subject and predicate *signify the same concept*.[26] Self-predicative judgment exemplifies this form of judgment, for it expresses the moment when the subject corresponds with itself in the predicate. When the 'concept' finally becomes 'conceptual' in the judgment, 'the concept is conceptual,' the concept is what it *ought* to be—it is *truly* conceptual. We will remember that as long as the concept labored under the opposition of identity and difference it could not truly be itself. Under the opposition of universality and particularity, the concept was *not* conceptual—it had to seek its being elsewhere, such as a naturalistic or psychological content. In such cases, the concept is *not* what it *ought to be*.

Of course, the self-predicative judgment is not just analytic; 'the concept is conceptual' is not just a tautology. The subject is identified with the predicate 'conceptual,' and so it is *analytic*. But it is also synthetic, for the subject is *different* from the predicate, since the subject *qua subject* is not the same as the predicate *qua predicate*. On the whole, it is a unity of identity and difference (synthesis and analysis). The concept, *qua subject*, is both different from its predicate (which is not a subject), and identical to the predicate, for the conceptual content of the predicate is the same as that of the subject. This identity of identity and difference is expressed in the judgment 'the concept is conceptual.' Indeed, because the apodictic judgment (and thereby self-predicative judgment) expresses the truth of judgment by undermining the difference between subject and predicate, it is just as much the *end* of judgment, for it spells the end of the difference between subject and predicate and the mutual exclusion of negations.[27]

Although it is the case that for Hegel syllogism develops out of judgment, for Hegel, objectivity can only arise by means of the self-negation of judgment as well as syllogism. Although we must go *through* judgment, as long as we refuse to go *beyond* judgment which cannot express the unity of opposition without *destroying itself*, we cannot grasp what it is for the concept to exist 'in and for itself' or to exist objectively.

More recently, Robert Brandom has famously read Hegel as a 'Rational Expressivist' in terms almost no one had thought to read him before, namely by emphasizing the 'holistic system of inferentially correlated judgeables' as the most 'minimal unit' of conceptual content:

> Rationalist expressivism understands the explicit—the thinkable, the sayable, the form something must be in to count as having been expressed—in terms of its role in inference. I take Hegel to have introduced this idea, although he takes the minimal unit of concep-tual content to be the whole holistic system of inferentially correlated judgeables, and so is not a propositionalist.[28]

Brandom takes the primacy of inference over judgment to be the central distinguishing factor that characterizes the development of German thought from Kant to Hegel.[29] Hegel, according to Brandom, understands concepts to be 'inferentially articulated.'[30] The identity of synthesis and analysis in Schelling may be one of the deeper Schellingian legacies in Hegel, but that revolution which Schelling unwittingly brought to philosophy lead to Hegel's *uncompromising view*, contra Brandom, that philosophy ought *not* proceed by means of inferences, argumentation, proofs, or demonstra-tions. In paragraph 58 of the *Preface* to *Phenomenology*, Hegel proclaims that philosophy ought not proceed by *argumentation*.[31] When we appeal to arguments, we are giving up on the *freedom* of the self-determining science:

> At the opposite extreme, argumentation is freedom from all content, and a sense of vanity towards it. What is looked for here is the effort to give up this freedom, and instead of being the arbitrarily moving principle of the content, to sink this freedom in the content, letting it move spontaneously of its own nature, by the self as its own self, and then to complete this movement.

Philosophical thought does *not* consist in 'giving reasons':

> This pattern of giving reasons and stating conditions belongs to the method of proof which differs from the dialectical movement, and belongs to external cognition.[32]

Hegel can certainly agree with Sellars that the Given is a myth. Hegel, like Sellars, gives up on the concept that knowledge 'rests on a foundation of non-inferential knowledge of matter of fact.'[33] Unlike Sellars, however, Hegel does not turn to Coherentist vision of a 'space of reasons' as a solution to the problem of the Given. The reason is simple: Hegel is beyond *reasons*. For this reason too, Hegel's account of contradiction cannot be properly accounted for in terms of reduction to the absurd. As Rosen points out, the logic is not a study of abstract patterns of inferential reasoning.[34] Hegel is clear that we ought not mix up the conceptual with the ratiocinative methods.[35] It is for this reason that Houlgate is exactly right to emphasize that Hegel's method is not syllogistic.[36] Because syllogism is constituted by judgment, and judgments cannot successfully express speculative truths, so do syllogisms fail to express speculative truths. In the syllogism, the concept is 'outside itself' just as it is in judgment. Just as one can safely reject syllogism as the method of philosophical science, one can also reject inference. Syllogisms fulfill their speculative potential by negating themselves as the true methodology of philosophical knowing.[37] What was formerly the proof is now the dialectical method.[38] For these reasons, it becomes clear that the 'most minimal unit' of conceptual content cannot be any kind of inference or inference-holism and that Hegel cannot be a Rational Expressivist.[39]

Although early Fichte and Schelling *proclaim* that the first principle is self-determining and free, they continue to give demonstrations of the principle. But were the principle self-determining, it would not require any independent demonstrations. Schelling's demonstration of the identity of synthesis and analysis at the outset of *STI*—despite its brilliance— is such an external reflection. Schelling demonstrates the essential features of the first principle, and therefrom investigates what could in principle instantiate such features. Rather, the first principle ought to establish its own truth.

As we mentioned earlier in our discussion of the ontological argument, it is not only the foundational dimension of argumentative reasoning that is problematic for Hegel's method. Because the principles of argumentation can be formulated separately from what it is one is arguing about, argumentation supposes a fundamental division between form and content. Given that such thinking proceeds by means of applying separate principles of inference, the formal principles of inference cannot supply the content that is thought by those principles. Thus, the division of form and content endemic to a science of 'giving reasons' undermines itself as the legitimate method for conceptual thought. If we mean to read Hegel charitably, for the same reason logic cannot proceed quantitatively, logic should not proceed by way of arguments either. Naturally, this does not entail that Hegel's logic is *without* method or rhapsodic. Rather, for Hegel it is only in avoiding appeals to given principles of inference that are distinct from the contents to which they apply that one can in principle avoid rhapsodic thinking.

One of Hegel's most profound revolutions is to rob the thinker of her traditional role as the principle and source of reasons. The role of the individual thinker is *not* to give reasons; it consists in *forgetting one's reasons* so that one can follow the self-development of the concept (and thereby the science) itself.[40] Although the true conception of the Absolute in *Realphilosophie* requires minds that think the Absolute, the mind that thinks the Absolute follows the determinations of the concepts and is subordinated to the movement of the concept. Just as we speak of our passions 'possessing us,' so thought functions the same way:

> It is all the less possible, therefore, to believe that the thought determinations that pervade all our representations—whether these are purely theoretical or hold a material belonging to sensation, impulse, will—that such thought determinations are at our service; that it is we who have them in our possession and not they who have us in theirs. What is there of more in us as against them? How would we, how would I set myself up as the superior universal over them—they that are the universal as such?[41]

Again, Hegel never tires of emphasizing that we are at the service of the concepts, not that the concepts are at our disposal:

> but still less shall we say of the concepts of things that we dominate them, or that the thought determinations of which they are the complex are at our service. On the contrary, our thought must accord with them, and our choice of freedom ought not to want to fit them to its purposes.[42]

As Houlgate points out, the philosopher must possess a readiness to be passive.[43] Indeed, this is the sense in which Hegel speaks of the 'vanity' of arguments.[44] Without transcending arguments philosophy cannot conceptually grasp what it would mean for the concept to be a *self-subsistent totality*. Conceptualizing this aspect of the concept would require a method other than that of applying rules of inference to a separate content—it requires dialectics. To put it polemically, *inference is not the moving force of Hegel's logic.*

Both McDowell and Brandom, the 'two different paths to Hegel from Sellars' myth of the Given,'[45] overplay the role and importance of the empirical in Hegel's thought. In his essay *Sketch of a Program for a Critical Reading of Hegel: Comparing Empirical and Logical Concepts*, Robert Brandom appears to read the function of speculative concepts as that which is to 'make explicit the process of making explicit.'[46] Accordingly, he argues that the difference between empirical and logical concepts is merely an *expressive* one.[47] For Brandom, the goal of the logic is 'to develop conceptual tools that are necessary and sufficient to express explicitly the essential structures that are implicit in our use of ordinary concepts (including those of the empirical sciences) in judgment and action.'[48] As he claims in *Some Pragmatists Themes in Hegel's Idealism*,

> The point of developing an adequate understanding of these categorial concepts is so that they can then be used to make explicit how ordinary empirical concepts work.[49]

In his most recent work, *A Spirit of Trust*, Brandom claims that logical concepts have the function to make explicit the function of 'ground level' concepts like 'blue' and 'sour':

> Speculative or logical concepts are theoretical philosophical metaconcepts, whose distinctive expressive role is to make explicit features of the conceptual contents and use (semantics and pragmatics) of those ground level concepts.[50]

Unfortunately, such a description of the *Logic* fails to track the radical conflict between empirical processes and logical ones. Hegel makes it *explicit*, as it were, that (speculative or logical) concepts proper are not explications of *how* ordinary empirical concepts work.[51] To the contrary, our ordinary empirical concepts, such as that of the $100, do not have the form of the concept proper: self-reference and existential implication, as the concept of God does, for example. The 'how' of empirical concepts is not 'self-reference' and 'existential implication'; the logic cannot be making explicit an empirical process of making explicit. The relationship cannot be one of *mere expression* when the form of the concept is *radically* at odds with what it is purported to express.[52] As Houlgate argues, logic does not address the empirical:

> Logic does not clarify all concepts—it does not address empirical concepts, nature or history.[53]

Of course, Hegel's elucidation of 'determinate being' shows the structure of determinate beings, just as the elucidation of 'quantity' shows the structure of quantities. But the mastery of ordinary experience and first order concepts requires a significant *deviation* from those concepts.

McDowell too, it seems, overplays the role of the empirical in Hegel's account of categories when he claims that

> It [the standpoint of Absolute knowledge] is not a standpoint at which we have somehow removed ourselves from the empirical world.[54]

Although the Absolute, which includes logic, nature, and spirit, certainly includes the empirical world, the categories of the logic *per se* are in fact *divorced* from the empirical world, since each is a concept of the Absolute, and their content is not in any way indebted to the empirical world. McDowell claims that the 'free movement of the concept' corresponds to and 'fits, for instance, the development of empirical inquiry.'[55] This certainly cannot be true of the concept as such, however, since it is self-predicative and existentially implicative, whereas empirical concepts are not.

In our analysis of Kant, we showed how his inability to identify an independent conceptual content *distinct* from predicates in possible judgments is the source of the vicious circularity of his account of categories. Hegel, by contrast, develops and elucidates the concept of the concept *independently* of judgment. Upon developing an account of the concept that is independent of judgment, Hegel shows how this independent content creates judgment in virtue of that very content. Pippin, in his book *The Satisfaction of Self-Consciousness*, identifies the conceptual content of judgment with that of the concept. He writes:

> The determinacy of the concept is not (or is not wholly and not fundamentally) a function of such abstraction, according to Hegel; instead the concept's determinacy (its own particularity or content) is primarily a function of the role it can and cannot play in judgments, judgments that originally determine the particular as the distinct particular that it is. Hegel is following Kant here in understanding concepts as 'predicates of possible judgments' and likewise insisting that to understand a concept is not to represent some abstracted common quality, but to understand how to use it in a variety of judgments.[56]

Pippin does indeed contrast the concept with abstraction, yet this ought to also entail a strong contrast of the concept with the 'predicate of possible judgments.' Further, Pippin proclaims that Hegel follows the Kantian conception of concepts as predicates of possible judgments.[57]

Although Pippin avoids making the error of over-emphasizing the role and importance of the empirical for Hegel's logic of concept, I would argue *contra* Pippin, that Hegel is not following Kant here, for the concept cannot be identified with a predicate of possible judgments. Judgments, for Hegel, follow from the concept. Hegel is giving *the condition for the possibility of any judgment whatever*: the self-differentiating concept. As Hegel points out, speculative truths, and in this case the concept, cannot be properly expressed in judgment. In judgment, the particular has been separated from its concrete unity with the universal and singular, and if anything, *fails* to express the concept proper. Bowman's critique of Pippin is *not misguided* when he argues that

> Hegel's speculative Idealism is not only not ultimately concerned with determinate judgment about determinate objects, but committed to

the thesis that orientation toward such judgments as the paradigmatic case of knowledge is itself misguided.[58]

Of course, it is true that judgment expresses the determinacy of the concept. But judgment can only express relative determinacy—for it places
the concept in a position of opposition with its negation. Accordingly,
judgment is not capable of expressing *absolute determinacy*, or where
it does, this absolute determination is only present in a relative form—
a *relativized absolute*. Judgment—like the category of particularity—
occupies the *middle* position. Because it determines the subject with a
predicate, it cannot convey the truth of the absolute indeterminacy of
Being with which logic begins. Likewise, it cannot express Absolute
determinacy in which oppositions are identified. *Judgment cannot be
absolutely grounded on judgment.* Rather, judgment truly expresses its
speculative truth in its self-demise, for there in its self-demise is its role
revealed as that which hides the Absolute concept.

Because the particular is also Absolute, one can legitimately look upon
the whole of Hegel's philosophy in terms of *particularity*. Particularity is
the form of the concept in which universality is in the form of self-negation.
In one sense, this means that the concept *qua* particular is expressed in
a one-sided manner, in which the concept is treated as distinct from its
negation. The one-sidedness of such determinations is codified in the
PNC and is the essential aspect of the illusion. Of course, empirical concepts also exhibit this one-sided character—they are not principles of
their own development, for they do not exhibit the self-developing character of self-predication and existential implication. Accordingly, they
must be connected to each other by means of some external principle of
thought, such as judgment or inference. Because inference and thereby
judgment which constitutes it articulate the form of empirical thinking,
one could legitimately look upon *this dimension* of the *Science of Logic*
as an attempt to articulate the rules for the employment of empirical
concepts. By turning one's gaze toward the judgment and empirical content, one misses the higher calling of logic: to conceive the Absolute—
itself by itself. When Brandom claims that the 'ultimate point of studying
meta-concepts' lies ultimately in what they can tell us about 'ground-level
concepts'[59] (like 'blue' and 'sour') he has missed the call to think the
Absolute. The self-thinking thought of Absolute knowing has no concern
for empirical determinations. Indeed, in *Logic* it is a mere *afterthought*,
if it is even a thought at all.

Just as one misses the Absolute determinacy of the concept by locat-
ing the determinacy of the concept in judgment, so one can also miss the
Absolute determinacy of the concept by construing determinacy in terms
of 'modally robust exclusion.'[60] Brandom argues that for Hegel determinate negation consists in the 'material incompatibility' of concepts, such
that 'the applicability of one concept precludes the other.' He provides

the example that a red patch of paint is not green.[61] Naturally, given this restricted view of determinacy, Brandom argues that Hegel endorses the PNC.[62] Indeed, green cannot be not-green. But the problem, of course, is the fact that Brandom's construal of Hegel's concept of determinacy in terms of 'material incompatibility' and 'material consequence' only acknowledges *relative* determinacy. The concept *of absolute* determinacy does not appear.[63] Instead, we only find determinate contents that are *relative* to one another—relative in the sense that they mutually exclude one another. As such, none of these contents count as absolute. Yet, the Absolute is exactly what Hegel is concerned with in the *Science of Logic*, for each and every category is a category of the Absolute.

If we return to the matter of judgment, we discover that judgment is one form of the *particularization* of the concept, under which the concept exists in a one-sided way such that it is distinct from its negation. Given the Absolute character of particularity, Hegel is not wrong at all to raise judgment to an absolute category of the logic or to proclaim that 'everything is a syllogism.'[64] Every concept of the logic is a definition of the Absolute—even judgment and syllogism. Nonetheless, the Absolute is here exemplified in its Absolute Self-Negation, for Hegel teaches us that judgment cannot express the form of speculative truths. Thus, the Absolute Truth of judgment and inference is the Absolute Truth of the element of the hiddenness of the Absolute. One must be able to look behind the form of judgment and inference—otherwise one will not appreciate them for what they really are: the Absolute in hiding.

Because it is a mistake to privilege the particular over the universal or the singular, it would certainly be a mistake to privilege the particular over other forms of totality, such that one would fail to remember the very reason for Hegel's proclamation that 'everything is a judgment.' Because the Absolute is just as particular as it is universal and singular, one can look at the text and *only* see the *clothes* in which the speculative has hidden its identity. By proclaiming that the determinacy of the concept lies in judgment, what one is really proclaiming is that what is real is the clothing, not the body which it covers. Even Hegel's own claim to the contrary—that speculative thinking ought *not* be understood in terms of judgment—can be read in terms of judgment, for the claim that speculative thinking is not exemplified in judgment itself *takes the form of judgment*. Thus, one can fall into the error of never really taking such claims about the limit of judgment with much seriousness. But if we do take them with seriousness, we need to re-think any reading that relies too heavily on judgment, inference, or empirical thought. If we read Hegel's logic as a totality of judgments and arguments we will have missed the form as well as the content of the text. Indeed, we will have taken the illusory reference inwards and outwards to be the conceptual determination of the concept without having acknowledged that they are *illusory references*.

One of the lessons about which the Chicago and Pittsburgh schools have reminded us is that *error can be instructive*. Their error consists in *privileging particularity at the cost of singularity*. This error teaches us, we *metaphysical* non-foundationalists (and perhaps more traditional readers), about our own tendencies to read Hegel in a one-sided way. Were one to claim, for example, that Hegel's logic ought *not* be understood in terms of substance or Essence, such a claim would be true, but would nonetheless be significantly qualified. Of course, Essence is overcome, just as inference and judgment are overcome, but Essence is a *true category* of the Absolute, just as every category of the logic, such as syllogism and judgment, is a true category of the Absolute. Just as one can fall into the trap of over-emphasizing judgment, one can just as much *underplay* its significance and deny it its rightful place in Absolute thinking, which would be equally foolhardy. The Absolute, as a conceptual system of self-determination might remain hidden in merely Essential determinations (as well as in judgment and syllogism, for example), but that form of hiddenness is itself an Absolute Truth of the Absolute.[65]

Long before Heidegger and Derrida taught us about the necessity of error, Hegel already understood that in order to succeed one must err. In order to arrive at the Absolute, one must wander from it—one must err in the sense of *errare*. Just as the function of the hammer is revealed when it breaks, the Absolute can only be revealed in its Absolute character because it went missing. Accordingly, the traditional problems of Nihilism and the Missing Difference should not be viewed as mere mistakes that lack all truth, but rather as necessary mistakes. Without wandering from our home, we could never have understood it.

The Resurrection of Finite Universality

The question, 'what is the concept?', demanded that any legitimate answer be both self-predicative and existentially implicative. Each of these characteristics is engendered in Hegel's concept of 'self-particularization.' Unlike the dogmatic appropriation of the concept as a formal principle that abides by the PNC, self-particularization abides by and fulfills the conditions of the question concerning universality. The self-contradiction of self-particularization in virtue of which the concept becomes singularity is not possible without the self-referring activity of self-differentiation. The self-referential feature of self-predicating universality necessitates that the concept particularize itself. Through its self-particularization, the concept achieves singularity. Without self-particularization, there would be no singularity whatever.

Our historical and systematic investigation into the question 'what is the concept?' lead us to a dualistic and finite conception of universality from which a number of paradoxes followed. The PNC, finitude of the concept, the separation of principles of universality and particularity, the denial of self-predication and existential implication, and the appeal to foundations all constituted the form of finite universality. From these we showed that a number of paradoxes followed: the problem of Nihilism, the problem of Instantiation, the Missing Difference, the problem of Third Man, the problem of Absolute Empiricism, and Onto-theology. Because the paradoxes follow from absolutizing finite universality, any solution to the problem of the missing Absolute must show why finite universality cannot achieve truth independently of the self-particularizing universal.

On the face of it, it appeared that Hegel's construal of the universal as self-particularization solved all of the paradoxes of finite universality in one single blow. Because the self-differentiating universal is both the principle of its universality and its particularity, self-differentiation is no longer beholden to the separation of the principles of universality and particularity. Moreover, it undermines the PNC, for as the principle of universality and particularity it is identical to itself only in its differentiation from itself. Since it is the principle of its own difference, there is no difference outside of itself to which it must appeal in order to be differentiated. For this reason, self-differentiation eschews the appeal to foundations. Last, as that which is identical to what it is not, there is no difference outside of the universal that could in principle limit it. For this reason, it is also infinite. Because the concept is true in virtue of itself, it is not indebted to an external principle of truth. Having elucidated the universal, we appeared to have already achieved our goal: to discover an account of the concept of the concept that did not fall victim to structural constraints of finite universality.

Upon closer inspection, however, we discovered that the self-differentiating universal differentiated itself into particularity. Insofar as the universal self-differentiated itself into particularity, we discovered that finite universality was not merely other to the self-particularizing concept, but endemic to it. Because the particular is self-differentiation in the form of negation, the particular is that which is not self-differentiating. Naturally, since the separation of universality and particularity entails the rejection of self-differentiation, the features of finite universality are constitutive of particularity. Both the universal and the particular, as particular species of the concept, are self-identical concepts that exclude their negations. As such, each is a finite determination governed by the PNC. In addition, since the universal and the particular species exclude each other, particularity is defined by the separation of the principles of universality and particularity. Finally, since neither is the principle of its own difference, the origin of the content is outside itself in two ways: in the very act of self-differentiation as well as in another universal or particular distinct from itself. This is the self-externality of the particular, in which the content of the particular is determined by another particular external to it.

Indeed, since particularity is constituted by the differentiation of the concept into the difference between the universal and the particular, particularity appeared to *re-instate* the very assumption of the separation of the principles of universality and particularity that Hegel's introduction of self-differentiation sought to undermine. Accordingly, because the various features of finite conceptual determination give rise to six problems (Nihilism, Instantiation, Missing Difference, Absolute Empiricism, Onto-theology, and the Third Man) and the particular contains finite universality, the self-differentiation of the universal into the particular inadvertently raised the threat that those same problems, such as the problem of the Third Man, that follow from the finite universal, would undermine the intelligibility of the concept. Indeed, in virtue of its very self-particularization, the concept necessarily posits a concept that is true in virtue of another, such that contingent determinations are necessitated by the self-particularizing form. For this reason, the initial argument that self-particularization solves the six problems of finite universality by undermining the traditional construal of universality in terms of finitude cannot be sufficient. These reflections indicate that we must go further to show that the various features constitutive of particularity are undermined by the development of the Absolute as conceptual singularity. Most worryingly, since Hegel integrates the finite features of universality that give rise to the problem of the disappearance of the Absolute, which is most clearly formulated in the problems of Nihilism and Onto-theology, one might raise the concern that the Absolute disappears again in his system of philosophy.

Although our initial motivation of Hegel's solution was not sufficient to allay all concerns regarding the classical paradoxes of Instantiation, the Missing Difference, *et alia*, already in our analysis of particularity some concerns had already been put to rest. First, because the separation of the principles of universality and particularity, the finitude of the concept, the PNC, and the appeal to foundations are structures of particularity that follow from the self-differentiation of the concept, they cease to be *ungrounded* assumptions. Because they are results of the creative activity of the concept, they are freed from any indebtedness to an absolute foundation and become instances of *presuppositionless science*. Though the specter of the six paradoxes of finite universality raised its head again in the element of particularity, with the rise of singularity Hegel lays to rest any concern that the self-particularizing universal could in principle be threatened by those various problems. To the contrary, the resurrection of universality out of singularity signals the salvation of the Absolute. By returning to universality out of its self-loss, the Absolute life of the concept has put an end to absolute death.

Singularity arose from particularity in virtue of the self-negation of particularity. Because particularity, as the self-negation of universality, had to remain itself, it necessarily negated itself. By negating itself, the self-negation of universality removed its own negation of universality. Through its self-negation, or differentiation of itself from itself, universality was restored to particularity. This restoration of self-particularization to particularity or the unity of universality with particularity is singularity. As we pointed our earlier, singularity is not a mere repetition of universality, for singularity is only universal in and through the very self-negation of particularity. Because the distinction between the universal and particular that is constitutive of particularity is undermined in the development of singularity, the self-differentiating concept undermines, once again, the assumptions that give rise to the six problems of finite universality. At the outset, the universal was simply given as self-differentiating and had not yet overcome the structural features of finite universality in virtue of its own activity, but was simply *given as that which overcomes them*. Unlike the moment of universality, in singularity it is *the very activity of the concept*, the very self-negation of particularity, in virtue of which the difference between universal and particular is overcome. If the self-differentiating universal did not overcome the finite universal on its own terms, then the self-differentiating universal would have only overcome the finite universal in a *stipulative* way, which would have undermined itself. This internal overcoming of the classical construal of universality in terms of finitude is important, for it shows that the self-differentiating universal overcomes them *within itself* on its own terms, and that the rejection of finite universality is not itself a merely stipulative act as it may have appeared at the outset. Like the resurrection of Christ, the Absolute *rescues itself* from non-existence.

Self-particularization is that which remains itself in all of its self-differentiations. Accordingly, upon contradicting itself, self-particularization remains itself even at the point at which it admits its negation. For this reason, self-contradiction does not just explode into everything and nothing upon its self-particularization. When the PNC is taken as an absolute principle, namely as the *unconditioned* form of universality, it contradicts itself. As an absolute principle, the PNC is not self-differentiating. Because it is not self-differentiating or subservient to a self-differentiating principle, when it is taken as the absolute principle of conceptual determination, the contradiction that follows from the six problems of finite universality does *not* result in the *preservation* of the conceptual content, but a complete explosion of that content into everything and nothing.

Just as the characteristic features of finite universality are contradictory, so is particularity contradictory. Because finite universality has been integrated into particularity in the *Doctrine of the Concept*, finite universality (and the PNC that governs it) no longer stands by itself but constitutes a moment of the concept that follows from the self-differentiation of the universal. As a moment of the concept, the particular is not just that which is not self-differentiating, but *that which is not self-particularizing is itself a differentiation of self-particularization*. In virtue of being what it is, the self-negation of self-differentiation negates itself, and this is nothing more than the self-contradiction of the PNC. Because particularity is a moment of the concept, the self-contradiction of particularity (and the PNC) does not lead to everything and nothing, but back to the concept itself as singularity. In virtue of being what it is, particularity contradicts itself. Without the concept of self-particularization, which is what it is only in virtue of its self-contradiction, we cannot give an account of what it is to be a universal.

Seen in this light, the universal is the singularity in virtue of the self-contradiction of particularity. The self-contradiction of particularity, as we have labored to show earlier, *resuscitates* the unconditionally universal concept as singularity. Simply put, only as singularity can the Absolute be Absolute. By integrating the structural characteristics of finite universality into the structure of particularity, the contradiction endemic to the finite construal of universality no longer explodes into nothing, but is the very means by which the concept achieves its singularity. Ironically, the very source of the problem itself becomes the principle of development from which one can escape the problems plaguing finite universality. As Hegel put it, the abstract universal is the 'soul'—without the abstract and finite, the concept would not have any content. This is indeed one of the most surprising results of the inquiry: without the disappearance of the Absolute in finitude, the Absolute could not exist at all. The Absolute can only be if it disappears and returns out of its disappearance in finitude. As Hegel's old compatriot, Hölderlin, would have it:

But where danger is, grows the saving power also.

The various features of finite universality govern the three forms of particular universality: the abstraction, the class, and the genus. Each of these particular universals is immanent in the concept itself, though they are inseparable from the concept. Upon achieving singularity, each form of the difference between universal and particular expressed in the forms of determinate universality were determined to be *illusory* differences, namely differences that disappeared into the concept per se or singularity. Because each of these particular universals exemplify the features of finite universality, and each of the particular universals only has an indeterminate or illusory being in the concept, so too then, must the finite universal only have an illusory being, that is a being that cannot be separated from singularity. On their own they are absolutely *nothing*. They too, as relative determinations, *only* subsist in the self-differentiation and self-particularization of the Absolute concept.[66]

To put this in the most general terms, the concept only solves the six problems of finite universality by integrating the fundamental assumptions from which they are generated, for example the PNC, into the very structure of the concept itself. By depriving the finite construal of universality its unconditionally absolute status, and thereby making it relative to the moment of particularity, the contradiction inherent in the concept ceases merely to be explosive, and the universal is able to achieve determinate content in virtue of its self-contradiction. Only through the self-differentiation of the universal into the particular and the self-negation of particularity can singularity arise. By integrating the finite universal into the concept, Hegel has breathed new life into an ancient city. By injecting the dead material of logic with the organizing principle of self-particularization, the difference between the principles of universality and particularity becomes enlivened with the power and life of the Absolute Concept.

The Resurrection of Conceptual Singularity

On its face, one might find the identification of the concept with the singular strange, especially since the singular appears in Hegel's *Phenomenology* as an indexical this that is *devoid of universality*. Upon following Hegel's dialectic in the *Phenomenology*, we discover, however, that the singularity with which one begins is not a counter-example to Hegel's account, but exemplifies his logical account in the *Science of Logic*. The *Phenomenology* instantiates Hegel's singular concept of self-particularization by performing a reductio on the supposition that sensual singularity could be independent of the singular concept. On the whole, the *Phenomenology* shows the spiritual truth of conceptual singularity—first in sense certainty and last in Absolute Knowledge.

In the *Phenomenology*, Hegel's account of self-knowing begins with the positing of an absolute singularity. But this singularity is not just the concept of singularity, for it is a *sensual singularity for consciousness*. This sensual singularity is *the indexical* here and now. Here Hegel famously shows that any attempt to posit a sensual singularity devoid of universality negates itself and gives rise *not only* to abstract universality, but a *concrete universality that contains its instances*. This universal to which the sensual singularity gives rise is a self-particularizing universal. In Kant, the form of unity that contains its instances is called *intuition*; in Hegel the concept becomes the sole constituent of truth and thereby transforms the intuition into the singular concept, or the 'concrete' universal. Thus, the absolute separation of sensual singularity from conceptual singularity is overturned at the outset. *Phenomenology* demonstrates, at the very beginning, that *the sensual this is impossible without the conceptual this*.

As Redding points out, McDowell's work has shown that the world 'is made up of the sort of thing that one can think.'[67] The indexical 'this' of sense certainty is 'the idea of a singular presence as knowable in its singularity.'[68] Redding is right to formulate the 'this' of sense certainty as the 'to de ti' or 'this such.'[69] The 'this,' rather than stand in conflict with or be opposed to thought, turns out to be an instance of a universal, such that the 'this' is simultaneously a universal and singular.[70] Accordingly, it is true that McDowell, in *Mind and World*, follows Hegel in 'affirming the conceptual nature of perceptual experience.'[71] However, McDowell does not seem to reconstruct the fully Hegelian sense in which the 'this' such and such embodies the Heglelian concept. Redding is right that regarding McDowell and Brandom:

> One does not find much in the in the work of either that engages with the aspect of Hegel's logic for which he is probably most well known—the so-called 'dialectical' nature of his logic with tis controversial claims about the nature of contradiction.[72]

The absence of such an engagement with the dialectical and contradictory dimensions of Hegel's method reflects a lack of engagement with *logical content*, since method can never be divorced from content in Hegel's logical thought. In addition, without such an engagement, we cannot appreciate how the 'this such' instantiates Hegel's logic of the concept, which as self-particularizing, is both contradictory and dialectical.

Indeed, for Hegel the conceptual this, the *this such and such*, is the *self-particularizing, singular* concept. The development of sense-certainty into perception is merely the first stage in the self-particularization of the concept in consciousness. Simply put, sensual singularity is an *instantiation* and self-externalization of logical singularity, which particularizes itself in consciousness. In order to work out the full sense in which singularity embodies the concrete universal in Hegel's science, we require recourse to Hegel's *Science of Logic* and those dimensions of Hegel's thought that, as Redding pointed out, remain neglected by the Pittsburg school, for example dialectic and contradiction.

Hegel states that 'what exists is the Now, and is universally (in every case) Now, but not always the same (particular) now.' *What justifies this distinction?* Phenomenologically, I can point to what the Now is, and say that 'Now is day.' 'Now is day' becomes false when 'Now is night.' In each case, the Now is present, though what is now changes. Thus, we can say that there is a now that is universal across all instances of the now, the Universal Now. The Universal Now is what it is irrespective of the changing content, that is the changing (particular) now-moments. This is an abstract universal. Instead, as Heidegger points out in the *Concept of Time*, in the abstract universal, I must point to *what is happening now* in order to differentiate one particular Now from another. This means that I must employ something other than the moment as an instance of time in order to distinguish the moments of time.

Again, if we consider the distinction phenomenologically, though we may separate them logically, keeping them *ontologically separate* seems problematic. If I only focus on the particular nows as instances of the Universal Now, every particular now, *qua* Now, is indistinguishable from every other particular now. Each is simply 'Now.' If 'as Now' any particular now is indistinguishable from any other 'particular now,' we cannot tell the time by the Now itself. In this respect, The Universal Now appears *formal* and empty of any particular nows. Time itself, as the Universal Now, does not tell what particular time it is. But again, this just motivates the distinction between The Universal Now and particular nows: the Universal Now does not seem to differentiate itself into particular nows (moments).

Every time I point to a now, this now (1) ceases to be, and another now, now (2) supplants now (1), *ad infinitum*. I cannot help but encounter some particular now. What seems obvious is that I *never* encounter the Universal Now as a particular now. I only encounter the Universal Now *as the Universal Now* in virtue of the Now *not being reducible* to the particular now. It seems that though there is a significant difference between universal and particular nows, it is unclear that they can be held apart on phenomenological grounds. If Time just is the Now, any specification of the Now, '*this* moment,' means 'this Now.' The question 'what time is it now?' implies the following answer: *'The Now is this now.'* *'The Now is this now'* is an example of *self-reference*, that is, the Universal Now is *a* particular now. Every time I answer the question 'what time is it Now? I must put the answer in the form of 'this now.' Since no particular now can be distinguished from any other now as a now, and *the Now is a particular now, we cannot distinguish the Universal Now from the particular nows*. If the Universal Now is just a particular now, we must posit *another* Universal Now that contains the particular now, *ad infinitum*.[1] Accordingly, by re-iteration of self-predication we build an ever expanding Now that incorporates the particular moments indefinitely. To say this phenomenologically, upon pointing to 'this now,' 'this now' ceases to be, and is *not now*, since *as what has been it no longer is*. But in the ceasing to be of 'this now,' the Now re-appears again as 'this now.' The Now, as the Universal Now, *constantly re-occurs as a different instance of itself.*

If the Universal Now were an instance of itself, it would contain itself. The Universal Now would be both the whole and the part of itself. Thinking in terms of *mereology*, if now (1) is divided into now (a) and (b), now (1) could not be distinguished from now (a) or (b), and so on. *The Universal Now, as Now, would be Now (1–n)*. Instead of being 'thin' or just one moment, the Now, *insofar as it is just one moment, appears to be constituted by an infinite series of moments*. Though the Universal Now appeared opposed to the particular now, it appears that if we apply self-reference to the Now, the Universal Now may be constituted by the series of particular nows. Accordingly, the Universal Now would not be *formal*. The Now, as one moment, appears to be constituted by an infinite series of moments, *Now (1–n)*. So we can treat the day as 24 hours, an hour as 60 minutes, and so on. The *Now itself* appears to be *constituted* by the coming-to-be and passing-away of the particular nows. Insofar as the Now is constituted by the coming-to-be and passing-away of the particular nows, neither is the Universal Now differentiated from the succession of the particular nows. This Now is a concrete universal, which combines particulars into a *successive* serial order.[73]

As is evident from the progress of sensual singularity in the *Phenomenology*, sensual singularity begins as a this devoid of all universality and develops into an abstract universal and finally into a concrete universal that exhibits the self-particularizing feature of Hegel's concept of the singular concept in the *Science of Logic*. In the final stage of the development of the Now, the *self-same universal* appears both as the *totality* as well as each *instance* of that totality and thereby exemplifies Hegel's definition of the concept in the *Lehre von Begriff*. The universal now becomes this now—it is *this such and such*. What is more, it is the self-development of the consciousness of the Now in virtue of which the self-particularization proceeds. Although singularity in the *Phenomenology* may begin as devoid of universality, that absence of universality negates itself and shows itself to be the *self-alienation* of self-particularizing singularity, *not its truth*.

The self-particularization of the concept can be well exemplified in other aspects of the *Phenomenology* as well and develops as the text proceeds. Although the singular concept arises already in sense-certainty, the concept *as such* is explicitly acknowledged first in consciousness *as Reason*, which is identified with the category. In *Reason*, consciousness thinks itself to be conceptual, but the concept *has not yet determined itself to be conceptual* or has not yet *conceptualized itself*. Because Reason first arises within the *Phenomenology* from a stage that is not identified with Reason (namely self-consciousness), and is thereby not yet rational, Reason has not yet determined by itself—it is not yet a result of the rational process.

Only in *Spirit* does Reason finally becomes true or determined by Reason. In other words, Spirit is the conceptual consciousness that has determined itself to be conceptual.[74] Thereby in the domain of mind Spirit instantiates the *Idea*, which is *the singular concept that is true*.[75]

> Reason is Spirit when its certainty of being all reality has been raised to truth.[76]

Spirit, or the concept raised to truth in the domain of mind, is nothing other than the 'I that is We and the We that is I':

> What still lies ahead for consciousness is the experience of what Spirit is—this absolute subsistence which is the unity of the different independent self-consciousness which, in their opposition, enjoy perfect freedom and independence: 'I' that is 'We' and 'We' that is 'I'.[77]

When the I is also We, and the We is also the I, the member of the whole, the I, is also the whole itself. As is evident, this structure instantiates the form of the concept in which the singular concept is both the whole and its element, wherein the concept preserves itself in its particularizations.

In Absolute Spirit, conceptual self-consciousness has not only raised itself to truth, *but knows itself to be Spirit.* It is

> Absolute knowing, or spirit that knows itself as spirit.

Finally, Absolute Spirit instantiates the *Absolute Idea.* In Absolute Spirit, Spirit recollects the forms of Consciousness, Self-Consciousness, Reason, and Spirit that have preceded it, and know them to be stages in its own self-knowing. Just as it is in virtue of the Absolute Idea that all the preceding thought determinations acquire their status *as categories* of the one logical system, it is in virtue of Absolute Spirit that all the stages of self-knowing are determined to be stages of Spirit, or Spirit's Absolute Knowledge of itself.[78] The goal of the logic is to discover the categories that are at work in *Phenomenology*, but which in that work were not yet grasped as logical contents *per se*:

> As impulses the categories do their work only instinctively; they are brought to consciousness one by one and so are variable and mutually confusing, thus affording to spirit only fragmentary and uncertain actuality. To purify these categories and in them to elevate spirit to truth and freedom, this is the therefore the loftier business of logic.[79]

One could easily read the logical categories of the subjective logic, such as 'concept,' 'Idea,' and 'Absolute Idea' as mere abstractions from their spiritual embodiment in Reason, Spirit, and Absolute Spirit. Indeed, the metaphor of logic as the 'realm of shadows' might indicate that the being of the *logic qua logic* is completely dependent upon the existence of these categories in other domains, such as nature or spirit. Nonetheless, this would be a mistake. Logic may be a 'realm of shadows' *in respect to* the non-logical domains in which logical categories are realized, but this metaphor by no means revokes or qualifies Hegel's explicit assertion and defense of his logic as an *ontological argument* which is *self-objectifying*. As Hegel says elsewhere, it is logic that is the *animating* spirit:

> the profounder foundation is the soul standing on its own, the pure concept which is the innermost moment of the objects, their simple life pulse, just as it is of the subjective thinking of them. To bring to consciousness this logical nature that animates the spirit, that moves and works within it, this is the task.[80]

The Logic is also shadow like insofar as it is devoid of natural and spiritual content—it appears empty in comparison to the colorful domains of nature and spirit and certainly logic cannot exist in nature of spirit without non-logical content. But were we to think of the logical categories as *being mere abstractions* from the domains of nature and spirit, then we would fail to see how the concept, grasped *by itself*, is the power of self-particularization, and what is more, we would fail to see how the various other domains of science are particularizations of the singular concept.

Logical categories are without presupposition—they cannot come to be or exist by abstraction from another stratum of existence, such as consciousness or nature. Although the mind is an enabling condition that makes the conceptualization of logic by the philosopher possible, this does not entail that logic is epistemically justified by mind. Instead, logical categories are self-determining and are responsible for their own *logical* existence. While *Phenomenology* is the propaedeutic to the *Science of Logic*,[81] the *Science of Logic* provides the scientific groundwork for the science of nature and mind that Hegel develops in his *Encyclopedia of the Philosophical Sciences*. As Hegel points out, the *Phenomenology of Spirit* gives us *one example* of the method of philosophy, which must be worked out in logic.[82]

Importantly, the transformation of sensual singularity into the concrete universal is a *back-turning*, for sensual singularity in the indexical *this* is only possible on account of the logical structure of singularity developed in *presuppositionless* logic. Thus, without an account of logical singularity, we cannot establish the possibility of sensual singularity. To understand the 'this such' as an instance of the self-particularizing concept, one requires recourse to the *Science of Logic* and in particular to the logic of the self-particularizing concept in the *Lehre von Begriff*.

Further, the categories of Consciousness, Self-Consciousness, Reason, Spirit, and Absolute Spirit all *re-appear* in the third volume of the *Encyclopedia*, but here they are now grounded on the *Science of Logic*, on the pure concept of self-determination.[83] Phenomenological forms re-appear in the *Encyclopedia* as the instantiation and the completion of science—no longer as its mere propaedeutic. This highlights how the content of the *Phenomenology* is both *the propaedeutic to science and science itself*.

By negating itself, the phenomenology is 'turning back' to the presuppositionless science from which it proceeds. The self-refutation of the opposition of consciousness in the phenomenology is not merely the self-removing propaedeutic, but also constitutes the *science of spirit* that is realized in virtue of the self-negation of relative knowing. Wendy Lynn Clark and J. M. Fritzman raise the objection against the non-foundationalist school that the phenomenology cannot only be read as the self-collapse of representational knowing. If it were *only* to consist in the self-collapse of representational knowing, the *Phenomenology* ought not require each stage of development, but ought only to consist in one page.[84] They are indeed correct that the reductio on the opposition of consciousness that gives rise to the *Science of Logic* cannot (in the end) only be a negative propaedeutic but must now be *re-integrated* into the science itself. But this re-integration of the forms of spirit (such as consciousness and self-consciousness) into the science does not undermine the foundation free character of the system, but rather *embodies its radical autonomy*.

Just as the forms of finite universality in the *Science of Logic* are not only to be overcome but to be integrated into Hegel's logic of the infinite concept, so is the finite opposition of consciousness in the *Phenomenology* not merely something to be overcome, but to be integrated into philosophical science. Thus, the reductio on the opposition of consciousness also constitutes the *resurrection* of finite universality constitutive of the opposition of consciousness (as well as its *self-overcoming* in Absolute Knowledge) *as* an integral and necessary dimension of philosophical science. Having been integrated into the science of philosophy proper as the spiritual self-particularization of logical singularity, the development of philosophical science as a whole constitutes a back-turning—the turning back of *Phenomenology* to its ground and the fulfillment of the *Science of Logic* and *Philosophy of Nature* by means of its self-particularization in Absolute Spirit.

Notes

1. Hegel, *SL*, trans. Giovanni, 282–283, 536 (Suhrkamp).
2. Keiji Nishitani, *Religion and Nothingness*, trans. Jan Van Bragt (Berkeley: University of California Press, 1983), 116.
3. See Clark and Fritzman, "The Nonfoundational Hegelianism of Dove, Maker, and Winfield," 10–12.
4. De Boer, "Hegel's Account of Contradiction in the Science of Logic Reconsidered," 365.
5. Ferrarin, *Hegel and Aristotle*, 182.
6. See Houlgate, *The Opening of Hegel's Logic*, 246.
7. John McDowell, *Mind and World* (Cambridge: Harvard University Press, 1996), 44. Also see his discussion of the indexical and its conceptual content, *Mind and World*, 57.
8. See McDowell, "Having the World in View," 466, 490.
9. McDowell, *Mind and World*, 7.
10. Hegel, *Hegel's Philosophy of Nature*, paragraph 246. Westfall claims that 'philosophy is grounded on the empirical sciences' and he draws this conclusion from the same paragraph, in particular 246R. But when the whole text is read, we discover that Hegel never indeed proclaims *science itself* to be grounded on anything empirical. Rather, it is the concept that grounds all science (including the science of nature.) See Kenneth Westfall, *Hegel's Epistemology, A Philosophical Introduction to the Phenomenology of Spirit* (Indianapolis: Hackett, 2003), 52.
11. Hegel, *PS*, trans. Pinkard, 4.
12. Also see Rosen, *The Idea of Hegel's Science of Logic*, 408.
13. See Houlgate, "Why Hegel's Concept is not the Essence of Things," 27. Because the concept 'preserves itself' in its differentiations, I would argue that

even though the Idea determines itself to be nature at the close of the Logic, the Logic *preserves itself (in its purely logical form) even though it gives rise to nature* and determines itself to be nature. Houlgate claims that 'concept and idea do not precede nature' and it turns out that 'there is actually no concept or idea prior to nature at all.' See Houlgate, "Why Hegel's Concept is not the Essence of Things," 27. Were the logic not to maintain its own identity apart from and prior to nature, we could not recover the purely logical truths that give rise to nature independently of an inquiry into nature. In addition, the non-temporal dimension of the logic indicates that logic is *eternally giving rise to nature* and *determining itself to be nature*, without exhausting its own content as a purely logical determination. Finally, it seems to me that although Houlgate is exactly right that the concept is not to be identified with essence or essential determinations, the essence is nonetheless a true concept of the Absolute, such that the whole of Hegel's system can be looked upon in terms of essence. This view would be incomplete, but it would allow us to see how the logic can *retroactively posit itself* as the cause of nature, in the manner of the categories of the logic of essence. For these reasons I would contend that Hegel's logic is a logic of 'immanence *and transcendence*' rather than just a logic of 'immanence.'

14. Hegel, *SL*, trans. Giovanni, 286–287, 539 (Suhrkamp).
15. Haas rightly points out that only through intellectual intuition can approach the living contradiction of the concept. See Haas, *Hegel and the Problem of Multiplicity*, 173.
16. Hegel, *SL*, trans. Giovanni, 539.
17. Grey points out that Hegel 'makes judgment the first installment on the promise of intellectual intuition' which is the 'ability of God to think things into existence.' See Carleson, *A Commentary to Hegel's Science of Logic*, 460. I would only amend this by positing the concept as the first installment, not judgment, and I would be careful to clarify that here in logic we are not yet dealing with mind, such that the kind of thinking involved evokes no subjectivity except *the agency of conceptuality by itself*.
18. Hegel, *SL*, trans. Giovanni, 533.
19. Also, Hegel's discussion in the Absolute Idea, Hegel, *SL*, trans. Giovanni, 744.
20. Hegel, *SL*, trans. Miller, 90.
21. Also see Hegel, *PS*, trans. Pinkard, 38, where Hegel is clear that the judgment and the proposition are 'destroyed by the speculative (conceptual) proposition.'
22. Hegel, *SL*, trans. Giovanni, Remark 2 of the logic of Being, 67.
23. Hegel, *SL*, trans. Giovanni, 586.
24. Ibid, 585–586.
25. Ibid, 629.
26. Ibid, 585.
27. See Ibid, 585–587.
28. Robert Brandom, *Articulating Reasons* (Cambridge: Harvard University Press, 2000), 35. Also see Brandom's claim in "Some Hegelian Ideas of Note for Continental Analytic Philosophy" where he writes that

> Hegel didn't just start in the middle of the traditional order, with judgment rather than the concept; he fully turned it on its head, not only understanding concepts in terms of judgments, but understanding judgments in terms of their role in inferences.

Robert Brandom, "Some Hegelian Ideas of Note for Continental Analytic Philosophy," Hegel Bulletin 35, no. 1 (2014): 1–15, 2.

29. Brandom, "Some Hegelian Ideas of Note for Continental Analytic Philosophy."
30. Robert Brandom, "Some Pragmatist Themes in Hegel's Idealism," *European Journal of Philosophy* 7, no. 2 (1999): 164–189, 174.
31. Hegel, *PS*, trans. Pinkard, 35–36.
32. Ibid, 40.
33. Sellars, *Empiricism and the Philosophy of Mind*, I.2, 128.
34. Rosen, *The Idea of Hegel's Science of Logic*, 408.
35. Hegel, *PS*, trans. Pinkard paragraph 64.
36. Houlgate, *The Opening of Hegel's Logic*, 30.
37. Also see Hegel's *SL*, trans. Giovanni, 738 in which the syllogism is identified as 'formal': 'the syllogism is therefore always the formal syllogism.'
38. Hegel, *PS*, trans. Pinkard, 39–40.
39. Houlgate has already shown that Brandom's reading of Hegel undermines the self-developing and autonomous feature of the concept. See Houlgate, "Phenomenology and De-Re interpretation: A Critique of Brandom's Reading of Hegel," 30–47, 32.
40. Hegel, *PS*, trans. Pinkard, 45. Here he is clear that the nature of science demands that the individual forget himself.
41. Hegel, *SL*, trans. Giovanni, 15.
42. Ibid, 16.
43. Houlgate, *The Opening of Hegel's Logic*, 67. This is not a presupposition, but an enabling condition.
44. Houlgate offers a similar critique of Brandom's account of the development of categories in *Phenomenology*, Houlgate, "Phenomenology and De-Re interpretation: A Critique of Brandom's Reading of Hegel," 31–32.
45. Redding, *Analytic Philosophy and the Return of Hegelian Thought*, 17.
46. Robert Brandom, "Sketch of a Program for a Critical Reading of Hegel: Comparing Empirical and Logical Concepts," in *German Idealism and Contemporary Analytic Philosophy*, ed. Ameriks, Karl, 131–161 (Berlin: De Gruyter, 2005), 155.
47. Ibid, 133–134.
48. Ibid, 134.
    Ibid. A similar attitude towards Hegel also seems to have been taken up by A. S. Pringle-Pattison, who argued that Hegel is best 'read backwards.' See W. J. Mander, *British Idealism: A History* (Oxford: Oxford University Press, 2011), 357. Pattison reads Hegel as offering an analysis of the ordinary processes of common experience. Importantly however, Pattison complained that Hegel tried to construct the world out of abstract thought, and so insisted on reading Hegel 'backwards.' Mander, *British Idealism: A History*, 111.
49. Brandom, "Some Pragmatist Themes in Hegel's Idealism," 165. Brandom also claims that the 'content of these concepts presupposed by experience is derived from their role in experience.' Ibid, 168. Certainly this cannot apply to logical concepts, which do not derive their content from experience, for they are without presupposition.
50. Robert Brandom, *A Spirit of Trust: A Reading of Hegel's Phenomenology* (Cambridge: Harvard University Press, 2019), 103.
51. See Hegel, *SL*, trans. Giovanni, 64–65.
52. De Laurentiis, in "On Hegel's Concept of Thinking," makes an important point that in order for any serious discussion of Hegel's *Realphilosophie* to take place, such as the issue of recognition that fascinates the Pittsburgh school, Hegel's concept of thinking as self-determination must first be recognized. Indeed, Rather than conceive of the logic as a product of another process, (see Brandom, "Sketch of a Program for a Critical Reading of Hegel:

Comparing Empirical and Logical Concepts," 157) it should rather be conceived as autonomous and self-determining. See Allegra De Laurentiis, "On Hegel's Concept of Thinking," in *Societas Rationis: Festschrift in honor of Burkhard Tuschling*, 263–285, ed. D. Huening, G. Stiening, and U. Vogel (Berlin: Duncker & Humboldt, 2002).

53. Houlgate, *The Opening of Hegel's Logic*, 11.
54. McDowell, "Hegel's Idealism as a Radicalization of Kant," 87.
55. Ibid, 86.
56. Pippin, *Hegel's Idealism: The Satisfaction of Self-Consciousness*, 237–238.
57. Ibid, 238.
58. Bowman, *The Metaphysics of Absolute Negativity*, 124 (see 124–125).
59. Brandom, *A Spirit of Trust*, 675.
60. Brandom, "Some Pragmatist Themes in Hegel's Idealism," 49.
61. Ibid, 174.
62. Ibid, 179.
63. Houlgate is right to identify singularity as absolutely indeterminate. See Houldgate, "Why Hegel's Concept is not the Essence," 25.
64. Hegel, *Hegel's Logic*, paragraph 181, 216.
65. By my lights, this reading of contradiction in Hegel's logic appears *close* to Brown's substitution interpretation of contradiction, whereby according to Brown, 'contradictions really do exist,' but 'they can only be expressed through substitutions such as contraries, essences, life, death, secrecy, movement, etc.' I would discuss such substitution, however, as *self-substitution*, such that the contradiction, insofar as it has substituted what is not contradictory for what is contradictory, has therefore preserved the contradiction even in the substitution as *the contradiction that is not contradictory*. This is close to what Brown means when he says that the 'contradictions appear through their disappearance.' See Brown, *Hegel on Possibility*, 75.
66. One might speculate that one reason philosophers have constantly identified the concept with one of these forms of determinate universality is because each presents itself as the whole concept, as singularity.
67. McDowell, *Mind and World*, 27–28. See Paul Redding, "The Analytic Neo-Hegelianism of J. McDowell and Brandom," in *A Companion to Hegel*, ed. S. Houlgate and M. Baur, 576–593 (Oxford: Wiley-Blackwell, 2011), 578.
68. Redding, "The Analytic Neo-Hegelianism of J. McDowell and Brandom," 578.
69. Ibid.
70. Ibid, 582. Redding draws some very interesting parallels to Quine here that would be worth further development. See 583. In Analytic Philosophy and the Return of Hegelian Thought, 90, Redding points out that both the medievals and Quine treated singulars as universals.
71. Redding, "The Analytic Neo-Hegelianism of J. McDowell and Brandom," 579–580.
72. Ibid, 587.
73. This short reconstruction of Sense Certainty can be found in Moss, *Ernst Cassirer and the Autonomy of Language*, 94–95, and is further elaborated upon in connection with Ernst Cassirer's philosophy of symbolic forms.
74. Hegel, *PS*, trans. Pinkard, 141.
75. Also see Rosen, *The Idea of Hegel's Science of Logic*, 392.
76. Hegel, *PS*, trans. Pinkard, 263.
77. Ibid, 110.
78. I do not mean to imply that the development of the categories in nature and spirit must proceed in the very same way that they proceed in logic.

Rather, the inseparability of form and content demand that we refrain from abstractly imposing a logical form on some non-logical matter.

79. Hegel, *SL*, trans. Giovanni, 17.
80. Ibid.
81. See Hegel's claim that *Phenomenology* is the 'coming to be of science as such.' See Hegel, *PS*, trans. Pinkard, 15. As he points out however, 'it is quite different from an absolute "foundation" of science,' Hegel, *PS*, trans. Pinkard, 16.
82. Hegel, *SL*, trans. Giovanni, 33.
83. See, for example, Hegel's discussion of 'consciousness as such' in *EL*, paragraph 418, in which sense-certainty re-appears, alongside self-consciousness, reason, and other categories already developed in the phenomenology.
84. Clark and Fritzman, "The Nonfoundational Hegelianism of Dove, Maker, and Winfield," 15.

15 The Singular Absolute

Earlier we established the only possible answer to the problem of the disappearance of the Absolute: *Absolute Dialetheism*. Either the concept is raised to an Absolute status or the Absolute transcends all conceptual determination. Each position requires the *complete abandonment of all first principles*. Because of the self-undermining character of all first principles, Absolute Dialetheism engenders an *anarchical* attitude towards the Absolute. Insofar as Absolute Knowing is without principle, it becomes *anarchical*. Nonetheless, in Hegel's system, although the *Logic* begins without any principles, the anarchical beginning undermines itself and establishes the concept as the one true principle. In other words, Hegel's philosophy does not remain anarchical, for self-thinking thought negates its initial indeterminacy and establishes the concept as *the singular self-determining* principle of the system of logic. In his own way, therefore, Hegel follows Aristotle's dictum 'Let there be one Lord,' with the caveat that this Lord must eternally determine itself to be the singular Lord from an initially indeterminate state. In Hegel, the death of God (or the first principle) initiates its resurrection.

Because the concept is raised to an Absolute status *on its own* by means of the self-negation of finite universality, the concept is not posited as Absolute in advance. Rather, it establishes itself as Absolute. In virtue of the self-establishing of the concept as the Absolute principle of all logical being, the concept determines itself to be *singularity*. The Absolute is not just the universal or the particular, but the *singular unity of universality and particularity*. The self-transformation of the Absolute into the self-particularizing concept is also the *self transformation* of the Absolute into the *singular* truth. Were the singular to owe its truth to another, it would not be *the singular truth*. Only what is singular has its truth in virtue of itself. Like Aristotle's concept of Form, Hegel's concept of the concept is *existentially implicative*. For the Ancient Greeks the concept of Form contained a paradox: on the one hand, each Form is both particular, or one in number, and universal, or one in kind. As an avid student of Ancient Greek philosophy, Hegel took the paradox to be *instructive*, for only by unifying the universal and particular in the concept of singularity could the paradox be transformed into a solution to the problem of the missing Absolute. The singularity of the Ancient Form, namely its character as 'this such and such,' is cancelled and preserved in Hegel's concept of singularity.

The dogmatic separation of the principles of universality and particularity has engendered a re-occurring complaint against philosophy, namely that it cannot think what is singular or the Absolute, with concepts. As long as the concept remains imprisoned in this division, the only recourse for philosophy is some form of *mysticism*, a view to which we have returned time and again in our investigation. Traditionally, because the concept is not singular, the singular was understood as *that which transcends the concept*. In mysticism, philosophy conditions the Absolute by excluding it from the domain of what can be revealed in language.

Mysticism can take a more sophisticated form, for mysticism can abandon absolute silence and begin to *speak* about the Absolute in contradictory utterances, such as in certain forms of poetic or ecstatic speech. In this way, mysticism ceases to constrain the Absolute to one side of an opposition, for it brings the Absolute into unification with speech and mediation. Still, for Hegel with the loss of any *necessary* measure by which to determine the truth of what is said about the Absolute in the ecstatic or poetic utterance, representations of the Absolute become *radically contingent* and arbitrary. When God inspires his vessel, God speaks through her—*Geistesblitz* does not itself have a measure. Hegel levies the critique that completely divorced from the power and development of reason, any Romantic poeticizing of the Absolute becomes itself just as arbitrary as any other speech about the Absolute. Hegel's self-particularizing universal appears to be the only alternative to total mysticism, in which the Absolute might be rescued, but only at the cost of sacrificing *absolute necessity* in philosophical thinking. The absence of any rational measure in mystical inspiration is a form of anarchism— the contingency of speech denies the *a priori* elevation of any utterance over the other. Each falls into equality with the other—all without rule, each claiming equal legitimacy as the other, each with its own spontaneous inspiration to guard its claim to truth. In stark contrast to the mystical form of anarchical thinking, Hegel's *resurrection of God* out of complete indeterminacy overcomes the anarchism with which it began. Unlike Hegel's self-overcoming of anarchic thought, mysticism *remains anarchical*—both in the immediacy of its feeling and in its articulation of Absolute Singularity.

In order to overcome the contingency of mysticism, Hegel takes a radical turn. Since the universal and the particular cease to be separated in singularity, in order to make Absolute Singularity conceivable, and make its existence possible, Hegel recognized the need for re-thinking how the concept could be conceived as a unity of universality and particularity. If we follow Hegel, we can avoid the objection that the concept cannot grasp the singular. Because the concept is itself singularity, and we know the concept, we can know singularity. Indeed, we know singularity just insofar as we know what the concept is. Because the concept is the Absolute, the self-conceptualizing of the concept is nothing less than Absolute Self-Knowledge. Because the concept is identical to singularity, the singular is no longer beyond the concept, for anything that is singular must be conceptual.

One of the perennial objections to Hegel's thinking is the accusation that Hegel has deified human thought. The objection proclaims that human reason is finite and further proclaims that by imbuing reason with infinite powers, Hegel has not only misunderstood but also failed to appreciate the limits of human reason. If we read Hegel closely, however, Hegel is very attuned to human frailty. His attentiveness to the frailty of the human being is accentuated by his proclamation in the *Phenomenology* that we ought no longer think for the concept, but we ought to allow the concept *to think for itself and for us*. Rather than imbuing the human being with powers that he does not have, Hegel calls on the philosopher to *forget herself* in order to 'think God's thought after him,' to use a famous expression from Kepler. It is true that for Hegel, by *detaching* herself from her own thinking, the philosopher can think the self-conception of Absolute thought, but this consists in tracing a movement of thought for which she is not responsible. This thought is constituted by the progression of categories in the *Science of Logic*—it is Absolute Self-Thinking-Thought, to which the human being does not contribute. Rather than deify the human being, Hegel has endowed God, so to speak, with infinite powers, not the human being. By giving all the power over the divine concept, whose thought we follow, Hegel systematized the radicalization of the omnipotence of God that is characteristic of the thought of the *protestant* reformation. For protestant thought, the omnipotence of God demands that the human being does not contribute to her salvation. The freedom we experience in thought is not one that we have independently of the Absolute, but we attain freedom in thought by participating in God's freedom. By following the thought of the logos (rather than one's own proclivities), Hegel's philosophy is also characteristically Greek, for it calls us to heed *the logos of the cosmos*.

Thus, Hegel's philosophy can overcome such objections.[1] Given the radicalization of the power of the *divine Logos* that is constitutive of the protestant revolution, one might have the opposite worry—that Hegel does not endow the human being with sufficient agency. This objection can be met by recognizing the role of the rational animal plays in transforming the Absolute into *Absolute Spirit*. Hegel's critique of mysticism is instructive for this point. By denying that the Absolute is conceptually determined, the Absolute ceases to be Absolute. Without existing in knowledge, the Absolute cannot be Absolute. Thus, in order for the

Absolute to be Absolute, it must exist in discursive knowing. Because the human being is a discursive thinker, the human being can think the Absolute by following its self-particularizing conceptual activity in logic, nature, and mind. Since the Absolute comes to exist in knowledge when the human being knows the self-particularizing concept, the Absolute achieves Absolute status only in the human knowledge of the Absolute. Thus, Hegel's thought of the Absolute in his threefold system of philosophy is the self-knowledge of the Absolute of itself:

> God is God only insofar as he knows himself: his self-knowledge is, further, a self-consciousness in man and man's knowledge of God, which proceeds to man's self-knowledge in God.[2]

In order to become a vessel of *Welt-Geist*, one must efface oneself, as Hegel makes clear in his famous preface to the *Phenomenology of Spirit*. One must forgo abstract thinking in order to *realize* the identity of Absolute with relative knowing. One must cease to think that true thought is reducible to one's own thought as a separate finite agent. Rather, true thought is the reconciliation of God's thought with human thought: it is the self-knowing of God through me. What is more, because the Absolute engenders its own non-being and self-alienation, one can know the Absolute because the self-alienation and other of the Absolute is engendered in the Absolute itself. This is reflected in Hegel's insight that the human being is *the mind of God*: through the self-particularizing of the Absolute, the Absolute takes a human form and is alienated from itself, from which and through which it knows itself. For Hegel truth is not the correspondence of a concept with a separate object, but *the self-correspondence* of the concept with itself engendered in the reconciliation of particular with the universal, the reconciliation of the human being with God. In and through this reconciliation, one can recognize one's own Absolute and self-determining singularity.

What this indicates is that Hegel's endorsement of the synthetic unity of apperception (or self-consciousness) as the being of the concept, at the outset of the logic of the concept, is not at all an indication of a deflated metaphysics. Rather, Hegel demands that Kant's project can only be fulfilled if the concept becomes the principle of its own existence. In *the final synthesis*, this means nothing less than *absolutizing self-consciousness*. Since the Absolute comes to be Absolute by coming to exist in the mind of a knower of the Absolute, by *knowing one's own knowing of the Absolute*, one knows *the Absolute itself*. Knowing the Absolute itself means nothing other than knowing one's own knowing of the Absolute. In terms of self-consciousness, by taking the Absolute as *the object* of one's knowledge, the subject knows oneself. Or the other way around: by knowing oneself, the *subject* of knowing, one knows the object of one's knowing. Hegel's Kantianism therefore is nothing less than the absolute overcoming of Kantianism. For absolutizing self-consciousness is ultimately nothing less than an affirmation of the very intellectual intuition Kant meant to guard against. Transforming the relativity of the concept (at work in *relative* self-consciousness) into an Absolute Principle of its own existence requires the transformation of relative self-consciousness into an absolute self-consciousness that achieves knowledge of its Absolute Object by means of the Absolute Concept.

In giving up all foundations, Hegel's philosophy also gives up the intellectual intuition of the early Fichte and Schelling as the ground of philosophy. But this does not mean that the concept of intellectual intuition never re-appears. Instead, it only requires that it not be taken for granted as the foundation of philosophy. Because the Absolute can be Absolute only by existing in knowledge, by knowing the Absolute the Absolute overcomes its relativity and *exists absolutely*. This is nothing less than the intellectual intuition of the Absolute in Kant's sense, for *the conceptualizing of the Absolute engenders its existence*. Hegel recognizes that just as the identity of synthesis and analysis arises only upon the completion of the logic in the Absolute Idea, so the intellectual intuition of the Absolute can only arise upon the very completion of the whole system of philosophy.

Accordingly, upon the completion of his system of philosophy, Hegel invokes Aristotle's definition of God, thought thinking itself—*nous that intuits itself*. This self-intuition of the Absolute, however, cannot succeed without us and is not devoid of all potentiality and plurality as in Aristotle's case, but is constituted by the manifold determinations of logic, nature, and spirit. Given that the self-intuition of the Absolute *cannot succeed without us*, and the Absolute Being of the Absolute depends upon its being known by means of that self-intuition, quite unlike McDowell's Absolute Idealism, Hegel's Absolute Idealism does indeed, in an important and highly qualified sense, 'threaten common sense that the world does not exist without us.'[3] Independently of the absolute self-knowing of Absolute existence, the Absolute is like a seed that has not yet blossomed into full maturation. Looking *from* the position of Absolute Knowledge *back* at the ancestral past of Absolute Existence, one can say that anterior to the absolute self-knowing of Absolute existence, the Absolute exists *as* that which is *on the way* to Absolute Being—as that which is complete in the sense that the character of being *not-yet* Absolute is realized in each and every stage of its development. Its *potential to be* Absolute is carried along with each stage of development and fully actualized in philosophical self-knowledge.

Since the Absolute becomes absolutely Absolute by means of the Absolute *Knowledge* of a rational species, the *correlation* between rational self-knowing and Being is the *final stage* of the development of the Absolute. Although at the level of logic alone, there is only a correlationism of being with *the agency of the concept*, the Absolute Existence of the Absolute demands a correlationism of being and a real rational agency (such as the human being). This developmental correlationism can account for the ancestral (what exists anterior to givenness), since it is not posited at the beginning, but at *the end* of the system. Instead, by completing the system with correlationism, one can account for the ancestral (and the *ancestral aspects of the Absolute*) with simultaneously giving an account of our knowledge of it.[4]

The development in the *Science* of *Logic* is the process by which the concept determines itself to be the singular principle of logic, nature, and spirit. This three in one—the singularity of logic, nature, and spirit, constitutes the complete scientific transformation of the Holy Trinity into scientific form. For Hegel, the Absolute is constituted by a *Theogony*. God or the Idea, as long as it remains merely logical, is not *absolutely* Absolute, for insofar as it is a non-natural or non-spiritual way of being, it excludes nature and spirit. Accordingly, it is only in virtue of its self-particularization in nature and spirit that the Absolute can be absolutely Absolute. Simply put, unlike in the Christian tradition, God remains incomplete before he enters the world of nature and spirit. For Hegel, the Absolute certainly is *logically* complete in its conceptual self-development *independently* of the creation of nature and spirit and the existence of nature and spirit certainly do depend upon the existence of logic. Nonetheless, the Absolute is not *absolutely* complete independently of its instantiation in nature and spirit. For logic does not sufficiently constitute all domains of existence. Patricia Marie Carlton tracks this distinction with the concepts of the 'internal' and 'external' Trinity. Whereas universality, particularity, and singularity constitute a purely 'internal' Trinity, the unity of logic, nature, and spirit all constitute an 'external Trinity'[5] whereby the Son constitutes the moment of nature.[6] The Absolute concept becomes absolutely Absolute only *in virtue of its natural and spiritual history*. The ontological 'argument' constituting Hegel's *Science of Logic* is only one element of a three-part development, the complete articulation of which requires following the self-particularizing concept in the domains of nature and spirit.

As Hegel points out in his Lectures on the *Philosophy of Religion*, what is needed is a 'self-elevation to God.'[7] Our knowing of God, ala Hegel, is nothing other than this very self-elevation to the divine.[8] Accordingly, it is not wrong to insist that human reason is 'co-extensive' with divine reason.[9] For this reason, Hegel's ontological argument is not a dialectical sequence performed by a human being about a separate being. Rather, as Harrelson puts it, the 'ontological argument' is a dialectical activity that is known because the human knowledge of God 'participates' in God's self-knowledge.

> Whoever 'grasps' or comprehends that being is the concept, i.e. whoever gazes from the summit of absolute knowledge and thereby

understands the inferences of the Hegelian logic, also perceives the existence of God via participation in God's self-knowledge.[10]

The Christian tradition—like the Greek one that preceded it—offered Hegel further resources for re-conceiving the Absolute as singularity.[11] As Magee points out, Hegel had no hesitations identifying himself as a Christian.[12] In the Christian tradition, the word becomes flesh (in the person of Immanuel), and it becomes flesh solely on its *own initiative*. In Hegel's system, the self-particularizing God freely particularizes itself in virtue of its own initiative. By re-thinking universality as singularity and infusing conceptual life into the pictorial vision of the self-particularizing God that is characteristic of Christian belief, Hegel freshly engages both Ancient Greek and Christian philosophy. As he writes concerning the ontological argument:

> Our present standpoint is that of Christianity. Here we have the concept in all its freedom. . . . The concept of spirit is the concept that has being in and for itself; but what has been thus distinguished, though it may at first appear as something external, devoid of spirit, extra-divine, is identical with the concept. Absolute truth consists in the development of this idea. In the Christian religion it is known that God has revealed godself, and the very being of God consists in revealing godself. Revealing is self-distinguishing; what has been revealed is precisely that God is revelatory.[13]

Just as the Christian religion recognizes that true monotheism requires a *self-particularizing* God, so Hegel recognized that no true conception of the Absolute is possible without recognizing the singularity of the self-particularizing concept.[14]

In the course of our reconstruction of Hegel's concept of the concept, we have painstakingly reconstructed Hegel's argument that the universal individuates itself. In virtue of its self-differentiating character, the universal differentiates itself into two distinct forms: the particular and the universal. Upon differentiating itself into these distinct forms, self-differentiation differentiates itself once again. This time, however, self-differentiation negates the separation of universality and particularity that is constitutive of particularity, thereby giving rise to singularity. This process of self-particularization endemic to the life of the singular universal constitutes Hegel's appropriation of the ontological 'argument.' No longer an argument, and no longer indebted to foundations, the concept becomes the source of its own existence. What is absolutely true—*itself by itself*, is the principle of its own existence, such that even our own self-knowledge must be conceived as a function of the free concept. Its truth does not depend upon anything except itself. Hegel's defense of the ontological argument against Kant's critique places him squarely in the tradition of a modern, rationalist metaphysics that proceeds by means of ontological arguments. Indeed, Hegel's endorsement of the ontological argument places him squarely in the long and distinguished tradition of that argument from the scholasticism of Anselm to Descartes, Spinoza, and Leibniz, whose concept of the Monad Hegel invokes in order to clarify his concept of the object in the *Encyclopedia Logic*.[15] Hegel's metaphysics, however, has fulfilled the promissory note of freedom initiated but not completed by the revolution of thinking that constitutes modern rationalist thought. The endorsement of the ontological argument is systematically connected to the concept of a self-particularizing God that is constitutive of Christian thought.

As this role of the human being indicates, Hegel cancels and preserves Christian thinking in his own system. The systematization of the protestant reformation in which the human being's role is diminished to zero initiates a dialectical process in which the human being's role is maximized. As the scriptures have it, by losing oneself one finds oneself:

> For whoever wants to save their life will lose it, but whoever loses their life for me will find it.[16]

Hegel systematizes the dialectical aspect of the reformation: by eliminating human freedom, human freedom is realized. Because the Absolute does not know its Absolute being without minds that have the potential to know, the Absolute can only achieve Absolute Self-Knowledge in the mind of the philosopher who knows the Absolute. Simply put, the philosophical knowledge of the Absolute is the self-knowledge of the Absolute of itself. In this sense, Hegel's philosophy is not 'disenchanted' in the usual way that people use this term. Instead, Hegel means to returned the human being, and human history to the absolute center of Being, since the self-particularization and self-completion of the Absolute only comes to fruition in her self-knowledge. Hegel's heterodoxy consists in making God's self-knowledge dependent upon the knowledge of a particular being. Since this particular being is herself an instantiation of the self-particularizing Absolute concept, the human being can be absolutely self-determined without sacrificing the omnipotence and freedom of the Absolute. Although the Absolute Idea is logically complete without the aid of human knowing, human knowing (or at least some form of mind capable of rational knowing) is not only a necessary self-particularization of the concept but also necessary for the self-realization of the Absolute Idea *as* Absolute Spirit. In the self-knowledge of philosophy, Spirit absolutizes itself. Although the Absolute Idea as a logical category does not require Absolute Spirit to be what it is (or any phenomenology for that matter), the knowing of the Absolute Idea in the mind of the philosopher becomes a necessary condition for the Absolute Idea to *exist* as a *stage* in the development of Absolute Spirit. Without a knower that exists in the domain of *Realphilosophie*, the Absolute concept could not come to exist in *the form of science* and its species—the *Science of Logic*, the science of Nature, and the science of Spirit.

Our analysis enables us to see that Hegel is not only a revolutionary thinker but a *reconciler*: his thinking reconciles Greek, Christian, Medieval, and Modern thought, among others, into the story of the self-particularizing concept. But the various dimensions of Hegel's thought which he acquires from the tradition, including the existentially implicative power of Ancient Form, the ontological argument for God's existence, and intellectual intuition, all require liberation from a finite conception of universality and a systematic grounding in the concept of self-particularizing singularity. Because the Absolute achieves its Absolute self-relation in knowing, the history of philosophy as the 'age of the world picture,' as Heidegger described it, is not contingently related to systematic philosophical thinking. Rather, the history of the philosophical engagement with the absolute, the problem of the disappearance of the Absolute, and with it the turn to mysticism, all become necessary to the very development and completion of the Absolute itself.[17] Hegel understood himself as not only having transformed the age of the world picture into 'the age of the world concept' but also having built that very transformation into the system of philosophy. For this reason, on these Hegelian terms it only seems fitting that a systematic investigation into the concept of the concept and its relation to Absolute Knowing and Being be investigated within the context of an inquiry in the history of philosophy.

It is often said that Hegel's critique of Kant is actually an effort to complete Kant's critique of reason. Certainly, it is true that Hegel radicalizes Kant's critique of reason. The radicalization of the critique of pure reason leads to the end of transcendental philosophy. Far from leaving metaphysics behind, the critique of transcendental philosophy constitutes a return to metaphysics—albeit a *critical metaphysics*. As Bernasconi puts it, any Hegel without metaphysics can only be the 'corpse of Hegel.'[18] This is nowhere more obvious than Hegel's invocation of *Nous* upon the completion of his system. Hegel returns to metaphysics by means of the self-overcoming of transcendental thought. But this return does not leave metaphysics unchanged. Rather, the return to metaphysics not only brings an end to all foundations once and for all, but transforms the Absolute into self-particularizing singularity. The Absolute must die in order to live, and God must be crucified in order to be resurrected—the historical good Friday must become speculative.[19] In the words of Richard Dien Winfield, 'Death to Metaphysics, Long Live Metaphysics!'[20]

Notes

1. Since this text is not primarily concerned with ethical objections, such as Levinas' accusation that Hegel's 'totalization' is violent, of course I do not mean

to imply that there are not other important objections to Hegel's thought that require significant attention.

2. Hegel, *Hegel's Philosophy of Mind,* 298. See Magee, *Hegel and the Hermetic Tradition,* 13.
3. McDowell, *Mind and World,* 17.
4. The transformation of correlationism in a new form at the end of the system raises a difficult modal problem concerning the existence of the human being. If the concept realizes itself with necessity in the domains of nature and spirit, then one might raise the worry that Hegel must be committed to the *necessary existence* of rational animals. This seems to imply that integrating the evolutionary teaching of the origin of rational life into Hegel's system would require the transformation of the content of that empirical teaching *from a contingency into a necessity.* Because Hegel himself seems to proclaim that the goal of philosophy is to give 'the validation of necessity' to *the content* of the empirical sciences, this implication of Hegel's system does not seem to be too far from his own self-conception of his system. See Hegel, *EL,* 12r.
5. See the discussion of the external and internal Trinity in Carlton, *Hegel's Metaphysics of God,* 8, 91.
6. Magee, *Hegel and the Hermetic Tradition,* 39.
7. Hegel, *Lectures on the Philosophy of Religion,* 167.
8. See Carlton, *Hegel's Metaphysics of God,* 64.
9. Ibid, 58.
10. Harrleson, *The Ontological Argument from Descartes to Hegel,* 220.
11. Rosen claims that Hegel's concept of the Absolute is indebted to Christian, but not to Greek rationalism, which he claims is dead: 'The absolute shows or as we can say, "speaks" itself to itself; it is divine logos of Christ and not the dead or abstract logos of Greek rationalism.' See Rosen, *The Idea of Hegel's Science of Logic,* 405. Although Rosen is right about the self-relation of the Absolute, Hegel had a higher evaluation of Greek rationalism than Rosen himself.
12. Magee, *Hegel and the Hermetic Tradition,* 16.
13. Hegel, *Lectures on the Proofs of the Existence of God,* 191–192.
14. Hegel also employs Christian language for educational purposes. See Introduction to Hegel, *Hegel's Philosophy of Mind,* paragraph 383, 17.
15. See Hegel, *Hegel's Logic,* 260, paragraph 194.
16. See "Matthew," in *Bible,* New International Version (Grand Rapids: Zondervan, 2017), 16:25.
17. Robert Brandom is right that Hegel's concept of recollection is a 'key concept articulating the historical dimension of his account of discursive normativity.' But recollection is even more than this. It is also a key concept articulating the historical dimension of his account of the *absolute existence* of discursive thought. See Brandom, *A Spirit of Trust,* 371.
18. Robert Bernasconi, "Hegel's Faith and Knowledge and the Metaphysics that Takes the Place of Metaphysics," in *Hegel and Metaphysics: On Logic and Ontology in the System,* ed. Allegra de Laurentiis (Berlin: De Gruyter, 2016), 135–148, 146.
19. Ibid, 144. Bernasconi also notes that Hegel's phrase 'God is dead' comes from a Lutheran hymn and is certainly not meant to indicate that God does not undergo resurrection. Ibid, 144.
20. See Winfield's recent piece in the edited volume on Hegel's metaphysics, originally presented at the HSA in 2014. Winfield, "Hegel's Overcoming of the Overcoming of Metaphysics," 59–70, 69.

References

Aquinas, Thomas. *Summa Theologica*. Edited by Anton C. Pegis. Indianapolis: Hackett, 1997.

Aristotle. "Categories." In *The Complete Works of Aristotle: Vol.1*, edited by Jonathan Barnes, 3–24. Princeton: Princeton University Press, 1984.

Aristotle. *Metaphysics*. Translated by Joe Sachs. Santa Fe: Green Lion Press, 2002.

Aristotle. "Nicomachean Ethics." In *The Complete Works of Aristotle: Vol. 2*, edited by Jonathan Barnes, 1729–1867, translated by W. D. Ross. Princeton: Princeton University Press, 1984.

Aristotle. "On the Soul." In *The Philosophy of Aristotle: Vol. 1*, translated by A. E. Wardman and J. L. Creed. New York: Penguin Books, 1963.

Aristotle. "Physics." In *The Complete Works of Aristotle, Vol. 1*, edited by Jonathan Barnes, translated by R. P. Hardie and R. K. Gaye. Princeton: Princeton University Press, 1984.

Aristotle. "Posterior Analytics." In *The Complete Works of Aristotle, Vol. 1*, edited by Jonathan Barnes, 114–167, translated by Jonathan Barnes. Princeton: Princeton University Press, 1984.

Armstrong, D. M. *Universals: An Opinionated Introduction*. Boulder: Westview Press, 1989.

Athanasius. *On the Incarnation*. Translated by John Behr. New York: St. Vladamir's Seminary Press, 2012.

Badiou, Alain. *Being and Event*. Translated by Oliver Feltham. London and New York: Continuum, 2005.

Badiou, Alain. *Logics of Worlds*. Translated by Alberto Toscana. London and New York: Continuum, 2009.

Barnes, Jonathan. *Early Greek Philosophy*. Suffolk: Penguin Books, 2002.

Barnett, Stuart, ed. *Hegel After Derrida*. London: Routledge, 1998.

Baugh, Bruce. *French Hegel*. New York: Routledge, 2003.

Beall, J. C., and Bradley Armour-Garb. "Should Deflationists be Dialetheists?" *Noûs* 37, no. 2 (2003): 303–324.

Beall, J. C., and David Ripley. "Analetheism and Dialetheism." *Analysis* 64, no. 1 (2004): 30–35.

Behler, E. *Frühromantik*. Berlin: Walter de Gruyer, 1992.

Beiser, F. "Hegel, a Non-Metaphysician? A Polemic Review of H T Engelhardt and Terry Pinkard (eds), *Hegel Reconsidered*." *Hegel Bulletin* 16, no. 2 (32) (1995): 1–13.

Beiser, F. *The Romantic Imperative: Concept of Early German Romanticism.* Harvard: Harvard University Press, 2006.

Berlin, Isaiah. *The Magus of the North.* Edited by Henry Hardy. London: John Murray, 1993.

Berman, Robert. "Ways of Being Singular: The Logic of Individuality." In *Hegel's Theory of the Subject*, edited by David Gray Carlson, 85–98. New York: Palgrave Macmillan, 2005.

Bernasconi, Robert. "Hegel's Faith and Knowledge and the Metaphysics that Takes the Place of Metaphysics." In *Hegel and Metaphysics: On Logic and Ontology in the System*, edited by Allegra de Laurentiis, 135–149. Berlin: De Gruyter, 2016.

Berto, Francesco. "Is Dialetheism an Idealism? The Russellian Fallacy and the Dialetheist's Dilemma." *Dialectica* 61, no. 2 (2007): 235–263.

Blumenberg, Hans. *The Legitimacy of the Modern Age.* Translated by Robert M. Wallace. Baskerville: MIT University Press.

Bordignon, Michela. "Contradiction or Not-Contradiction? This is the Problem." In *Hegel Jahrbuch*, Vol. 19, Issue 1, edited by Andreas Arndt, Brady Bowman, Myriam Gerhard, and Jur Zovko, 163–171. Berlin: Akademie Verlag, 2013.

Bordignon, Michela. "Hegel: A Dialetheist? Truth and Contradiction in Hegel's Logic." *Hegel Bulletin* 40, no. 2 (2017): 198–214.

Bowman, Brady. *Hegel and the Metaphysics of Absolute Negativity.* Cambridge: Cambridge University Press, 2013.

Bradley, Armour-Garb, and J. C. Beall. "Further Remarks on Truth and Contradiction." *The Philosophical Quarterly* 52, no. 207 (2002): 217–225.

Brandom, Robert. *Articulating Reasons.* Cambridge: Harvard University Press, 2000.

Brandom, Robert. "Holism and Idealism in Hegel's Phenomenology." In *Tales of the Mighty Dead.* Harvard: Harvard University Press, 2002.

Brandom, Robert. "Sketch of a Program for a Critical Reading of Hegel: Comparing Empirical and Logical Concepts." In *German Idealism and Contemporary Analytic Philosophy*, edited by Karl Ameriks, 131–161. Berlin: De Gruyter, 2005.

Brandom, Robert. "Some Hegelian Ideas of Note for Continental Analytic Philosophy." *Hegel Bulletin* 35, no. 1 (2014): 1–15.

Brandom, Robert. "Some Pragmatist Themes in Hegel's Idealism." *European Journal of Philosophy* 7, no. 2 (1999): 164–189.

Brandom, Robert. *A Spirit of Trust: A Reading of Hegel's Phenomenology.* Cambridge: Harvard University Press, 2019.

Brient, Elizabeth. *The Immanence of the Infinite: Hans Blumenberg and the Threshold to Modernity.* Washington: Catholic University of America Press, 2002.

Brown, Nahum. *Hegel on Possibility.* New York: Bloomsbury, 2020.

Bruno, Anthony. "Determinacy, Indeterminacy, and Contingency in German Idealism." In *The Significance of Indeterminacy*, edited by Robert Scott and Gregory S. Moss, 67–84. New York: Routledge, 2018.

Bungay, Stephen. "The Hegelian Project." In *Hegel Reconsidered: Beyond Metaphysics and the Authoritarian State*, edited by H. Tristram Engelhardt Jr. and T. Pinkard, 19–43. Dordrecht: Kluwer, 1994.

Burbidge, John. "Concept and Time in Hegel." *Dialogue: Canadian Philosophical Review* 12 (1973): 403–422.

Burbidge, John. *On Hegel's Logic, Fragments of a Commentary*. New York: Humanities Press, 1995.

Cantor, Georg. *Briefe*. Edited by Herbert Meschkowski and Winfried Nielsen. Berlin and Heidelberg: Springer, 1991.

Carlson, David Gray. *A Commentary to Hegel's Science of Logic*. New York: Palgrave Macmillan, 2007.

Carlton, Patricia Marie. *Hegel's Metaphysics of God: The Ontological Proof as the Development of a Trinitarian Ontology*. Burlington: Ashgate, 2001.

Cassirer, Ernst. *The Philosophy of Symbolic Forms. Vol. Two: Mythical Thought*. New Haven: Yale University Press, 1955.

Cassirer, Ernst. *Substance and Function*. Translated by William Curtus Swaby and Marie Swaby. New York: Dover Publisher, 1953.

Clark, Wendy Lynn, and M. Fritzman. "The Nonfoundational Hegelianism of Dove, Maker, and Winfield." *The Philosophical Forum* 34, no. 1 (Spring 2013): 91–113.

Collingwood, R. G. *An Essay on Philosophical Methodology*. Edited by James Connelly and Guiseppina D'oro. Oxford: Oxford University Press, 2005.

Copenhaver, Brian, trans. *Hermetica*. Cambridge: Cambridge University Press, 1995.

Cotnoir, A., and A. Bacon. "Non-Well-Founded Mereology." *Review of Symbolic Logic* 5 (2012): 187–204.

De Boer, Karin. "Hegel's Account of Contradiction in the Science of Logic Reconsidered." *Journal of the History of Philosophy* 48, no. 3 (2010): 345–374.

De Boer, Karin. *On Hegel: The Sway of the Negative*. New York: Palgrave Macmillan, 2010.

Deguchi, Yasuo, and Jay L. Garfield. "The Way of the Dialetheist: Contradictions in Buddhism." *Philosophy East and West* 58, no. 3 (2008): 395–402.

De Laurentiis, Allegra. "On Hegel's Concept of Thinking." In *Societas Rationis: Festschrift in Honor of Burkhard Tuschling*, edited by D. Huening, G. Stiening, and U. Vogel, 263–285. Berlin: Duncker & Humboldt, 2002.

Denyer, Nicholas. "Dialetheism and Trivialization." *Mind*, New Series 98, no. 390 (1989): 259–263.

Derrida, Jacques. *Glas*. Translated by Richard Rand. Lincoln: University of Nebraska Press, 1990.

Descartes, Rene. *Meditations on First Philosophy*. Translated by John Cottingham. Cambridge: Cambridge University Press, 1999.

Desmond, William. "Overdeterminacy, Affirming Indeterminacy, and the Dearth of Ontological Astonishment." In *Significance of Indeterminacy: Perspectives from Asian and Continental Philosophy*, edited by Robert Scott and Gregory S. Moss, 51–66. New York: Routledge, 2018.

Diego, Bubbio, Paolo, Allessandro De Cesaris, Maurizio Pagano, and Hager Weslati, eds. *Hegel, Logic, and Speculation*. London: Bloomsbury, 2019.

Dümont, Jürgen, and Frank Mau. "Are There True Contradictions? A Critical Discussion of Graham Priest's 'Beyond the Limits of Thought'." *Journal for General Philosophy of Science/Zeitschrift für allgemeine Wissenschaftstheorie* 29, no. 2 (1998): 289–299.

Duns, Scotus. "Ordinatio." In *Five Texts on the Medieval Problem of Universals*, edited and translated by Paul Vincent Spade, 57–113. Indianapolis: Hackett Publishing, 1994.

Echo, Umberto. "Some Remarks on a New Realism." www.wcp2013.gr/files/items/6/649/eco_wcp.pdf.

Ederheimer, E. *Jakob Böhme und die Romantiker. I und II Teil: Jakob Böhmes Einfluß auf Tieck und Novalis*. Heidelberg: Carl Winter's Universitätsbuchhandlung, 1904.

Everett, Anthony. "Absorbing Dialetheia?" *Mind* 103, no. 412 (1994): 413–419.

Ferrarin, Alfredo. *Hegel and Aristotle*. Cambridge: Cambridge University Press, 2004.

Fichte, Gottlob. *Concerning the Conception of the Science of Knowledge Generally (1794)*. Translated by Adolph Ernst Kroeger. Witthorn: Andos Books, 2017 [1794].

Fichte, Gottlob. *Fichtes Idealismus und die Geschichte: Kleine Schriften Werke Band I*. Edited by Emil Lask. Jena: Dietrich Schegelmann Reprintverlag, 2002.

Fichte, Gottlob. "First Introduction to the Science of Knowledge." Translated by A. E. Kroeger. *Journal of Speculative Philosophy* 1, no. 1 (1867): 23–36.

Fichte, Gottlob. "Grundlage der Wissenschaft der Praktiken." In *Fichte's Sämmtliche Werke, Erster Band*. Berlin: Verlag von Veit und Comp., 1845.

Fichte, Gottlob. *Science of Knowledge*. Edited and translated by Peter Heath and John Lachs. Cambridge: Cambridge University Press, 1982.

Findlay, J. N. *Hegel, A Re-Examination*. New York: The Macmillan Company, 1958.

Foster, M. B. "Christian Doctrine of Creation and the Rise of Modern Natural Science." *Mind* 43, no. 172 (October 1934): 446–468.

Foster, M. B. "Christian Theology and Modern Science of Nature (I)." *Mind* 44, no. 17 (1935): 439–466.

Foster, M. B. "The Concrete Universal: Cook Wilson and Bosanquet." *Mind* 40 (1931): 1–22.

Frank, Manfred. *Philosophical Foundations of German Romanticism*. Translated by Elizabeth Millan Zaibert. Albany: SUNY, 2004.

Franke, William. *On What Cannot Be Said, Vol. 1: Classic Formulations, University of Notre Dame Press*. Notre Dame: University of Notre Dame Press, 2014.

Frege, Gottlob. "On Concept and Object." In *Collected Papers on Mathematics, Logic, and Philosophy*, edited by Max Black et al, 187–194, translated by Brian McGuinness. New York: Blackwell, 1984.

Gabriel, Markus. *Fields of Sense*. Edinburgh: Edinburgh University Press, 2015.

Gabriel, Markus. *Sinn und Existenz*. Berlin: Suhrkamp, 2016.

Gabriel, Markus. *Transcendental Ontology*. New York: Bloomsbury, 2013.

Gabriel, Markus. *Why the World Does Not Exist*. Translated by Gregory S. Moss. Cambridge: Polity Press, 2015.

Gillespie, Michael Allen. *Nihilism Before Nietzsche*. Chicago: University of Chicago Press, 1995.

Halfwassen, Jens. *Hegel und der patentlike NeuPlatonismus*. Bonn: Bouvier Verlag, 1999; Hamburg, 2005.

Halper, Edward. "Hegel and the Problem of the Differentia." In *Form and Reason: Essays in Metaphysics*, 197–209. Albany: SUNY, 1993.

Harrelson, Kevin J. *The Ontological Argument from Descartes to Hegel.* New York: Humanity Books, 2009.

Harris, H. S. *Hegel's Development: Toward the Sunlight 1770–1801.* Oxford: Clarendon Press, 1972.

Haas, Andrew. *Hegel and the Problem of Multiplicity.* SPEP Studies in Historical Philosophy. Evanston: Northwestern University Press, 2000.

Hegel, G. W. F. *The Difference Between Fichte's and Schelling's System of Philosophy.* Translated by H. S. Harris and Walter Cerf. Albany: SUNY, 1977.

Hegel, G. W. F. *Elements of the Philosophy of Right.* Edited by Allen W. Wood, translated by H. B. Nisbet. Cambridge: Cambridge University Press, 1991.

Hegel, G. W. F. "Eleusis." In *Language and Death: The Place of Negativity,* edited by Giorgio Agamben, translated by Karen E. Pinkus and Michael Hardt. Minneapolis: University of Minnesota Press, 2006.

Hegel, G. W. F. "Excerpt on Love." In *Early Theological Writing,* edited and translated by T. M. Knox, 302–309. Chicago: University of Chicago Press, 1996.

Hegel, G. W. F. *Faith and Knowledge.* Translated by Walter Cerf. Albany: State University of New York Press, 1977.

Hegel, G. W. F. "Fragment of a System." In *Early Theological Writings,* edited by T. M. Knox, 309–321, translated by Richard Kroner. Chicago: University of Chicago Press, 1996.

Hegel, G. W. F. *Hegel: The Letters.* Translated by Clark Butler and Christine Seiler with Commentary by C. Butler. Bloomington: Indiana University Press, 1984.

Hegel, G. W. F. *Hegel's Logic.* Translated by William Wallace. Oxford: Clarendon Press, 1975.

Hegel, G. W. F. *Hegel's Philosophy of Nature.* Translated by A. V. Miller. Oxford: Oxford University Press, 2004.

Hegel, G. W. F. *Introduction to the Philosophy of History.* Translated by Leo Rauch. Cambridge: Hackett Publishing Company, 1998.

Hegel, G. W. F. *Lectures on the History of Philosophy: Greek Philosophy to Plato.* Translated by E. S. Haldane. Lincoln: University of Nebraska Press, 1995.

Hegel, G. W. F. *Lectures on the History of Philosophy: Plato and the Platonists.* Translated by E. S. Haldane and Frances H. Simpson. Lincoln: University of Nebraska Press, 1995.

Hegel, G. W. F. *Lectures on the Philosophy of Religion.* Translated by R. F. Brown, P. C. Hodgson, and J. M. Stewart. Berkley: University of California Press, 1984.

Hegel, G. W. F. *Lectures on the Proofs of the Existence of God.* Edited and translated by Peter C. Hodgson. Oxford: Oxford University Press, 2007.

Hegel, G. W. F. *Nürnberger Schriften, Werke 4.* Frankfurt am Main: Suhrkamp Verlag, 1970.

Hegel, G. W. F. *The Phenomenology of Mind, Vol II.* New York: Routledge, 2013.

Hegel, G. W. F. *Phenomenology of Spirit.* Edited and translated by Terry Pinkard. Cambridge: Cambridge University Press, 2018.

Hegel, G. W. F. *Phenomenology of Spirit*. Translated by A. V. Miller. Oxford: Oxford University Press, 1977.

Hegel, G. W. F. *Science of Logic*. Translated by A. V. Miller. Amherst: Humanity Books, 1969.

Hegel, G. W. F. *Science of Logic*. Translated by George Di Giovanni. Cambridge: Cambridge University Press, 2015.

Hegel, G. W. F. "Vorlesungen 10." In *Vorlesung über die Logik Berlin 1831*. Hamburg: Felix Meiner Verlag, 2001.

Hegel, G. W. F. "Vorlesung Über Logik und Metaphysik: Heidelberg 1817." In *Ausgewählte Vorlesungen und Manuskripten, Vol. 11*. Hamburg: Meiner Verlag, 1992.

Hegel, G. W. F. *Wissenschaft der Logik II*. Frankfurt am Main: Suhrkamp, 1986.

Heidegger, Martin. *Being and Time*. Translated by John Macquarrie and Edward Robinson. New York: Harper and Rowe, 1962.

Heidegger, Martin. "Language." In *Poetry, Language, Thought*, translated by Albert Hofstadter, 185–209. New York: Harper Collins, 2001.

Heidegger, Martin. "The Thinker as Poet." In *Poetry, Language, Thought*, translated by Albert Hofstader. New York: Harper and Row, 1971.

Heidegger, Martin. "What Is Metaphysics?" In *Basic Writings*, edited by David Farrell Krell, 89–111. New York: Harper Collins, 1993.

Henrich, Dieter. *Between Kant to Hegel*. Edited by David S. Pacini. Harvard: Harvard University Press, 2003.

Henrich, Dieter. *Hegel Im Kontext*. Frankfurt am Main: Suhrkamp Verlag, 1971.

Henrich, Dieter. "Hegels Grundoperation. Eine Einleitung in die Wissenschaft der Logik." In *Der Idealismus und der Gegenwart*, edited by Guzzoni, Ute, Bernhard Rang, and Ludwig Siep, 208–231. Hamburg: Meiner, 1976.

Hoesle, Vittorio. *Hegels System Der Idealismus der Subjektivitaet und das Problem der Intersubjektivitaet*. Hamburg: Felix Meiner Verlag, 1987.

Hölderlin, Friedrich. *Patmos*. http://gutenberg.spiegel.de/buch/friedrich-h-262/132.

Houlgate, Stephen. *The Opening of Hegel's Logic*. West Lafayette: Purdue University Press, 2005.

Houlgate, Stephen. "Phenomenology and De-Re Interpretation: A Critique of Brandom's Reading of Hegel." *Hegel Bulletin* 29, no. 1–2 (57–58) (2008): 30–47.

Houlgate, Stephen. "Schelling's Critique of Hegel's Science of Logic." *Review of Metaphysics* 53, no. 1 (September 1999): 99–128.

Houlgate, Stephen. "Why Hegel's Concept is not the Essence of Things." In *Hegel's Theory of the Subject*, edited by David Gray Carlson, 19–29. New York: Palgrave Macmillan, 2005.

Husserl, Edmund. *Shorter Logical Investigations*. Edited by Dermot Moran, translated by J. N. Findlay. London: Routledge, 2001.

Ibn, Al Arabi. "The Wisdom of Divinity in the Word of Adam." In *The Bezels of Wisdom*, translated by R. W. J. Austin. Mahwah: Paulus Press, 1980.

Jacobi, Friedrich Heinrich. *The Main Philosophical Writings and the Novel Allwill*. Translated by George Di Giovanni. Montreal: McGill-Queen's University Press, 2016.

Jacobi, Friedrich Heinrich. *Über die Lehre des Spinoza in Briefen an den Herrn Moses Mendelssohn*. Berlin: Hoffenberg, 2017.

Kallestrup, Jesper. "If Omniscient Beings Are Dialetheists, So Are Anti-Realists." *Analysis* 67, no. 3 (2007): 252–254.

Kant, Immanuel. *Critique of the Power of Judgment*. Edited by Paul Guyer, translated by Paul Guyer and Eric Matthews. Cambridge: Cambridge University Press, 2001.

Kant, Immanuel. *Critique of Pure Reason*. Edited and translated by Paul Guyer and Allen Wood. Cambridge: Cambridge University Press, 1998.

Kant, Immanuel. *Grounding for the Metaphysics of Morals*. Translated by James W. Ellington. Indianapolis: Hackett, 1981.

Kant, Immanuel. *Kritik der reinen Vernunft*. Hamburg: Meiner Verlag, 1998.

Kant, Immanuel. *Opus Postumum*. Edited by Paul Guyer. Cambridge: Cambridge University Press, 1998.

Koch, Anton. "Die Selbstbeziehung der Negation in Hegels Logik." *Zeitschrift für Philosophische Forschung* 53, no. 1 (January 1999): 1–29.

Kojeve, Alexandre. *Introduction to the Reading of Hegel*. Edited by Allan Bloom, translated by James Nichols. Ithaca: Cornell University Press, 1980.

Kreines, James. "Fundamentality Without Metaphysical Monism." *Hegel Bulletin* 39, no. 1 (May 2018): 138–156.

Kreines, James. "Hegel's Metaphysics: Changing the Debate." *Philosophy Compass* 1, no. 5 (September 2006): 466–480.

Kreis, Guido. *Negative Dialektik des Unendlichen: Kant, Hegel, Cantor*. Berlin: Suhrkamp, 2015.

Lakebrink, Bernard. "Der Begriff des Einzelnen und die Hegelsche Metaphysik." *Studien zur Metaphysik Hegels*, 89–120. Freiburg: Verlag Rombach, 1969.

Lau, Chong-Fuk. "A Deflationary Approach to Hegel's Metaphysics." In *Hegel and Metaphysics: On Logic and Ontology in the System*, edited by Allegra de Laurentiis, 27–41. Berlin: De Gruyter, 2016.

Longuenesse, Beatrice. *Hegel's Critique of Metaphysics*. Cambridge: Cambridge University Press, 2007.

Lowe, E. J. *More Kinds of Being: A Further Study of Individuation, Identity, and the Logic of Sortal Terms*. Oxford: Wiley Blackwell, 2009.

Magee, Glenn. *Hegel and the Hermetic Tradition*. Ithaca: Cornell University Press, 2008.

Magee, Glenn. "Hegel as Metaphysician." In *Hegel and Metaphysics: On Logic and Ontology in the System*, edited by Allegra de Laurentiis, 43–57. Berlin: De Gruyter, 2016.

Maimonides, Moses. *Guide for the Perplexed*. Translated by Michael Friedlander. New York: Cosimo Classics, 2007.

Maker, William. *Philosophy Without Foundations*. Albany: SUNY, 1994.

Mander, W. J. *British Idealism: A History*. Oxford: Oxford University Press, 2011.

Mann, Gottfried. "Zum Begriff des Einzelnen, des Ich, und des Individuellen bei Hegel." Dissertation, Heidelberg, 1935.

Marion, Jean-Luc. "Is the Ontological Argument Ontological?" In *Cartesian Questions: Methods and Metaphysics*. Chicago: Chicago University Press, 1999.

Martin, Christian Georg. *Ontologie der Selbstbestimmung, Eine operationale Rekonstruktion von Hegels "Wissenschaft der Logik."* Tübingen: Mohr/Siebeck, 2012.

Maybee, Julie E. *Picturing Hegel: An Illustrated Guide to Hegel's Encyclopaedia Logic*. Plymouth, UK: Lexington Books, 2009.

McCumber, John. *Company of Words: Hegel, Language, and Systematic Philosophy*. Evanston: Northwestern Press, 1993.

McDowell, John. "Hegel's Idealism as a Radicalization of Kant." In *Having the World in View*. Harvard: Harvard University Press, 2009.

McDowell, John. *Mind and World*. Cambridge: Harvard University Press, 1996.

McTaggart, John, and Ellis McTaggart. *A Commentary on Hegel' Logic*. Cambridge: Cambridge University Press, 1910.

Meillassoux, Quentin. *After Infinitude*. Translated by Ray Brassier. London: Bloomsbury, 2015.

Meister, Eckhart. "On Detachment." In *The Essential Sermons, Commentaries, Treatises, and Defense*, translated by Edmund Colledge, O. S. A. and Bernard McGinn. Mahwah: Paulist Press, 1981.

Meister, Eckhart. "Sermon 6." In *The Essential Sermons, Commentaries, Treatises, and Defense*, translated by Edmund Colledge, O. S. A. and Bernard McGinn. Mahwah: Paulist Press, 1981.

Meister, Eckhart. "Sermon 48." In *The Essential Sermons, Commentaries, Treatises, and Defense*, translated by Edmund Colledge, O. S. A. and Bernard McGinn. Mahwah: Paulist Press, 1981.

Meister, Eckhart. "Sermon 52." In *The Essential Sermons, Commentaries, Treatises, and Defense*, translated by Edmund Colledge, O. S. A. and Bernard McGinn, 199–203. Mahwah: Paulist Press, 1981.

Meister, Eckhart. "Sermon 83." In *The Essential Sermons, Commentaries, Treatises, and Defense,* translated by Edmund Colledge, O. S. A. and Bernard McGinn. Mahwah: Paulist Press, 1981.

Mill, John Stuart. *A System of Logic, Ratiocinative and Inductive*. Charleston: Biblio Bazaar, 2009.

Milne, Peter. "Omniscient Beings are Dialetheists." *Analysis* 67, no. 295 (2007): 250–251.

Moss, Gregory S. "Absolute Imagination: The Metaphysics of Romanticism." *Social Imaginaries* 5, no. 1 (2019): 57–80.

Moss, Gregory S. "Annihilating the Nothing: Hegel and Nishitani on the Self-Overcoming of Nihilism." *Frontiers of Philosophy in China* 13, no. 4 (2018): 570–600.

Moss, Gregory S. "Dialetheism and the Problem of the Missing Difference." *Northern European Journal of Philosophy* 19, no. 2 (August 2018): 1–22.

Moss, Gregory S. "The Emerging Philosophical Recognition of the Significance of Indeterminacy." In *The Significance of Indeterminacy*, edited by Robert Scott and Gregory S. Moss, 1–38. New York: Routledge, 2018.

Moss, Gregory S. *Ernst Cassirer and The Autonomy of Language*. Lanham: Lexington Books November, 2014.

Moss, Gregory S. "Four Paradoxes of Self-Reference." *Journal of Speculative Philosophy* 28, no. 2 (2014): 169–189.

Moss, Gregory S. "Free Thinking in Schelling's Erlangen Lectures." In *The Significance of Indeterminacy: Perspectives from Asian and Continental Philosophy*, edited by Robert Scott and Gregory S. Moss, 84–103. New York: Routledge, 2018.

Moss, Gregory S. "The Paradox of Representation in Nishitani's Critique of Kant." In *Kant on Intuition: Western and Asian Perspectives on Transcendental Idealism*, edited by Steve Palmquist, 275–283. New York: Routledge: 2018.

Moss, Gregory S. "The Problem of Evil in the Speculative Mysticism of Meister Eckhart." In *The Problem of Evil: New Philosophical Directions*, edited by Benjamin McCraw and Robert Arp, 35–51. Lanham: Lexington Books, 2016.

Moss, Gregory S. "The Schellingian Heritage of Cassirer's Philosophy of Symbolic Forms." In *Ernst Cassirer's Philosophy of Symbolic Forms: The Method of Culture*, edited by Anne Pollok and Luigi Filieri. Piza: Edizioni ETS, 2020.

Moss, Gregory S. "The Synthetic Unity of Apperception in Hegel's Logic of the Concept." *Idealistic Studies* 45, no. 3 (2016): 279–306, 280–281.

Muratori, Cecelia. *The First German Philosopher: The Mysticism of Jakob Böhme as Interpreted by Hegel*. Dordrecht: Springer, 2016.

Nagarjuna. *The Fundamental Wisdom of the Middle Way*. Translated by Jay Garfield. New York: Oxford University Press, 1985.

Nassar, Dalia. *The Romantic Absolute: Being and Knowing in Early German Romantic Philosophy 1795–1804*. Chicago: University of Chicago Press, 2013.

Ng, Karen. *Hegel's Concept of Life: Self-Consciousness, Freedom, Logic*. Oxford: Oxford University Press, 2019.

Nishitani, Keiji. *Religion and Nothingness*. Translated by Jan Van Bragt. Berkeley: University of California Press, 1983.

Norman, R. Routley, and Graham Priest, ed. *Paraconsistent Logic: Essays on the Inconsistent* (Analytica). Oakland: University of California Press, 1989.

Novalis. *Aphorismen und Fragmente 1798–1800*. Edited by Michael Brucker. Insel Verlag, 1992. https://gutenberg.spiegel.de/buch/aphorismen-5232/6

Novalis. *Fragmente. Ernste Vollstängide geordnete Ausgabe*. Edited by Ernst Kamnitzer. Dresden: Jess Verlag, 1929. https://gutenberg.spiegel.de/buch/fragmente-i-6618/1.

Oppy, Graham. "Ontological Arguments." *Stanford Encyclopedia of Philosophy*. https://plato.stanford.edu/entries/ontological-arguments/

Parsons, Terence. "True Contradictions." *Canadian Journal of Philosophy* 20, no. 3 (1990): 335–353.

Peacocke, Christopher. *A Study of Concepts*. Cambridge: MIT University Press, 1993.

Philo. "Who Is the Heir of Divine Things." In *The Works of Philo*, translated by C. D. Yonge. Peabody: Hendrickson Publishers, 1993.

Pinkard, Terry. "How Kantian Was Hegel?" *Review of Metaphysics* 43, no. 4 (June 7, 1990).

Pippin, Robert. "Hegel and Category Theory." *Review of Metaphysics* 43 (June 1990): 839–848.

Pippin, Robert. *Hegel's Idealism: The Satisfaction of Self-Consciousness*. Cambridge: Cambridge University Press, 1989.

Pippin, Robert. *Hegel's Realm of Shadows: Logic as Metaphysics in the Science of Logic*. Chicago: University of Chicago Press, 2019.

Plato. *Parmenides*. Translated by Albert Keith Whitaker. Newburyport: Focus Philosophical Library, 1996.

Plato. "Parmenides." In *Plato: Complete Works*, edited by John M. Cooper, 359–398. Indianapolis: Hackett Publishing, 1997.

Plato. *Phaedo*. Translated by Eva Brann, Peter Kalkavage, and Eric Salem. Newburyport: Focus Philosophical Library, 1998.

Plato. "Philebus." In *Plato: Complete Works*, edited by John M. Cooper, 398–457. Indianapolis: Hackett Publishing, 1997.

Plato. "Republic." In *Plato: Complete Works*, edited by John M. Cooper, 971–1224. Indianapolis: Hackett Publishing, 1997.

Plato. "Seventh Letter." In *Plato: The Collected Dialogues*, edited by Edith Hamilton and Huntington Cairns. Princeton: Princeton University Press, 2005.

Plato. "Sophist." In *Plato: Complete Works, Plato: Complete Works*, edited by John M. Cooper, 235–294. Indianapolis: Hackett Publishing, 1997.

Plotinus. *Enneads 7 Vols*. Loeb Classical Library. Translated by A. H. Armstrong. Cambridge: Harvard University Press, 1988.

Poeggeler, Otto. *Hegel's Kritik der Romantik*. Paderborn: Wilhelm Fink Verlag, 1999.

Porphyry. *Isagoge*. Translated by Edward W. Warren. Toronto: Pontifical Institute of Mediaeval Studies, 1975.

Priest, Graham. *Beyond the Limits of Thought*. Oxford: Oxford University Press, 2003.

Priest, Graham. "Dialectic and Dialetheic." *Science & Society* 53, no. 4 (1989/90): 388–415.

Priest, Graham. "Everything and Nothing." Presented at the University of Bonn on July 17, 2017.

Priest, Graham. "Logic of Paradox." *Journal of Philosophical Logic* 8, no. 1 (1979, 1986): 219–241.

Priest, Graham. "The Logical Structure of Dialectic (Draft)."

Priest, Graham. *One: Being an Investigation into the Unity of Reality and of its Parts, Including the Singular Object Which is Nothingness*. Oxford: Oxford University Press, 2014.

Priest, Graham. "What Is so Bad About Contradictions?" *The Journal of Philosophy* 95, no. 8 (1998): 410–426.

Pseudo-Dionysius. "The Divine Names." In *The Complete Works of Pseudo-Dionysius*, translated by Colm Luibheid, 47–133. Mahwah: Paulist Press, 1987.

Quine, Willard L. "On What There Is." *Review of Metaphysics* 2, no. 5 (1948): 21–38.

Radler, Charlotte. " 'In Love I Am More God': The Centrality of Love in Meister Eckhart's Mysticism." *The Journal of Religion* 90, no. 2 (April 2010): 171–198.

Redding, Paul. "The Analytic Neo-Hegelianism of J. McDowell and Brandom." In *A Companion to Hegel*, edited by S. Houlgate and M. Baur, 576–593. Oxford: Wiley-Blackwell, 2011.

Redding, Paul. *Analytic Philosophy and the Return of Hegelian Thought*. Cambridge: Cambridge University Press, 2007.

Redding, Paul, and Paulo Diego Bubbil. "Ontological Argument: Hegel and the Ontological Argument for the Existence of God." *Religious Studies* 50, no. 4 (December 2014): 465–486.

Rockmore, Tom. "The Pittsburgh School, the Given, and Knowledge." *Social Epistemology, Review and Reply Collective* 2, no. 1 (2012): 29–38.

Rosen, Stanley. *The Idea of Hegel's Science of Logic*. Chicago: University of Chicago Press, 2013.

Russell, Bertrand. "On the Relations of Universals and Particulars." *Proceedings of the Aristotelian Society*, New Series 12. 1–24.

Sainsbury, R. M. *Paradoxes*. Cambridge: Cambridge University Press, 2015.

Schaefer, Alfred. *Der Nihilismus in Hegel's Logik: Kommentar und Kritik zu Hegel's Wissenschaft der Logik*. Berlin: Verlag Arno Spitz GmbH, 1992.

Schelling, F. W. J. *Ages of the World*. Translated by Jason Wirth. Albany: SUNY, 2000.

Schelling, F. W. J. *The Grounding of Positive Philosophy*. Translated by Bruce Matthews. Albany: SUNY, 2007.

Schelling, F. W. J. *Historical-Critical Introduction to the Philosophy of Mythology*. Translated by Mason Richey and Markus Zisselberger. Albany: SUNY, 2007.

Schelling, F. W. J. *On the History of Philosophy*. Translated by Andrew Bowie. Cambridge: Cambridge University Press, 1994.

Schelling, F. W. J. *Outline for a System of the Philosophy of Nature*. Translated by Keith R. Peterson. Albany: SUNY, 2004.

Schelling, F. W. J. *System of Transcendental Idealism (1800)*. Translated by Peter Heath. Charlottesville: University Press of Virginia, 2001.

Schelling, F. W. J. "Über die Philosophie als Wissenschaft." In *Schelling's Werke, Fünfter Hauptband*, edited by Manfred Schroeder. München: D.H. Beck'sche Buchhandlung, 1927.

Schelling, F. W. J. "Vom Ich als Prinzip der Philosophie." In *Werke. Auswahl in drei Bänden*, edited by Otto Weiß. Leipzig: Fritz Eckardt, 1907.

Schick, Frederike. *Hegels Wissenschaft der Logik-metaphysische Letztbegruendung oder Theorie logischer Formen?* München: Verlag Karl Aber, 1994.

Schick, Stefan. *Contradicto est regula veri. Die Grundsätze des Denkens in der Formalen, Transzendentalen und Spekulativen Logik*. Hamburg: Meiner Verlag, 2010.

Schlegel, F. *Dialogue on Poetry and Literary Aphorisms*. Translated by E. Behler and R. Struc. Philadelphia: Pennsylvania University Press, 1968.

Schlegel, F. *Kritische Friedrich-Schlegel Ausgabe: Vol. 35*. Edited by Ernst Behler, in Collaboration with J. Anstett and B. Eichner. Paderborn: Schönigh, 1958.

Schleiermacher, Friedrich. *On Religion*. Translated by Richard Crouter. Cambridge: Cambridge University Press, 1996.

Schubert, Alexander. *Der Strukturgedanke in Hegels "Wissenschaft der Logik*. Band 232 (Meisenheim: Glan Hain Verlag bei Athenaeum Monographien zur philosophischen Forschung, 1985.)

Schwab, Philipp. "The Crisis of the Principle. Schelling's Ages of the World and Erlangen Lectures in Light of the Debate with Hegel." Presented at the Conference *Schelling: Crisis and Critique*, 21–25 of February, 2017 in Mexico City.

Schwab, Philipp. "Die Aporie des Anfangs. Zur Bestimmung des Systemprinzips bei Fichte, Schelling und Hegel." Presented at *Das Problem des Anfangs*, at the Southern University of Denmark in Odense, February 2016.

Sellars, Wilfred. *Empiricism and the Philosophy of Mind*. Edited by Andrew Chrucky. http://selfpace.uconn.edu/class/percep/SellarsEmpPhilMind.pdf

Spinoza. "Ethics." In *Complete Works*, edited by Michael L. Morgan, 213–383, translated by Samuel Shirley. Indianapolis: Hackett Publishing, 2002.

Stern, Robert. *Hegelian Metaphysics*. Oxford: Oxford University Press, 2009.

Trisokkas, Ioannis D. "Hegel on the Particular in the 'Science of Logic'." *Owl of Minerva* 43, no. 12 (2011–2012).

Trisokkas, Ioannis D. *Pyrrhonian Skepticism and Hegel's Theory of Judgment: A Treatise on the Possibility of Scientific Inquiry.* Leiden: Brill, 2012.

Trisokkas, Ioannis D. "The Speculative Logical Theory of Universality." *Owl of Minerva* 40, no. 2 (2009).

Vico. *New Science.* Translated by D. Marsh. London: Penguin Books, 2013 [1725].

Vlastos, Gregory. "The Third Man Argument in Plato's Parmenides." In *Philosophical Review* LXIII (1954): 319–349.

Westfall, Kenneth. *Hegel's Epistemology, a Philosophical Introduction to the Phenomenology of Spirit.* Indianapolis: Hackett, 2003.

White, Alan. *Absolute Knowledge: Hegel and the Problem of Metaphysics.* Athens: Ohio University Press, 1983.

Winfield, Richard Dien. *From Concept to Objectivity: Thinking Through Hegel's Subjective Logic.* Burlington: Ashgate, 2006.

Winfield, Richard Dien. "Hegel's Overcoming of the Overcoming of Metaphysics." In *Hegel and Metaphysics: On Logic and Ontology in the System*, edited by Allegra de Laurentiis, 59–71. Berlin: De Gruyter, 2016.

Winfield, Richard Dien. *Hegel's Science of Logic, A Critical Rethinking in Thirty Lectures.* Plymouth: Rowman and Littlefield Publishers, 2012.

Wittgenstein, Ludwig. *Tractatus.* http://tractatus-online.appspot.com/Tractatus/jonathan/D.html.

Wittgenstein, Ludwig. *Tractatus.* Translated by C. K. Ogden. Mineola: Dover, 1999.

Woody, Melvin. *Freedom's Embrace.* University Park: Penn State University Press, 1998.

Zizek, Slavoj. *Less than Nothing: Hegel and the Shadow of Dialectical Materialism.* London and New York: Verso, 2012.

Index

abstract universal 2, 8, 127, 137–142, 184, 196, 331, 346, 374, 384, 401–402, 419, 421, 423, 424, 427, 431–432, 434–438, 441, 443, 452, 470, 471, 472, 474

analysis 5, 7, 16–22, 27, 32, 36–37, 39, 45, 54–55, 57–59, 61–64, 73, 86, 88, 94, 99–101, 135, 137, 140, 147, 166, 178, 192, 234, 248, 255–256, 269–272, 274, 277, 283–284, 288, 310–311, 316, 333, 346, 348, 365, 373, 378, 393–394, 397, 403, 405, 418, 426, 429, 433, 458–460, 463, 468, 479, 486, 490; Analytic Unity of Apperception 39

Anselm 350, 356, 489

Aristotle 4, 13–15, 17–20, 23, 32, 40, 64–65, 74–76, 78–81, 85, 88–90, 92–95, 108–133, 135–140, 142–143, 146–149, 151–158, 160, 162–166, 176, 179–180, 184–186, 189, 194, 196, 205, 209–225, 230–233, 247, 249–250, 258, 263, 276, 282, 289–290, 317, 322–326, 328, 337–338, 355, 369, 382–383, 386, 392, 444, 453–454, 477, 482, 486, 492, 495

Aquinas, Thomas 88, 157, 194, 198, 209, 212, 215–221, 224–225, 492

Auto Kath Auto 6, 87, 102, 194, 195, 222, 228, 322, 351

back-turning 102, 193, 307, 316–318, 321–322, 359, 371, 422, 457, 476–477; *Palintropos* 221, 307, 315–317, 321–322, 371, 392; *Rückkehre* 307, 316–317

Badiou, Alain 286–287, 304–305, 492

Begriff 5–6, 63, 74, 88, 138, 277, 327, 351, 381–382, 387, 409, 420, 439, 443–444, 474, 476, 498

being-at-work 212, 214, 220, 225, 231, 322, 324; being-at-work-staying-itself 214

Berkeley, George 174–175, 179–180

Böhme, Jakob 52, 70, 250, 495, 500

Bordignon, Michela 280–281, 284–285

Bowman, Brady 308, 313, 327, 334, 352, 354, 358, 463, 480, 493

Brandom, Robert 277, 285, 459, 461, 464–465, 472, 478–480, 491, 493, 497, 501

Burbidge, John 440, 494

Cassirer, Ernst 65, 174–175, 178, 181, 183, 186, 187–188, 223, 480, 494, 499–500

Christianity 1, 50, 81, 218, 243, 283, 352, 410, 487–491, 495, 498

class-membership 2, 133, 141–142, 176, 179, 181, 183–184, 187–188, 286, 312

Conceptual Eliminativism 237

contrariety/contraries 109, 119, 125, 153, 192, 210, 213–215, 221, 224, 257–258, 275

correlationism 374, 486–487, 491

creation 35, 38, 49, 52, 68, 73–74, 77, 88, 92, 178, 197–199, 202, 217–218, 261, 335, 352, 413–414, 420, 441, 455–456, 487, 495; *Ex Nihilo* 74, 88, 198, 207, 414

De Boer, Karin 285, 335, 355, 421, 441, 477, 494

deduction: metaphysical 17–18; transcendental 17, 19, 129

Descartes, Rene 65, 99, 129, 210, 349, 350, 355–357, 453–454, 455, 489, 491, 494, 496

Desmond, William xi, 244, 250, 494

development (*Entwicklung*) 272, 332, 342, 350, 360, 367–368, 371–372, 375, 380, 387, 388, 391, 393, 401, 405, 407, 422–424, 432–433, 446

dialectic 5, 8, 32–33, 71, 98, 106, 164, 190, 193, 201, 207, 242, 248–249, 255–258, 260, 263, 271–273, 279–280, 282, 284–285, 303–304, 311, 313–314, 316–319, 325–328, 340, 346, 348, 350, 351, 353, 362, 371–372, 379, 388, 393, 405, 416, 423–424, 430, 433, 435, 450, 460, 461, 471, 472, 487, 489, 493, 501, 503

dialetheism 3–4, 8, 185, 234–239, 242, 248–249, 255, 275–282, 293, 306, 320, 492–494, 499; absolute 3–5, 7–8, 156, 226, 239, 241–243, 246–247, 268, 286–287, 294, 301, 304, 333, 343, 482; relative 286–287, 294

Eckhart, Meister 4, 197, 200–201, 223–224, 499–501

emanation ix, xiii, 25, 27, 73–91, 93, 352

empiricism 40, 141, 174–175, 178, 182, 184, 284, 337, 346, 445, 479, 502; absolute empiricism (problem of) 2, 94, 142, 147, 156, 159, 168–185, 193, 226, 239–241, 260, 309, 448, 467–468

epistemology 11–12, 16, 93, 135, 194–195, 218, 237, 262, 273, 283, 303, 306, 311, 339, 353, 477, 501, 503

existential implication 6, 99, 126–129, 137, 145–146, 148–149, 157, 233, 241, 247, 262–263, 268, 303, 307, 309, 310, 323–324, 338, 340, 350, 413, 415, 417, 427, 430, 433, 446, 456, 462, 467

existentialism 243

equivocity/equivocal 193, 197–201, 211–213, 215–216, 221, 219

faith 47–51, 69, 71, 74, 92, 164, 198, 200, 218, 220, 357, 491, 493, 496

Fichte, Gottlieb 15–25, 27–28, 30, 35–36, 38–39, 42–48, 51–55, 60–62, 64–73, 75, 88, 172, 263, 269–270, 274, 308, 329, 333, 442, 454–454, 460, 486, 495–496, 502

First Principle 36, 59

form (*Eidos*) xiii, 13–20, 23, 26, 65, 74–81, 85, 89, 102–127, 130–133, 138, 143, 146, 149, 157, 162–163, 175, 180, 185, 191–192, 213–215, 219–222, 224, 225, 228–234, 247, 259, 321–326

foundations (foundationalism) 25, 143, 309, 402, 273, 284, 309, 348, 413–414, 448, 467–468, 486, 488, 490, 495, 498

Franke, William P. 244, 495

Frank, Manfred 69, 495

freedom 46, 54, 55, 74, 242, 270, 273, 305, 324, 325, 333, 369, 380, 397–398, 404, 413, 440, 442, 459–461, 475, 484, 488, 489, 500, 503

Frege, Gottlob 138, 157, 186, 249, 495

Gabriel, Markus 68, 194, 250, 304, 286–307

genus 2, 4, 75, 78, 81–84, 90, 105, 110–113, 117, 121, 123, 125, 127, 130–133, 135–137, 140–142, 148–149, 155–163, 176, 179, 187, 189, 196, 198, 200, 209, 210–221, 224–225, 232, 240–241, 250, 261, 289–290, 297–298, 303, 310, 312, 396, 415, 419, 441, 445, 446, 470

(the) given xiii, 40, 48, 71, 92, 97, 137, 143, 145–146, 195, 266, 284, 309, 334, 349, 353, 364, 394, 402, 450, 460, 461, 501

God 6, 14, 38, 68, 73–74, 76, 86, 98–99, 101, 129, 193, 197–200, 203, 208–210, 215–221, 224–225, 228, 243, 245, 250, 259, 303, 308, 330–357, 400, 414, 441, 456, 462, 478, 482–491, 494, 496, 501

Halper, Edward xi, 163–168, 186, 248, 283, 315, 327, 358, 495

Hamman, Johann Georg 50–51

Heidegger, Martin 11, 195, 198, 200, 201, 203, 206–209, 222–224, 228, 250, 287, 305, 439, 466, 472, 490, 497

Heine, Henrich 350

Heraclitus 4, 108, 130, 153, 191, 193, 203, 222, 317–318, 322, 328, 457

history 35, 40, 65–66, 92, 101,
   137–138, 140, 142, 156, 174, 186,
   221, 228, 244, 247–248, 258–259,
   274, 289–291, 313, 328, 337, 340,
   342, 350–351, 356–358, 419, 441,
   462, 479, 487, 489–490, 494, 496,
   498, 502
Houlgate, Stephen 269–270, 280,
   284, 285, 334, 354, 452, 460–462,
   477–480, 497, 501
Hume, David 47, 49–51, 70, 175,
   178–179, 181
Husserl, Edmund 138, 157, 181, 186,
   188, 288, 497

idea 101, 208, 266–267, 283, 328,
   330, 340–341, 347, 355–356,
   377–378, 420, 440, 452–453,
   454, 455–456, 475, 479, 480, 491,
   501; absolute idea 270, 281, 313,
   218, 340, 341, 346, 355, 373, 376,
   377–380, 439, 441, 456, 475, 478,
   486–487, 489
idealism: German 4, 11–73, 13, 21,
   23–25, 27–28, 45, 46, 65, 73, 83,
   86, 88, 93–94, 146, 214, 274, 291,
   329, 454, 479, 493; objective 30;
   speculative 47, 69, 333, 463–465;
   subjective 24, 30; transcendental
   36, 54, 62, 66–67, 70, 177, 240,
   274, 500, 502
ideality 6–7, 280, 316–317, 329,
   359–379, 387, 393, 398, 403, 405,
   423, 442
Inclosure Schema 162, 185, 249, 250
indeterminacy 65, 76, 77, 87, 154,
   158, 205, 208–209, 244, 250,
   268–269, 272–273, 276, 288,
   305, 313, 325, 344, 389–390,
   394, 398, 414, 464, 482–483,
   493, 494, 499
induction: empirical 15; intuitive 15
inference x, 7, 44, 111, 114, 126, 132,
   177–180, 201, 229, 248, 263, 270,
   290, 294, 305, 312, 332, 346, 350,
   381, 445, 457, 459–461, 464–466,
   478, 488
infinitude: bad/false (quantitative)
   53, 174, 293, 313–315, 375, 442;
   indeterminate (*see* indeterminacy);
   intensive 85–87, 90, 394; true 313,
   314, 387, 426, 442
instantiation (problem of) 2, 6, 94,
   98, 101–108, 127–128, 145–146,

148, 152–153, 156, 162, 170,
   175–177, 186–187, 214, 228,
   240–241, 259, 260, 262, 306, 308,
   319–321, 324, 333, 336, 392, 441,
   467, 468, 472
intuition: intellectual 20–24, 36,
   38–39, 41–42, 48, 51, 64, 66–68,
   98, 100–101, 117, 127, 145, 167,
   328, 332–333, 339, 348–349, 376,
   453–456, 478, 486, 490; sensual/
   sensible 19–20, 41, 129, 453

Jacobi, Friedrich Heinrich 36, 39,
   46–52, 54, 69, 70, 71, 239, 245,
   303, 308, 329, 333, 340–342, 497
judgment 7, 17–19, 36–37, 39, 41,
   43–45, 53, 56–59, 68, 70, 95–96,
   115–117, 122, 132, 149, 150–152,
   154, 178, 180, 193, 244, 261, 267,
   271, 278, 281, 283, 292, 312, 316,
   327, 332, 333, 346, 373–376, 381,
   391, 393, 417, 419, 422, 432, 433,
   436, 438, 439, 441, 443, 444, 445,
   448, 453, 457–466, 478, 498, 503;
   analytic 36–41, 45, 56, 68, 149,
   151; synthetic 36, 37, 43, 57–59,
   150, 151, 346; thetic 43–44, 53

Kant, Immanuel 4, 6, 13, 15, 16–21,
   23–24, 27, 32–45, 48–49, 55, 62,
   65–68, 72, 74–75, 92–101, 108,
   111, 117, 122, 125–129, 134–138,
   142–143, 145–146, 148–158,
   166–168, 177, 180, 185–186, 197,
   205, 207–209, 223–224, 232–236,
   240, 249–250, 263, 265–267,
   269, 276, 282–285, 312, 325, 328,
   333–339, 343–349, 354, 356,
   369, 376, 382, 392, 452–455, 459,
   463, 471, 480, 485–486, 488, 490,
   497–498, 499–500
Kreis, Guido 277, 280, 285, 498

Leibniz, Gottfried Wilhelm 99,
   350, 489
life 6, 71, 90, 113, 117, 119–120, 124,
   199, 230, 307, 317, 326, 327, 341,
   342, 352, 374–376, 380, 413–414,
   420, 434, 441, 451, 456, 468, 471,
   475, 480, 488–489, 491, 500
Locke, John 119, 157, 175
logic: of being 6, 7, 272, 313, 331,
   335, 356, 359, 360–363, 365–367,
   369–372, 378, 383, 385–386, 390,

393, 395, 399, 401, 407, 412, 424,
478; of the concept (+doctrine of
the concept) xiii, 6–7, 64–65, 135,
136, 173, 255, 258, 263–264, 301,
304, 307–308, 314, 316, 318, 320,
321, 330, 332–333, 336–337, 346,
349, 352–354, 359, 360–362, 366,
367, 369, 371–378, 385, 401, 403,
405, 413, 421, 441, 454–456, 470,
472, 485, 500; of essence 6, 255,
272, 279, 301, 331, 351, 360–362,
365–371, 375, 378–379, 380, 385,
393, 403, 405, 410, 441, 443, 478;
formal 36, 95–96, 98, 125–126,
129, 136, 247, 249, 250, 341, 384,
393, 448; foundation free 265,
340, 349; presuppositionless 476;
transcendental 33, 41, 95–97, 129,
137, 335
Lowe, E.J. 138, 157, 498

Magee, Glenn 250, 334, 335–336,
342, 354–356, 488, 491, 498
Maimonides 65, 198–201, 223,
283, 498
mereology 80, 300–301, 306,
473, 494
metaphysics xiii, 1–2, 5–6, 8, 11–12,
13, 16, 35, 49, 80, 88, 93, 101,
109–110, 113, 115, 126, 128–132,
135, 146, 153, 154, 157–158, 186,
189, 194–195, 210, 214, 218,
221–225, 230, 237, 247, 249–251,
258, 273, 284, 287, 289, 290, 291,
304, 311, 323, 326–328, 330,
333–340, 346–348, 354–355,
357–358, 380, 439, 480, 485,
489–495, 497–502, 503; critical
490; foundation free xiii, 1, 2, 5,
8, 339–340; general 334–335;
Hegelian 304, 334, 336–337, 357,
502; meta-metaphysics 11–12;
special 334–335, 338
McDowell, John 334, 345, 354, 356,
450, 462–463, 471–472, 477, 480,
486, 491, 499, 501
Meillassoux, Quentin 374–375, 380, 499
metaphor 14, 76, 82, 84–86, 230,
276, 284, 322, 326, 336, 338–340,
352, 377, 413, 419, 434, 449, 456,
475
Mill, J.S.157, 174, 178–180, 187, 499
missing difference (problem of) 2, 94,
133, 137, 147, 156, 159–188, 193,

219, 234–235, 239, 240–241, 246,
260, 290, 309, 327, 466–468, 499
monism 189–191, 193, 210, 226,
284, 334, 341, 356, 498
mysticism 4, 8, 52, 70, 88, 92, 201,
223, 241, 243–246, 250–251, 259,
267–268, 295–296, 483–484,
490, 500–501; hermetic 245, 250,
491, 494, 498; monochromatic
245–246, 250

naturalism 174
nature 28, 30, 31, 35, 46, 48–51, 62,
67, 74, 128, 192–193, 221–222,
246, 270, 278, 284, 340–343, 348,
352–353, 356, 358, 375, 376, 379,
422, 445–454, 456–462, 472,
475–478, 480, 485–487, 490, 495,
496, 502; philosophy of 28, 30–31,
67, 128, 340–341, 343, 356, 379,
477, 478, 496, 502
Neo-Kantianism 174, 181
Neo-Platonism ix, 27, 73–94, 214,
328, 352
Nietzsche 69, 243, 250, 495
nihilism (problem of) 2, 11, 36–54,
69, 71, 93, 156, 185, 201, 204,
239, 241, 244, 260, 290–291,
303–304, 308–309, 327, 329,
333, 340, 342, 440, 466–468, 495,
499, 502; meta-metaphysical 290;
metaphysical 201, 244, 291
Nishitani, Keiji 66, 69, 477, 499–500
nominalism 141, 176–177, 182, 184
Non-well Founded Set theory 247
Noumenon 22, 101, 117, 325, 328
Nous 22, 78, 101, 107, 117, 127, 192,
215, 324–325, 328, 337, 486, 490
Novalis 51–52, 70, 202, 223, 495,
500
no-world view x, 286–307, 293–294,
301, 306

objectivity 28, 30–32, 38–41, 47, 59,
61, 70, 74, 134–135, 232, 259,
329–332, 335, 338, 342, 347, 350,
354, 357, 358, 373, 375, 376, 380,
451–452, 459, 503
Ockham, William of 176–177
One and All 1, 3, 23, 27, 194, 239
ontological argument 21, 42, 99,
168, 243, 303, 326, 329–358,
451–452, 460, 475, 487–491, 496,
498–501

ontology xiii, xiv, 21, 66, 175, 291–293, 295–296, 298, 299, 304–305, 334, 339, 342, 354, 355, 357, 491, 493–494, 495, 498, 503

onto-theology (problem of) 2, 94, 126, 147, 156, 189–225, 226–227, 240, 268, 287–290, 298, 302, 309, 310, 467–468

parameterization 238

Parmenides (the Philosopher) 102, 191–193, 198, 221, 291, 317

participation (problem of) xiii, 102, 104, 130, 228, 230, 232, 259, 318–319, 321, 323, 488

perception 14–15, 143, 164, 175, 344, 472

Pippin, Robert B. 333, 334, 336–339, 346, 354–355, 364–365, 480, 500

Plato 14, 27, 74–75, 77–79, 81, 85–94, 101–113, 118, 120, 122, 123, 128–131, 136, 138, 141, 147, 157, 162, 175, 185, 191–193, 213–214, 222, 224, 226, 228, 232, 233, 240, 247, 258–259, 263–264, 270, 317, 318–322, 328, 338, 352, 357, 361, 392, 439, 456, 496, 500–501, 503

positing (*Setzen*) 7, 52–53, 62–63, 68, 71, 277, 322, 330, 362–372, 379, 385–387, 394, 395, 403–405, 435

post-modernism 1

potency (*Dunamis*) 14, 114, 122, 124, 212, 214, 219–220, 231, 322

Priest, Graham 3, 159, 162, 185–186, 226, 234–238, 242–243, 247–250, 279–282, 285, 287, 294, 298–299, 300–301, 306, 494, 500–501

principle of identity 32, 33, 38–39, 42, 44, 45, 47, 61–62, 69, 87, 92, 93, 128, 135–136, 143, 156, 166, 204, 221, 227, 255, 260, 274, 282, 298, 308–309, 330

Principle of Non-contradiction (PNC) 2–5, 8, 13, 62, 83, 86, 95, 102, 105, 137, 144, 149–156, 169–170, 189–191, 196, 201, 203, 206, 210, 220, 222, 226–228, 234–237, 239, 241–242, 249–250, 255, 258, 263, 268, 273, 276, 278, 294, 307–308, 382–384, 397, 418–421, 433, 447–448, 464–466, 467–470

Pros Hen 4, 126, 206, 209, 210, 212–225, 250, 290

psychologism 382, 448, 174, 183–184, 186

Ramsey, Frank 296

realism 6, 13, 48, 51, 291, 294, 350, 495; new 1, 294, 495

Realphilosophie 454, 456, 461, 479, 490

reason (*Vernunft*) 6, 15–16, 18, 22–23, 36, 38–39, 43, 47–52, 55, 65, 69, 70, 79, 83, 85, 89, 94–96, 98–99, 104, 112, 114, 149, 171–174, 177, 179, 180, 186, 194–195, 207, 208, 220, 222–223, 244–245, 267, 270, 304, 312, 332, 337, 341–342, 345, 346, 348, 351, 357, 377, 381–382, 424, 426, 442, 449–452, 460–461, 474–476, 483–484, 487, 490, 495, 498

recollection 14, 204, 491

Redding, Paul 251, 350, 357, 444, 472, 479–480, 501

Reinhold, Karl Leonhard 24, 42, 45, 66

Romanticism 52, 69, 243, 284, 493, 495, 499

Russell, Bertrand 138, 157, 237, 248–250, 286, 493, 501

self-predication 77, 79, 80, 82, 97, 104, 122–123, 125–126, 129, 130, 137, 148–149, 157, 162, 163, 190–191, 220–221, 230–233, 240, 262–263, 268, 303, 307, 413, 415, 422, 427, 430, 433, 446, 456, 464, 467, 473

self-reference 104, 156, 159, 162, 230, 232, 234, 248, 256, 257, 264, 306, 309, 315–316, 321–323, 327, 335, 344–345, 355, 388, 394–396, 434, 462, 473, 499

self-referential predication 6, 80, 82, 279, 280

Sellars, Wilfrid 284, 349, 460, 461, 479, 502

sense-certainty 164, 472, 474, 481

sensibility 17, 36, 41, 94, 97–98, 126, 129

Schelling, F.W.J. 23, 25, 27–39, 42, 46, 51–72, 73, 75, 88, 93, 146, 168, 196, 222, 242, 246, 257, 259, 263, 269–274, 284, 304, 305, 333, 340, 342, 356, 442, 454–455, 459–460, 486, 496–497, 500, 502

Schema (Schematism) 41, 98, 162, 232, 97
Schlegel, Karl Wilhelm Friedrich 4, 46, 51–52, 70, 502
Scotus, Duns 141, 157, 197, 200–201, 222, 495
self-consciousness 11, 20, 24, 32, 35, 40, 42, 55–56, 59–62, 64, 66, 171, 172, 270, 272, 304, 334, 346, 354, 355, 380, 455, 463, 474–475, 476, 480, 481, 485–486, 500
singularity (Einzelheit) xiii, xiv, 1, 3–5, 7, 8, 139, 265, 301, 310, 312–313, 315, 318, 321–322, 326, 332, 347, 351, 353, 360, 373, 375, 377, 378, 381–444, 446, 447–449, 456, 466–472, 474, 476–477, 480, 482, 483–485, 487–488, 490
Socrates 102–109, 113, 115, 117–119, 123, 125, 129, 130, 133, 139, 141, 143, 146, 160, 179, 185, 196, 215, 228–231, 233, 247, 321, 328
Spinoza 46, 49–51, 70, 99, 157, 210, 349, 350, 356, 489, 497, 502
spirit (*Geist*) 246, 318, 340, 341, 342, 342–343, 345, 348, 352, 353, 356–358, 420, 424, 426, 441–442, 445, 449–452, 456, 462, 471, 474–477, 480, 484, 485–490, 491
Stern, Robert 357
subjectivity 5, 13, 15, 19, 21–23, 28–32, 35, 39, 47, 56, 59, 61, 74, 96, 134–135, 143, 148, 266, 336–338, 341, 346–347, 355, 374, 375, 376, 377, 443, 478
sublime 266–267, 284
sufism 200, 243
syllogism 114, 116, 126, 132, 137, 149, 157, 179–180, 187, 323, 332, 354, 373–376, 380–381, 393, 433, 459–460, 465–466, 479
synthesis 32, 36, 38–45, 53–55, 58–59, 61–64, 68, 86, 97, 100, 147, 166–168, 208, 232, 255, 256, 260, 269–274, 333, 337, 346, 348, 431, 459, 460, 485, 486; Synthetic Unity of Apperception 35, 39, 40, 64, 65, 98, 346, 485, 500

theology: negative (apophatic) 3, 6, 199, 228; positive (kataphatic) 197
thing-in-itself 22, 38, 68–69, 208
trinity 351, 487, 491

transcendental: aesthetic 16–17; analytic 16–17, 98; ideal 208, 209; idealism (*see* idealism)
transition (*Übergehen*) 6, 272, 360–361, 366, 368, 370–372, 379–380, 399, 401, 405, 407, 424, 426
truth: coherentism 100, 101, 134, 206, 279, 280, 313, 377; Correspondence Theory 28–31, 41–42, 57, 96–97, 100, 106–107, 115, 117, 127, 134–136, 145, 147, 152, 167, 172, 204, 223, 248, 262, 315, 374, 376–377, 392, 439, 450–452, 485; dual principles of 92–93, 185; general criterion of 27, 32, 34–35, 39, 57, 150; truth logic 95–96, 125–126, 135–136, 143, 146, 148, 180, 242, 258, 263, 308, 374
third man (problem of) 2, 89, 94, 104, 129, 147–148, 156, 226–241, 247, 259–260, 261, 268, 290, 310, 315, 320–323, 391–392, 467–468, 503

understanding (*Verstand*) 17–19, 22, 36, 40–42, 49–51, 64, 94, 96–99, 101, 127, 129, 145, 167, 233, 266, 276, 284, 285, 312, 323, 381, 382, 384, 393, 397, 421, 424, 426, 447, 448, 454, 455
univocity/univocal 6, 29, 193, 197, 200–201, 211–212, 215–216, 218–219, 221, 250

Vicious Circle Principle 237–238

Winfield, Richard Dien ix, xi, xiv, 280, 283–284, 354, 358, 490, 503
Wittgenstein, Ludwig 244, 266, 283, 296, 503
world 1, 3, 5, 8, 13, 25, 33, 47, 48–49, 54, 66, 69, 70, 73–77, 82, 87–89, 93, 120, 144, 194, 196, 198, 204, 218, 221–223, 225, 242–243, 250, 258, 266–267, 275–277, 279, 284–291, 293–307, 318, 333–338, 341–343, 348, 351–352, 354, 356, 358, 463, 471, 477, 479–480, 486–487, 490–492, 495, 499, 502

Žižek, Slavoj 71, 327, 503